Library of
Davidson College

CHALLENGES TO A LIBERAL INTERNATIONAL ECONOMIC ORDER

A conference sponsored by the
American Enterprise Institute for Public Policy Research

CHALLENGES TO A LIBERAL INTERNATIONAL ECONOMIC ORDER

Edited by
Ryan C. Amacher, Gottfried Haberler,
and Thomas D. Willett

American Enterprise Institute for Public Policy Research
Washington, D.C.

Library of Congress Cataloging in Publication Data

Main entry under title:

Challenges to a liberal international economic order.

    (AEI symposia ; 79C)
    1. International economic relations—Congresses.
2. International business enterprises—Congresses.
3. International finance—Congresses. I. Amacher, Ryan C. II. Haberler, Gottfried, 1900-
III. Willett, Thomas D. IV. Series: American Enterprise Institute for Public Policy Research. AEI symposia ; 79C
HF1410.C45   382.1   79-11687
ISBN 0-8447-2151-4
ISBN 0-8447-2152-2 pbk.

AEI Symposia 79C

© 1979 by the American Enterprise Institute for Public Policy Research, Washington, D.C. All rights reserved. No part of this publication may be used or reproduced in any manner whatsoever without permission in writing from the American Enterprise Institute except in the case of brief quotations embodied in news articles, critical articles, or reviews.

The views expressed in the publications of the American Enterprise Institute are those of the authors and do not necessarily reflect the views of the staff, advisory panels, officers, or trustees of AEI.

"American Enterprise Institute" is the registered service mark of the American Enterprise Institute for Public Policy Research.

Printed in the United States of America

The American Enterprise Institute for Public Policy Research, established in 1943, is a publicly supported, nonpartisan, research and educational organization. Its purpose is to assist policy makers, scholars, businessmen, the press, and the public by providing objective analysis of national and international issues. Views expressed in the institute's publications are those of the authors and do not necessarily reflect the views of the staff, advisory panels, officers, or trustees of AEI.

Council of Academic Advisers

Paul W. McCracken, *Chairman, Edmund Ezra Day University Professor of Business Administration, University of Michigan*

Robert H. Bork, *Alexander M. Bickel Professor of Public Law, Yale Law School*

Kenneth W. Dam, *Harold J. and Marion F. Green Professor of Law, University of Chicago Law School*

Donald C. Hellmann, *Professor of Political Science and International Studies, University of Washington*

D. Gale Johnson, *Eliakim Hastings Moore Distinguished Service Professor of Economics and Provost, University of Chicago*

Robert A. Nisbet, *Resident Scholar, American Enterprise Institute*

Herbert Stein, *A. Willis Robertson Professor of Economics, University of Virginia*

James Q. Wilson, *Henry Lee Shattuck Professor of Government, Harvard University*

Executive Committee

Herman J. Schmidt, *Chairman of the Board*
William J. Baroody, Jr., *President*
Charles T. Fisher III, *Treasurer*

Richard J. Farrell
Richard B. Madden
Richard D. Wood

Edward Styles, *Director of Publications*

Program Directors

Russell Chapin, *Legislative Analyses*

Robert B. Helms, *Health Policy Studies*

Thomas F. Johnson, *Economic Policy Studies*

Sidney L. Jones, *Seminar Programs*

Marvin H. Kosters/James C. Miller III, *Government Regulation Studies*

Jack Meyer, *Special Projects (acting)*

W. S. Moore, *Legal Policy Studies*

Rudolph G. Penner, *Tax Policy Studies*

Howard R. Penniman/Austin Ranney, *Political and Social Processes*

Robert J. Pranger, *Foreign and Defense Policy Studies*

Periodicals

AEI Economist, Herbert Stein, Editor

AEI Foreign Policy and Defense Review, Robert J. Pranger and Donald C. Hellmann, Co-Editors

Public Opinion, Seymour Martin Lipset, Ben J. Wattenberg, Co-Editors; David R. Gergen, Managing Editor

Regulation, Antonin Scalia and Murray L. Weidenbaum, Co-Editors; Anne Brunsdale, Managing Editor

William J. Baroody, Sr., *Counsellor and Chairman, Development Committee*

MAJOR CONTRIBUTORS

Bela Balassa
Johns Hopkins University and the World Bank

Robert E. Baldwin
University of Wisconsin

Jacob S. Dreyer
United States Treasury

Richard D. Erb
American Enterprise Institute

J. M. Finger
United States Treasury

Malcolm Gillis
Harvard University

Gottfried Haberler
American Enterprise Institute

Robert G. Hawkins
New York University

I. M. D. Little
The World Bank

Gordon W. Smith
Rice University

Jan Tumlir
General Agreement on Tariffs and Trade, Geneva

Ingo Walter
New York University

Thomas D. Willett
Claremont Men's College

CONTENTS

PREFACE
   The Editors

INTRODUCTION AND SUMMARY OF THE CONFERENCE 1
   Ryan C. Amacher, Gottfried Haberler, and Thomas D. Willett

PART ONE
OVERVIEW AND HISTORICAL PERSPECTIVE

Major Challenges to the International Economic System 17
   Thomas D. Willett

The Liberal International Economic Order in Historical
   Perspective 43
   Gottfried Haberler

Commentary
   Peter B. Kenen   66
   Hollis B. Chenery   70
   Ronald Findlay   73
   Paul Craig Roberts   80

Discussion 83
Postscript 85
   Gottfried Haberler

PART TWO
COMMODITIES PROBLEMS

Commodity Instability: New Order or Old Hat? 91
   Gordon W. Smith

Commentary
    A. I. MacBean   137
    Richard James Sweeney   141
    Dragoslav Avramovic   152

Discussion 154

PART THREE
INTERNATIONAL INVESTMENT

The Multinational Corporation 159
    Robert G. Hawkins and Ingo Walter

Multinational Corporations and a Liberal International
    Economic Order: Some Overlooked Considerations 199
    Malcolm Gillis

Commentary
    Thomas Horst   214
    Paul P. Streeten   215

Discussion 220

PART FOUR
TRADE POLICIES

Protectionist Pressures in the United States 223
    Robert E. Baldwin

The New Protectionism, Cartels, and the
    International Order 239
    Jan Tumlir

The Developing Countries and the International Order 259
    I. M. D. Little

The New Protectionism: An Evaluation and
    Proposals for Reform 279
    Bela Balassa

Commentary
    Jagdish N. Bhagwati   303
    Nat Weinberg   307

Discussion 313

PART FIVE
THE LIBERAL'S DILEMMA:
POLICY RESPONSES TO FOREIGN MONOPOLIES

Countervailing Foreign Use of Monopoly Power 317
    Jacob S. Dreyer

Commentary
    Franklyn D. Holzman 348
    Robert D. Tollison 353
    Richard E. Caves 357
    Carlos F. Diaz-Alejandro 362
    Roger E. Shields 364
    Edward Tower 369

Discussion 378

PART SIX
STRATEGIES FOR A MORE LIBERAL AND
EQUITABLE INTERNATIONAL ECONOMIC ORDER

International Resource Transfers: The International Financial
    System and Foreign Aid .... 383 ✓
    Richard D. Erb

Trade Liberalization: A Public Choice Perspective 421
    J. M. Finger

A Survey of Proposed Changes in World Trade Institutions:
    An Appendix to J. M. Finger's Paper 454
    Stephen Golub and Joanna Shelton

Commentary
    Peter T. Bauer 462
    Kenneth W. Dam 467
    William R. Cline 471
    Juergen B. Donges 476

Discussion 483

List of Participants 487

PREFACE

This conference was organized by Gottfried Haberler and Thomas D. Willett at the suggestion of Thomas F. Johnson, Director of Economic Policy Studies at the American Enterprise Institute. In editing the conference volume, the organizers were joined by Ryan C. Amacher, who took primary responsibility for preparing summaries of the conference discussions. In the development of the conference, the organizers were fortunate in being able to draw upon the advice of an informal planning group that included Sven Arndt, Jacob S. Dreyer, Richard D. Erb, William Fellner, J. M. Finger, Thomas F. Johnson, and Richard J. Sweeney. We should like to express our gratitude to this group and to the other conference participants for contributing to what we believe was a very successful conference. We hope that the publication of these conference papers and discussions will prove useful to a wider audience interested in the current challenges facing the application of liberal economic principles to the operation of the international economic order.

THE EDITORS

CHALLENGES TO A LIBERAL INTERNATIONAL ECONOMIC ORDER

INTRODUCTION AND SUMMARY OF THE CONFERENCE

Ryan C. Amacher, Gottfried Haberler, and Thomas D. Willett

During the 1970s the international economic system has faced increasingly serious challenges. Accelerating inflation and huge U.S. balance of payments deficits caused the breakdown of the system of pegged exchange rates adopted by the international community at Bretton Woods at the end of World War II. This was followed in short order by the oil embargo and subsequent sharp increases in oil prices, which put a heavy strain on international payments, drove inflation still higher, and led to rapidly mounting debts by the oil-importing countries. It is hardly surprising that these events triggered widespread fear of a disruption of the Western industrial economies and the international economic order, reminiscent of the economic disasters of the 1930s when depression spread across the world and national protectionist policies strangled world trade.

The international economic order has not collapsed, however. The framework of international economic cooperation and the commitment to basically liberal international economic policies developed by the major industrial countries over the postwar period have proved sufficiently strong to prevent wholesale reversion to the shortsighted economic nationalism of the 1930s. The new system of flexible exchange rates has proven to be consistent with the basic principles of international monetary cooperation adopted at Bretton Woods and to be capable of allowing the international community to manage the severe financial strains resulting from the oil shock without major defaults and adoption of beggar-thy-neighbor policies. Yet, it would be dangerous to allow the avoidance of the most extreme possible disasters to lull us into a false sense of security. In almost every country today, pressures for the adoption of protectionist policies are strong. Even governments committed to liberal economic principles have at times made concessions to protectionist pressures, and the general thrust over the postwar period toward more liberal trade policies in the industrial countries has been slowed and even reversed. In the face of the frustrations of both high inflation and high unemployment at home, national governments seem

INTRODUCTION AND SUMMARY

to be finding it increasingly difficult to maintain liberal policies, much less continue the progress toward reducing trade barriers. Both the AFL-CIO in the United States and representatives of the negotiating bloc of the developing countries have become increasingly vocal in challenging the basic principles of a liberal international economic order (LIEO).

In Europe, too, there is increased discussion of the possibilities of establishing international cartels and adopting "better organization of fair trade," a euphemism for protectionist government control of trade patterns. Proposals for greater government control of international commodity markets abound, and the difficulties faced by liberally organized economies in dealing with state-controlled entities have multiplied as the volume of East-West trade has expanded. Even for those who reject the attacks from the developing countries on the principles of liberal economic order, there remain the very real problems of the acute poverty of millions in the developing countries and the effects of international economic activities on income distribution within the industrial countries.

Overview

This volume presents the papers and proceedings of a conference sponsored by the American Enterprise Institute to assess the major challenges facing the essentially liberal international economic order and to discuss proposals for reforming the structure and operation of the system. The conference was held December 1 and 2, 1977, at the American Enterprise Institute and was attended by a group of more than fifty international economic experts from the United States and abroad.

Far too often, discussions of the international economic order are merely shows in which advocates of different points of view talk past one another in rhetorical flourishes as they attempt to win debating points with the audience. Many examples of such critiques are already widely available, and the organizers of this conference sought to minimize further contributions to the proliferation of such confrontational posturing. The purpose was rather a working conference in which the participants could attempt to cut through the traditional rhetoric to consider substantive issues such as the operation of the international economic system, the major challenges it faces, and various proposals for improving its operation. Almost all the participants in the conference adopted a liberal economic framework as a basis for analysis, but they varied widely in their assessments of many aspects of the operation of the international economic system and its possible improvement.

As the conference participants made abundantly clear, the adoption of liberal economic principles does not require a belief in laissez-faire under all circumstances, nor does it imply a blanket defense of current international economic institutions and national economic policies. These are among the common misconceptions fostered by much of the exaggerated rhetoric surrounding discussions of the New International Economic Order (NIEO).

The main (economic) proposals for an NIEO are to be found in the Charter of Economic Rights and Duties of States approved in December 1974 by the General Assembly of the Sixth Special Session of the United Nations. These proposals call for:

- adoption of an "integrated" approach to price supports for an entire group of commodity exports of less developed countries (LDCs)
- the "indexation" of LDC export prices to tie them to rising prices of developed countries' manufactured exports
- the attainment of official development assistance to reach the target of 0.7 percent of gross national product (GNP) of the developed countries
- the linkage of development aid with the creation of special drawing rights (SDRs) by the International Monetary Fund (IMF)
- the negotiated "redeployment" of some developed countries' industries to LDCs
- the lowering of tariffs on the exports of manufactures from LDCs
- the development of an international food program
- the establishment of mechanisms for the transfer of technology to LDCs separate from direct capital investment.

Of special interest in light of the success of the Organization of Petroleum Exporting Countries (OPEC) are two provisions of the charter: (1) It affirms each state's "full permanent sovereignty" over its natural resources and economic activities, which was specifically intended to include the right to nationalize foreign property in disregard of existing international laws. (2) Primary product producers have the "right" to associate in producers' cartels, and other countries have the "duty" to refrain from efforts to break these cartels.

Most of the conference participants felt that a liberal international economic order was in the interests of the developing countries. Hence, they rejected major components of these NIEO proposals that were critical of current trade policies in both the developing and the industrial countries, as well as of immigration and foreign aid policies in many of the industrial countries. Rejection of Marxist beliefs that multinational corporations are inherently exploitative does not imply

INTRODUCTION AND SUMMARY

that multinationals can do no wrong. Similarly, reasonable assessments of international commodity issues must accept that both private markets and government organizations may behave imperfectly. The liberal economic approach entails a preference for market solutions to economic problems, but it realizes that there are circumstances in which the private market cannot or does not work well and in which government activity is required to achieve economically desirable outcomes. But government interventions are usually less than perfect. This means that the appropriateness of various government policies and activities must be judged carefully case by case. Generalizations that market or government activities are always ideal or are always evil may make potent political rhetoric, but they are a poor guide to sensible policies.

In the following section, a brief summary of each of the conference sessions is presented. It is difficult to offer a short overall summary of the major conclusions of the conference because, as the organizers intended, it focused on developing a better appreciation of the nature of the most important problems facing the international economic system and on discussing better ways to analyze such problems and to develop guidelines for policy. We believe the conference was highly successful in achieving these objectives.

We believe it is fair to say that a substantial majority of the participants judged that our current economic difficulties, such as stagflation, are primarily a reflection of governments' failure to apply liberal economic principles consistently, rather than a failure of the liberal economic order. Perhaps the strongest consensus among the vast majority of the participants was concern over the potential danger of recent tendencies among governments committed to liberal principles: they reluctantly adopt politically expedient protectionist compromise measures in hopes of heading off pressures for even stronger protectionist measures. In the short run, such compromises may often be successful. Over the longer term, these well-intentioned compromises are likely to undermine the operation of the international economic system, and the exceptions of protectionism may come to outweigh the general rule of liberal policies. This is particularly true of such expedients as voluntary quota and market-sharing arrangements that can be much more destructive of the efficient operation of the economic system than is the traditional protectionist measure of tariffs.

Although there was much thoughtful discussion at the conference of ways to reverse the tide of protectionism, no major solutions surfaced. The best hope of stemming protectionist policies would still seem to be continued efforts by all concerned parties to make and keep government officials, business, labor, and the general public aware of the longer-term dangers of such strategies. This awareness needs to be combined with improved policies for reducing the economic hardship of the minorities who are harmed by international trade.

Perhaps the most important message for industrial countries was that they should be wary of treating the developing countries as a monolithic entity. In particular, they should not take the strident and hostile rhetoric coming from some political leaders and bureaucrats of developing countries as representing all developing countries. The explosive rhetoric of some should not blind industrial countries to the much more moderate and responsible positions being taken by many other negotiators and representatives. Nor should the hardship and the very real problems of many developing countries be ignored in reaction to the atmosphere of confrontation being fostered by some. Tolerance and cooperation are necessary to preserve and strengthen the operation of the international economic order according to liberal principles.

Summary of the Individual Sessions

The conference was divided into six sessions. Session I, chaired by Fritz Machlup of New York University, provided a historical framework and an overview for the following sessions. In the first paper Thomas D. Willett of Claremont Graduate School and Claremont Men's College discussed the meaning of a liberal international economic order and outlined some of the major challenges facing it. Some of these challenges stem from the difficulties of managing economic interdependence in an imperfect world. These questions include the management of international externalities and the common property resources of the world's oceans, international commodity problems, and the proper response of countries embracing a liberal philosophy to the illiberal actions of others.

A second major set of challenges comes from protectionist pressures within the industrial countries. Willett stressed the long-run dangers of giving in to protectionist pressures as short-run political expedients and offered an optimistic prognosis that a resurgence of economic warfare such as occurred in the 1930s was not likely. He was much less optimistic, however, that the industrial countries would avoid a continued escalation of "cooperative" protectionism.

A third set of challenges concerns the developing countries. The basic principles of a liberal international economic order are being attacked in proposals for an NIEO by some of the most radical of the developing countries. Another major challenge questions the desirability of a liberal approach in alleviating poverty and accelerating human and

INTRODUCTION AND SUMMARY

economic development in the less developed countries. Willett was critical of many of the proposals for an NIEO and expressed concern that much of the NIEO rhetoric and negotiating tactics may be likely to retard rather than to promote the welfare of those in greatest poverty in the developing countries.

In the second paper Gottfried Haberler of the American Enterprise Institute considered the basically liberal post–World War II system of freer trade, which is institutionalized by the General Agreement on Tariffs and Trade (GATT) and the IMF. Haberler argued that challenges to this liberal order are based on assertions that it has not performed well, particularly for developing countries. He then examined the historical record of the liberal order with respect to less developed countries and concluded that, contrary to frequent assertions, it has performed extremely well. The first quarter century after World War II was a period of unprecedented growth and prosperity, not only for the industrial countries but also for the LDCs. The recession of 1973–1975 and the somewhat sluggish recovery thereafter in the industrial world had unfavorable repercussions on the LDCs, but they have weathered the setback better than the industrial countries themselves.

Haberler maintained that it is not a liberal order but serious deviations from the free market economy that has produced stagflation. Stagflation poses a particularly difficult dilemma for macro policy. Haberler argued that monetary restraint will not solve the problem of stagflation without structural reform designed to make the economy more competitive and flexible..

In the commentary that followed these papers, Peter B. Kenen of Princeton University disagreed with Haberler's contention that the most significant threat to the liberal order comes from the LDCs. He argued that the main threat comes from the response in the developed world and from the illiberal domestic policies in developed and underdeveloped countries. Ronald Findlay of Columbia University agreed with Kenen that the greatest threat to the present system is from the developed countries. Findlay argued that a truly liberal system never existed, indeed, could never exist. He did not view the future of liberal trade policies with optimism and expressed fears that the developed world will become more regulated and restrictive and that countries of the developing world will maintain extensive control of their economies.

Hollis B. Chenery of the World Bank agreed with both Willett and Haberler that many of the proposals for the NIEO would not represent helpful reforms for the underdeveloped countries, but he stressed that this does not mean that changes in the present system are unwarranted.

Chenery disagreed with Haberler's assumption that the internal distribution of income is the internal problem of each country.

In the final comment, Paul Craig Roberts from the office of Sen. Orrin G. Hatch concentrated in the New International Economic Order as the major threat to liberal trade. He saw many of the calls for a new system as the self-seeking demands of international bureaucrats.

In a postscript prepared for this volume, Gottfried Haberler examined and partly accepted the points made by the discussants. Haberler concluded with the argument that freer trade can still serve as a stimulus to growth in underdeveloped countries. As evidence of this, he indicated pairs of countries that are similar in most respects except that one has pursued liberal trade policies and the other has not.

Session II, chaired by Robert M. Stern of the University of Michigan, concentrated on commodity problems. The background paper was presented by Gordon W. Smith of Rice University, who argued that programs to stabilize commodity prices have been severely oversold by their proponents. Yet, there are at least three reasons why these programs must be taken seriously. First, the NIEO proponents are increasing their demands for commodity stabilization, and Western diplomats feel some need to accommodate them. Second, many people in the industrial countries accept the idea of promoting greater commodity price stability as a tool for antiinflationary policy. Third, for some commodities, international agreements are seen as an attractive alternative to domestic action. Smith found that the empirical evidence supporting various views of market failures in the major commodity markets is inconclusive. He concluded that the deleterious macro effects of commodity price fluctuations on the LDCs are best offset through compensatory financing. The benefits of stabilized prices could, in fact, be gained by domestically financed domestic buffer stocks. He also concluded that any buffer stock scheme now under consideration would be underfinanced and should not be pursued since it would raise commodity costs and would likely be ineffective at price stabilization.

A. I. MacBean of the University of Lancaster (England) agreed with Smith on the main issues and suggested that price stability could be improved by better information on production and by reform of agricultural production in Europe, Japan, and the United States. He discounted the argument that inflation in the West is in any significant degree caused by commodity price instability. MacBean agreed that the main issue is how commodity price instability affects growth in the LDCs. He argued that only a few countries seem to be candidates for help in this regard, and those candidates are better aided by other types of economic aid than by specific commodity agreements.

INTRODUCTION AND SUMMARY

Dragoslav Avramovic of the World Bank presented what he called a different conceptual framework. His remarks and his prepared statement, which is reproduced here, presented the case for a common fund to stabilize commodity prices as proposed by the United Nations Conference on Trade and Development (UNCTAD). He emphasized his belief that the markets for many primary commodities do not work well. Avramovic's framework is very similar to the framework of proponents of the NIEO.

Richard J. Sweeney of Claremont Men's College strongly endorsed Smith's conclusion that proposals for commodity price stabilization have been greatly oversold. Sweeney concentrated his remarks on efficient information processing, arguing that the idea of separable micro and macro problems was invalid. He noted that filter rules indicate that commodity markets are processing information very efficiently. He argued that the markets are performing well and that, where this is so, there are no additional arguments for government intervention on macroeconomic grounds.

The third session, chaired by Gary C. Hufbauer of the U.S. Treasury, concentrated on the multinational corporation (MNC). In the main paper for the session, Robert G. Hawkins and Ingo Walter of New York University documented the growing significance of the multinational corporation, attempted to distinguish among successful and unsuccessful behavioral characteristics of multinationals, assessed the effects of multinationals on the international economy, and examined their benefits and costs to host and home countries. The main conflict, they argued, centers on the global objective function of the multinational and the national objective function of host countries. This conflict gives rise to pressure for new rules of the game.

In the discussion that followed the presentation of this paper, Malcolm Gillis of Harvard University made extensive comments. We invited him to turn these comments into a paper, which appears in this volume following the paper by Hawkins and Walter. Gillis viewed the New International Economic Order as a challenge to the status quo, not to the liberal order. His case rests on the belief that in many respects the present system is not liberal. Gillis examined the various constituencies for the NIEO, the LIEO, and the status quo and argued that multinational corporations are in the constituency for the status quo.

Paul P. Streeten of the World Bank raised once more the question of what a liberal treatment of multinationals means. He questioned whether liberal treatment means laissez-faire treatment or intervention to make the MNCs conform to a competitive order. He also took issue with the concept of global welfare and argued that since the term is meaningless it is useless for judging MNC performance. Streeten argued that few investments are Pareto-optimal, and even if they were we might still legitimately be concerned with the distribution of benefits.

Thomas Horst of the U.S. Treasury reemphasized a few of Malcolm Gillis's points. He thought the most interesting issue was whether the multinationals themselves are part of the constituency of a liberal economic order and cited some evidence to show that they often are not. Horst felt that the background paper failed to put the evidence into a critical perspective and felt the authors should have considered whether, on balance, multinationals are good or bad.

Session IV, chaired by Wilson E. Schmidt of Virginia Polytechnic Institute and State University, began with a discussion of trade policy. The first paper by Robert E. Baldwin of the University of Wisconsin focused primarily on protectionist pressures in the United States. Baldwin characterized the U.S. government as being caught between the great authority to reduce tariffs granted the president by Congress for the Tokyo Round and the rising pressure for domestic protectionism. He felt that substantial progress is necessary in this round of negotiation because Congress is unlikely to give the president such broad negotiating power as it did in the Trade Act of 1974. He also pointed to the necessity of improving resource adjustment mechanisms as a way of reducing protectionist pressure.

The second paper, by Jan Tumlir of GATT, characterized the strengthening of protectionist pressure as the "new protectionism" because of its recent appearance as a broadly based political phenomenon in both Europe and the United States. Tumlir distinguished the European brand of new protectionism as a renewal of the belief that cartels can solve the problems of resource adjustment. He felt we are approaching a phase in which a ruling paradigm is being replaced. He also discussed adjustment assistance policies in Europe, pointing out that they often fail to distinguish between attempts to facilitate adjustment and attempts to prevent it.

The third paper, by I. M. D. Little of the World Bank, focused on the trade policies of the developing countries. Little argued that LDCs have been firmly wedded to the idea of a controlled international economic order since 1945. The LDCs were anti–free trade because international trade did not fit well into planning mentality. He argued that this anti–free trade posture used the declining terms-of-trade argument as a rationalization and that this bias became less pronounced in the mid-1960s. The whole UNCTAD approach is wrong, according to Little; the developing countries should enter the international political arena and lobby for aid and freer trade.

INTRODUCTION AND SUMMARY

In the commentary that followed, Bela Balassa of Johns Hopkins University and the World Bank was concerned that several important issues were not addressed because most of those in attendance were in general agreement concerning the benefits of a liberal order. These issues included arguments against the new protectionism in developed countries, an answer to labor's claims, and the question of how LDCs should deal with inadequate growth rates in developed countries. Balassa has since expanded on these ideas, and we have included his expanded version as the fourth paper of this session.

Jagdish Bhagwati of the Massachusetts Institute of Technology concentrated on Little's paper. Although basically in agreement, he felt a need to distinguish between those LDCs where overvalued exchange rates play a central role in determining import substitutes and those where overvalued exchange rates are used to accommodate the obsession with a certain type of industrialization and to define the degree and pattern of import substitution. He felt the real challenge to a liberal order comes from the LDCs' belief that developed countries do not subscribe to the liberal order when it does not serve their interests.

Nat Weinberg, a Washington-based labor consultant and former labor union official, spoke for what he called the victims of trade. His views were probably, he stated, closest to the views of the United Auto Workers. He favored free trade as an ideal, but he argued that certain conditions are necessary for free trade to be desirable. Since these conditions are not met, labor unions view trade policies on the basis of their practical consequences on people. He argued that many of the assumptions underlying comparative advantage theory are irrelevant to the realities of the modern world. Only with full employment can displaced labor be fully and equitably absorbed into the economy. He also advocated much more generous compensation for workers whose jobs are displaced by imports.

The fifth session of the conference, chaired by William Fellner of the American Enterprise Institute, was devoted to the problems of responding to the use of monopoly and monopsony power by other countries. Jacob S. Dreyer of the U.S. Treasury presented the one background paper, which concentrated on the challenge that deliberately created governmental monopoly poses to liberal trade policy. He examined the consequences of monopoly power in international markets and of policies to counteract this power. He discussed U.S. antitrust policy and its application to the problem of foreign monopolies. Dreyer concluded by enumerating some basic guidelines for dealing with foreign monopoly. The difficulty of the subject is highlighted by the fact that most of the benefits of trade are still present when dealing with foreign monopoly. The only complaint is that these benefits are less than they would be in the absence of the monopoly. Dreyer's own preference was to proceed with great caution in deciding to institute countervailing policies against foreign monopolies.

Franklyn Holzman of Tufts University concentrated his comments on the threat posed by centrally planned economies. He argued that it is incorrect to assume that because the Russians have a monopoly in their home market they can transfer that monopoly power to international markets. He felt that the conclusions of a General Accounting Office study of East-West trade were badly overstated and that we should not attempt to countervail Soviet power by increased governmental activity.

Robert D. Tollison of Virginia Polytechnic Institute and State University examined the ways in which the United States might respond to antisocial behavior on the part of other governments. The United States can ignore the behavior and set a good example or react and hope that retribution will lead the offending country to change its behavior. Tollison advocated a middle ground determined case by case.

Richard E. Caves of Harvard University presented a widely ranging criticism of Dreyer's paper and cataloged the retaliatory measures open to U.S. policy makers. Caves pointed out that unilateral action to make markets more competitive would not be sufficient because some of the benefits would spill over to other countries. He argued that the proper direction for study was to devise scenarios for reciprocal monopoly busting.

Carlos F. Diaz-Alejandro of Yale University pointed out that the discussions of the new international economic order have become a debating game. He hoped to make a few points for the side that he felt was not widely represented at the conference. He viewed much of the LDC action as countervailing the developed countries' restrictions on the flow of labor. He argued that the fight is between the rising oligopolists and the old, established oligopolists.

Roger E. Shields of Chemical Bank picked up Dreyer's emphasis on the need to examine the externalities of East-West trade. He argued that the departure from the rules of the game in dealing with state trading monopolies created some important problems, particularly in sales of arms and high-technology items. If a particular technology is not unique to a firm but is unique to the country, the only way to internalize the economies or diseconomies is through state action.

In the discussion that followed, Edward Tower of Duke University made detailed comments on the Dreyer paper and on Caves's remarks. We asked him to formalize his comments, and they are included here.

INTRODUCTION AND SUMMARY

Tower suggested rules for an optimum world commercial policy system that would internalize the externalities associated with illiberal policies. He proposed auctioning import and export licenses in competitive markets and remitting some part of quota and tariff revenues to trading partners.

The last session of the conference was chaired by Marina v. N. Whitman of the University of Pittsburgh and was concerned with strategies for achieving a more liberal and more equitable international order. The first paper, by Richard D. Erb of the American Enterprise Institute, focused on international financial issues and resource transfers to the developing countries. Erb began on an optimistic note by asserting that the international financial system is now consistent with the workings of a liberal international order. He then went on to examine some challenges to the efficiency and equitable character of the international financial system. He argued that the system must continue to service a high level of resource transfers and that the amount of resource transfers to poorer countries must be increased. Erb argued for increased U.S. development aid. He felt that aid strategy should serve U.S. objectives and that the promotion of a liberal international economic order should be a primary objective.

In the second background paper, J. M. Finger of the U.S. Treasury examined trade liberalization from the perspective of the public choice literature. Finger concluded that the larger the number of participants, the less likely the negotiating process is to work well. He suggested returning to the format of the old reciprocal trade negotiations but concentrating on exchanges between a major developed country and its major LDC trading partners to achieve greater liberalization.

The first of the four commentators for this session was Peter T. Bauer of the London School of Economics. Bauer expressed the belief that the NIEO proposals were more of a threat to free trade than most of the participants had felt. He argued that the demands for an NIEO should be resisted. He was skeptical of aid programs in general, but he advocated bilateral aid as an alternative far superior to the wealth transfer mechanisms of the NIEO.

Kenneth W. Dam of the University of Chicago concentrated on trade issues. He called for institutional changes to stem the protectionist pressures. In particular, Dam spoke against adjustment assistance that works to prevent adjustment. He pointed to early tariff reductions that were legislated before it was clear who the specific gainers and losers would be. He ended on the pessimistic note that the best we may be able to achieve in trade liberalization is a stalemate with current protectionism.

William R. Cline of the Brookings Institution suggested that the free-rider problem mentioned by Finger is not as great as is the problem that certain products are labor intensive and hit sensitive industries. Cline felt that the conference should have given more emphasis to concessional transfers, which he termed a primary concern of the NIEO. He called for a return to U.S. leadership of the postwar period.

Juergen B. Donges of the Kiel Institute of World Economics concentrated on trade liberalization. He argued that protectionist pressure will be more successful where governments have to set trade policy in a democratic setting. He advocated a gradual reduction of tariff barriers in order to lessen the impact on labor in selected industries. Donges called on LDCs to adapt themselves to a more liberal trading order, arguing that developed countries would regard such action as an application of reciprocity. Economists easily recognize the benefits of trade liberalization, but the difficulty lies in selling these programs to policy makers. To this end he called for a steady supply of careful, empirical work on the beneficial aspects of a liberal trade regime.

Marina v. N. Whitman closed the proceedings with the observation that the conference, like most successful conferences, served more to raise questions than to offer solutions. This observation sits well with the purpose of the conference—to develop a better appreciation of the nature of the problems facing a liberal international economic system. We hope these papers and the discussions that follow will interest others in analyzing and finding solutions to the challenges posed by the conference participants.

PART ONE

OVERVIEW AND HISTORICAL PERSPECTIVE

Major Challenges to the International Economic System

Thomas D. Willett

The purpose of this conference is to analyze the major challenges to the operation of the international economic order on liberal principles and to consider possible ways of strengthening the functioning of our current international economic system. This first paper will present an overview of the performance of the international economic system over the postwar period, offer some observations on several of the major challenges currently facing the system, and give a partial characterization of what is meant (at least by the organizers of this conference) by liberal economic principles. Its purpose is to initiate discussion, and it in no way purports to represent a comprehensive analysis. The accompanying paper by Gottfried Haberler offers a historical review of the operation of the international economic system against which we may compare alternative analyses and proposals for change. After a series of papers on more specific issues, we shall return to broader considerations in Part 6 and discuss general strategies for improving the equity and efficiency of the operation of the international economic system and for minimizing changes that are likely to conflict with these objectives.

Introduction

The basic framework of our postwar international economic system developed from a series of negotiations between the United States and the United Kingdom. With progressively broadened participation, these negotiations culminated in the Bretton Woods Agreements, which established the International Monetary Fund and the International Bank for Reconstruction and Development (the World Bank). More important, Bretton Woods represented a deliberate decision by the participating countries to reestablish a liberal international economic order based on a strengthened framework for international cooperation as opposed to

PART ONE: OVERVIEW

a reversion to a system of economic nationalism and heavy state control of international transactions.[1]

During the postwar period we have come to take a fairly high degree of international economic and financial cooperation for granted, but the blatant economic nationalism of the 1930s still rested heavily on the minds of the Bretton Woods negotiators. There was strong sentiment in many quarters in the United Kingdom that, with all the destruction and dislocation of the war, the country could not afford to adopt a liberal economic strategy and that survival required a wall of special protective agreements with the Commonwealth countries. In large measure, however, final victory in the negotiations went to the advocates of a liberal economic order, and the resulting international economic order provided a solid foundation for postwar economic recovery.[2]

Over the past decade, however, both the principles and the institutional arrangements of the postwar economic order have come under increasing attack, and the social contract established at Bretton Woods has begun to show alarming signs of disintegration. Inspired by such dramatic events as the U.S. termination of the gold convertibility of the dollar and imposition of an import surcharge in 1971, the subsequent widespread adoption of floating exchange rates among the major industrial countries and failure of efforts to restore a pegged rate system, and the prospective economic and financial repercussions of the huge increase in oil prices, many commentators questioned the very viability of a cooperative international economic order.

In my view, such predictions of a wholesale collapse of international economic cooperation and a repetition of the trade wars of the 1970s were greatly exaggerated. Certainly, to date they have not proven correct. Many confused the basic principles of international financial cooperation that were the heart of the Bretton Woods system with the

---

[1] The classic study of these negotiations is Richard N. Gardner, *Sterling-Dollar Diplomacy: The Origins and the Prospects of Our International Economic Order*, rev. ed. (New York: McGraw-Hill, 1969). Also of particular interest are the discussions in Roy F. Harrod, *The Life of John Maynard Keynes* (New York: Harcourt Brace, 1951). A recent, quite useful addition to the literature on the negotiations is Alfred E. Eckes, *A Search for Solvency: Bretton Woods and the International Monetary System, 1941–1971* (Austin: University of Texas Press, 1976).

[2] It should be noted in fairness to the critics of rapid liberalization that the initial U.K. effort to dismantle its system of exchange controls as part of the U.S.-sterling loan provisions was a failure. Massive capital impact quickly drained the United Kingdom's international reserves, and widespread exchange controls were reestablished. The programs of gradual exchange liberalization and restoration of convertibility over the following decade, however, may be judged much more favorably, as may the U.K. decision not to surround itself with a high wall of tariff barriers against countries outside the Commonwealth.

specific procedures of "fixed" exchange rates,[3] fearing that the breakdown of the pegged rate system and widespread adoption of floating rates would be accompanied by a resurgence of economic nationalism and beggar-thy-neighbor policies reminiscent of the 1930s. On the contrary, the adoption of floating rates has facilitated cooperative policies and reduced on balance the pressures for illiberal trade and balance of payments restrictions.[4]

However, even if the crises facing the international economic system have been greatly exaggerated at times, there can be little question that there are serious challenges facing the preservation of a basically liberal international economic order. The dangers of an outbreak of trade warfare and collapse of the fabric of international welfare should not be overlooked, but I believe that the greater danger may well be a gradual but progressive retreat from liberal policies as the result of one "special case" exemption after another.

It should be emphasized, however, that the adoption of a liberal economic philosophy and the advocacy of a liberal international economic order are not the same as a philosophy of complete laissez-faire, nor need they imply the objective of achieving maximum economic output without regard to distributional and environmental concerns. Neither do they imply opposition to all proposals for changes in the international economic system. For example, while some aspects of the various proposals from the developing countries for a New International Economic Order clearly run counter to a liberal economic order, others, such as the reduction of trade barriers by the industrial countries, do not.

The liberal, at least in my definition, is characterized by a desire to utilize the operation of competitive markets to the extent feasible, as contrasted with a general distrust of the market evidenced in some other political and social philosophies. The liberal does not see the operation of the market as being generally exploitative as does the Marxist, nor does he assume that competitive markets are the ally of the strong against the weak. He sees competitive market transactions as leading to mutual gains.

Not all markets are even workably competitive, however. The

---

[3] This is discussed in some detail in my study, *Floating Exchange Rates and International Monetary Reform* (Washington, D.C.: American Enterprise Institute, 1977).

[4] This point will still be disputed by some, for there have certainly been many instances in which countries have adopted or tightened restrictive measures while their currency was floating. In my judgment, however, there is little question that without greater flexibility of exchange rates the adoption of restrictive policies would have been greater still.

PART ONE: OVERVIEW

liberal approach favors the operation of free markets where significant deviations from competition or important externalities are not present but recognizes a case for government intervention where these conditions do occur. In looking at actual market circumstances, the liberal is likely to emphasize that bigness is not necessarily synonymous with monopoly power. Thus, for example, he will find unconvincing arguments that, because some large multinational corporations have greater revenues than some of the governments of the developing countries with which they deal, the multinational will necessarily be able to strike a bargain that gives it a disproportionate share of the gains. The liberal would stress that large corporations do often compete quite forcefully against one another, and he would consider the circumstances of the particular situation.

The liberal is dubious of the assumption that governments work perfectly. Thus he does not take a finding of less than perfect operation of the private market as a per se case for government intervention. Realistic alternatives must be considered. Thus, for example, in the case of commodity price instability, many liberals might conclude that the private market had provided insufficient stabilizing speculation for some commodities and that a well-run, government-operated buffer stock might aid overall performance, yet be quite skeptical that in practice a government-run buffer stock would actively perform better or that its objectives would be limited to stabilizing prices.

At this point, however, the liberal must be careful not to let his skepticism lead to an assumption of the necessity of substantial government failure, paralleling the Marxist hostility toward the operation of the market. Liberal economic principles can provide a valuable perspective for analyzing such issues, but one cannot legitimately conclude from such a perspective alone that any type of commodity agreement is inconsistent with a liberal economic system. The question must be what types of agreements would appear to be desirable or undesirable and what types of formal and informal safeguards can be established. These are issues that must be analyzed case by case.

Before turning to more detailed discussion, let me briefly outline some of the major challenges facing a liberal international economic order. One of course is the possible unpremeditated collapse of international cooperation as events outrace the reasoned reactions of national authorities. The possibility of complete breakdown of the Bretton Woods social contract and degeneration into the economic nationalism of the 1930s cannot safely be ignored. As indicated above, however, I do not view such a catastrophe as likely. Despite all of the strains that have appeared, I believe that the fabric of international cooperation among the industrial countries remains strong and that the mistakes of the 1930s are unlikely to be repeated.

A more likely threat comes from those who repudiate the very principles on which a liberal economic system is based. This position has long been held by Marxists, who view the market system as inherently exploitative. Today a considerable portion (although clearly not all) of the supporting argumentation for the developing countries' proposals for an NIEO adopts such a perspective.

Within the industrial countries, the most serious challenge comes from pressure groups who by and large favor the general operation of a market system but argue that special circumstances require special government measures to improve their economic positions (or keep them from worsening). Thus the governments of the industrial countries face pressure for antiliberal concessions both from the representatives of the developing countries' bloc in international negotiations and from domestic interest groups seeking protection or other government support. Both in dealing with domestic interest groups and in international negotiations, governments find it extremely difficult to adopt a longer-run time perspective. The tendency is to think of how one can reduce the pressures of the moment, and it is easy to start a series of seemingly individual decisions that have a cumulative impact not envisioned at earlier stages. Enough marginal concessions can change the basic character of the system. Far too often, recent international economic decision making in the industrial countries has focused primarily on short-run tactical questions, to the neglect of considerations of long-run strategy. As shown in Gottfried Haberler's paper, the problems of stagflation have given rise to short-term political pressures for greater government intervention in the economy, when a strong case can be made that a major portion of stagflation is itself due to the effects of various government policies.

The gradual proliferation of illiberal policies in turn generates a major dilemma for the liberal. In what instances should he advocate countervailing government actions to discourage or offset the effects of illiberal government intervention abroad?

International regulatory policies pose another challenge. Increasing international economic interdependence in many areas has increased the potential desirability of many types of formal and informal international regulatory policies. The danger of course is that in practice regulatory bodies frequently operate in ways grossly inconsistent with liberal economic principles. The challenge is to establish formal or informal international machinery to deal effectively with market failures and common property resources while keeping to a minimum the extent to which special interests gain control over the determination of regulatory policies. The Law of the Sea negotiations offer a prime example of this type of challenge.

Still another major challenge concerns distributional considerations. One may reject many of the charges levied by third world representatives against the operation of the international economic system and still be concerned both about particular policies in the industrial countries that harm the developing countries (for example, the high levels of effective protection facing LDC exports) and about the cruel problems of poverty that plague many areas of the world. It is not necessary to believe that people have been exploited to have humanitarian concerns about poverty. Unfortunately, many of the proposals put forward in the name of aiding the poor take the form of illiberal measures, which do little to aid the poorest in the developing countries. Proposals to raise commodity prices are a case in point. To the liberal concerned about third world poverty, there is a need for substantial reorientation of both the North-South discussions and negotiations and of many industrial country policies that affect the third world.

In the following sections, I shall offer some observations on these challenges.

Domestic Protectionist Forces

Considerable progress has been made over the postwar period in reducing trade barriers, but in recent years the rate of progress has slowed, protectionist pressures have mounted rapidly, and U.S. leadership in the movement toward freer trade has faltered. In the early postwar years, much of the emphasis was on the elimination of currency restrictions, quotas, and other nontariff barriers to trade erected during the worldwide depression and international economic chaos of the 1930s. Since then, trade liberalization has come primarily through reductions in tariff barriers. Much of this reduction in some countries has been the result of membership in a free trade area or customs union, such as the European Free Trade Association (EFTA) or the European Communities (EC). But for the United States and many other countries the principal vehicle of trade liberalization in recent years has been the successive multilateral trade negotiations conducted under the aegis of the General Agreement on Tariffs and Trade.

GATT originally allowed trade policy to be relegated to the realm of low politics. Rules governing international trade made it possible to resolve trade issues in a separate forum from other issues of low and high politics. Richard N. Cooper has termed this a two-track system, "with trade issues traveling along their own track, not interfering with traffic elsewhere."[5]

During the 1960s, when the most significant trade negotiations took place, the United States was a leader in the movement for free trade. There was a strong momentum toward liberalization. Trade policy was used as an instrument of foreign policy. For example, the United States was willing to bear the economic costs of the Common Market as a reasonable price for strengthening Europe. Specific trade and investment issues seldom impinged on the high politics of foreign policy.

With the decline in the cold war and reassessments of international political and security situations, the status of trade relations was fundamentally changed. While the foreign policy check on protectionist trade policies in the United States was weakening, a number of factors were contributing to a resurgence of protectionist pressures. Beginning in the mid-1960s, there was a gradual erosion of the most-favored-nation (MFN) principle (Article 1 of GATT). This principle stated that all trading partners were to be treated on the basis of nondiscrimination—that is, there would be no preferential treatment.[6] The MFN principle, along with the agreements to keep trade issues on a separate track, worked well until the mid-1960s. At least from the U.S. point of view, the causes of the erosion lay in the establishment of a Common Agricultural Policy and preferential trading agreements by the EEC, the erection of nontariff barriers to trade in all major economies, and quotas blocking imports into Japan.[7]

The loss of momentum toward further liberalization at the end of the Kennedy Round was jumped on by protectionists. Increased competition from foreign producers has particularly affected many of the traditional manufacturing industries, where the U.S. comparative advantage has long been eroding. These industries are unusually heavily unionized, many by unions affiliated with the politically potent AFL-CIO. And the AFL-CIO's recent abandonment of its traditional liberal

---

[5] Richard N. Cooper, "Trade Policy Is Foreign Policy," *Foreign Policy*, no. 9 (Winter 1972–73).

[6] There was some allowance for giving preferences under MFN, but the conditions were stringent. Where trade preferences were granted among two or more countries, the movement between the countries had to be to complete free trade. External barriers to trade with other countries could remain the same or would be standardized among the free-trade countries. In the European Free Trade Area, each country kept its external barriers, while the Common Market adopted common external barriers. The opportunity costs to countries for deviations from MFN were therefore not trivial. This procedure is a good example of how scope for individual deviations from international agreements can be accommodated, but under tough conditions so that such actions will not be undertaken frequently.

[7] See Cooper, "Trade Policy," p. 49.

trade position and its new support for restrictive legislation have been a great help to the protectionist cause. C. Fred Bergsten discusses the causes of this shift in position in some detail.[8] He argues essentially that organized labor opted for a protectionist stance because members were willing to give up some income that could be generated through freer trade in order to avoid the accompanying dislocation costs. Thus, as income levels of union members go up, the tendency is toward avoiding shifts in geographic location.

The increase of foreign competition for particular influential industries was accompanied by an unprecedented deterioration in the U.S. merchandise trade-balance position beginning in the mid-1960s. This has made the case of protection more plausible to many, and some even argue that foreign competition was a major overall cause of domestic unemployment. Such arguments do not stand up to careful economic analysis,[9] but their political potency should not be underestimated.

Another economic factor related to increased protectionism is the diminution in agricultural exporter support for freer trade, in part because of the European agricultural trade barriers mentioned above. The easing of cold war pressure and the restoration of economic prosperity in Europe reduced the power of arguments within the United States that overriding national security concerns required liberal trade policies and acceptance of European restrictive measures. Many in this country became increasingly critical of U.S. failure to exert economic interests more strongly in dealings with Europe. Complaints about defense burden sharing, trade, and exchange rate policies became more prevalent. This increased dissatisfaction was an important factor underlying the international portions of the August 1971 New Economic Policy and Secretary Connally's "strong-arm" tactics with the Europeans in attempts to link trade, monetary, and national security issues so as to improve overall U.S. bargaining positions.[10]

Finally, issues (such as investment conflicts, nontariff barriers, and export rather than import restrictions) not covered effectively in the

---

[8] C. Fred Bergsten, "Crisis in U.S. Trade Policy," *Foreign Affairs*, vol. 49, no. 4 (July 1971), pp. 619–35. As Peter Kenen points out in his discussion below, it is also possible that real income for labor as a whole could rise from protectionism at the expense of other factors of production.

[9] See, for instance, Lawrence Krause, "How Much Current Unemployment Did We Import?" *Brookings Papers on Economic Activity*, no. 2 (1971); Larry Hays and Thomas D. Willett, "Two Economists' View of the Case for Trade Liberalization," *Columbia Journal of World Business*, Fall 1973, pp. 20–25; and Thomas D. Willett, "International Trade Theory Is Still Relevant," *Banca Nazionale del Lavoro Quarterly Review*, September 1971.

[10] See, for instance, C. Fred Bergsten, *Toward a New International Economic Order* (Lexington, Mass.: Lexington Books, 1975), chapters 25, 26.

GATT arrangements have assumed greater importance, thus complicating efforts to maintain momentum toward freer trade and keep protectionist pressures in check.

In industrial countries, this new protectionism has been labeled neomercantilism and differs from the old mercantilism in that it is not primarily engineered by a national elite to secure power rather than plenty; rather, it reflects an increase in the influence of domestic economic elements in securing policies that have important international repercussions.[11] Neomercantilism is less concerned with trade surpluses per se and more concerned with the adjustment problems and economic positions of particular groups. It is motivated more by the aggregation of a number of special interests seeking political protection than by general feelings that national prosperity and prestige require trade surpluses. Of course, interest in achieving trade or current account surpluses has far from disappeared. There are still important elements of old-style mercantilism left in the minds of both government officials and the general public in many countries, especially the LDCs, and neomercantilists still find old-style mercantilist arguments useful at times.

Still, there is much more economic sophistication today about alternative means of expanding domestic employment. Also, as rates of inflation have risen, countries have recognized the need to balance concern about inflation and unemployment through increased restraint in trying to run large trade surpluses because of the increased inflationary pressures that would result. To be sure, countries still frequently show concern about securing strong trade balances and assert the need for greater economic expansion abroad so that increased exports will increase domestic economic activity, but despite the strong adverse pressures resulting from the oil price increases and consequent deterioration in the trade positions of most countries, there are many reasons to be optimistic that the experience of the 1930s will not be repeated.

Neomercantilism today will probably continue to take the form primarily of sector-specific actions rather than the general across-the-board protectionist trade and exchange actions so widespread in the 1930s. But even apart from the danger that a series of specific protectionist measures will snowball into a general trade war, a pro-

---

[11] See, for instance, Harold B. Malmgren, "Coming Trade Wars: Neomercantilism and Foreign Policy," *Foreign Policy*, no. 1 (Winter 1970–71); and C. Fred Bergsten, Robert O. Keohane, and Joseph S. Nye, Jr., "International Economics and International Politics: A Framework for Analysis," in C. Fred Bergsten and Lawrence Krause, eds., *World Politics and International Economics* (Washington, D.C.: Brookings Institution, 1975), pp. 3–36. It should be added, however, that the old mercantilism in practice often catered to special interests as well.

liferation of such policies is a serious threat to the functioning of the international economic system.

There is a basic dilemma here. As we have become more successful in developing methods of domestic protection that minimize the danger of generating uncontrolled foreign retaliation, the propensity to adopt such solutions has likewise been increased. The proliferation of "voluntary" export restraint programs and orderly marketing agreements highlights this problem. This approach has considerable short-run political attraction in that it provides domestic relief without provoking retaliation, but such agreements generally tend to take the form of quotas, which encourage cartel-type practices abroad and which generally have substantially greater adverse effects on economic efficiency than do tariffs.[12]

To liberals who accept the view that a relatively affluent society can and should afford to take measures to help ease some of the difficulties of those facing particular economic hardships, adjustment assistance is an attractive strategy. It is clear, however, that adjustment assistance can only reduce and not eliminate this dilemma. To what extent should those who suffer from foreign competition receive more favorable treatment than those who suffer from increased competition from domestic sources? Beyond temporary compensation to reduce income losses following job losses, my impression is that retraining programs for workers and encouragement of innovation and diversification for firms have not been notably successful in general. It is important to explore possible ways to improve adjustment assistance programs; this will be one of the major topics for discussion in Part 4. But I am not optimistic that generous adjustment assistance policies will succeed in substantially reducing the pressures for protectionist measures.

The Liberal's Response to Illiberal Actions Abroad

How to respond to the illiberal policies of others presents a particular difficulty for the liberal. In general, I have found little substance to the arguments that the basic assumptions of liberal trade policies are no

---

[12] For a very useful analysis of the effects of voluntary exports restrictions, see C. Fred Bergsten, "On the Non-Equivalence of Import Quotas and Voluntary Export Restraints," in C. Fred Bergsten, ed., *Toward a New World Trade Policy* (Lexington, Mass.: Lexington Books, 1975), pp. 239–72. For references to the extensive economic literature on the effects of tariffs versus quotas, see Richard J. Sweeney, Edward Tower, and Thomas D. Willett, "The Ranking of Alternative Tariff and Quota Policies in the Presence of Domestic Monopoly," *Journal of International Economics*, vol. 7, no. 4 (1977), pp. 349–62.

longer relevant to the current world.¹³ (This of course has been a popular theme of the AFL-CIO in its attempts to justify its shift away from advocacy of liberal trade policies.) It is easy to exaggerate the extent to which the adoption of liberal trade and investment policies makes sense only if similar policies are followed abroad. But there can be little question that the adoption of illiberal policies abroad necessitates much more careful analysis of one's own trade and investment policies on grounds of both efficiency and equity. For example, considerably more analysis is needed of the key factors influencing the response of policy makers in basically competitive economies to situations in which their citizens and firms are dealing with noncompetitive buyers or sellers abroad.

The issue of competitive disadvantage has been raised most often with respect to unfair foreign competition and import policy. In what circumstances should domestic industries be protected against unfair subsidization and predatory pricing of foreign firms, and what form should this protection take? Especially difficult are the problems involved in competition from state-owned or state-controlled enterprises such as are prevalent in the steel industry, for example, and the problem of subsidization resulting from regional development policies within countries (for example, the Michelin plant in Canada). In many instances, countries can "artificially" improve their terms of trade by exploiting the potential monopoly power of the state. For example, in the great Russian grain deal of 1972, it has been argued that because of state control the Russians were able to purchase huge quantities of wheat without bidding up the price, as would normally have occurred with such large aggregate purchases by competitive buyers.

In areas of high technology, there have been numerous instances in which foreign governments, by controlling terms of transactions, have been able to play one firm off against another for access to a particular foreign market, thus improving their terms of trade at the expense

---

[13] I have specifically addressed the AFL-CIO arguments in my paper, "International Trade Theory Is Still Relevant," pp. 3–19. On the assumptions of liberal trade policies and their relevance, see also Richard N. Cooper, "Economic Assumption of the Case for Liberal Trade," in Bergsten, *Toward a New World Trade Policy*, pp. 19–32; and Lord Robbins, "The Classical Theory of Trade Policy," in his *Money, Trade, and International Relations* (London: Macmillan, 1971), pp. 187–209. Robbins points out that the classical economists wrote primarily from a national point of view, and most would have been hesitant to advocate policies that improved world welfare at the expense of their own country, but he points out that they also would have been hesitant to advocate policies that brought gains to their country at the expense of others and that "most of them would certainly have held that there was no essential contradiction between enlightened national self interest and the welfare of the world as a whole" (p. 188).

of the exporting country. In general, governments have increasingly placed conditions on the types of foreign investment allowed into their country and have placed requirements on operating procedures. Clearly, there is no prospect for outlawing such policies; they are an integral part of national sovereignty. But such policies can involve beggar-thy-neighbor practices just as much as can protectionist actions in the trade area, and they may give rise to legitimate pressures within the capital-exporting countries to take retaliatory actions.[14] The preservation of a basically liberal approach would be impossible for a country like the United States if the government intervened in every international transaction involving state regulations or state activities abroad. On the other hand, in many instances a hands-off policy would involve serious costs to the domestic economy and would stimulate strong pressures for countervailing actions.

In Part 5, discussion will focus on methods of deciding when there is sufficient provocation to make countervailing government intervention desirable, strategies for intervention, and policy strategies for preserving domestic autonomy while avoiding beggar-thy-neighbor provocations. For example, with respect to limitations on foreign investment, when do the actions of host governments have sufficiently little effect on the home countries' welfare to ignore them? It is presumed that in a competitive world market the actions of a single small country could do little to affect the terms of trade, while in the case of a high-technology item with a very limited market, the actions of a major industrial country could have a major impact on the terms of trade. But it must also be remembered that the impact of many small countries can be quite significant if they act in concert. To what extent can we rely on competition among countries to eliminate the generation of substantial "excess" profits to state activities? And to what extent can the formulation of general policies toward foreign investment by host countries instead of discretionary negotiations on a purely case-by-case basis serve to minimize the danger that "legitimate" policies designed to preserve aspects of national autonomy will be used in fact to extract beggar-thy-neighbor gains?

International Regulation

Another important challenge to the efficient operation of a liberal international economic system comes from the possible need for international regulation to control international externalities. Improvements in transportation and communication have greatly increased the degree of inter-

---

[14] See, for example, C. Fred Bergsten, "Coming Investment Wars?" *Foreign Affairs*, vol. 53, no. 1 (October 1974), pp. 135–52.

national economic interdependence in many areas. Although the effects of such increased economic interdependence are most often discussed in terms of the rapid expansion of international trade in relation to GNP for most countries, whole new issues have been generated that complicate the task of operating the international economic system on liberal principles. Advances in technology in many areas have raised major operational issues of national and international property rights with respect to our great global commons, the oceans. Pollution, overfishing, and ocean mining have all become important issues of international economic management.

Clearly, important cases of externalities and public welfare are involved here. Complete laissez faire is not a tenable solution. But analysis of the types of management policies and institutional arrangements called for can be complex. Not only is there disagreement over methods of economic management, but the nature and significance of the externalities vary considerably with different ocean uses.[15] Devising sound ocean management policies would be difficult enough even if a liberal approach were universally adopted, but failure to date to secure agreement in the Law of the Sea negotiations has stemmed more from differences in objectives than from disagreements about what policies would be most efficient.

For example, many developing countries, for greatly varying reasons, are attempting to outlaw private enterprise in the ocean-mining industry of the future. For the land-based producers of the major ocean metals—copper, nickel, cobalt, and manganese—the motive is fairly clear: limitation of future competition. But for most of the LDCs, the view that the oceans should be mined only by an international authority is hard to understand in terms of the economic well-being of their citizens. It seems highly unlikely that acceptance of the LDC proposals in this area would not result in limitations on ocean mining and increased costs greatly exceeding anything that would be justified in terms of normal principles of economic regulation. The vast majority of LDCs are net importers of these materials; yet there is considerable support for these proposals throughout the developing countries.

---

[15] See for example, Dennis E. Logue and Richard James Sweeney, *The Economics of the Law of the Sea Negotiations* (Los Angeles: International Institute for Economic Research, March 1977); Richard J. Sweeney, Robert D. Tollison, and Thomas D. Willett, "Market Failure, the Common Pool Problem, and Ocean Resource Exploitation," *Journal of Law and Economics*, vol. no. 17 (April 1974), pp. 179–92; and Robert D. Tollison and Thomas D. Willett, "Institutional Mechanisms for Dealing with International Externalities," in Ryan C. Amacher and Richard James Sweeney, eds., *The Law of the Sea: U.S. Interests and Alternatives* (Washington, D.C.: American Enterprise Institute, 1976).

PART ONE: OVERVIEW

Demands for a New International Economic Order

A considerable part of the solidarity of the LDC position appears to be the result of an antiliberal ideological perspective focused on the elevation on the "status" of the governments of the developing countries and their negotiators, even at the expense of the economic welfare of their citizens.[16] As is emphasized in the literature on bureaucratic and public choice theory, even in highly developed political structures there is substantial scope at times for government officials to follow policies that favor their own interests at the expense of the general public.[17] It is a well-known political axiom that one of the best ways to secure domestic political support is to focus on foreign affairs. For example, John Spanier has argued that, "The leaders of new states confront problems that are so vast that rather than concentrate on their domestic needs they may prefer to play a dramatic role on the international stage. (See Seymour Martin Lipset, *The First New Nation* [New York: Basic Books, 1963], p. 45.) This may, in fact, help them 'nationalize' their people. Since the only force that united the people was hatred of the former colonial power—and this 'reactive nationalism' tends to lose its force as a socially cohesive factor soon after independence—the only way of arousing the people and keeping them united is to continue the struggle against European colonialism or 'imperialism' in general. The

---

[16] Robert W. Tucker argues, for example, that "from the vantage point of the new states, the inequalities development is expected to correct are also inequalities of power and status. Indeed, they are probably *above all* inequalities of power and status. As such, the redress of inequalities in income and wealth is not only ranked lower in significance than is the redress of inequalities in power and status; the prime purpose perhaps of redressing the former inequalities is to redress the latter." *The Inequality of Nations* (New York: Basic Books, 1977), p. 106. See also Karl Brunner, "The New International Economic Order: A Chapter in Protracted Confrontation," *Orbis*, vol. 19 (1976), pp. 102ff.; and Herbert G. Grubel, "The Case against the New International Economic Order," *Weltwirtschaftliches Archiv*, vol. 2 (1977), pp. 284–307. For further discussions of the NIEO proposals, see the following studies: Jagdish N. Bhagwati, ed., *The New International Economic Order: The North-South Debate* (Cambridge: M.I.T. Press, 1977); Mahbub ul Haq, *The Poverty Curtain* (New York: Columbia University Press, 1976); Albert Fishlow, Carlos Diaz-Alejandro, Richard Fagen, and Roger D. Hanse, *Rich and Poor Nations in the World Economy* (New York: McGraw-Hill, 1978); Alasdair MacBean and V. N. Balasubramanyam, *Meeting the Third World Challenge* (New York: St. Martin's Press, 1976); Rachel McCulloch, "Economic Policy in the United Nations: A New International Economic Order?" in Special Supplement to the *Journal of Monetary Economics*, conference vol. no. 6 (1976), pp. 17–52; and W. Howard Wiggins and Gunnar Adler-Karlsson, *Reducing Global Inequities* (New York: McGraw-Hill, 1978).

[17] Thus it is frequently misleading to assume that international economic policies are always based on aggregate national economic interests. This is a major theme of the book Robert Tollison and I are preparing on "Economic Interdependence: A Public Choice Perspective."

more tenuous the bonds uniting the members of the society, the more ardent will be the campaign against the 'vestiges of imperialism.' "[18] This may explain much of the rhetoric of the governments of the developing countries against the operation of the postwar liberal international economic system and proposals for the adoption of an NIEO.

In this respect, the LDC challenge to a liberal international economic order is reminiscent of old-style mercantilism with its emphasis on national power and prestige rather than the neomercantilism prevalent in the industrial countries. To some extent, this is a normal and perhaps healthy reaction to the colonialism of the past and to the problems of creating some degree of political solidarity in newly independent states.[19]

Of course, the exaggerated rhetoric of some should not be taken as reflecting the views of all. In many quarters, there is much more substantive discussion of possible deficiencies in the operation of various aspects of the international economic system and of ways in which improvements could be made. It is certainly not a legitimate logical step to lump together all of the concerns and demands of the developing countries and dismiss the whole bundle because of the overstatements and unsound or unrealistic proposals of some.

Unfortunately, however, logical consistency is not always highly valued in the real world of public affairs. It is not surprising that the most blatantly excessive rhetoric of the developing countries is sometimes used as an excuse for dismissing all of their concerns. I fear that much of the LDC rhetoric on the NIEO proposals may have become an expensive luxury for the gratification of political and social objectives of elites in the developing countries at the expense of improvement of the economic well-being of their general population. Of course, the acceleration of LDC demands has resulted in some concessions from the industrial countries that have improved the economic well-being, but too often the concessions won have done little for those who are worst off in the developing countries. And they have resulted in increased resistance to further aid by some groups in the industrial countries.

The negotiators for the developing countries should remember that in many areas the policies and programs they seek must be approved

---

[18] *Games People Play: Analyzing International Politics* (New York: Praeger, 1972), pp. 392–93. Henry Kissinger has made a similar argument in *American Foreign Policy: Three Essays* (New York: Norton, 1969), pp. 40–42.

[19] See, for example, the discussion of defensive nationalism by Carlos F. Diaz-Alejandro, "North-South Relations: The Economic Component," in Bergsten and Krause, *World Politics and International Economics*, pp. 221–23.

ultimately by domestic legislatures in the industrial countries as well. Unfortunately, this point is often insufficiently appreciated by negotiators from the industrial countries themselves. The escalation of LDC rhetoric, both threats and demands, has played into the hands of those in the industrial countries who wish to reduce their countries' international involvement. While threats or strident rhetoric may increase one's bargaining position with international negotiators, just the opposite is likely to be the effect on a nation's legislature and the general public. At least in the United States, policies that smack of tribute may be expected to face considerable opposition and stimulate greater pressures both for reductions in foreign assistance and for illiberal actions in return. International negotiators should not forget that in the United States it has traditionally been Congress rather than the executive branch which has lowered the levels of foreign assistance programs and has been the most reluctant to grant other economic concessions to the developing countries.

At times, of course, concessions may be a rational attempt to head off an intensification of illiberal actions by others. For example, it has become fashionable in some quarters to advocate various commodity agreements as being in consumer-country interests as a means of heading off unilateral cartel actions by producer countries.[20] This approach should not be dismissed out of hand. As in the case of the voluntary export restraint policies discussed above, there are times when small illiberal steps will head off large ones. In practice, however, I am skeptical that there is much scope for such a strategy in dealing with the third world.

There is little question that the propensity and ability of third world countries to take actions that impose economic costs on the industrial countries have increased, but the magnitude of this shift in potential "bargaining" strength has often been greatly exaggerated.[21] And I am

---

[20] See, for example, C. Fred Bergsten, "The Response to the Third World," *Foreign Policy*, no. 17 (Winter 1974–75). I find more attractive the strategy of trying to trade tariff reductions, rather than commodity price floors, for assurances against supply descriptions and control pricing. See Robert M. Stern, "The Accommodation of Interests between Developed and Developing Countries," *Journal of World Trade Law*, September-October 1976, pp. 405–20. My pessimism, discussed below, about how much can be bought with concessions in this area would apply to Stern's proposal as well, however.

[21] Thus, in the exchange between Bergsten and Krasner on this issue, I found myself much more in agreement with Krasner. See C. Fred Bergsten, "The Threat from the Third World," *Foreign Policy*, no. 11 (Summer 1973), and Stephen D. Krasner, "Oil Is the Exception," *Foreign Policy*, no. 14 (Spring 1974). See also Roger D. Hansen, "The Political Economy of North-South Relations: How Much Change?" *International Organization*, vol. 29, no. 4 (Autumn 1975), pp. 921–47; and Raymond F. Mikesell, "More Third World Cartels Ahead?" *Challenge*, November-December 1974, pp. 24–31.

not very optimistic about the effectiveness of such arrangements in deterring future cartel-type actions if producers decide this is in their interest. Of course, concessions can at times produce goodwill and reduce militancy, but one cannot always count on this type of response, or on how long it will last. The scope for successful economic concessions is also limited by the extent to which the LDC policies are determined more by the political and status considerations discussed above than by direct economic interests.

Foreign Assistance and Resource Transfers

Foreign assistance programs and the extent of U.S. participation in international organizations such as the United Nations have been in serious difficulties in Congress for many years. The old arguments that foreign aid was essential to combat communism and secure world peace have worn thin, as have the initial unrealistic expectations that foreign aid would lead to results in the developing countries paralleling those of the reconstruction of Europe after World War II. The net flow of U.S. official development assistance as a percentage of GNP has fallen steadily from 0.49 percent in 1965 to 0.31 percent in 1970 to only 0.20 percent in 1975. I believe that increased militancy by the advocates of an NIEO would be more likely to contribute to a continuation than to a reversal of this trend.

Despite the considerable degree of disillusionment with foreign aid brought about by the many instances of abuse (by both industrial and developing countries) and the relatively modest success of aid flows in stimulating economic development, a continued decline in support for foreign assistance is not inevitable. To expect aid programs to close the gap between the average per capita incomes in the industrial and developing countries in the near future would not be realistic. But most liberals would not accept that the focus of North-South discussion should be primarily on income gaps and inequality per se. The liberal is likely to be much more concerned about the alleviation of individual hardship than about the general degree of inequality of income distribution.[22] I

---

[22] For recent general discussions of whether the focus of social policy should be to provide minimum levels or to focus on inequality per se, see Ryan C. Amacher, Robert D. Tollison, and Thomas D. Willett, eds., *The Economic Approach to Public Policy* (Ithaca N.Y.: Cornell University Press, 1976), Part 4; and Colin D. Campbell, ed., *Income Redistribution* (Washington, D.C.: American Enterprise Institute, 1977), Part 1. For an interesting discussion within the North-South context, see Jagdish N. Bhagwati, "Economic and World Order from the 1970s to 1990s: The Key Issues," in Jagdish N. Bhagwati, ed., *Economics and World Order* (New York: Macmillan, 1972), pp. 10–15. Bhagwati concludes on practical grounds that focusing on income gaps may be counterproductive and that at present emphasis should be placed on securing minimum standards of living.

share Gunnar Myrdal's hope that, if the case for foreign aid were made more forthrightly in humanitarian terms and if aid programs were oriented more in this direction, then public support in the industrial countries might be more forthcoming.[23] Some progress has been made in this direction in recent years. For example, in the Foreign Assistance Act of 1973, Congress directed the U.S. foreign aid program to move in this direction. I should add, however, that it is easy to overestimate the responsiveness of the general public to humanitarian appeals for aid to those beyond their own borders. As Tucker has argued, "What evidence we have points to the conclusion that the great majority persists in drawing a sharp distinction between the welfare of those who share their particular collective and the welfare of humanity, and to assume that the collective is quite entitled to what its members have created."[24] Any significant chance of reversing current trends would require a major initiative by the executive branch.

It should be stressed that humanitarian rationales for aid focus on improving the position of individuals in adverse circumstances. As has been often pointed out, many of the transfers of funds to the governments of countries with lower average incomes have done little to help

---

[23] See Gunnar Myrdal, *Against the Stream: Critical Essays on Economics* (New York: Vintage Books, 1975), pp. 44–51 and 126–32. Myrdal argues that "the discovery that aid—of the type and magnitude actually awarded—cannot be seen to have promoted democracy, peace, and development, not to speak of the false baits of gratitude and political sympathy—has tended to breed cynicism and even a biased pessimism about the development prospects of underdeveloped countries.... On the other hand ... in the few, mostly smaller, developed countries where aid has been increasing ... aid has had to be argued far more simply as motivated by human solidarity with, and compassion for, the needy. And I state my firm conviction as an economist having studied these problems, that this is the only motivation that holds, and it is this we must stress if we want to reduce the global trend toward decreasing aid to underdeveloped countries" (pp. 129–30). On the "glib" theories of relationships between democracy, economic development, and peace, see his chapter, "Politics and Economics in International Relations," pp. 167–81, and Robert W. Tucker's discussion of "Equality and Order," chapter 3 of *The Inequality of Nations*. For a useful review of the objectives of the U.S. aid programs through the mid-1960s, see Goran Ohlin, "The Evolution of United States Aid Doctrine," chapter 2 of *Foreign Aid Policies Reconsidered* (Paris: Organization for Economic Cooperation and Development, 1966); reprinted in Benjamin J. Cohen, ed., *American Foreign Economic Policy* (New York: Harper and Row, 1968). Ohlin concluded that humanitarian concerns had played a relatively minor role in U.S. aid programs.

[24] Tucker, *Inequality of Nations*, pp. 139–40. Tucker goes on, however, to point out that "The distinction does not preclude acts of humanitarian assistance taken in response to both natural and social catastrophes" (p. 140). He does argue that such assistance is seen as a "matter of grace or bounty," rather than as duty. Another cogent analysis of the various rationales for international resource transfers is given in Richard N. Cooper, "A New International Economic Order for Mutual Gain," *Foreign Policy*, 1977, pp. 66–120.

the most needy in such countries. The humanitarian rationale dictates transfers for specific purposes, not general unconditional transfers to the governments of lower-income countries. Thus, for example, general debt relief would be a very inefficient mechanism for aid on this rationale, both because, on average, higher-income LDCs would receive more of the implicit transfer than lower-income ones and because there is no assurance that the resources transferred would be used primarily for humanitarian purposes.

I do not want to enter here into a philosophical debate over whether support for humanitarian aid is a duty or a preference,[25] but I should like to record my strong agreement with Richard Cooper's argument that "The illegitimacy extending natural rights principles to nations . . . makes it difficult for those who want to claim rights to transfers [to nation states] on ethical grounds."[26] The humanitarian rational for aid may conflict with two basic tenets of the "new egalitarianism" (Robert Tucker's term) of the advocates of a new international economic order, the emphasis on the "rights" of states rather than individuals, and the principle of total noninterference in their national affairs.[27] Unfortunately, some of the most desperately needy live in countries whose own governments will do little to aid themselves or to facilitate aid from others.

Another rationale for resource transfers is the claim for compensation because of the alleged discriminatory operation of the international economic system. I personally do not find such arguments compelling in general. The notion that such biases must exist because there is considerable inequality of average incomes among countries has no logical foundation. I do not find persuasive the various arguments put forward by Raul Prebisch, Gunnar Myrdal, Hans Singer, and others that the world economy has generally operated to the disadvantage of the developing countries.[28] The various patterns of development among the

---

[25] In this connection, considerable attention has been given to the recent work by John Rawls, *A Theory of Justice* (Cambridge: Harvard University Press, 1971). For criticism and analysis of Rawls's theory, see Robert Amdur, "Rawls' Theory of Justice: Domestic and International Perspectives," *World Politics*, vol. 29, no. 3 (April 1977), pp. 438–61; James M. Buchanan, "Review of Rawls' Theory of Justice," *Public Choice*, Fall 1972; and Dennis C. Mueller, Robert D. Tollison, and Thomas D. Willett, "The Utilitarian Contract: A Generalization of Rawls' Theory of Justice," *Theory and Decision*, vol. 4, no. 3, pp. 345–69; reprinted in Amacher, Tollison, and Willett, *Economic Approach to Public Policy*.

[26] Cooper, "A New International Economic Order," p. 78.

[27] For further discussion of these issues see ibid., pp. 75–81, and Tucker, *Inequality of Nations*, pp. 154–58.

[28] A number of the major papers in this debate are conveniently collected in James D. Theberge, ed., *Economics of Trade and Development* (New York: John Wiley, 1968).

PART ONE: OVERVIEW

third world countries give little support to the Marxian view that the prosperity of the industrial countries has come at the expense of the developing countries and that the latter would have been better off with autarkic policies. Although often overlooked in debates on the NIEO, the experiences of the third world countries with respect to economic development have been far from homogeneous. A theory that the growth of the industrial countries occurred at the expense of the developing countries cannot explain these differences among the experiences of the third world countries. Indeed, many of the areas in the third world that are least developed economically are also those that have had the least contact with the industrial countries.[29]

It is quite true that at the time of the establishment of the postwar international economic system relatively little attention was paid to the developing countries. But a strong case can be made that they have been major economic beneficiaries of the system, as is extensively documented in the accompanying paper by Gottfried Haberler.[30] As was

---

[29] See, for example, P. T. Bauer, "Western Guilt and Third World Poverty," *Commentary*, vol. 61, no. 1 (January 1976), and P. T. Bauer and B. S. Yamey, "Against the New Economic Order," *Commentary*, vol. 63, no. 4 (April 1977), pp. 25–31. There is some presumption that Western prosperity would have been more likely to have occurred at LDC expense under colonialism than over the postwar period, but even for the former period the evidence of net disadvantage to the developing countries is far from strong. Undoubtedly, many instances of "exploitation" did occur, but many economic benefits were also generated. As Richard N. Cooper has recently observed; "That much poverty remains is not in question. That economic poverty exists, directly or indirectly, *because* of past colonial rule is highly doubtful" ("A New International Economic Order for Mutual Gain," p. 86). In his paper, Cooper presents a useful, brief review of some of the studies on this subject (see pp. 81–90).

[30] As Haberler points out, there has not been a persistent deterioration in the terms of trade of the developing countries. (Nor are the terms of trade a necessary indicator of changes in economic welfare and the gains from trade.) It is true that the developing countries have on average faced considerably more export variability than the industrial countries, but a number of recent studies by, for example, A. I. MacBean, Peter B. Kenen, and Constantine S. Voivodas, and Odin Knudsen and Andrew Parnes have found that on average export instability has had much less impact on economic growth rate than had generally been believed, and D. J. Mathieson and Ronald I. McKinnon have found that openness has had a stabilizing influence for developing countries. As Robert Stern points out, "The fact that openness may be associated with greater stability in LDCs means that relatively greater LDC trade with the advanced countries has not exposed the LDCs to unfavorable transmission effects arising from fluctuation in domestic economic activity in the advanced countries. The policy implication to be drawn is that LDC movements towards autarky may expose them to relatively greater instability" ("World Market Instability in Primary Commodities," *Banca Nazionale del Lavoro Quarterly Review*, June 1976, p. 9). Stern's paper gives extensive references to the literature. See also Gordon W. Smith, "Commodity Instability and Market Failure: A Survey of Issues," in F. Gerald Adams and Sonia Klein, eds., *Stabilizing World Commodity Markets* (Lexington, Mass.: Lexington Books, forthcoming), and his paper herein. It should also be noted that the industrial

pointed out by Robert McNamara at the recent annual meeting of the IMF and World Bank, "If one looks objectively at the developing world's economic record during the past quarter century, it is impressive. It surpasses the performance of the present industrial nations for any comparable period of their own development."[31]

Of course, this historically high average rate of growth has not touched all countries and individuals equally. Widespread poverty remains in many quarters of the earth, and all too often the current prospects for economic progress for the most needy are not great. Discouragingly little from the vast array of proposals for a New International Economic Order addresses specifically the problems of the most needy, however. Indeed, many of these proposals would lead to redistribution from the poorer to the more affluent within the developing countries.[32]

All of this is not to say that there are no specific market situations in which the developing countries suffer economic losses from dealings with firms from the industrial countries. Although their prevalence is frequently vastly overstated, some monopoly elements do exist, which can give rise to exploitation in the technical economic sense. And there have certainly been times when strong inequalities in information and expertise have caused representatives of the developing countries to make poor deals with firms from the industrial countries.

To the liberal, such situations call for correction on a case-by-case basis. My impression is that the small countries have made great strides in securing the expertise necessary to bargain effectively with the big companies. This of course is the liberal's preferred solution. There may be instances where further LDC government intervention is justified to counter monopoly or monopsony power, but I suspect such instances

---

countries have provided and recently substantially enlarged a special financing facility within the IMF to help reduce the balance of payments impact of LDC export instability. Indeed, Finger and Kreinin have recently suggested that the size of this facility may be above optimal size, that is, that the developing countries would be better off if some of the funds from the facility were reallocated to other forms of assistance. See Mordechai E. Kreinen and J. M. Finger, "A Critical Survey of the New International Economic Order," *Journal of World Trade Law*, vol. 10 (November/December 1976), pp. 493–512. These issues will be topics for discussion in Part 2.

[31] Robert S. McNamara, Address to the Board of Governors at the Annual Meeting of the International Monetary Fund and World Bank, Washington, D.C., September 1977; excerpted in the *Money Manager*, October 3, 1977, p. 11.

[32] Proposals for price-raising commodity agreements are a prime example. Indeed, for many commodities the major producers are developed countries. For an interesting analysis of some of the distributional aspects of the NIEO proposals, see Sidney Weintraub, "The International Economic Order: The Beneficiaries," U.S. Department of State, External Research Study, July 1977.

are now outnumbered by cases where LDC governments use their own national monopoly position in an active rather than defensive manner.[33]

In this regard, it is also important to recognize that countries are not monolithic. As Theodore Moran has pointed out, frequently "exploitation" of consumers and workers in the developing countries has resulted from collusion between domestic officials and foreign economic actors.[34] In such instances, the preferred liberal solution would be domestic political reforms.

In summary, while the charges that the market forces of international trade and investment have operated to the disadvantage of the developing countries have validity in some particular instances, the arguments that this is a general tendency that justifies a radical restructuring of the international economic system and substantial reparations from the industrial countries lack strong support.

Policy Discrimination and International Decision Making

Another strand of the arguments for a New International Economic Order asserts that the developing countries have been discriminated against by policy measures of the industrial countries and by the operation of the international economic and financial organizations. Again, however, there seems to me to be insufficient support for such assertions as a general tendency. Rather than operating systematically against the LDCs, many policies of the industrial countries and the international economic institutions have been deliberately skewed in their favor. For instance, although the LDC share of world trade has fallen somewhat over the past decade, their share in IMF quotas has been raised significantly, not to mention the special financing facilities that have been created for the LDCs. Before the most recent quota revisions, the less developed countries had a 26.7 percent share of quotas, roughly 50 percent greater than the 17.4 percent share which would be given by

---

[33] There is of course a voluminous literature on the costs and benefits of direct investment and multinational corporations. A sometimes overlooked factor in such discussions is that the willingness of the industrial countries to credit taxes paid abroad provides a substantial fiscal transfer to the developing countries which tilts the distribution of mutual gains in their direction and would tend to offset specific cases of negative economic effects due to externalities and noncompetitive situations. See, for example, Grubel, "Against the New International Economic Order," pp. 295–97; and Thomas D. Willett, "The International Firm and Efficient Economic Allocation: Discussion," *American Economic Review*, May 1970, pp. 449–50.

[34] Theodore H. Moran, "The Theory of International Exploitation in Large Natural Resource Investments," in Steven J. Rosen and James R. Kurth, eds., *Testing Theories of Economic Imperialism* (Lexington, Mass.: Lexington Books, 1974).

application of the original Bretton Woods formula. By contrast, the U.S. share was actually 23.3 percent, in comparison with a 28.4 percent share implied by the Bretton Woods formula. The most recent revision continues this trend. Likewise, when applying capital controls, the industrial countries have frequently adopted special provisions to lessen the impact on developing countries.

Representatives of the developing countries have argued that they have been disadvantaged by the move from pegged to floating exchange rates among the industrial countries, but such arguments have frequently tended to compare an idealized fixed-rate world, which would operate without deflationary policies and controls, with the real-world operation of flexible exchange rates. In practice, I believe that the substantial majority of developing countries have benefited on balance from the adoption of more flexible exchange rates among the industrial countries.[35]

There are important areas, however, where the policies of the industrial countries have imposed costs on the developing countries. Immigration policy is a prime example.[36] And in the trade area, the structure of protection in most industrial countries is biased against the developing countries, in the sense that there is generally higher effective protection on processing and manufacturing than on raw material imports. It is also true that the developing countries did not participate to a great degree in the Kennedy Round of tariff negotiations. The result, not surprisingly, was that tariff reductions were biased toward making the largest cuts in those areas in which the industrial countries had the greatest mutual interest. Although the industrial countries have adopted special tariff preferences for the developing countries, offsetting policy changes have resulted in much less net liberalization.[37] But while the reductions made by many of the industrial countries were biased toward themselves, the developing countries, on average, were not making any reductions at all.

---

[35] For discussion of the impact of reform of the exchange rate system on the developing countries, see William Cline, *Flexible Exchange-Rates and the Developing Countries* (Washington, D.C.: Brookings Institution, 1975); and Diaz-Alejandro, "North-South Relations," pp. 235–37. Additional references are given in Willett, *Floating Exchange Rates*, p. 31.

[36] For discussions of immigration policy and the brain drain, see Walter Adams, ed., *The Brain Drain* (New York: Macmillan, 1968); Jagdish N. Bhagwati and Martin Partington, eds., *Taxing the Brain Drain* (Amsterdam: North-Holland, 1976); Jagdish N. Bhagwati, ed., *The Brain Drain and Taxation* (Amsterdam: North-Holland, 1976); and Diaz-Alejandro, "North-South Relations," pp. 218–20. Bhagwati makes a strong case that compensation should be paid to developing countries from which skilled labor and professionals emigrate.

[37] For a useful review of the studies in this area, see Kreinin and Finger, "New International Economic Order."

PART ONE: OVERVIEW

Over the postwar period as a whole, there has been a substantial reduction in the level of industrial-country import barriers to the exports of developing countries, which has not, on average, been matched by a reduction in the levels of import barriers existing in developing countries. Thus, in a world in which there are still widespread trade barriers, there is some ambiguity in judging whether the developing countries have been treated unfairly in the trade area. To the liberal, of course, even "fairly" balanced trade barriers are usually objectionable. The case for reducing the trade barriers facing developing countries' exports need not rest on arguments about discriminatory policies.

There are definitely areas in which, on liberal economic principles, policy changes are needed that would benefit the developing countries (and benefit many industrial countries as well). And there may be particular cases where a strong case for compensation can be made. But I do not find persuasive the argument that the developing countries have been systematically discriminated against and disadvantaged by the policies of the industrial countries and international economic organizations so that generalized compensation should be paid.

Although I would conclude that the developing countries have not been seriously adversely affected by lack of representation in international economic organizations, I must note that there are difficult points at issue concerning the weight of representation the developing nations "should" receive in such organizations. Mahbub ul Haq has argued:

> The basic objective of the emerging trade union of the poor nations is to negotiate a new deal with the rich nations through the instrument of collective bargaining. The essence of this new deal lies in the objective of the developing countries to obtain greater equality of opportunity and to secure the right to sit as equals around the bargaining tables of the world.[38]

The developing countries have consistently favored one nation–one vote rules, which give them a substantial majority of votes, as opposed to the weighted voting schemes based on various economic variables such as are used by the IMF. As noted above, a substantial redistribution of voting weights within the IMF has given the developing countries a voting share that is disproportionate in terms of the traditional

---

[38] Mahbub ul Haq, "Negotiating a New Bargain with the Rich Countries," in Guy F. Erb and Valeriana Kollab, eds., *Beyond Dependency: The Developing World Speaks Out* (Washington, D.C.: Overseas Development Council, 1975), p. 158.

IMF formulas. However, the developing countries are of course still tremendously underrepresented in terms of number of nations or population. The one nation–one vote criterion does have considerable appeal from the standpoint of traditional democratic theory, but recent work in the theory of public choice has emphasized that there are desirable normative aspects to weighted voting schemes.[39] As a normative issue, there are many complicated aspects to the question of how much voting power the developing countries should have and how this should perhaps vary for different questions. For example, on questions of income redistribution, should the prospective recipients receive full votes? And on allocative decisions, where the strength of "interest" varies from one area to another, it can be argued that voting strengths should vary correspondingly. The really difficult issue, of course, would be measuring the strength of interests.

Turning to positive analysis, I see considerable danger to the effectiveness of international organization from the one nation–one vote rule. Problems of the tyranny of the majority are well known in democratic theory, and in the international context those who view themselves as being tyrannized rightly or wrongly have greater options to withdraw from the process than in domestic politics. It is quite possible that the developing countries could attempt to push too far, thereby substantially reducing the extent to which the industrial countries are willing to operate through broadly based international organizations as opposed to various formal and informal "rich men's clubs." With respect to a large number of international economic issues, attempts to define equality of bargaining status as one nation–one vote could well end in reducing rather than increasing the effective representation of the developing countries. The Law of the Sea negotiations are a case in point.

A major issue concerns the possibility of meeting the developing countries' desires for a greater voice in international economic negotiations while preserving the effectiveness of our major international economic organizations. It may be that the proliferation of special-purpose conferences and organizations, though an administrative nightmare, is the most promising way of reconciling these two potentially conflicting objectives.

---

[39] See, for example, Dennis C. Mueller, "Fiscal Federalism in a Constitutional Democracy," *Public Policy*, Fall 1971, pp. 567–93, and "Constitutional Democracy and Social Welfare," *Quarterly Journal of Economics*, February 1973; and Dennis C. Mueller, Robert D. Tollison, and Thomas D. Willett, "Solving the Intensity Problem in Representative Democracy," in Amacher, Tollison, and Willett, *Economic Approach to Public Policy*, pp. 444–73. For a discussion of these issues in an international context, see Tollison and Willett, "Institutional Mechanisms," pp. 82–84.

PART ONE: OVERVIEW

Concluding Comments

In this paper I have briefly commented on what I see as some of the major challenges facing the operation of a liberal international economic order. As noted earlier, I have not attempted a comprehensive analysis of the challenges enumerated, nor have I covered all significant challenges facing the international economic system.[40] It is hoped, however, that these introductory comments will help to provoke discussion both of their nature and seriousness and of ways of responding to them.

---

[40] I might note in particular the omission of the problems raised by stagflation. This topic is treated in Gottfried Haberler's paper herein.

The Liberal International Economic Order in Historical Perspective

Gottfried Haberler

By liberal economic order we mean the order of the market or capitalist economy, of the modern mixed variety, relying predominantly on private enterprise and competition (in the broad sense that producers compete for consumers' dollars), although there may exist monopolies, oligopolies, or government enterprises in some areas. The liberal order does not imply a policy of strict noninterference on the part of government.

More specifically, the liberal *international* economic order is the largely American-inspired post–World War II system of freer trade, of low, nondiscriminatory tariffs (most-favored-nation clause and absence of quantitative restrictions), and of currencies freely convertible into each other in the exchange market at either fixed or variable exchange rates (absence of exchange control)—the system symbolized and institutionalized by the GATT and the IMF.

This liberal order is being challenged from different sides. It is being frontally attacked by Socialist and Communist parties and other advocates of comprehensive central planning inside Western countries, and it is being challenged from the outside by the Communist (centrally planned) economies—the latter attack is, however, not the subject of this conference. The main theme is not the East-West but the North-South problem (or better, the temperate zone–tropics problem). Some of the problems posed for the market economies by the existence of centrally planned economies will be discussed in Part 5.

We are concerned with the challenges to the existing liberal international order in the West, both in the industrially developed countries (DCs) and in the developing or less developed countries.

In the DCs, after a period of very successful liberalization of trade and payments under the auspices of the GATT and IMF, the liberal international order is facing increasingly serious challenges. In recent years, largely as a consequence of high unemployment during the recession of 1973–1975 and the subsequent sluggish recovery, protectionist

---

Note: A shorter version of this paper appeared in the *Zeitschrift für Nationalökonomie* (Vienna), vol. 38 (1978), pp. 145–160.

PART ONE: OVERVIEW

pressures have become very strong in practically all industrial countries. Higher import duties and quantitative import restrictions (quotas) are being demanded with increasing urgency and granted in many cases. New nontariff methods of import restrictions, such as the so-called voluntary restraints that importing countries put on foreign exports (also called "orderly market agreements," OMAs), are being applied with increasing frequency. Continuing a tradition of favoring substitution of cartels for import duties, the French government recently made proposals for "organized free trade." These and other protectionist tendencies in the DCs will be taken up in subsequent papers.

A more serious and more far-reaching challenge to the liberal order comes from the LDCs' increasingly urgent demands for a New International Economic Order. These demands have led to a continuing North-South dialogue and at times to confrontation, played out in a succession of international conferences.

This challenge to the liberal order is based on the assertion that the existing LIEO has not performed well, or at any rate is no longer performing well, especially with respect to the LDCs. The first task is therefore to try to form a judgment about the performance of the market or capitalist system and its alleged shortcomings.

Performance and Alleged Shortcomings of the Liberal Order

From the Nineteenth Century to World War I. There is fairly general agreement that in the nineteenth century the liberal order performed extremely well, especially as far as the now-developed countries are concerned, all of which were less developed early in the nineteenth century. The most glowing description of the productive achievements of capitalism in the nineteenth century has been given by Karl Marx himself in the *Communist Manifesto*.[1]

---

[1] First German edition, 1847; authorized English translation with a preface and comments by Friedrich Engels, London, 1888. Following are a few samples of Marx's description of the productive achievements of capitalism, of "the bourgeoisie," as Marx called it in the *Manifesto*: "It [the bourgeoisie] has been the first to show what man's activity can bring about. It has accomplished wonders far surpassing the Egyptian pyramids, Roman aqueducts, and Gothic cathedrals; it has conducted expeditions that put in the shade all former migrations of nations and crusades. . . . All old-established national industries have been or are daily being destroyed. They are dislodged by new industries, whose introduction becomes a life and death question for all civilized nations, by industries that no longer work up indigenous raw materials, but raw material drawn from the remotest zones; industries whose products are consumed, not only at home, but in every quarter of the globe. . . . The bourgeoisie, by the rapid improvement of all instruments of production, by the immensely facilitated means of communication, draws all nations, even the most barbarian, into civilisation. The cheap prices

The work of modern economists and economic historians analyzing and measuring the operation and results of the liberal economic order in the nineteenth century has fully confirmed Marx's judgment. Let me mention only two names. On the theoretical side, Joseph A. Schumpeter has given a classic analysis of the process of capitalist economic development, stressing the innovational role of the private entrepreneur.[2] Modern economists have become used to defining and measuring the performance of an economy or an economic system in terms of economic growth, that is, growth of aggregate output or, better, output per capita of goods and services (GNP).[3] Simon Kuznets in several impressive volumes has summarized and synthesized the enormous amount of work that he and others (many under his guidance or inspiration) have done to quantify the growth of total product and per capita product (as well as many structural characteristics) of all the major economies from the early nineteenth century up to the present period.[4]

Kuznets's figures clearly show the high and sustained rates of growth in the now-developed countries after "the beginning of modern growth," in other words, after the liberal, capitalist order had taken hold. Accord-

---

of its commodities are the heavy artillery with which it batters down all Chinese walls, with which it forces the barbarians' intensely obstinate hatred of foreigners to capitulate. It compels all nations, on pain of extinction, to adopt the bourgeois mode of production, it compels them to introduce what it calls civilisation into their midst, i.e. to become bourgeois themselves. In a word, it creates a world after its own image. . . . The bourgeoisie, during its rule of scarce one hundred years, has created more massive and more colossal productive forces than have all the preceding generations together. Subjection of nature's forces to man, machinery, application of chemistry to industry and agriculture, steam navigation, railways, electric telegraphs, clearing of whole continents for cultivation, canalisation of rivers, whole populations conjured out of the ground—what earlier century had even a presentiment that such productive forces slumbered in the lap of social labor?"

[2] See Joseph A. Schumpeter, *The Theory of Economic Development: An Inquiry into Profits, Capital, Credit, Interest, and the Business Cycle* (1912), trans. Redvers Opie (Cambridge: Harvard University Press, 1934); *Business Cycles: A Theoretical, Historical, and Statistical Analysis of the Capitalist Process*, 2 vols. (New York: McGraw-Hill, 1939).

[3] In this paper I accept GNP per capita as a measure of economic performance and do not discuss the questions of long-term "cost of growth," of pollution in the broad sense of deterioration of the environment, of the alleged eventual limits to growth, let alone the doomsday prophecies of the Club of Rome and other doomsayers. I have expressed my views on these problems elsewhere. See Gottfried Haberler, "Disenchantment with Growth," in *Economic Growth and Stability: An Analysis of Economic Change and Policies* (Los Angeles: 1974), pp. 30–37, 199–204.

[4] See especially Simon Kuznets, *Modern Economic Growth: Rate, Structure, and Spread* (New Haven: Yale University Press, 1966), and *Economic Growth of Nations: Total Output and Production Structure* (Cambridge: Harvard University Press, 1971).

ing to Kuznets, the date of entry into modern economic growth was roughly the end of the eighteenth century in Great Britain, the 1830s in France and the United States, the 1850s in Germany, the 1860s in the Scandinavian countries, and so on.

Marx, of course, was not an ardent supporter of capitalism, although he gave the devil his due. An integral part of his vision was the theory of "increasing misery" of the working classes, of the proletariat (*Verelendungstheorie*).[5] But the polarization of society through the increasing misery of the working classes that Marx had forecast did not materialize. Because it really makes no sense now to say that the American, the European, the Japanese, or even the Brazilian or Mexican workers are getting poorer all the time, either in absolute terms or relative to other classes, modern Marxists have given up applying the theory of increasing misery to developed countries. But it has survived and flourishes in the international sphere. Thus, the past master of American Marxism, Paul Sweezy, concedes that in the developed countries workers have a "tolerable if degraded life" but that the advanced countries "increasingly impose the burdens on the people of the colonies and the raw material producing countries."[6]

In the Marxian scheme, this exploitation of the raw material-producing countries, what we now call the LDCs, by the developed industrial countries is the consequence of colonialism. But the theory of exploitation has survived the demise of colonialism. It now comes in the form of the Prebisch-Singer theory, which asserts that there is a secular tendency of the terms of trade to move against the LDCs.[7] In an extreme form, this theory has been put forward by Gunnar Myrdal. He asserts that "trade operates (as a rule) with a fundamental bias in favor of the rich and progressive regions (and countries) and in disfavor of the less developed countries." His thesis is not only that the

---

[5] This theory was essential for Marx's thesis of the inevitable overthrow of the capitalist system. Actually, contrary to Marx's theory, the Communist revolution came first in a backward country, Russia, not in a mature capitalist country.

[6] Paul Sweezy, "Marxism: A Talk of Students," *Monthly Review*, October 1936. Actually, the theory that capitalism can survive only as long as there exist "noncapitalist spaces" to exploit goes back to Rosa Luxemburg's theory of imperialism. See Rosa Luxemburg, *The Accumulation of Capital* (1913), translated from the German with an introduction by Joan Robinson (New Haven: Yale University Press, 1951).

[7] This theory can be called a theory of exploitation because it attributes the adverse change in the terms of trade largely to DC protectionist policies (tariff escalation) and to monopolistic price setting by large firms, national and multinational, as well as by labor monopolies (unions) in the DCs. As a result of these anticompetitive policies, the LDCs are hampered in their drive for industrialization, and the benefits of technological advance are largely kept by the DCs for themselves instead of being passed on to the LDCs.

poor derive less benefit from trade than the rich but that the poor as a rule become poorer if and because the rich get richer.[8]

The secular tendency of the terms of trade to deteriorate for the LDCs has remained an article of faith for the supporters of the NIEO. I shall return to this subject below. At this point I want only to indicate the historical roots of the theory.

From World War I to World War II. The period between the two world wars bears the scars of those wars and of the Great Depression of the 1930s. However, reparation of physical war damage, rebuilding of destroyed capital equipment and buildings, replenishment of inventories, and reopening of disrupted channels of communication, transport, and trade between the warring countries were achieved amazingly quick, much faster than most people, including many economists, had expected. This was true not only after the First World War but also after the second, which was much more destructive than the first. But the speed of reconstruction would not have surprised the classical economists. Alfred Marshall wrote: "Ideas whether those of art and science or those embodied in practical appliances are the most 'real' of the gifts that each generation received from its predecessors. The world's material wealth would quickly be replaced if it were destroyed but the ideas by which it was made were retained."[9]

The Great Depression of the 1930s was a major disaster. It was a case of disintegration of the world economy. Under the combined influence of high unemployment, steep decline in output, and a protectionist explosion (high tariffs, quotas, and exchange control), world trade shrank by about two-thirds in nominal terms (dollars) and one-third in real terms. As always in depressions and recessions, prices of primary products fell much more sharply than prices of manufactured goods, turning the terms of trade violently against the LDCs.

In the 1930s, the economic nature and causes of the Great Depression were widely misunderstood. For Marxists, the catastrophic slump was confirmation of the master's theory that under capitalism depressions were bound to become more and more severe until the capitalist system came crashing down in a final big bang. But many non-Marxist economists, too, put forward explanations that did not hold out much hope for the survival of the liberal market economy—for example, the

---

[8] Gunnar Myrdal, *Development and Underdevelopment*, Fiftieth Anniversary Commemoration Lecture (Cairo: National Bank of Egypt, 1956).

[9] Alfred Marshall, *Principles of Economics*, 5th ed. (London, Macmillan, 1907), p. 780. See also a similar statement by John Stuart Mill, *Principles of Political Economy*, 1. 5. 7.

PART ONE: OVERVIEW

widely held Keynesian theory of secular stagnation due to a lack of investment opportunities and chronic oversaving.[10]

From the present vantage point, the explanation of the exceptional virulence of the Great Depression is much simpler. Whatever the forces, monetary or nonmonetary, that caused the downturn of the cycle in the summer of 1929 (well before the crash on the New York Stock Exchange), the depression would never have become so severe if there had not been a sharp contraction—destruction—of money. One need not be an extreme monetarist to recognize that a reduction in the money supply of about 30 percent, as happened in the United States, was bound to depress the economy or, if it was already sliding, to push it down into the abyss. (Today many economists are scared stiff when the money supply fails to rise for a couple of months.) The monetary contraction, in turn, was due to institutional weaknesses (collapse of the American banking system) and horrendous mistakes of monetary and fiscal policy, mistakes of commission (outright deflationary moves) as well as omission (failure sufficiently to counteract the deflation by monetary expansion).

Furthermore, one need not be an enthusiastic advocate of floating exchange rates to realize that under fixed exchanges (gold standard) a severe depression in the world's leading economy was bound to spread to all other countries that pegged their currencies to the dollar and to gold, with special intensity to the raw material–exporting countries, the LDCs. However, the United States was not the only sinner. Similar mistakes, deflationary policies or failure to counteract deflation, were made in other leading countries, notably in France and Germany. And the international currency system of fixed exchanges, the gold standard under which exchange rates were rigidly fixed and could be changed only spasmodically in extremis, was calculated to maximize the pains of adjustment.[11]

The upshot is that these institutional defects and horrendous policy mistakes on the national and international level had nothing to do with basic weaknesses or internal contradictions of the liberal market system, and nothing to do with a tendency toward secular stagnation, lack of

---

[10] For further discussion of these and other explanations of the extraordinary severity of the Great Depression that were popular in the 1930s, see my essay, *The World Economy: Money and the Great Depression, 1919–1939* (Washington, D.C.: American Enterprise Institute, 1976).

[11] For details, see ibid. The statement that under the exceedingly unfavorable circumstances of the 1930s—a severe depression in the leading economic country—the gold standard operated to spread the depression around the globe does not imply and is not meant to imply that the gold standard did not work satisfactorily under more favorable circumstances.

TABLE 1

PERCENTAGE DECLINE IN U.S. DEPRESSIONS AND RECESSIONS

	Jan. 1920–July 1921	Aug. 1929–Mar. 1933	Nov. 1973–Mar. 1975
Industrial production	− 32.4	− 53.4	− 14.0
GNP in constant dollars	n.a.	− 32.6	− 6.6

investment opportunities, chronic oversaving, or a propensity of the market economy to develop gigantic real maladjustments.

Proof of all this is that in country after country, as soon as monetary deflation was stopped by orthodox, liberal methods (monetary-fiscal expansion combined with devaluation or floating of the currency) or by unorthodox, illiberal methods (monetary fiscal expansion combined with exchange control as in Nazi Germany), the depression lifted, output and employment quickly expanded, and the alleged real structural contradictions and weaknesses, lack of investment opportunities, and maladjustments disappeared as quickly as they seemed to have appeared a few years earlier.

Further proof is that after World War II, when the deflationary mistakes of the 1930s were avoided, there was no postwar depression despite the much greater destruction of the second war. There were mild recessions, inflation, and later stagflation but no depression comparable to the so-called first and second depressions after World War I. The figures in Table 1 show that even the last, most severe recession of 1973–1975 was a far cry from the severe interwar depressions. The 1973–1975 recession, stagflation, and the sluggish recovery since 1975 will be more fully discussed below.

The Post–World War II Period. There is virtually general agreement that the first twenty-five or thirty years after World War II were a period of unprecedented growth and prosperity. Compared with the interwar period, the entire postwar period, including the last recession and the somewhat sluggish recovery, must be judged a great success, although the unusual coexistence of inflation and unemployment—stagflation—that developed in the early 1970s should cause anxiety for the future.[12]

---

[12] Stagflation on the recent scale is a new phenomenon. There have been periods of stagflation earlier but not of the same magnitude and duration as in the 1970s. See below.

PART ONE: OVERVIEW

World trade grew by leaps and bounds, although it declined slightly during the last recession.

As far as the DCs are concerned, these statements will hardly be questioned. Even in West Germany, the industrial country hardest hit by the Great Depression, war destruction, and immediate postwar dislocations (dismemberment, 10 million refugees from the East), real GNP per capita passed the highest prewar level in the middle 1950s and has since soared to the fifth or sixth highest level in the world, surpassed only by the United States, Switzerland, Sweden, Kuwait, and the United Arab Emirates.

There is a striking contrast between Germany, where liberal policies —the policy of the so-called social market economy (*Soziale Marktwirtschaft*)—have been pursued, and Britain, with its socialist policies. According to World Bank statistics, in 1975 German GNP per capita was almost twice that of the British (US$6,670 against US$3,780),[13] while before the war British per capita GNP was much greater than the German.

To what extent did the LDCs participate in the extraordinary prosperity and growth of the world economy since the war? The first thing to stress is the enormous differences that exist with respect to wealth, income, and other characteristics of development among the countries constituting the third world. The LDCs are a much more heterogeneous group than the DCs. Apart from the superrich oil countries, there are the middle-income countries such as Argentina, Brazil, Mexico, and Taiwan and, at the other end of the spectrum, the very poor countries of the fourth world. The third world is a hierarchy of countries ranging from the very poor and backward to the fairly rich and progressive, those on the verge of entering the club of the developed industrial countries.

In fact, the world as a whole, developed and less developed, is a hierarchy of countries ranging from the richest with the highest per capita GNP (United Arab Emirates and Kuwait, followed by Switzerland, Sweden, and the United States) to the very poor. There is no clear-cut gap separating two distinct, more or less homogeneous groups.

---

[13] See *World Bank Atlas: Population, per Capita Product, and Growth Rates* (Washington, D.C.: World Bank, 1977), p. 7. World Bank figures exaggerate the contrast because they are based on unadjusted or slightly adjusted exchange rates. But there can be no doubt that the contrast would remain substantial, even if detailed adjustments of local currency estimates for purchasing power parity were made. On the problems and results of such adjustments, see the elaborate study by Irving B. Kravis, Zoltan Kennessey, Alan Heston, and Robert Summers, *A System of International Comparisons of Gross Products and Purchasing Power* (Baltimore: Johns Hopkins University Press for the World Bank, 1975).

Thus the classification of countries into DCs and LDCs is essentially an arbitrary one.[14]

It also follows that the concept of a unique, allegedly widening gap between the DCs as a group and the LDCs as a group is wholly arbitrary and devoid of any useful meaning. There are of course any number of gaps between individual countries, DCs as well as LDCs. Some of these gaps are widening, others shrinking, still others reversing themselves (as, for example, the gap between Britain and Germany mentioned above). But there is no single, unique gap between DCs and LDCs in general.

The *World Bank Atlas* lists many LDCs with very high growth rates of GNP per capita for two periods, 1960–1974 and 1965–1974, in many cases higher in the second period than in the first. Among the high-growth countries are South Korea, Taiwan and Malaysia, Brazil and Colombia, Greece and Portugal (before the revolution), Rhodesia and Malawi, not to mention Hong Kong and Singapore. It is hardly by chance that these are the countries that have pursued relatively liberal, that is, market-oriented, policies, both domestically and in foreign trade.[15]

Simon Kuznets in his magisterial lecture, "Two Centuries of Economic Growth: Reflections on U.S. Experience," summed up the results of the enormous amount of research done in recent years:

> Even in this recent twenty-five year period of greater strain and danger, the growth in peace-time product per capita in the United States was still at a high rate; and in the rest of the world, developed *and less developed* (but excepting the few countries and periods marked by internal conflicts and political breakdown), material returns have grown, per capita, at a rate higher than ever observed in the past.[16]

In his paper, "Aspects of Post–World War II Growth in Less Developed Countries," Kuznets had this to say: "For the LDCs as a

---

[14] GNP figures, aggregate as well as per capita, along with growth rates of population and per capita real GNP for literally all countries in the world (including, for example, Albania, Mongolia, and the Maldive Islands), can be found in the *World Bank Atlas*.

[15] On this point, see the paper by I. M. D. Little below, in Part 4.

[16] Richard T. Ely Lecture, *American Economic Review*, vol. 67 (February 1977), p. 14 (emphasis added). Kuznets's findings about growth in the LDCs are reported at some length in *Economic Growth of Nations*, chapter 1; and in "Aspects of Post–World War II Growth in Less Developed Countries," in *Evolution, Welfare, and Time in Economics: Essays in Honor of Nicholas Georgescu-Roegen*, A. M. Tang, E. M. Westfield, and James E. Worley, eds. (Lexington, Mass.: Lexington Books, 1976), chapter 3.

group, the United Nations has estimated annual growth rates of total and per capita GDP (gross domestic product at constant factor prices) from 1950 to 1972. The growth rates of per capita product . . . for the twenty-two years was 2.61 percent per year. . . . Such growth rates are quite high in the long-term historical perspective of both the LDCs and the current DCs." These high growth rates are largely a recent phenomenon, the result of the post–World War II period of comparative liberalism and liberalization. "While the historical data for LDCs rarely provide a firm basis for judging their long-term growth," it can be established indirectly that in earlier periods the growth rates must have been lower: for applying the recent growth rates to earlier periods "would have meant impossibly low levels of per capita product and consumption at the beginning of the preceding quarter of a century." Kuznets further points out that for the current DCs for which we have long-term growth rates "the observed rates (for well over half a century of their modern growth) are generally well below those cited for the LDCs."[17]

Kuznets is, of course, fully aware of the danger of using broad aggregate measures of growth for the LDCs as a group, given the great diversity among the countries in the third world. He discusses and carefully evaluates possible biases in the procedures. But after everything has been said and done, he stands by the basic soundness of his findings and is puzzled that, despite the "impressively high" growth rates "in the per capita product of LDCs over almost a quarter of a century," the general sentiment in the LDCs is one of dissatisfaction and gloom that "seems to ignore the growth achievements." He conjectures, and gives ample reasons for this conjecture, that "a rise in expectations has produced a negative reaction to economic attainments which otherwise might have elicited litanies of praise for economic miracles."[18]

Three factors have aroused excessively optimistic expectations. The apparent early economic successes of Soviet Russia—rapid industrialization and growth and immunity from the depression that engulfed the West in the 1930s—made a deep impression in the LDCs as well as in the DCs. It engendered the belief that governments have it in their power by comprehensive central planning to lift backward countries, in one great leap, to a higher level of development. It took a long time for the persistent conspicuous lag of the centrally planned countries behind the

---

[17] Kuznets, "Aspects of Post–World War II Growth," pp. 40–41. From 1960 to 1972 the average growth rate of per capita GNP of some sixty-seven LDCs with over 1 million population each, and omitting major oil exporters, was 2.6 per year (p. 42).

[18] Ibid., p. 41 and passim.

market economies to shake confidence in the superiority of central planning. This issue cannot be further discussed here. I confine myself to asking a simple question: How is one to explain the glaring gap in the per capita GNP and standard of living between such pairs of countries as East and West Germany, Austria and Czechoslovakia, Yugoslavia and Greece—pairs of countries that enjoyed about the same standard of living in the pre-Communist period?[19]

Two later events have fostered unrealistic, overoptimistic expectations: the success of the Marshall Plan to speed up European recovery after the war and the effectiveness of the oil cartel. Unfortunately, the task of developing backward countries is much more difficult than those two successes suggest. It is one thing to use foreign aid to help a developed country that has been thrown back by a destructive war to replenish its capital stock and so to get back on its customary living standard; it is a much more time-consuming and difficult task to help less developed countries to introduce far-reaching reforms, develop a suitable infrastructure, and adopt habits of work and policies conducive to modern economic growth. As regards the success of OPEC, there are few, if any, important raw materials that offer the same chances for effective cartelization as does crude oil; and if there were such opportunities, mutual monopolistic exploitation would not be an effective way to speed up the growth of LDCs as a group.

The conclusion that the LDCs as a group had an impressive growth performance in the post–World War II period does not, of course, change the fact that many of them are very poor. Almost all of them entered the stage of modern economic growth with a much lower level of per capita GNP than the current DCs did a century or so ago (with the exception of Japan, which also started from a very low level). Therefore, the gap between LDCs and DCs, however this essentially ambiguous and arbitrary concept is defined, has not appreciably declined and will not disappear in the foreseeable future, even if the growth of the LDCs as a group continues to exceed that of the DCs. But the very respectable growth performance does show that, contrary to what is often said, the liberal international economic order does not prevent the LDCs from showing impressive progress and that, again contrary to widely held views, prosperity and growth in the DCs do spread to the LDCs.

Furthermore, satisfactory overall growth does not change the fact that the internal income distribution in most or many LDCs is widely

---

[19] The comparative performance of different economic regimes can be profitably studied in other pairs of countries with roughly similar resource endowments and at a similar stage of economic development: North Korea and South Korea, Sri Lanka and Taiwan, Burma and Malaysia.

regarded as unsatisfactory. It is well known that the contrast between rich and poor, in particular, is much greater in most LDCs than in DCs. This clearly is the consequence of internal social and economic structure, resource endowment, institutions and policies; it has nothing to do with the international economic order. If, however, a liberal international economic order improves the overall situation and growth performance of the LDCs, that should make it easier for them to pursue policies and adopt measures of structural reform to alleviate poverty and reduce the inequality of income distribution.[20]

The Terms of Trade and the Growth of LDC Trade

As mentioned earlier, the critics of the liberal international economic order accept the Prebisch-Singer theory of the secular tendency of the terms of trade to deteriorate for the LDCs. They rightly regard this deterioration as essential for their case because without it they could hardly uphold the thesis of the failure of prosperity and growth in the DCs to spread to the LDCs. In other words, a failure of DC growth to benefit the LDCs would have to reveal itself in a change in the terms of trade against the LDCs.

It is hardly necessary to discuss why there is a strong presumption that DC growth will spread to the LDCs. For classical as well as Keynesian economics, in rare harmony, teach that the demand of the DCs for the exports of the LDCs will strengthen when the DCs' GNP grows—in other words, the marginal propensity to import is positive (barring the most unlikely case that DC imports largely consist of inferior goods, the Giffen case). It is, of course, possible and it often happens that progress in DCs may reduce demand for *particular* imports from LDCs: synthetics take the place of natural materials, rayon replaces silk, nylon substitutes for jute, and synthetic rubber reduces the demand for natural rubber. Such cases have been often cited to help explain the alleged secular change in the terms of trade against the LDCs.[21] Individual industries may suffer from technological discoveries and changes, but not a single case comes to mind where a whole country has come to grief for that reason. It would have to show, at any rate, in a change in the terms of trade.

---

[20] On the problem of income distribution and growth, see Hollis Chenery and others, *Redistribution with Growth* (London: Oxford University Press for the World Bank, 1974).

[21] Exactly the same type of arguments were used in the 1940s and 1950s by well-known economists, especially in Britain, to establish the case of the permanent dollar shortage.

What, then, are the facts about the alleged tendency for the terms of trade to change against the LDCs or for prices of primary products to fall in relation to manufactured goods?[22] Fortunately, a definitive answer can be given, for this is one of the most thoroughly analyzed and researched areas in international economics. There has been no long-term trend for or against the LDCs. There have been and there still are cyclical fluctuations, in the past at times violent and destructive. Prices of primary products typically exhibit more pronounced swings in the business cycle than prices of manufactured products, and the terms of trade of individual countries, of DCs as well as LDCs, are occasionally subject to change for special reasons unrelated to the business cycle. But no long trend in the terms of trade for broad groups of countries, DCs or LDCs, or of primary against manufactured products has been established.

The most thorough statistical analysis of price trends in international trade can be found in Robert E. Lipsey's important book, *Price and Quantity Trends in the Foreign Trade of the United States*.[23] This study, carried out with the careful attention to basic data and statistical methods that one expects in a National Bureau publication, reaches the following conclusions:

> Two widely held beliefs regarding net barter terms of trade found no confirmation in the data for the United States. One is that there has been a substantial long-term improvement in the terms of trade of developed countries, including the United States; the other, that there has been a significant long-term deterioration in the terms of trade of primary as com-

---

[22] There exists—or existed—a school of thought that teaches the exact opposite of the Prebisch-Singer thesis. British economists especially have been very concerned that the terms of trade must turn against the industrial countries because of the operation of the law of diminishing returns in agriculture and mining. This theory goes back to Ricardo and earlier writers. Marshall and Keynes worried greatly about the British terms of trade. In our time, Austin Robinson took up the theme. Gloomiest of all was W. S. Jevons. (References to the literature can be found in my paper, "An Assessment of the Current Relevance of the Theory of Comparative Advantage to Agricultural Production and Trade," in *International Journal of Agrarian Affairs*, vol. 4, no. 3 [May 1964], p. 139.) Ricardo's pessimism, Marshall's and Keynes's worries, not to mention Jevons's forebodings of disaster have proved to be entirely groundless.

[23] A study by the National Bureau of Economic Research (Princeton, N.J.: Princeton University Press, 1963). The coverage of Lipsey's volume is more comprehensive than the title suggests. The book also contains price, quantity, and terms of trade indexes for the United Kingdom and continental industrial Europe. References to earlier, less comprehensive statistical analyses, which reached the same conclusions as Lipsey, can be found in the paper cited in n. 22 above. It should be noted that Lipsey's conclusions are based not only on U.S. terms of trade figures but also on those of other industrial countries.

PART ONE: OVERVIEW

pared to manufactured products. Although there have been very large swings in U.S. terms of trade since 1879, no long-run trend has emerged. The average level of U.S. terms of trade since World War II has been almost the same as before World War I.[24]

Lipsey goes on to say that the U.S. terms of trade improved steadily from 1951 until 1960, the last year in his series. However, this improvement, which reflects a deterioration of the terms for the LDCs, was not the beginning of a trend but the reaction to the exceptionally high commodity prices caused by the Korean War and massive U.S. stockpiling during and immediately after the Korean War.[25]

According to IMF statistics, the U.S. terms of trade and those for the industrial countries as a group have exhibited mild parallel fluctuations since 1960.[26] In the 1970s the terms of trade of the industrial countries deteriorated from 100 in 1970 to 88 in 1976. This evidently reflects the oil price rise, because the terms of trade for the LDCs as a group (excluding the major oil exporters) have deteriorated by almost exactly the same amount. Both the DCs and the LDCs suffered at the hands of OPEC.

It is extremely important to note that in the post–World War II period, when the cyclical fluctuations were very much milder than in the interwar period, the fluctuations in terms of trade too were much milder. We have no terms of trade figures for the LDCs as a group in the interwar period, but the U.S. figures (and those for other industrial countries) indicate the order of magnitude of the enormous changes that occurred during the Great Depression. With 1913 equal to 100, the index of the U.S. terms of trade (export prices/import prices) stood at 99.8 in 1927 and improved by over 40 percent in the depression (1934 = 141.4), reflecting a corresponding sharp deterioration in the terms of trade of the LDCs.[27] In the post–World War II and Korean War period, in contrast, the range of variation was between 102 in 1948 and 82 in 1951; two decades later the range was between 101 in 1968–

---

[24] Lipsey, *Price and Quantity Trends*, p. 76.

[25] The problem was once again considered by an Expert Group on Indexation, sponsored by UNCTAD, which met in spring 1975. The group, under the chairmanship of Hendrik Houthakker, reported that "there was general agreement that the statistics presented to the Group did not provide any clear evidence of a long-term deterioration in the net barter terms of trade of developing countries, although they did suggest that these terms of trade were subject to substantial short-term fluctuations" ("Summary of Main Conclusion," mimeographed).

[26] See IMF, *International Financial Statistics*, which presents indexes for export and import prices for most countries and groups of countries, such as industrial countries and less developed areas with and without the oil-exporting countries.

[27] Lipsey, *Price and Quantity Trends*, p. 443.

1969 and 89 in 1974. The extreme swings of the terms of trade during the Great Depression of the 1930s have not been repeated, but they have unduly colored later discussions.

World trade has grown during the post–World War II period as almost never before. The recession of 1973–1975 caused a slight decline (from 1974 to 1975), as was to be expected, but rapid growth resumed in 1976. Much has been made of the alleged fact that the trade of the LDCs has grown less rapidly than that of the DCs. It is true that from 1943 to 1963, according to IMF statistics, the exports of "less developed areas" fell from 30 percent to 22 percent of world exports.[28] Since then, however, according to GATT statistics, exports of the DCs and the non-oil-exporting LDCs have grown at approximately the same pace.[29] The lag in the rate of growth of LDC trade behind that of DC trade from 1948 to 1963 is easily explained by the fact that the remarkable European recovery from the war slump hit its stride around 1948 and that the even more impressive revival of the Japanese economy started at about the same time. These developments gave a strong boost to the growth of intra-DC trade. The European economic resurgence was spearheaded by the rapid expansion of the German economy after the currency reform of 1948 and Ludwig Erhard's simultaneous dash for liberalism—the abolition overnight of all wartime and postwar controls. The beneficial effects on the world economy, including the LDCs, of the assorted European (not only German but also French, Italian, and so on) and Japanese economic miracles can hardly be exaggerated.[30] They stimulated the world economy both directly by providing rapidly expanding markets, especially for neighboring countries, and indirectly by demonstrating dramatically that (to use Keynes's phrase) "the classical medicine" of liberal policies still works. The German example encouraged other countries to pursue liberal policies. Later, the creation of the European Common Market gave another strong boost to intra-DC trade. All this greatly increased demand for raw materials and other imports, manufactures, and services such as tourism and thus redounded to the great benefit of the LDCs, although it raised the DC share and reduced the LDC share in world trade.

Since the LDCs pursue on the whole much more protectionist

---

[28] IMF, *International Financial Statistics*, 1972 Supplement, pp. xxxii–xxxiii.

[29] See GATT, *International Trade, 1975/76* (Geneva, 1976), Table F, "Network of Total International Trade, 1963, 1968–1970." IMF, *International Financial Statistics*, no longer publishes the percentage figures.

[30] From 1959–1960 to 1970–1971, average annual growth of real GNP was 4.9 in Germany, 5.8 in France, and 5.5 in Italy. See *OECD Economic Outlook*, no. 14 (December 1973), p. 23.

PART ONE: OVERVIEW

policies than the DCs, a certain lag of their trade growth behind that of the DCs would not be surprising. But it is hardly necessary to argue at length that any such lag would not imply that the stake of the LDCs in liberal trade policies is not great. It is true that LDC exports are hampered by restrictions (cascaded tariffs, nontariff barriers, and so on) in the DCs (as they are by the highly protectionist policies of the LDCs themselves).[31] Obviously, it is not liberal policies that hurt the LDCs but deviations from liberalism.

Despite protectionist tendencies in the DCs and LDCs, the export of manufactured goods from developing countries has grown steadily and rapidly during the last twenty years. In 1955 exports of manufactures were 10 percent of total nonoil merchandise exports of developing countries. In 1976 and 1977 they were 41 percent, while the share of agricultural exports fell from 76 percent to 45 percent and that of ores and minerals rose slightly from 13 percent.[32] About 80 percent of LDCs' manufactured goods go to Western industrial (Organization for Economic Cooperation and Development, OECD) countries and Middle East oil-exporting countries. Of the remaining 20 percent, by far the largest part is accounted for by intra-LDC trade and a tiny fraction by exports to Communist countries.

The Last Five Years: 1972–1977

The Changing Mood: From Optimism to Gloom. The comparatively optimistic appraisal of the world economy, including the LDCs, will perhaps not be strongly challenged for the first quarter century after the Second World War, although it runs counter to the voices of gloom that have been emanating from the Economic Commission for Latin America (ECLA), UNCTAD, and the chorus of supporting voices in the DCs. What about the last four or five years? Has not the world recession of 1973–1975, the somewhat sluggish recovery, chronic unemployment, stagflation, and the breakdown of the Bretton Woods system given the lie to the rosy optimism of the 1950s and 1960s?

The general mood in the industrial countries has certainly changed since around 1973. Optimism has given way to pessimism and doubt, and the prophets of doom for the third world find themselves confirmed in their gloomy convictions.

---

[31] On the high rates of protection in the LDCs, see Bela Balassa et al., *The Structure of Effective Protection in Developing Countries* (1971), especially Table 3.1.

[32] See "Prospects for Developing Countries, 1978–85," World Bank document, November 1977; (processed), p. 44.

The recession is indeed a reality. In the United States, it lasted from November 1973 to March 1975, making it the longest of the six postwar recessions. On most measures, it was also the deepest recession since the war. In Europe and Japan, the contrast between the last and the earlier postwar recessions was even greater than in the United States: Unemployment went much higher than in the earlier recessions, and the cyclical recovery has been slower and seems to lag behind U.S. recovery in most European countries. Two major industrial countries, Britain and Italy, still suffer from very high rates of inflation which make their cyclical recovery especially precarious.[33]

But it must be stressed again that both in Europe and in the United States the recent decline was definitely a recession and not a depression, if by depression we mean a slump comparable to what happened in the 1930s or even in 1920–1921, the so-called first and second post–World War I depressions. Thus, in the United States, industrial production declined by 14 percent from November 1973 to March 1975. The corresponding figures for three interwar depressions—June 1920–July 1921, August 1929–March 1933, and May 1937–June 1938—were 32, 53, and 32 percent, respectively. Other measures of the depth of the cyclical decline, such as GNP (in constant dollars) and unemployment, tell the same story. The same is true of other leading industrial countries.

It is true that during the current recovery unemployment has remained high compared with earlier cyclical recoveries. In the United States in June 1977, after more than two years of cyclical upswing, unemployment, although down from the 8.9 percent recession peak, was still 7.1 percent. In other industrial countries, too, unemployment is much higher than in earlier upswings.

However, the structure of unemployment has greatly changed since the 1930s. Socially and economically, unemployment is a much less serious problem than it used to be. It is very significant that in the United States, while unemployment has remained on a high level, employment has been increasing steadily and substantially. This pattern reflects a rising labor-force participation rate, especially among women. Women and young people represent a much greater share in the labor force than formerly, and these groups are much less firmly attached to their jobs than adult male workers. This in turn means that the high unemployment reflects less durable and more intermittent unemployment than in the past. Moreover, it is well known that in all industrial countries unemployment benefits have become so generous in size, duration, and

---

[33] Since this was written inflation in the United States has increased and inflation in Britain has decreased (author's note added in March 1978).

PART ONE: OVERVIEW

availability that the statistically recorded number of jobless persons contains an unknown but increasingly large number of people who do not care to work, who are "voluntarily" unemployed in the Keynesian sense.[34]

The upshot of this discussion is that the unemployment situation, although far from satisfactory, is not nearly so serious, either in absolute terms or in comparison with earlier postwar business cycles, as the figure of 7.1 percent suggests. What is true of the United States is also true of other industrial countries, including Germany and Japan.

The most troublesome feature of the current expansion is the persistent high rate of inflation. The 1973–1975 recession was the first highly inflationary recession. Unlike the "classical" recessions and depressions of the prewar era, the price level did not decline (or even remain stable) but accelerated to a two-digit level in 1974, eight months after the recession had started. Later, the inflation rate came down sharply, but the cyclical recovery in 1975 started with an inflation rate of about 10 percent. It was—and still is—a case of pronounced stagflation, that is, coexistence of high unemployment and high inflation. On that scale, stagflation has never happened before.[35]

As far as the DCs are concerned, the fact that the ongoing expansion started with a high rate of inflation that probably will go higher makes the outlook much less favorable than it otherwise would be. In other words, the inflation will probably shorten the duration of the upswing and will reduce its peak level of employment and capacity utilization. If attempts are made to prolong the expansion by stimulative fiscal-monetary policies, inflation will accelerate and the next recessions will be all the more intractable.

What is the implication of all that for the LDCs? We can, I believe, start from the assumption that what matters basically for the LDCs is the *real* performance of the DC economies. The lower the unemployment, the higher the capacity utilization and the growth rate of real GNP in the DCs, the better the outlook for the LDCs for two reasons: first, DC demand for LDC exports is stronger, and second, protectionist pressures in the DCs are weaker.

Whether a given real performance of the DC economies—real growth, unemployment, and capacity utilization—is accompanied by

---

[34] The distinction between voluntary and involuntary unemployment has been criticized as useless. To my mind the distinction is essential and conceptually not difficult, although the statistical separation of voluntary and involuntary unemployment inevitably is rough and inexact.

[35] In some earlier postwar recessions, prices continued to creep up slowly or failed to decline, which was then regarded as an alarming development.

stable or rising prices is of minor importance for LDCs. It could even be argued that an inflationary real expansion in the DCs is better for the LDCs than an equal noninflationary real expansion for the following reason: Since most LDCs have high rates of inflation, with a given real rate of expansion in the DCs, the higher the DC inflation, the easier it is for the LDCs to stabilize their currencies in terms of DC currencies and to avoid exchange control. Since many LDCs try to peg their currencies to a DC currency (most of them to the dollar) or to a basket of such currencies, this is not an unimportant matter.

However, if it is true that inflation in the DCs tends to reduce the duration and amplitude of the real cyclical upswing in the DCs, the problem appears in a different light. That is to say, the real long-term interest of the LDCs would be best served if the DCs were able to solve their stagflation problem without endangering long-term real growth.

The Dilemma of Stagflation. We should take a closer look at stagflation, because the coexistence of high inflation and persistently high unemployment is often regarded as a striking malfunction of the liberal market economy and an embarrassing failure of liberal economics (of both the Keynesian and monetarist varieties). I shall try to show that in a truly liberal order—in other words, in a highly competitive market economy—stagflation of the recent scale and duration would not be possible. It is not the liberal order but the increasingly serious deviations from the free market economy and the ensuing price and especially wage rigidities that cause the stagflation dilemma.

It is true that no industrial country has been completely successful in eliminating inflation and unemployment at the same time.[36] Stagflation, indeed, poses a nasty dilemma for macroeconomic policy. On the one hand, unlike an old-fashioned (classical) recession or depression characterized by falling prices, in an inflationary recession (or in a highly inflationary cyclical expansion such as the present one) a Keynesian policy of monetary or fiscal expansion is bound to accelerate inflation. It is now fairly generally recognized that in such an environment, despite high unemployment and slack, monetary expansion, although it may produce more employment and higher output in the very short run, would soon be followed by a higher rate of inflation which in

---

[36] Switzerland is no exception. True, inflation has been reduced from a peak of about 10.0 percent in 1974 to about 1.5 percent in 1977, and unemployment is less than 1.0 percent of the labor force. But Switzerland is a special case because the low unemployment rate has been made possible by a substantial decrease in the number of foreign workers. If the departed foreign workers are counted as unemployed, the unemployment percentage is substantial.

PART ONE: OVERVIEW

turn would sooner or later lead to a new recession.[37] On the other hand, an antiinflationary policy of tight money and fiscal restraint is apt to lead to higher unemployment and slack. What is the explanation of this dilemma, and how can it be resolved? Two explanations and two corresponding policy prescriptions have been proposed. Fortunately, the explanations can be reconciled, and the policy prescriptions complement each other.

The explanation of the monetarists is simple and their policy prescription straightforward. Stagflation, they say, is the predictable outcome of a long-drawn-out inflation. Inflationary expectations have become very sensitive to expansionary measures. Therefore, Keynesian policies have lost their potency, except in the very short run. Stagflation, like any other inflation, can be subdued only by reducing monetary growth. It is acknowledged that this cannot be done without initially creating more unemployment. But monetarists are confident that if the rate of monetary expansion is reduced gradually, inflationary expectations will subside, labor unions will moderate their wage demands, and the economy will gradually settle into a sustainable growth path with stable prices and substantially full employment.

The other view (which is shared by the present writer) accepts the monetarist proposition that no inflation, including stagflation, is possible without permissive monetary expansion and that stagflation cannot be cured without monetary restraint; but it insists that inflationary expectations alone cannot explain stagflation of the present scale and duration, the stubborn coexistence of rapidly rising prices and wages on the one hand and severe unemployment on the other. Concretely, in a truly liberal economy—that is to say, in a more competitive economy

---

[37] Some diehard Keynesians and politicians with a time horizon extending merely to the next election still argue, despite the experience of prolonged stagflation, that monetary expansion is safe and not inflationary as long as there is substantial unemployment and slack. There are, however, convincing reasons for assuming that Keynes himself would not have taken that position. T. W. Hutchison, in his pamphlet, *Keynes versus the "Keynesians" . . . ?: An Essay on the Thinking of J. Keynes and the Accuracy of Its Interpretation by His Followers* (London: Institute of Economic Affairs, 1977), shows that in 1937 Keynes was already greatly concerned about inflation, although at that time the rate of inflation was much lower and unemployment much higher than in recent years.

Disenchantment with inflationary policies has been expressed with surprising bluntness by the Labor prime minister of Britain. In a speech to the Labor Party Conference on September 28, 1976, James Callaghan said, "We used to think that you could just spend your way out of a recession and increase employment by cutting taxes and boosting Government spending. I tell you, in all candour, that that option no longer exists, and that insofar as it ever did exist, it only worked by injecting bigger doses of inflation into the economy followed by higher levels of unemployment as the next step. This is the history of the past twenty years."

than we have now—stagflation on the recent scale could not occur. If there were more competition in commodity and labor markets, the spectacle of prices and wages rising in the face of high unemployment and low capacity utilization would be impossible.[38] While monetary restraint is an absolutely necessary condition, it alone is not an economically efficient and politically feasible solution of the stagflation dilemma. If a policy of monetary restraint is not supplemented by structural reform, that is, by measures designed to make the economy more competitive and flexible, so much transitional unemployment will be created that politically the policy of monetary restraint could not be carried through. Or if it is assumed, unrealistically, that the process of disinflation was carried through and a noninflationary equilibrium reached, the residual unemployment ("natural" unemployment, as the monetarists call it) would be higher and the level as well as the growth rate of per capita GNP (standard of living) lower than in a competitive environment. Consequently, if it is not possible to remove at least the worst impediments to competition that have been put in place since the Great Depression, it would be very difficult, perhaps politically impossible, to prevent a relapse into attempts to increase employment and speed up growth by inflationary policies that would inevitably lead to a new recession.

This is not the place for a thorough discussion of structural reform measures.[39] Among the measures designed to bring the economy closer to the competitive ideal are deregulation of industry; restraint of union power; elimination of minimum wages, which have greatly contributed to youth unemployment; freer international trade (free trade is the most effective and, economically as well as administratively, though not politically, the easiest antimonopoly policy); vigorous antitrust policy; and many others. A bundle of such measures would reduce the "natural" rate of unemployment and improve what Keynesians call "the trade-off between inflation and unemployment."[40]

---

[38] Competition cannot of course prevent prices and wages from rising if the supply of money is being inflated. What is impossible under effective competition is the combination of rising prices and wages on the one hand and persistent excess supply of labor (unemployment) and excess supply of commodities (low capacity utilization) on the other hand.

[39] Elsewhere I have discussed the stagflation problem, indicated possible cures in greater detail, and given references to the literature. See Gottfried Haberler, "The Problem of Stagflation," in *Contemporary Economic Problems, 1976* (Washington, D.C.: American Enterprise Institute, 1976), and "Stagflation: An Analysis of Its Causes and Cures," in *Economic Program, Private Values, and Public Policy*, Essays in Honor of William Fellner, Bela Balassa and Richard Nelson, eds. (Amsterdam: North-Holland, 1977); available also as AEI reprint no. 64.

[40] Acceptance of this phrase is not meant to be an endorsement of the Phillips curve. By now it should be clear that no long-run trade-off exists between infla-

Even in a much more competitive economy than the one we have now there would presumably occur mild fluctuations in economic activity. The business cycle would still be there, but the cyclical ups and downs in output and employment would be milder and would not play around a steep upward trend of the price level as is now the case. The long-run economic growth rate would be higher because recessions would be shorter and milder, and out of a larger GNP a larger amount would be saved and invested.

In summary, we can say that stagflation of the recent magnitude and duration is a very serious problem. But it does not signify a failure of the liberal economic order or the market economy; on the contrary, in a truly liberal (that is to say, more competitive) economy than the one we have now, the dilemma of stagflation would not exist or would exist only in a mild and innocuous form.

The Outlook for the Future. What are the implications of all this for the LDCs? From their point of view, it is to be hoped that the DCs will pull themselves together and get out of the stagflation quagmire. Greater stability, lower unemployment, and more rapid growth in the DCs would expand markets for LDC exports and reduce protectionist pressures.

Perhaps it is unrealistic to assume that the DCs will in fact pursue a policy of structural reform, of restoring a greater degree of competition, with sufficient vigor and comprehensiveness to eliminate stagflation completely. Halfhearted measures here and there will not do much good. If this is the prospect, we must reconcile ourselves to higher levels of "natural" unemployment and lower rates of growth than in the past. This is often regarded as the most likely prospect—for example, when it is said that at the present time in the United States full employment should be defined as 5 or 6 percent measured unemployment and not 4 percent as used to be the case before the recent recession.[41]

What are the implications of that outcome for the LDCs? Of course,

---

tion and unemployment. But macroeconomic policies to reduce unemployment would be far more effective and the transition to a noninflationary growth path would be much less painful (transitional unemployment would be lower) in a competitive environment than under present conditions of rigid wages and prices. On that Keynesians and monetarists should be able to agree.

[41] A more dismal scenario, which unfortunately cannot be dismissed as entirely out of the question, would be an attempt to deal with the problem of stagflation by tinkering with symptoms—by means of direct price and wage controls, consumer rationing, and similar measures. The dismal prospects of this outcome, not only for economic growth (standard of living) but also for the liberal order and for democracy itself will not be further discussed in the present essay.

they would be much better off if the DCs were able to eliminate stagflation altogether. But even in the present situation, with a growth rate of 4.5 percent in the OECD area forecast for 1977 and 1978, the situation of the LDCs is not hopeless or even bad. World trade, including that of the LDCs, has resumed its rapid growth after the decline in the recession of 1974 and 1975. It is not generally realized that, contrary to earlier expectations, the LDCs as a group have weathered the recent recession better than the DCs. According to World Bank figures, the annual real rate of growth of GNP per capita of a representative group of LDCs (excluding oil-exporting countries) was 5.6 percent in 1973, 3.7 percent in 1974, 2.9 percent in 1975, and 3.7 percent in 1976, as compared with 3.7 percent in 1966–1972. The figures for the industrial countries for the same years are 5.0, —0.6, 4.2, and 3.5 percent.[42]

At any rate, if the internal economic policies of the DCs fall short of the optimum and if therefore their growth rate is lower than it could be, it would be irrational for the LDCs to make things worse by retreating further from the liberal international economic order that has served the whole world, including the LDCs, so well.

---

[42] See World Bank, *Annual Report, 1977*, p. 104. The figures for 1976 are preliminary. These high growth rates were facilitated by large borrowing abroad, whose tapering-off from the present, probably unsustainable level will present difficult adjustment problems.

COMMENTARY

Peter B. Kenen

The preceding papers have dealt with two groups of challenges—those arising in developed countries and those coming from less developed countries. I will make my comments under these same rubrics, rather than discussing the papers individually.

Gottfried Haberler suggests that the demand of the less developed countries for a New International Economic Order is the "more serious and far-reaching" challenge. In response to that demand, he carefully documents the gains made by less developed countries partly, perhaps largely, as a consequence of the prosperity conferred on developed countries by the liberal international economic order and transmitted to the less developed countries by trade and investment. Strategic to his argument, moreover, is his detailed refutation of the Prebisch-Singer thesis that the terms of trade must go against the less developed countries.

Were one to take seriously *all* of the demands and threats made by the less developed countries a few years ago, especially those that would have impaired the contractual claims of investors and creditors, it would be hard to disagree with Haberler's judgment. The liberal order as we now know it does not sanctify property rights per se, but it cannot function effectively when contracts are not worth the paper on which they are written.

As Haberler points out, however, the less developed countries are not homogeneous, and sane minds appear to have prevailed. The demands pressed most forcefully today may not constitute a "serious and far-reaching" challenge to a liberal international order. To turn Thomas Willett's thought around, a half-dozen buffer fund or buffer stock agreements would not be disastrous, even if they were badly managed. (A more serious challenge to the liberal order resides in the responses of certain developed countries to the demands from less developed countries. Proposals to "organize" commodity markets seem always to strike a sympathetic chord in at least one European capital, where a passion for Cartesian rationality sometimes manifests itself as detestation for the disorderly commotion of the marketplace and the unpredictability of price flexibility.)

If the less developed countries threaten the liberal international order, it is not because of their demands for a New International Economic Order but rather because of what many of those countries have already done to themselves and what some of them have done to others and to us. What they have done to themselves is, of course, to stultify their own economies by illiberal trade regimes and ill-conceived domestic policies. The irrationalities of economic policies in many LDCs impair more seriously the prospects for growth, especially for export-led growth, than the trade barriers imposed by developed countries on the exports of LDCs. To put the point strongly, too strongly perhaps, few less developed countries are properly positioned to take advantage of new export opportunities. Few would benefit quickly or substantially even if developed countries were willing or able to accede immediately to demands for unilateral trade liberalization and a new international division of labor.

To stay with the same point for a moment more, allow me to suggest that the preceding papers are themselves peculiarly illiberal in one way. They delineate too narrowly the sets of policies and institutions that define the character of the international economic order. From a liberal point of view, it makes little sense to talk about trade policies in isolation. The international order cannot be liberal, even with liberal trade policies, if domestic policies are illiberal. The challenge to a liberal international order can come from domestic policies that interfere with the efficient functioning of markets, within and between countries, as well as from trade policies that segregate markets. I make this statement with particular reference to the domestic policies of less developed countries, but it is no less germane to the domestic policies of developed countries.

The same point is made obliquely by Thomas Willett when he talks about challenges posed by the growth of state enterprises and state-subsidized enterprises in steel and other industries. The challenges are novel and difficult to answer in traditional ways, because the degree to which such enterprises engage in "unfair" trade practices is hard to measure. Their practices may be "unfair" even when they do not involve explicit discrimination between home and foreign markets. Governments and governmental enterprises bulk large both as sellers and as buyers in many markets, and the degree to which their practices depart from those of profit-maximizing private sellers and utility-maximizing private buyers may be the most difficult problem for measuring and also for preserving a liberal international economic order.

As I said earlier, the present practices of some LDCs have already impaired the effective functioning of the liberal international economic order by the damage they have done to others. The increase in the price of oil imposed by a handful of LDCs is damaging because it has distorted relative prices and, therefore, the allocation of resources, because it has redistributed income within and between countries in most unfortunate ways, and because it has compounded the problems of macroeconomic management in developed countries—and this in turn threatens the preservation of liberal policies.

Two further comments may be made about the preceding papers. First, I want to suggest to Gottfried Haberler that his refutation of the Prebisch-Singer thesis, while thoroughly persuasive to me, is increasingly irrelevant to the rhetoric of North-South relations. Forecasts of secular deterioration in the terms of trade or attempts to prove deterioration do not figure importantly in the case most often made today for improving the terms of trade of less developed countries. The case made now, as I understand it, is that the terms of trade are worse than they *should be*, not worse than they were, because they have been depressed artificially by unequal bargains between small, weak countries and big, strong multinational companies, by monopolistic practices in the pricing of manufactured goods, and by price support programs for temperate-zone agricultural products.

These arguments run from reasoned statements by producers of raw materials that multinational firms have chosen to process those materials in the consuming countries, and have thus deprived producing countries of their "proper" share in added value, to vulgar Marxist theories of imperialistic exploitation that would cause Rosa Luxemburg acute embarrassment. I do not endorse these theories. Neither do I know how to refute them. Like Willett, I am tempted to dismiss them because I find it so hard to understand them. But they are not answered by demolishing, deductively or statistically, the Prebisch-Singer thesis.

Second, I want to endorse and extend Willett's point that politics, internal and international, explain much of what we hear from the spokesmen for the less developed countries. The demand for a larger share of the action is louder and clearer than the demand for a larger share of the pie. At times, indeed, the demands reflect the aspirations of the spokesmen themselves for more influence within their own governments. The larger their countries' decision-making roles in the international system, the larger their own roles within the decision-making communities of their countries.

COMMENTARY

I have less to say about the papers' comments on challenges from the developed countries, but I would like to add to what I said earlier about the macroeconomic situation and its implications for the liberal order.

Both papers express concern about the recrudescence of strong protectionist sentiment in developed countries. I share that concern. In Willett's paper, moreover, I detect a sense of helplessness, and I share that too. Improvements in adjustment-assistance programs will not change the minds of labor unions, although significant improvements are possible, especially if the emphasis is shifted from enhancing worker mobility to redevelopment of communities affected by import competition.

But I must disagree with the way Willett puts labor's case for protection. He cites with apparent approval C. Fred Bergsten's suggestion that workers have decided "to give up some income that could be generated through freer trade in order to avoid the accompanying dislocation costs." May I remind him—and Bergsten—that workers may suffer *permanent* income losses on account of movements to freer trade. All factors of production are quasispecific to particular occupations, and those employed in import-competing industries may lose even in the long run from a movement to freer trade. The point was made by A. O. Krueger in a brilliant article[1] and has been rediscovered by a number of others who have been reworking the Stolper-Samuelson analysis of the relationship between trade and income distribution. (The point, of course, goes back to Haberler's own work on the determination of trade patterns when factors of production are truly or quasispecific to particular activities.)

I must also disagree with Haberler on remedies for protectionist pressures. In a footnote to his comments on stagflation, he says that "some diehard Keynesians and politicians with a time horizon extending merely to the next election still argue, despite the experience of prolonged stagflation, that monetary expansion is safe and not inflationary as long as there is substantial unemployment and slack." While I am not one who would say that it is safe, I would venture to suggest that it may be less risky than deferring or forgoing expansion. For as long as there is idle capacity and much unemployment in the industrial world, the liberal international economic order will be vulnerable to dangerous protectionist pressures. On the one hand, the situation invites resort to competitive practices by firms and governments that are likely to provoke protectionist reactions. On the other, it makes more difficult

---

[1] A. O. Krueger, "The Political Economy of the Rent-Seeking Society," *American Economic Review*, vol. 64, no. 3 (June 1974), pp. 291–303.

the reallocations of resources, human and material, required to adjust to import competition.

Furthermore, I do not share Haberler's belief that we have the will, skill, or time to improve by piecemeal changes in policies and institutions the prospects for reconciling price stability with high levels of economic activity. There may be no "economically efficient and politically feasible solution" for the stagflation problem—none that is available in time to turn back the protectionist challenge.

My own view—with which many will probably disagree—is that we may have to take greater risks on the side of inflation or to minimize those risks as best we can, even by resort to direct wage and price restraints. Otherwise, we may be unable to prevent a serious disintegration of the liberal order, economic and political. I dare to suggest, moreover, that the inefficiencies of incomes policy—against which economists complain so loudly—may be smaller and less permanent than the inefficiencies with which we would be saddled by capitulating to or compromising with protection demands.

As it is the role of a discussant to provoke discussion, I have emphasized my disagreements with Haberler and Willett. Permit me, then, to close by saying emphatically that I agree with most of what they say and admire greatly their manner of saying it. They have given us much to think about.

Hollis B. Chenery

While I agree with much of what both Gottfried Haberler and Thomas Willett have put forth, I think the purpose of a commentator is to indicate those areas where he finds the analysis insufficient or where he disagrees. Because these first papers are setting the general framework, I would like to add a bit to the overview and suggest some questions. Perhaps some of these questions can be pursued in more detail in later papers.

To sharpen the issue, I would like to draw a parallel between the analysis of a federal system, such as that of the United States, and the international order. Look at the problems of New York City, for example. Are they the fault of the system or the fault of mismanagement of New York City? That is the first question. Second, what does one do about it? However one answers the first question, I think, is more or less irrelevant to what one does about it. Certainly, what is learned from the past is useful as a guide to what to do about it. But few people would say that, given the initial conditions of New York City, the solution lies entirely within the power of New York City.

Nor can one say the opposite, that it is entirely a problem for the federal government, in this case for the system. It is obviously a problem for both. And, I think all constructive solutions that are being proposed have elements from both.

Essentially the same is true about the role of the developing countries within the international system. We can argue endlessly about how they got where they are. But how do we find constructive solutions? It is hard to say that the only step necessary is to make the system more liberal, and in an unspecified time, which might be two or three hundred years, the mess poor countries are in will be solved by their own efforts. The alternative is a somewhat mixed set of policies that would involve some changes in the system as well as some actions on the part of the countries themselves.

I would like to sketch briefly the way the present system works, as we see it in the World Bank, in regard to poverty. It has become a recognized fallacy to take countries as the unit of analysis instead of human beings. When people are taken as the units and grouped within as well as between countries, a striking paradox is revealed. In the last twenty-five years, although the world has grown at its fastest rate and per capita income all over the world—averaged in the usual way—has grown at more than 3 percent, the income level of the poorest 40 percent has grown something less than 1 percent. Although middle-income countries in the developing world have grown in per capita terms at about the same rate as the advanced countries, the poorest countries have grown at about half that rate. Unlike middle-income countries whose growth rates have been accelerating, the growth rates of the poor countries have been declining. The problem is not getting better; instead, at least for the last ten years, it has been getting worse.

Within countries, the income distribution does follow the Kuznets hypothesis, according to the best cross-section and time-series evidence now available. This means that in middle-income countries something like 80 percent of any increment of growth goes to the top 40 percent of income recipients. This would be true of Mexico, Brazil, and all countries on the Kuznets curve. Those happen to be quite typical of cross-country measurements. There are some exceptions, such as Taiwan, where a considerably higher proportion, incrementally, has been going to the lower-income groups.

World income distribution is getting worse over time not only because of differences in growth rates of countries but also because of the structure of income distribution within countries.

Turning to the present debates about the New International Economic Order, I agree with both papers that the developing countries have not picked very useful reforms to advocate. Those they have picked, I think, would not do much for the poorest people; they would do more for the middle-income countries and for the countries with more unequal income distribution. They would do something for India, for example, if India were to follow good trade policies. The poorest countries are aware that such reforms would not benefit them, but they see the advantage of sticking together. I do not propose to pursue this line of thought, except to say that it seems to me that we cannot discuss actual proposals without some reference to the political framework.

I would assume that it would be possible to have a consensus of relatively liberal policies as a starting point, if one did not take the extreme position that all that is needed is to make the market system work. The specific areas that do not work well and that prevent the poorer people within poor countries from benefiting, even where governments are relatively favorable to doing that, would make a fairly long list; I shall do no more than give a few examples.

It is certainly true that the financial system operates to provide capital to those countries that need it less and not to those countries that need it most. The failure of the international financial system to provide a sufficient increase in public capital after the crisis of 1973–1974 has meant that the middle-income countries with good export prospects have done quite well. The poorest countries, which cannot borrow significantly because of their poor credit rating, have been limited by the smaller increase, in real terms, in public capital. It is in these countries that the changes of the last five years have had the most serious effects.

The same thing operates, of course, within countries. The middle-income groups have access to credit, public facilities, and so forth, and the poor do not. One can extend the analogy within and between countries.

I cannot agree with Haberler that internal distribution is the problem of the poor countries. I think that much of the internal distribution we now see is the effect of modern technology and emulation of Western living standards. We may believe that we should not intervene in such a situation, but we should at least recognize that, whether we intervene or not, the international system does have a great deal to do with internal income distribution. It is probably a more important factor in many countries than the external effects of trade and aid. We cannot just walk away from the problem and say that the multinational corporations, technology, and so forth, have nothing to do with internal distribution.

The area of greatest potential benefit to the poorest people in the poorest countries, unfortunately, is still the aid field, and this is the area that is politically most difficult. The decline in aid relative to everything else is well known. The only solution I see is to ration it much more strictly, in accordance with need and performance.

Most aid still goes to middle-income rather than poor countries. In any rational system of allocating aid, a high proportion would go to India and the subcontinent. The United States, of course, cut off aid to India several years ago for totally irrelevant reasons and is having a difficult time even starting up a $50 million aid program. As a result, the United States is far from following an allocation policy that relates aid to areas of poverty. The World Bank has put a ceiling on its allocation of soft aid to India, which in effect means that India gets about half as much as other countries of its income level. India has the misfortune of being a big country and following unpopular policies.

I think that the present moment is a very favorable time for India, and India can do a great deal without aid. Only if it starts to succeed will it need an increase in aid. But the Indian government seems to be so discouraged by its poor performance of the last twenty years that it is very cautious about expanding; 4 percent growth seems to be optimism in India, whereas it would be pessimism in most other developing countries.

To what extent does one intervene? Of the many liberal dilemmas, this is perhaps the most important. The U.S. government has invented a system of intervention on the basis of human rights, which is playing havoc with intervention on the basis of human needs. And some reconciliation between human rights, as defined by the State Department and, I presume, the Central Intelligence Agency, and human needs, as now defined by most international organizations in terms of access to potable water, nutrition, and so forth, clearly needs to be worked out. Otherwise, the conflict is going to be used as a pretext for reducing aid on the human rights basis. Since we already have political reasons for limiting aid to countries that basically need it, it will be easy to argue that there is not much need for aid from the United States or from other Western countries. This will only serve to sharpen, or make more shrill, the claims of the developing countries.

Ronald Findlay

Gottfried Haberler has presented us with a vigorous and learned defense of the desirability of a liberal international economic order. I share his attachment to the goal of achieving and preserving an LIEO and applaud the theoretical acumen and breadth of historical knowledge with which he refutes once again the many hoary myths perpetuated by its critics.

PART ONE: OVERVIEW

It would, however, be superfluous for me to dwell on the many virtues of his paper, which are apparent to any reader. Instead, I shall concentrate on the points at which I differ from him—not about the desirability of an LIEO but about the extent to which it has been realized in the past and the relative strength of the dangers to which it is exposed at present.

If a liberal international order is taken to mean one in which there is free movement of goods, capital, and people across national frontiers, then it is clear that the world economy has never experienced a time when this ideal was ever realized fully, even to a reasonable approximation. The 1870–1914 period, which most liberals see as a golden age, perhaps came close to achieving these conditions in a technical sense, but it should never be forgotten by any true liberal that this was also the era when the industrially developed countries of the West dominated the peoples of Asia and Africa by means of armed force. Goods were free to move, but it was manufactures and capital that went "south" and primary products that went "north." The massive migrations of this period consisted largely of redistributions of people of European stock within the temperate zones and of Asians within the tropics. Even this movement, however, was severely restricted early in the interwar period, and controls on immigration were never again relaxed to any appreciable extent.

Benjamin Disraeli apparently once said that "liberalism is an expedient and not a principle." He is undoubtedly right for the vast majority of mankind—politicians, businessmen, trade unionists, and bureaucrats. It is only in the economics profession that there appears to be a genuine attachment to liberalism as a principle. In the "real world," liberalism unfortunately functions as an "ideology," in Marx's or Mannheim's sense of a rationalization of special interests. Manchester, the Mecca of liberalism in the days of Cobden and Bright, became a hotbed of protectionism when the Lancashire textile industry could no longer stand up to foreign competition.

No less distinguished a liberal than Lord Robbins, in his essay on "Liberalism and the International Problem," argues that the nineteenth-century liberals were hopelessly naive in imagining that a liberal international order could ever come about.[1] Within a nation, it takes the strong and visible hand of the state to create the framework of law and order within which the invisible hand of the price mechanism can do its work. In the absence of a supranational authority, there is nothing to prevent the system from breaking down when each nation pursues

---

[1] See Lord Robbins, *Money, Trade, and International Relations* (London: Macmillan, 1971), chapter 11.

its individual self-interest. The benefits of free trade to consumers tend to be sacrificed to protect the losses that would be inflicted on the few who are engaged in import-competing production, for the familiar reason that a localized group facing a large potential loss can lobby more effectively than the many who each would gain only a little. Substantial protection for agriculture now seems a permanent political feature in all the major industrial countries, and the same seems likely to become the case for textiles and footwear, and perhaps for steel as well, in the United States and Europe.

The world economy has come closest to approximating a liberal order whenever a single power was strong enough to exercise "hegemony" or "leadership" and confident enough to permit rising powers to emerge. This was the case with Britain during the pre-1914 period and the United States during the last three decades. The Robbins problem is solved in each case by the hegemonic power acting as an "enforcer" of the rules of the game, which may be stacked in its favor but which nevertheless permit lesser powers to improve their relative positions, as was the case with the United States and Germany vis-à-vis Britain and Germany and Japan vis-à-vis the United States. The world economy as a whole seems to reach a crisis whenever the hegemonic power's industrial and financial base is eroded while the rising new powers as yet lack the experience and institutions with which to take over the leadership role. Charles P. Kindleberger's analysis of the 1930s in these terms seems to me to be a valuable supplement to Haberler's explanation, which stresses the blunders in U.S. monetary policy.[2]

The three decades since 1945 have been a period of unprecedented growth in world trade and production. The contrast with the interwar period could not have been greater and is well symbolized by the contrast between German reparations and the Marshall Plan. The economies of Japan and Western Europe grew at a particularly rapid rate as their technological gap with the United States was narrowed, if not altogether closed. The removal of trade barriers through the promotion of the European Common Market and as a result of the Kennedy Round made world trade grow even faster than world production. In the last few years, however, a number of disturbing features have cast doubt on the prospects for a continuation of these favorable trends. The oil cartel is one, but I do not think that this factor alone would be a serious impediment to growth. It of course creates a substantial redistribution of income and wealth, but this should not by itself necessarily produce any decline in growth.

---

[2] See Charles P. Kindleberger, *The World in Depression, 1929–1939* (Berkeley and Los Angeles: University of California Press, 1973).

PART ONE: OVERVIEW

As I stated earlier, a liberal international system can only be created and maintained when the dominant country in the world economy is sufficiently confident of its technological and financial superiority. There are now increasing signs that the U.S. commitment to liberal principles is being seriously weakened as major segments of its industrial sector are becoming less able to stand the pressures of foreign competition and fears mount about the value of the dollar. The U.S. dominance in science and technology, as measured by a number of indicators, also shows signs of being eroded. Under these circumstances, the thrust toward an LIEO in the last three decades that has taken place under American inspiration and leadership has been blunted and may even be reversed, while the strong new industrial exporters such as Germany and Japan show little sign of having the desire or ability to assume the responsibilities of world economic leadership.

I therefore join Peter Kenen in disagreeing with Haberler when he says that the most serious threat to an LIEO comes from the demands of the less developed countries for a new international economic order. The challenge here appears to contain more rhetoric and bombast than substance. The bulk of world trade takes place between OECD members, and the proponents of an NIEO can do little or nothing to alter that basic fact. There were times during this conference when the charismatic eloquence of Peter Bauer had me imagining that the Saracens were at the Pass of Roncesvalles, the Golden Horde at the Vistula, and Suleiman the Magnificent just outside Vienna, such was the enormity of the danger to Western civilization posed by the NIEO. To phrase my point somewhat melodramatically, it is not the barbarians at the gate that threaten the liberal citadel but the traitors within the walls.

The interests of the developing countries would best be served if their spokesmen would challenge the major industrial powers to abide truly by the oft-repeated liberal slogans, to prove that their attachment is to liberalism as a principle rather than as an expedient. In a world of highly mobile capital, rapid transfer of technology, and low transport costs, the relative abundance of labor in the developing countries is an enormous asset. The phenomenal success of Korea, Taiwan, Hong Kong, and Singapore and, to a lesser extent, of other countries as well in promoting manufactured exports attests to this. Extensive and incontrovertible evidence is available of the close correlation between growth of GNP and of exports in the less developed countries. The familiar old arguments about stagnant markets for LDC exports were clearly shown to be false by the experience of the last two decades. It would therefore be tragic if the rise of protectionism in the advanced countries should breathe new life into those tired old arguments.

COMMENTARY

In his list of possible bilateral comparisons to demonstrate the superiority of "outward looking" development strategies, Haberler includes Burma and Malaysia. I would rather compare Burma with Thailand, since these two neighboring countries are very similar in size of population, religion, culture, and natural resource endowments. In 1940 Burma was the world's leading rice exporter, and her total exports exceeded those of Thailand in value. Throughout the postwar period, and particularly after the left-wing military takeover in 1962, Burma has followed a policy of stringent trade controls and exclusion of foreign investment. A state monopoly purchases rice from farmers at prices well below world levels, while extremely low quotas on imported consumer goods make their domestic prices much higher than world levels. There is consequently a drastic squeeze on the internal terms of trade of the peasants, who naturally respond by reducing the amount they plant in excess of their own subsistence needs. In 1975 Burma's exports amounted to $167 million while Thailand's exports were $2.3 billion. There has been no substantial expansion of domestic industrial production to offset this, since the chronic self-induced shortage of foreign exchange makes it impossible to import capital goods on the necessary scale. Those who extol the virtues of "delinking" and following a path of "inward development" would do well to look at the Burmese case.

The widespread hostility to externally oriented development strategies and to the notion of an LIEO throughout much of the third world is a phenomenon that most Western economists find difficult to understand. The historical roots of this phenomenon, however, are interesting to explore. It should be remembered that modern economics and the liberal philosophy and approach to policy with which it is associated reflect its origins in the English experience of the last two centuries. In those conditions, the cause of free trade was bound up with political reform and general social progress, because the middle classes stood to gain on all these points by comparison with the aristocratic landed interests. As Ricardo argued in his pamphlet on the Corn Laws, free trade would reduce rents and increase the rate of profit, and thereby the rate of growth. The growth of manufacturing production in turn would tip the political and social balance in the nation increasingly in favor of the progressive cities and away from the conservative countryside.

The other side of the same Ricardian model, however, implies for England's trading partners an increase in the relative preponderance of the landlord class as against the urban and industrial interests. Rents go up and the profit rate goes down and with it the rate of growth. The symmetry of the model dictates this result as a logical necessity, and there would seem to be historical support for it as well, in the experience of the primary producing regions of the periphery.[3] Should a good liberal in the United States before the Civil War have been in favor of free trade, knowing that it would increase the power of the slave South relative to the democratic, industrial North?

These considerations are manifestations of the underlying Stolper-Samuelson theorem that links the patterns of income distribution and international trade. It is therefore puzzling that Haberler should say that trade has nothing to do with inequality in the distribution of income. Perhaps what he has in mind is that trade may affect the degree of inequality in the distribution of income in either direction, depending upon exogenous factors such as the system of property ownership and so on, which is certainly correct. Another and not so familiar link between trade and income distribution is the so-called Kuznets curve, which states that the curve relating per capita income to the degree of inequality in the distribution of income is in the shape of an inverted U, rising to a peak and falling thereafter. If we accept the hypothesis that trade promotes growth, then it follows that trade enhances inequality to the left of the critical turning point on the Kuznets curve and reduces it to the right. These connections, however, can only be regarded as highly tentative in the present state of our knowledge. Resistance to an LIEO is associated with the belief that the role for the less developed countries envisaged within it is one of perpetuating their existence as "hewers of wood and drawers of water" while the more glamorous industrial occupations are reserved for the North. The reason for this identification is perhaps that the theory of comparative advantage, on which the intellectual case for an LIEO rests, has traditionally been expounded within too static a framework. Factor proportions and technology can change and the pattern of comparative advantage with them.[4] Once it is realized that the theory of comparative advantage does not assign eternal and immutable roles in the international division of labor, resistance to acceptance of an LIEO should decrease, though this consideration probably will not count for much in practice.

---

[3] For interesting discussions of some possible social and political implications of specialization on primary production, see M. M. Postan, "Economic Relations between Eastern and Western Europe," chapter 6 of his *Medieval Trade and Finance* (Cambridge: At the University Press, 1973); Immanuel Wallerstein, *The Modern World-System* (New York: Academic Press, 1974); Celso Furtado, *The Economic Development of Latin America* (Cambridge: At the University Press, 1970).

[4] For an examination of comparative advantage in dynamic contexts, see my *International Trade and Development Theory* (New York: Columbia University Press, 1973), chapters 7 and 8.

Hostility to an LIEO in the developing countries also stems from its identification on their part with the period of colonial rule from which most of them have only recently emerged. It is possible to argue that this colonial experience, bitter though it certainly was in many cases, was a necessary stage in the creation of an integrated world economy that would ultimately benefit all mankind. This was the view of Karl Marx himself. In his well-known *New York Daily Tribune* articles on the British rule in India, he saw the historical role of Western imperialism as shattering the basis of the "Asiatic mode of production" that had kept India and China stagnant for millennia, in spite of a high level of civilization.[5] While colonial rule did make possible the participation of the Asian masses in the world economy, it certainly did not result in substantial and sustained economic development. Those who attribute all recent difficulties with development to excessive government interference should not forget that India and many other less developed countries had several decades of more or less laissez-faire economic policies under colonial rule.

While the state can undoubtedly cause considerable harm by arbitrary intervention with the free play of economic forces, it also has a crucially important positive role to play in the promotion of economic development. In Japan, for example, the state on the whole followed a liberal trade regime but was actively and extensively involved in the economy in many ways, such as pioneering in key industries, organizing banking and finance, and providing social overhead capital in education, power, and transport.[6] The colonial regimes did little or nothing beyond the maintenance of law and order. The problem with contemporary developing economies appears to be not so much an excess or deficiency of overall state intervention but too much of the wrong kind, in the sense of suppressing and distorting activities best left to the private sector, and too little of the right kind, in the sense of providing an appropriate social and physical infrastructure for sustained development to take place.[7]

In conclusion, let us briefly consider the prospects for an LIEO. They do not appear to me to be too bright. It is unlikely that the newly developing nation-states of the third world will give up lightly the extensive control of their economies that they have been seeking to establish,

---

[5] These are conveniently available in Shlomo Avineri, ed., *Karl Marx on Colonialism and Modernization* (New York: Anchor Books, 1969).

[6] See W. W. Lockwood, *The Economic Development of Japan* (Princeton, N.J.: Princeton University Press, 1968), chapter 10.

[7] See Stanislaw Wellisz, "Lessons of Twenty Years of Planning in Developing Countries," *Economica*, May 1971, for a convincing analysis of this theme.

however unfortunate the results might be in most cases. In the advanced industrial countries, it would seem that the power of pressure groups and special interests will result in increasing suppression of market solutions to economic problems in favor of regulations and restrictions of various sorts. Karl Polanyi was of the opinion that it was only a peculiar combination of circumstances that made possible a free market economy in the late nineteenth century.[8] Societies usually subordinate their economic transactions to processes of social and political control, from the ancient empires of Babylonia and Egypt to the modern welfare states. For those of us to whom liberalism is a principle and not an expedient, the outlook appears to be a bleak and lonely one, but the reader of this volume can take comfort in the fact that Haberler and Willett, much wiser men than I, are far more cheerful. Cassandra may not always be right.

Paul Craig Roberts

To the extent that the fine papers by Gottfried Haberler and Thomas Willett have any faults, they fall into the following categories: (1) an assumption that facts are relevant without explanation of what would cause people to accept empirical facts contrary to their self-interest just because they are objectively true, and (2) a failure to deal directly with the political entrepreneurship of the third world rulers or the incentive structure in our own international bureaucracies. The third world rulers, the international bureaucrats, and the Western academics who are staging the NIEO are not poor. They have been remarkably successful in transferring resources to themselves from people with much lower incomes. What we have here is just another case of concentrated gains and dispersed costs, and entrepreneurs have moved in to take advantage of the situation. Willett shows that he very well understands the situation when he concludes, "It may be that the proliferation of special-purpose conferences and organizations . . . is the most promising way of reconciling these two potentially conflicting objectives." It is certainly a promising way of furthering academic travel to exotic places.

I should like to have prepared a paper on this theme; that would have given me an opportunity to be sufficiently obnoxious to promote an offer to sell out to an international bureaucracy for one of those $70,000-plus, tax-free salaries with diplomatic privileges. I would hope to be shipped to Geneva, where I might become one of those who, to quote the *Washington Post*, "over lunch in the agreeable and expensive

---

[8] See George Dalton, ed., *Primitive, Archaic, and Modern Economies: Essays of Karl Polanyi* (New York: Anchor Books, 1968), particularly chapters 1–4.

eighth-floor restaurant of the Palais and in Geneva's nightspots decides who shall be in charge of rigging markets for rubber, copper, cocoa and much more."

I have observed that fighting third world poverty pays better than fighting U.S. domestic poverty. Having worked for the Congress, I can juggle statistics as well as anybody, but I do not know whether I can compete with the civil servant quoted by Oscar Morgenstern in his book, *On the Accuracy of Economic Observations*, who said: "We shall produce any statistics that we think will help us to get as much money out of the United States as we can. Statistics which we do not have, but which we need to justify our demands, we shall simply fabricate."[1] I hope the representatives of the international organizations and the third world know how to buy off their critics. I really do not want to have to go through with the bill I am drafting that would require our academic specialists in development economics and our international bureaucrats, including those in the Treasury and the State Department, to register as foreign agents.

Peter Bauer and others have told the story of the West African marketing boards that were set up ostensibly to stabilize the prices received by agricultural producers but served instead to transfer between one-third and one-half of the commercial values of the producers' crops to cover current operating expenses of the governments involved. This could explain why some third world governments might be vociferous consumers of the anti-Western imperialist diatribes that originate in Western universities. It is always in the interest of indigenous imperialists to support the argument that the country is exploited by foreigners.

The real beneficiaries of foreign aid, reparations, or whatever the transfers are called, are the international organizations, those who control political power in the recipient countries, those who staff the foreign aid agencies of the giving countries, and the Western professors who advise on economic development schemes. I once served in a state university as the academic replacement for a professor who had just purchased a $60,000 home and gone on an Agency for International Development (AID) mission to India for two years. This was back in the 1960s and it was not in the Washington, D.C., area, so $60,000 would pay for a nice house. His pay for his mission to the poor was $30,000 per year plus expenses, which allowed him to pay off his mortgage on his return. One of his colleagues had gone on a similar mission to South America and bragged to me that he had "salted away $30,000." Such "missions," which let academics save at annual rates

---

[1] Oscar Morgenstern, *On the Accuracy of Economic Observations*, 2nd ed. (Princeton University Press, 1963), p. 21.

PART ONE: OVERVIEW

equal to their normal incomes, explain the great popularity among professors of foreign aid and all arguments that justify it. He who has not yet got his can hope to in the future. Western taxpayers who are assuaging "guilt" for the poverty of underdeveloped countries are fattening the pocketbooks of others, but the others are not the exploited farmers of West Africa.

There may be some who are too earnest, and others who feel too guilty, to see the humor in my remarks, and they may interpret them as scathing criticism. To the contrary, my remarks betray my admiration for the political skill of third world governments who have used our tax dollars to hire our citizens as spokesmen for their interests.

We really should not be fooled into believing that there is any kind of academic issue here, such as the terms of trade, or any moral issue. At the same time, no one should ever take it personally if he goes to the Hill to testify on North-South issues and a staffer or a senator gives him a hard time. The Congress is used to hired lobbyists and sees through the moral veils that are used. I suppose everyone has noticed that senators and representatives consult with staff during hearings. Some people are so ungracious as to think they are asking what to say next, but usually what they are asking is: "Who is paying this one? What interest does he represent?" Occasionally, a really bright country comes along and, instead of hiring academics, buys the congressmen themselves.

It does not upset me that people take advantage of opportunities to maximize their wealth. As an economist, I expect them to do so. But individuals maximizing their private welfare may generate external diseconomies and social costs. The private success of the NIEO entrepreneurs may reduce world social welfare. This is because our policy of reassurances and accommodation has raised the rate of return on aggressive demands and attracts resources to the generation of political conflicts. The social opportunity costs of these resources are high, and the private participants in the NIEO operation do not bear all the risks inherent in the conflicts they generate.

DISCUSSION

Bela Balassa disagreed with Peter Kenen that the Prebisch-Singer argument on the terms of trade has no importance. He felt that the argument is still put forward to change the present terms of trade. Balassa also pointed out that one must be careful (as Hollis Chenery was) to realize that we are not dealing with a monolith of developing countries, that there is a wide range of successes and failures. He expanded on this idea, pointing out that there is a wide range in economic performance, and this range is produced by the economic policies of the individual countries.

Peter Bauer agreed with Kenen that one must examine domestic policies in both developed and less developed countries. He disagreed with Chenery's argument that it is not important to determine why the poor are poor. If they are poor because their governments pursued such policies as expelling and annihilating minorities, aid will simply allow them to continue these policies and reduce income still further. Bauer agreed with Paul Craig Roberts that much of the pressure for a new order comes from special interest groups, namely, international politicians who stand to gain from growth in the international bureaucracy.

Jagdish Bhagwati argued that the threat to an LIEO from the developing countries was stronger than Peter Kenen and Ronald Findlay had implied. The developing countries viewed the basic question as one of distributive justice rather than efficiency. The performance criterion of economics is not the answer. The policies of the developing countries should be viewed as second-best or nth-best ways of replacing or getting more mileage from their dwindling aid programs. What is needed are guidelines for the granting of aid. Without the incorporation of some sort of welfare criteria, the call for liberal trade is perceived by the developing countries as a self-serving mechanism of the developed countries. Bhagwati strongly disagreed with Bauer's attack on the leadership in developing countries. He argued that aid must be channeled through the leadership of nation-states, in the hope that it will trickle down to those in greatest need.

PART ONE: OVERVIEW

Juergen Donges viewed the challenge to liberal policies as both political and economic. The political challenge comes from a zero-sum game mentality. In this view someone has to lose, and the third world is politically determined to win. He thought that the challenge to economists is to develop a positive-sum game description that the politicized world will accept. The economic challenge is that the third world countries need to change to a more diversified output mix. Donges pointed out that a liberal system does not have to mean one in which the developing countries export raw materials.

Peter Kenen regained the floor to clarify some misunderstanding surrounding his earlier (partial) statement. In his comment that the terms of trade arguments are irrelevant to the current debate, he meant that arguments concerned with the trend of the terms of trade are irrelevant. The call for a new order claims that the terms of trade are worse than they should be regardless of any historical record. He also denied any suggestion that he was dismissing as unimportant the demands of the developing countries. What he was suggesting was that we can live with these demands and still have a liberal order far more readily then we can live with many other challenges to the liberal order. He concluded by pointing out that it is insulting to dismiss the integrity of the demands of the developing countries *and* that the demands of the Group of 77, in their present form, are equally insulting to the integrity and intelligence of many in the developed countries. He added that he felt that the hostile response of those in the developed world is in part due to the fact that they have been angered.

The authors of the papers were given an opportunity to respond. Thomas Willett reemphasized the necessity of looking at one country at a time instead of viewing the developing countries as a monolith. He argued that there is a need to continue to move the emphasis of development programs into areas where one can be more sure of favorable distributional effects. He argued that negotiators from the developing countries should recognize that ultimately they must appeal not only to the government negotiators but also to Congress and the general public. He argued that one of the most serious dangers to the successful pursuit of humanitarian objectives was the militancy of the developing countries, and he expressed concern that the rhetoric surrounding the NIEO could play into the hands of those who would prefer no aid for the less developed countries.

POSTSCRIPT

Gottfried Haberler

I am very grateful to the discussants for their constructive comments and criticism, which give me an opportunity to clarify and in places to modify my paper. In general, I was a little surprised—and gratified—by the large area of agreement that emerged, and I shall try to show that some points of disagreement are semantic rather than substantive.

Ronald Findlay and Peter Kenen questioned my statement that NIEO presents a greater threat to LIEO than protectionism in the industrial countries. They may well be right in saying that "all the demands and threats made by the LDCs" in connection with NIEO should not be taken "seriously" (Kenen) and that "the challenge [to NIEO] appears to contain more rhetoric and bombast than substance" (Findlay). Protectionism in the DCs, in contrast, is quite real. That is what I really had in mind: NIEO, in principle, *if taken seriously*, is the greater threat.

Kenen says that Willett's and my papers are "themselves peculiarly illiberal" because they do not deal with domestic policies. "The international order cannot be liberal, even with liberal trade policies, if domestic policies are illiberal." We all know that if there are domestic distortions, policy induced or otherwise, trade regulations of some sort are justified. If, for example, domestically some commodities are subject to excise taxes or safety or health regulations, imports too must be subject to similar taxes and regulations. If trade restrictions were confined to such cases, I would not call it an illiberal trade policy. In a short paper certain things have to be taken for granted. That does not make the paper "illiberal." It would require a book to spell out everything in detail. As far as government enterprises are concerned, which Kenen rightly mentions as a complicating factor, a special session of this conference is devoted to some of these problems.

In a similar vein, Findlay states that a truly liberal international order should provide free movement not only of goods and capital but

---

This Postscript incorporates and expands the authors' concluding remarks at the end of the first session of the conference.

also of people. If this is accepted, he says, a liberal order has never existed, not even in approximation. Perhaps Willett and I should have said something about migration. I, for one, simply took it for granted that there is no free migration from the LDCs to the DCs, and only in a few rare cases between the DCs, nor is there free migration between the LDCs for that matter. One may deplore this, but it would be unrealistic to expect a change.

It is even doubtful whether a greater international mobility of labor can be regarded as desirable from the standpoint of international peace and harmony, despite the economic benefits for all participants that may be expected. Mixing of people of different cultural, religious, and racial backgrounds often leads to strife, tension, and violence. Witness the ugly reactions in Britain to the influx of "colored people" or the treatment of Asians in black African countries, not merely in Amin's Uganda.

As for trade, it is one of the basic tenets of classical trade theory that international immobility of labor does *not* invalidate the case for free trade in commodities.

This brings me to the related problem of internal income distribution in the LDCs (or elsewhere) and its relation to the international order. In my paper I said that the great inequality of incomes, the stark contrast between the rich and the poor in most LDCs (compared with the internal income distribution in the DCs) is the consequence of deep-seated internal factors (social structure, resource endowment, institutions, and policies) and has nothing to do with the international economic order. This statement has been challenged by several speakers, Findlay and Hollis Chenery among them. "Nothing" is perhaps too strong a word; "very little" would be better.

International trade clearly has some influence on income distribution. For one thing, we all know that factors of production specific to import-competing industries will suffer from freer trade. As Kenen reminds us, even some workers are specialized to such a degree that they may incur a permanent income loss when cheap imports replace home production. This has been known at least since Cairnes's theory of non-competing groups (1879). But it does not tell us whether freer trade can be bad for labor *as a whole* or for the lower-income strata or for the poor as a group, however these ambiguous terms are defined. Before I turn to that question, it should perhaps be pointed out that the possible income loss suffered by some specific factors is not a strong argument against free trade. For there probably exists no policy change, however desirable, that does not inflict an income loss on some people. For example, general disarmament, even if efficiently managed without causing *general* unemployment, may permanently hurt specialized factors, including some workers, in the armament industry. Nobody would argue that for that reason mutual disarmament is of doubtful value and should not be attempted.

Findlay invokes the Stolper-Samuelson theory to suggest the possibility that LIEO may operate to hurt labor or the poor as a group in the LDCs. But he—rightly—is very cautious. Both he and Chenery mention the Kuznets curve to suggest, very tentatively, that in some cases the income distribution in the LDCs may be influenced unfavorably by freer trade. Chenery even presents some statistical findings that seem to show that in some cases the lower-income classes may have benefited less from free trade than the upper echelons or that low-income countries have benefited less than higher-income countries among the LDCs. It is not that poor countries or the poor in some countries have suffered an absolute loss but merely that they have benefited less than the better off. At any rate, the proper policy response in such cases would not be to restrict trade but to try to change the income distribution by tax measures, retraining of displaced workers, or some other domestic policies. As far as the Stolper-Samuelson theorem is concerned, I would say that it is ingenious from the purely theoretical standpoint but is of no help in the present context, because it is based on a two-factor model and breaks down, as Stolper and Samuelson recognize, when we introduce, as we surely must, more than two factors and two types of income, different types of labor, salaries, profits, interest, and so on.

I therefore conclude that my statement that inequality of income distribution has very little to do with the international order has emerged pretty much unscathed from the discussion. And the little systematic influence trade may have on income distribution may, as Findlay himself suggests, "go in either direction"; in other words it may make the income distribution in some sense either more or less "equal" or desirable.

On the other hand, the presumption that freer trade and LIEO are good things overall, that they stimulate GNP growth, remains as strong as ever. I am glad that Chenery agrees with me "that growth is a necessary condition for doing anything about poverty."

I suggested in my paper that comparisons between pairs of countries with liberal and illiberal policies, both in the domestic and international trade area, clearly show the superiority of liberal policies. As examples among the LDCs, I mentioned Malaysia and Burma. I accept Findlay's statement that a comparison of Thailand and Burma is even more telling. And Bela Balassa has added the example of Ghana and the Ivory Coast.

Kenen thinks that the refutation of the Prebisch-Singer thesis, a

PART ONE: OVERVIEW

criticism he finds "thoroughly persuasive," is "irrelevant to the rhetoric of North-South relations." One can, of course, take the somewhat cynical view that the LDCs are out to get valuable concessions and that, if some of their arguments are demolished, they will not be prevented from pressing their claims. But I do not believe it is true that the Prebisch-Singer thesis is no longer used. As Balassa has said, it is still bandied about in support of all sorts of measures for changing the terms of trade.

Kenen disagrees with what I said about how to deal with stagflation. He says we should take some "risks on the side of inflation" and recommends using incomes policy to bring down inflation and unemployment, despite the admitted inefficiencies of that approach. However, incomes policy means different things to different people. Unfortunately, Kenen did not say what type of incomes policy he has in mind. Frankly, I am unhappy that he mentions "direct wage and price restraints" as a possibility. This type of incomes policy has never worked for any length of time. However, I have expressed my views on these problems in greater detail in several publications (see my paper for references), and since this topic is not of central importance to our conference, I refrain from pursuing it further.

PART TWO

COMMODITIES PROBLEMS

Commodity Instability: New Order or Old Hat?

Gordon W. Smith

The United States seems to be moving inexorably toward wider participation in international arrangements to control primary commodity markets. The list of moves during the past two years appears impressive. The United States finally joined the Tin Agreement in 1976 after twenty years on the sidelines; it has indicated its willingness to participate in the newly negotiated Sugar Agreement. It has continued its membership in the new Coffee Agreement and is pushing for some form of more effective Wheat Agreement. For the future, administration spokesmen are somewhat optimistic about agreements in natural rubber and tungsten; the prospects for copper seem less favorable, although discussions are continuing. Topping it all, the United States has gradually pulled back from full opposition to UNCTAD's Common Fund proposal and currently supports a much reduced and considerably modified common funding for commodity agreements.

The main support for this apparent change in policy orientation is threefold. (1) The Integrated Commodity Programme with its $6 billion Common Fund has been the centerpiece of proposals for the New International Economic Order. In diplomatic circles, there is felt to be a somewhat greater need to attend to the demands of the Group of 77 for a better deal in commodity trade. Lurking in the background is the threat of "oil diplomacy" and raw materials cartels unless something more positive is done. (2) For the industrial countries, the main direct economic attraction of commodity agreements is their supposed ability to reduce the impact of commodity instability on inflation while at the same time softening the damage inflicted by price instability in many LDCs. (3) Finally, for commodities such as grains and sugar, international agreements are sometimes viewed as valuable extensions of or substitutes for domestic programs to support or stabilize prices in the industrial countries. If properly negotiated, they could presumably serve to reduce the destabilizing effects which such policies as the EEC's variable levy have upon the world market and more open agricultural economies. A fourth, older, and currently less prominent basis for public

PART TWO: COMMODITIES PROBLEMS

intervention in commodity markets has been the supposedly gross microeconomic inefficiencies such markets are said to exhibit, particularly in smoothing price fluctuations over time.

This paper argues that the entire price stabilization package has been severely oversold by its proponents. True, as the following discussion will suggest, there is evidence that private markets in many commodities fall short of the ideal of microeconomic efficiency. And a case certainly can be made that commodity instability interferes severely with development in many LDCs, although the inflationary effect of commodity price fluctuations is less certain. However, the review of operating and prospective commodity arrangements, which concludes this paper, strongly suggests that most of them have done or will do little to improve matters significantly. Some (coffee, cocoa, sugar, and, until recently, tin) rely mainly on export quotas for price support at the price bottoms. In the past, these agreements have usually meant inadequate protection for consumer interests during periods of shortage. Indeed, as in the case of coffee, the consumer-producer agreement during excess supply may serve as a prelude to producer-cartel type of actions during periods of short supply. Other agreements such as copper and tin would rely more upon buffer stocks in the future. No one really knows how large a stock would be required for what kind of stabilization. Empirical results thus far suggest buffer stocks may be discouragingly large when account is taken of their impact on private stockholdings. Certainly, UNCTAD's estimates of the required financing for a broad spectrum of buffer stocks fall far short of any reasonable total.

My general policy conclusions from all this are quite unremarkable. (1) Compensatory finance should be the primary mechanism used to mitigate the macro impact of commodity fluctuations on LDCs. If particular LDCs find that they prefer greater stability of production than the world market allows, they can use the counterpart of these IMF loans (or the buffer stock facility) to form their own domestic buffer. (2) Underfinanced commodity agreements should not be negotiated. Their buffer stocks will be ineffectual at best, while recourse to export quotas to support floors will raise average costs to consumers.

One point that should come through clearly to the reader of this paper is the *inconclusiveness* of the empirical evidence in this area. In part this is a reflection of the unsettled state of economic theory. On the other hand, it probably is one more illustration of a wise remark made by James Tobin in 1977 in response to a hostile question: The idea that we can throw away our theory and look at the facts ignores fifty years of econometric frustration.

Are Commodity Markets Inefficient?

Short-Term Informational Efficiency. It has long been argued that commodity markets do not generate and process information efficiently, that they are periodic victims of overly optimistic and pessimistic speculative waves, and that they are excessively myopic in their vision. Such inefficiencies could amplify significantly the underlying and irreducible instability of commodity markets. Speculators might systematically discount the likelihood of shortages far down the line and thereby hold suboptimal stocks.[1] Producers may give too much weight to recent price behavior in forming their expectations of the future and thereby generate excessive cycles in output unwarranted by the best available information.[2]

The actual extent of informational inefficiencies is far from clear. Many observers purport to see signs of gross inefficiencies in particular market episodes. For example, experts have claimed that the late 1960s and early 1970s witnessed (avoidably) poor market forecasting by producers of nonferrous metals and by those who could have counterbalanced producers' errors through larger carry-overs of the metals.[3] The extraordinary price increases of 1972–1974 following on the heels of the large declines in the previous few years were at least partially a result of this inefficient generation and use of longer-term information by market participants. The short-run dimension is probably less important but has received more attention. There is some consensus that by early 1974 most commodity markets were dominated by excessive speculative fever.[4] Long-run mistakes produced short-run overshoot or overreaction, even though the best information should have indicated that such extraordinarily high prices were sustainable only briefly. The bottom-line conclusion often drawn is that public buffer stocks should

---

[1] The opposite is also possible, particularly after a period of high prices; speculators may overestimate the likelihood of shortages and stock too much. Record stocks in copper may be a case in point.

[2] The long-gestation tree crops seem to exhibit the results of this myopic behavior most clearly in apparent fifteen-to-twenty-year price cycles.

[3] Interview by the author and J. Michael Finger with James Burrows and others from Charles River Associates. Memo summarizing the interview is available from J. M. Finger of the U.S. Treasury.

[4] See, for example, Walter C. Labys and Harman C. Thomas, "Speculation, Hedging, and Commodity Price Behavior: An International Comparison," Graduate Institute of International Studies, Geneva, December 1974; Charles Piggott and Gordon W. Smith, "A New Era of Commodity Trade?" U.S. Treasury/OASIA-Research, Washington, D.C., April 1975; Richard N. Cooper and Robert Z. Lawrence, "The 1972–75 Commodity Boom," *Brookings Papers on Economic Activity*, no. 3 (1975), pp. 671–715; Nicholas Kaldor, "Inflation and Recession in the World Economy," *Economic Journal*, vol. 86 (December 1976), pp. 703–14.

be formed to prevent excesses rooted in poor information and speculation.[5]

Unfortunately, rigorous and systematic tests of such assertions (which do, after all, benefit from a good deal of hindsight) have been sorely lacking. "Weak form" tests of spot and futures price behavior have been performed, but with mixed results. And though inability to pass such tests is good evidence of inefficiency, grossly inefficient markets of the type described in the previous paragraph may still emerge unscathed.

Be that as it may, in evaluating the empirical tests that have been made it is useful to keep in mind Eugene Fama's version of the efficient markets hypothesis. "Market efficiency requires that in setting the prices of securities at any time $t-1$ the market correctly uses all available information."[6] More specifically, at any time $t-1$ there is assumed to exist an objective, correct probability density function that maps information available at that time into the probabilities associated with security price outcomes in period t. An efficient market, in effect, forms its price expectations for period t by plugging all available information into this objective density function in $t-1$.[7] Symbolically, let F be the objective density function and Φ the set of all available information. Then,

$$E(P_t) = E[F_{t-1}(\phi_{t-1})].$$

The efficient market hypothesis asserts that

$$F^m_{t-1} = F_{t-1}$$

and

$$\phi^m_{t-1} = \phi_{t-1},$$

where m refers to market-related terms. It follows that

$$E^m(P_t) = E[F_{t-1}(\phi_{t-1})] = E(P_t).[8]$$

---

[5] Cooper and Lawrence, "Commodity Boom," pp. 711–15; Kaldor, "Inflation and Recession," p. 713.

[6] Eugene Fama, "Reply," *Journal of Finance*, vol. 31 (March 1976), p. 143.

[7] Ibid.

[8] Evidently the term "all available information" skirts the fact that much information, including knowledge of the appropriate economic model, is not costless to market participants. *Economically* rational expectations, which take into account the benefits and costs of additional forecasting precision, need not correspond to the costless rational expectations of the Fama approach. See Edgar L. Feige and Douglas K. Pearce, "Economically Rational Expectations: Are Innovations in the Rate of Inflation Independent of Innovations of Measures of Monetary and Fiscal Policy?" *Journal of Political Economy*, vol. 84 (June 1976), pp. 499–522.

An efficient market then uses this information by setting "the prices of securities at t–1 so that it perceives (true) expected returns to equal their equilibrium values."

$$r_t \equiv P_t - P_{t-1},$$
$$E(r_t) = E(P_t) - P_{t-1},$$
$$E(r_t) = r^*_t,$$

where $r \equiv$ one period returns and $r^* \equiv$ equilibrium one period returns.[9] That is to say, in an efficient market only equilibrium returns are earned, and assets are correctly valued.

A complete empirical test of informational efficiency would compare the "true" next period forecast with the "market's expectations."[10] This approach is obviously impossible, and actual tests have been much weaker. All those with which I am familiar for commodities are of the so-called weak-form hypothesis.[11] That is, they seek to determine whether one part of the information set, past price behavior, has been fully milked of its useful content and incorporated into market prices. If it has, as in an efficient market, it should be impossible to find buy-sell rules based on price movements that earn systematically higher profits than buy-hold in the same security, or alternatively in other assets of the same risk category. Other weak-form tests assume the more restrictive random walk model. In this case, the sequence of one-period returns is assumed to be generated by a frequency distribution identical for each moment in time and independent of the sequence of information.[12] In other words, each element of any n-period sequence of returns is seen as having been drawn independently, but from an identical frequency distribution.[13] This is a very strong assumption. One impli-

---

[9] Fama, "Reply," pp. 143–44.

[10] The meaning of "market expectations" when individual participants in fact differ in their assessments has long plagued theorists of speculative markets. For an excellent attempt to nail down more precisely the notions of market efficiency and expectations, see Mark Rubinstein, "Securities Market Efficiency in an Arrow-Debreu Economy," *American Economic Review*, vol. 65 (December 1975), pp. 812–24.

[11] In the finance literature, the weak form is that all information obtainable from past price history is fully reflected in market prices. The semistrong form, of greater importance, is that *all* publicly available information is so reflected in prices.

[12] See Fama, "Reply," pp. 144–45; and Eugene Fama, "Efficient Capital Markets: A Review of Theory and Empirical Work," *Journal of Finance*, vol. 25 (May 1970), pp. 400–404.

[13] Although the error is of minor practical import, Fama's characterization of the random walk is overly restrictive. If spectral techniques are employed to detect the intertemporal dependence, identical variances of the distribution of returns

PART TWO: COMMODITIES PROBLEMS

cation, that returns (and if these are zero, the changes in prices) should be intertemporally independent, has been the basis of the voluminous literature that tests for serial correlation in first (and second) differences in prices, uses spectral analysis to detect phase relations, and employs runs and other tests in attempts to discover evidence of nonindependence over time.

To turn first to the various mechanical buy-sell rules, even though none has approached the complexity of "advanced chartism," they still raise considerable doubts about the efficiency of the commodity markets examined. A typical procedure runs x percent "filter rules" of many different bandwidths.[14] Hendrik Houthakker's is the simplest.[15] In his rule, May, September, and December futures were bought once a year on different fixed dates. The contracts were held until maturity unless they fell to a stop-loss level x percent below cost of acquisition, in which case they would be sold. Percentages ranging from 0 to 100 were used. In a solid majority of cases for wheat and corn, the two commodities examined, these stop-loss rules outperformed buy-hold. Houthakker is unable to assess the statistical significance of the results; even so, he concludes that his results "indicate the presence of price behavior that would not be present if price changes were random." Roger Gray also found that filter rules were profitable in both Chicago corn and wheat futures,[16] while Richard Stevenson and Robert Bear reject randomness in part because of the superiority of their 5 percent filters over buy-hold in Chicago corn and wheat.[17]

Seymour Smidt used filter bands around moving averages of soybean futures prices ranging from one to ten days prior.[18] After subtracting trading commissions, sixteen of the twenty rules tested gave positive

---

over time are not required, although the mean of the distribution of returns must remain fixed. See Walter C. Labys and Clive W. J. Granger, *Speculation, Hedging, and Commodity Price Forecasts* (Lexington, Mass.: D. C. Heath, Lexington Books, 1970), pp. 63–64.

[14] Although there are many variants, in essence these rules say, "Buy (sell) when the price rises x percent above some level, sell (buy) when it falls by x percent below some level." The procedure filters out small changes in prices, which are thought to have no information content. If such rules are profitable, future price changes depend on previous changes in ways not fully reflected in current price—a violation of the weak-form hypothesis.

[15] Hendrik S. Houthakker, "Systematic and Random Elements in Short-Term Price Movements," *American Economic Review*, vol. 51 (May 1961), pp. 164–72.

[16] Roger W. Gray, "The Search for a Risk Premium," *Journal of Political Economy*, vol. 69 (June 1961), pp. 250–60.

[17] Richard A. Stevenson and Robert M. Bear, "Commodity Futures: Trends or Random Walks?" *Journal of Finance*, vol. 25 (March 1970), pp. 65–82.

[18] Seymour Smidt, "A Test of the Serial Independence of Price Changes in Soybeans Futures," *Food Research Institute Studies*, vol. 5 (1965), pp. 117–36.

returns. These and other filter tests led Smidt to reject randomness, but since he did not compute the comparable buy-hold returns, he did not in fact test the efficient information property.

Peter Praetz ran twenty-four filter sizes on the Sydney wool exchange futures contracts.[19] Less than half did better than buy-hold, a number that Praetz concluded was insufficient to reject the fair-game hypothesis. However, he later showed that profitability comparisons in such tests are heavily biased in favor of buy-hold if the underlying process is a random walk, the bias increasing with the proportion of time that the filter is operating in a short position.[20] Were this bias to be taken into account, Praetz might have had trouble drawing support for market efficiency from his filter tests.

Charles Cox examined the spot prices for six commodities.[21] His trading rule was to buy for sale one week later if current price was below a weighted moving average of past prices. It sold spot and replenished one week later if current price was above the moving average. These rules earned substantial profits in all six commodities when no futures markets were operating, while only two of six (potatoes and orange juice) showed profits when futures trading was active.

Unfortunately, mechanical buy-sell rules have not been published for most of the commodities in the UNCTAD Integrated Programme or, indeed, for most of the commodities now covered by or seriously considered for international agreements. The coffee, cocoa, sugar, tin, rubber, and copper markets are all a good deal "thinner" than the wheat, soybean, and corn markets tests in the United States, so that a priori they would appear less likely candidates for informational efficiency.

Time and resources precluded extensive testing of mechanical rules specifically for this paper. However, for London copper I was able to run the simplest of rules, similar to those tested by Houthakker: buy-hold except for a simple stop-loss order to sell when price falls by a certain percentage below original purchase price, in this case 5 percent. The rule bought ninety-day copper on the first and fifteenth of every month during 1973–1974 and early 1975—the big boom and bust months.[22] If the ninety-day price fell by 5 percent or more below

---

[19] Peter D. Praetz, "Testing the Efficient Markets Theory on the Sydney Wool Futures Exchange," *Australian Economic Papers*, vol. 14 (December 1975), pp. 240–49.

[20] Peter D. Praetz, "Rates of Return on Filter Tests," *Journal of Finance*, vol. 31 (March 1976), pp. 71–75.

[21] Onions, potatoes, pork bellies, hogs, cattle, and orange juice. Charles C. Cox, "Futures Trading and Market Information," *Journal of Political Economy*, vol. 84 (December 1976), pp. 1216–38.

[22] Or the nearest day to the first or fifteenth when markets were closed on those days.

PART TWO: COMMODITIES PROBLEMS

TABLE 1

Profits on London Metal Exchange (Copper) Transactions:
January 1, 1973, to February 15, 1975

	Number of Buys	Number of Sells	Profits Net of Commissions[c] as Annual Percentage of Average Value of Contracts Held
Buy-hold[a]	52	0	11.7
5 percent stop-loss[b]	52	21	28.0

[a] Buy one ninety-day contract on the first and fifteenth of each month and hold until maturity.
[b] Same as buy-hold, except sell if ninety-day price falls by 5 percent or more.
[c] .50 percent of value of transaction.
NOTE: All transactions occur at closing wirebar prices, London Metals Exchange.

purchase price, the rule sold at the spot or ninety-day price, whichever was lower.[23] Otherwise, it held until maturity. One variant on this rule commonly used by commodity traders would ratchet the stop-loss upward with any increase in the ninety-day price. I did not test this variant.

As Table 1 indicates, the stop-loss rule outperforms buy-hold substantially during the period in question. While this is by no means a conclusive statistical test, it is certainly consistent with the overreaction stories recounted above.

Finally, D. Gale Johnson has argued that the soybean market for much of 1973 was speculative and did not reflect the best available public information.[24] Thus, I ran a similar rule for the November 1973 Chicago soybean contract from November 1, 1972, to its expiration. Again, the simple 5 percent stop-loss rule outperformed buy-hold by a substantial margin (see Table 2), a result consistent with Johnson's contention and with previous filter tests.

Curiously, in light of the filter test results, the random walk version of market efficiency has emerged almost unscathed from the various attempts to detect intertemporal correlations in price movements. By far the most complete study of the random walk hypothesis in commodity

---

[23] Thus, the test is biased against the stop-loss rule, since the sale price during the lifetime of the ninety-day contract will always be between the current ninety-day price and the spot price. Unfortunately, the London Metals Exchange publishes only spot, sixty- and ninety-day prices.

[24] D. Gale Johnson, "Fluctuating Supplies and Prices of Major Grains and the International Economic System," paper funded by Departments of State, Treasury, and Labor and the Council of International Economic Policy, June 1977, pp. 50–51.

TABLE 2
November 1972 Chicago Soybean Contract Transactions: November 1, 1972, to October 31, 1973

	Profits as an Annual Percentage of Average Value of Contracts Held
Buy-hold[a]	16.3
5 percent stop-loss[b]	30.9

[a] Buy one November 1972 contract on the first and fifteenth of every month.
[b] Same as buy-hold, except sell if contract price falls by 5 percent or more below purchase price.
NOTE: All transactions occur at closing prices, Chicago Board of Trade.

markets, that of Labys and Granger (L-G), concluded that "most series obey a random walk or near random walk."[25] L-G hypothesized a random walk in which the series of gross returns is a "fair game."[26] They then applied spectral analysis to daily, weekly, and monthly prices for several futures contracts.[27] With the monthly data, there was a little evidence of an annual component and its harmonic. Weekly and daily data, however, almost uniformly did not permit rejection of the randomness hypothesis.[28] The results for selected commodities appear in Table 3.

Labys and Thomas (L-T), 1974, update and expand on L-G for the period January 1970 through June 1974. The daily prices of nine commodities in London and five in New York (including copper and coffee in both locales) were subjected to spectral analysis. *Again*, the evidence did not permit rejection of the random walk (see Table 3) even though price instability was violent during those years.

Complementing L-T, I performed runs tests on the daily three-month-forward London Metals Exchange (LME) copper price for the period February 16, 1973, to January 27, 1975—the big boom and bust period—and on the November 1973 Chicago soybean contract for November 1, 1972, to October 31, 1973, a speculative market if there ever was one, according to Johnson. With randomness assumed, the

---
[25] Labys and Granger, *Speculation, Hedging*, p. 84.
[26] That is, $E(P_t) - P_{t-1} = 0$.
[27] Sixteen for monthly data, six for weekly observations, and ten for the daily price series. The number of observations varied between 186 and 260 taken from the 1950s and 1960s. L-G worked with cash prices, but the results are irrelevant for informational efficiency unless something further is known about the costs of holding physical commodities.
[28] Cocoa and cotton futures daily prices showed negative autocorrelation.

TABLE 3

Results of Spectral Analysis of Commodity Futures Prices (First Differences)

	Labys-Granger			Labys-Thomas	
	Daily	Weekly	Monthly	London	New York
Cocoa	N	—	R	R	S″
Coffee	R	—	—	R	—
Corn	R	R	S	—	—
Copper	—	—	S	R	R
Rubber	R	—	—	R	—
Sugar	R	—	—	S″	S″
Tin	—	—	—	R	—
Soybeans	R	R	—	—	—
Wheat	R	R	S′	—	—

NOTE: R = random walk; N = negative serial correlation; S = slight trace of annual, not significant; S′ = moderate trace of annual, sometimes not significant; S″ = slight seasonal; dash (—) signifies that no analysis was performed.
SOURCES: Walter C. Labys and Clive W. J. Granger, *Speculation, Hedging and Commodity Price Forecasts* (Lexington, Mass.: D. C. Heath, Lexington Books, 1970); and Walter C. Labys and Harman C. Thomas, "Speculation, Hedging, and Commodity Price Behavior: An International Comparison," Graduate Institute of International Studies, Geneva, December 1974 (processed).

number of runs turned out to be almost exactly what one would have expected. Further analysis of the two series indicated that the direction of daily price changes was completely independent of the signs of the changes in the previous two market days.

Finally, Praetz reported on the efficiency of the Sydney wool futures exchange. He assumed a random walk in which the gross rate of return to holdings futures is constant. He concluded that the "correlation coefficients, runs tests and spectral analysis [of daily futures] provide only small departures from a model in which price changes are uncorrelated. Clearly, this model stands as a good first approximation to the underlying stochastic process generating price changes."[29]

The conflict in the evidence is clear. On the one hand L-G, L-T, and Praetz, using spectral analysis, have been unable to reject the random walk version for a broad range of commodities, while the weight of the filter rules is against a less stringent hypothesis. And it is surely suggestive that in copper and soybean markets, supposedly dominated

---

[29] Praetz, "Testing the Efficient Markets Theory," p. 248.

by speculative fever and where a simple stop-loss rule outperformed buy-hold by a wide margin, price changes seemed about as random as one could wish.

At least two interpretations are possible. First, spectral analysis, runs tests, and the like may not be sufficiently powerful techniques to detect the less obvious forms of randomness in price series. This is a position taken recently by Dennis Logue and Richard Sweeney.[30] The second interpretation emphasizes the very loose association between randomness and informational efficiency, as do L-G and L-T. For L-G, randomness means unpredictability, instability, and market disequilibrium, and they felt their findings should support the formation of commodity agreements. Either way, market interventionists will find significant support in the commodity market tests published so far.

In conclusion, it should be noted that even had the informational efficiency hypothesis emerged unscathed from the tests, the further premise that "all available information" or economically rational information is also *socially* optimal would have remained untested. There are reasons to believe that the information about commodities that is readily available and diffused is suboptimal: (1) International data on stocks and production are often very scanty and of dubious quality; (2) The volume of serious modeling of commodities outside American agriculture has been small until recently. If nothing else, suboptimal information will raise the risk premium required by private stockists, thus increasing market instability.

Long-Term Informational Efficiency. Longer-term inefficiencies are potentially far more important than the day-to-day variety in generating fundamental instability. Indeed, most serious proponents of intervention have tended to concentrate on them to the extent that microeconomic efficiency is a consideration at all. In particular, it is argued that the private market generally performs the buffer stock or carry-over function ineffectively, while investment and production decisions, especially those with longer gestation periods, tend to be informed by overly myopic forecasts. For propositions with such widespread acceptance, empirical testing has been remarkably sparse.

As to the adequacy of private buffer stocks, at least three factors may generate suboptimal carry-over or buffer stocks of commodities: informational inefficiencies, inadequate diffusion of the considerable risk involved in holding stocks for long periods, and noncompetitive

---

[30] Dennis E. Logue and Richard J. Sweeney, " 'White Noise' in Imperfect Markets: The Case of the Franc/Dollar Exchange Rate," *Journal of Finance*, vol. 32 (June 1977), pp. 761–68.

market structures. It is difficult in practice to separate the impact of the three. If, however, competition can be assumed and "the" private discount rate is known, then it would be possible to test for information efficiency through some form of longer-term filter rule or more directly (and much less feasibly) through calculation of privately optimal storage rules, given what might be assumed to be the best information.

Many people believe that a public buffer stock that reduces instability by buying low and selling high could actually earn profits above and beyond interest, storage, and other costs. If this were true, and the rate of interest were reckoned correctly, it should be possible to introduce profitable buffer stocks into good econometric commodity models and thereby reduce market instability—prima facie evidence for information inefficiencies. This exercise has been performed several times in the past few years. I experimented with many buffer-stock-decision rules of thumb within the Wharton Econometric Forecasting Associates, Inc. (EFA) tin model and the Charles River Associates–Wharton EFA copper model.[31] While a well-financed buffer stock could indeed reduce market instability dramatically, none of the rules investigated earned positive profits, even at interest rates below those usually available to private firms. Behrman's is the most complete study so far of the UNCTAD Common Fund proposal.[32] In it he simulated buffer stocks that maintained price bands ±15 percent around known long-run trends. Of eleven serious candidates for buffer stocks, four showed a profit (coffee, cocoa, tea, and rubber). The rest were losers, using 5 percent real discount rates. Taylor, Sarris and Abbott simulated similar rules for the international wheat market, and again the buffer stock lost money.[33] All of the models simulated have significant limitations, particularly in the way the private storage sector is assumed to behave. Furthermore, all the rules simulated are quite mechanical, and the tests are not very powerful. Still, the results do suggest that the view that private markets are grossly inefficient in performing the buffer stock function is overly simplistic. Interestingly, governments, not the private

---

[31] Gordon W. Smith and George R. Schink, "The International Tin Agreement: A Reassessment," *Economic Journal*, vol. 86 (December 1976), pp. 715–28; Gordon W. Smith, "An Economic Evaluation of International Buffer Stocks for Copper," Department of State, Intelligence and Research, October 1975.

[32] Jere R. Behrman, *International Commodity Agreements: An Evaluation of the UNCTAD Integrated Commodities Programme*, Monograph, no. 9 (Washington, D.C.: Overseas Development Council, 1977).

[33] Lance Taylor, Alexander H. Sarris, and Philip C. Abbott, *Grain Reserves, Emergency Relief, and Food Aid* (Washington, D.C.: Overseas Development Council, 1977), prepublication version.

sector, manage the bulk of the stocks in two of the four commodities for which Behrman's rules earned profits: coffee and cocoa.

Filter rules operating over long time horizons are probably a better way to detect inefficiency in the buffer stock function. I am unaware of any published results along this line. In an admittedly limited test, I applied the following rule for copper purchases and sales: calculate the five-year lagged moving average of deflated LME spot prices; sell one lot at the current year's average if it exceeds the moving average by more than 15 percent; buy one lot if current price is more than 15 percent below the moving average. The main limitation of this rule is that it permits one to trade at annual average prices, something never known in advance. With more detailed observations—say weekly or daily—this difficulty could be corrected, probably without any great change in the outcome. Time and resources did not permit such detailed analysis for this survey.

In any case, the results appear in Table 4. If we assume an 8 percent real discount rate (and basically negligible storage costs),[34] positive discounted profits were earned in the two periods in which the rule was active: 1957–1966 and 1971–1974, while the higher 10 percent discount rate incurred slight losses in the earlier period and substantial gains in the second. These discount rates are fairly high and allow risk premiums which themselves are larger than the average short-term interest rates charged to businesses in the United States.[35]

Obviously, no firm conclusions can be drawn from one test of this limited nature,[36] except perhaps that together with the previous filter test on copper it does suggest the LME copper market is *not* informationally efficient. More complete tests for most of the UNCTAD commodities could resolve this question once and for all.

With accurate models of market behavior outside the storage sector, it may be possible to test for efficiency more directly in a manner suggested by Robert Gustafson for agricultural products.[37] Stockists

---

[34] In LME warehouses, storage costs are on the order of 0.5 percent per year.

[35] *Economic Report of the President*, 1976.

[36] No other rules were tested. A 15 percent band was selected because it was obvious that with 8 and 10 percent discount rates, narrower bands were almost certain to lose money.

[37] Robert L. Gustafson, "Carry Levels for Grains: A Method for Determining Amounts That Are Optimal under Specified Conditions," *USDA Technical Bulletin*, no. 1178 (1958). D. Gale Johnson, "Increased Stability of Grain Supplies in Developing Countries," University of Chicago, Office of Agricultural Economics Research Paper, no. 76:14, April 1976; D. Gale Johnson and Daniel Sumner, "An Optimization Approach to Grain Reserves for Developing Countries," April 1976; and John P. Stein and Rodney T. Smith, *The Economics of United States Grain Stockpiling* (Santa Monica: Rand, 1977) have used this approach to determine optimal stock levels.

PART TWO: COMMODITIES PROBLEMS

TABLE 4

Results of ±15 Percent Rule around
Five-Year Lagged Moving Average
(current dollars)

Year	Activity	8 Percent Real Discount Rate	10 Percent Real Discount Rate
1957	Buy		
1958	Buy		
1959	Buy		
1964	Sell		
1965	Sell		
1966	Sell		
1957–1966		$1.131	$0.9855
1971	Buy		
1972	Buy		
1973	Sell		
1974	Sell		
1971–1974		$1.252	$1.2050

NOTE: Buy one lot of copper if real LME average is at least 15 percent below five-year lagged moving average; sell one lot if price is at least 15 percent above the lagged moving average.
SOURCE OF PRICES: Wharton Econometric Forecasting Associates, Inc.

would be assumed to know the behavior of planned supply and demand over time. Random shocks (such as weather) would be introduced in supply, based on past yield fluctuations, and in demand via the export sector. Dynamic programming could then be used to determine for each year the optimal storage level that would maximize the total expected value of discounted (at market rates) consumer surplus and export revenue. This optimal stock would then be compared with actual stocks held. While this approach has been used for normative purposes, that is, to determine optimal stock levels, the author knows of no published attempt to use it to test the positive hypothesis of market efficiency.[38] It has some promise for wheat, where—in the United States, at least— excellent data are available. The optimal storage norm is much more difficult to apply for industrial raw materials, because the primary disturbances appear as activity variables—investment, GNP, and so forth—

---

[38] Bruce Gardner of Texas A. & M. University is currently using this approach to test the hypothesis of market efficiency.

on the demand side of the market. Their probability distributions are not nearly so simple to determine as those of agricultural yields.

The Efficiency of Producer Decisions. Many commodities require long gestation periods between the decision to produce and actual output. Coffee trees, until recently, began to yield only in their fifth year. It may take five years to bring a copper mine on line. The most important source of price instability—which stockists can only partially mitigate—is often miscalculation by producers of expected price or future demand.

In this context, John Muth's rational expectations hypothesis is a useful standard, at least in competitive markets.[39] It asserts that economic agents use the appropriate economic model in forming their expectations. Furthermore, since it is known that the rest of the market is also rational and therefore uses the same good model, expected price will equal the equilibrium price (if the model is correct and the right information is plugged into it).[40]

None of the commodity models with which I am familiar incorporates the rational expectations assumption. Producer-expected price is some kind of average of recent past prices, either a naive projection of last year's price or some form of adaptive expectation, as in the best coffee and cocoa models. In the Wharton EFA models, stockists are also assumed to have regressive expectations around some "normal" price. If these assumptions are correct, neither producers nor stockists are acting "rationally," because their predictions are wrong on the average, and market stability could be improved by more extensive diffusion of information or by government interference with the price mechanism in such a way as to induce irrational decision makers to produce rational outcomes.

However, econometric models were estimated not to test rational expectations but to simulate historical experience of the principal variables accurately in a statistical sense. As such, they probably do not constitute a fair test of the efficiency hypothesis. In some cases, it may

---

[39] John F. Muth, "Rational Expectations and the Theory of Price Movements," *Econometrica*, vol. 29 (July 1961), pp. 315–35.

[40] I know of only one empirical application of rational expectations to commodity production decisions: Thomas F. Cooley and Stephen J. DeCanio, "Rational Expectations in American Agriculture, 1867–1914," *American Journal of Agricultural Economics*, vol. 59 (February 1977), pp. 9–17. Using Muth's original model, they cannot reject rational expectations for U.S. cotton and wheat producers. Since this version is empirically indistinguishable from adaptive expectations, the result hardly constitutes a strong test. On this last point, see Charles R. Nelson, "Rational Expectations and the Predictive Efficiency of Economic Models," *Journal of Business*, vol. 48, no. 3 (July 1975), pp. 331–43.

PART TWO: COMMODITIES PROBLEMS

be possible to include rational expectations in new models, so that fair tests could be made against the alternative hypothesis.

Having said this, I may be stretching a point to argue that Brazilian coffee producers or Ghanaian cocoa producers have the faintest idea of the longer-run supply and demand models generating prices or enough information to make extended forecasts. There is certainly no denying that the rush to plant when prices are high is feverish; given the lags, it is equally obvious that lust for extraordinary profits is usually frustrated. More fundamentally, it is not at all clear what the "rational" expectations of oligopolists should be, particularly if cartels, collusion, and communication are ruled out. The strategic uncertainty becomes most serious for long-term investment decisions, such as whether to open a new mine. Even for seemingly competitive industries, a few governments, by manipulation of incentives, may be in de facto control. Governments in effect become the oligopolists. The classic case of this type is coffee, with Brazil (decreasingly) the dominant "firm."

On balance, the proposition that producers follow "rational" expectations appears very suspect for many key commodities in the world as it is structured today.

Risk, Myopia, and Private Stockpiles. Many advocates of publicly supported buffer stocks from Keynes to Houthakker have rested their cases upon the supposed divergence between the social and the private aversions to the very large risks entailed in maintaining large stocks for long periods.[41] Private stockists are held to be overly myopic and to require excessive ex ante risk premiums. As a result, private stocks are too small and price instability too large. The implied remedy is either a subsidy to storage or publicly held buffer stocks. The risk would then be spread over the entire taxpaying population. Since each citizen would bear only a minuscule share of the total risk, the social risk premium would be very low indeed. This argument is not completely correct and must be recast.[42]

Potential sources of private risk aversion include the following: (1) An individual or company may face a cash-flow problem as a re-

---

[41] John M. Keynes, "The Policy of Government Storage of Foodstuffs and Raw Materials," *Economic Journal*, vol. 68 (September 1938), pp. 449–60; and Hendrik S. Houthakker, *Economic Policy for the Farm Sector* (Washington, D.C.: American Enterprise Institute, 1967).

[42] Arrow and Linder show that even for public investments with no private counterparts (for example, pure public goods) the government should use the risk-free rate only when the returns from the project are uncorrelated with past government investments and with national income. K. J. Arrow and R. C. Linder, "Uncertainty and the Evaluation of Public Investment Decisions," *American Economic Review*, vol. 60 (June 1970), pp. 364–78.

sult of losses on inventories. This may force bankruptcy, even though over the long haul the storage activity may be profitable. In this case, risk aversion is rooted in capital market imperfections. (2) The separation of ownership from control, to the extent that it creates discretionary behavior possibilities for management, may also lead to excessive risk aversion. Large losses could threaten the control of existing management, while large gains might be unnecessary for the maintenance of the status quo. Hence, corporations may be overly timid from a social viewpoint, another market failure. (3) The costs of being wiped out in the market are surely felt by most individuals to be more severe than the gains from doubling net worth. Although the example is extreme, it is generally felt that diminishing marginal utility of income is a common attribute, and this is sufficient to generate risk aversion without market failure.

In principle, risks could be transferred and optimally pooled through "risk markets" in which shares in each individual "project" could be bought and sold by consumers.[43] Obviously, these markets do not exist to nearly the extent required for optimality, if for no other reason than the transactions and informational costs their operation would entail. Still we are far from the world in which no risks are pooled in the private sector.[44] Corporations, conglomerates, mutual funds (even in commodity futures), pension funds, insurance companies, and so on, all reduce risks to individuals by pooling projects and by spreading the risk of any particular project over large segments of the population.

The Keynes-Houthakker school must be arguing, in effect, that far from optimal pooling occurs in storage activities. Or, more precisely, government intervention in storage is desirable, while control of most other investment is not, because whatever imperfections result from the absence of explicit risk markets are likely to generate more costly distortions in very risky activities, such as commodity storage, over longer time periods.

Empirical literature on the degree of excessive risk premiums is

---

[43] A proof of this proposition for a simplified economy appears in Agnar Sandmo, "Discount Rates for Public Investment under Uncertainty," in J. H. Dreze, ed., *Allocation Under Uncertainty: Equilibrium and Optimality* (London: 1974), pp. 192–212, which is also an excellent treatment of the differences between Jack Hirshleifer, "Investment Decision under Uncertainty: Choice-Theoretic Approaches," *Quarterly Journal of Economics*, vol. 79, no. 4 (November 1965), pp. 509–36, and "Investment Decision under Uncertainty: Application of the State-Preference Approach," *Quarterly Journal of Economics*, no. 2 (May 1966), pp. 252–77, and Arrow and Linder, "Uncertainty."

[44] Sandmo, in "Discount Rates," analyzes the adverse consequences of an economy made up wholly of unincorporated businesses so that individuals have *no* possibility of diversifying their portfolios.

nonexistent. It seems reasonable to believe that the truth lies somewhere between the poles of optimal pooling and no pooling at all, but where on the continuum it is impossible to say.

Summary and Conclusions. The signs of microeconomic inefficiency in many commodity markets are too numerous to ignore. The many studies in which simple mechanical trading rules dominate buy-hold, even in the "best" of commodity markets, call into question their short-term informational efficiency. My admittedly limited longer-run rule suggests that, for copper at least, the market is not performing the buffer stock function efficiently. Common sense suggests that even the wisest farmers in many LDCs will fall far short of the rational expectations norm, if for no other reason than that they do not possess the necessary knowledge and information. And, clearly, economic theory does not suggest that the time profile of investment in uncoordinated oligopolistic industries will be in any sense socially optimal or equivalent to that which would have been generated by competitive industries following rational expectations. Finally, risk aversion in storing commodities may well be excessive. Surely no empirical study with which I am acquainted has shown the contrary.

None of this, however, suggests that the proper remedy is a whole set of internally negotiated commodity agreements or a common fund. Informational inefficiency may or may not require more extensive public involvement in generating and disseminating commodity information. Excessive risk aversion may or may not counsel subsidies to private storage. Uncoordinated oligopoly may or may not benefit greater coordination. But initiatives along the lines now being considered will have to seek grounds other than microeconomic inefficiencies for convincing support.

Macroeconomic Consequences of Commodity Instability

Although a microeconomic allocational case can be made for some kind of intervention in commodity markets, the main thrust of the economic arguments has emphasized the potentially far more serious macroeconomic spillovers of fluctuations. In the words of Assistant Secretary C. Fred Bergsten,

> Both exporting and importing countries face important problems under the current regime for commodity trade. Excessive price fluctuations can ratchet up inflation in importing countries. Unstable earnings from commodity exports can disrupt

... development. Inadequate investment in productive sources of raw materials has an inflationary effect on the world economy over the longer run.[45]

That is to say, the main benefits from more stable commodity markets will be less inflationary pressure for the developed countries, healthier development in the LDCs, and steadier investment in primary production. This is the intellectual core supporting commodity agreements at the present time.

Inflation and Commodity Price Fluctuations. The linkage of commodity price fluctuations to net increases in the price level or to acceleration in the pace of inflation is not very novel, certainly not for those with experience in the LDCs. One of the tenets of the 1950s Latin American structuralist school of inflation was the idea that harvest failure, through higher food prices and subsequently higher wage demands and monetary expansion, can set off an inflationary spiral.[46] The model seemed plausible enough for those LDCs in which food represented a big portion of urban workers' budgets, in which unions had significant bargaining power, and in which governments were unwilling to permit free importation of foodstuffs.

However, before 1972 few American economists took seriously the inflationary threat that commodity supply shocks could pose to the United States. The primary sector as a whole accounted for much less than 10 percent of total value added, farmers received less than 30 percent of the consumer's food dollar, and so forth. Seemingly, it would have taken an extremely unlikely conjuncture of supply shocks and bottlenecks in many commodities to make a significant ripple in the cost of living.

The unlikely occurred in 1972–1974. During 1973—before the oil price increase—as much as 45 percent of the rise in the consumer price index (CPI) was "due to" increases in the input prices of crude

---

[45] Speech before a conference of business executives sponsored by the Council of the Americas, June 27, 1977.

[46] An excellent statement of this line of reasoning is Richard C. Porter, "The Inflationary Implications of Crop Failure," *Pakistan Development Review*, vol. 2 (Spring 1962), pp. 1–22. In its simplest form the hypothesis rules out substantial imports of food and assumes that carry-over stocks are inadequate. More complex versions analyze the impact of food imports on foreign exchange availability for other uses. The structuralists tended to emphasize the constant inflationary pressure arising from lagging agricultural production and the inflation-propagation sequence by which declines in exports become reflected in higher inflation rates. See, for example, Werner Baer and Isaac Kerstenetsky, *Inflation and Growth in Latin America* (Homewood, Ill.: Richard D. Irwin, 1964).

materials above their trend values.[47] By early 1974 the food price component of the CPI stood 15 percent above the general index (1967 = 100), while in the nineteen years prior to 1973 it had fluctuated in a narrow band from 4 percent above to 3 percent below the general index.[48] According to World Bank data, the real prices (in 1967–1969 U.S. dollars) of thirty-four primary commodities (excluding petroleum) had risen 40 percent during 1972–1974 before plummeting back to 1972 levels a year later.[49]

The explanations put forth for this turn of events were multifaceted: Russian harvest failure, inadequate grain stocks,[50] the EEC's Common Agricultural Policy,[51] Japanese speculation in soybeans, copper, and other raw materials,[52] the fear that inflation would erase much of money's value, exchange controls in Great Britain (where many commodity exchanges are based),[53] hedging against the possibility of cartels similar to OPEC, and so on. One thing is clear: many of the price increases that occurred cannot be explained by (then) current production shortfalls in food and minerals. Rather, contingency hoarding (in fact or through futures contracts) against further adverse events played a large role. Unfortunately, we will never be able fully to disentangle the factors involved, but the events did make structuralists of a sort of many American economists.

Few now seriously doubt the economywide impact of increases in relative prices of commodities arising from supply shocks and production bottlenecks. (But the shocks do have to be large and spread over large groups of commodities, for according to one estimate it takes fully a 14.5 percent increase in crude materials prices, excluding petroleum, to produce a 1.0 percent rise in the CPI.)[54] Furthermore, it should be clear that had stocks of food and raw materials been substantially larger than in fact they were, much of the price run-up could not have occurred,

---

[47] Joel Popkin, "Commodity Prices and the U.S. Price Level," *Brookings Papers on Economic Activity*, no. 1 (1974), pp. 255–56. The standard of comparison overstates the autonomous contribution of relative commodity prices since general inflation was also above trend in 1973. On the other hand, feedback through higher wages was not included.

[48] Dale E. Hathaway, "Food Prices and Inflation," *Brookings Papers on Economic Activity*, no. 1 (1974), p .65.

[49] World Bank, "Price Prospects for Major Primary Commodities," Report no. 814/76 (Washington, D.C., June 1976).

[50] Philip H. Tresize, *Rebuilding Grain Reserves* (Washington, D.C.: Brookings Institution, 1976), p. 1.

[51] Johnson, "Fluctuating Supplies," pp. 24–28.

[52] Ibid., p. 50; Piggott and Smith, "A New Era," p. 18.

[53] Labys and Thomas, "Speculation, Hedging," pp. 21–26.

[54] Popkin, "Commodity Prices," p. 254.

and we would have been spared an important part of the subsequent inflation-unemployment spiral. Finally, it is also evident that private firms cannot be expected to hold socially adequate stocks for such unlikely contingencies as the 1972–1974 rise in prices, if for no other reason than that they capture almost none of the macroeconomic gains.

From all this it follows that publicly held or subsidized stocks accumulated slowly and then released in extraordinary circumstances might have substantial macro payoffs. However, the design and implementation of such specifically antiinflation shock contingency stockpiles are quite complicated and to my knowledge have never been attempted.[55] The inflation argument has been used instead to bolster the case for traditional buffer stocks operating within price-stabilizing commodity agreements.

Why would a buffer stock that dampens fluctuations symmetrically around equilibrium prices tend to reduce the overall rate of inflation over the cycle? Enter now the ratchet hypothesis. Simply put, oligopoly industries are quick to raise prices when materials costs go up but are very reluctant to reduce prices when materials costs fall back to lower levels.[56] Hence, support for commodity prices when they are falling will not prevent reductions in final goods prices—they would not have occurred in any case—while buffer stock sales will indeed prevent some inflation. All this, even though on average commodity prices are unaffected by buffer stock activity.

If this view is correct and the inflation-unemployment trade-off is stable, the gains for the industrial countries from buffer stocks can be impressive indeed. Behrman, for example, simulated buffer stocks that stabilized the prices of UNCTAD's ten core commodities within bands of ±15 percent around long-run trends during 1963–1972. Assuming the full ratchet (no additional inflation when prices are supported), such stabilization could have brought the United States alone gains of at least $15 billion (in 1975 dollars) in GNP over ten years with no increase in the pace of inflation.[57] More impressively, all this would have

---

[55] The social cost entailed a particular percentage increases in the relative price of any one commodity should be an increasing function of the rate of general inflation and the rate of relative increase in commodity prices generally. Even to make a rough estimate of the "required" stocks for each commodity would be extremely difficult, if not impossible.

[56] Casual empiricism in the supermarket often seems to support this contention, particularly for downwardly sluggish sugar and coffee prices. For statements of this hypothesis, see Cooper and Lawrence, "Commodity Boom," pp. 707–09; Behrman, *International Commodity Agreements*, p. 46.

[57] Behrman, *International Commodity Agreements*. The gain arises from a reduction of the amount of unemployment necessary to offset higher commodity prices, p. 46. Behrman employs lower-bound Phillips curve estimates and Okun's law in reaching his conclusion.

been achieved with a maximum investment in such stocks of between $6 billion and $10 billion.

Unfortunately, the rationale for such a ratchet is far from clear.[58] The kinked demand curve hypothesis, the administered pricing literature,[59] and Okun's more recent theory of customer markets[60] all suggest oligopoly prices will be adjusted infrequently but in no way imply an asymmetry in adjustment. That is, oligopolies should delay the pass-through of materials price but not alter the direction of change. When materials costs are rising, oligopolies will tend to dampen the inflation by adjusting more slowly; when costs are falling, they should tend to dampen the deflationary forces.

The ratchet is even less plausible when the general rate of inflation is appreciable, as it is now. Oligopoly firms are now forced by other cost changes to adjust prices more frequently. Why they should insist on ignoring materials cost declines when deciding upon the magnitude of the price change is not at all clear.[61]

Empirically, there is very little if any support for a generalized ratchet. Econometric pricing studies have concluded that the response to changes in unit labor costs is symmetrical.[62] And as Finger and DeRosa point out, "it would be very difficult to rationalize a ratchet effect on materials costs when there is none on labor costs."[63]

Ratchet pricing may not end the story, however. If the costs from higher commodity prices are greater during boom periods than during recession, a broad group of buffer stocks might still bring macroeconomic benefits to the industrial countries. The group is likely to act in a

---

[58] An interesting review of the ratchet effect is J. Michael Finger and Dean A. DeRosa, "Commodity-Price Stabilization and the Ratchet Effect," *World Economy*, vol. 1 (January 1978), pp. 195–204.

[59] A recent testing of the hypothesis that finds some support for it is Leonard Weiss, "Stigler, Kindahl, and Means on Administered Prices," *American Economic Review*, vol. 67 (September 1977), pp. 610–19. A very useful survey of hypotheses concerning oligopoly and inflation and some empirical tests appear in Steven Lusgarten, *Industrial Concentration and Inflation* (Washington, D.C.: American Enterprise Institute, 1975).

[60] Arthur M. Okun, "Inflation: Its Mechanics and Welfare Costs," *Brookings Papers on Economic Activity*, no. 2 (1975), pp. 360–65.

[61] This point is much less compelling for products where materials costs are a high proportion of total value, such as coffee.

[62] Frank C. Ripley and Lydia Segal, "Price Determination in 395 Manufacturing Industries," *Review of Economics and Statistics*, vol. 55 (August 1973), pp. 263–71; James Tobin, "The Wage-Price Mechanism: Overview of the Conference," in Otto Eckstein, ed., *Econometrics of Price Determination* (Washington, D.C.: Board of Governors of the Federal Reserve System and the Social Science Research Council, 1972), p. 10.

[63] Finger and DeRosa, "The Ratchet Effect," p. 201.

fairly uncoordinated fashion during normal times. That is, some buffer stocks will be buying, others selling, and still others will be inactive, mainly because the price movements of different commodities, particularly movements far from trend or equilibrium levels, should not be highly correlated most of the time.[64] These supposedly low correlations are one reason, according to UNCTAD, for pooling the financing of buffer stocks, and they find some support in the Behrman analysis.[65] One reason for suspecting that the correlation may be low is that aggregate economic activity in the industrial countries tends to drive industrial raw materials prices,[66] while food crops are influenced more by product-specific factors—weather, gestation periods, and so on.

Buffer stocks are likely to be highly coordinated, if ever, only during extreme booms and recessions that also happen to coincide with unusual weather or the extreme phases of some of the longer-term agricultural price cycles. 1958–1962 was probably one such period on the down side, while 1972–1974 qualified on the up side.

If this general picture is not far wrong, then the industrial countries might indeed expect positive net macroeconomic benefits from buffer stocks. During "normal" times, the buffer stocks would have a negligible effect on the industrial countries. During an unusual boom, they would bring a significant reduction in inflationary pressures, much in the manner of the antiinflation contingency stocks described above. Finally, during unusually slack periods they would allow prices to fall significantly below trend, while still preventing extreme and probably functionless declines.

The benefits of price supports to primary producers are obvious, but the industrial countries do pay higher than free market prices during support periods.[67] Before 1975 one could have argued that inflation would be a relatively minor problem during severe recession, so that the real costs of somewhat higher commodity prices would likely be less than the real gains from lower commodity prices during inflationary booms. This line does not carry much force, however, for the recent recession when inflation continued almost unabated for many months. About all one can say at this point is that, if the pre-1975 inflation-recession relations gradually reassert themselves, buffer stocks might bring the macroeconomic benefits traced above. If not, then the whole effect becomes dubious.

---

[64] It is the extreme movements that would trigger a buffer stock's entry into the market.

[65] Behrman, *International Commodity Agreements*, pp. 40–41.

[66] Cooper and Lawrence, "Commodity Boom," pp. 679–95.

[67] The discussion is highly oversimplified, since many industrial countries supply the bulk of their primary goods, while others are leading exporters.

PART TWO: COMMODITIES PROBLEMS

In conclusion, it should be noted that buffer stocks over a broad range of commodities are required to make a dent in the macro picture. We are still far from this point in international negotiations, and for a variety of reasons to be discussed later none of the proposals under consideration seems adequate for such a task.

Impact on the LDCs. In the last analysis, attention has again focused on commodity instability, mainly because of the demands articulated by LDCs in various international forums. LDCs depend more upon primary commodities for their exports, and their export earnings also fluctuate substantially more than those of the industrialized world.[68] For example, at least twenty-five LDCs depended upon one commodity for at least 50 percent of their export earnings during 1970–1972. Thirteen more depended on two primary commodities for more than 50 percent of their export receipts in the same period.[69] The problem is particularly severe for nations depending on exports of industrial raw materials, since their price and quantity movements over time tend to reinforce each other and may in turn provoke declines in capital flows. In some cases, for example, Chile, there can be no doubt that in the context of actual economic policy responses export instability has played havoc with economic performance.[70]

Foreign exchange instability and the second best. The principal macroeconomic "externality" of commodity instability occurs through the foreign exchange market, as autonomous foreign exchange earnings fluctuate over the cycle. It is of little use to point out that in a perfect market foreign exchange speculators could iron out these fluctuations to some extent. First, speculators would probably do no better in this respect than those operating in commodity markets. Second, even if they could, the institutional market conditions required for such efficiency do not exist, if for no other reason than that LDC governments will not permit them to develop. This may be totally wrongheaded on the part of LDC governments, but it is usually the reality.

Uncompensated by private or public action, fluctuations in exchange earnings may give rise to substantial adjustment costs. If aggre-

---

[68] For recent surveys on this point, see Robert M. Stern, "World Market Instability in Primary Commodities," *Banca Nazionale del Lavoro Quarterly Review*, June 1976, pp. 175–95; Mordechai E. Kreinin and J. Michael Finger, "A Critical Survey of the New International Economic Order," *Journal of World Trade Law*, vol. 10 (November/December 1976), pp. 493–512; Behrman, "International Commodity Agreements," pp. 37–44.

[69] From World Bank data supplied to the U.S. Treasury Department.

[70] See, for example, Clark W. Reynolds, "Domestic Consequences of Export Instability," *American Economic Review*, vol. 65 (May 1963), pp. 65–74.

gate demand is lowered to bring payments back into balance, excess capacity and unemployment will result. If exchange rates are allowed to clear the market freely so that payments remain in balance, the real losses from adjustment to high and then low exchange rates may be substantial.

It is to reduce the adjustment problem that governments hold foreign exchange reserves. A substantial literature devoted to the choice of optimal reserve holdings has developed in the last ten years.[71] The various models differ mainly in the policy options assumed available to deal with adjustment problems. Even if optimal reserves are held by a given LDC, export instability should be accompanied by some cost and hence should reduce potential GNP below what it otherwise would have been. The greater the instability of foreign exchange earnings, other things being equal, the greater will be the average level of optimal foreign exchange reserves held by the central bank. Savings are thus diverted to a liquid form, which is almost certain to have a lower direct return than investment in real capital. At the very least, then, one cost of instability is the earnings forgone by having more foreign exchange holdings. To this should be added the adjustment costs entailed even when optimal reserves are held.

With suboptimal reserves, the costs of instability will be greater, showing up as excessive compression and expansion of imports and concomitant costs of adjustment, which may include alternating inflation and unemployment.

The foreign exchange externality arises in a second-best framework. First, LDCs may not be following optimal adjustment policies. Thus, global waste could probably be reduced by dampening foreign exchange fluctuations. Buffer stocks might help for countries highly dependent upon particular commodities (coffee, cocoa, and copper are three important cases). This second-best externality is not captured by private market participants.

Second, LDCs may be following optimal policies but may face imperfect capital markets. For some reason, the differential between their

---

[71] See, for example, H. R. Heller, "Optimal International Reserves," *Economic Journal*, vol. 76 (June 1966), pp. 296–311; Peter B. Clark, "Optimum International Reserves and the Speed of Adjustment," *Journal of Political Economy*, vol. 75 (March/April 1970), pp. 356–76; Michael G. Kelly, "The Demand for International Reserves," *American Economic Review*, vol. 60 (September 1970), pp. 655–67; M. J. Flanders, *The Demand for International Reserves*, International Finance Section Studies, no. 27 (Princeton, N.J., 1971); J. A. Frenkel, "The Demand for International Reserves by Developed and Less-Developed Countries," *Economica* (February 1974), pp. 14–24; E. M. Claasen, "The Otimizing Approach to the Demand for International Reserves," *Weltwirtschaftliches Archiv*, vol. 110 (1974), pp. 354–98.

borrowing and their lending rates may be too large from a global-efficiency standpoint.[72] Since instability leads governments to hold more reserves (lend to foreigners), actions that reduce instability (and hence reserves) will raise global output to some extent. Again, these gains are external to private market participants.

Finally, if LDCs hold optimal reserves and also face perfect capital markets, moves to reduce instability beyond the efficiency optimum will generate global waste but probably transfer income to LDCs as the burden of instability is shifted from them to whoever finances the stabilization program.

Remedial distorting actions in particular commodities for the purpose of reducing the external costs of foreign exchange fluctuations can be at most only third best. Indeed, price stabilizing policies may actually destabilize foreign exchange revenues, if price and quantity movements are negatively correlated. In most of the buffer stock simulations performed thus far, destabilization has not occurred, however.[73] The foreign exchange problem can be dealt with directly through the IMF's compensatory finance facilities, which have recently been expanded and liberalized,[74] while the global losses associated with overly stable markets could be avoided. If particular LDC governments should choose greater stability, they would still be free to manipulate internal buffer stocks, subsidies, and so on, to achieve their goals.

Export instability and growth. Although there is no compelling reason why waste of the types set forth above should imply lower average growth rates, in the empirical literature the cost of export instability has often been identified with this result. A substantial effort has been expended to determine whether there is some correlation between various measures of export instability and the rate of economic growth.[75] International cross-sections have usually been used. This prac-

---

[72] Substantial distortions in the allocation of capital also exist in the industrial countries. Diversion of investment from the private sector to commodity stocks may involve indirect costs even greater than the benefits accruing to LDCs.

[73] See, for example, Behrman, *International Commodity Agreements*, pp. 62–63; Smith and Schink, "The International Tin Agreement," pp. 719–23; Smith, "An Economic Evaluation."

[74] For a recent analysis of these facilities, see Jos deVries, "Compensatory Financing: A Quantitative Analysis," World Bank Staff Working Paper, no. 228 (Washington, D.C., 1975).

[75] Alistair MacBean, *Export Instability and Economic Development* (Cambridge: Harvard University Press, 1966); Peter B. Kenen and Constantine S. Voivodas, "Export Instability and Economic Growth," *Kyklos*, fasc. 4 (1972), pp. 791–804; Constantine S. Voivodas, "The Effect of Foreign Exchange Instability on Growth," *Review of Economics and Statistics*, vol. 56 (August 1974), pp. 410–12; Odin Knudsen and Andrew Parnes, *Trade Instability and Economic Development* (Lexington, Mass.: D. C. Heath, 1975); David Lim, "Export Instability and

tice requires that all other important factors affecting growth across countries be correctly specified if the tests are to be unbiased. Since the models have not succeeded in this respect, some skepticism about the statistical results is warranted.

Still, almost no one has turned up a significant relation between export instability and growth of the sign predicted.[76] Indeed, some—including MacBean and Knudsen and Parnes—even find a positive relation between the two. Instability apparently generates more investment and growth! The Knudsen-Parnes analysis provides an explanation: export instability apparently increases the average savings rates out of permanent income. The savings are converted into higher investment and growth rates; hence, the paradox is explained.[77]

While ingenious, the Knudsen-Parnes analysis is inconclusive. Their measure of export instability, the sum of the ratios of squared deviations from trend to the square of the trend value, is significantly correlated across their sample with the growth rate of exports.[78] Since export growth nowhere appears explicitly as an explanatory variable for GNP growth, savings, and investment (as it would, for example, in gap models), one may wonder whether it is instability or merely its correlation with export growth that produces their results.[79]

Probably the most warranted conclusion from this cross-sectional literature is "that the case has certainly not been proven that export instability is a serious deterrent to growth in LDCs."[80] But this in no way invalidates the conclusions given above, since the costs of instability are likely to show up in ways other than lowered average growth rates.

Economic Growth: A Return to Fundamentals," *Oxford Bulletin of Economics and Statistics*, vol. 38 (November 1976), pp. 311–33.

[76] Voivodas, "The Effect of Instability," found a relationship but not in his two-gap formulation, which was an attempt to model the structure of the relationship.

[77] Of course, higher savings may take the form of financial investments in foreign assets, for example, foreign exchange. The relation of export instability to investment is fairly weak in Knudsen and Parnes's equations.

[78] At the 5 percent level for the sample of twenty-eight countries, at the 1 percent level if Paraguay is excluded, using the Spearman rank correlation coefficient. The correlation is probably not accidental and arises from the nature of the measure itself. If high growth rates fluctuate in the same proportion as low growth rates, a positive correlation between the growth rates and the Knudsen-Parnes instability index will be observed.

[79] Unfortunately, Chile, the worst case of export and growth instability according to Mathieson and McKinnon, is excluded from the Knudsen-Parnes sample. See D. J. Mathieson and Ronald I. McKinnon, "Instability in Underdeveloped Countries: The Impact of the International Economy," in P. A. David and M. W. Reder, eds., *Nations and Households in Economic Growth* (New York: Academic Press, 1974), pp. 325–26.

[80] Stern, "World Market Instability," p. 180.

PART TWO: COMMODITIES PROBLEMS

In a promising recent development, some researchers have begun to analyze the impact of export and foreign exchange fluctuations through models of individual countries. Presumably, this procedure controls, as the cross-sections have not, for country-specific influences on growth, instability, and so on. The results thus far have been inconclusive. Rangarajan and Sundararajan estimate simple Keynesian models for eleven primary exporters.[81] When stable export growth is substituted for the actual pattern, five countries experience higher average growth rates, and six lower rates. One of the six countries was Ghana, for which Acquah, with another country model, concluded that fluctuations in the cocoa market generated internal fluctuations and reduced growth potential.[82] The Economic Research Group at the University of Pennsylvania has begun an analysis of the effects of export instability, using several LDC country models incorporated in Project Link. This should help considerably to clarify these issues.

Commodity Agreements: A Review

Since 1973 a flurry of proposals and negotiations has centered on commodity stabilization. Perhaps the catalyst was the UNCTAD Integrated Commodity Programme and the $6 billion Common Fund proposal floated in December 1974. The United States, the EEC, and Japan have resisted such a sweeping approach and have insisted that each commodity be dealt with individually. Several agreements have been subsequently negotiated or renewed: cocoa, coffee, sugar, and tin. Other commodities are now under discussion: rubber, tungsten, copper, wheat, and feed grains. Parallel to the individual negotiations have been the North-South "negotiations" over the form of a common fund.

Below, I consider some of the policy issues currently centered on commodity agreements and their financing. First, international commodity agreements (ICAs) are examined briefly in general terms. Then, the operation of agreements now in force and under discussion is evaluated in some detail. Finally, I turn to the question of common funding for buffer stocks.

Who Gains from Trend Neutral Stabilization? Assume for the moment that a buffer stock agreement could be negotiated and that the agree-

---

[81] C. Rangarajan and V. Sundararajan, "Impact of Export Fluctuations on Income: A Cross Country Analysis," *Review of Economics and Statistics*, vol. 58 (August 1976), pp. 368–72.
[82] Paul Acquah, "A Macroeconomic Analysis of Export Instability in Economic Growth: The Case of Ghana and the World Cocoa Market" (Ph.D. dissertation, University of Pennsylvania, 1972).

ment acted only to reduce fluctuations in prices around their trend (long-run equilibrium?) values. Assume further that the additional stabilization is globally efficient. Who is likely to gain from such an agreement? With linear supply and demand functions and additive disturbance terms (and no feedback of price fluctuations on planned production),[83] the answer is simple: it all depends on the source of the disturbance. If supply shocks generate the instability, producers gain unambiguously both in total revenue and in producers' surplus, while consumers may lose. Demand disturbances reverse the situation, because producers' revenue will fall unambiguously with stabilization.[84]

Using the linear supply, demand, and additive disturbance assumptions, a World Bank staff study recently concluded that over the long haul stabilization would cost LDCs export revenue over a large set of products, ranging from copper to corn. Producer revenue gains would likely occur only in coffee, cocoa, jute, and wool.[85] Whatever else might be its merits, commodity price stabilization is not a very promising vehicle for increasing resource transfers.[86]

Unfortunately, these clear-cut results are sensitive to changes in initial assumptions, as Turnovsky has shown in several papers.[87] If the disturbances are multiplicative instead of additive, the source of the market instability becomes irrelevant, and the slopes of the supply and demand curves are the critical variables.[88] If producers follow adaptive

---

[83] In the original Massell model, this was guaranteed by the assumption that the stockpiles would always maintain price at expected equilibrium values. Benton F. Massell, "Price Stabilization and Welfare," *Quarterly Journal of Economics*, vol. 34 (April 1969), pp. 285–97.

[84] See Massell, "Price Stabilization"; Ezriel M. Brook, Enzo R. Grilli, and Jean Waelbroeck, "Commodity Price Stabilization and the Developing Countries: The Problem of Choice," World Bank Staff Working Paper, no. 262 (Washington, D.C., July 1977), provides a useful review of the literature on the gains from stabilization and estimates of commodities where stabilization is likely to benefit LDCs.

[85] Brook, Grilli, and Waelbroeck, "Commodity Price Stabilization," p. 29. The estimates do not, of course, include any macro gain, nor do they assume risk aversion.

[86] Greater price stability might, however, increase user demand for products with close substitutes, for example, natural rubber.

[87] Stephen J. Turnovsky, "Price Expectations and the Welfare Gain from Price Stabilization," *American Journal of Agricultural Economics*, vol. 56 (November 1974), pp. 706–16; and "The Distribution of Welfare Gains from Price Stabilization: The Case of Multiplicative Disturbances," *International Economic Review*, vol. 17 (February 1976), pp. 133–48.

[88] The presumption is that multiplicative disturbances are most likely for annual agricultural crops—total output being the product of area planted and yields. Log-linear demand functions are often used in the econometric work, and these implicitly assume multiplicative disturbances.

rather than rational expectations in the unstabilized market, it is impossible to tell whether producers will lose from stabilization of a demand-shock market and whether consumers lose if the source of instability is on the supply side. No doubt mixtures of these various ingredients occur in practice.

Under the circumstances, it might seem best to rely upon simulations of structural econometric models of the individual commodity markets. (Even here, it is often difficult to distinguish the competing hypotheses statistically.) Buffer stocks introduced into the Charles River Associates–Wharton EFA copper models and the Wharton EFA tin model produced slight declines in producer revenues over the period simulated, 1956–1973.[89] This is basically in accord with a priori expectations and agrees with the World Bank staff's conclusions, which were based on the sign of the historical correlations between price and quantity fluctuations around trends. Behrman's buffer stock simulations of thirteen UNCTAD commodities show substantial increases in producer revenues for all commodities except sisal, copper, and tin, which lose, and tea, which breaks even.[90] These results are particularly sensitive to the period simulated (1963–1972), since it encompassed only ten years.[91] Ten billion dollars' worth of stocks were carried out of 1972 for later sales, far more than the buffer stocks were assumed to hold at the beginning of 1963. Taylor, Sarris, and Abbott find that wheat producers and exporters would be the losers if an international buffer stock were to stabilize prices within certain bands.[92] This result is also consistent with the World Bank's results, but it arises from the nonlinearity of the demand curves rather than from the dominance of demand shocks.

To summarize, the evidence strongly suggests that metals and wheat producers can expect a decline in revenue with buffer stocks. The tropical beverages would be the main gainers, while the outcome for the other commodities is more or less indefinite. Ironically, agreements in the beverages have relied or will rely more on export quotas for their implementation. Buffer stocks are more likely in the metals and in wheat. That is to say, LDC producers are likely to lose revenue in those commodity agreements that do or are likely to rely on some form of buffer stock.

---

[89] See Smith, "An Economic Evaluation," and Smith and Schink, "The International Tin Agreement," for further details.

[90] Behrman, *International Commodity Agreements*, table 5. I subtracted the value of the buffer's terminal stocks in making this calculation.

[91] Stocks were carried into 1963 for copper and tin, while stocks were carried out in 1972 for most of the other products.

[92] Taylor, Sarris, and Abbott, "Grain Reserves," pp. 43–54.

Commodity Agreements in Practice: Some General Points. The negotiation and financing of commodity agreements are not trivial matters; they involve a great deal of political compromise. What prices should be defended? Obviously, costs differ considerably across countries, and accurate comparisons are made even more difficult by inappropriate exchange rates. The long-run equilibrium price is generally unknown (even if it could be defined). As a result, there is no price which by its nature could compel acceptance by all members of an agreement, even if everyone's goal were only stabilization. And mistakes can be costly.

Obviously, producers would prefer stabilization around higher prices. Many agreements, particularly of the North-South variety, should be biased in favor of producers, even if consumers' votes carry equal weight. Coffee and tin, for example, are far more important to exporting countries than they are to the United States and West Germany. The cost to the latter of prices that are many cents "too high" is slight, while the perceived benefit to the LDCs in question should be much more intense. Perceived political benefits or indirect economic benefits may lead consumers to accede more readily to producer demands for higher prices.

Agreements that rely upon export quotas can be strongly biased in favor of producers. First, quotas tend to raise average price over the cycle by restricting total supply. Second, such agreements may be a breeding ground for cartels, giving producers the necessary experience in hammering out their differences on market sharing.

Commodity agreements have a way of being not very binding on the participants. For example, some rely on export quotas on the down side and nationally held stockpiles on the up side.[93] There is no guarantee that during periods of shortage producers will in fact release their stocks as required by the agreement. They may prefer instead to act as a producer cartel.

Even if the agreement were only for stabilization purposes and even if the long-run trend or equilibrium price were known and accepted by all, the problem of determining the "required" buffer stock size would remain. Simply put, how much money should be appropriated for the agreement, or what should its borrowing limits be? Many have reasoned as though private stocks could effectively be ignored in this exercise. This procedure almost surely underestimates the magnitude of the effort required of the buffer stock, as public stocks merely substitute to some extent for the private. Underfinanced

---

[93] The sugar and coffee agreements are of this type.

PART TWO: COMMODITIES PROBLEMS

buffer stocks, however, may not only fail to achieve their goal but even add to the instability.

Most of these points will be illustrated below.

Current and Proposed Commodity Agreements. The international tin, coffee, and cocoa (inactive thus far because of high prices) agreements are prototypes of North-South ICAs. All the main producers are LDCs, and export quotas have been the principal weapon used to prevent price declines. The coffee and tin agreements have done a much better job of maintaining floor prices than of preventing extremely high ones, and on this count there is no reason to expect that the Cocoa Agreement will be much different. All three agreements are likely to be biased in favor of producers for many of the reasons summarized above.

The International Tin Agreement. The International Tin Agreement (ITA), in operation continuously since 1956, is the grandfather of ICAs.[94] After "standing aside" for twenty years, the United States finally joined the fifth agreement in 1976, primarily, it would seem, as a political gesture. Within the government it was generally believed that the economic benefits or costs would be small but that the political gains would be worth the effort.

Prior to 1976, the Tin Agreement was a relatively mild affair. It defended fairly low floor prices, mainly through export quotas. Its buffer stock, never much larger than 20,000 tons, was far too small to be of much consequence and was far outweighed in its market impact by sales (120,000 tons net, 1956–1974) from the U.S. General Services Administration (GSA) strategic stockpile of tin. The United States, in an effort not to antagonize producers, concentrated its sales during periods of market scarcity and high prices (1964–1966 and 1973–1974). Yet, in spite of GSA sales, which must be considered massive in relation to tin consumption, prices soared far above the Tin Agreement's ceiling levels during most of those years. In effect, the ITA and U.S. stockpile together constituted an informal commodity agreement; the ITA defended known floors through export quotas (when necessary), and the GSA defended high but unknown ceiling prices. The whole operation maintained prices within bands of ± 20–25 percent around trends, not exactly a paragon of stability.

If there had been no U.S. stockpile and the ITA had been designed from the beginning mainly as a buffer stock to reduce price fluctuations, at least 100,000 tons of tin at the peak would have been necessary, judging from simulations of the Wharton EFA world tin

---

[94] The standard work is William Fox, *Tin: The Working of a Commodity Agreement* (London: Mining Journal Books, 1974).

model over the period 1956–1974.[95] This stock is far larger than has been heretofore contemplated for tin and is considerably more in relation to world consumption than has been recommended for other metals, such as copper.[96] It is unlikely that such a sizable package could have been negotiated.

The year 1977 saw tin prices again penetrate and remain far above the ITA's ceiling, as the buffer stock's 20,000 tons were exhausted to little avail in a matter of months. The U.S. government certainly did nothing to help the situation. Producers and consumers had every reason to believe that the GSA would sell tin if very high prices threatened. No doubt this expectation reduced privately held stocks and held back producers in their production plans. As of this writing (April 1979), Congress has yet to approve further disposals of the declared 160,000-ton surplus of tin.

The Tin Agreement is now taking on more substantial powers. With probable consumer contributions and borrowing on tin warrants, the buffer stock will have the potential of perhaps 70,000 tons, an amount sufficient to achieve its stabilization goals except in the most extreme circumstances.[97] If some additional help from the GSA can be anticipated, tin will have the resources to become a model commodity agreement.

Unfortunately, as the agreement gathers real power internal conflicts are mounting. Producers have pushed aggressively for higher prices since 1974 and have succeeded in getting real support prices fixed considerably above long-run trends.[98] The "hard-line" countries in the agreement, the United States, West Germany, and Japan, could have vetoed such increases had they chosen. Rather than arouse producers' animosity, they abstained from the key vote in the July 1977 Tin Council meeting, although they have resisted subsequent efforts to raise prices even further. The agreement has taken on a definite pro-producer cast, more or less as one would have expected. The price of tin is not that critical to consumers, and the four main tin producers are Thailand, Malaysia, Indonesia, and Bolivia, all of some political importance to the United States.

The Tin Agreement also illustrates the problems created by stiff

---

[95] For a more complete description of the simulations and of this line of reasoning, see Smith and Schink, "The International Tin Agreement."

[96] See, for example, Behrman, *International Commodity Agreements*, tables 6–8 for his and UNCTAD's recommendations.

[97] On these points see Gordon W. Smith, "U.S. Commodity Policy and the Tin Agreement," Rice University, September 1977.

[98] Smith, "Commodity Policy," p. 32. A semilog trend was calculated for 1961–1975 and projected to 1977.

PART TWO: COMMODITIES PROBLEMS

marginal export taxes and social policies that raise costs or reduce production.[99] Higher prices on the average result. Should these prices be reflected in higher ceilings and floors? Should the producers be pushed to change their social policies? The potential for political conflict is great.

The International Coffee Agreement. The first two coffee agreements in the 1960s were designed mainly to transfer resources to Latin American and African producers. The consumers, led by the United States, agreed to police the export quotas, a move that made them fairly effective. The agreements showed the usual conflicts between the well-established and newer producers when it came to the allocation of quotas. Brazil was forced to cut back most, in part because it had the most to gain from higher prices. Buffer stocks played no role in the first two agreements, and price stabilization in the sense of the Tin Agreement was far from the focus of the Coffee Council. It has been estimated that during the mid-1960s $500–$600 million per year was transferred from consumers to producers through the higher prices permitted by export controls.[100]

When the supply surplus finally eased in the late 1960s and early 1970s, consumers received little consideration, and the second agreement fell apart during 1971 in a dispute over price adjustments to the devaluation of the dollar. Brazil then led the move to form a coffee cartel outside the agreement, based on the April 1972 Geneva Pact, which instituted more severe export controls than those in effect at that time. Brazil also formed a coffee trading firm, Café Mundial, to support prices in world markets. None of these moves was particularly successful, and real green coffee prices actually declined in New York from 1972 to 1975.

Apparently, producers had second thoughts about going it alone, and a new Coffee Agreement with U.S. participation took effect in 1976, again with export quotas but no international buffer stock. The 1975 Brazilian frost, the most severe in history, brought spectacular increases in coffee prices just as the third agreement was taking effect. In recent months, green coffee prices have fallen back from well over

---

[99] Bolivia uses COMIBOL, the state mining enterprise, as a residual employer, while Malaysia's indigenization policy is holding back new investment by Chinese Malaysians in gravel-pump tin mining.

[100] B. S. Fisher, *The International Coffee Agreement: A Study in Coffee Diplomacy* (New York: Praeger, 1972), p. 153. The U.S. share alone was about $314 million annually, 1964–1967, according to a General Accounting Office report cited in the International Trade Commission report to the Senate Finance Committee, *International Commodity Agreements* (Washington, D.C.: Government Printing Office, 1975), p. 12.

three dollars a pound to less than two dollars, still about triple the levels of 1972 and ridiculously above anybody's cost of production. Producers are not content, however, and again led by Brazil, the Latin Americans have agreed to hold back exports until prices have been pushed up further.[101]

The experience with coffee makes clear that commodity agreements based on export quotas will be severely biased in favor of producers. Consumer nations cannot count on good will to protect them when supplies are short. Export-quota ICAs may well become export-quota cartels during times of shortage, particularly during this period when many LDCs are struggling to service an external debt that has ballooned since 1973.

With the new Sugar Agreement and the discussions of wheat and copper agreements, we enter a different terrain. These commodities are produced in many industrial countries, including the United States, so that, unlike the typical North-South commodity, producers' interests in the principal consumer countries are also involved. The United States, at least, seems to be moving toward the internationalization of domestic policies, toward an attempt to avoid the relative isolation of the quotas, tariffs, and subsidies of the past while at the same time minimizing the impact that freer trade in these commodities could bring (and has brought) to domestic producers. In some ways, then, the ICA is an operational alternative to other forms of trade intervention that may preserve domestic producers' interests. In some cases, the ICA may on balance be preferable to domestic protectionism, particularly if a significant portion of world exports is accounted for by LDCs. These points are seen most clearly in the recently negotiated International Sugar Agreement (ISA).

The International Sugar Agreement. Until the end of 1974, the domestic U.S. sugar market was mostly isolated from world market developments. High support prices were maintained for domestic sugar through strict import quotas. The annual congressional allocation of these quotas to the various exporting nations became notorious for lobbying and political pressures—no small wonder, since the quota was the gift of the right to sell at premium prices.[102] The Sugar Act was allowed to expire at the end of 1974 during a period of extremely high world market prices for sugar. Imports were no threat to domestic producers, and in the post-Watergate era the spectacle of the annual

---

[101] *Wall Street Journal,* November 7, 1977, p. 19; various issues of the *Journal of Commerce.*

[102] Pre-Castro Cuba received the largest import quota. Curiously, pro-Castroites argued that this was merely a tool used to keep Cuba backward.

PART TWO: COMMODITIES PROBLEMS

struggle for quotas was too suggestive of corruption to be easily tolerated. The United States went free market in sugar—for a while.[103]

The 1953, 1958, and 1968 sugar agreements were relatively minor affairs. They covered only the free market for sugar, which made up perhaps 10 percent of world production.[104] Most of the trade was governed by such preferential arrangements as the U.S. Sugar Act and the Commonwealth Sugar Agreement. The United States was a member of the first two postwar agreements, but membership was meaningless since the United States rarely dealt in the market covered by the agreements. They established ceiling and floor prices, maintained by variable export quotas. Although there was no provision for an international buffer stock, targets were set for maximum and minimum national stocks, which were to serve as a buffer against severe upward price pressures.

The agreements were not notably successful. Inappropriate quotas often were set, chiseling was common, and national stocks sometimes exceeded the maximums and at other times were insufficient to defend ceiling prices. "For long periods during the agreements, free market prices remained below the minimum of the objective range, but in . . . 1954, 1972, and 1973 . . . were well above the maximum."[105] Curiously, the average annual price fluctuation was considerably larger during the twelve most recent years of the agreements than during the eleven earlier noncontrol years.[106]

The main U.S. objective in the new ISA is to prop up the world market to levels that with the normal sugar tariff and transaction costs would allow domestic producers to receive about thirteen cents a pound without deficiency payments. Hence, the floor price for the ISA has been fixed at eleven cents a pound, equivalent for "technical" reasons to the thirteen-cent domestic price sought by U.S. producers.[107] The ceiling was fixed at twenty-one cents. As in previous agreements, variable export quotas, along with nationally held target stockpiles, will be used to achieve price objectives. A minuscule international stock is also contemplated.

If it works, which it has not thus far, the new ISA should be very similar in its narrow economic impact to the old quota system. Domestic prices will be supported at thirteen cents, but the differential between

---

[103] Aggregate quotas, too large to be binding, have been set.
[104] International Trade Commission, *International Commodity Agreements*, p. 18.
[105] Ibid., p. 19.
[106] Alton D. Law, *International Commodity Agreements: Setting, Performance, and Prospects* (Lexington, Mass.: D. C. Heath, Lexington Books, 1975).
[107] *Wall Street Journal*, October 6, 1977.

U.S. and world market prices will be eliminated by the export quotas of the ISA. Congress will be spared the quota exercise, and the consumer need pay no more for sugar than under the old scheme. Unfortunately, free trade in sugar does not appear to be a viable political alternative,[108] given the apparent influence of domestic sugar-producing interests and the budgetary costs of sugar deficiency payments under the free trade regime. Relying on the ISA should yield a small political payoff with some of the LDCs, but if the ISA fails to operate effectively the United States can always revert to the tariff.

There is some chance that the ISA could turn into another coffee affair if prices should firm considerably. Significantly, Brazil is also one of the largest sugar exporters.

Copper. The world copper market is among the most unstable. Ten years ago, the violent free market oscillations were of less economic importance, since most transactions in the United States and Europe occurred at "producers' prices," which were considerably more stable. In recent years, however, the Europeans have abandoned the list price system entirely, and the American companies, in the face of import competition, have found it necessary to adjust their prices much more in sympathy with world prices. To a degree never before experienced, the London Metals Exchange indeed represents world transactions prices.

Copper would seem to be one of the strongest candidates, both politically and economically, for an effective ICA based on the buffer stock principle. As we saw earlier in this paper, there is some evidence that the LME market is not an efficient one and that the industry does not perform the buffer stock function adequately. Physical storage costs are very low. Furthermore, copper looms large in the foreign exchange receipts of several LDCs—Chile, Zaire, and Zambia most of all. There is strong evidence that export instability rooted in copper has interfered with development in several of these countries. The multinational banks have clear reason to be concerned about the ability of Chile, Zaire, and Peru to service their debts during the current period of extremely low prices.[109] The U.S. industry has been in considerable difficulty since mid-1977, and if things do not improve soon, it appears that some form of remedial action may be taken (tariffs, GSA purchases of copper, and so on).[110] Given all this, one would think that industry support for a

---

[108] It lasted in the United States only as long as world market prices were quite high.

[109] On this point, see Gordon W. Smith, *The External Debt Prospects of the Non-Oil-Exporting Developing Countries: An Econometric Analysis*, Monograph, no. 10 (Washington, D.C.: Overseas Development Council, 1977).

[110] See, for example, *Wall Street Journal*, October 21, 1977, p. 1.

PART TWO: COMMODITIES PROBLEMS

copper agreement would be fairly strong. It is not. Apparently, industry spokesmen are concerned that in such an agreement their interests might be sacrificed for diplomatic gains with certain LDCs. They prefer action that does not carry such a threat.

Preliminary copper discussions under the auspices of UNCTAD have not progressed very far. Perhaps the biggest obstacle (besides industry opposition) has been the sheer size of buffer stock that may be required to achieve stabilization goals. For example, buffer stock simulations for the period 1955–1974,[111] using the Charles River Associates–Wharton EFA copper model, required a maximum stock valued at well over $3 billion (in 1977 dollars) to maintain prices within a band of ±15 percent around long-run equilibrium levels.[112] (By comparison, the entire UNCTAD Common Fund was targeted for only $6 billion.) One explanation for this magnitude is that the model allows, albeit crudely, for substitution *between* public and private stocks,[113] a possibility sometimes ignored in such exercises. Even if we allow for an overestimate of 100 percent, we are still talking about a 1.4-million-ton maximum during that period. At a floor price of sixty-five cents a pound, the cost today would be $1.8 billion, with no allowance made for increases in copper consumption since its 1955–1974 averages.

Behrman, using different target prices and the period 1963–1972, estimated a maximum of only 500,000 tons for ±15 percent stabilization.[114] This estimate is extremely misleading as an order-of-magnitude for future stockpiles. Behrman's simulations, unlike the first set, did not remove the GSA from the copper market. The GSA alone sold over 730,000 tons during 1965–1967 in an effort to keep down copper prices. Obviously, one cannot count on the now nonexistent GSA copper stockpile for such help in the future. Furthermore, Behrman's buffer stock ends 1972 with only 219,000 tons of copper. This sum would have been totally inadequate to contain prices during 1973 and 1974. When these factors are taken into account, Behrman's stabilization targets would have required something closer to a 1.5-million-ton buffer stock at a maximum.[115]

---

[111] This was a full twenty-year cycle for copper in the sense that the buffer stock began and ended with zero stocks of copper.

[112] For details of these simulations and their limitations, see Smith, "An Economic Evaluation."

[113] When the buffer stock purchases copper to raise prices to floor levels, a substantial proportion comes out of stocks that otherwise would have been held privately at lower prices.

[114] This is *not* a complete cycle.

[115] The remaining differences between the two sets of simulations probably arise from differences in the models, particularly in the elasticity of price with respect to the stock-consumption ratio, and differences in the way target prices were set.

Changes in the structure of the world copper market suggest that even these figures could be insufficient if some form of export restraint were not imposed on producing countries. Copper mines have been nationalized in Chile, Zaire, and Zambia and have large government participation in Peru. The objective of these companies may well be to maximize net foreign exchange revenues rather than economic profit per se. Three of the four are under severe debt-servicing pressures, and indeed Chile and Peru are said to be exporting currently at capacity in spite of extremely low prices.[116] In these conditions, a copper buffer stock could easily be overwhelmed with offers to sell. The bottom line is that, although buffer stocks may make good sense for copper, they will be extremely difficult to negotiate because of the size of the financial commitment. One can imagine the difficulty in obtaining congressional approval for the U.S. contribution, particularly if the U.S. industry opposed such an action.

Wheat and grain reserves. Certainly no commodity issue has received more attention in recent years than the management of grain reserves.[117] As an offshoot of its price support program, the U.S. government (through purchase or loan) used to carry the bulk of the world's grain reserves. The price stability guaranteed by these large stocks was so great that private carry-over of grains was minimal during the 1960s and early 1970s. When the American reserves were largely run down in 1972–1974, the world was left in precarious balance. Serious and widespread harvest failures at that time could have been extremely costly in terms of human welfare.

Since the U.S. government claimed to be out of the storage business and clearly wanted to avoid the persistent farm surpluses of the past, how could "adequate" grain reserves be provided? Adequate for what purposes?

The simplest answer relies on the free market.[118] The goal of grain reserves should be to raise the sum of consumer and producer surplus to a maximum. Since the private storage sector is competitive (so the reasoning goes) and suffers from none of the inefficiencies analyzed above, and since inflation is a monetary phenomenon unrelated to relative prices, private stocks will normally be socially optimal. Of course, the United States may perceive political gains from even greater market

---

[116] See the *Wall Street Journal*, October 24, 1977, p. 30.

[117] On this topic, see Tresize, *Rebuilding Grain Reserves*; Taylor, Sarris, and Abbott, "Grain Reserves"; Johnson, "Fluctuating Supplies"; Stein and Smith, *Economics of Grain Stockpiling*.

[118] Stein and Smith, *Economics of Grain Stockpiling*, pp. 15–26.

stability. In that case, storage subsidies to the private sector are the indicated response.

This point of view, while highlighting many salient issues, will not carry the day. Rightly or wrongly, too many are too skeptical about too many of its premises. Furthermore, it ignores the fact that governments and their decisions, not the private market, dominate grain storage and trade throughout much of the world. It may be preferable to negotiate international agreements that interfere with market operations to some extent in exchange for a reduction in the uncertainty and destabilization resulting from government intervention in other countries. Even so, the free market outcome in grain reserves is a very useful reference for judging the benefits and costs of interference.

Another simple answer, which leaves many issues unresolved, entirely divorces quantities stored from their economic net value. Stein and Smith somewhat uncharitably call this the "mechanical" approach.[119] In the words of Taylor, Sarris, and Abbott:

> The standard deviation of world production of either major class of grains has been about 12 to 15 [million metric tons] over the past 20 years. Having two standard deviations' worth of both crops in storage [25 or 30 million metric tons of both wheat and feed grains] would allow the world to make up for bad harvests in all but the worst year or two in a century.[120]

Individual countries would set or be given targets for grain stocks, based perhaps upon some criteria of burden sharing. Presumably, these stocks would be accumulated in periods of low prices, but the actual operation of such a scheme is generally left fairly vague.[121]

Not only does this approach ignore the economic costs of stabilization, it implicitly assumes free trade in grain, a worldwide pooling of grain reserves that is far from reality today. Johnson and Sumner illustrate the dramatic economies in reserve stocks that free trade could in fact bring.[122] Applying Gustafson's optimal storage approach, they find that in only one year out of twenty would worldwide grain reserves reach as high as 18 million tons. Half of the time there would be no

---

[119] Ibid.

[120] Taylor, Sarris, and Abbott, "Grain Reserves," p. 6.

[121] Tresize, *Rebuilding Grain Reserves*, seems to favor two positions. Early on (pp. 14–20), he establishes world stock targets without considering their price duals. Later he writes as if the targets could be reached by some floor-ceiling price stabilization arrangement (pp. 41–45).

[122] D. Gale Johnson and Daniel Sumner, "An Optimization Approach to Grain Reserves for Developing Countries," in *Analysis of Grain Reserves: Proceedings*, compiled by David J. Eaton and W. Scott Steele, Economic Research Service Report no. 634, August 1974, pp. 56–66.

reserve grain in stock at all, and reserves would exceed a mere 2 million tons only one year in four! These figures are far below typical carry-over levels even in most recent years. One reason for the small stocks is that the optimal rule allows an instability that many countries now find unattractive. More important, the difference between optimal reserves with trade and actual stocks seems to be rooted in the many restrictive policies affecting international grain trade.

Taylor, Sarris, and Abbott (TSA) do recognize the importance of government intervention in affecting the grain reserves required for various stabilization targets. They recommend an international buffer stock to reduce price fluctuations in the world market by defending floor and ceiling prices, a proposal that seems closer to the current U.S. policy orientation. TSA base their argument upon Monte Carlo simulations of fairly detailed demand-supply models for wheat and feed grains. Unfortunately, trade restrictions are incorporated in fairly mechanical fashion. The only policy variable is the proportion of the difference between trend consumption and actual production' that governments in different countries will allow to be imported in a given year. This proportion may vary with price. Time series are used to estimate the parameters. The EEC's variable levy system cannot adequately be approximated in this fashion, and the model implies a constancy of policy clearly belied by the Soviet Union's behavior in the mid-1960s and in 1972. Private stocks are excluded entirely from the model, a potentially serious defect with the wide price bans they simulate. (See the Appendix to this paper for a discussion of this problem.) Nor is it clear from the TSA presentation what was assumed in the simulations about the domestically held public stocks in the various countries.

In any case, TSA consider 15 million tons of wheat a reasonable ceiling on the buffer stock. This would reduce expected world price fluctuations by more than a third (in their simulations), and in only one year in twenty (instead of three in twenty) would prices rise above $200 per ton. (The assumed long-run equilibrium price was $140 per ton.)

The novelty of the TSA results is the small stock size requirement. Since U.S. wheat stocks alone were run down by more than 17 million metric tons in 1972–1974,[123] one may feel justified in doubting that 15 million tons would have brought greater stabilization. It seems likely, then, that the TSA stock would still have permitted the violent price run-ups that originally forced policy makers to consider once again the questions of grain stockpiling. The TSA model has too many uncer-

---

[123] Taylor, Sarris, and Abbott, "Grain Reserves," p. 18.

PART TWO: COMMODITIES PROBLEMS

tainties, so that Johnson's conclusion is still valid: "Given the agricultural and trade policies followed by the nations of the world no one knows what appropriate reserve rules should be."[124]

Apparently, U.S. policy makers agree, to judge by the recent rather loose general proposal made by the American delegation to the International Wheat Council's Preparatory Group.[125] Lower and upper "trigger prices" would be set along with target reserves for each country[126] and would take into account such factors as wheat production, consumption, trade, GNP, and the variability of wheat production. In essence, target reserves would be accumulated when market prices were near or at the low trigger, and at the same time each country "would limit the use of any prevailing export subsidies or other destabilizing measures." If the price fell below the floor, countries would take steps, particularly reductions in import barriers, to increase consumption. At very low prices, production cutbacks would be negotiated. Symmetrical steps would be taken at the high end of the range.

The United States opposes the EEC proposal of rigid floor and ceiling prices within which prices should be maintained. It also leaves open the exact manner in which prices will be defended. But the United States is pushing for a large target stockpile, 30 million metric tons, double the figure proposed by the EEC. It also is pressing for some easing of some of the trade restrictions that destabilize the world wheat market.

Wheat agreements have never worked well in the past.[127] It remains to be seen whether the United States will be successful in this attempt to internationalize a more liberal domestic farm policy.

Another reason sometimes put forward for grain stockpiling is that it is a reserve against famine. Somewhat related to this is Johnson and Sumner's provocative proposal for a grain insurance program for LDCs.[128] The United States and perhaps other industrial countries would for a small fee (possibly zero) agree to supply all shortfalls in

---

[124] Johnson, "Fluctuating Supplies," p. 33.

[125] "Possible Elements of an International Wheat Agreement," PREP(77)7 International Wheat Council Preparatory Group, September 28, 1977.

[126] Agricultural Secretary Bergland has stated that a $2.1 billion band will later be proposed by the U.S. along with an international buffer stock. *Journal of Commerce*, June 6, 1978, p. 7.

[127] For an excellent summary of previous failures, see "Introductory Statement by Dr. Dale E. Hathaway, United States Delegate," PREP(77)8, International Wheat Council Preparatory Group, September 30, 1977.

[128] D. Gale Johnson, "Increased Stability of Grain Supplies in Developing Countries: Optimal Carryovers and Insurance," in Jagdish N. Bhagwati, ed., *The New International Economic Order: The North-South Debate* (Cambridge: MIT Press, 1977), pp. 252–72.

grain production greater than, say, 3–4 percent below trend. This would become the principal form of food aid. It would avoid most of the production disincentive effects of the past and would still provide some incentive for LDCs to stock grain on their own for even greater stability. Notice that it would also mean substantial pooling of grain reserves for LDCs, with concomitant savings in stock costs. The expected annual costs of such a program would be 4 million tons of grain ($560 million at $140 a metric ton). Thus far this proposal has not made much of an impact on policy makers here, but it should.

The Common Fund. One of the stranger curiosities in North-South relations during the past three years has been the tenacity with which the Group of 77 has pushed for a $6 billion common fund to finance commodity buffer stocks and other somewhat vague initiatives in the primary commodity area. Equally strange has been the goodwill and effort wasted in discussions of what is essentially a negotiating dead end. The United States has worked itself into the position of supporting "common funding"—thus preserving the UNCTAD jargon—but in an innocuous form that is far from the third world proposals.

The problems with the UNCTAD version are fatal. First, everyone who has seriously examined the proposal agrees that $6 billion would be far too small a sum to achieve reasonable stabilization (for example, ±15 percent around long-term trends) for the core commodities.[129] Behrman puts the minimum figure at $10.4 billion, based on his simulations, and this is almost surely an underestimate. Behrman did not remove the GSA sales from the tin and copper markets,[130] nor did he allow for the fact that Brazil and other coffee producers accumulated and then sold large stocks of coffee in the period he simulated. These national stockpile actions could not be counted on in the future to reduce the burden on the UNCTAD Common Fund.

Second, contributions would be made to the fund before their exact usages are determined. That is, no one knows exactly what buffer stocks could be organized "effectively" or what each would "require." Buying a pig in a poke is not very popular with most governments.

Third, because of involuntary pooling some governments might end up financially supporting buffer stock activities they would otherwise have opposed.

Fourth, the proposition put forward by UNCTAD that pooling would reduce the financial requirements of the core group of buffer

---

[129] Kreinin and Finger, "A Critical Survey"; Behrman, *International Commodity Agreements*.
[130] See the section on copper, above.

stocks seems of marginal importance at best. Some writers have found some pooling economies, but they have not been large.[131] The problem is that commodity portfolios have been treated in isolation. In fact, if individual buffer stocks are guaranteed by governments, their risks will already be spread over the taxpaying population. It is not clear that adding other commodities to the taxpayers' portfolio will improve the situation. Furthermore, if buffer stocks borrow to finance stock purchases, the lending institutions themselves should perform the necessary pooling. If the UNCTAD combination is optimal, we might expect banks to recognize this without recourse to the Common Fund.

The current U.S. negotiating approach makes some sense. Individual agreements would contribute to the fund. It would then use the paid-in capital to borrow in private markets for the individual buffer stocks. That would be the extent of the Common Fund. The Group of 77 is not impressed, and one may be justified in wondering what the real need is for another international fund of the type favored by the United States. It is not at all clear that it is superior to separate financing by each buffer stock.

Summary. It would seem that international agreements, while feasible for some commodities, are unlikely to bring the benefits claimed for them by their supporters. For diplomatic reasons, the North-South agreements are likely to be biased in favor of producers. Export quotas turn out to be much more important in the existing agreements than one would have expected, given the public emphasis on buffer stocks. Apparently, one reason is that international buffer stocks for important commodities would be far too expensive for governments seriously to consider. Wheat and other grains may be exceptions, if the past is any guide. Far from the package of stabilizing buffer stocks evisaged by Kaldor, we seem to be constructing or maintaining the ineffective institutions of the past. Under the circumstances, it is fortunate that other steps, such as an expansion in the IMF's compensatory finance facility, have been taken to lessen the impact of instability on LDCs.

Appendix: Private Storage and Buffer Stocks

A problem that plagues all simulations of buffer stocks in econometric commodity models is the reaction of private speculators who also hold stocks. Clearly, if public stocks are large enough, private speculation ceases entirely. And if both private and public stockpiles are following

---

[131] Behrman, *International Commodity Agreements*, pp. 68–69.

optimal rules with the same storage costs and information set, public stocks will substitute one for one for private. With buffer stocks that defend price ceilings and floors, the substitution effect will be larger, the narrower the width of the effective band. Some, such as TSA and UNCTAD, have ignored this substitution effect entirely. Others, such as Smith and Schink and Behrman, allow some substitution through the form of the stock demand equation: the lower the price, the higher the ratio of stocks demanded in relation to current consumption. Thus, when a buffer stock buys, raising prices to the floor, some private stocks will be dumped on the market for sale to the buffer stock. This is probably not too inaccurate at the floor. Things are worse at the ceiling. When prices are driven down by the buffer stock's sales, some of the added supply is absorbed by private stocks because stock demand rises with a fall in price. But if the buffer stock is large enough to defend the ceiling, no speculator would add to stock, since his expected gain is negative. This procedure, then, overstates the substitutability of the two stocks at ceiling level prices. At some point below ceiling prices, private and public stocks must enter the pricing equation, because the public stock will act exactly as the private in limiting further price increases. That is, the two increasingly become substitutes for each other before buffer stock sales are actually made. Assuming an adequate buffer stock, we would expect the private sector to act to contain prices somewhat below the ceiling as they disgorge increasingly unprofitable stocks. Then prices should shoot rather quickly to ceiling levels, at which point they would be contained by buffer stock sales.

At least two attempts, both for wheat, have been made to approximate the effect of floor-ceiling buffer stocks on private storage behavior.[132] Both assume optimal storage behavior in the private sector, using simple market models with supply disturbances. A floor-ceiling buffer stock is imposed on top of this. This problem for the private sector becomes enormously more complicated to solve, since the price bands, the ceiling on the buffer stock size, and the actual size of the stock all must be added to the usual market items in determining the expected value of an additional increment to private stocks. Gardner's Monte Carlo results are interesting in that the differences between subsidized private storage and public buffer stocks are not that large, either

---

[132] Bruce L. Gardner, "Optimal Stockpiling and the Effects of Public on Private Grain Storage," Technical Article, no. 13638 of the Texas Agricultural Experiment Station, Texas A. & M. University, 1977; John P. Stein, Emmett Keeler, and Rodney T. Smith, *U.S. Grain Reserves Policy: Objectives, Costs, and Distribution of Benefits* (Santa Monica: Rand, 1977).

PART TWO: COMMODITIES PROBLEMS

in relation to the degree of stabilization permitted or in net costs.[133] The main difference is that even with a ±20 percent band, private storage declines dramatically, from an average 2.4 percent of mean production to 0.2 percent. Wheat storage costs are high in relation to the product's value, so that comparable effects of private stocks of metals, coffee, and the like should not be expected. But considerable substitution is bound to occur.

---

[133] The buffer stock was ± 20 percent around the market clearing price. The subsidy program was designed to defend the band.

COMMENTARY

A. I. MacBean

Gordon Smith's paper is an excellent survey of the main issues, and I agree generally with his conclusions. Such differences as there are between us are largely questions of emphasis. Accordingly, my comments are intended to supply a few extra points that may reinforce his critique of the case for substantial and wide-ranging intervention in commodity trade through international commodity agreements.

Market Efficiency

The major concern here is whether the market system in which the eighteen UNCTAD primary commodities are bought and sold performs well. Two basic questions are involved: (1) Do the spot and futures markets operate so as to reduce excessive swings in prices, or do they tend to encourage destabilizing as opposed to stabilizing speculation? (2) Do they operate unfairly toward the producers so that the prices they receive are too low and profits are transferred to the intermediaries or final buyers?

It would not surprise me in the least if the markets were far from perfect. As Smith shows, the statistical analyses of much more sophisticated and better-informed markets in the United States suggest that they are less than efficient. The markets relevant to the UNCTAD commodities are much thinner and less well informed. We know that destabilizing speculation also occurs in foreign exchange markets, which are much wider and much more sophisticated than commodity exchanges. After detailed questioning of a large number of participants in such markets—traders, sellers, and buyers—the House of Lords Select Committee on Commodity Prices concluded that, imperfect though they were, the markets did not perform too badly most of the time. Most speculative activity probably was rational and well informed and tended to be stabilizing. Occasionally, however, quite strong destabilizing

PART TWO: COMMODITIES PROBLEMS

activity could occur, and the 1973–1974 commodity boom was one such occasion. The general spread of rapid inflation, the various supply shocks, and the oil crisis combined to produce a high degree of uncertainty, resulting in excessive purchases. It was believed that there were many new entrants into the commodity markets who had no previous experience there.[1]

However, in relation to the general experience of price fluctuations and their effects on producers and consumers, the importance of destabilizing speculation in the commodity exchanges can easily be exaggerated. The quantities of commodities that pass through the markets are often small. A great deal is bought and sold in contracts that bypass the exchanges and, even if the commodity market prices are used as a guide, these contracts are unlikely to be tied to extreme highs and lows. The volumes actually traded in the markets at extreme prices are probably small. As far as the countries that export the goods are concerned, annual export unit values (EUVs) represent a much better guide to effects than week-to-week changes in spot or future market prices. Changes in EUVs do not correlate very well with changes in commodity market prices.[2]

The reasons for fluctuations in commodity prices are quite genuine and are well analyzed in standard economics in terms of low elasticities and large random disturbances on either supply or demand. The uncertainty about when, if ever, a turnaround in prices will occur is a sufficient explanation of why private stock operations are insufficient to prevent wide swings in prices. The commodity markets probably in general do act to smooth them. Occasionally, they exaggerate, but the speculation is froth upon the waves and unlikely of itself to have much impact upon resource allocation or on macroeconomic variables.

Some improvement in price stability could be achieved in the following ways. Some, probably minor, improvement can be made in information flows on such issues as the age structure of tree populations and acreage planted. Better knowledge of technology in irrigation and plant protection would also tend to reduce supply fluctuations. Liberal reforms in agricultural protection systems in Europe, Japan, and the United States would enormously widen the free markets and reduce their instability.

There seems little concrete evidence that buyers in the developed countries are able to exploit sellers in the developing countries, as it is often alleged. Most markets seem to involve sufficient competition from

---

[1] House of Lords, Select Committee on Commodity Prices (Her Majesty's Stationery Office, May 1977), vol. 1, chapter 8.
[2] Ibid., annex 1, table 3.4*b*.

buyers from many countries, including the nations of the Council for Mutual Economic Assistance (COMECON), to prevent collusive actions to lower prices in most commodities. Bananas and aluminum are obvious possible exceptions. It would be interesting to hear of any evidence that average prices received by producers have been lower than the long-run equilibrium prices because of monopsony or other market imperfection.

In my view, government policies, in protecting temperate-zone agriculture in Europe, North America, and Japan, have had a much more damaging effect by restricting demand for sugar, meat, grains, and oil seeds. This and the effects of the stagnation in the growth of the OECD nations are much more significant causes of low volumes and prices for LDC commodity exports.

Effect of Commodity Price Instability

The view that fluctuations in primary commodity prices are a major cause of inflation in the OECD nations has recently gained wide acceptance, particularly in official pronouncements. Both the previous British prime minister, Harold Wilson, and U.S. government officials seem to endorse it, and it appears to have become a major argument in support of ICAs. Apart from Berhman's pamphlet, the main academic support comes from Nicholas Kaldor's recent article in the *Economic Journal*.[3] Prima facie, the case for some impact should be stronger in the United Kingdom, which has a much higher trade ratio than the United States. But even for the United Kingdom, the eighteen UNCTAD commodities suggested for ICAs amounted to at most 10 percent of U.K. imports.[4] A 10 percent increase in all import prices for Britain produces about a 2.5 percent increase in the cost of living. This suggests a 0.25 percent effect attributable to an average 10 percent rise in the price of the eighteen UNCTAD commodities, and they seldom all move up and down together. The causes of inflation are complex, but it seems improbable that ratchet effects stemming from this small group of commodities could be a significant factor in OECD inflation. The market structures for passing on cost-push elements of national origin such as rising wages may be not uncommon, but given the open nature of most OECD economies it seems likely that cost reductions through falling food and raw material prices would also be passed on to consumers. The ratchet effect may exist, but it is unlikely that exogenous fluctua-

---

[3] Nicholas Kaldor, "Inflation and Recession in the World Economy," *Economic Journal*, vol. 86 (December 1976), pp. 703–14.

[4] House of Lords, Select Committee on Commodity Prices, annex 1, table 4.9.

tions in the prices of the UNCTAD commodities would play a significant part in generating inflation in consuming nations. I find myself even more skeptical on this issue than Gordon Smith. In any case, could the suggested remedy of buffer stocks ever be enough to deal with exceptional swings such as 1973–1974, where the inflationary impact has some plausibility? Given the high financial and other costs of storage, who would accumulate the stocks and hold them long enough to meet this fairly rare contingency?

Other macro effects, such as the reduction in LDC demands for industrial nations' exports during a commodity price slump, are much more directly and effectively dealt with by compensatory finance than by the perilous accumulation of buffer stocks.

Macro Effects on LDCs

The main issue has always been the macro effects of commodity price fluctuations on growth in LDCs. Extensive reading of the literature from Coppock to Knudsen and Parnes leads me to agree heartily with Smith's quotation from Stern expressing the not-proven verdict. However, if our interest is focused on what may be the more important question of whether many of the people who live in the third world are significantly affected by export instability, we can see that the importance of the problem is generally exaggerated. Most third world citizens live in several large countries—Brazil, China, India, Indonesia, and Pakistan, where exports account for a very small part of national income. Moreover, export proceeds in these countries have been relatively stable (apart from Indonesia, where the post-1973 surge in petroleum export proceeds has jerked its instability index to a fairly high level in recent years).[5]

The countries likely to suffer most are those that combine a high export ratio to national income with high export instability. In thirty-five out of a sample of ninety LDCs, exports form at least 20 percent of national income. Ten of these are mainly oil exporters; three export mainly manufactures. Of the remainder, ten—Barbados, Jamaica, Ivory Coast, Mauritius, Sierra Leone, Rhodesia, Zambia, Malaysia, Fiji, and New Caledonia—show more than average export instability.[6] Their populations are relatively small, and several have relatively high per capita incomes. Their problems could be solved much more simply by measures directed toward their specific difficulties than by ICAs for commodities that may have little relevance to them.

---

[5] Ibid., table 4.3.

[6] Ibid., table 4.5.

Of course, many LDCs already have national policies, such as marketing boards and progressive export taxes, that reduce the impact of export fluctuations on their domestic economies. Moreover, in recent years they have drawn heavily on the IMF's compensatory finance scheme (up to about $2.7 billion).

International Commodity Agreements

One of the many problems with ICAs is that, even if the long-run equilibrium price could be predicted or if a successful adaptive forecasting model could be built into such a scheme, there would still remain the difficulty of deciding which targets to go for: price stabilization, revenue stabilization, or maximization of the present value of the stream of revenues minus costs. Each national producer government might have a different objective function. No wonder it can take over ten years to negotiate an agreement.

The Common Fund

If buffer stocks would not work, the Common Fund is an irrelevancy. Even if they would work, it does not make a great deal of sense. Its main gains come from pooling of risks and offsets from price movements. But the biggest pool of cash around is the IMF. Why not simply borrow from it to finance buffer stocks? If its rules are not suitable, then reform them.

Another aspect of the Common Fund put forward by LDCs involves the use of funds to finance rationalization and diversification. This makes little sense outside of a complete consideration of investment alternatives. Diversification for its own sake is irrational. It can actually lead to increased export revenue instability as well as to low social rates of return on the resources invested in it. Of course, it is sensible to consider the effects of investment in export production on other LDCs and to share information about expansion plans for commodities where world demand elasticities are low, but this can be handled with the help of such organizations as the World Bank, the Food and Agriculture Organization (FAO), and the commodity study groups.

In short, I find Smith's conclusions well justified, not only by the evidence he has examined but by such additional evidence as I have seen in recent years.

Richard James Sweeney

It is a pleasure to discuss the fine paper by my friend and former colleague at the U.S. Treasury, Gordon Smith. I admire the paper, and

PART TWO: COMMODITIES PROBLEMS

though the discussant's role requires emphasis on areas of disagreement, let me start by stressing my agreement with some of Smith's principal conclusions. He notes that "the entire price stabilization package has been severely oversold" and that "the review of operating and prospective commodity arrangements . . . strongly suggests that most of them have done or will do little to improve matters significantly. . . . One point that should come through clearly," he says, "is the *inconclusiveness* of the empirical evidence in this area." It may be that my discussion of tests of market efficiency will add to the confusion regarding the empirical evidence—but that is the opposite of my intention.

The tests of market efficiency seem to me to be the core of Smith's paper, and I shall devote my attention to these tests. He deals, first, with efficiency questions; second, with macro problems; and, third, with institutional arrangements. I do not subscribe to a macro/micro split, except in certain limited cases such as the Great Depression; macro effects are usually the sum of micro effects. If the system of micro markets behaves efficiently, there are rarely separate macro problems to worry about (and conversely, if there are micro inefficiencies, curing these will also cure the accompanying—reflected—macroeconomic ills).[1]

Let me make clear at the beginning that there are two sorts of inefficiencies: conventional, static inefficiencies, such as externalities, free riding, or common property problems; and dynamic inefficiency—failure to process information efficiently over time. In the absence of stochastic shocks, the system would presumably settle down to a long-run equilibrium where the effects of informational inefficiencies have vanished, though any static inefficiencies would remain. Consequently, skepticism about the existence of informational inefficiencies is skepticism about a whole class of dynamic problems but not about the existence or relevance of possible inefficiencies of the more usual static kind.[2]

---

[1] It seems quite plausible that the Great Depression should be represented as an "income constrained" process, to use the terminology of Robert Clower, "The Keynesian Counterrevolution: A Theoretical Appraisal," in *The Theory of Interest Rates*, F. Hahn and F. P. R. Brechling, eds. (London: Macmillan, 1965). As is argued persuasively by Axel Leijonhufvud, *Keynes and the Classics* (London: Institute of Economic Affairs, 1969), such processes have relevance only when income falls so low that people have a hard time selling off assets so as to consume on the basis of their permanent income (see Milton Friedman, *A Theory of the Consumption Function* [New York: National Bureau of Economic Research, 1955]). This was probably so in the Great Depression, but in the recession of 1974–1975 it seems likely that the large majority of households acted on their permanent income and thus made decisions wholly explicable in terms of microanalytical principles, and that there is no necessity to explain their behavior in terms of additional macro states of the world.

[2] Some possible third world responses to the static problem of buying from a monopolist are considered by R. J. Sweeney, "Monopoly, the Law of Comparative

COMMENTARY

Efficient Information Processing

What is meant by market efficiency, informational efficiency, or (as I prefer) efficient processing of information? A great deal has been written on this topic,[3] but I find it useful to begin discussions of the subject by thinking in terms of Figure 1.[4] In the absence of stochastic disturbances, demand is D' and price is P'. In some periods demand falls to D'' and price to P'', but in the next period demand and price tend to return to D' and P'. (The process also works for demand and price increases to D''' and P'''.)

Depending on interest, transactions, and storage costs, there is a good deal of money to be made in the market as it has been described so far. A speculator who sees price fall to P'' knows there is an excellent chance that it will revert to P' in the next period, and he will tend to buy the good and store it when P begins to fall toward P''. He will tend to sell the stored goods when P starts to rise toward P'''. These speculative actions will tend to limit price fluctuations to a relatively narrow band around P', the size of the band depending on interest, transactions, and storage costs. (For this reason, the fifteen-to-twenty-year cycles in long-gestation tree crops that Smith mentions in his footnote 2 do not seem puzzling or worrisome—to me.) Note that this discussion can refer to any good at all (though storage, interest, transaction costs, and so on, are clearly more important for fresh strawberries than for bonds).[5]

Note carefully that the fall in price toward P'' and its subsequent tendency to return to P' would lead to correlations among price changes (as would upward fluctuations toward P'''). However, the actions of speculators described above would tend to eliminate these correlations. Thus, if information is efficiently processed in a market, we would expect to see speculative activity eliminate from price changes any serial correlation (that cannot be explained in terms of interest, transactions, storage costs, and so on).

Advantage, and Commodity Price Agreements: A Simple General Equilibrium Analysis," *Weltwirtschaftliches Archiv*, vol. 110, no. 2 (1974), pp. 259–87.

[3] See, for example, Eugene Fama, "Efficient Capital Markets: A Review of Theory and Empirical Evidence," *Journal of Finance*, vol. 25 (May 1970), pp. 383–417; and for a nontechnical introduction, see James H. Lorie and Mary T. Hamilton, *The Stock Market: Theories and Evidence* (Homewood, Ill.: Irwin, 1973).

[4] The following is a condensed version of the argument in R. J. Sweeney, "Introduction to Efficient Processing of Information by Markets," in R. J. Sweeney and T. D. Willett, eds., *Studies on Exchange Rate Flexibility and International Monetary Stability* (Washington, D.C.: American Enterprise Institute, forthcoming). This sort of discussion is often aimed at the identifiability of the supply curve.

[5] See R. J. Sweeney, "Efficient Information Processing in Output Markets: Tests and Implications," *Economic Inquiry*, July 1978, pp. 313–32, for an application of this discussion to output markets.

PART TWO: COMMODITIES PROBLEMS

FIGURE 1

THE RELATION BETWEEN PRICE AND DEMAND FLUCTUATIONS

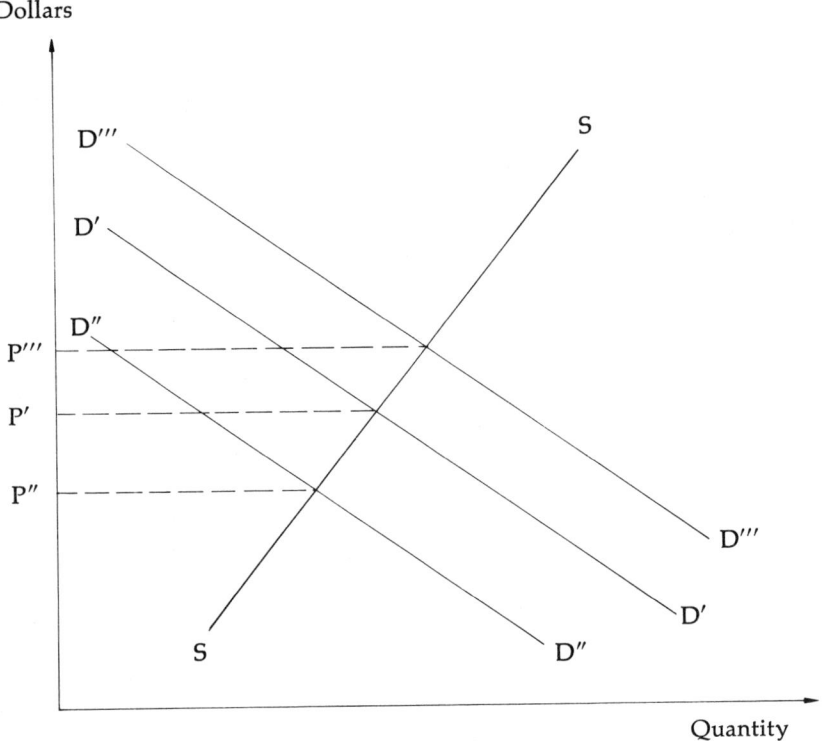

In addition, in the absence of other speculators, one could make up rules based on current and past price changes in order to forecast and profit from future price changes. Such rules are called "filter" rules and work similarly to the following example. "Buy when price rises x percent above its previous local minimum, and sell when price falls y percent below its previous local maximum."[6] The idea here is that upward movements larger than x percent are likely to be significant upward trends that can be profitably exploited—x percent is supposed to "filter

---

[6] This is one rule, based on S. S. Alexander, "Price Movements in Speculative Markets: Trends or Random Walks," *Industrial Management Review*, May 1961, pp. 7–26. There are an infinite number of possibilities; see, for example, Sweeney, "Efficient Information Processing."

out" random movements (y percent works in the same way on downward trends). It should be clear from the discussion surrounding Figure 1 that all profitable information will be removed by speculation that is based on efficient information processing. This does not mean that speculators as a class do not make money stabilizing such fluctuations. They should, and the evidence in financial markets is that they do. But an additional or marginal speculator—say, a governmental body—that tries to use a filter rule should not be able to make profits if the market has already exploited such rules efficiently. Put another way, if a rule could make profits, this would be prima facie evidence that the market is inefficient in processing information and that intervention could perhaps usefully remedy the inefficiency.[7] Conversely, lack of any profits, or actual losses, would be evidence that intervention would not be justified—at least on efficiency grounds.

If self-reversing price fluctuations, as described above, would be inconsistent with informational efficiency, permanent changes that are not self-reversing would be consistent. For example, suppose the mean equilibrium price suddenly rose to P''' in Figure 1—people now demand more of the good, on average, and there are tendencies for price to fluctuate around P''' as it did around P'. Any speculator who sold goods when P started to rise from P' to P''' would find that he had made a costly mistake. Consequently, all speculators would try to sort out the transitory from the permanent shocks, and would offset the transitory effects while hastening the incorporation of permanent effects, by refusing to sell (in fact, by buying) when price is below its permanent level. Further, if any of these permanent changes are correlated, the market should recognize this and eliminate the correlation. For example, if a permanent upward shift today is often followed by an equal shift tomorrow, price should jump today to include the average increase to be expected tomorrow.

Thus, we see that Smith's reports on serial correlation (random-walk) tests and filter rule tests are not esoterica but are at the heart of the very serious question of how well commodities markets behave over time and whether there is reasonable scope for government intervention on efficiency grounds.

---

[7] Governments can, of course, act in suboptimal ways, so that even in the face of market failure it is not at all clear that proposed government intervention would not result in even more serious government failure. In the context of information-processing failures, one must ask why governments would have better information or would be quicker or more likely to act on it. Indeed, it is standard to argue that governments with superior information could simply release it to the public and allow markets (optimally) to react to it.

PART TWO: COMMODITIES PROBLEMS

The Conflict between Serial Correlation and Filter Rule Tests

Alas, as Smith strongly emphasizes, the serial correlation and filter rule tests in the literature often give conflicting results. The serial correlation results for spot and forward commodities markets by, for example, Labys and Granger are all more or less consistent with informational efficiency as laid out above.[8] The changes in price are random, save for some seasonal elements not unreconcilable with efficiency when costs of storage, et cetera, are accounted for.[9]

Smith, however, reports on filter rule tests he did for the copper spot and future forward markets on the London Metals Exchange for 1973–1975. For copper and tin markets, he used a simple "stop-loss" filter rule. He "bought" a ninety-day-forward contract every two weeks and held this contract to maturity—unless the spot or ninety-day-forward rate fell x percent below the price specified in the forward contract, in which case the contract was sold (at perhaps a smaller loss than if the contract had been held to maturity). As he reports, he made substantial profits by using this rule, as did Houthakker.[10]

How do we reconcile the conflicting serial correlation and filter rule results? Smith cites work by Logue and myself that argues that serial correlation and filter rule tests on a single series might give differing results because serial correlation tests might miss nonlinear intertemporal relationships that filter rules will perhaps detect, and we discuss a case in exchange markets where this seems to have happened.[11] Another possibility is that, unless two tests are logically equivalent, we will sometimes get conflicting results simply by chance, especially in the case of filter rules, which do not have statistical confidence bounds as they are currently formulated.[12] However, in the case of Smith's results, I suspect another reason for the difference, one involving the fact that he used a spot and forward rate.

I believe that his filter rule results may not be surprising given the data sample he chanced upon—or, more strongly, that even if the markets

---

[8] See Walter C. Labys and Clive W. J. Granger, *Speculation, Hedging, and Commodity Price Forecasts* (Lexington, Mass.: D. C. Heath, Lexington Books, 1972).
[9] This is, for example, the case for U.S. consumer goods markets; see Sweeney, "Efficient Information Processing."
[10] See Hendrik S. Houthakker, "Systematic and Random Elements in Short-Term Price Movements," *American Economic Review*, vol. 51 (May 1961), pp. 164–72.
[11] See Dennis E. Logue and Richard J. Sweeney, " 'White Noise' in Imperfect Markets: The Case of Franc/Dollar Exchange Rate," *Journal of Finance*, vol. 32 (June 1977), pp. 761–68.
[12] Peter D. Praetz, "Rates of Return on Filter Tests," *Journal of Finance*, vol. 31 (March 1976), pp. 71–75, discusses this problem.

COMMENTARY

FIGURE 2

HYPOTHETICAL REALIZATION FROM EFFICIENT SPOT AND FUTURES MARKETS

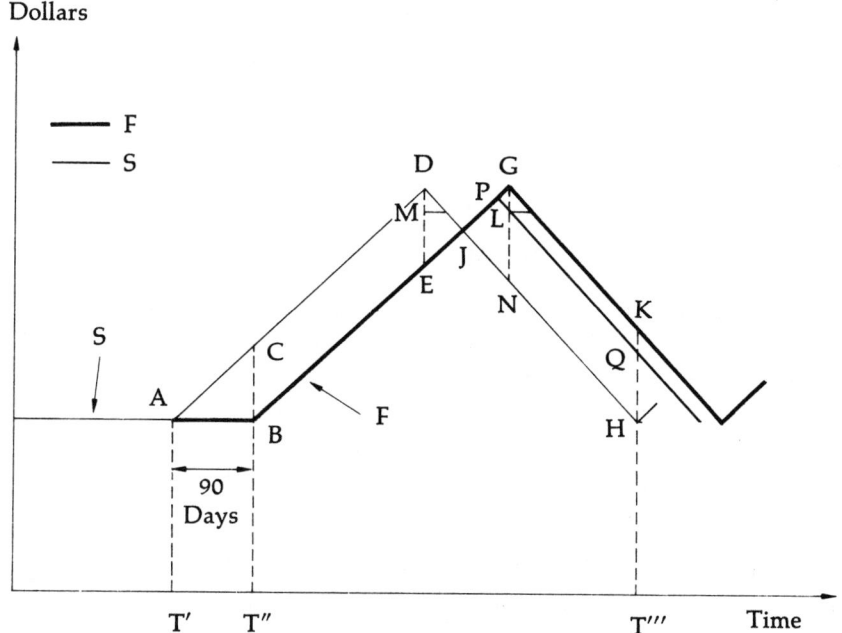

(spot and forward) are efficient, the actual data examined should make us *expect* results similar to Smith's. Let me spell this out in some detail, because it is the core of what I have to say and, as pointed out above, it bears vitally on Smith's arguments.

Note, first, that price series that do a random walk—where changes in price are purely random (aside from, possibly, a nonzero mean)—will sometimes show a pattern such as is schematically sketched with the curve S in Figure 2. (S is to be a spot or "cash" price for the time t.) All the price changes are random, but price itself seems to display up-and-down trends (as some call them, or cycles, as others call them). These "trends" are easily picked out by the eye—but they simply are not in the statistical process that generates the price series or changes. Any one realization of this process tends to show such trends, even though the day-to-day expected change is simply a constant.

147

PART TWO: COMMODITIES PROBLEMS

Nevertheless, these spurious trends are entirely to be expected. Their apparent existence has called forth a great deal of stock market research by "practical" people in the market (chartists, technicians, and so on)—and the discovery that such trends were (statistically, at least) spurious is what gave the power to the initial efficient markets literature.[13] These spurious trends cannot be expected to make money in the spot market (by buying and holding, with an eye toward reselling), except for the chance of getting in on a market that ex post was "rising."

Second, Smith's data looks (in a very rough way) like the segment of S_t from A to D to H—boom and then bust (see Figure 2). The question is whether there is something statistically spurious about these results based on the particular realization Smith used from the stochastic process.

To investigate this possibility, we assume a highly simplified world of efficient markets. Suppose that the expected rate of change of the spot commodity price is zero, or $E(S_{t+j}) = S_t$ for all $j \geq 0$, where E is the mathematical expectation operator. This simply says that the mean rate of change is zero—in the U.S. stock market it is positive; for the dollar price of Italian lira, negative. Further, we adopt for illustration the stringent hypothesis that efficiency requires that F_{t+90}, the forward rate at time t on a contract to mature in ninety days, equal the spot rate expected to hold in ninety days, or $F_{t+90} = E(S_{t+90})$. (This relationship could fail to hold—for example, because of risk aversion[14] —even if the market is efficient, so this is all rather more stringent than necessary.)

Begin by assuming S_t is constant for $0 \leq t < T'$. At time T', S begins to rise, though this is simply a segment of a random-walk series that only ex post has a trend, while the stochastic process generating changes in S involves no trend at all for S—the "trend" is an accident. F also begins to rise at the same time—since $F_{t+90} = E(S_{t+90}) = S_t$ —but the F curve is displaced ninety days to the right. Thus, F at the maturity of the contract appears to start to rise at T'' (where $T'' - T' = 90$ days). This allows us to see that the profit on the ninety-day contract taken out at T' is CB when the contract comes due at time T''. In other words, the forward contract taken out at T' has a price $B = A$,

---

[13] See Paul H. Cootner, *The Random Character of Stock Prices* (Cambridge, Mass.: M.I.T. Press, 1964).

[14] For example, B. H. Solnik, *European Capital Markets* (Lexington, Mass.: D. C. Heath, Lexington Books, 1973), argues, in the context of an international version of the capital asset pricing model, that the forward exchange rate should be a biased predictor of expected future spot rates because of risk aversion.

since $E(S_{t+90}) = S_t$ (no upward or downward tendency ex ante for S to change) and $F_{t+90} = E(S_{t+90})$. (Recall that F_{t+90} is the forward contract taken out at t that is due to mature in ninety days, so the contract maturing at T' is $F_{T'-90}$.) Profits due to this rising trend are then given by the area $CBED$. At D, we suppose the random-walk series S begins one of those downward "trend" segments. F of course also starts down, but because of the ninety-day displacement, the F curve rises until point G. Even though S starts down at point D, profits are made until point J, and these profits are given by the triangle DEJ. Beyond point J, losses for the downward trend in S (but S turns up before F) are given by the area $GJHK$. Net profits from taking out the future contracts are then the area $CBEJD$ minus the area $GJHK$.

Let us now suppose that we impose an x percent stop-loss filter rule, whereby if $F_{t''} - F_{t'} < (1-x) F_{t'}$, for $t'' > t'$, the contract that matures at t'' is sold. This requires of course that $t'' - t' < 90$ days; otherwise, the contract would have matured. If S declines over this period at an average rate of a percent per day, then any $x < a \cdot 90$ (approximately) will serve to activate the stop-loss rule. In other words, there is a whole range of $x > 0$ that will cause the forward contracts to be sold before maturity.

Figure 2 illustrates one such rule. When S falls from D to M, F does also, and this activates the stop-loss rule. The forward contract that would mature at a price D ($= G$) is instead sold early, for the loss DM. But if it had been held to maturity, the loss would have been GN. Hence, the stop-loss rule saves LN. The losses with the stop-loss rule, from point J to point H, are given by the areas $JGN + GLQK$, which is a saving of $NLQH$ (> 0) in losses as compared to buy-and-hold over this segment. In this example, then, the stop-loss rule beats buy-and-hold by $NLQH$.

After T''', S turns up again. In the same way that losses were made by the stop-loss rule around the turning point D, so there will be forgone profits around the turning point H. The stop-loss rule will have the speculator selling off some contracts that could have been profitably held to maturity. Whether these lost profits (as compared to buy-and-hold on the upward segment after T''') would exactly (or more or less) offset the losses saved beyond point J depends on how the graph is drawn—or on how the stochastic realization falls out. The point is, over the time range from points J to H, we expect the stop-loss rule to make $NLQH$ more profits than buy-and-hold. Consequently, we would have to find profits from the stop-loss rule of *more* than $NLQH$ in order to believe that they reflected inefficiencies.

My stylized straight-line diagrams might lead one astray. In par-

PART TWO: COMMODITIES PROBLEMS

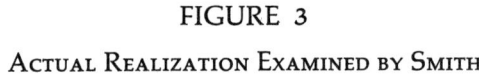

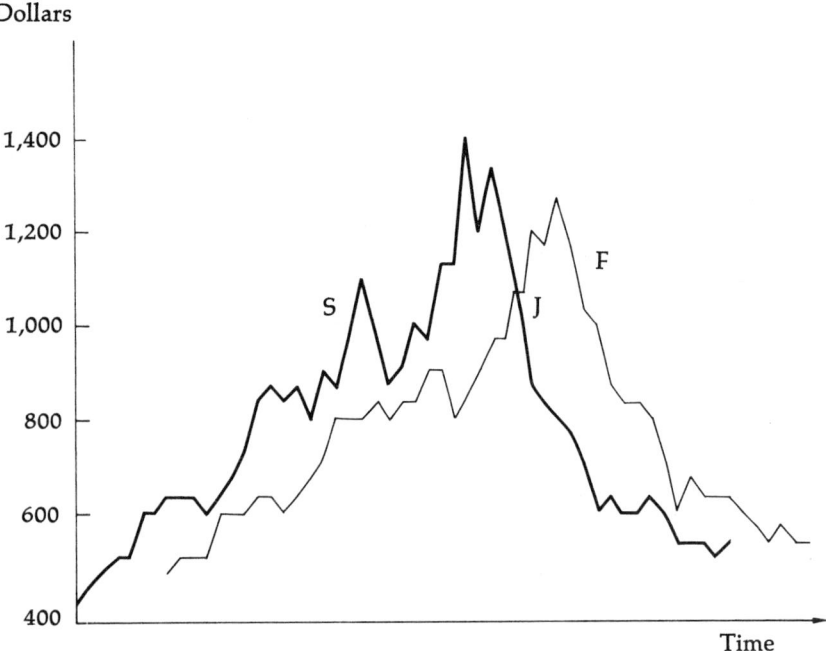

ticular, as they are drawn, it is clear that a stop-loss rule where $x \to 0$ would maximize the savings ($NLQH \to NGKH$ as $x \to 0$). However, though random-walk series appear to have up-and-down trend segments they also have "ripples" along these "trends." Up-ticks in the ripples could induce one to hold on to contracts, even though the ex post trend is down, if the filter is small enough. Consequently, for any particular realization, there is likely one (or more) x such that $0 < x < a \cdot 90$ is the optimum filter.

Figure 3 plots the data used by Smith. The curves are rougher than the S and F curves in Figure 2, but the general pattern certainly seems similar. Even if the spot and future markets are efficient, we should expect the stop-loss rule to save a great deal of losses beyond point J in Figure 3. (Whether we should expect the stop-loss rule to beat buy-and-hold by as much as it did is another question, and one that would require more work.) If the speculator stumbles by chance onto a single boom-bust sequence, as Smith essentially did, a stop-loss rule will clearly tend to look good. As always, the real problem is to tell at the time that one is in a boom-bust sequence.

Analyzing Filter Rule Results

What is the lesson in all this? First, filter rules can indicate inefficiency even when there is none—just as can more formal tests, such as serial correlation tests.[15] Second, we ought to perform filter rule tests on series of "sufficient length." This raises the question of what "sufficient length" is. Somewhat crudely put, the problem with Smith's sample is that it contains only one boom-bust sequence, rather than several, over which filter results would tend to balance out. The same small-sample problem arises in filter tests on a single series. Even if the process generating changes in the series has a positive mean, the sample mean may be negative. In this case, filter rules will tend to look good because they kick the speculator out of what is ex post a down market.

Third, we should seriously consider examining the realization of one series—here S—and inquiring what we would expect of profits in a spot-forward filter rule under the hypothesis that the market is efficient. Concretely, if S and F are generated in an efficient context, and efficiency is taken to require that $F_{t+90} = E(S_{t+90})$, then we can compute from S what F "should" be (before we even examine F); and from S and this computed series F^*, we can calculate profits Π_x^* for a given x percent filter rule. We can then compare Π_x^* with the actual profits we find, Π_x. We would expect that if the market is efficient, for some x, $\Pi_x^* - \Pi_x > 0$ and for other x, $\Pi_x^* - \Pi_x < 0$ just by chance, but we would tend to find $\Pi_x^* - \Pi_x = 0$.

This points up two conceptual failings of the Smith test. He does not specify the relationship between F_{t+90} and $E(S_{t+90})$, or the relationship between S_t and $E(S_{t+90})$. Yet without these two key links, we cannot tell what level of profits to expect from filter rules.

The purpose of this discussion has been to show that Smith's filter rule results are not at all necessarily in conflict with the serial correlation tests he reports. This is so for two reasons: (1) given the spot realization, the stop-loss rule would have a good chance of beating an

---

[15] In Philip Cummins, Dennis E. Logue, Richard J. Sweeney, and Thomas D. Willett, "Aspects of Efficiency in U.S./Canadian Foreign Exchange Markets," in Arthur Laffer and Ernst Tanner, eds., *Studies in U.S./Canadian Economic Relations* (New York: Marcel Dekker, 1978), tests of a series on forward exchange rates apparently show significant serial correlation, though filter rules make no profits. This leads the authors to conclude that the detected serial correlation is not economically serious.

efficient market, and (2) the hypothesis of efficiency is not well enough specified in his paper to let us judge whether the filter rule profits are larger than should be expected. In turn, this conclusion is significant, since the question of how well commodity markets process information is of central importance for judging the economic case for intervention.

Dragoslav Avramovic

Developing countries have two major concerns in their primary product exports: a tolerable income and access to markets. The need for price support becomes acute in periods of excess supply or demand shortfall when prices and producers' incomes decline sharply. This need is also critical in cases where the price decline has been protracted over a long period. Another important concern of developing countries is excessive fluctuation of commodity prices and supplies, which affects adversely long-run demand and in many products generates investment cycles that lead to resource waste.

As matters now stand, the many financially weak producing countries, mostly low income, have limited staying power in the market. Financially unable to carry stocks and in urgent need of foreign exchange, the low-income countries are frequently compelled to sell competitively on a falling market the inevitable commodity surpluses that periodically arise, because most commodity production is highly variable and cannot be quickly adjusted to changing demand. This pressure for distress sales occurs in the face of a limited number of buyers in developed countries who postpone purchases in the expectation of still lower prices, apprehensive of losses in inventory if they buy prematurely. These circumstances frequently lead to extremely sharp price falls and to associated declines, sometimes disastrous, in producers' incomes. Specific instances of enormous losses to the poor producers, caused by such distress sales, are known. Even under normal circumstances, when crops are near average, the bunching of competitive sales in the face of a limited number of buyers will lead to erosion of the market price and protracted declines in export revenue.

In the present international financial system, no organization has the responsibility of providing financial aid to the developing countries to improve their market staying power. If international public funds were available to help absorb temporarily the surpluses and give the producers breathing space to adjust their production and deliveries, distress sales would be avoided. The low-income countries would be able to time their sales properly and thus improve their bargaining position in relation to financially strong buyers.

The Common Fund proposed by the developing countries would fill the present void. To meet the actually experienced needs, it should have broad powers of intervention to protect the export commodity price interests of all developing countries; sufficient resources at its command, subscribed by governments and available for prompt use in most LDC markets; and the capacity to undertake other measures, in addition to price support, aimed at avoiding the chronic overcrowding of export markets and at improving the competitive position of primary products.

Establishment of a limited number of commodity agreements—five or six have been mentioned, including those already existing—is a step forward, but it is not a substitute for the Common Fund. Such agreements would help those developing countries that export the commodities concerned, and they would also meet the specific economic interests of some developed countries. A financial confederation of those five or six agreements, if feasible, would result in budgetary savings for the countries concerned, depending on the precise arrangements made. But "common fund" is a misnomer for such an arrangement. It would not be the common fund the developing countries as a group need. In such a financial confederation, there would be no catalytic effect; little change in the present pattern of market finance and therefore market control; no possibility of taking initiative in more than five or six markets and therefore no protection for the many producers of other commodities. In the New International Economic Order, a common fund should be able to respond promptly and efficiently to the distress signals of all developing countries.

Stabilization of export commodity prices of developing countries on a broad front would be in the interest of developed countries and of the world economy as a whole. It would support effective demand and protect employment in the face of the present recession, and by maintaining investment it would help assure supplies of scarce primary products and avoid price increases when accelerated economic activity resumes. An effective common fund would also make a major contribution to stability of the international credit system. By setting a floor to prices of commodity exports of developing countries, it would help improve their debt-servicing capacity and their prospects for sustained growth, which in turn will benefit the international economy.

DISCUSSION

Hendrik Houthakker complimented Gordon Smith on his paper. Houthakker, referring to his earlier work on corn and wheat markets in the United States, said the results showed less than perfect efficiency because speculators who carry the risk are financially weak. He therefore thought there was justification for government intervention because large governmental funds would not face the liquidity problems of private speculators. Houthakker felt that this is Avramovic's basic position and that it is really not new, having been put forward by Keynes decades ago. He felt the real question for further research concerned whether or not the government could do much better than private speculators.

Malcolm Gillis pointed out that the Tin Agreement is a story of price ceilings pierced and floors breached while the members to the agreement could do little about it. He disagreed with Smith that tin producers cut back production in the face of quotas. Gillis argued that Indonesia and Bolivia both continue to produce in the face of quotas, because the tin is produced by state enterprise and it is impossible to fire workers. Gillis was sympathetic to Smith's conclusion that export instability probably does not adversely affect growth, but he argued that export earnings instability can lead to domestic inflation through ratcheting up governmental expenditures. When the boom is in progress, tax revenues rise rapidly and the expenditure side adjusts. Civil servants' salaries rise, new projects are started, and the budget in general grows. When the boom is over and revenues drop, the expenditure side remains where it was. The result is the export instability that leads to inflation in a boom *and* in the subsequent bust.

Helen Junz felt that Smith was correct in his assessments of the past experience with commodity agreements but said that the reason the Tin Agreement had not worked well is that it was underfinanced. Junz predicted that the international political pressure for a Common Fund will grow. She argued that such activities as diversification are better undertaken by the World Bank or other institutions than by individual commodity agreements. William Cline found the Common Fund proposals particularly interesting because they offer real potential for mutual gain. He cautioned against too quickly rejecting the benefits of stabilization. He argued that the private market will not do the optimal amount of stockpiling because of the divergence between private and social discount rates in what is essentially a time-consuming process. Even if this private stockpiling were optimal, Cline felt there would still be distributional problems. He argued that these windfall gains could be transferred to the LDCs via a common fund without jeopardizing the efficiency of the system. Cline felt that $10 billion for a common fund was not too high a price for stability and was in the range of other World Bank programs.

Juergen Donges questioned the ability of any commodity agreement to cope with periods of exceptional price instability such as the Korean boom and the 1972–1974 period. He picked up on Junz's argument that we should look at history and pointed out that the history of Europe's common agriculture policy shows that such programs do not work. Donges argued that agreements are not needed to forestall cartels but that the integrated commodity agreements are being requested precisely for those primary commodities that are not suitable for cartelization. The producing countries want the consuming countries to participate because cartels without them do not work. In any event, he pointed out that cartels could be less costly in terms of welfare loss than commodity agreements.

Peter Bauer argued that it is necessary to distinguish between commodity agreements that are meant to smooth fluctuations and those meant to transfer resources. He felt that governments cannot smooth fluctuations better than the private market, and, as a mechanism for transferring resources, governments are very regressive in that some producers are restricted from producing in order to restrict supply. In concluding, Bauer took issue with Cline's attention to the imperfections of the private market, to the neglect of the potential imperfections in government intervention.

In the time given to respond, Gordon Smith said that he agreed with many of the comments and indicated that a number of them emphasized points covered in his paper but not in the oral summary. He argued that the problem of distress sales of commodities could easily be handled through the compensatory finance provisions of the IMF and that the problems of internal marketing, which Avramovic pointed out, are domestic problems that would not be helped by international agreement. Smith emphasized that, contrary to what had been asserted, he had not begun his paper with the assumption of perfect competition

PART TWO: COMMODITIES PROBLEMS

and perfect markets. He had in fact emphasized the possible inefficiencies in these markets but had concluded that the actual inefficiency was probably not large. In conclusion, he argued that the most promising solution to the problem of commodity instability is compensatory finance, a scheme already in place.

PART THREE

INTERNATIONAL INVESTMENT

The Multinational Corporation

Robert G. Hawkins and Ingo Walter

Facilitated by postwar improvements in international communications and transportation, foreign investment and production by multinational corporations (MNCs) have become central elements shaping international economic interdependence. Major questions have been raised, however, about the relevant benefits and costs from foreign direct investment, about national regulation, and about possible international control of MNCs. International investment has witnessed periodic departures from a generally liberal policy toward MNC activities, but governmental restrictions have been steadily easing since World War II. Liberalization of controls has been embraced by most of the major industrial countries, as reflected in the articles and objectives of the OECD, IMF, and GATT. With the return to convertibility among the major currencies in the late 1950s, most of the advanced industrial countries embarked on a sustained relaxation of controls over direct foreign investment—both inward and outward. The major exception has been Japan.

The rapid growth of international direct investment and of MNC activity, made possible by certain advantages and characteristics of such firms and facilitated by liberalized national policies, has inevitably led to conflicts in objectives and attitudes among the various companies, groups, and countries involved, whose interests frequently point in fundamentally different directions. Although the most visible conflict is between the host developing-country governments and the multinational firms, serious threats to liberal investment policies exist in the advanced home countries of MNCs as well. And the very size and economic power of large MNCs themselves may present challenges to liberal economic ideals as economic decisions are made without reference to or constraint by market forces.

There are thus increasingly vocal challenges to liberal government policy toward MNCs in both home and host countries. The rhetoric of the New International Economic Order, which would seek to reduce

PART THREE: INTERNATIONAL INVESTMENT

the role of foreign direct investment and MNCs in the developing countries, is but one example.

This paper adopts a broad definition of the MNC and direct investment. A company that manages, owns, or controls production facilities in several foreign locations qualifies as an MNC. The specific share of equity ownership or the specific number of foreign locations involved is given no special relevance despite their possible effect on international allocation of resources or on conflicts with home and host countries and with interest groups. Although much of the discussion applies to MNCs that are wholly or partially public enterprises, as well as to private enterprises, public enterprises raise additional issues of regulation and control not dealt with here.

The current challenges to an essentially liberal treatment of foreign direct investment and MNC activities are described below. The paper seeks to identify the source and rationale of policy initiatives to restrict or control MNCs at the national and international levels. It attempts to set out the actual or potential economic benefits and costs of MNC activity from various perspectives—world economic welfare, home- and host-country national interests, and objectives of particular groups and industries.

First, a brief indication of the growing importance of MNC activities in the international economy will be presented. Second, we shall examine several alternative explanations of the success and behavioral characteristics of MNCs, in order to provide a basis for understanding how their objectives conflict with those of nations and interest groups. Third, the effects of MNCs on the international economy, which in large measure determine whether or not such firms make a positive contribution to world economic welfare, will be identified. We shall then assess the benefits and costs of MNC activities for home and host countries, respectively, and discuss the possible sources of gain, the policy issues and conflicts that result from actual or perceived harm, and the recent trends in control of MNCs by home and host countries. Finally, an attempt will be made to synthesize the pressures for closer control and scrutiny of MNC activities, including their consistency and effectiveness.

The Multinational Firm in the World Economy

The role of foreign direct investment in the integration of the international economy has been growing in the postwar period.[1] It has been

---

[1] The quality of data sources on MNC foreign activity is quite uneven. Extensive data on U.S. MNCs can be found in U.S. Tariff Commission, *Implications of*

estimated that the foreign production of MNCs accounted for as much as 20 percent of world output in 1970 and that intracompany trade of these firms now accounts for almost 25 percent of international trade in manufactures. The relative importance of the MNC as an international integrative force is reflected in comparative growth rates after 1960 in world trade, output, and activity. Foreign production of MNCs grew at a rate of well over 10 percent, world trade grew at a rate of about 9.5 percent, and growth of world output was in the 8 percent (nominal terms) range. MNC international activities have played a growing role in international interdependence.

Structure and Growth of Foreign Activities. U.S. companies dominate the aggregate figures for worldwide foreign direct investment. In 1967 the U.S. share in world foreign direct investment was approximately 55 percent. By 1975 it still accounted for approximately 50 percent of the total, although the share of European and Japanese firms rose significantly in the 1970s. Following the United States in order of importance, the major foreign direct investment "source" countries were the United Kingdom (14 percent), France (6 percent), West Germany (5 percent), and Switzerland (4 percent), followed by the Netherlands, Canada, Japan, Sweden, and Italy. Some, such as Switzerland, Canada, and Sweden, serve as home countries for several major worldwide multinational companies and thus, together with the United States, are especially susceptible to policy measures relating to foreign direct investment.

Since data on foreign activities by U.S. firms are the most complete available, they are used to indicate the structure and growth of MNC activities. The most striking feature is the growth in the size of foreign investment (and production) activities relative to the growth of domestic investment in MNC home (and host) countries. As shown in Table 1, the growth of U.S. capital outflows for direct investment purposes was not only sizable and fairly consistent from 1960 to 1975 but also consistently higher than the growth of domestic plant and equipment expenditures (column 3), except for the modest decline of 1975.

The evidence in column 1 does not fully reflect the investment by controlled affiliates of U.S. companies financed from abroad. Columns

---

Multinational Firms for World Trade and Investment and for U.S. Trade and Labor: Report to the U.S. Senate Committee on Finance (1973); U.S. Department of Commerce, *U.S. Direct Investment Abroad, 1966: Final Data*; and J. W. Vaupel and J. P. Curhan, *The Making of Multinational Enterprise* (Boston: Harvard Business School, 1969). Current flow and stock data for the United States are published in the *Survey of Current Business* annually. The best source of comparative data on MNCs, by nationality of base, is United Nations, *Multinational Corporations in World Development* (New York, 1973).

PART THREE: INTERNATIONAL INVESTMENT

TABLE 1

FOREIGN INVOLVEMENT OF U.S. COMPANIES RELATIVE TO FIXED INVESTMENT IN THE UNITED STATES, 1960–1975

Annual Average	Foreign Direct Investment Flow (billions of dollars) (1)	Fixed Capital Expenditure by Majority-Owned Foreign Affiliates of U.S. Companies (billions of dollars) (2)	U.S. Business Investment (billions of dollars) (3)	(1) as Percent of (3) (4)	(2) as Percent of (3) (5)
1960–1962	2.77	4.0	48.7	5.7	8.6
1966–1968	5.30	9.1	84.3	6.3	10.8
1970–1972	7.88	15.0	107.1	7.1	11.7
1973	13.13	20.6	136.5	9.6	15.1
1974	15.26	25.8	147.9	10.3	17.4
1975	14.35	27.0	148.7	9.7	18.2

SOURCE: U.S. Department of Commerce, *Survey of Current Business*, various issues.

2 and 5 of the table reflect total fixed investment expenditures by majority-owned foreign affiliates of U.S. firms. The growth by this measure was higher than U.S. capital outflows for direct investment purposes—reflecting an increasing tendency to finance capital expansion offshore and the expanding importance of joint ventures in overall MNC activities. But more important, the external capital expenditures of U.S. MNCs expressed as a percentage of total fixed capital formation in the United States rose consistently from 8.6 percent in 1960–1962 to 18.2 percent in 1975.

The changing sectoral and geographic distribution of U.S. foreign direct investment can be seen in Table 2. Manufacturing has become the largest single sector for foreign investment, accounting for almost half the total stock and new investment flows. Petroleum has tended to fall as a share of the total, from about 30 percent in the 1960s to 20–25 percent in recent years. And the share of the services sector has risen, reflecting the rapid growth of international banking, business services, and communications.

As for geographic distribution, MNC activities among advanced industrial countries remain by far the most important part of international direct investment flows. The shares of the stock or flow of U.S. direct investment in advanced countries has remained in the vicinity of 75

TABLE 2

U.S. Foreign Direct Investment by Industry and Region, Recent Years

Industry and Region	Stock Outstanding at End of 1976	Average Annual Flows, 1973–1976[a]
Total foreign direct investment (billions of dollars)	137.2	11.8
Percentage distribution by industry		
Manufacturing	45	48
Petroleum	22	13
Mining and smelting	5	4
Services and other	28	35
Percentage distribution by region		
Developed countries	74	81
Canada	25	22
Europe	40	51
Other	9	8
Developing countries	21	16
Latin America	16	20
Other	5	— 4
International and unallocated	5	3

[a] Net capital outflows plus reinvested earnings.
SOURCE: U.S. Department of Commerce, *Survey of Current Business*, October 1975 and August 1977.

percent for an extended period (heavily focused on Canada and Great Britain); less than 25 percent resides in developing countries. Other MNC home countries have a somewhat higher share in the developing countries than the United States does, but even so, only about one-third of the total stock of foreign direct investment from all countries is in the developing world. For MNCs based in European countries, the United States appears to be the largest single host country, despite some interregional investment concentration within the European Community.

MNC investment activity has risen in importance relative to total domestic capital spending in several host countries. For decades, almost half the plant and equipment expenditures in manufacturing in Canada was carried out by affiliates of U.S. firms; over 15 percent of British investment in manufacturing is made by foreign firms. And despite the fact that only one-third of MNC investment takes place in LDCs, MNCs account for large shares (over half) of total fixed capital investment in some of them—in Brazil, South Korea, Mexico, and others, foreign direct investment accounts for very significant (20 percent or more) and growing shares of capital formation.

Shifting Forms of Activities. Historically, the predominant form of U.S. foreign business involvement was either to export or to serve foreign markets with wholly owned foreign affiliates. The licensing of products and technology to unaffiliated foreign producers occurred relatively infrequently and tended to be either for special technological arrangements, for small overseas markets, or for use in the early stages of corporate internationalization.[2] MNCs based in other countries have made somewhat less intensive use of the wholly owned subsidiary, although it is the predominant type of organization for them as well.

Over the last decade, largely as a result of policy initiatives of many developing- and a few industrial-country governments, the forms of international involvement by MNCs have been changing to some extent. Although still predominant among the industrial countries, the wholly owned foreign subsidiary has declined in relative importance, especially in developing countries and in the petroleum and mining sectors. On the other hand, control- and equity-sharing arrangements are increasing in frequency. These include joint ventures, management and design contracts, marketing agreements, and turnkey construction arrangements, each of which purports to leave some degree of decision making, oversight, and equity ownership in the hands of host-country entities. This change in the relative importance of forms of involvement by MNCs reflects the changing aspirations of LDC host-country governments, their greater sophistication in negotiating arrangements with MNCs to their own advantage, and the growing competition among MNCs for the opportunities offered by the host countries. One indication is the increasing relative importance of license fees, royalties, and business service receipts in national balance of payments accounts.

The Competitive Strength of Multinational Firms

The multinational enterprise has been analyzed in great detail in recent years.[3] Its development during a rather short time span into probably

---

[2] See Mira Wilkins, *The Maturing of Multinational Enterprise* (Cambridge: Harvard University Press, 1974), for various examples of the evolution of U.S. companies from exporters to MNCs with extensive subsidiary networks.

[3] For a recent survey of the literature, see Robert G. Hawkins, ed., *Economic Issues of Multinational Firms* (Greenwich, Conn.: JAI Press, 1978). An earlier survey is contained in John H. Dunning, ed., *Economic Analysis and the Multinational Enterprise* (London: Allen and Unwin, 1975). See also Raymond Vernon, *Sovereignty at Bay* (New York: Basic Books, 1971).

the preeminent form of international economic organization is based on competitive power—power that derives from an ability to organize systematically a wide variety of international transactions and that is not necessarily dependent on the operation of free and efficient markets. Multinational companies can often provide consumers with better and cheaper products or services, react faster to changing economic conditions, and more adroitly overcome or capitalize on market distortions created by governments than can national firms that must deal with independent foreign customers, suppliers, and sources of useful knowledge.

Several explanations have been offered for the multinational's competitive strength or oligopolistic advantages. First, the MNC is viewed as a superior alternative to the market at a time when the classical requirements for efficient markets seem to be increasingly violated in the real world of international trade. The profile of international transactions has evolved from one of many buyers and many sellers, relatively homogeneous products, relatively low transactions and information costs, and few prospects for cheating to one where exchange is much more concentrated in highly sophisticated product groups, semifinished goods, and even disembodied know-how where the attributes of competitive markets are absent. Under such circumstances, it is argued, intrafirm transactions may be less costly and less risky than either spot markets or long-term (forward) contracts between independent buyers and sellers. This may be one source of the "institutional comparative advantage" of the MNC and its competitive power.[4]

Second, the MNC is viewed as possessing a significant degree of monopoly power deriving from the "appropriability" of technology. The firm absorbs useful knowledge from its home and host environments—product, process, applications, management, and marketing know-how—and generates additional knowledge itself through internal research and development (R&D) efforts. Shielded by industrial property conventions, corporate secrecy, and the sheer difficulty of replicating complex technologies, the firm develops market advantages that competitors find difficult to match and that represent real proprietary assets of the firm.[5]

Third, the multinational enterprise can be considered an "informa-

---

[4] A comprehensive exposition of this view is contained in Jean-Pierre Hennart, "A Theory of Foreign Direct Investment" (Ph.D. dissertation, University of Maryland, 1977).

[5] See Stephen P. Magee, "Information and the Multinational Corporation," in Jagdish Bhagwati, ed., *The New International Economic Order: The North-South Debate* (Cambridge: M.I.T. Press, 1977).

tion factory" that systematically gathers and organizes information about market developments, comparative costs, technologies, and other competitive elements through its global operating network. Its efficiency and speed in utilizing that information in decision making may simultaneously provide the MNC with a competitive edge and improve the operations of markets (which require knowledge). The MNC can act and react faster than its national competitors, and its affiliates are continually updated on the state of play in input and output markets and technologies. In industries where technical progress is rapid or where markets undergo rapid change, this information advantage can explain a great deal of the MNC's versatility, adaptability, and competitive strength.

Fourth, scale economies are available to the MNC that may not be accessible to national firms. By subdividing the production process internationally to achieve lower input costs, the firm may be able to reap scale economies by concentrating entire plants on just a part of the overall production process. In much the same way, MNCs can achieve scale economies in management and R&D because they can increase staffs beyond the critical mass needed to generate cross-fertilization of ideas, specialization of function, and an adequate support infrastructure.

Competitive advantages may also be derived from the sheer size of multinational firms. Capital requirements for large projects may be beyond the capabilities of smaller national firms. Access to international sources of capital not as easily tapped by national firms may be a source of oligopsony advantage to MNCs in some industries. Larger firms may be better able to attract and hold superior talent in scientific, engineering, management, and marketing ranks because of the lower perceived risk of such employment. Various centralized functions, such as public relations, advertising, and market intelligence, may likewise be accomplished with greatest efficiency and effectiveness only in large-scale organizations.

Another explanation may be the multinational firm's ability to monopolize markets.[6] In order to widen price-cost margins, the firm may engage in horizontal and vertical acquisitions which, on the whole, may reduce the level of competition. MNC affiliates, furthermore, can engage in predatory competitive practices if there is cross-subsidization among operating units of the international corporate structure. Once the local competition has been destroyed, effective prices can be raised and the permanent monopoly gains can accrue to the multinational

---

[6] See Richard E. Caves, "International Corporations: The Industrial Economics of Foreign Investment," *Economica*, vol. 38 (1971), pp. 149 ff.

enterprise. This foreign-investment equivalent of "predatory dumping" in international trade is viewed as the province of multinationals because of their unique cross-subsidization and transfer-price capabilities in the private sector. Survivors may mainly be multinationals in national markets characterized by a significantly greater degree of concentration.

Perhaps the most widely accepted explanation of the MNC's competitive strength is its "packaging" of a wide variety of services, which may include financial capital, inputs, capital equipment, specialized manpower, product technology, process and adaptation know-how, management and marketing know-how, access to export markets through the firm's own distribution channels, or some combination of these. The MNC's links with its affiliates thus encompass international trade, factor flows, and technology transfers. The links are continuous, and the MNC typically has a permanent stake in the profitability of its affiliates, providing them with technological updates, managerial troubleshooting, new capital infusions, and the like, which maintain the affiliate's competitive edge through time. It is the package, as distinct from its constituent parts, that is credited with the MNC's power in the marketplace.[7]

These explanations of MNC competitive strength are not mutually exclusive, but they carry certain common implications. One is that the MNC will tend to have a competitive edge over strictly local (national) firms. National firms possessing some of these same advantages can and do eventually become multinational—emulating the leaders and attempting to establish and exploit the same sources of competitive power. The longer-term result may involve a relatively small number of large oligopolistic multinational firms in a given industry, a characteristic often cited in industries in which MNCs are dominant.

Each explanation is also consistent with various economic theories of MNC management. It is presumed that the objective function of management places a high priority on optimization of long-term shareholder wealth and that this basic objective is pursued more or less consistently by headquarters and affiliates. In pursuit of this objective, a fairly predictable pattern of MNC managerial behavior emerges. The firm, first of all, will seek to exploit large and growing markets for its products, which means heavy corporate emphasis on new-product development and alignment of production locations to the sources of final demand. The firm will also attempt to minimize input costs—labor and capital, raw materials and intermediates, and environmental resources—and this may trigger sometimes abrupt shifts in the location of pro-

---

[7] See J. M. Stopford and L. G. Wells, *Managing the Multinational Enterprise* (New York: Basic Books, 1962); and Wilkins, *Multinational Enterprise*.

duction to obtain an edge over competitors or to prevent rivals from encroaching on the firm's market share.

Furthermore, the firm will try to operate in markets that are less than perfectly competitive, where higher returns or lower risk and uncertainty are possible. This will include the risk associated with exchange-rate fluctuations, policy changes due to political shifts, and business or economic risk related to diverse national economies. The firm will try to protect itself as best it can by shifts in production, diversification of assets, subdivision of production processes, financial and foreign-exchange manipulations, and attempts to alter the public policy framework within which the MNC operates.[8] Indeed, in certain circumstances MNCs may seek to establish or perpetuate departures from liberal economic policies in their own self-interest.

But the firm will also try to avoid artificial barriers to international trade and payments. Tariffs and quotas can be avoided by shifting production inside the protected area. Exchange restrictions can sometimes be similarly avoided through intercompany transfer pricing. Finally, some of the same vehicles may be used to reduce the overall tax burden of the firm by taking profits in low-tax countries or deferring the incidence of taxation into future time periods.[9]

The objectives of MNC management give rise to patterns of operating behavior that may produce the benefits of the multinational firm as an institution and at the same time create conflicts between it and national governments and interest groups. The conflicts are attributable to differences in objectives and involve the distribution of the joint benefits of MNC activities. When set off against differences in the leverage of each party, policies of MNCs and host governments may threaten the gains from the complex interactions of multinational firms and national economies.

The Effects of Multinational Firms: A Global View

Given the competitive strengths and market power of MNCs relative to indigenous firms and the resulting barriers to entry for locally owned competitors, do MNC activities on the whole enhance or reduce world economic welfare? Both positive and negative effects on economic wel-

---

[8] MNC efforts in these directions have been characterized as "internalizing transactions" to reduce risk and uncertainty and as a principal cause of MNCs' resort to production abroad rather than licensing or exporting. See Peter Buckley and Mark Casson, *The Future of Multinational Enterprise* (London: Macmillan, 1976), especially chapters 2–3.

[9] See Thomas Horst, "The Theory of the Multinational Firm: Optimal Behavior under Different Tariffs and Tax Rates," *Journal of Political Economy*, vol. 79 (June 1971).

fare may result from MNC activities. Advocacy of a liberal international investment regime is based on the supposition that the net global impact of MNCs is significantly positive. But there is also the question of the distribution effects between the host and home countries.

The Volume of World Investment. MNCs may affect the international allocation of capital investment and its overall volume as well. The volume of global real capital formation is enhanced by the presence of MNCs if investment in host countries rises more than investment falls in home countries as a result of MNC activity. It is plausible that MNCs indeed raise capital formation on a worldwide basis. They tend to have access to more sources of financial capital and superior information systems with which to apply the funds, perhaps in activities with higher expected yields or lower risk, than strictly national companies. To the extent that projects are identified and undertaken by MNCs sooner and at higher returns than they would have been otherwise, multinationals raise the amount of worldwide savings and investment.[10] On the other hand, large MNCs with substantial market power may block the entry of new competitors in local markets, restrict investment and output in their own activities, and thus seem to reduce total capital formation.

Hard and convincing evidence is difficult to establish. Several studies have attempted to discover whether inward foreign investment by MNCs in host countries supplements or substitutes for indigenous investment.[11] They generally conclude that some MNC investment supplements domestic savings in the host country while some serves to substitute for it. Estimates show that the outcomes differ widely among countries and through time, although the evidence is quite strong that export-oriented investment is largely supplemental to domestic investment.[12] On the other side of the investment flow, there is meager evidence on whether MNC outward investment reduces or leaves unaffected home-country capital formation. Some studies have shown that foreign direct investment by U.S. MNCs in advanced industrial countries is closely asso-

---

[10] This case would be defined as "anticlassical" in the taxonomy of Hufbauer and Adler. See G. C. Hufbauer and M. H. Adler, *Overseas Manufacturing Investment and the Balance of Payments* (Washington, D.C.: U.S. Treasury Department, 1967), pp. 4–10.

[11] See the surveys in James Riedel, "Economic Dependence and Entrepreneurial Opportunities in the Host Country–MNC Relationship," in Hawkins, *Economic Issues*; Kaj Areskoug, "Private Foreign Investment and Capital Formation in Developing Countries," *Economic Development and Cultural Change*, vol. 24 (April 1976); and John Dunning, "Multinational Enterprises and Domestic Capital Formation," *Manchester School of Economic and Social Studies*, vol. 38 (June 1973), pp. 283–310.

[12] Riedel, "Economic Dependence and Entrepreneurial Opportunities."

ciated with changes in market size (GNP) and financial variables in the host countries but that foreign variables have relatively little effect on corporate investment in the United States.[13] This limited evidence is at least consistent with the view that foreign investment activity does not fully substitute for domestic capital formation in the home country.

To the extent that MNC foreign investments do not substitute for (displace) investment in home countries *and* do supplement (not displace) investment by indigenous firms in host countries, world capital formation will be enhanced by MNC activities—that is, the "anticlassical" assumptions of Hufbauer-Adler would partially hold. This implies a higher rate of real savings worldwide with MNCs than without. While it is certainly conceivable that this has occurred in the postwar period, it must be borne in mind that the coopting and nonexploitation of investment opportunities by MNCs with market power is extremely difficult to observe in available data.

Whether a higher level of global investment enhances world economic welfare remains a matter for debate. If we ignore second-order or indirect effects and cross-national effects on income distribution, higher levels of world investment would tend to involve an intergenerational redistribution of income, which would have a positive welfare impact only if the social productivity of the marginal investment exceeds the real rate of social time preference worldwide. If it does, then the loss in current consumption would be more than offset by the present value of higher consumption in the future. It could then be said that MNC activity improves resource allocation among generations.

Still, the argument assumes full employment of available resources. If inputs into the production process are idle—for example, labor or natural resources—increasing world capital formation no longer would involve a strict trade-off between current real consumption and real investment but would result in increases in both. The "activation of idle resources" by MNC investment activity presumably occurs in many LDC "export platform" investments and in the more traditional investments in natural resource extractive industries. This line of reasoning would predict that MNC activities tend to increase worldwide real income and welfare.

---

[13] See, particularly, Alan Severn, "Investment and Financial Behavior of American Direct Investors in Manufacturing," in Fritz Machlup, Walter Salant, and Lorie Tarshis, eds., *The International Mobility and Movement of Capital* (New York: National Bureau of Economic Research, 1972), pp. 367–97. Additional evidence is cited in Guy V. G. Stevens, "The Determinants of Investment," in Dunning, *Economic Analysis and the Multinational Enterprise*, pp. 47–84. Dunning has emphasized the distinction between factors that determine where production is carried out and those that determine who owns or controls the activities.

International Allocational Efficiency. To the extent that MNC activities affect the international allocation of resources and location of production, they may improve or harm the efficiency of world resource utilization. The concern is not simply with an MNC's allocation of capital; perhaps more important are those elements of proprietary know-how, including technology and managerial expertise, that carry with them a monopoly element and remain with the firm in a private enterprise system.[14]

All else being equal, the application of the "package" of MNC services in a foreign location will tend to improve international allocational efficiency because the services being transferred are combined with indigenous inputs in the host country that are cheaper than similar inputs in the home country. The productivity of either the MNC resources being transferred or the local resources being utilized (or both) would normally tend to be higher as a result of international application of MNC services. This net efficiency gain might be manifested in lower-cost products on the output side, higher returns to the MNC for inputs or economic rent, or higher returns to local resources.

Similar gains in allocational efficiency may of course be secured with free trade in products under neoclassical assumptions, but they would be equal only if the elements in the MNC package are perfectly separable. Yet the sources of benefit in MNC activities arise (1) from the "jointness" of two or more of the service inputs contributed by the MNC; (2) from the superior efficiency with which these inputs are combined in the MNC package; and (3) from the proprietary nature of one or more of its services. These advantages provide the MNC with the aforementioned monopoly-element advantage over local national firms and a potential source of economic rents to the elements in the MNC package. But even with the existence of the monopoly elements and exploitable rents, MNC international production activities do save inputs, that is, they improve allocational efficiency. This is not to say that if there were no monopoly elements in the MNC package and proprietary technology a superior allocation could not be achieved without MNCs. But that would assume away the topic of the paper.

The processes by which MNC activity may contribute to international allocational improvement are several. Product or process technology may be transferred sooner and more cheaply if the complementary managerial techniques for applying that technology in a new location can be transferred as well. Successive repetitions of similar

---

[14] John Dunning, "International Trade Theory, Location of Production, and the Multinational Enterprise," University of Reading Discussion Paper in International Investment and Business Studies, no. 39 (March 1977).

PART THREE: INTERNATIONAL INVESTMENT

transfer processes can be achieved. Market access in export markets via an MNC marketing network is often superior to alternatives available to indigenous firms.[15]

MNC activity also may improve the quality (productivity) of local factor inputs. When the quality of factor supplies in host countries is substantially below that of the same factors in the home country, the allocation of factor improvement services (such as manpower training) to the host country by the MNC may raise the return per unit of expenditure for factor improvement. MNC training programs for employees in host countries tend to be more extensive than those carried out by local firms and are more productive than the same expenditures in the home country. While not all MNC efforts to increase factor quality in host countries have been successful, the evidence suggests that activities such as training employees, establishing technology-transfer linkages with local suppliers and customers, and bringing new resources on stream in extractive industries have considerably improved factor (or input) use in host countries and have often tended to equalize the quality of productive factors across national boundaries.[16]

The international allocative effects of MNCs may be characterized as follows: Because of the MNCs' advantages in information, decision making, and risk reduction through diversification, production activities are likely to be broken up into small steps with differing input-mix requirements. The steps are then allocated to affiliates in host countries on the basis of the relative factor input costs, differential transport costs, international trade barriers, and the like. National specialization, reflecting comparative advantage of factor endowments, factor qualities, or production functions, is carried further than would occur without MNCs. While the underlying economic forces might in any case guide the international economy toward a similar allocation of production, existence of the MNC network surely accelerates and enhances specialization of production and gains from international trade.

An additional point about the allocative attributes of MNCs in-

---

[15] The marketing role of MNCs for developing countries has been emphasized in José de la Torre, "Foreign Investment and Export Dependency," *Economic Development and Cultural Change*, vol. 22 (October 1974), pp. 133–50; and Gerald Helleiner, "Manufactured Exports from Less Developed Countries and Multinational Firms," *Economic Journal*, vol. 83 (March 1973), pp. 21–47.

[16] See, particularly, G. L. Reuber and others, *Private Foreign Investment in Development* (Oxford: Clarendon Press, 1973), chapter 6; and Walter A. Chudson and Louis T. Wells, Jr., *The Acquisition of Technology from Multinational Corporations by Developing Countries* (New York: United Nations, 1974). A survey of the issues in natural resource industries is also found in Carlos F. Diaz-Alejandro, "International Markets for Exhaustible Resources, Less Developed Countries, and Transnational Corporations," in Hawkins, *Economic Issues*.

volves the "portfolio effect" of diversified national locations on the risk of the MNC as a business enterprise. Risk may be divided into two types: the risk that the foreign affiliate will not prove economically viable (commercial failure) or that, because of political change, the capital value of the affiliate will not be realized (nationalization without appropriate compensation); and the risk of variability of future earnings and their capitalized value. The variance of the expected capital value of the MNC is reduced by investment in projects in some countries whose earnings will be imperfectly correlated with the earnings of projects located in other countries (reduction of diversifiable risk and hence enhanced shareholder welfare).

A favorable portfolio effect can be attributed to MNC activities only if the firm can achieve international diversification via a portfolio of projects that the individual investor cannot himself achieve by investing in the securities of national companies in several countries. This implies that capital market segmentation exists for *indirect* (portfolio) investment to a greater extent than for *direct* investment. In addition to differing national securities laws and disclosure requirements, there is some likelihood that MNCs have more information about their foreign projects than indirect investors in portfolios of securities have about their foreign companies. To the extent that this is true, MNCs may make a net contribution to world welfare by reducing the risk in the portfolio of its shareholders, a reduction not achievable through other investment strategies if capital markets are segmented.[17]

Other Sources of Potential Benefit. Aside from improving the efficiency of international resource allocation, MNC activities may produce other results affecting world welfare.

One such result may be a favorable impact on competition in host-country markets. If the local industry is competitively lethargic, an MNC affiliate may inject a new competitive force into the local market and shock it into adopting improved production techniques or reducing its economic rent to meet the competitive threat. In the view of some, an important element in enhancing the efficiency of European firms was investment by U.S. companies (including banks) in Europe during the 1950s and 1960s.[18] Moreover, the evidence suggests that the competitive overlap in products effectively supplied by major national firms has

---

[17] On this point, see the paper and literature cited therein by Wayne Y. Lee and Kanwal S. Sachdeva, "The Role of the Multinational Firm in the Integration of Segmented Capital Markets," *Journal of Finance*, vol. 32 (May 1977), pp. 479–91.
[18] See Bela Belassa, "American Direct Investment in the Common Market," *Banca Nazionale del Lavoro Quarterly Review*, no. 77 (June 1966).

increased significantly since 1960.[19] MNC activity may thus strengthen competition and reduce monopolistic influences in some cases.

But there may be a negative aspect as well. Through strategic predatory pricing and denial of access to inputs or technology, MNCs may eliminate competition so as to enhance the degree of monopoly in their competitive position in the industry. In addition, they may seek to influence government policy or the terms of their collaborative arrangement with a host government to secure exclusive or sheltered access to the local market. Such competition-reducing behavior is not unexpected, since it serves either to increase return or to reduce risk. To perpetuate shelters against competitive forces is in the interest of all firms, including MNCs, and is in opposition to many liberal international economic policies.

Another result associated with the competitive strength of the MNC is economies of scale. These may arise from the optimization of the size of individual production units or the centralization of certain types of systemwide activities such as R&D, liquidity and foreign exchange management, corporate planning, and the like.[20] Evidence on the optimization of size remains ambiguous, although the realization of economies of scale through centralization of specific activities seems less so. R&D is normally tightly centralized in countries with the most ample resources, including scientific and technical personnel.[21] For many industries, this means the United States, the United Kingdom, France, Germany, and Japan. To the extent that MNCs are able to achieve economies of scale in managerial functions and R&D, global economic welfare is of course enhanced. This represents an additional dimension of the breaking up of the production process by the MNC to take advantage of differing national endowments and characteristics.

Firms with multiple foreign production locations and a network of

---

[19] For a review of some of the evidence relating to increased competition in national markets, see F. T. Knickerbocker, *Market Structure and Market Power Consequences of Foreign Direct Investment by Multinational Corporations*, Occasional Paper, no. 8 (Washington, D.C.: Center for Multinational Studies, 1976); and Thomas G. Parry, "Competition and Monopoly in Multinational Corporation Relations with Host Countries," in Hawkins, *Economic Issues*.

[20] This appears to be the case in Canada and the United Kingdom. See John Dunning, *The Role of American Investment in the British Economy* (London: Political and Economic Planning, 1970); and Thomas G. Parry, "Technology and the Size of the Multinational Corporation Subsidiary: Evidence from the Australian Manufacturing Sector," *Journal of Industrial Economics*, vol. 22 (December 1974), pp. 125–34. See also Caves, "Corporations," pp. 132–33; and Parry, "Competition and Monopoly."

[21] For a review of the evidence, see Edwin Mansfield, "Technology and Technological Change," in Dunning, *Economic Analysis and the Multinational Enterprise*, pp. 147–83.

communications are frequently in a position to exploit rapidly and on a worldwide basis product or process innovations. One may hypothesize that the potential return to R&D may thus be higher in an MNC than in independent national firms that must rely on international trade or licensing agreements. If, further, corporate expenditures for R&D are positively related to expected return, the multinationality of firms may result in higher levels of R&D worldwide, which would tend to enhance economic growth. This set of hypotheses has yet to be tested.

Detractions from World Economic Welfare. This section has focused mainly on those effects of MNC activity that would tend to raise world economic welfare. In several ways, however, MNC actions can be viewed as resulting in "costs," or reductions in world welfare. As already noted, MNCs may in the final analysis turn out to be anticompetitive and may harm either international allocational efficiency or host-country market performance. Such behavior may arise from within the MNC when various components of the MNC package (such as technology) associated with a high monopoly element are supplied only in combination with other parts of that package for which alternative cheaper sources of supply are available. Such tie-ins, designed to maximize the economic rent accruing to the MNC, may well distort the allocation of peripheral resources so that high-cost MNC-related suppliers substitute for lower-cost alternative suppliers. There is a definite possibility that the "bundling" of the MNC service package may bring about an anticompetitive resource misallocation as a result of attempts to maximize the rent of the total package.

In addition, the market power of the multinational may serve as an effective barrier to the entry of competitors lacking the MNC's advantages. This could lead to growing concentration and monopolization in world markets as the multinationals further exploit superior competitive positions. Yet, as noted, the evidence suggests that world markets, although still oligopolistic in many manufacturing industries, have in fact become *less* concentrated through time.

A related aspect of MNC behavior is also important. MNCs have been quick to respond to governmental measures to induce (or restrict) investment in particular industries in particular nations. Such measures may include, among others, highly protected markets, tax and other incentives, and prohibitions on foreign investment. The result, in many cases, has been distorted and inefficient resource allocation.[22] MNCs

---

[22] See, for instance, the examples and estimates in Constantine Viatsos, "Transfer of Resources and Preservation of Monopoly Rents," Economic Development Report, no. 168, Harvard Center for International Affairs, 1970.

do not themselves establish the distortive measures, but they have frequently encouraged and facilitated them, since they have a direct interest in the establishment or preservation of governmental policy measures that favor their own interests. Given their size, market, and financial advantages, MNCs have sometimes been in a position to wield substantial policy-making influence in host as well as home countries, leading to measures contrary to liberal competitive solutions.

Another possible cause of reduced world welfare is the MNCs' capacity to accelerate the adjustment process among nations and among industries. Sophisticated information-processing, screening, and decision-making systems enable MNCs to observe changes in market conditions, and to respond by rapid shifts in market shares, demand for inputs, and supplies of outputs. These rapid shifts often place additional pressures on the adjustment processes in countries where MNCs operate. Labor-market disruptions and technological obsolescence in competitive firms, for example, may result in more unused resources and less adjustment through attrition than would occur at a somewhat slower pace of change. Although there is no unequivocal reason that rapid adjustment is more costly than slow adjustment, it may well be that it is.

Finally, the flexibility of MNCs may allow them to impose external costs on the world economy that purely national firms could not. For example, if their activities have environmental effects (water or air pollution), MNCs may shift location to "pollution havens" in other countries where environmental control requirements are not stringent. The world as a whole may then bear the social costs of higher levels of environmental damage as a result of the MNCs' ability to move operations across national boundaries.[23]

To summarize, the multinational firm carries both gross positive and negative implications for global welfare. Given its capacity to mobilize resources and its flexibility in international production, it may not only improve the allocation of world resources but also raise the level of investment and the pace of technological change. But negative aspects may detract from this positive contribution. Whether MNCs have been, on balance, positive or negative contributors cannot be definitively proven, but the indications are strong on the positive side. In a rapidly changing world of complex technologies and giant projects, the alternatives to the MNC are even more uncertain. The global welfare effects are important and need to be considered carefully in weigh-

---

[23] See Ingo Walter, *International Economics of Pollution* (London: Macmillan, 1975); and Thomas N. Gladwin and Ingo Walter, "Multinational Enterprise, Social Responsiveness, and Pollution Control," *Journal of International Business Studies*, vol. 7 (Winter 1976).

ing the pros and cons of public policies that challenge liberal policies toward international investment and MNC operations. But policies are made by nations, according to perceived national and group interests. The following sections will therefore discuss effects of MNCs on home and host countries, respectively, in order to identify pressures for control of international investment and challenges to liberal policies in this area.

The Effects of Multinational Firms: A Home-Country View

Ultimately, the case for a liberal policy toward outward foreign investment must rest on some net benefit—economic or political—to the home country. The sources of such benefits can be analyzed from two perspectives: a general-equilibrium, essentially long-term view and one that is basically partial equilibrium and short term in nature.[24]

Potential Benefits. In a general-equilibrium (Pareto-optimal) context, the benefits of MNCs' foreign activities may take two forms. The returns to the owners of the factors of production will tend to be either higher or less risky than in the absence of foreign activities. These higher real rewards may be distributed to stockholders in the form of dividends, to management and technical employees in higher salaries, or to the labor force in higher wages. Neoclassical trade theory predicts that the relative rewards to the abundant factors in the home country will tend to benefit from MNC foreign operations while scarce factors may be harmed. Overall, the gains of the winners are likely to exceed the losses of the losers, as long as the host-country economy is Pareto-optimal.

Benefit to the home country may also be reflected in lower-cost final products manufactured abroad by the MNC. In dividing the production process more finely, some activities are transferred to lower-cost foreign facilities producing for export back to the home country. The resulting gain thus goes partly to the purchasers of the final products. For foreign investments in the extractive sector, this particular source of benefit is obvious.

An additional source of potential long-term benefit to the home country arises when MNCs plan R&D activities on a worldwide basis but centralize their execution in the home country. This may result in higher levels of locally conducted R&D than would occur in the absence of the MNC foreign affiliates. This, in turn, would result in greater tech-

---

[24] This distinction has been emphasized in Stephen Magee, "Jobs and the Multinational Firm," in Hawkins, *Economic Issues*.

nological change. This benefit is difficult to quantify, but the presence of more professional and scientific jobs and workers in the MNC home countries is a positive manifestation.

From a shorter-term (and partial-equilibrium) perspective, there are at least three possible sources of benefit of MNC activities to the home economy. First, private foreign direct investment is a substitute for higher levels of official financial and technical assistance to MNC host countries, and this should be viewed as a benefit, given government fiscal constraints.[25]

Second, if the balance of payments effects of MNC activities are positive, then the nation's terms of trade are more favorable or the required balance of payments adjustments to deficits are smaller than without foreign investment. Although there has been much debate over the net impact of MNC operations on the home-country balance of payments, some strong indications suggest that it is in fact positive for many industries.[26] In a world of floating currencies, of course, the weight of the balance of payments issue is less than in the earlier period of generally pegged currencies.

Third, MNC activities may stimulate the demand for home-country workers—create jobs—which can be a positive contribution in periods of unemployment. This effect, too, can be either positive or negative, depending upon the linkages between foreign production and trade. A positive contribution to the demand for home-country workers is possible and would represent a distinct and separate gain to national welfare in addition to that arising from a shift in the composition of the jobs available. As noted above, these gains may be viewed as part of a general-equilibrium "gain from foreign investment."

Home countries may also perceive a benefit in the spread of its culture, mores, and business attitudes and practices through the network of its MNC affiliates. Increased awareness and understanding of the way private-sector firms operate may be gained from offshore MNC activities, redounding to the political and perhaps strategic advantage

---

[25] The idea that the United States has sought to stimulate foreign direct investment to supplement U.S. development assistance is implicit in several policy measures relating to U.S. foreign investment. These include: the deferral of U.S. income taxes on foreign earnings until repatriated to the United States; the Western Hemisphere Trading Corporation for additional tax relief on profits from investments in LDCs in Latin America; and the Overseas Private Investment Corporation program for insuring political risks of foreign investment.

[26] See, for example, Hufbauer and Adler, *Overseas Manufacturing*; and R. G. Hawkins, "U.S. Multinational Investment in Manufacturing and Domestic Economic Performance," Occasional Paper, no. 1 (Washington, D.C.: Center for Multinational Studies, 1972).

of the home country. But this effect can also be a two-edged sword, as the intrusion of foreign firms may also damage home-country interests in host countries.

Sources of Conflict. Concern over foreign direct investment and technology transfer by MNCs arises mainly from short-term adjustment problems facing the home country. As a result, the principal pressures for regulation and control of foreign operations address *domestic* economic ills, problems, or alleged injustices. Among the more important concerns that have arisen in the United States, and in other major MNC home countries, are job displacement through foreign production, the erosion of national competitive advantages, the avoidance of a "fair" share of local tax burdens, the suppression of competition, and the undermining of domestic policy goals.

Job displacement. By far the most persistent and intense issue relating to home-country effects of foreign direct investment in the United States, West Germany, and Sweden (among others) is the impact of overseas production by national MNCs on the local labor market. Despite the fact that multinationals span the spectrum of industries from services to the extractive sector, this issue is focused almost exclusively on manufacturing. Even within manufacturing, the narrower focus has been on the actual or potential displacement of production workers in activities that are labor intensive and not technology, capital, or skilled-worker intensive. The jobs issue underlies the most probable political rationale for a major departure from a liberal policy toward foreign investment by home-country governments, already experienced in some European nations.

The evidence on labor-market effects of foreign investment is now plentiful.[27] There is no doubt that some home-country jobs are eliminated by foreign production of MNCs. Production that could have been carried out at home may be transferred abroad, making redundant the production workers affected. There is offsetting job creation as well, however. It has been shown that a positive and causal relationship exists between U.S. exports to a particular foreign market and local

---

[27] See, among others, R. G. Hawkins, "The Multinational Corporation: A New Trade Policy Issue," in R. G. Hawkins and Ingo Walter, eds., *The United States in International Markets* (Lexington, Mass.: D. C. Heath, Lexington Books, 1972), chapter 7; Tariff Commission, *Implications of Multinational Firms,* chapter 7; Duane Kujawa, ed., *American Labor and the Multinational Corporation* (New York: Praeger, 1973), chapters 6–8; and R. G. Hawkins and Michael Jedel, "U.S. Jobs and Foreign Investment," in Duane Kujawa, *International Labor and Multinational Enterprise* (New York: Praeger, 1977), pp. 47–92.

production by U.S. firms.[28] Hence, some production jobs—and certainly nonproduction jobs—owe their existence to MNC facilities abroad.[29]

The net impact of MNCs on home-country labor demand thus depends on the relative size of the effects of job elimination and job creation. The job elimination effect, in turn, depends on the international competitive situation faced by the MNC in the various markets it serves. If, in the absence of MNC investment, the markets would have been lost to a foreign competitor, no loss in jobs can be attributed to the foreign production decision—the foreign activity is "defensive." If the firm could have retained these markets and still supplied them from the home country without foreign investment but instead engaged in overseas production to raise profits or reduce risk, then the home-country production jobs are destroyed—the foreign activity is "aggressive."

While there is a wide range of estimates on the net number of U.S. jobs destroyed (up to 2 million) or created (up to 600,000), depending upon the assumptions as to what proportion of MNC activity abroad is defensive, they yield relatively small net impacts on domestic labor demand compared with all effects on labor demand. The macro adjustment required in the labor market to move to a new general long-term equilibrium is quite small.

Still, a job is not necessarily a job. The skill, location, and industry characteristics of the jobs created are not the same as those of the jobs eliminated. The micro (structural) adjustment burdens placed on the labor market can be significant. The jobs eliminated—both directly in the affected industry and indirectly in supplier industries—tend to have higher proportions of semiskilled (predominately unionized) operatives while the jobs created have higher proportions of managerial, professional, technical, and clerical workers.[30] While the required macro adjustment is relatively small, the micro adjustment and "churning" in the labor market are not trivial. Again, as with international trade, the problem is one of adjustment associated with the less competitive productive factors and with the issues of equity and efficiency involved in accomplishing or blocking that adjustment.

Erosion of capital and technological advantages. An extension of the argument that MNCs transfer home-country jobs abroad has been

---

[28] Both theoretical and empirical evidence for U.S. manufacturing can be found in Thomas A. Horst, "American Exports and Foreign Direct Investment," Harvard Institute of Economic Research Discussion Paper, no. 362 (Cambridge, May 1974).
[29] Some rough estimates of this effect are found in Hawkins, "The Multinational Corporation."
[30] See Elizabeth Webbink, "U.S. Foreign Trade in Manufactured Goods, 1966–1970, and the Structure of the Domestic Labor Market" (Ph.D. dissertation, New York University, Graduate School of Business Administration, 1977).

offered in the United States.³¹ It is argued that, in the process of expanding activities abroad, MNCs transfer abroad domestic capital and technology to be combined with cheaper labor in host countries. In the process, the capital and technological advantage of the United States is eroded; the international competitiveness of its manufacturing base is compromised; manufacturing activities (and the associated jobs) shrink, thus robbing the economy of a formerly highly productive and dynamic sector; and the rising share of national income coming from abroad in the form of MNC earnings increases the vulnerability of the economy to foreign economic performance and causes an adverse shift in domestic patterns of income distribution. In short, the U.S. economy could follow the path of the United Kingdom and become a "rentier," services-oriented economy with slow growth and massive displacement of output and production workers in the manufacturing sector.

There is no effective way to substantiate or disprove this sort of prognosis, which is made basically within a partial-equilibrium framework. Suffice it to say that this scenario is a genuine concern to some and an important source of distrust of the liberal international investment policies that have been followed in most of the MNC home countries in the past two decades.

Inequitable and inefficient taxation. A directly related source of conflict in several MNC home countries is the tax treatment of foreign-source income. For one thing, multinationals, through the sophisticated use of tax havens abroad, transfer pricing, and tax holidays and incentives offered by host countries, are able to escape their fair share of home-country fiscal burdens. This point applies specifically in the case of the United States as a result of the income tax deferral provisions.

There is also the question of whether the tax treatment by the home country of MNC foreign revenues provides a differential incentive to make investments abroad rather than at home. There has been considerable debate over whether both the U.S. provision for credits against foreign taxes paid and the deferral provision constitute an implicit subsidization of foreign investment.³² It is commonly agreed that foreign

---

[31] For a concise statement of the position of U.S. organized labor on this point, see Gus Tyler's testimony in U.S. Congress, House, Subcommittee on International Economic Policy of the Committee on International Relations, *U.S. Jobs and American Multinationals*, 94th Congress, 2d session, February 4, 1976. The general argument is also made in R. E. Muller and R. J. Barnett, *Global Reach* (New York: Simon and Schuster, 1975), chapter 3.

[32] On this point, see G. C. Hufbauer and others, *U.S. Taxation of American Business Abroad* (Washington, D.C.: American Enterprise Institute, 1975), especially the exchange between Norman Ture and Wilson Schmidt, pp. 67–75. The argument that the U.S. tax system encourages foreign activity at the expense of

tax credits are relatively neutral in their effects but that the deferral provision constitutes a marginal incentive favoring foreign investment. On the other hand, denial of the investment tax credit and some other tax benefits to foreign activities of U.S. MNCs provides a counterinducement for U.S. companies to invest at home. Indeed, the net incentives from the U.S. tax system favor domestic expansion rather than foreign investment. Yet the deferral provision provides an incentive for U.S. MNCs to lodge earnings abroad (via transfer pricing) to postpone tax liability and thus reduce the current balance of payments and tax shares of the United States in those operations. This incentive, together with such government measures as subsidized insurance against certain risks associated with foreign investment, may stimulate the expansion of foreign operations of U.S. MNCs and accelerate the domestic production and job displacements described above. Thus, the neutrality and the equity of tax treatment of MNC activities abroad are sources of conflict and debate in the home countries mainly because they are related to the jobs question.

Anticompetitive implications. Relatively little studied is the impact of MNC foreign activities on market structure and the degree of monopoly in home countries. International expansion by MNCs may serve as a source of domestic market strength and monopoly, either through their segmentation of final product markets or through vertical integration.[33] As noted earlier, simple indexes of producer concentration in most industries, nationally or internationally, do not tend to support the view that additional monopolization of markets is related to MNC external expansion—although more subtle increases in market power may in fact occur.[34]

Complication of domestic economic policies. The existence of MNC

---

domestic activity is also made in Peggy B. Musgrave, "Direct Investment and the Multinationals: Effects on the United States Economy," Committee Print of U.S. Senate Committee on Foreign Relations (Washington, D.C., 1975), pp. 53 ff. See also Thomas Horst, "American Multinationals and the U.S. Economy," *American Economic Review*, vol. 66 (May 1976), pp. 150–52. A general description of U.S. tax policies in this area can be found in Tariff Commission, *Implications of Multinational Firms*, pp. 68 ff.

[33] This potential negative aspect ("monopoly capitalism") of MNC activities has surfaced frequently in the radical critiques of MNCs. The point is made, with special reference to banking-industrial connections, in Muller and Barnett, *Global Reach*, chapter 4.

[34] The evidence is examined in some detail in R. G. Hawkins, "Are Multinational Corporations Depriving the United States of Its Economic Diversity and Independence?" and J. F. Weston, "Do Multinational Corporations Have Market Power to Overprice?"; both in Carl Madden, ed., *The Case for the Multinational Corporation* (New York: Praeger, 1977); and in Vernon, *Sovereignty at Bay*, chapter 6.

networks of foreign affiliates may frustrate the implementation of both micro and macro national policies in the home country. The home country's antitrust policies may sometimes be made more difficult, and income maintenance and minority employment policies may be compromised as MNCs transfer labor demand abroad and away from the high costs of minimum wages and social insurance imposed by home governments. Also, technological exclusivity in certain fields may be reduced, and policies to limit the supply of certain products to specific foreign countries may be eroded as MNCs locate their facilities worldwide on a cost/risk basis. MNCs thus add an additional layer of difficulties to the implementation and enforcement of several areas of micro objectives.[35]

At the macro level, MNCs' access to foreign sources of financial capital may provide an escape from restrictive domestic monetary policies of home countries, thus complicating stabilization measures. In addition, balance of payments or exchange rate objectives may be rendered more difficult to achieve with the additional trade and financial interconnections resulting from MNC activities.[36] Although these macro issues may not be of major concern for large countries such as the United States, for smaller base countries of large MNCs (Switzerland or Sweden), the problem may be less trivial.

Policy Responses in Home Countries. Home-country political pressures have been mobilized in response to MNC concerns and conflicts mainly in the areas of employment and balance of payments. Although most OECD countries maintain a relatively liberal stance toward their international firms' outward investment activities, almost all have had or still impose some limits or conditions on the expansion of foreign MNC activities. In the earlier postwar period, these tended to be mainly for balance of payments purposes. In the 1970s, limiting adverse effects on domestic production and employment has been the most important objective.

From 1965 to 1974, the United States instituted capital outflow restrictions for portfolio investments, bank lending, and new outflows of direct investments by U.S. MNCs, all for the purpose of improving the balance of payments in the short run. Other countries, including the United Kingdom, France, Japan, and Italy, have also limited or

---

[35] For an excellent review of several such issues for the United States, see Tariff Commission, *Implications of Multinational Firms,* chapter 8.
[36] See Geoffrey Maynard, "Monetary Policy," in Dunning, *Economic Analysis and the Multinational Enterprise,* pp. 234–49.

discriminated against foreign expansion by their MNCs for similar purposes.

In the more recent past, pressure by organized labor has surfaced in several countries to limit the freedom of expansion abroad by MNCs. Worker participation laws in some countries such as West Germany and Sweden bring representatives of home-country workers directly into the managerial decision-making process. Job protection of home-country employees has been guaranteed as a price for expansion of foreign production in a number of recent cases of foreign investment by MNCs. In the United States, the same pressure has surfaced in the protectionist posture of the AFL-CIO and various individual national unions. The most serious legislative thrust to screen and regulate MNC activities was the Burke-Hartke bill, which would have subjected foreign-investment and technology-transfer decisions by American MNCs to a test of U.S. employment effects before they could be carried out.[37] This legislation failed to gain approval, although in every congressional session since 1971 the AFL-CIO has urged similar legislative programs to restrict the activities of U.S. MNCs when jobs were likely to be eliminated—regardless of whether additional jobs were created elsewhere—and this issue will continue to be debated.

Home-countries' efforts to regulate foreign direct investment can be traced to problems of macroeconomic adjustments and adjustments to structural change in the labor market. International macro disequilibrium, as with a long-term balance of payments deficit and overvalued currency, not only contributes to excess imports and suppression of exports but also encourages foreign expansion of the country's MNCs and limits the attractiveness of inward investment by foreign-based MNCs. For almost two decades, this was the situation in the United States. Despite the currency realignments of 1971–1973 and currency floats since, foreign exchange market intervention by some countries has served to perpetuate exchange rate incentives for U.S. capital outflows and disincentives for capital inflows. Since this has occurred at a time of high unemployment and structural labor market problems, it serves to increase receptivity to arguments for controlling MNC operations and foreign investment. The implication, of course, is that a country that does not have factor-market flexibility or effective adjustment assistance policies is likely to face strong pressures to block the source of the disturbance—that is, the production and technology transfer activities of its firms abroad. This may result in negative welfare effects

---

[37] For extended discussion of the Burke-Hartke bill and labor's position on foreign investment, see Kujawa, *American Labor*, chapters 3–5.

for the international economy and for the home country as well in the long run.

The Effects of Multinational Firms: A Host-Country View

Economic conflict between the MNC and its home-country environment exists in magnified form between the multinational firm and host countries. The sharpness of such conflict frequently gives rise to policies that restrict trade, capital flows, and technology transfers as host countries try to capture a greater share of the joint gains from MNC activities or to reduce what they regard as negative economic or social effects of international investment.

Sources of Gain. The gains generally anticipated by host countries from foreign direct investment include at least the following: enhanced capital formation, increased income and employment, technological advancement, and a net contribution to the balance of payments. The national objectives underlying these expected gains tend to have different weights, depending on the particular circumstances involved. It may be, for example, that the employment objective overrides all the others, so that the MNC as an institution will be viewed positively even if its contributions in some of the other areas are only marginally positive or even negative. Or balance of payments problems may represent a critical constraint on national economic progress, so that positive balance of payments contributions dominate judgments about the social usefulness of foreign direct investment. The point is that the economic gains from MNC operations in each host country have to be viewed in the light of specific local objectives. What is considered a generally favorable economic contribution in one country may be viewed quite differently and give rise to restrictive policies in another—or in the same country at a different time.

With respect to capital formation, the question is whether foreign direct investment in fact enhances the national capital stock. As noted above, the answer depends on what would have happened if the investment had not been made by the MNC. Would a rival MNC have undertaken the investment? Would local entrepreneurs have done so? If the answer is yes, then there may be no net increase in capital formation. If not, then the MNC can be credited with the full amount of the gain, assuming the transfer problem is taken care of. This is true whether there are actual inflows of financial capital from abroad or whether part or all of it is raised locally. In some cases it seems plausible to argue that if local entrepreneurs or rival MNCs could have undertaken the investment in question they presumably would have done so. If they in fact did not, then one can point to a gain in capital formation.[38] This, in turn, leads to positive conclusions about the effects of foreign direct investment on host-country employment and income.

The argumentation on balance of payments gains or losses runs along similar lines. Such gains or losses depend on initial inflows and their respective time profiles of financial capital, induced imports of capital equipment, intermediates and raw materials, induced exports, and repatriation of earnings. What would have happened if the investment had not been made? Would the finished goods in question have had to be imported? Would alternative ventures have been undertaken with more favorable balance of payments effects? Again, there can be no definitive answers; assumptions play a critical role in assessing net balance of payments effects and possibly in shaping policies to deal with them.[39]

The same is true of income and employment gains, which often represent the principal criteria on which foreign investment is judged, particularly in developing host countries. But here the assessment becomes even more difficult. The human resource effects depend not only on the reduced levels of unemployment and underemployment that can be attributed to foreign direct investment but also on the implications for the quality of the labor force. Formal training programs and on-the-job training routinely carried out by MNC affiliates at all levels of employment benefit labor-force efficiency both immediately and over the longer term as normal turnover releases higher-quality workers into the national labor pool.

There is perhaps less question about the gains from technology infusions by the MNC, although the issue is hardly free of conflict. At least in the short run, if no technologies comparable to those supplied by the MNC are available locally, the technology component of the MNC package may make available new or better products or boost the efficiency of productive factors. If comparable technology had been available locally, it presumably would already have been put into production.[40] Managerial know-how, in particular, represents a form of technology that may be difficult to supply locally, and, as discussed

---

[38] See Kaj Areskoug, "Private Foreign Investment and Capital Formation in Developing Countries," *Economic Development and Cultural Change*, vol. 24 (April 1976).

[39] Reuber, *Private Foreign Investment*.

[40] See Philip L. Swan, "The International Diffusion of Innovation," *Journal of Industrial Economics*, vol. 21 (September 1973). See also Mansfield, "Technology and Technological Change"; and Keith Pavitt, "The Multinational Enterprise and the Transfer of Technology," in John H. Dunning, ed., *The Multinational Enterprise* (London: Allen and Unwin, 1971).

earlier, continuous technological updating through the MNC umbilical can provide benefits that might not otherwise materialize.

Entrepreneurship and risk taking are particularly critical elements often in scarce supply in host countries. As an institution, the MNC is geared to an entrepreneurial role.[41] It scans the international environment for profit opportunities based on both supply and demand factors. Having found one, it assesses the economic and political (sovereign) risks in relation to the expected returns. Because of the MNC's diversification across many projects in many countries it may be able to take economic risks in host countries that local entrepreneurs do not wish to incur—that is, in any given instance, the MNC may be less risk-averse than local entrepreneurs. At the same time, the MNC may be exposed to greater sovereign risk because of its "foreignness," which may partly or wholly offset its advantage with respect to economic risk even if it, too, can be ameliorated through international diversification. Alternatively, exposure to sovereign risk can trigger risk-reducing behavior on the part of the MNC—for example, domestic financing of capital requirements—that may serve to reduce the net benefits to the host country concerned.

The gains to the host country associated with foreign direct investment are enhanced by an essentially permanent linkage of the MNC to its affiliate in a host country. Corporate headquarters is interested in profitability, and this means maintaining the competitive advantages of its affiliates. Besides providing continuous infusions of useful knowledge, the MNC may supply access to markets and sources of inputs abroad, periodic doses of additional capital investment, and the like, thereby from time to time renewing the basis on which its economic contribution rests. The local affiliate is permanently plugged into the international economy, and the MNC makes its local operating decisions according to international economic conditions. It is arguable whether the continuous updating of technology and market conditions occurs most readily in the wholly-owned-subsidiary form of MNC involvement. A lag in updating affiliates that are joint ventures or management contracts, some argue, may be expected because of the lesser degree of control and safety these forms carry with them. Also, turnkey plants involve a once-and-for-all injection which, to be updated, requires frequent negotiations of new agreements.

Unless national policy measures or other distortions interfere, MNC involvement can thus promote the "static" gains from efficient production at the national level. The "dynamic" or growth benefits are

---

[41] This is dealt with in detail in Riedel, "Economic Dependence and Entrepreneurial Opportunities."

more difficult to predict, since the continuity gains associated with the MNC have to be set against what the host country could have done on its own given enough time.

Sources of Conflict. Each of the foregoing benefits ascribed to MNC involvement in host countries has its reverse side: costs and conflicts associated either with the external effects of the foreign direct investment itself or with the distribution of the gains between the firm and the host country.

For example, the balance of payments effects of foreign direct investment are frequently subject to debate. At the outset of an MNC-related project, host countries like to see a maximum inflow of capital from abroad, while MNCs prefer to limit their net capital commitment by as much local debt-financing of the project as possible. Host governments may recognize the need to import capital equipment, but they are interested in minimizing the import bill associated with material inputs and may try to pursue this objective using trade restrictions, exchange controls, or "local content" regulations. The policy measures applied by the host country may conflict with MNC objectives, such as minimizing costs, achieving product-quality targets, and remitting profits. At the same time, the host-country government may try to pressure the MNC into expanding exports, which in turn may conflict with the firm's plans for efficiently serving different national markets from specific production facilities around the world. Direct restrictions on earnings repatriation may also be motivated by a balance of payments objective. Sometimes the various dimensions of the problem will be linked—for example, in schemes that permit a company to import one dollar in inputs (or remit one dollar in profits) for every five or ten dollars in exports generated.

Closely related are the income and employment effects of foreign direct investment. Even if these are acknowledged to be positive—and not simply substitutes for activity that would have occurred in any case—there is always the argument that they could be improved. This applies particularly to the use of local sources of intermediate inputs and the creation of backward linkages into the host economy. It also applies to forward linkages and the creation of distribution and service networks and additional processing within the national economy. Particularly in the latter area, countries attracting foreign investment in the extractive industries are often vitally interested in forward processing and increased value added, while the MNC is interested in minimizing cost and risk—which may well require undertaking downstream processing offshore in closer proximity to the sources of final demand.

Technology is perhaps even more subject to conflict. MNCs are regularly accused of bringing into host countries "inappropriate" technology that is not well suited to local factor endowments—for example, the use of advanced labor-saving process technology in highly labor-abundant host countries plagued by chronic unemployment.[42] Such projects may not only fail to absorb much unemployed labor but may also drive out of business local competitors who produce more labor intensively but at higher cost or lower quality, thus exacerbating the employment problem. Such allegations remain an important source of conflict despite often justified claims by MNCs that standard technologies cause them to be "locked" into capital-intensive production, with little scope for substitution within competitive cost constraints.

Another important source of conflict is the transfer of product-related technology incorporated in goods sold by the MNC in host countries, and this, once again, involves the "appropriateness" of the technology to local conditions.[43] Recent conflicts involving Coca-Cola in India and Nestlé in West Africa are cases in point. The imported technology is alleged to have harmful effects on social or economic objectives in the host country which may outweigh benefits in other areas.

In a related area, MNCs are accused of failure to do research and development in host countries, leading to underemployment or emigration among skilled, research-oriented individuals, thus contributing to a permanent national dependence on imported technology. MNCs are also alleged to overprice technology and to enforce various restrictive practices that further reduce the benefits to the host country. The fact that multinational firms spend only about 6 percent of their R&D budgets outside their home countries (less than 1 percent in developing countries) and generally amortize their R&D costs over global sales raises their vulnerability to such criticism.[44] Host countries have tried with mixed success to encourage local research and development, but the

---

[42] See, for example, Jack Baranson, *Industrial Technologies for Developing Countries* (New York: Praeger, 1969); W. A. Chudson, "The International Transfer of Commercial Technology to Developing Countries," UNITAR Research Reports, no. 113 (New York: United Nations, 1971); and R. R. Nelson, "Less Developed Countries in Technology Transfer and Adaptation," *Economic Development and Cultural Change*, vol. 20 (October 1974).

[43] See A. F. E. Wing, "UNCTAD and the Transfer of Technology," *Journal of World Trade Law*, May-June 1976; Hal Mason, "The Multinational Firm and the Cost of Technology to Developing Countries," *California Management Review*, vol. 15, no. 4 (1973).

[44] See M. G. Duerr, *R&D in the Multinational Company* (New York: Conference Board, 1970). See also Edith Penrose, "International Patenting and the Less Developed Countries," *Economic Journal*, vol. 83 (September 1973).

existence of economies of scale in R&D and the need to maintain close managerial oversight have limited the international spread of R&D within MNC networks.

Developing host countries have been particularly vigorous in attacking industrial property conventions as exploitative and monopolistic in their protection of MNCs. Reduced protection of proprietary know-how could of course worsen the terms under which technology is made available to them. Nevertheless, the conflicts arising over technology have stimulated calls for action against industrial property conventions that protect technical innovations, for codes of conduct to govern corporate behavior on the appropriateness of technology, and even for technological "decoupling"—the creation of national or regional R&D centers designed to reduce dependence on imported technology and improve adaptation of imported know-how to local conditions.

Host-country fiscal and financial objectives represent another area where conflicts with MNCs can easily arise. Tax avoidance and avoidance of exchange controls through intracompany transfer pricing are two obvious areas where the objectives of the host government and the MNC management often conflict. A related argument is that MNCs have the ability to set prospective host countries against each other in a competitive bargaining context and thus negotiate operating arrangements (tax holidays, subsidies, and other concessions) that represent de facto subsidies and result in the bulk of the joint gains from foreign investment going to the company rather than the host country. Less apparent is the possibility of "escape" by multinationals from the dictates of domestic monetary policies.[45] It is argued that, whereas local firms must cut back on investment spending during periods of national monetary restraint, affiliates of MNCs are in a position to resist the policy through intracompany loans and access to international financial markets. Besides causing slippage in the effectiveness of monetary policy, MNC affiliates could in this way gain a competitive advantage over domestic competitors forced to toe the line.

There is also the problem that MNCs may introduce greater instability into the host economy. Especially in highly labor-intensive, export-oriented activities such as assembly of electronic components (the so-called screwdriver industries), the possibility of abrupt withdrawal by firms as economic or political conditions change has to be taken into account by host-country governments. This can have the

---

[45] See R. G. Hawkins and Donald Macaluso, "Multinational Corporate Operations and Domestic Credit Restraint," *Journal of Money, Credit, and Banking*, vol. 9 (November 1977).

effect of locking them into suboptimal policies with respect to foreign investment, creating constant apprehension that large foreign employers will move out. A quite different risk of instability is associated with heavy concentration on export production, the demand for which may decline dramatically in times of recession in major markets, leading to selective or wholesale plant shutdowns in the foreign subsidiaries. Aside from the constraints on domestic policy, the risk of such "micro" and "macro" instability has to be considered carefully by host countries when the costs and benefits of foreign investment are reviewed. For a given level of host-country gain, foreign investment projects embodying lower levels of instability risk are clearly to be preferred.

On the question whether the presence of MNC affiliates increases or reduces the degree of competition in host-country markets, the evidence is ambiguous.[46] Examples of enhanced competition attributable to foreign investment abound, but so do examples of predatory behavior to drive out local firms and negotiation of monopoly positions in local markets as a condition for entry. Moreover, conflict often arises over restrictive business practices, such as refusal of an MNC affiliate to export because the foreign markets have been assigned by corporate headquarters to affiliates in third countries. MNCs have also been accused of causing "excessive" competition, as a kind of bandwagon effect that produces entry of a large number of different MNC affiliates serving an inadequate market at inefficient levels of production—the result of decisions taken by the respective corporate headquarters on the basis of global market share rather than on host-country market conditions.

Various additional conflicts emerge between MNCs and host countries. Regional development policy, for example, may be at variance with the multinational's locational preferences. Host governments may have specific structural policies to promote particular sectors or industries, and a firm's investment or operating plans may conflict with them. Public policy may favor certain racial or ethnic groups in employment or ownership of business, which again may not coincide with MNC activity in the host country concerned. Then there is the question of expatriate managers, whom the firm may need to provide adequate administrative and supervisory services as well as communication with the parent organization but whose presence conflicts with host-country goals of indigenization of higher-level jobs. Foreign-owned projects may conflict with host-country environmental or other social goals. Finally, there is the more general issue of foreign ownership of business and industry (or private ownership in general), which often represents a major source

---

[46] See Caves, "Corporations," and Parry, "Competition and Monopoly."

of potential or actual conflict between MNCs and host countries, even if the relevant arguments are usually more political than economic.

Another "cost" usually associated with foreign ownership of affiliates in host countries is a perceived loss of control over local economic decisions. Extraterritoriality of managerial decision making is the issue here, with fundamental choices affecting local operations allegedly being made at MNC headquarters by individuals who know or care very little about local conditions or the effects of their actions on the host-country economy. Political extraterritoriality, often a sensitive issue, involves the application in host countries of MNC home-country laws in such areas as antitrust, trade boycotts, and business conduct. Not to be ignored is the view that the local MNC affiliate may act as an agent for the home-country government and, in turn, that local political representatives of the home country can be used to further the firm's ends at the expense of host-country interests. Each of these issues raises the level of discomfort, justified or not, about foreign ownership of business in host countries.[47]

In all of these conflict areas, the differences between host-country and MNC objectives frequently represent the surface manifestation of fundamental intercountry conflict. To the extent that the investing firm is hurt, of course, so are its shareholders and others in the MNC's home country. But in areas such as taxation, the resolution of MNC conflict depends fundamentally on resolution of intercountry conflict. It should be remembered that conflict can also arise between actual or prospective host countries vying with each other for the benefits of foreign investment, with the MNC caught in the middle.

Nor is conflict necessarily the product of clashes between corporate and national goal structures. What is good for host countries with respect to foreign direct investment is not necessarily good for particular groups within those countries. Local firms, for example, often claim that MNCs tend to skim the cream off the local labor force by paying higher wages or providing better working conditions, leaving them with the less productive end of the quality spectrum and impairing their competitiveness. As noted, they also argue that local MNC affiliates have preferential access to financing through intracompany loans and through the superior standing of the parent firm in domestic and international credit markets. Other charges of "unfair" MNC advantages include cross-subsidization of affiliate operations, facilitation of entry into local markets, survival in periods of slack demand, and predatory competitive behavior.

---

[47] For a survey, see Ingo Walter, "A Guide to Social Responsibility of Multinational Corporations," in Jules Backman, ed., *Social Responsibility and Accountability* (New York: New York University Press, 1975).

Despite the fact that host-country labor may be one of the principal beneficiaries of foreign direct investment, conflict between MNCs and local labor groups is common. It generally involves the standard issues of wages and working conditions, recently including worker participation in management, where foreign ownership may raise the level of conflict. Also at issue are the MNCs' ability to shift production to foreign plants in the event of a strike, the local affiliate's ability to withstand longer strikes because of MNC financial support, management's unwillingness to adapt to local labor practices, and similar points that raise the firm's bargaining power in negotiations with organized labor in individual host countries.

National Control. Conflicting objectives invariably lead to attempts at national control of multinational corporate operations. Only in a very few highly industrialized host countries is such control relatively minimal. There are essentially five ways a host country can attempt to control the operations of multinational companies within its borders over the life cycle of foreign investment projects.[48]

First, it can apply "entry controls." This involves ex ante assessment of the prospective impact of each project on national objectives and on those of politically significant domestic interest groups. A registration and screening procedure may be set up to administer the entry controls, and various actions may be taken. Entry may be denied if the prospective effects of the proposed foreign investment are considered harmful or if no significant contribution is expected—for example, when existing domestic firms accomplish essentially the same thing at reasonable levels of efficiency. Or entry may be permitted under market conditions, with the MNC affiliate left to sink or swim as best it can. Or some form of "pioneer industry" status may be accorded highly desirable projects, including grants, low-interest loans, tax holidays, tariff exemptions, or other incentives deemed necessary to attract the investment.

Second, the host country may limit the forms of participation the MNCs are allowed to engage in, or particular industries may be considered off limits to foreign investment. Majority-owned affiliates may be prohibited, thus mandating local joint-venture partners. Or ownership positions in fixed capital assets may be banned completely, with participation limited to turnkey plants, management contracts, and the like.

---

[48] A detailed discussion of these alternatives is contained in Thomas N. Gladwin and Ingo Walter, *Multinationals on the Firing Line* (New York: John Wiley, forthcoming).

The intent generally is to utilize limited foreign equity ownership to permit an effective local voice in management of the enterprise.

Third, the host country can apply operating controls of various types once the foreign investment has been made. These may or may not be different from rules governing domestic enterprise and can involve domestic-content rules limiting the maximum share of imported inputs, price and wage controls of various types, selective credit controls, local-ownership requirements, environmental regulations, and the like. Operating controls may reduce the profitability of the local MNC affiliate and influence future investment behavior—at the limit, they may cause the firm to pull out. For the host country, the effectiveness of operating controls depends on understanding their effects on MNC behavior and this, in turn, is highly dependent on the firm's available options.

Fourth, the host country can apply financial controls on the remission of profits by MNC affiliates. This may be based on a maximum rate of remitted profits as a proportion of invested capital. Such controls frequently run up against alternative ways of remitting profits, as noted earlier, as well as techniques like inflated book values of invested capital, if this represents the base on which allowable earnings remissions are calculated. Exchange controls may also be used to give unfavorable rates of exchange on profit remissions.

Finally, the host country can apply terminal controls. That is, it can force nationalization or expropriation to terminate an MNC's local activities, or it can purposely make operating or profit-repatriation controls so onerous that the firm is induced to sell off its assets to local interests and depart. Often, terminal controls are applied in an atmosphere of crisis and tension with respect to a given foreign-investment project, or as part of a systemic political change favoring national control of enterprises. Often, too, they are applied gradually to phase out the MNC's involvement in the local economy.

These five control techniques can represent alternatives, or they may be used together. For example, the Philippine government relies primarily on entry controls; Canada has attempted to move in this direction in recent years. Various countries ban such industries as banking, mining, and telecommunications from foreign ownership. Japan will generally accept only joint ventures. India is heavily involved with all types of controls but is particularly notable for its myriad operating controls. Brazil represents a relatively free entry and operating environment for foreign investment but focuses especially on financial controls applied to earnings remissions. Cuba and Chile have gone through periods of extensive use of terminal controls, while Indonesia and several Latin

American countries rely on gradual phase-out. Most approaches to host-country control of MNCs represent interferences with international investment according to free-market criteria, since they affect either capital flows directly or the earnings on invested capital. The only exception is a policy imposed to correct market distortions created by the MNCs themselves. Hence, one can say that the allocational gains from international investment are diminished accordingly. But maximum global gains from efficient capital allocation are not necessarily what individual countries are after. The question is: How much of these allocational gains will be sacrificed, and how will they be redistributed, as a result of host countries' pursuit of their own economic and social objectives?

Conclusions

As in international trade, the bottom line on international investment is the optimal global allocation of resources in accordance with the dictates of free trade in goods and services and free markets for factors of production. Yet national markets are not free, being subject to myriad private and public distortions of competitive conditions. Nor is international trade free, as countries seek to achieve patterns of international production other than those dictated by the economics of comparative advantage. This means that the allocation of capital internationally through foreign investment has not in the past and cannot in the future develop solely according to the dictates of the market but will also be distorted. At the same time, the distortions arising in other sectors can in part be overcome by international capital flows. Traditional trade theory teaches that trade and factor flows tend to substitute for one another, and that when trade is blocked capital flows can serve at least in part to restore the allocational gains forgone.

The real-world analysis of international direct investment thus involves not only an assessment of the underlying economic variables related to relative factor and resource endowments and efficiencies but also an assessment of existing domestic and international distortions. Both contribute incentives and disincentives which tend to motivate the operations of multinational corporations that dominate flows of foreign direct investment.

Also, as with international trade, both the gains from international investment and the division of those gains are of interest. In trade, the players among whom the gains will be shared are the importing and exporting countries, each seeking to achieve improved terms of trade. In international investment there is a third actor, the multinational firm, whose actions can influence the allocation of gains between home and host countries and sometimes can prevent either from capturing some of the benefits (at least for a time) by directing them to third countries.

Quite apart from the intercountry division of the gains, there is the additional question of the amount the MNC can appropriate unto itself for the exclusive benefit of its shareholders or managers.[49] The multinational firm is generally interested in long-run shareholder wealth, an interest that sometimes coincides with the operation of free markets and sometimes does not. Home and host countries are interested in maximizing complex objective functions that again are sometimes served by the operation of free markets and sometimes not. Economic conflict between countries and companies is inevitable—whether the issue is job displacement, income distribution, capital formation, anticompetitive behavior, balance of payments improvement, or tax avoidance. Economic leverage—what can the country offer that the multinational firm needs (and vice versa), and what are the options that each of the two parties has available?—is thus the principal determinant of the outcome. Company leverage will be stronger, the greater the economic value of the package of services it can provide, the broader the options it has at its disposal, and the fewer the options available to the home or host country involved. A host country's leverage will be greater, in turn, the larger its national market and the more rapid its growth, the more valuable the local resources and the more conducive the local policy climate, the larger the number of viable options it has available, and the smaller the number of options open to MNC management.

"Options" are especially important in a bargaining context for both the nation and the MNC. A host country may be able to "unbundle" the package of services provided by the multinational enterprise. It may be able to raise the required capital abroad on its own, to acquire the physical capital facilities through outright purchase or construction on a turnkey basis by an international engineering firm, to license the necessary technology abroad, to train its own labor and management, to search out its own export markets and sources of material inputs, and to maintain all of these elements at international standards through time. If unbundling is possible, the host country's bargaining power will be that much greater and the capacity of the MNC to appropriate a disproportionate share of the joint gains correspondingly less. But frequently the ease of unbundling is greatly overstated, especially in terms of its effectiveness over long periods in industries where technical progress is relatively rapid.

Similarly, the MNC may or may not have good alternatives avail-

---

[49] For a recent thoughtful discussion, see Raymond Vernon, *Storm over the Multinationals: The Real Issues* (Cambridge: Harvard University Press, 1977).

able. If it depends on local sources only for manpower for labor-intensive export manufacture, this can be done in any number of host countries. On the other hand, the MNC may be dependent on local supplies of raw materials for which no good alternatives are available, at least in the near term. Or it may be that the local market for the MNC's products is particularly large or rapidly growing, by international standards. And there are always competitor MNCs willing to take on projects the firm turns down, with possibly significant implications for its global competitive position.

In a bargaining context, outcomes depend in large part on both parties' assessments of each other's objectives, alternatives, and probable responses. Mistakes in such assessments can lead to exacerbated conflict—the outcome of which often involves further barriers to international investment and the efficient international allocation of production. In particular, developing host countries have often had an exaggerated idea of the power of the MNC to achieve its own objectives at their expense. For their part, MNCs have often done poorly in identifying host-country goals and adapting their operations accordingly on a voluntary or anticipatory basis, although there is some evidence that this has been changing.[50]

The fact remains, however, that the multinational firm maximizes its objective function globally while countries are forced to maximize nationally. For this reason, there has been increasing pressure to establish rules of international investment that transcend national political frontiers. Whether in regard to tax avoidance, foreign ownership, technology transfer, restrictive business practices, or other conflict points, the aim is to set international constraints on the behavior of the multinational firm. Recent initiatives include regional arrangements such as the EEC competition policy and the "fade-out" approach to indigenization in the Andean Pact, as well as much broader approaches such as the proposed UNCTAD code of conduct on transfer of technology, the OECD code on MNC behavior, and a similar code now under development by the Commission on Transnational Corporations of the U.N. Economic and Social Council.

The problem with international approaches to regulating international investment is that they assume broad coincidence of interest among those doing the regulating. We have already indicated that economic conflict surrounding the MNC often simply reflects more fundamental conflict between countries or groups in those countries. For example, the perceived international trade and investment interests of

---

[50] A managerial view is contained in Gladwin and Walter, *Multinationals on the Firing Line*.

U.S. and Korean labor point in fundamentally different directions—both sides might agree on the ultimate desirability of free trade and investment, but no agreement exists on appropriate ways of getting there. Similarly, what is viewed as good for Singapore is not necessarily considered good for India. And so the international control mechanisms attempted thus far are often honored more in the breach than in the observance. It will be difficult to get agreement on international MNC control systems, let alone assure their effectiveness once promulgated.

This means that control of international investment and multinational corporate behavior will—with the possible exception of cohesive regional economic groupings—ultimately boil down to a matter of national policy. For home and host countries, this means developing an accurate assessment of the effects of foreign direct investment with respect to each of the relevant national economic and social objectives. What does international investment mean for employment, income, income distribution, taxation, the balance of payments, the natural environment, competitive structures, business conduct, and all the rest? Such an assessment, in turn, means constructing the inevitable "alternative scenario," sketching out in a defensible way what would have happened in the absence of foreign investment. Because of the critical role of assumptions, the outcome of such an assessment will be subject to controversy. And even if agreement were possible on the nature of the alternative scenario, there is still the problem of setting off the effects against the specific national preference—which may itself be subject to intense controversy and rapid change.

Assuming countries have a reasonably good idea where their real interests lie with respect to foreign investment, national policies designed to enhance the benefits and reduce the costs can be readily devised, but not without running the risk of serious international spillovers. For instance, investment incentives in one country may draw production away from others and give rise to shifts in trade flows and the demand for offsetting restrictions abroad. Nationalization or expropriation in a given host country may be viewed as sufficiently serious for MNC home countries to take action. Actions that encroach on foreign-owned technologies may likewise trigger reactions abroad. National policies aimed at national enterprises that happen to be affiliates of foreign-owned MNCs, while perhaps in the national interest, can lead to "investment wars" not too dissimilar to the conflicts that have developed periodically in the trade sector—conflicts over the specific terms and effects of international investment.[51]

---

[51] See C. Fred Bergsten, "The Coming Investment Wars," *Foreign Affairs*, vol. 54 (June 1976).

Multinational Corporations and a Liberal International Economic Order: Some Overlooked Considerations

Malcolm Gillis

Introduction

Not too many years ago the governor of the central bank in a faraway land concluded that the prime barrier to faster economic growth in his country was the lack of a viable organized capital market. I was asked to advise on measures to encourage the development of such a market. I arrived in this distant land clutching under both arms the collected works of Edward S. Shaw and Ronald McKinnon, with a copy of Raymond Goldsmith in my briefcase. In the office of the governor, I was informed that my terms of reference had been changed. It was no longer necessary to bother with policies for development of the capital market. Rather, it was expected that I would devote my short visit to the task of updating estimates of the credit expansion multiplier. After asking the reason for this change, I was told that the problem of capital market development had already been overcome: just the week before, the governor had himself laid the cornerstone for a new building to house a newly created stock exchange and had decreed that the stock market was to "open" on October 1 of that year. Thus, the problem of inadequate capital markets had been solved by resort to two venerable devices: the stroke of a pen and the erection of an institution.

Much of the debate in international forums over the New International Economic Order in the early 1970s struck me as bearing strong earmarks of the type of thinking that underlay the central bank governor's attitude toward capital market development: if a mechanism is not performing according to expectations, it is sufficient to decree new rules of the game and, while doing so, create a new institution or two, such as commodity stabilization organizations or agencies to police codes of conduct for multinational firms, to service these aims. In that way, by some predetermined date, a New International Economic Order will come into being.

This is not to say that there is nothing amiss in the workings of what has come to be called the international economic system nor to imply that claims of inequitable results in the operation of the system —particularly those charges leveled by the poorest nations—are without foundation. But it does seem that a good many of the proposals for reform emanating from UNCTAD and elsewhere may have been based on unrealistic expectations of the extent to which the system may be improved by fiat rather than through an evolutionary process. It also seems fair to say that in recent forums where the debate over the system has been aired (as in the Paris Conference in March 1977) creeping realism appears to have set in among some proponents of a New International Economic Order. The level of discussion has, in my view, thereby been perceptibly raised. This conference should serve the purpose of raising the level of discussion still further. In order to do this, however, realism on the part of supporters of a liberal international economic order is also required. And a realistic discussion of the prospects for an LIEO cannot be usefully undertaken without first examining the constituencies that may be expected to line up behind it.

The Need for Identification of the Constituency

I would argue that there are perhaps three principal standards around which different constituencies could rally, insofar as debate over the "reform" of the international economic order is concerned—the NIEO, an LIEO, and the status quo. The characteristics of the NIEO have been well described in a number of other papers and need not be treated in detail here. Basically, proponents of NIEO perceive grave inequities in the present workings of what has come to be called the international system and have, through UNCTAD and other vehicles, prepared a formidable list of proposed reforms that would expand developing country access to private and official international capital, to international reserves, to technology, and to markets for manufactured products. Ironically, these proposals have reached full bloom just at the moment when the arguments of the adherents of the "dependency school" have gained some currency among developing country leaders and economists. In its least extreme form, dependency theory is interpreted to mean that the dependency of developing nations upon the capitalistically dominated world economy is merely a major obstacle to their development.[1] In its more extreme form, dependency theory is interpreted to mean that dependence is the *cause* of underdevelopment and involves a categorical denial of benefits from trade with rich countries. In this view, poor countries (far from seeking the incremental re-

---

[1] "Dependency" in this sense includes dependence not only upon trade with advanced nations but upon their capital, technology, and managerial methods.

forms in the international economic order typified in UNCTAD proposals) should take major steps to insulate themselves from the workings of capitalistically organized world markets.[2]

Supporters of LIEO may be identified, as in Thomas Willett's characterization, as those who seek to "utilize the operation of competitive markets to the extent feasible," and who view competitive market transactions as leading to mutual gains rather than exploitation.[3] This view is fully consistent with the standards against which liberal definitions are best measured, to wit, those in Henry Simons's *Economic Policy for a Free Society*.[4] Whereas the international economic system as modified after Bretton Woods may have, in the early postwar years, approximated something that Simons might have recognized as a "liberal" order,[5] I would argue that as it has evolved over the past twenty-five-odd years, the international economic order does not now merit such a label, given the maze of trade and exchange restrictions and the pervasive anticompetitive pressures and preferences that have developed.

Rather, I would tend to view the NIEO demands as a challenge not so much to a "liberal" order as to the status quo and to a set of institutions that may qualify only as distant relatives to a liberal order. Each of the three arrangements for an international system has its own constituency. The constituency for NIEO is fairly easy to identify. It is vocal and tends to cloak its demands in the name and best interests of the poor of the world, even if it has yet to be demonstrated that NIEO measures would benefit the poor rather than the elite groups in poor countries. The constituency for the status quo speaks in more muted tones and in any case has few proselytizers willing to carry its standard openly. As to the constituency for a liberal order, I will argue that, notwithstanding repeated and forceful demonstrations of the benefits (to rich and poor alike) of freer mechanisms for trade, payments, and factor movements, the membership of this constituency has likely been greatly overestimated. In particular, a significant share of the most

---

[2] For a critical review of many significant aspects of dependency theory, see Michael Roemer, "Dependence and Industrialization Strategy," Development Discussion Paper, no. 37 (Harvard Institute for International Development, February 1978). For a skeptical view of dependency theory (as theory) from a sympathetic reviewer, see Thomas E. Weisskopf, "Dependence as an Explanation of Development," Discussion Paper, no. 66 (Center for Research on Economic Development, February 1977).

[3] Thomas D. Willett in Part 1, above.

[4] Henry C. Simons, *Economic Policy for a Free Society* (Chicago: University of Chicago Press, 1948).

[5] This view is expressed by Gottfried Haberler in Part 1, above.

potent members often presumed to be in this constituency may owe their allegiance elsewhere.

The Constituency That Was Not. More than one proposal for liberalizing (in the Henry Simons sense) domestic or international policies has foundered because presumptions regarding its constituency proved unfounded. A recent case in point on the domestic front is the fate of Secretary William Simon's 1975 proposals for integration of the personal and corporate income tax. The impetus for integration has been based on three considerations: (1) recognition of inequities involved in the "double taxation" of corporate-source income; (2) more recently, concern over the welfare costs of capital income taxation and, in particular, the effects of heavy capital taxes on the national rates of saving and investment; and (3) concern over the effects of the corporate tax on corporate financial policy.

Nearly all the serious proposals for income tax integration would result in less tax liability for corporations or their shareholders than is now the case. Thus, it would appear reasonable to expect that corporations would flock en masse to the integration banner, but until now, this has not happened. Clearly not all corporations support this measure that for so long has been identified with liberal principles. In a recent article, Charles McLure and Stanley Surrey sought to identify the business constituency that might favor integration.[6] This constituency is rather smaller than the set of all corporations, and a surprising number of major corporations have strong incentives for actively opposing likely forms of integration. In particular, firms characterized by one of the following four features would not be favorably inclined toward integration: (1) high debt-equity ratios, (2) low dividend-payout ratios, (3) substantial tax preference income, or (4) substantial foreign tax credits.[7] Managers of such firms would not tend to find integration

---

[6] Charles E. McLure, Jr., and Stanley S. Surrey, "Integration of Income Taxes: Issues for Debate," *Harvard Business Review*, September-October 1977, pp. 169–82.

[7] Any one of these characteristics would, by itself, tend to cause corporations to oppose integration. But it should be noted that to the extent that a firm has a high payout ratio (a factor normally predisposing firms in favor of integration), and also has substantial tax preference income or foreign income, the firm's interests would be threatened by integration. Firms with substantial tax preferences or foreign tax credits would not necessarily oppose integration if pass-through of these items were allowed. See ibid., p. 178. But given the very great administrative difficulties inherent in allowing pass-through, and given that European countries do not allow pass-through under their integration systems, it is more likely that such items would be "washed out" in the event of integration here.

favorable to their interests, and the numerous firms having at least one of these characteristics may be counted as among the largest and most influential in the economy. But throughout the long discussion of the pros and cons of integration, academics and policy makers have mistakenly assumed that the corporate community as a whole represented a major part of the constituency for integration.

The Constituency That Almost Is Not. As noted, the identities of the constituencies for a New International Economic Order are rather widely known and are identified in conference papers by Thomas Willett and Robert Baldwin, among others. But what groups comprise the constituency for a liberal international economic order? Clearly, the members cannot be defined as the set of all interest groups not found in the constituency for NIEO, for a substantial portion of that set appears to favor neither "new" nor "liberal" international economic institutions. For example, heavily unionized industries in the United States cannot by any means be numbered as staunch supporters of proposals for an UNCTAD-style NIEO, and, as Willett observes, their strong recent support for the protectionist cause puts much of organized labor squarely outside the liberal constituency.[8] Other authors identify some of the constituents for a liberal order. Thus, Baldwin maintains that the major organizations representing business as a whole appear to favor trade liberalization, subject to some provisos.[9] I would add that a significant percentage of the academic constituency for a liberal order may be found at this conference.

Is it reasonable to expect multinational firms, or most of them, to line up solidly within the constituency for a liberal international economic order? Many authors writing on such firms implicitly assume that the bulk of multinational corporations lie within the liberal constituency.[10] Is this a reasonable assumption, particularly given the non-homogeneity of MNCs as a group?

I take the definition of liberalism offered earlier to mean that any special preferences and privileges offered to direct investment by particular multinational firms, and not available to all other firms, should be grouped under the heading of *illiberal* practices, alongside such devices as exchange controls, high tariff and nontariff barriers to trade, and preferential trading agreements. To the extent that such preferences and privileges secured (by whatever means) by multinational firms are

---

[8] Willett, herein.
[9] Robert E. Baldwin in Part 4, below.
[10] See, for example, Robert G. Hawkins and Ingo Walter, Part 3, above.

made at their behest, then MNCs should be viewed as *sources* of illiberalism, along with ill-conceived policies of home- and host-country governments, organized labor in the United States, and cartel-type arrangements among European and Japanese firms. To put this observation in its proper perspective, it is important to identify the underlying sources of policy initiatives to restrict or control MNCs at either the national or the international level. Commonly, specialists in this area focus on only two sources of threats to liberal investment policies: host developing-country governments and policies in the advanced home countries of MNCs.[11] But, as suggested above, there may be a third source—perhaps not as significant and certainly not as obvious as the other two—the multinational firms themselves. That is to say, perhaps a substantial number of MNCs, whether American, European, or Japanese, have a very large stake in preserving and promoting illiberal policies. In any case, this hypothesis merits serious consideration.

In particular, it is not inconceivable that some of the illiberal policies adopted by governments—particularly developing-country host governments—toward multinational firms had their origins in responses to illiberal policies of multinational firms headquartered in the United States, Japan, and Europe. Or perhaps, in many cases, illiberal actions by host-country governments may be viewed as belated but largely futile efforts to correct distortions that may arise from the market power and noncompetitive behavior of MNCs, behavior that is often incorrectly lumped under the heading of the "competitive" strength of multinational firms.[12]

But there is ample evidence that MNCs do often engage in practices to eliminate competition and thereby enhance their monopoly power. Examples abound. Economists unwilling to believe that Japanese MNCs carve up export markets in such a way as to reduce competition among themselves in particular countries have clearly not been abroad recently to observe this practice, particularly in Southeast Asia. Another such practice is the refusal of MNC affiliates in a host country to export, even when the host-country government attempts to facilitate such exports. They refuse because the foreign markets have already been assigned either to affiliates in other countries or to the head office. Such anticompetitive practices might conceivably help provoke adoption by host governments of illiberal policies toward foreign investment.

One practice usually attributed to host-country illiberalism is that of entry controls, which may be used by governments to deny invest-

---

[11] See, for example, ibid.
[12] Ibid.

ment privileges to foreign firms.[13] One might think that MNCs as a group would strongly favor the speedy dismantling of such controls. But it is not generally realized that cases abound in which entry restrictions against MNCs have been activated by governments at the behest of multinational firms that arrived earlier. This type of illiberal policy has been all too common in automotive assembly, pharmaceuticals, tires, and a host of other product lines. In most cases of which I am aware, the pressure for closing off particular fields to foreign investment has come from domestic firms in the host country. Further, cases could be cited in which domestic affiliates of some U.S.- and European-based MNCs have insisted upon (and received) monopoly privileges in the host-country market (for example, tire production in Indonesia).

Indeed, as these few examples indicate, many MNCs may find it quite comfortable to operate in an illiberal world. One might argue that over the years many, if not most, MNCs have become relatively more adept than their non-MNC brethren at taking advantage of the opportunities for spoils offered by illiberal policies toward not only foreign investment but trade and international payments. Given the devices that many have developed over the years to extract maximum rents from restrictive policies, would it be sensible to include MNCs as a group in the constituency for a liberal order? If not, would it be possible to develop a typology that would enable identification of those that *do* belong in the constituency?

Many perceptive observers of the international economic system have argued that much MNC activity can be explained by the high premium such firms place upon maintaining stability.[14] Any major move toward a more liberal international economic order might be viewed as a threat to that stability, although perhaps not nearly so great a threat as a move toward an UNCTAD-type international economic order. For this reason we might be well advised to place MNCs squarely in the constituency for the status quo, not for liberalization.

Conceptions and Misconceptions

A familiar stereotype is that the multinational firm tends to be (1) American-based, (2) privately owned, and (3) "efficient." All three features may have been common in bygone years but, like most stereotypes, this one has long outlived whatever usefulness it may once have had. In recent years the form and sources of international investment

---

[13] Ibid.

[14] See, for example, Raymond Vernon, *Storm over the Multinationals: The Real Issues* (Cambridge: Harvard University Press, 1977), chapter 4.

have changed in ways that are as yet but dimly perceived in home and host countries. Not the least of these changes has been the rise of MNCs with bases other than in the United States and the more recent appearance of substantial involvement by state-owned multinational enterprises. At the same time, it has become increasingly clear that "efficiency" does not mean the same thing to everyone (indeed, not even to all economists), so that claims of the superior "efficiency" of MNCs must be heavily qualified if they are to be taken seriously.

The MNC as an American Creature. Many official pronouncements from international organizations—and indeed, not a few academic studies—concerning the need for reforming host-country policies toward MNCs implicitly (and sometimes explicitly) view the MNC as basically an American creature. This concept is understandable from the point of view of host countries, since in most instances the U.S. firms arrived first and, outside Africa, have usually been most visible, particularly before 1970. The persistence of the view is understandable in academic efforts, particularly American, since U.S. firms are easier to study because data on their foreign activities are the most detailed and extensive available. But this tendency to use U.S. direct foreign investment experience and data as representative of worldwide activities of MNCs serves to obscure a number of recent developments that may be particularly noteworthy and that could conceivably provide further impetus for illiberal policies toward MNCs in general.[15]

One of the most significant of these phenomena has been the much more rapid rate of expansion by MNCs based in the other industrialized countries relative to expansion by U.S.-based firms. Another little-appreciated (until very recently) development has been the rapid growth in investments by developing-country firms in other developing countries.[16] Although it is probably true that U.S.-based firms still account for as much as 50 percent of direct foreign investment, the overseas involvement of Japanese and Western European (particularly German) firms has from all accounts been growing much faster.[17] It has been argued that, among other considerations, this development will contribute to the ability of LDC host countries to harness MNCs to

---

[15] For an illustration of this tendency, see Hawkins and Walter, above.

[16] Among the first to recognize this development, and particularly its implications for technology transfer, was Louis T. Wells. See his "Internationalization of Firms from the Developing Countries," in Agmon Tamir and Charles P. Kindleberger, eds., *Multinationals from Small Countries* (Cambridge: M.I.T. Press, 1977).

[17] C. Fred Bergsten, "An Analysis of U.S. Foreign Direct Investment Policy and Economic Development," AID Discussion Paper, no. 36 (Bureau for Program and Policy Cooperation, November 1976), p. 9.

promote their national objectives, because LDCs wanting foreign direct investment now face a much wider choice of multinationals with which they can do business. Thus, LDC host countries can presumably now do a better job of playing off multinational firms against one another in the process of negotiating terms and conditions for entry.

If this development does in fact serve to improve the bargaining power of LDCs vis-à-vis the multinational firms, we might expect on this account a somewhat lesser degree of uncertainty in the environment for foreign direct investment than has been the case in the past. To some extent, much of the impetus for overturning or renegotiating terms for foreign investment in LDCs has come from the belated realization that many such arrangements have been negotiated from positions of weakness and unequal bargaining abilities on the part of LDCs. Thus, it might be argued that anything that places LDCs in a better position to negotiate initial bargains with multinational firms will tend to reduce the scope for future renegotiation or expropriation, thereby adding an element of predictability and certainty in an investment climate that has in the past often been characterized by periods of marked political uncertainty.

Therefore, on the one hand, the growing role of European- and Japanese-based MNCs may reduce pressures for restrictive policies toward foreign direct investment. On the other hand, this development might also contribute to an even greater degree of conflict between MNCs and host-country governments, particularly LDCs, over the next few years. There are some grounds for a hypothesis that many relative newcomers to the multinational arena lack the capacity for anticipating and resolving conflicts with host-country interests that some of their American- and British-based counterparts have developed over the past thirty years, often through bitter and costly experience. If so, would those firms be expected to repeat many of the mistakes in dealing with host-country governments that U.S.-based firms frequently made when they first began to be involved internationally on a grand scale in the 1950s? And, would firms that are relatively new to the game be expected to respond to host-country reactions to their mistakes in the same counterproductive way that U.S. firms responded in earlier years,[18] thereby provoking further restrictive measures by host-country governments?

The scenario outlined above may not be all that farfetched. It could be argued that most U.S.-based MNCs have, as a result of greater

---

[18] Such counterproductive moves by U.S. firms included (1) pressure to enact and enforce the Hickenlooper agreement; (2) embargoes against trading with firms nationalized by foreign governments; and (3) outright bribery of LDC officials.

PART THREE: INTERNATIONAL INVESTMENT

experience, developed a greater degree of sophistication in dealing with LDC host-country governments. Rarely do U.S. MNCs now believe it reasonable to expect success in efforts to tie up potential sources of raw materials in LDCs through long-term contracts negotiated on terms grossly unbalanced toward the firm. And it could be argued that few U.S.-based (and, to a great extent, British-based) firms are particularly surprised or disturbed by LDC demands for renegotiation of entry terms once agreements are signed. Indeed, in some recent cases such firms have themselves taken the initiative to reopen foreign investment agreements in which LDC interests were particularly poorly protected. The impetus has come not from altruism but from MNC self-interest in preventing renegotiation from becoming a political football later on.

But what of French-, Japanese-, Italian-, and Australian-based MNCs? If recently signed agreements in minerals and in some manufacturing fields are any indication, one might conclude that many foreign-based MNCs, to a significantly greater extent than their American counterparts, still tend to focus on the short-term gains that can be extracted when negotiating entry conditions with host countries unable to recognize or exploit their bargaining positions. Thus, continental minerals enterprises often tend to view minerals concessions negotiated with LDC governments as inviolate for all time, while many of their American and British counterparts have come to the conclusion that periodic renegotiation of such contracts is virtually inevitable. Further, while still in the euphoric flush of the largest single order of capital equipment in European history (by a Southeast Asian state steel enterprise in 1972), a German firm, inexperienced in such matters, recently discovered that one-sided contracts concluded by host-country officials clearly lacking legal authority to conclude them are agreements that no responsible government can honor, in spite of the most explicit threats mustered to enforce them.

Finally, the rapid rise of European- and Japanese-based MNCs is not irrelevant for the future effectiveness, not to mention the consequences, of tighter codes of conduct imposed on or contemplated for U.S.-based MNCs by Congress and the Securities and Exchange Commission. The lesser the degree of recognition within Congress of the growing importance of non-American MNCs, the greater the tendency to assume that strict enforcement of such codes will eradicate questionable activities (including large-scale bribery to secure contracts) of multinational enterprises without corresponding adverse effects on the market shares, exports, and domestic employment of and in U.S. multinationals. However, there is little if any effective pressure upon governments in other important bases for MNCs (in Japan and Europe) to follow suit. Indeed, it is questionable whether any significant mechanisms even exist through which some of these governments could enforce such codes, even if they were of a mind to do so. Since overseas business practices branded as unfair and immoral have never been less prevalent in Japanese- and European- than in U.S.-based firms, the latter will remain subject to intense pressures to continue utilizing such methods to secure business. This is not to say that Congress should not impose restrictions. Rather, it is only to say that expectations of greater morality in international business practices imposed via American fiat may be largely based on wishful thinking. If not, then the costs, in terms of American exports and lost market shares, of enforcing morality may have been significantly underestimated. The task of the observing economist is not to judge a legislative action but to ensure that legislators are aware of all costs.

The MNC as a Private, Profit-Seeking Entity. At least one safe generalization about multinational firms in the 1950s and early 1960s was that, as private firms, they could be expected to pursue profit maximization more or less consistently, whether on the scale of an individual foreign investment project or, more likely, in terms of global profitability. While the overwhelming majority of direct foreign investment generally remains in the hands of privately owned firms, a different type of enterprise has come on the scene unheralded and largely unnoticed. These are the state-owned enterprises of Europe (and, to a lesser extent, of prosperous developing countries) that may only incidentally seek profits in their pursuit of more cosmic objectives.

The extent of state ownership of firms that qualify as multinationals is not generally appreciated, partly because this is a relatively new phenomenon. There are numerous examples, quite apart from the state-owned airlines, in Western Europe, and there are even a few rising state-owned multinationals in such places as Brazil and Iran.

The French government owns a large share of equity in TOTAL, which has worldwide interests in oil, gas, and uranium deposits. COGEMA, a natural resource firm wholly owned by the French government, is active in uranium exploitation in no less than five LDCs. Also in France, Renault is a state-owned firm with activities in a number of Western European nations and installations in several. In Italy, ENI has significant foreign interests in hydrocarbons and, through its subsidiary AGIP, in uranium exploration in South America. In Britain, the government owns a controlling interest in British Petroleum, a multinational firm under any taxonomy, and British Leyland has far-flung interests in Africa, including South Africa. In West Germany, the government has had effective control of Volkswagen since 1945.[19] In Brazil, the rapidly growing natural resources state enterprise, CVRD, has begun to cast its net well beyond Brazilian shorelines, and the state-owned National Iranian Oil Company has had significant and diverse overseas investments for a number of years.

The rise of state-owned firms in the multinational arena is only part of the story. Increasingly, traditional multinational firms may find it necessary to contend with state-owned firms in the host-country domestic markets they seek to penetrate and for the host-country natural resource endowments they wish to develop. Nowhere is this more apparent than in the mineral industry. For example, in Canada no less than four new state-owned enterprises in mining have been created in the last five years. In Latin America it has been estimated that fully three-quarters of planned investment in mineral extraction and processing from 1976 to 1982 is scheduled to be undertaken by state-owned firms alone or in joint ventures with foreign firms.[20]

The implications of a growing role for state-owned firms in the international economic order are difficult to assess. But there are reasons for believing that this development may give rise to new forms of conflict and thereby provide additional impetus for illiberal policies toward direct foreign investment. For example, more than one European government has been known to employ heavy diplomatic pressure through official and unofficial channels when other countries undertake changes in tax laws that would affect the interests of their state-owned multinational firms. This type of official advocacy of home-country-enterprise interest has gone well beyond the lobbying for home-country private firms traditionally performed by commercial attachés and carries with it a greater potential for transformation of low-level economic disputes into full-fledged political conflicts between sovereign governments.

In any case, state-owned firms already play a substantial role in the international economic system. If their role expands further, what is the assurance that the existing rules of international investment will prove adequate to accommodate state-owned enterprises? Several potentially significant questions may arise. In particular, will home-country governments themselves respond to host-country threats to their own

---

[19] Even in 1973, 40 percent of the shares of Volkswagen were publicly held (20 percent by the central government and 20 percent by the government of Lower Saxony). See Louis T. Wells, "Automobiles," in Raymond Vernon, ed., *Big Business and the State* (Cambridge: Harvard University Press, 1974), p. 240.

[20] Malcolm Gillis, "Taxation, Mining, and Public Ownership," in Lincoln Institute, University of Arizona College of Mines, *Non-Renewable Resource Taxation in the Western States* (Tucson, May 1977).

state-owned enterprises in about the same fashion and intensity as they have reacted to host-country policies toward private firms? Or will countermeasures by home-country governments move in more ominous directions when the state's own equity is threatened? In cases where state-owned multinational enterprises are involved in restrictive arrangements, will governments be as willing and as able to break up these arrangements as they would when only private firms are involved?

A related question has to do with the growing role of state enterprises in host-country markets. This too could also have unforeseen, and perhaps illiberal, consequences for foreign direct investment by privately owned multinationals. For example, perhaps host-country governments will be more inclined to grant monopoly privileges in the domestic market to their own progeny, further reducing the scope for foreign direct investment by privately owned MNCs. This tendency will be greater if such arrangements are viewed as the political prerogatives of a sovereign state rather than as restrictive business practices. In this case, efforts to curb such illiberal measures may prove even less fruitful than in the past.

MNC Efficiency. Detractors of multinational enterprises, from the dependency theorists to a variety of homegrown critics, are prone to attribute to the firms responsibility for a wide variety of social ills in countries where they operate. These include income inequality, unemployment, political disruption, warped consumption patterns, and poverty in general.[21] Anecdotal evidence forms the basis of most such assertions. More sanguine observers of the multinational phenomena acknowledge many of these costs but are far less inclined to attribute blame for them to multinational firms exclusively.[22] In any case, many writers tend to view such costs as partial offsets to the contributions to global welfare that are thought to flow from the economic "efficiency" of multinational activities abroad.

For both critics and defenders, it is typically the case that the term "efficiency" is applied as if there were a universally accepted definition of the word.[23] Unfortunately, "efficiency" means different things to different people; authors rarely specify what efficiency criterion they are

---

[21] See Ronald Muller, "Poverty Is the Product," *Foreign Policy*, no. 13 (Winter 1973–1974), p. 97.

[22] See Raymond Vernon, "Does Society Also Profit?" *Foreign Policy*, no. 13 (Winter 1973–1974), pp. 107–10; and Bergsten, "Analysis," pp. 3–55.

[23] See, for example, R. J. Barnett and R. E. Muller, "Global Reach," Part 2, as published in the *New Yorker*, December 2, 1974. Here the authors make use of a "contemporary definition of efficiency," which they do not bother to identify.

applying to multinational firms, and when they do, they often utilize definitions of efficiency that few economists would accept as valid. For example, efficiency in multinationals is sometimes defined in terms of output maximization, independent of costs and preferences.[24] Application of such an efficiency concept could tell us everything about the implications of MNCs for global welfare. More likely, it could tell us nothing.

Failure to define the efficiency criterion also materially reduces the comparability, if not the credibility, of the conclusions of many otherwise very useful studies of the implications of MNC behavior. This is not a plea for adoption of a single efficiency standard, such as the economists' concept of "allocative efficiency," in all such undertakings. This definition (lying as it does at the very core of neoclassical economics) has a very specific meaning for economists and may not always be universally serviceable in efforts (particularly empirical approaches) to understand and assess the behavior of multinational firms and their implications for society.[25] In any event, claims that MNCs improve "international allocative efficiency" have yet to be satisfactorily substantiated.[26] Moreover, given the oligopolistic climate in which MNCs operate and which they have helped to nurture (partly through success in securing anticompetitive privileges from host governments), it is doubtful that such claims could ever be fully substantiated. In any case, the proof would be forbiddingly arduous. Nonetheless, it is not difficult to accept Vernon's conclusion that in many industries (oil, aluminum, copper, automobiles) the multinational trend has, by weakening the position of established leaders, probably freed most national markets a little.[27] This development should reduce the scope for the inefficiencies associated with exercise of market power, but this more modest claim is a far cry from the assertion that MNCs improve allocative efficiency.

Fortunately, not all studies intended to assess the implications of MNC performance for global welfare fail to specify workable criteria of efficiency. In fact, some employ an efficiency standard that most analysts, including economists, would find provisionally acceptable: that

---

[24] This was the case in the earlier version of the paper by Hawkins and Walter, above.

[25] A number of useful ways of defining "allocative efficiency" are acceptable to economists. In the context of a given distribution of income, one may speak in terms of satisfaction of a number of basic marginal equivalences, or allocative efficiency may be more prosaically defined as a situation in which the social costs of producing a given level of output desired by consumers is at a minimum.

[26] Hawkins and Walter, above.

[27] Vernon, "Does Society Also Profit?" p. 109.

of efficiency in the sense of private cost minimization.[28] Indeed, success in minimizing costs is what is usually meant in reference to the relative "efficiency" or "inefficiency" of enterprises, whether multinational or state-owned.[29] While efficiency judgments based on a cost-minimization efficiency criterion would reveal less about the welfare consequences of multinational firms than would conclusions based on an allocative efficiency criterion, the former is at least readily recognizable to both neoclassical economists and specialists in business behavior. In addition, it is much more likely that, compared with studies using idiosyncratic concepts of efficiency, a study employing this measure of performance for multinationals will yield results that would allow useful comparisons with conclusions of other investigations. In turn, this would help reduce the extreme difficulty now encountered in trying to draw useful generalizations from the mountainous literature on multinationals. While there is little merit in the Procrustean view that a single efficiency criterion should be employed to the exclusion of all others, it may be argued that lack of a common measure of efficiency has been an important factor in rendering the literature on multinationals unnecessarily contentious. Even if the cost-minimization criterion is not the one adopted, analysts should at a minimum identify which efficiency concept forms the basis for their assessments of the efficiency implications of multinational firms.

---

[28] See, for example, Robert O. Keohane and Van Doorn Ooms, "The Multinational Firm and International Regulation," *International Organization*, vol. 29, no. 1 (Winter 1975), pp. 172–75. The authors provide a heuristic discussion of the implications of MNCs for allocative efficiency but correctly refrain from making unsubstantiable claims as to the net impact of the firms on global efficiency.

[29] This point is developed in Malcolm Gillis, "Uses and Abuses of Concepts of Efficiency in Public Enterprises," paper presented at the Joint Workshops in Public Finance and Latin American Development, University of Chicago, March 10, 1978.

COMMENTARY

Thomas Horst

The question raised by Malcolm Gillis, whether the multinational firms are part of the constituency for a liberal international economic order, is very interesting. Because it is so often assumed that they *are* part of the constituency, let me cite two further instances where they are not. The first is the area of commodity cartels and agreements. M. A. Adelman argues rather persuasively that the success of OPEC was due in no small degree to the cooperation of the large multinational oil companies.[1] Similarly, General Foods and other coffee processors are often instrumental in the development of international commodity agreements. Although one should be cautious about generalizing from a few cases, the success or failure of a commodity cartel or agreement may hinge on the role played by the multinational producers or processors of that commodity.

Second, the support of the multinational firms for a liberal international economic order is less than clear-cut in the area of reducing tariff and nontariff barriers to international trade. One case in point is cited by Herbert Marshall, Frank A. Southard, Jr., and Kenneth W. Taylor, who note that a number of the firms lobbying at the Ottawa Conference in 1932 were American subsidiaries anxious that "Empire content" rules be stiffened and that other protection be maintained or increased in order to protect the subsidiaries' position in Canadian and other British Empire markets.[2] A more recent case is the role played in current trade issues by the Special Committee for U.S. Exports, a lobby consisting of many large and medium-sized U.S. corporations with substantial export businesses. In the Zenith case before the Supreme Court, the issue was whether the United States had an obligation under its do-

---

[1] M. A. Adelman, "Oil Import Quota Auctions," *Challenge*, vol. 18 (January-February 1976), pp. 17–22.

[2] Herbert Marshall, Frank A. Southard, Jr., and Kenneth W. Taylor, *Canadian American Industry* (New Haven: Yale University Press, 1936).

mestic countervailing duty statute to impose an additional duty to offset the rebate of Japanese excise taxes. If the Supreme Court had upheld Zenith's contention that the U.S. government did have such an obligation, our international trading relations could have been severely disrupted. Rather than supporting the government's position that countervailing duties applied in this instance would have clearly violated our GATT obligations, the committee strongly supported the Zenith position. The committee believed that U.S. exporters are at a competitive disadvantage in international markets and welcomed a more active role for the U.S. government in protecting their position.

I believe that Hawkins and Walters attempt too high a level of generality in their paper. They appear to be looking for rather simple conclusions about difficult issues. For example, they would like to know what impact multinational firms have on the balance of payments. While I believe there is much that one can say about this issue, I do not think it lends itself to easy generalizations. The problem is that the impact will differ according to the particular situation. Rather than trying to add up all the pluses and minuses, I think it would be more useful to try to characterize those situations where the impact is positive and those where the impact is negative.

Furthermore, I believe Hawkins and Walters could do more to integrate their findings. For example, their conclusions about the impact on the balance of payments should be related to their conclusions about exports and imports and, thus, about domestic and foreign employment. Likewise, the balance of payments for any one country may be in deficit or in surplus, but for all countries taken together the aggregate deficits must be matched by the aggregate surpluses. This point is important. When one has drawn a conclusion about the impact of multinational firms on the balance of payments of home countries, by implication one has also drawn a conclusion about the implication for host countries. The authors have made an extensive survey of the literature and could provide an exceedingly useful service for their readers by relating the conclusions to one another.

Paul P. Streeten

I shall confine my comments to three main points, following precedent in concentrating on areas of doubt or disagreement and omitting areas of agreement and minor queries. The first point raises the question of what is meant by a liberal treatment of transnational corporations (TNCs); the second makes a plea for the abandonment of such concepts as "global economic welfare," and the third questions the assumption of smooth, continuous trade-offs between the objectives of host countries and TNC investment.

First, I should like to ask: What does a "liberal" treatment of TNCs mean? It can be interpreted in two ways. It might mean laissez faire (and laissez-passer), with minimum regulation and maximum freedom to conduct business. Alternatively, it might mean intervention in order to make TNCs conform to a desirable competitive liberal order. If competition is a way to achieve equal opportunities, regulating TNCs so as to make them conform more closely to it is a basic principle of the New International Economic Order.

It has been emphasized repeatedly that the liberal order does not mean laissez faire and that competition and free trade have to be enforced through antitrust legislation and rules for international trade. It is, of course, in the nature of TNCs that they are oligopolies. The special advantage that makes it possible for a foreign company to set up local affiliates may derive from large-scale operation or from a spreading of risks, as in the case of mining companies; from advertising and the creation of goodwill, as in the case of branded food; or from expenditure on research and development, as in the case of pharmaceuticals. Whatever the source, a monopolistic advantage is the essence of the TNC. Its relationship with the host country therefore is one of bilateral monopoly or oligopoly.

Moreover, the restrictive practices adopted by TNCs, in violation of the principles of a liberal order, are well known. They cover such activities as agreements between firms for the allocation of territorial markets; pooling and allocation of patents, trademarks, and copyrights; fixing of prices or of price relationships; allocation of total exports and export restrictions; establishment of reciprocal exclusive or preferential dealing; and others.

The existence of a monopoly element and of restrictive practices is, however, not the only reason that TNCs themselves constitute a challenge to the liberal order or that their regulation, as called for by advocates of the NIEO, is part of a liberal order. TNCs extend the area of planning to intrafirm transactions, which raise quite distinct issues. The existence of a wide range of intrafirm transactions is not in itself a manifestation of monopoly power, but it does constitute an interference with the liberal market economy. Although there are good reasons for some decisions to be taken within a firm and others by independent firms, it is not obvious that in delimiting these areas private and social costs and benefits coincide. The decision about what area to leave to intrafirm transactions is itself one of public policy. The large and growing volume of international intrafirm transactions appears to constitute another challenge to a liberal economic order.

Advocates of the NIEO are often criticized for wishing to interfere with freely and competitively determined prices and markets. But TNCs themselves manage and administer a wide range of prices. The transactions conducted within the firm are based on administrative considerations. The residual open market is often a small fraction of total transactions, and the prices in this thin market are distorted because of the large volume of intrafirm trade. If the NIEO is a call to planning, the TNCs have anticipated this call and have replaced market forces by planning within the firm. In fact, TNCs do many of the things advocated by the NIEO, but not necessarily in the interests of any particular nation or even the world community. By accumulating and running down inventories, they stockpile; they stabilize prices; they secure supplies and markets; they attempt to ensure themselves against inflation, and so on. Is it proper for these things to be done within a company and improper if done by governments?

A third challenge to the liberal order arising from the spread of TNCs is the prevalence of differential factor mobility. In a world of laissez faire and laissez-passer, *all* goods and *all* factors of production are mobile across national frontiers. From some points of view, this may be a highly desirable state of affairs. In the theory of comparative advantage, only goods, not factors of production, are mobile internationally. This again can be shown to have all-round advantages, on certain assumptions, if free trade is adopted. But what if some factors—namely, capital, know-how, and management—are highly mobile internationally, while unskilled and semiskilled labor is relatively immobile? Moreover, the total supply of management, know-how, and capital is relatively inelastic, though elastic for any particular country, so that it earns rents, quasirents, and monopoly profits, while the domestic supply of labor in many poor countries is highly elastic, though inelastic internationally, pushing remuneration down to the subsistence minimum. Is this then a situation in which some free movement is better than none, or are we in the world of the second best, where partial mobility may make things worse, compared with complete immobility (or perfect mobility), by skimming off the rents and monopoly profits for the home countries and leaving the host countries with only the wages of labor, often female labor that withdraws from the labor force after marriage.

My second point is a plea to abandon such terms as "world economic welfare," "global income," "world efficiency," and so on. They are meaningless and therefore quite useless for judging TNC performance. Worse, by suggesting actions for which there is no logical, moral, or political basis, they can be highly misleading and are open to abuse.

Very few investments leave everyone better off—or at least no one worse off. Even if there were such investments, we should still be concerned with the distribution of the gains and with the question of whether the improvement might not preclude an even better alternative.

If some countries, and people within countries, are harmed, the question of compensation arises. Actual compensation for all losers is ruled out for both political and technical reasons—for political reasons, because the losers may be voteless or unpopular or undeserving or in safe seats; for technical reasons, because benefits are often diffused and it is difficult to identify all beneficiaries. Even if identification is possible, it may be difficult to squeeze out the last ounce of consumers' surpluses. Already complicated tax systems may not stand the strain of additional complications. In any case, no one has yet devised a costless system of lump-sum taxes that has no distorting effects.

Even if all these objections could be dismissed and it was argued that governments are the guardians of the social conscience and are willing and able to correct any ill effects arising from foreign investment, the argument would collapse for international investment because there is no world government. Therefore, the international distribution of gains and losses—and the distribution of the gains themselves—is crucial. If United Brand gains $100 while a poor Central American banana grower loses $90 because the company bribed the president of a republic to break the banana cartel and thus increased competition, is the net profit from the bribery strictly to the point? Can we really say that world welfare has increased?

I would therefore plead that we rule out such expressions. Gunnar Myrdal spoke of the "Communistic Fiction," which presupposes a harmony of interests in the case of a single country. If the assumption is false for a single country, it is absurd for the world as a whole.

My third point questions the assumption of a smooth, continuous, steadily downward-sloping marginal productivity of investment curve. This model leads to the conclusion that a host country has to weigh the advantages of imposing controls on a foreign company against the disadvantage of losing some of the investment or the whole project. Anything that reduces the net rate of return—whether taxation or restrictions on repatriation or remittance, conditions of local participation or the use of local materials, or price controls—will tend to reduce the investment. It may drive away whole projects and firms. On this assumption, there is a trade-off between the host country's objectives and allocational gains. All controls diminish these allocational gains.

COMMENTARY

This model is not only empirically but analytically false. As I have already emphasized, it is in the nature of the TNC to enjoy a monopolistic advantage (which may be only temporary). It follows that there is often a large gap between average costs and marginal (local operating) costs. The use of already existing knowledge is costless or involves only low costs. For any given price and quantity, there will then exist a rent or quasirent that can be divided in different proportions between the company and the country. This is the bargaining range without trade-offs. A bargain settled within this range will not affect the allocation of resources, at least the short-run allocation. With adequate information and skilled bargaining, the host country can impose its conditions upon the company without reducing the company's commitment or affecting allocational efficiency.

It might be objected that this cannot hold for the long run. If all quasirents were to be appropriated, nothing would be left for reinvestment, for exploration, for research and development, for goodwill creation, and for all other fixed, joint, or overhead costs. As for investment for expansion, there is no reason the TNC should not go to the capital market to raise capital. As for continuing activities to maintain the special advantage, the developing countries, constituting normally a small share of the total market, enjoy the benefit of the importance of being unimportant. It is unlikely that, in deciding on R&D expenditure, the lower quasirents earned from operating in developing countries will be an important deterrent. Developing countries, in bargaining for a larger share in the quasirents of the TNCs, therefore need not be afraid of killing the goose that lays the golden eggs.

DISCUSSION

I. M. D. Little expressed concern that the discussion was unnecessarily complicating the analysis. The important question is whether a firm coming into a developing country is a good or a bad thing, not whether the developing country gets the most possible out of it. A multinational brings in capital, employs people, pays taxes, and generates spin-offs. In general, Little felt that the multinationals provide more good than harm to the developing countries. The only argument for keeping them out that makes sense, Little argued, is that they will pervert the host country in a political way.

Peter Bauer agreed with Little and questioned the basis for the idea that multinationals are monopolies. Some have monopoly power, but many do not. The fact that these companies have tried to restrict competition should not upset us, Bauer argued; all firms try to restrict competition, and the multinationals are no different in this regard from domestic firms. Wilson Schmidt underscored Bauer's point and argued that this tendency to try to restrict competition demonstrated the importance of deciding who should set the rules of the game.

In the time given Robert Hawkins and Ingo Walter to respond, they agreed with Malcolm Gillis's comment that the multinationals were not interested in a completely liberal international economic order. Multinationals are interested in an optimal international economic order for themselves. Often, they argued, multinationals are interested in promoting barriers to free trade. They agreed with Paul Streeten that "global efficiency" may not be a useful concept from the point of view of international investment, but if it is not, it is also not useful for trade theory or trade policy. They also argued that there is not enough commonality of interests among the developing countries for common national policies by host countries to be developed.

PART FOUR

TRADE POLICIES

Protectionist Pressures in the United States

Robert E. Baldwin

The U.S. government presently finds itself in a perplexing position with respect to trade policy. It is actively engaged in a multilateral trade negotiation (the Tokyo Round) in which it possesses the greatest authority ever to reduce tariff and nontariff distortions of international trade. At the same time, however, the administration is facing protectionist pressures from particular industries and labor groups that are stronger than at any time since the early 1930s.

The broad powers to reduce trade distortions are, of course, derived from the Trade Act of 1974. Not only does this law permit the government to reduce U.S. tariffs up to 60 percent (100 percent for duties 5 percent or less) and extend duty-free treatment on a wide range of products to developing countries, but it urges the president to enter into agreements (subject to congressional approval) that reduce or harmonize nontariff trade barriers. These latter barriers are now recognized as the most important sources of trade distortions.

Evidence that protectionist pressures are very strong and that protectionists are achieving some of their goals is apparent. In the spring of 1977 the U.S. government entered into orderly marketing agreements with South Korea and Taiwan for shoes and with Japan for color television sets. Under such arrangements, foreign countries agree to quantitative limits on their exports to the United States. Pressures for a similar arrangement for steel are now very strong, as this industry has undertaken a highly successful public relations campaign to call attention to its problems. In June of 1976 quotas were imposed on special steel (stainless steel and alloy tool steel), and the odds seem to favor considerably broader quantitative restrictions. The textile industry is another sector arguing for greater protection. The Multi-Fiber Arrangement (MFA) already quantitatively limits textile imports, but the industry wants a tightening of existing controls.

Two other examples of protectionist pressures under the current administration relate to cargo preference and subsidies to sugar producers. The president backed a bill requiring the share of oil imports

PART FOUR: TRADE POLICIES

carried by U.S.-flag tankers to rise from the current rate of about 3.5 percent to 9.5 percent by 1982. The bill cleared the Senate but was defeated in the House after various consumer-oriented groups called attention to the high costs involved in its passage. With respect to sugar, the president did not, as the industry wished, decrease existing import quotas, but he did approve the granting of producer subsidies when the price of sugar falls below a specified target level.

Although most internationalists are much concerned about the currently prevailing mixture of protectionism and liberal trade policies, this situation actually is quite typical of post–World War II U.S. trade policy. Every administration since President Truman's has felt it necessary to make protectionist concessions, either to obtain congressional acceptance of bills permitting further tariff reductions or to ward off what are regarded as even less acceptable protectionist policies. President Truman, for example, accepted a peril-point provision and an explicit escape clause in the 1951 extension of the reciprocal trade program as the solidarity of Democrats in Congress for a liberal trade policy began to break down in the early 1950s. At the same time, the protectionist attitude of the Republican party began to change, and by 1958 President Eisenhower was able to obtain a four-year extension of the reciprocal trade program with an additional 20 percent tariff-cutting authority. However, voluntary constraints on exports of cotton textiles were accepted by the Japanese in 1955, and voluntary import quotas in oil were introduced in 1958 and made mandatory in 1959 under a national security provision in the trade bill.

President Kennedy continued the practice of yielding to particular protectionist interests when he agreed to the negotiation of a formal international agreement permitting the general use of import quotas on cotton textiles. The rationale was that this step was necessary to obtain passage of the Trade Expansion Act of 1962, under which a significant degree of trade liberalization did in fact occur. The Johnson administration faced protectionist pressures that rival those of the present—a fact not unrelated to the recession in late 1969 and 1970. By that time the trade program did not have to be periodically renewed in order to maintain the tariff concessions already made. Thus, by threatening to use his veto powers, President Johnson was able to prevent passage of legislation permitting the wide application of import quotas, but he was not successful in obtaining new tariff-cutting authority. Moreover, even to maintain the status quo, he felt it necessary to negotiate a voluntary restraint program on exports of steel from Japan. President Nixon's main concession to protectionist interests was the negotiation of the MFA, which added wool and man-made fibers to the list of cotton textiles and apparel subject to quantitative restrictions. The requirements for obtaining import relief under "escape clause" actions were also weakened considerably in the Trade Act of 1974.

Although those favoring the reduction of world trade barriers have generally regarded the postwar period as one in which trade liberalization has dominated, this proposition is by no means evident in the post–Kennedy Round period. Most of the nontariff trade barriers (NTBs) introduced as concessions to the protectionists are still with us. The most important NTB in the manufacturing field is the MFA, first introduced as a device for dealing with market disruption.[1] If protection on these grounds has any meaning, it implies that quotas should be gradually increased until they are eliminated and the necessary adjustment in the use of domestic resources is made. Yet it is apparent from the past fifteen years of controls that the agreement is not being used as a means to reduce textile production in the more industrialized countries to levels where the textile sector can compete effectively in world markets. The U.S. textile industry talks about the need for domestic production to grow at a rate that will provide sufficient funds for capital modernization and research activities. Gradual retrenchment is simply not in the game plan, and there is no reason to believe that textile industries in other developed countries do not share this position. Moreover, though representatives from developing countries frequently complain about their market share, producers in these countries can often be silenced when they are given a guaranteed share of the market. Cartelization can be a corrupting influence on economic efficiency.

Among the several important issues that arise in connection with the present protectionist trend, three are selected for consideration here. The first deals with the impact on trade, employment, and social welfare of additional trade liberalization. What can be said, using the tools of economic analysis, of the probable impact of the kind of liberalization envisioned at the time of the adoption of the Trade Act of 1974? Existing protectionist pressures are based on more than fears of the consequences of the Tokyo Round, but an estimate of these possible effects provides a basis for better assessing the claims of the current protectionist groups. However, in addition to the question of the magnitude of the trade and employment effects of further tariff cuts, there is the matter of just how trade policy is determined in the actual political environment. We may hope that economists' projections carry some weight in public policy deliberations, but we would be foolish to think

---

[1] Gardner Patterson, *Discrimination in International Trade: The Policy Issues, 1945–1965* (Princeton, N.J.: Princeton University Press, 1966), pp. 307–17.

they have more than a marginal influence on policy makers. Thus, if we are to use our analysis most effectively, we must try to understand the political economy of U.S. trade policy. Finally, given economic estimates of the consequences of a particular trade policy, such as a significant multilateral tariff reduction, plus an analysis of how trade policy is determined in practice, the third issue to be raised is how, or even whether, a politically feasible compromise can be reached between the opposing sides on a trade policy that can achieve the goals for employment, growth, and income distribution loosely shared by the major political groups.

The Consequences of Further Liberalization

In connection with the first issue—the impact of additional trade liberalization—I should like to summarize the results of a study recently concluded by two colleagues, F. David Richardson and John Mutti, and myself, in which we estimated the consequences in the U.S. economy of a 50 percent duty reduction on most items by this country and the other industrial signatories to the General Agreement on Tariffs and Trade.[2] The analytical framework and data sources are described in detail elsewhere,[3] but briefly the procedures were as follows. U.S. exports to eighteen other industrial countries and the rest of the world and U.S. imports from all sources were reclassified on the basis of the 367 sectors covered by the 1967 input-output table published by the Department of Commerce. The trade figures together with the tariffs faced by U.S. exports in each of the eighteen countries and the duties levied on imports into this country were initially taken from a detailed matrix of world trade assembled by the GATT secretariat. Utilizing these trade data together with a set of import and export demand elasticities for the tradable sectors in the classification system as well as

---

[2] Certain items were excluded in making the estimates on the grounds that tariff cuts will not affect the volume of trade because of existing quotas, because they are not legally possible, or because they are highly unlikely for political reasons. These comprise crude oil and petroleum imports into the United States, products covered by the Multi-Fiber Arrangement, items covered by escape clause actions, and agricultural products subject to quantitative restrictions (QRs) or variable levies. The calculations were made prior to the introduction of quotas on shoes and color TV sets.

[3] Robert E. Baldwin, *U.S. Tariff Policy: Formation and Effects* (Washington, D.C.: U.S. Department of Labor, Office of Foreign Economic Research, June 1976); and Robert E. Baldwin, John H. Mutti, and J. David Richardson, "Welfare Effects on the United States of a Significant Multilateral Tariff Reduction: A Progress Report," Conference on Trade and Development, University of Wisconsin, Madison, Wis., November 11 and 12, 1977.

direct and indirect input-output coefficients, we estimated the trade and domestic output effects of the tariff-cutting simulation for each of the sectors. Under the assumption of a flexible exchange rate, the trade "impact effects" provided the basis for calculating any change in the exchange rate needed to maintain the initial conditions of the balance of payments. Next, estimates of the employment displacing or creating effects of the sectoral trade changes were made by multiplying the net output changes by labor coefficient measures for each industry.

A final step involved calculating changes in consumer and producer welfare in the various sectors. These estimates include the welfare losses (gains) associated with the labor displaced (added) by net import (export) increases in each industry. In an economic framework where wages as well as the returns to capital are rigid in a downward direction, the income forgone during the period that labor and capital facilities displaced by imports are idle represents a real welfare loss to the community. Advocates of greater protection rightly have argued that these costs should be taken into account in assessing the impact of any tariff liberalization.

In estimating the income lost because of unemployment, a U.S. Department of Labor survey of workers displaced by import competition was first analyzed to determine the length of time it took individuals to find other jobs, depending upon various socioeconomic characteristics—age, sex, race, and years of education. Using these relationships together with the socioeconomic characteristics and average earnings of the employees in each industry as taken from the 1/1,000 1970 Sample Census of Population, the average number of days of unemployment per worker was multiplied by the average daily wage in the industry and by the net number of displaced workers to yield the forgone income of the unemployed workers. A discount rate of 10 percent was used to calculate the present value of this income stream. If the net change in the industry's employment was positive, it was assumed that this reduced unemployment and increased income from a pool of workers with equivalent characteristics and previous earning opportunities.

There are several plausible scenarios for the manner in which tariff reductions affect the income accruing to capital owners. The simple one followed in making the estimates reported here was to assume that one-tenth of each industry's capital depreciates annually. Thus, if the tariff cuts reduced an industry's output by 1 percent, the capital made idle by the output reduction is assumed to wear out in 1.2 months or 36.5 days. In other words, the average number of day's worth of income lost by the capital is 36.5/2 or 18.25. Data on capital's

PART FOUR: TRADE POLICIES

income share in total output was taken from the U.S. input-output table.

The results of the various calculations are reported in Table 1. The initial "trade impact" effects from the 50 percent multilateral duty cut are so small that the exchange rate pressure is negligible. Similarly, the aggregate employment effects before and after the exchange rate change are minimal.[4] However, the net welfare gain of over $1 billion is significant, with the consumer gains overwhelming the losses as a result of some net unemployment and idling of capital facilities.[5] Moreover, consumer gains the first years (about $100 million) are larger than the total losses to labor and capital.

Although the overall employment impact is very small, there are some particular industries for which this is not true. In thirty-one of some three hundred traded-goods industries, for example, employment declines by 1 percent or more. The top fifteen of this list are: food utensils and pottery (20.6 percent); rubber footwear (13.1 percent); cutlery (12.4 percent); motorcycles, bicycles, and parts (12.0 percent); artificial flowers (11.3 percent); pottery products (9.7 percent); scouring and combing plants (4.6 percent); other leather products (4.0 percent); games and toys (3.1 percent); industrial leather tanning (3.1 percent); ceramic wall and floor tile (2.7 percent); jewelry (2.7 percent); nonrubber footwear (2.7 percent); sewing machines (2.6 percent); and radios and TV sets (2.5 percent). On the other hand, there are seven industries in which employment rises by 1 percent or more, namely: semiconductors (6.3 percent); computing machines (3.2 percent); tobacco (3.0 percent); office machines (2.3 percent); mechanical measuring devices (1.5 percent); electronic components (1.4 percent); and X-ray tubes and apparatus (1.1 percent).

Several of the above are industries in which the net benefits to the economy from the trade liberalization are among the largest. In twenty-six industries, the net change in welfare exceeds $10 million. The welfare changes are all positive and account for about 60 percent of the total net welfare gain for the economy. Seven of the industries with declining employment listed above are on this list, as are four of the employment gainers.

---

[4] It should be kept in mind that the major NTB items are omitted from the calculations. If the tariff equivalents of these items were reduced on a multilateral basis by 50 percent, the estimating procedure indicates that this would have a deficit-creating net effect of $710 million (−$964 million for textiles, +$320 million for agriculture, and −$66 million for all other sectors) and would result in a net loss of 108,000 jobs.

[5] The welfare effect of the 3/1,000 of 1 percent currency appreciation is negligible, amounting to an additional gain of only about $1.5 million.

TABLE 1

Trade, Employment, and Welfare Effects on the United States of a 50 Percent Multilateral Tariff Reduction

Effect	Exchange Rate	
	Fixed	Flexible
Trade changes (millions of dollars)		
Exports	+ 1,750	+ 1,747
Imports	− 1,746	− 1,747
Net trade effect	+ 4	0
Employment changes (man-years)		
Export-related	+ 136,000	+ 135,800
Import-related	− 151,200	− 151,200
Net employment effect	− 15,200	− 15,400
Exchange rate change (percent)	—	+ 0.003
Welfare changes (present value at 10 percent in millions of dollars)		
Consumer benefits plus tariff revenue on additional imports	+ 1,056	
Labor adjustment effects	− 37	
Capital adjustment effects	− 5	
Net welfare effect	+ 1,014	

SOURCE: Robert E. Baldwin, John H. Mutti, and J. David Richardson, "Welfare Effects on the United States of a Significant Multilateral Tariff Reduction: A Progress Report," Conference on Trade and Development, University of Wisconsin, Madison, Wis., November 11 and 12, 1977.

While the estimates made of the trade, employment, and welfare effects of a significant tariff liberalization involve a number of arbitrary assumptions, various sensitivity tests (not reported here) suggest that the kind of tariff-cutting exercise likely to come out of the Tokyo Round will not have significant aggregate effects in the U.S. economy. However, as noted, there are some industries for which deep tariff cuts would impose significant hardships on employees and capital owners, even though net welfare effects in many of these industries are positive.

How Trade Policy Is Determined

In many ways the results reported above are consistent with the political pressures currently observed in the trade field. Much of the protectionist pressure is industry specific and stems from sectors where the analysis suggests an appreciable adverse impact on labor and capital. The footwear and television industries have already succeeded in limiting imports, and the textile sector is arguing for even tighter controls. The steel industry (where the estimates indicate an employment decline of 0.65 percent) is another major group lobbying for the imposition of nontariff barriers to protect its interests. The major organizations representing business as a whole favor trade liberalization, provided certain alleged practices by foreign governments are modified. The AFL-CIO opposes liberalization in principle, but it would seem from its actions that this organization is much more concerned about the employment effects in particular industries than about the aggregate employment effect.

The political behavior of congresspersons also indicates that protectionism in the United States arises from the difficulties of particular industries rather than from a general opposition to expanding U.S. trade through reciprocal duty cuts. In a previous study, I found a significant positive relation between a congressperson's opposition to the Trade Act of 1974 and the proportion of voters in his or her district or state who were employed in the major "import-sensitive" industries.[6] Senators and representatives from areas where there seemed to be no serious import problem tended to follow the wishes of the president (to vote in favor of the bill) if they were Republicans or those of the AFL-CIO (to vote against) if they were Democrats. In the case of the Democrats, however, 112 of 233 representatives voted for the bill, whereas 160 of 179 Republicans voted in favor of the bill. This behavior, as well as similar patterns of response on previous trade bills, indicates the great influence the president has on those in Congress who are members of the same political party, especially when he strongly favors a particular piece of legislation.

The same relationships would seem to hold at the present time. A trade bill is not now under active consideration, but there are many ways for Congress to exert pressure in trade matters. Various members can combine either to threaten restrictive trade legislation or to issue statements of concern about import competition. Visits may be made to the president, and it may be suggested that favorable votes on other legislation desired by the president will be influenced by his actions in the trade field. Thus far, the main protectionist pressures from congresspersons come from those who represent areas where it is alleged that special import problems exist. The steel lobby in Congress is a good example. One difference now is that in the absence of a trade bill

---

[6] Robert E. Baldwin, "The Political Economy of Postwar U.S. Trade Policy," New York University *Bulletin*, no. 1976–4.

supported by the president and his party's leadership in Congress the individual congressperson is much more prone to champion the interests of import-sensitive industries in his or her district. The costs of doing so, in terms of possible retaliatory action by the president and the congressional leadership, are much less than when a bill is under active consideration.

The president also plays a much more important role in setting trade policy when the country is operating under existing trade legislation. While the president must obtain congressional approval to enter into agreements reducing nontariff trade barriers, he can act alone in making international agreements that introduce or raise such NTBs as quotas. It is apparent that much of the current political pressure for import restrictions is directed at presidential action of this type. Another route for seeking import protection is, of course, through actions brought before the International Trade Commission. This semijudicial body operates under very general guidelines—for example, imports must be a "substantial" cause of serious injury for a finding of import relief. Some objective standards might be developed even under vague instructions such as this, but the decisions of the commission seem to be heavily influenced by the strength of protectionist pressures at any particular time. In any event, since the decisions of the commission are advisory to the president (although they can be carried out if both houses of Congress favor them), the views of the president are still crucial if this procedure for obtaining greater protection is followed. However, one route to possible greater protection that bypasses the president is being followed more and more by industry: seeking relief through the courts. The recent court decision (later overturned by a higher court) that the export rebates by some foreign countries of domestic value-added taxes violated U.S. law represents an example of this approach.

Given the key role played the president, the question arises as to what factors seem to determine whether he adopts a liberal or a protectionist attitude. As mentioned above, he invariably pursues a mixture of these policies, but there is still a significant range of policies within this compromise position. The advice the president receives from within the executive branch is based upon interagency negotiations usually chaired by the Office of Special Trade Representative (STR).[7] Besides STR, the key agencies on such committees are State, Treasury, Commerce, Labor, and Agriculture. State has traditionally been the most

---

[7] The following remarks are personal observations based on my experience as a member and observer of interagency trade committees at various times as well as on discussions with members of such groups.

influential agency on trade matters, although Treasury has important influence in areas such as dumping. On agricultural issues, the Department of Agriculture plays the dominant role and, because of its very close relationship with Congress, is sometimes able to set the policy itself. Commerce and Labor, especially the former, exert considerable influence at times, but State, Treasury, and Agriculture generally appear to be the most influential of the traditional agencies. The Office of Special Trade Representative, which was established under the Trade Expansion Act of 1962, initially had little power, but it has steadily grown in influence, mainly at the expense of the State Department and the trade people on the White House staff. The authority of the STR, Ambassador Robert Strauss, seemed considerable, in part because of his political influence in Congress and his close relationship with the president.

The advice of the various members of the interagency committees usually reflects the interests of the groups they represent. The most consistently liberal spokesperson on such committees is the representative from the State Department, the one government agency concerned with foreign reactions to U.S. trade policies and with how they affect American foreign policy interests. Though short in background support, the State representatives are usually among the most able individuals in interagency groups. The Commerce Department often appears ambivalent in its views. Its representatives are keenly aware of the competitive difficulties faced by certain industries and often argue against significant duty cuts for these industries. On the other hand, the department must also be the spokesperson for large multinational firms, which generally favor export expansion through trade liberalization. The views of the Agriculture Department reflect this ambivalence even more sharply. Because the United States is a major exporter of agricultural goods, this department vigorously pushes for the reduction of tariff and nontariff trade barriers in foreign countries, but the American farmer is highly protectionist when it comes to lowering U.S. trade barriers. The position espoused by Agriculture in both the Kennedy and Tokyo rounds of trade negotiations is that cuts in U.S. duties on industrial products should be used as "payment" for achieving reductions in foreign agricultural trade barriers.

Until the late 1960s, the AFL-CIO favored trade liberalization, and in the Kennedy Round the Labor Department expressed concern only about duty reductions affecting particular import-sensitive industries. In interagency discussions within the current administration, the Labor Department represents the views of the AFL-CIO fairly closely. The views of Treasury and STR are generally somewhere between those of State and Commerce in favoring protectionism or trade liberalization.

Of course, the dominant factor in trade decisions from the executive branch is the attitude of the president himself. And it seems to me that the main variable influencing his views is the extent to which he is internationally oriented. Presidents Roosevelt, Truman, and Kennedy, for example, strongly believed that a lowering of artificial barriers to trade was a major means of preventing future political conflicts. They thought that the narrow, nationalistic economic policies of the 1930s were partly responsible for such conflicts as World War II. Concerned about avoiding future major wars, they placed trade liberalization high on their lists of domestic and foreign policy priorities. Moreover, their views were widely shared by most of the major political forces in the country.

The belief that trade liberalization was an essential part of U.S. foreign policy accounts in considerable part for the strong liberalization trend in the administrations of these presidents. An issue such as tariff liberalization may benefit many people but each only slightly, yet it may hurt a small number of groups considerably. When this is the case, as various writings on political decision making in a democracy suggest, pressure-group politics based on short-run economic self-interest usually leads to protectionist policies. It does not pay an individual who stands to gain only slightly to incur the costs of opposing protectionism or organizing group opposition. On the other hand, for those who would lose significantly under liberalization, it is worthwhile to expend large sums in an effort to obtain an antiliberalization outcome. The conviction of the aforementioned presidents and of many in Congress that trade liberalization was necessary for world political stability acted as an effective counterbalance to such protectionist pressures. The foreign policy argument was also used extensively in justifying the U.S. foreign aid program. Although the basic proposition has merit in my view, one must admit that it has not been confirmed by careful empirical testing and that its applicability seems sometimes to have been exaggerated, particularly in the days when the threat of communism was continually thrown at anyone who expressed hesitancy about the merits of an international economic program. Thus, one had the uncomfortable feeling that such international economic measures as trade liberalization were being implemented mainly for reasons of somewhat questionable validity.

The conviction that trade liberalization should be a key part of U.S. peace-promoting efforts has weakened considerably as the worst fears about communism have proved unfounded and the position of

PART FOUR: TRADE POLICIES

the United States as the super economic power has changed. This weakening raises serious concerns about the prospects for continued trade liberalization. The passage of the Trade Act of 1974 seems, for example, to be something of an aberration. In the early part of his administration, President Nixon did not give much evidence of the strong internationalist actions he later took. But, somewhat unexpectedly, he and his exceptional secretary of state were able to exploit a series of international political conditions in a highly successful manner. As he achieved these successes, the president adopted the internationalist policies of earlier leaders such as Presidents Truman and Kennedy, including those relating to trade. At the same time, opposition to trade liberalization lessened as the recession of the late 1960s passed and the United States devalued its currency. The AFL-CIO in particular did not vigorously oppose the trade bill until close to the end of its course through Congress. Thus, strong support by the president, coupled with weak opposition on the part of the Democrats, many of whom were still strong internationalists themselves, enabled the bill to become law.

President Carter's views seem to reflect the generally lessened short-run concern about the encroachment by non-U.S. political allies into foreign policy areas of vital concern to the United States, and consequently he does not appear to consider trade liberalization as important a foreign policy tool as did some of the earlier presidents mentioned. In my view, the old foreign policy argument still has sufficient validity to justify a higher priority for trade liberalization than it seems to be receiving. The developing countries can no longer be regarded as lightly as in the past. They are rapidly gaining the kind of political, economic, and military strength that requires serious consideration from such countries as the United States. Moreover, they feel deeply frustrated by the actions of the industrialized countries, who are taking steps to keep out the kind of products they can successfully produce and whose exportation is very important for raising their living standards. The recent clamor from the developing nations on the matter of the NIEO is but a small illustration of their frustration. To refuse to open up our markets at a reasonable speed to these countries will seriously endanger future world peace, in my view. But such an argument is not as yet accorded much influence in foreign policy decisions.

The Possibility of Compromise

Although political support for trade liberalization seems easier to attain when rather vague foreign policy arguments are used, there are also strong economic arguments for reducing world trade barriers. Estimates of the static welfare gains have already been presented. In addition, unless the industrialized countries are willing to shift resources from sectors where they lose their comparative advantage into new lines of comparative efficiency, not only will they find it more and more difficult to maintain adequate growth rates but their economies may be plagued by chronic unemployment and inflation. Already there are illustrations of these consequences. But economic adjustment is painful and thus politically difficult to achieve. Is it possible to maintain the resource flexibility needed for adequate long-run growth, especially if the foreign policy argument previously used to support the open-economy approach no longer has its former political force?

The answer to this question is by no means evident, but three steps can be taken to improve the chances for an affirmative answer. The first and most obvious step is to try to restore world economic prosperity. When domestic output and employment lag, it is politically easy to blame exports from foreign producers. Past experience indicates that a return to prosperity has an almost miraculous effect in muting protectionist pressures, even from some of the industries most out of step with world resource conditions.

A second and somewhat longer-run measure that will help hold protectionism in check is to bring about changes in the articles of GATT relating to nontariff trade barriers. Most business and labor groups in this country, whether they represent import-competing or export industries, believe that foreign governments engage in activities that subsidize and favor firms in their countries much more extensively than does the U.S. government. At the same time, they think that the U.S. government imposes much more onerous (in a cost-profit sense) regulations on American firms than foreign governments do on their domestic companies. While this view often seems to be overstated, there is, I think, much substance in it. For example, in most other developed countries where government ownership of industry is more significant than in the United States, purchasing policies giving preference to domestic producers, even though these policies may not be spelled out in explicit rules, seem more extensive than in this country. Extension of credit for sales of capital goods by their exporters at interest rates considerably below what is available to American exporters is another example of subsidization by foreign governments. Even more important are the various domestic aids provided by foreign governments to their industries, ranging from special wage, capital, and research subsidies to particular industries to overly generous regional development schemes that artificially stimulate exports or retard imports. U.S. antitrust and tax laws are frequently cited as illustrations of how the U.S. government imposes overly burdensome rules on American exporters. Business and labor groups in this country regard this type of intervention by foreign governments, as well as the various rules that must be followed to satisfy U.S. legislation, as "unfair" in terms of their ability to compete internationally.

Economists who consider the efficient allocation of resources to be the key objective of economic activity make the following points about such government practices. To the extent that there is a uniform element in various government subsidies, preferences, and regulations, movements in exchange rates and factor prices tend to offset any unfavorable balance of trade effects. Moreover, the differential effects among industries should be regarded in much the same way as the differential consequences of some underlying real factor affecting comparative advantage. The fact that a foreign government's subsidy policies place severe competitive pressures on certain U.S. industries, even after exchange rate changes resulting from the subsidies, is not in principle different from the fact that the existence of lower wages abroad puts severe competitive pressures on particular U.S. industries. If foreign governments want to use their own taxpayers' money to provide us with goods at lower prices than we can provide for ourselves, then we should welcome the addition to our living standards. Like predatory dumping, subsidizing actions that drive out competition and then result in higher prices are not in the importing country's self-interest, but this is quite different from condemning foreign subsidization in principle. Similarly, if such subsidization is of the "on again, off again" variety, the costs of shifting domestic resources in and out of the affected industries may be greater than the gains from lower prices.

Members of the business and labor communities listen to such arguments with incredulity and promptly write off any economist making them as hopelessly unrealistic. To them it is abundantly clear that such government actions are grossly "unfair." What this comes down to is that they place income distribution goals ahead of economic efficiency. They consider the income and employment loss in affected industries to be more important than the widely dispersed benefits of lower import prices, even when economists can show a net gain in consumer and producer surplus terms. They also note that the theoretical possibility that redistribution can make everyone better off is of little comfort to those who are actually harmed. However, when business and labor say they are prepared to accept "fair" foreign competition, it is not clear just where they consider "unfair" competition to end. One hears more and more from labor that the absence of rules requiring such conditions as the forty-hour week and fringe benefits covering health and retirement comparable to those in developed countries constitutes "unfair" practices by governments in low-wage countries. In short, when they are pressed, advocates of "fair" international competition often end by presenting the old protectionist argument that costs of production should be made equal among all countries by appropriate government actions. This, of course, would result in no competition from foreign producers.

Although there is a possibility that efforts to improve upon GATT's rules of "good behavior" in the nontariff field could become an exercise designed to protect those countries already industrialized, the likely payoffs in such areas as government subsidies to domestic firms seem worth the risk. However, long and hard negotiations among GATT members will be necessary to achieve meaningful improvements in the relevant articles of GATT. Furthermore, because of the lack of clear-cut answers concerning the appropriateness of such measures, it is important to establish semijudicial bodies for investigating charges that particular government actions violate a code. A possible concern with regard to the current reform efforts is that the administration will tire of the negotiations and settle for enough progress so that they can be officially declared a success. This might actually be a desirable course to follow, if we were confident that new trade legislation would be passed enabling future negotiations after the present act expires at the end of 1979. But the protectionist pressures of recent years suggest that it will not be nearly so easy in the future to obtain the broad powers given the president in the Trade Act of 1974. Thus, if we are to have the best chance of working out acceptable compromises on trade policy among various domestic interests, significant progress in the current round of negotiations is essential in the NTB area.

The third and most important step that is needed to help lessen long-run protectionist pressures is to improve upon our resource adjustment mechanisms. Foremost is the need to state explicitly in legislation dealing with the problem that, when an industry is not able to compete as effectively as other U.S. industries in world markets, its activity level must be reduced to the point where it can meet the kind of "fair" competition embodied in GATT rules. Most industries do not accept this notion and instead believe they should be able to maintain at least their present absolute size. Existing adjustment measures—tariffs, quotas, extended unemployment payments, and so forth—are second-best adjustment measures. Essentially, they try to maintain the status quo. The hope is that workers and capitalists will see that the future situation is likely to be even worse, and they therefore will seek alternative uses of their resources. But the political means for securing

PART FOUR: TRADE POLICIES

further protection coupled with existing adjustment and welfare aids are such that this is not a rational course to follow. Labor and management find it is better to stay where they are and devote their efforts to obtaining enough protection to ensure their existing employment.

Even if meaningful adjustment is recognized in trade legislation, the means of achieving it in a manner consistent with freedom of choice are by no means obvious. Our social values and income level are such that we should be able to reduce output in noncompetitive industries slowly enough to enable most of those currently employed in such industries to remain, if they wish. It seems essential, however, that such industries do not hire large numbers of new young workers, who become socially immobile as they become older. At the same time, of course, young workers must be provided with opportunities for gainful employment in other industries and regions. This is not the place to go into detail about how these results might be obtained and, in any event, I do not have anything unique to say about the possible means. It would seem that the use of wage subsidies and taxes (but not enough to constitute an uneconomic export subsidy) may be needed as well as various monetary incentives for industrial rationalization. The problem of maintaining resource flexibility in older economics is one that must somehow be successfully solved if we are to solve satisfactorily the economic growth problems facing both developed and developing nations.

The New Protectionism, Cartels, and the International Order

Jan Tumlir

At first sight, the new protectionism—for I shall maintain that it is a new political phenomenon—appears sufficiently homogeneous that a separate analysis of its European and American forms seems a nitpicking exercise.

The lists of products affected are long and varied, but products from four distinct categories appear most frequently on both sides: textiles and clothing, to which I would add shoes; steel; transport equipment, so far mainly ships but with rumblings from the automotive sector; and a motley group of such light engineering products as TV sets and tubes, ball bearings, dry-cell batteries, and cutlery. In all four groups, imports into Western Europe and North America from Japan and a group of developing countries (and, in the case of Western Europe, from the East European countries) have been growing considerably more rapidly than trade in the same products within and between these two large, industrially mature areas. But new sensitivities are being discovered almost daily,[1] the lists will no doubt grow, and, since the nature of the problem is clear, a product-by-product analysis would be tedious.[2]

The author is writing in a personal capacity; his views are not to be interpreted as representing the official position of the GATT secretariat. Thanks for critical comments and suggestions are due to Robert E. Hudec and Richard and Billie Blackhurst. None of them, of course, bears any responsibility for the result.

[1] Most recently, pulp and paper from Brazil seems to be disrupting the Western European market, according to the *Financial Times*, November 11, 1977.

[2] A quantitative assessment would be more to the point but is not possible, for practical as well as conceptual reasons. The chief practical reasons are: (1) our knowledge of the restrictive measures taken is far from complete; and (2) some of those we know about affect the products defined in such detail that statistics do not exist. The main conceptual difficulties are: (1) the volume of the trade affected tells nothing about the degree of restriction; (2) antidumping and subsidy-countervailing measures are in their nature not protectionist acts, yet in some cases these procedures may be abused for protectionist purposes; and (3) the uncertainty created by the measures actually taken, and by the political pressures for more, is itself a most effective means of protection, certainly in the long run.

PART FOUR: TRADE POLICIES

The nature of the common problem explains the similarity of the "solutions" on both sides of the Atlantic. In both areas, the preferred means of protection are bilaterally negotiated—hence, discriminatory—restraints. They are essentially of two types: the exporters' "voluntary" self-restraint and the orderly marketing agreement. (There is now some tendency to exaggerate the legal difference between them.)

Another point of similarity is that the commercial policies of the European Community and the United States contrast starkly with those of small countries such as Sweden and Switzerland. We can thus say that the two largest trading units find it most difficult to resist the new protectionist offensive. To point out that the small countries had less protection to begin with, that they are more dependent on trade, and that therefore their enterprise and labor must be more flexible in adjustment might be a sufficient explanation, but in my view it is incomplete. Recently, Hong Kong and South Korea were asked to cut back voluntarily their textile exports to the European Community by 9 and 7 percent, respectively. The EEC's negotiator was reported to have said that these exporters "appeared to take the attitude that their present shares of the EEC market were 'acquired rights' which could not be touched. This was a totally unacceptable position and showed a complete lack of understanding."[3] Under GATT, a country's share in another country's market indeed used to be an acquired right, to be challenged only by more efficient producers. In short, the new protectionism relies more than the old on the use of coercive power, and smaller countries have less of it.

Cartels as Instruments for Adjustment

The new protectionism in Western Europe differs from the North American version in a way that is important enough to be a major theme of this report. We have seen in Europe a surprising revival of the belief in the efficacy of cartels as instruments for solving the problems of adjustment and overcapacity. I say "surprising," although I know the tradition of European thought on that issue and the state of law as determined by that tradition. But in the 1960s, certainly in Germany, it seemed a dying tradition. Now, however, we see a relatively sudden change in political vocabulary, in effect a resumption of the speech patterns of the 1930s, featuring in particular an overuse of the word "rationalization" (used for its incantatory quality, no corre-

---

[3] *Times* (London), November 5, 1977.

sponding plan having been specified).[4] We also see that some cartels enjoy more, and more open, official support than did any cartels of the 1930s and that they seem to have been conceived from the beginning as international agreements. A final point is that, although the cartelization-rationalization movement of the interwar period was a disastrous failure, nobody refers to that experience, not even by a hint. It is as if it had never occurred.

The "salvation through cartel" idea animates two industries in particular, steel and shipbuilding. There is in operation a European Community steel cartel enforcing minimum prices for construction steels and recommending minimum prices for other kinds of steel (a distinction is being made, in other words, in the pricing of steel for the trading and nontrading sectors). The cartel may embrace producers from outside the EEC, since explicit export restraint agreements have been concluded with all the major external suppliers of steel to the EEC, except of course the U.S. producers.[5]

> Italy: The "Bresciani," northern Italy's small, fiercely independent ministeel mills, are bowing to the threat of European Community fines. They have been selling steel reinforcing bars to Germany, France, and Belgium below the EC's minimum of $225 per metric ton, a level set to prevent a price war among member nations during the present slump in steel and housing. The Bresciani, many of which were little more than village smiths in the early postwar years, have agreed to sell at the EC minimum on condition that EC members buy a fixed quota at that rate, but complain that they are being penalized for efficiency. They can produce a metric ton in less than four hours, compared with 7.6 hours for the French industry. And they can sell it economically for $176.[6]

Europe continues to be a large exporter of steel to the United States, having actually increased its share of that market in 1977 by almost ten percentage points, as the share of Japan declined by a corresponding amount. The cartel-enforced or recommended internal prices lie above those at which steel is traded internationally in the presently

---

[4] "The British knitting industry has asked the Government for help towards the rationalization of the tights manufacturing sector where massive over-capacity now exists across Europe." (*Financial Times* [London], November 9, 1977.)

[5] See Commissioner Vicomte Etienne Davignon's report to the European Parliament in *Débats* (Luxembourg), May 7, 1977, p. 93.

[6] *Business Week*, October 17, 1977.

depressed and fiercely competitive international market.[7] The issue of subsidies is also involved, with the losses of the nationalized British Steel Corporation in fiscal 1977 running to some 20 percent of sales. The proposition made by the European Commission for rationalizing the European steel industry and relieving the international market tension was reported in the following terms:

> The Davignon Plan . . . has three main elements: An undertaking by the European and Japanese steel producers not to upset the American market with their exports, or to "compete unfairly" in other markets; an end to the campaign by the US steel industry to get the Carter Administration—by way of the courts—to impose punitive antidumping duties on foreign steel imports; and coordinated steps to restructure the world steel industry including the phasing out of old plants and limits on the explosive growth of new steel-making capacity in Japan and many parts of the developing world.[8]

In shipbuilding, international pressure is being exerted, mainly on Japan, for a sharing of orders "on the basis of solidarity and equity." At a meeting of the OECD Working Party Six in February 1977, the Japanese agreed to raise their prices by 5 percent; but it turned out that this form of self-restraint benefited Brazil and Korea rather than European yards. At another meeting in Tokyo in early November, the Japanese were asked by the EEC to reduce their ship production forecast for 1980, as well as the shipbuilding industry's capacity. In Europe, the commission estimates, production capacity should be reduced by 46 percent by 1980.[9] This, however, is only a guideline, and no plan for implementation exists; more important, there is no agreement among countries on how the cuts should be distributed beyond the further guideline mandating "equality of sacrifice in the painful process of reducing capacity."[10] In addition, the Association of West European Shipbuilders has urged the OECD governments to ban economic aid to third world countries that might lead to an expansion of world shipbuilding capacity.

To sum up this peculiar official mood, let me quote the British secretary of state:

---

[7] For an analysis of the U.S. reaction to steel imports from Japan and Europe, concluding that the "reference price approach" cannot be more than a stopgap measure, see M. J. Marks, "Remedies to 'Unfair' Trade: American Action against Steel Imports," *World Economy*, vol. 1, no. 2 (January 1978), pp. 223–37.

[8] *Guardian* (London), November 7, 1977.

[9] *Financial Times* (London), December 3, 1977.

[10] Ibid.

> Externally, we and the other advanced industrialized countries should at least be starting to consider whether the present basically free market system can continue to cope in conditions of increasing interdependence and complexity in the world economy. . . . We all know that we need now . . . faster growth rates amongst many of the strong economies. Hitherto the conventional wisdom is that this is only possible within a generally open international trading regime. Equally, we must recognize that there could be increasing problems of over-production of some manufactures as developing countries move into the industrial era. They have not got the same ability to anticipate the potential market, and they will overproduce and they have overproduced in many areas. Overproduction in the past has tended to arise only with primary products. The worldwide organization of the tin, coffee, cocoa, sugar and even wheat markets has been tried with varying degree of success. . . . This does not mean that the markets for industrial products should be similarly organized. I think you face great difficulties if you try to do so, but there are a number of products—steel and ships, for example—for which international coordination of policies seems highly desirable at the present time.[11]

What sense can an economist make of all this? The first notion we should get into focus is that of overcapacity. Global steel production peaked in 1973, shipbuilding probably in the same year. Do we expect it to be falling from here to eternity? The problem labeled "overcapacity" is not much of a problem. All industries comprise productive facilities of widely varying vintages and productivity. When overlaid by excess aggregate demand, the fact may not have been clearly noticeable, but the ebbing of aggregate demand in the process of disinflation has wonderfully sharpened our powers of concentration on facts of this kind. Often an industry facing a growing demand fails to innovate, perhaps because it prefers to satisfy the wage demands of its unions. Eventually, demand slows down or declines, imports from more efficient producers abroad increase, and the industry faces a crisis. Of course, there are no fatal crises for large industries. Emergence of more productive facilities elsewhere reduces the social value of their installations, but they nonetheless remain capable of producing. The oldest and least productive facilities may have to be written off; the more modern ones can be improved. The labor they employ will have to be content for some time with real wage increases that fall somewhat short of labor productivity increase. As the profits (or at least the market prospects)

---

[11] The Right Honorable Dr. David Owen to the British National Committee, International Chamber of Commerce, November 1, 1977.

of the industry improve, it can borrow and invest to catch up with the newer facilities elsewhere. Given these and other considerations (for example, supply and cost of different forms of energy, and the development of technology), there is no way for an authority external to the industry reliably to estimate the total capacity needs a few years hence, although individual firms may be better able to determine the kinds of investments that will be profitable. It is equally impossible for a group of governments to distribute capacity cuts among their national industries by negotiation, at the same time safeguarding the economic efficiency of these industries as well as the broader efficiency of the economies in which they operate. All this was fully discussed in the 1930s.[12]

It is in other ways that the discussion of these industrial problems shows a distinctly contemporary quality. First, in the 1930s it may have been possible to organize an all-inclusive cartel; in the global industrial economy of the 1970s, it is not. The statements cited earlier indicate that the currently envisaged solutions require the support of official diplomacy to ensure that developing countries and Japan abstain from expanding those industries in which the Atlantic OECD members are experiencing excess capacity.[13] It is hard to imagine how political forces could be successfully brought to bear on this objective within the framework of even a rudimentary economic order indicating to nations the relative efficiency of different kinds of investment.

Second, there is now a general presumption that the government should take positive action to aid the industries in distress. The European discussion centers explicitly on the kind of public assistance—over and above toleration and enforcement of cartel agreements as to minimum prices and market shares—these industries need to shed the excess capacity plaguing them. To the average newspaper reader, such actions may appear plausible—but only because the most important issues remain undiscussed.

The condition of excess capacity, as I have said, is largely temporary. It is perhaps aggravated by unusually large differences in average cost of production between firms—differences not only between

---

[12] See, for example, F. A. Hayek, ed., *Collectivist Economic Planning* (London: G. Routledge, 1935), pp. 22–225; and Lionel Robbins, *Economic Planning and International Order*, 1937 ed., reprint (New York: Arno Press, 1972), chapter 6.

[13] William Diebold, Jr., reminds me that, like most ideas discussed at any time, this one is far from novel. A possibility of international agreements to this effect was discussed by Eugene Staley in *World Economic Development: Effects on Advanced Industrial Countries* (Montreal: International Labour Office, 1944), pp. 203–04.

but also within national industries.¹⁴ The current situation testifies to errors of foresight in the past: liquid funds were committed to specific forms of real capital in an overestimation of the growth of demand or an underestimation of the rate at which more efficient units of production would be established by other entrepreneurs.¹⁵ With respect to investment, the main lesson of economics is that bygones are bygones. There is nothing that a collectivity can do to recapture the level of social welfare that would have prevailed if errors of foresight had not occurred in past investment decisions. Efficient adjustment requires that these errors be acknowledged and the assets of the financially weakest firms revalued accordingly.¹⁶ Public assistance to firms loaded with excess capacity could only compensate their owners for past errors of judgment. Making such compensation a general principle of public policy would amount to a socialization of investment risk, transforming at one stroke a private enterprise into a full-fledged socialist economy.

Although there is a great deal of talk about saving jobs, the main purpose of cartels has always been to prevent the necessary correction of book values.¹⁷ This, I have already noted, can be done only at considerable cost to other industries and to society at large. The subsidy necessary to prevent bankruptcies in an industry with inflated capitalization can be given in many forms, including a permitted or imposed cartel arrangement combined with protection. If the subject happens to be an industry producing intermediate goods such as steel, steel-using industries (which provide much larger employment than does steel making) will be penalized, and corrective action will eventually be needed on their behalf. In all advanced countries, however, most steel-using industries are export industries. Should they obtain a subsidy in their turn?

Book values can be corrected in several ways, but even the most drastic correction, bankruptcy, is only an accounting operation with no opportunity cost. The real costs of avoiding that correction multiply

---

[14] Clearly so, if the EEC is taken as a single "national" market.

[15] Another failure of foresight may relate to the past behavior of wages. Its effects are reducible to the two specified in the text.

[16] Policy plans of this kind contain another undiscussed contradiction. The economic value of the capital goods constituting the "excess capacity" is less than their book value but, in many cases, exceeds their scrap value. What does "phasing out excess capacity" mean in these circumstances? The physical destruction of serviceable plants?

[17] Another advantage of the cartel, it is argued, is that it can allocate more equitably among the firms in the industry such book-value corrections as it cannot prevent. How this is done I cannot explain; I can only reflect on the sad decline of the once noble word "equity."

rapidly through time, however, by imitation and retaliation, and may eventually cause a crisis in the international order.

"Organizing" Foreign Trade

There are, of course, many other parallels between the present situation and the 1930s; it is the differences that are frightening. One parallel is the use of discriminatory protective devices. In that unhappy decade, however, discrimination was without a pattern. Governments discriminated in favor of or against other countries because of bilateral payments imbalances, misguided efforts to obtain better entry conditions for their own exports, or because the policy coordination possible between pairs or small groups of countries was more extensive than the concert of nations was willing to accept. In the present decade, a clear pattern to discrimination has emerged, which I have described elsewhere as a "siege-economy mentality spreading in Western Europe and North America . . . the illusion . . . that relatively unobstructed, liberal trade could be maintained among the old-industrialized countries if the dynamic 'disruptive' industrial newcomers could only be kept at bay."[18]

This is now changing. In early 1977, I could only speculate that the belief was an illusion. Subsequently, Raymond Barre referred to the virtual international monopoly that the United States and Japan enjoyed in the aerospace, nuclear, and electronic sectors by virtue of their far-flung multinationals. "Europe could not accept a situation," he said, "in which the existence of such large organizations deprived it of the right to develop its own industries on which its whole economic future depended."[19] Australia, asked to restrain her (minimal) steel exports to the EEC, threatened to embargo uranium exports to Europe. In October 1977, Austria took action to protect her balance of payments, imposing a tariff surcharge on all imports except those from the EEC and EFTA countries. In November, Italy imposed new restrictions on imports of textiles from all countries except other EEC members. Then came the steel restraints, affecting trade among the developed countries as well as their imports from the less developed ones.

The old protectionism, as practiced prior to the Great Depression, could be considered ordinary democratic politics. Centered on the tariff, it coexisted, with no apparent intellectual difficulty, with the acceptance of the market as a national as well as an international eco-

---

[18] Jan Tumlir, "Can the International Economic Order Be Saved?" *World Economy*, vol. 1, no. 1 (October 1977), p. 16.
[19] *Financial Times* (London), July 7, 1977.

nomic allocation and distribution mechanism. Indeed, protectionists as well as (if not more than) free traders stood for laissez faire. Now, as in the 1930s, protectionism is an expression of a profound skepticism about the market's ability to allocate resources and distribute incomes to society's satisfaction. Skepticism on this point seemed justified in the 1930s, in the midst of a nearly total and wholly incomprehensible economic collapse. It is difficult to explain it now, however, after a quarter-century in which the market economies performed with an unprecedented degree of success. Indeed, to explain the renewed skepticism at all we have to begin by noting that it is cultivated by the governments themselves.

Our political life consists largely of politicians making promises to organized groups. Because each promise entails a function for government, our political life consists largely of government's soliciting additional functions for itself. When we enumerate all the functions and responsibilities accepted by government in the last several decades, we can see (1) that they are general (for example, macroeconomic) as well as particular responsibilities (for example, group-income maintenance, regional distribution of income and industrial activity, promotion of high-technology industries, and other structural objectives); (2) that many of these goals are mutually incompatible; and (3) that since economics has not specified the terms on which they trade off for each other, there is no rational way for the political process to assign weights to them.[20] Their incompatibility manifests itself most clearly in the economy's external relations, which in turn compel governments to grope for an appropriate "organization" of foreign trade. This notion implies that government would determine the amount of imports to be admitted in each industrial sector. In this way, of course, the government would be determining the relative price structure of the economy, the relative sizes of individual import-competing industries and of the import-competing sector as a whole, thus also of the export sector and of the nontradables.[21] The concept of "organized liberalism"

---

[20] Economic jargon continues to mislead the profession as well as the politicians and the public. We talk about maximizing a social welfare function, written in the form $f(a, b, c, \ldots n)$, assuming that the weights attached to individual arguments are given to us by the political process. But the above form is only a symbol of a function we cannot specify, and without specification there is no possibility of a rational ordering of priorities. Indeed, "policy" without priorities is the order of the day as the current vacillation between employment and disinflation objectives clearly shows.

[21] It might be said that the Vanik, Mills, and Burke-Hartke congressional initiatives of the late 1960s and early 1970s were different in that they proposed a general scheme with little scope for administrative discretion: the share of imports in each domestic product market would simply be frozen. But it was precisely

PART FOUR: TRADE POLICIES

implies, on this showing, a degree of central planning never before attempted in Western societies. On the fringes of the economics profession an argument, eerily blending mathematics with theology, flickers on about the feasibility of this degree of centralized planning in societies desiring to maintain some vestige of individual freedom. The most curious feature of this argument is the resolute inattention it displays to the problem of how such sovereign, democratic, centrally planning societies would live with each other. Not only would national foreign trade plans have to be negotiated among them; since the planning (or "organization") of foreign trade logically implies domestic production planning, the latter plans, too, would be subject to international negotiation.[22] Can one imagine arrangements more propitious to the exercise of national power?

The desperate improvisation of the 1930s reflected the sincere—and, on the face of it, not implausible—belief that central planning could not do worse than the market. But few believe that today. That is the ominous difference. At least, the cabinet-level officials and legislative leaders know that there is no way in which a thorough organization of world trade, as a complement of national central planning for all the structural objectives in production and distribution that different organized interests may specify, can be combined with macroeconomic growth and stability, with individual freedom and property rights, and ultimately with an orderly political process and peace. It is not merely that no theory of such planning exists. Even if one were devised, it would not be practicable, given the tradition of constitutional rights in

---

in this sense that they were unrealistic. The shares to be frozen would have to be negotiated first, internally as well as externally, in order to minimize retaliation. Would we freeze the market share of imported oil? Could the negotiation ever be concluded? Thus, in practice these proposals come close to the more recent French initiative.

[22] Although we are still some distance from international negotiation of comprehensive national production plans, there have already been cases of intergovernmental negotiations not only of the amount of production but of the production techniques to be used by particular firms. The bilateral agreement on color television receivers concluded between the United States and Japan contains the following stipulation, confirmed by the Japanese ambassador in Washington: "I have the honor to confirm the intention of the Ministry of International Trade and Industry that it will guide Japanese firms which plan to make direct investment into the United States in color television receiver production during the effective period of the Notes exchanged, to adopt such production processes as add no less labor content in the United States than the Japanese-affiliated color television receiver manufacturers which are operating commercially in the United States at the time when the Notes exchanged enter into force." "Japan-United States: Orderly Marketing Agreement for Japanese Color Television Receivers" (Washington, D.C., May 20, 1977), *International Legal Materials: Current Documents*, vol. 16, no. 3 (May 1977), p. 641.

248

most industrial countries and the fact of sovereignty internationally. Even domestically, the alternative to the market is not scientific planning but political negotiation, an endless series of tests of power, the corporate state—a mutant incapable of survival because it cannot live in peace with its neighbors. All this is well known and explicit in our government and political party programs. Yet, planning without a theory or hope of success is being introduced—piecemeal, surreptitiously, stubbornly—into government practice, mainly, one gathers, for short-term expediency and to keep the growing administrative staffs occupied.[23]

Threats to the Legal Defense of Liberal Trade

> Indeed the major premise of the Sherman Act is that the suppression of competition in international trade is in and of itself a public injury; or at any rate, that such suppression is a greater price than we want to pay for the benefit it sometimes secures.
> Justice Stone (*United States* v. *Trenton Potteries*, 1927).

The law of the industrially advanced democratic countries as it has evolved over centuries embodies a different concept of economic organization than that of "organized liberalism." It is thus not surprising that the recent developments of governmental and administrative practice raise growing problems in law.[24] I believe that if the new protectionist offensive is dissipated before we have replayed the 1930s it will be due not to the governments having summoned what they call "political will," but to the law having caught up with them, so to speak, in self-defense. What is now threatened most is the integrity of the law itself.

Without professional expertise in this area, I can raise only two clusters of questions for discussion.

---

[23] Note how the distinctive form of the new protectionism, namely, the bilaterally negotiated restraint, appears calculated to maximize official activity, each importing country sending negotiating teams to all exporting countries and vice versa, with far-flung travel an important fringe benefit for the negotiators.

[24] The *Times* (London), May 30, 1977, quotes Sir Richard Marsh: "both parties in government, and I include myself when I was a minister, have totally ignored the law and encouraged the civil servants to do the same thing. The statutes are broken or not observed regularly as a matter of course. Many of the pressures which ministers have applied in nationalized industry pricing or in the settlement of industrial relations have been in flagrant breach of the statutes." This may be an exaggeration or an extreme case. It does, nonetheless, indicate that the overextended democratic executives do tend to have a problem with the law.

PART FOUR: TRADE POLICIES

Antitrust. Most of the OECD countries now have some antitrust, competition, or cartel-control laws on their statute books and have developed some jurisprudence and administrative practices under them. Although they vary widely in stringency, these laws have three features in common. First, they recognize more or less explicitly that competition among firms disperses economic, hence political, power and for that reason is a good thing. Second, they pay particular attention to those restrictions of competition that could raise the nation's import prices. In this respect, most are quite explicit in prohibiting agreements between domestic and foreign firms for that purpose. In each national jurisprudence, the treatment of import-price-raising agreements among foreign firms is a more or less moot point when no overt connection can be ascertained with domestic firms that might profit from the relative price change. The "impact doctrine" forged by U.S. courts is still far from graphic. It has given rise to considerable international ill will; all the same, other countries are in the process of forging impact doctrines of their own.[25] Third, the antitrust jurisprudence in the OECD countries, as well as in the non-OECD countries, is informed by the Webb-Pomerene doctrine in which associations, cartels, and group agreements formed for the sole purpose of exporting are exempt from the general laws, whatever they are, protecting and promoting competition. This is unfortunate because the 1919 U.S. statute (Webb-Pomerene Act) which seems on the surface so clearly to express the mercantilist attitude of its own period (now staging a comeback), is so narrowly circumscribed, in both its letter and its subsequent court interpretation, that it cannot be considered a threat to competition in U.S. export trade.[26] It has, however, had important symbolic effects abroad.

The distinguishing feature of the new protectionism is that it infringes on competition in more, and more drastic, ways than the old varieties. Its connection with cartelization is threefold. In some industries and countries or regions, protectionism assumes the form of defensive cartels in which the organized self-interest of an industry is backed by the coercive power of public authority, which enforces discipline among firms and grants the protection without which higher prices could not be maintained at home. In other situations, a public authority seeks protection for industries under its jurisdiction through

---

[25] In 1975, for example, the Federal German Cartel Office successfully prosecuted an export self-restraint concluded by a group of Japanese exporters of dry-cell batteries.

[26] See W. L. Fugate, *Foreign Commerce and the Antitrust Laws*, 2nd ed. (Boston: Little, Brown, 1973), chapter 7; and A. D. Neale, *The Antitrust Laws of the U.S.A.* (Cambridge: At the University Press, 1970), chapter 12.

agreements that, whether negotiated directly with the foreign export industry or with its public authority,[27] almost inevitably imply cartelization of the foreign suppliers.[28]

A third situation is only indirectly connected with the new protectionism. Liberal trade is also being encroached upon from the export side without protectionist motivation. The export restraint may be genuinely voluntary, agreed upon by firms possessing some market power or by their governments. OPEC is, after all, only an orderly marketing agreement. So were the uranium cartel—now subject to considerable legal and diplomatic misgivings in several countries—and the nickel cartel. The two motivations came together in the case mentioned above, when Australia threatened to embargo uranium exports to the EEC should its steel exports to the same destination be restricted.

What to do about foreign cartels beyond the reach of national law (or those able to resist the force of law) is a most serious question,[29] which should be discussed in the context of efforts, already mentioned, by several industrial countries to develop legal doctrines and practices to cope with such situations. So far, given the stringency of the U.S. law and the near ubiquity of U.S. multinationals (without whose active participation few cartels could maintain a substantial degree of effectiveness for long), this country has played the role of the global antitrust policeman. But surely it is anomalous that in this vital respect the international economic order should rely on a particular legal tradition

---

[27] Direct negotiation with a foreign export industry is not usually the case, but it was in the U.S. steel restraint of the late 1960s and early 1970s, attacked, in my view not unsuccessfully, in the courts. See *Consumer Union of U.S., Inc.* v. *Kissinger*, 506 F.2d 136 (D.C. Cir. 1974).

[28] An effort is now being made to draw a strict legal distinction between exporters' self-restraint and an orderly marketing agreement. The distinction emphasizes that the marketing agreement is between two executives, and, indeed, both executives may be legally "covered." In the case of both self-restraint and orderly marketing agreements, however, the motive and the effect are the same. The cautious phrase "almost inevitably" was inserted above for the following reason: there is only one way, seldom practiced, of administering quantitative restrictions in a nondiscriminatory way, namely, auctioning off the import licenses. Similarly, a government could restrain an export industry without encroaching on competition among its firms only by auctioning off export licenses toward the country with which export restraint had been negotiated. It is most difficult, however, to imagine a government of a minimally democratic state enforcing export restraint on an unwilling, fiercely competitive industry. Restraint *with* competition has nothing to recommend itself to the large export firms whose active cooperation is necessary if the agreement is to work to the satisfaction of the importing country.

[29] For a systematic discussion of this question, see Joel Davidow, "Extraterritorial Application of US Antitrust Law in a Changing World," *Law and Policy in International Business*, vol. 8, no. 4 (1976), esp. pp. 903–08.

PART FOUR: TRADE POLICIES

of a single country. There is a need for a more deliberate international coordination of the development of national antitrust laws as well as judicial and administrative practices.[30] The initial effort could be directed toward progressive restriction and eventual elimination of the Webb-Pomerene type of clauses from national law. (Without such a clause in its national law, the government of an exporting country could not be coerced into self-restraint by its trading partners.)

An indispensable condition of such a legal development is a more scrupulous observance by national executives in the core countries of the spirit of the existing antitrust laws. Good legislation presupposes electorates sensitive to the quality of law. The present practices invite the public to consider law itself a mere expedient. Such blunting of the sense of law must result, for example, "from the contradictions in national policies which maintain, on the one hand, that economic competition is a necessary condition of a decentralized political order ensuring individual freedom and, on the other hand, impose cartelization on competitive industries abroad."[31] Respect for law must diminish further when confronted with the spectacle of governments promoting cartels abroad when imports from a competitive industry are inconveniently cheap and trying to break cartels abroad when the supply from them is inconveniently expensive.

An overview of recent developments in this area drives me to the conclusion that decisions dictated by short-term exigencies of trade policy threaten to bring about, through their cumulative force, a major reversal in the antitrust policy of industrial countries. This would be a political change almost impossible to overestimate. Antitrust has decisively shaped the American economy (and polity) for close to a century, and I would maintain that its more recent development in other OECD countries (and, indeed, even in some less developed countries) has been an important factor in the highly successful performance

---

[30] The January 1978 decision of the U.S. Supreme Court allowing foreign governments to sue for punitive damages under U.S. antitrust law is an important step in this direction—not that it reflects negotiated international coordination, but it reduces the obstacles to it. The decision may be contrasted with the ruling of the British House of Lords (*In re Westinghouse Electric Corporation Uranium Contract Litigation MDL Docket 235, First-Fifth Appeal*), announced in December 1977, concerning the request of a U.S. court for testimony from the executives of a British company (Rio Tinto Zinc) in the case of the Canadian uranium cartel litigated in the United States. In refusing the request, Lord Wilberforce stated: "It is axiomatic that in anti-trust matters the policy of one state may be to defend what it is the policy of another state to attack" (p. 9).

[31] Richard Blackhurst, Nicolas Marian, and Jan Tumlir, *Trade Liberalization, Protectionism, and Interdependence*, GATT Studies in International Trade, no. 5 (Geneva, November 1977), p. 57.

of the world economy in the post–World War II period. It is remarkable that the reversal is occurring without any public, let alone legislative, discussion of its implications.

Fair (International) Trade Practices. Similarly endangered is the legal integrity of antidumping and subsidy-countervailing laws and administrative practices. Economists frequently have a problem with these rules: Why should a country outlaw activities that improve its terms of trade? The answer should, in my view, stress two points. Politically speaking, liberal trade has always been, in Robert Hudec's words, "an orphan in the household of democratic government."[32] In every country, it is supported by a loose, precarious coalition, which has to be assiduously cultivated and which could not be held together without rules ensuring visible, publicly defensible fairness in competition with foreign firms. It would be most difficult to overestimate the role played by these rules in the establishment and maintenance of the liberal trade order in the postwar period, particularly in its formative years, say, 1947–1955. The political role of these rules grows in importance, however, when increasingly organized interest groups force upon the government (or offer it an opportunity to assume) additional economic functions and responsibilities.

The economic answer is simpler but also less important. Because permanent dumping is not a realistic alternative, it is clear that the practical effect of such rules is to minimize the extent to which predatory dumping and excessive "distress sales" generate uncertainty for the domestic industry. Such uncertainty has a real economic cost that could outweigh the transitory gains to consumers. It should also be stressed that dumping problems are more likely to appear in areas where competition is weak. In the 1920s Jacob Viner pointed out that "dumping is likely to prevail as a systematic practice only if . . . [t]he exporting industry is trustified or syndicated."[33] Characteristically, in many recent invocations of antidumping laws on both sides of the Atlantic, the export industries accused of dumping indicated that they would prefer to satisfy the complaining industry through an export self-restraint or an orderly marketing agreement.

We may distinguish two threats to these legal defenses of liberal trade. First, the temptation to misuse and abuse them for protectionist purposes is constant but is particularly pronounced in periods of unem-

---

[32] Robert E. Hudec, "GATT or GABB? The Future Design of the General Agreement on Tariffs and Trade," *Yale Law Journal*, vol. 80, no. 1299 (1971), p. 1310.
[33] Jacob Viner, *Dumping: A Problem in International Trade*, 1923 ed., reprint (New York: A. M. Kelley, 1966), p. 348.

ployment. Simultaneously, subsidization and dumping, intermittent phenomena in the normal course of trade, tend to become more frequent and widespread in recessions. A scrupulous enforcement of the rules is time consuming, and when the recession is generalized, time will be of the essence for the complaining firms, which in those conditions suffer from intensified foreign competition as well as from a decline in total domestic demand. Yet, to try to expedite the administrative procedures at the cost of sacrificing some fairness toward the accused industries would have far-reaching consequences, both domestic and international.

While this particular threat may be said to be an immanent one, reappearing in every generalized recession, the second threat belongs among the new challenges to the international economic order that are the proper subject of this conference. The subsidy-countervailing laws have another important function, which they exercise at the exporting end. Their existence in other countries protects a government from political pressures to redistribute income via export and production subsidies. In other words, the rules are supposed to help governments that do not want more economic involvement; by the same token, there is a threat to these rules from governments that desire it. Several instances may be recorded.

Only a few years ago, strong international political pressure was exerted by and on behalf of developing countries to obtain a right to subsidize exports—in other words, to obtain a preferential immunity from countervailing duties. This is not the place to analyze the conditions under which export subsidization might be economically beneficial to a less developed country. In the face of mounting protectionism, to which it has contributed, the campaign has now lost much of its force. But so far, the bulk of manufactured exports from LDCs has been directed toward developed countries' markets. Many development theorists have been arguing in favor of efforts to intensify the mutual trade of less developed countries. In fact, there is now a rapidly growing trade in manufactures among the ten to fifteen less developed countries that are the largest exporters of manufactures to the developed areas. Would the less developed countries be willing to accept subsidized exports in their mutual trade? And if they were not, would it be possible for any exporting firm to sell subsidized exports to developed countries and exports free of subsidy to developing ones and to demonstrate this distinction convincingly to the public authorities in the latter markets? As Kant maintained, and as already seen in the preceding pages, the principles of social conduct should be such that, if everyone followed them, they would lead to no self-contradiction.

In most OECD countries, production (including investment) subsidies expressed in percentage of GNP have been on the rise since about mid-1960. This is why an early international agreement on a subsidy-countervailing code is urgent. A particularly difficult problem in this respect is posed by the practice, routinized in the United Kingdom but now spreading to other countries (for example, Sweden), of nationalizing lame-duck industries as a last-resort measure to preserve their employment. Most of these industries—steel, ships, automobiles—are to a significant measure export industries, and some of them, for the time being, are depressed worldwide.

Finally, dumping is bound to generate much more dangerous friction among governments when the idea of a rationalization cartel becomes public policy in one or more countries—and the cartel is also an exporter. The importing countries are then faced with a compounded legal problem, involving antidumping as well as antitrust.[34]

What these cases have in common is a frontal attack on the idea of a legal obligation to conform to fair international trade practices. Increasingly, export subsidization and dumping are claimed as sovereign rights, but the logic of the case is marred by the fact that the countries claiming these rights are themselves unwilling to accept subsidized or dumped exports.[35]

National Interest and Economic Interdependence

The possibility must be contemplated that the leaders of national executive departments and legislatures are already being carried by events,

---

[34] In February 1976, the U.K. government introduced a policy under which an industrial strategy would be determined by tripartite (government, management, and unions) sector working parties, with the ultimate objective of negotiating planning agreements. Reviewing the achievements of the policy in the past two years (under the headline, "Seeking Credibility for the Industrial Strategy"), *Financial Times*, January 18, 1978, writes: "Equally, individual companies and unions, worried about losing their traditional freedom of action, often show little enthusiasm for trying to take company-level decisions based on the broader sector working party discussions and shy away from anything such as planning agreements which smack of union power or socialist-inspired planning. Companies treasure their autonomy and, while they may be prepared in sector working parties to discuss common problems, especially on competing abroad, often they are not prepared to blur competition at home for the sake of any industrial strategy. As one managing director puts it: 'It's one thing to gang up on beating the Japanese but you don't want all this mateyness with your competitors at home all the while.'"

[35] "Brussels. Nov. 17. The EEC Commission has opened anti-dumping investigation on the sale of iron and steel tubes from Spain following French complaint of dumping on the European market, a Commission spokesman said." Ibid., November 18, 1977.

PART FOUR: TRADE POLICIES

pushed by the popular expectations they have aroused to a destination they can envisage and must fear. If this is so, it would be important to know the nature of the paralyzing illusion, the intellectual short circuit, that now condemns whole societies to this fateful drift.

This particular mental trap—a variant of the ancient "fallacy of sovereignty," the concept of sovereignty as unlimited power, virtual omnipotence—is very old.[36] Its contemporary version is best summarized by the following statement: "Economic interdependence is a two-edged sword . . . it involves costs as well as benefits."[37] In this form, it has become the ruling paradigm, in the full Kuhnian sense of an unexamined framework and methodology of analysis, for an influential school of political science as well as for several schools of political economy. By extension, the international order that promotes the growth of interdependence comes to be considered a similarly mixed blessing.

---

[36] Discussed by Sir Karl Popper in *The Open Society* (London: Routledge and Kegan Paul, 1952), chapter 7.

[37] L. B. Krause and J. S. Nye, "Reflections on the Economics and Politics of International Economic Organizations," in C. Fred Bergsten and Lawrence Krause, eds., *World Politics and International Economics* (Washington, D.C.: Brookings Institution, 1975), p. 334. See further: "The third basic reason . . . concerns the conflict between national security, social priorities or other internal goals, and the economic benefits of a liberal trade policy. It reflects the growing economic role of governments in all industrialized countries. . . . The policy objectives could include regional development, a higher degree of self-sufficiency for particular sectors of the economy . . . or environmental standards." (Ernest Preeg, *Economic Blocs and U.S. Foreign Policy* [Washington, D.C.: National Planning Association, 1974], p. 152.) "Interdependence . . . makes governments increasingly dependent upon actions taken by other governments for the achievement of both domestic and foreign policy goals. . . . Autonomy could also usually be reasserted if governments reduced the number of tasks that they have assumed, but that action would seriously jeopardize governmental legitimacy because it would result in a refusal to accept responsibilities expected by a highly politicized populace." (E. L. Morse, *Modernization and the Transformation of International Relations* [New York: Free Press, 1976], pp. 104–05). See also the quotations in the introduction to Blackhurst, Marian, and Tumlir, *Liberalization, Protectionism, and Interdependence*, pp. 2–3; and Robert Gilpin's article in Bergsten and Krause, *World Politics*. Analysis along these lines, whether positive or normative (the two being difficult to distinguish at times), seems to be a response to the observed rise of economic issues to the level of "high policy." Many of these writers appear to draw on a widely quoted statement by Richard N. Cooper: "The central problem of international economic cooperation . . . is *how to keep the manifold benefits of extensive international economic intercourse free of crippling restrictions while at the same time preserving a maximum degree of freedom for each nation to pursue its legitimate economic objectives.*" (*The Economics of Interdependence: Economic Policy in the Atlantic Community* [New York: McGraw-Hill, for the Council on Foreign Relations, 1968]; emphasis in original.) It is in my view wrong, however, to interpret this sentence in the sense I am criticizing here. Cooper's careful formulation only restates the central problem in law, namely, how to reduce to the necessary minimum the limitations that law imposes on the behavior of individuals so that freedom of all can be maximized.

The costs of interdependence to which this view draws attention are reckoned in terms of the legitimate national objectives that may conflict with and have to be sacrificed to the discipline of the international order.[38] National societies are thus seen to have two sets of goals: those for which international order is a necessary condition; and those for which it is an impediment. Clearly, something must be wrong here.

What should be immediately striking is the enormous difference in relative importance of the two sets of national goals. If those of the first set—including, above all, economic growth—are vital, is there a choice between them and the goals of the second set? Indeed, can the latter be called *national* goals? I have already touched on this issue in my discussion of the social welfare "function," which we can only symbolize but not specify. As long as the functional relationships between all the particular objectives remain unspecified, the political process has no rational way of assigning weights to them. Not knowing the relative prices, the public cannot decide how much to buy of this or that. It is not that a discussion of the legitimacy of objectives we do not know how to attain would be a scholastic exercise. The point is, rather, that the legitimacy of many so-called national objectives is questionable from the viewpoint of the process by which they were put on national agenda.

There is a more fundamental fallacy. The rules of the international order define the legitimate rights of all constituent states. It follows that a national objective that could not be attained *except* through an infringement of these rules could not be considered legitimate. In principle, of course, the international order does not prescribe or proscribe national goals (though it explicitly upholds the most general political ones, such as peace, justice, territorial integrity, and so forth); it only regulates the policies by which countries pursue their goals. Whatever domestic economic objective a nation may set itself is usually attainable in various ways, among which interference with international transactions (various forms of which *are* proscribed by the international rules) is—as Jagdish Bhagwati, Harry Johnson, and Max Corden have demonstrated—a second-best, third-best, or even a lower-order policy. There are ways of pursuing national objectives which are at the same time efficient and proof against protest from abroad. The international order

---

[38] This view has increasing influence on the present negotiations concerning the reform of the international economic order. Reform has become necessary because observance of the rules of the existing order has been progressively declining. The decline is attributed, in the view criticized here, to the unrealistic stringency of the rules themselves. Much of the reform effort is consequently directed at relaxing the rules, in the hope that in a looser and more permissive form the order will better commend itself to governments.

cannot be deemed costly because it constrains countries to use policies that are best from the national viewpoint.

The view that imputes to international order costs as well as benefits—and in which governments and nations pursue, characteristically, "arrays of objectives" rather than national interest—amounts to a specific, and rather passive, concept of democratic government. The government is there to make gestures of carrying out the wishes of politically organized groups, regardless of incompatibility: the economy itself, in which the sum of inputs must equal the sum of outputs, will in the end ensure compatibility, with inflation usually acting as the great reconciler. The process, however, is unsustainable, since it induces a cumulative deterioration of the economy's productivity. In the earlier concept of democracy, it was the function of the government to mediate between individual groups, explaining and persuading so as to modify their particular points of view and weld them into a national interest. Several of the political scientists and philosophers who have accepted the notion of two categories of legitimate national objectives have analyzed the concept of (a single) national interest and concluded that, with the decline of the security concern in the 1960s, it has lost most of its usefulness for policy guidance.

It seems that we are approaching the phase, so well described by Kuhn, of the dramatic *Gestalt* switch, the replacement of a ruling paradigm. For any branch of science in which it occurs, its effects are somewhat traumatic. The new paradigm to orient "normal policy" is unlikely to be entirely new. It will have to pick up again the notion of long-term national interest, defining it so that it can provide practical guidance to the policy maker. If the need is for principles of social conduct such that, if everybody followed them, they would lead to no contradiction, equating national interest with the maintenance and development of international order would do the trick.

The Developing Countries and the International Order

I. M. D. Little

The import trade of almost all LDCs has been dominated by controls since soon after 1945, or independence, whichever came first. For some countries in Latin America, controls started during the Great Depression or during World War II. Thus, the development challenge is not new and, except in the case of commodities with which I am not here concerned, cannot be considered in the context of the New International Economic Order. Almost invariably, controls were instituted as a result of a balance of payments crisis. In the 1930s the crisis may have been caused by worsening terms of trade, but since World War II the crisis in most countries has been the result of increased spending for development. In a few countries—Brazil, for example—the crisis was due to an overvalued exchange rate, a legacy of the war, which they were reluctant to change. In a few others, it was due to a total disruption of export markets and war damage (especially in Korea and Taiwan).

Of course, World War II also left most industrialized countries with almost complete import and exchange controls. But within a decade the import controls had been dismantled, as well as the exchange controls in many, though not all, countries. Japan is an exception, but it was scarcely thought of as a developed (albeit industrialized) country in 1955. Few economists would not agree that there was a case for controls as extreme disequilibriums occurred—for most countries as a result of World War II but for some, especially Latin American countries, as a result of the failure of exports in the Great Depression. Controls for these reasons are hardly a challenge to an LIEO. But controls in the postwar period can rarely be justified by the exogenous reasons of war or a long-drawn-out and severe worsening of export prices. The main reason for balance of payments problems became development expenditure.

While the Western industrialized countries got rid of controls, the

---

I am indebted to D. B. Keesing for several helpful suggestions.

developing countries intensified them.[1] Thus, reliance on controls, not tariff protection, is the bigger challenge. The intensification of controls for at least the first half of our thirty-year postwar period, long after extreme exogenous disequilibriums had vanished, is what demands explanation. My impression is that this reliance arose mainly from the conviction that a developing country could not manage its foreign affairs, including development, without controls. Of course, all controls protect—and sometimes protect absolutely. But the primary motive was balance of payments management, not protection.[2]

There are several reasons for the above contention:

- The timing of the institution of controls leads to this conclusion.
- Although industrialists might press for controls rather than tariffs, because controls are more securely protective (in the face of a possible fall in import prices, the control will tend to behave like an upwardly variable levy on imports), there were very few industrialists in many of the developing countries where controls were instituted.
- Governments, if bent only on protection, would surely prefer tariffs for fiscal reasons. In fact, they soon began to lose revenue by controlled import substitution and lost still more as they instituted export subsidies to counteract some of the worst effects of import controls.
- As we shall see, perusal of some of the writings of the first generation of postwar "challengers" suggests that management of the economy was the dominant reason.

The threat of protection—by quotas or tariffs—from established interests is forever with us and occurs in any industrialized or semi-industrialized country. No intellectual explanation of challenges to an LIEO is required.[3] But what I have said above suggests that this is not true of most LDCs. An intellectual challenge has probably played an important role in maintaining the control system but not so much in instituting it. Just as tariffs have been raised behind controls to mop up some of the premiums generated, so did the new intelligentsia, taught

---

[1] I shall not say much about the USSR—where trade was for a long time a sort of planning residual—or about Eastern Europe, where the Communist takeover resulted, if to a lesser degree, in the same kind of trade philosophy.

[2] This is not to deny, of course, that appeals to Hamilton and List, and the three-quarters of a century of high protection in the United States, played some role. A part was also played by the glamorization of import substitution, as a result of A. O. Hirschman's doctrine of linkages.

[3] However, in 1975 a group of former Treasury advisers in Cambridge, England, began to argue that import controls would be a less inflationary way of maintaining foreign balance than letting sterling fall, and that there was no hope of rejuvenating British industry without protection. This view was rejected by the chancellor.

by the development economists of the 1940s and 1950s, rise in support of the system. In many semiindustrialized countries, this has resulted in a strange meeting of the minds of intellectuals, businessmen, and bureaucrats.

Thus, the challenge to liberal (that is, control-free) trading is not at all new. Perhaps few components of the NIEO *are* new. But the modern intellectual opposition to free trading dates back to the 1940s and is not primarily concerned with the infant-industry argument.

This challenge is especially associated with Hans Singer and Raul Prebisch, although Thomas Balogh and Gunnar Myrdal and their protégés have also played a considerable part.[4] There are also more recent frills of a neo-Marxist character, but I shall do no more than glance at these. I do not aim to rival, for instance, the review of Carlos Diaz-Alejandro.[5] Nor can I pretend to all the doubts he expressed concerning an LIEO.

Singer's main thesis in 1949 was that LDCs had not much benefited from international investment and trade—above all, not in the way of industrialization.[6] There were dark hints that the benefits might have amounted to less than nothing, because activities were diverted from industrialization, which carried with it major externalities. He took up the alleged secular worsening of the terms of trade from the U.N. document, "Relating Prices of Exports and Imports of Underdeveloped Countries,"[7] and explained this "indisputable fact" essentially by an ever-increasing degree of monopoly (with labor sharing in it) in the production of manufactures, making little of it, however, as far as balance of payments management was concerned. What he did was to cast general doubt on the value of trade and foreign investment for LDCs.

Prebisch and the U.N. Economic Commission for Latin America (ECLA) emphasized the same "indisputable fact" from 1949 onward; the "fact" continued to have ready credence as a result of the worsening

---

[4] I shall not go into what might be called the negative challenge. The stress on nonhuman capital investment and on internal mobilization of resources for it—a dominant theme in the literature of the 1940s and 1950s (along with neglect of the fact that investment may be inefficient)—itself resulted in deemphasizing trade.

[5] Carlos Diaz-Alejandro, "Trade Policies and Development," in *International Trade and Finance*, P. B. Kenen, ed. (Cambridge: At the University Press, 1975).

[6] See H. W. Singer, "The Distribution of Grains between Investing and Borrowing Countries," *Papers and Proceedings* (American Economic Association, May 1950). This negative view conflicts strongly, as the title implies, with W. Arthur Lewis ed., *Tropical Development, 1880–1913*, Studies in Economic Progress (London: Allen and Unwin, 1970).

[7] United Nations, Department of Economic Affairs, 1949.

in the LDC terms of trade for a decade, after a peak in commodity prices at the time of the Korean War. It became enshrined in UNCTAD and in constant repetition by many development economists. The recovery after the early 1960s, the historically high levels of today, and the fact that all scholarly work, to my knowledge, denies any long-run trend have probably still not fully exorcised the myth created by the U.N. work (which was based on the United Kingdom's terms of trade from 1876 to 1946).[8]

Explanations of a nonexistent fact are not interesting to me, and so I shall not go into the variants on Singer's explanation. What is more interesting are the conclusions that were drawn. First, of course, there was the need for industrialization. But why does not the change in the terms of trade against primary commodities itself cause industrialization? Singer had explained this by saying that when times were good there was no incentive, and when they were bad there was no money. This was (necessarily for the argument) allied to the view that "all private activity tends to be governed by the price relations of the day"— a view that may do some injustice to the intelligence of entrepreneurs. While this argument clearly has some force in explaining the delay in LDC industrialization between 1913 and 1939, it would not be very apposite in the face of a *trend*, caused neither by war, by stagnation, nor by slump, in the industrialized countries.

More than the theory of declining terms of trade was, or should have been, needed to make ECLA and Prebisch believe that trade must be controlled. To the argument of declining terms of trade was added the view that the income elasticity of foreign demand for LDC exports was inevitably lower than that of LDC demand for imports—especially, of course, if domestic demand was to be steered toward investment goods for development. Added to this was the acceptable argument that the price elasticity was very low (at least for developing countries taken together). All this amounted to the thesis that exports of LDCs were virtually exogenous; therefore, total imports were also exogenous. Import controls or other restrictions were therefore not restrictive of trade; they served only to control the pattern of imports in the interest of development. And given the declining terms of trade, balance of pay-

---

[8] A recent article (G. F. Ray, "The 'Real' Price of Primary Products," *National Institute for Economic and Social Research Review* [London], August 1977) suggests a long, slow worsening of the purchasing power of manufactures over that of commodities in the final third of the nineteenth century, recovery before World War I, then a short boom and longer bust, leaving prices at historically very low levels in the early 1930s. But in the post–World War II period, commodities' purchasing power seems never to have fallen below the best levels achieved earlier.

ments trouble would be endemic, and frequent devaluation would result, with consequent inflation. Moreover, devaluation would further worsen the terms of trade in the face of an inelastic foreign demand. It all begins to look rather plausible.[9]

However, even if we accept the elasticity assumptions, this does not add up to a case. Export taxes could be used to prevent devaluation from reducing export proceeds. Luxury taxes can prevent low-priority imports. The externalities (if they exist) inherent in industrialization could be dealt with by tariffs (but see below). Finally, it is probably an illusion that reducing consumption is less inflationary if it is done by price rises resulting from controls than if it is done by price rises resulting from other policies. The argument could thus be fully convincing only to those who had acquired faith in planning—in the sense of trying to manipulate quantities with some end in view, with prices as a by-product, rather than vice versa.

This last theme in the symphony was not lacking. The USSR's apparent success, and that of the United Kingdom in wartime, was deeply influential in some quarters. ECLA itself was, of course, a proponent of planning. Indeed, to express a disbelief in planning in the 1950s was a confession of confusion or worse, at least for the LDCs. In Europe, Balogh and Myrdal were among the conspicuously successful teachers of the need for controls and planning and of the view that trade between unequal partners might damage the poor partner.

The emphasis on quantities is also connected with structuralism. But what is structuralism? I doubt if it can be closely defined, but it seems to involve the belief that a country's structure of production, and of imports and exports, is both inappropriate and almost unchangeable; except, in the long run, by investment, which must be controlled in order to produce eventually a more desirable structure. In regard to trade and its effect on the proper pattern of production, structuralism is, or was, essentially associated with export pessimism. This was one of the many rigidities that was supposed to exist. Export pessimism, plus a small or nonexistent capital goods industry, led to the two-gap model—the view, which was dominant until at least the second half of the 1960s, that the typical LDC's growth was limited by foreign exchange and not by savings (which logically required the view that savings could not be transformed into investment).

No doubt, structuralism was first born in Latin America. But like many ideas it appears to have had an independent genesis in India

---

[9] See A. O. Hirschman, "Ideologies of Economic Development in Latin America," in *Latin American Issues* (New York: Twentieth Century Fund, 1961).

PART FOUR: TRADE POLICIES

sometime before 1958. I certainly imbibed it, along with much else, in New Delhi. Export pessimism, India's lack of many minerals, the idea that India must become independent of aid within fifteen years and pay its debts, showed structurally that all necessities that could be made in India must be made in India. There was no choice.[10] The plan must therefore be optimal (if consistent, which, of course, it was not). It also followed that prices and most traditional economics were irrelevant. The argument was logical but hopelessly wrong.[11]

In particular, it was believed that investment goods must be made in India (it tended to be assumed that consumption-good demand could be satisfied by agriculture and traditional industries, with very little investment); otherwise, India could not grow.[12] Thus the two-gap idea (with foreign exchange dominating) was in place, though not baptized.[13] To me, India is living proof of the disastrous results of structural thinking.

Quite a few of the undesirable extravagances of the resultant import substitution policies had been recognized by Prebisch by 1964.[14] These included capital intensity, low value added at international prices (but not value subtracted!), loss of scale, lack of competition, and the growth of "inessential" production behind the barriers to trade. These

---

[10] See W. B. Reddaway, who wrote: "Virtually *every* kind of export increasing or import saving type of production which is even reasonably sensible seems to be needed to get the balance of payments on to a viable basis: indeed it seems to be necessary to press all of them forward about as fast as is permitted by the market or by practical considerations on the supply side. So that although the argument for favoring labour-intensive types of production is valid, provided it is stated with sufficient care, its practical importance seems to be very small." (W. B. Reddaway, *The Development of the Indian Economy* [London: Allen and Unwin, 1962].)

[11] Jagdish Bhagwati has argued that these arguments were mere rationalizations—the real explanation of the Indian strategy was simply that it was an imitation of the USSR. He may be right, but this does not, of course, imply that India's strategy was not a fine example of structural thinking.

[12] There was a particular Indian gloss to this thesis, the famous Mahalanobis argument that machines to make machines were better than machines, and so on—the argument for unlimited capital intensity.

[13] See I. M. D. Little, "The Strategy of Indian Development," *National Institute for Economic and Social Research Review* (London), May 1960. The two-gap idea was modeled and developed by Hollis B. Chenery, Michael Bruno, and McKinnon in the early 1960s and still plays an important role. Whether this development has been conducive to closed or to open policies is a moot point. On the one hand, it tended to suggest that the cure for undervaluation of foreign exchange lay only with development, and hence to condone policies that caused it. On the other hand, by pointing up the foreign exchange shortage, it may have helped to lead to export promotion policies.

[14] Raul Prebisch, *Towards a New Trade Policy for Development* (United Nations, 1964).

disadvantages were placed in the context of a plea for reducing barriers in the industrial centers. Some of this implied a rerecognition of the validity of comparative advantage, but in the meantime a generation of development economists had been taught to sneer at the idea.

There was, however, no recognition that protection inhibits exports, or any recognition that the LDCs' falling share of world trade was due either to this or to lagging agricultural production. The idea of the long-term decline in the terms of trade was still in place, and policies of import substitution continued. No distinction was drawn between protection by controls and by tariffs. The philosophy was still controlled trade. Neither then nor since has UNCTAD favored free trade—not even for industrialized countries. For how then could they give preferences? Any reciprocity was and has remained anathema and part of the asymmetry argument—what was bad for DCs was good for LDCs.

It is in a sense a mistake to think only of challenges to an LIEO, for this implies that the latter is the consensus or is established or, to use a horrible fashionable phrase, is the prevalent paradigm. The opposite is true. In the 1960s the great majority of LDCs were married to control systems and high protection. Indeed, they still are, though to a lesser extent. The erstwhile theoretical contenders, Gottfried Haberler and Jacob Viner, had been defeated; the Singer-Prebisch-Balogh-Myrdal team dominated. Thus, it is to the liberal challenge to the controlled-trade establishment that we must now turn. On a theoretical plane, the seeds had been sown by 1963. At the more influential applied level, the challenge did not acquire real force until 1970.

A year or so before the UNCTAD 1964 manifesto, Jagdish Bhagwati and V. K. Ramaswami had made the essential theoretical advance showing that protection might be a poor way of dealing with a domestic factor distortion or an externality—indeed so poor that it could make matters worse.[15] But the link between protection and lagging exports was not brought out, although it was implicit. As a result of the Bhagwati-Ramaswami article, it could easily be seen that protectionists were essentially advocating protection against their own agriculture or other primary tradable output. Some level of the exchange rate could

---

[15] Jagdish Bhagwati and V. K. Ramaswami, "Domestic Distortions, Tariffs, and the Theory of Optimum Subsidy," *Journal of Political Economy*, February 1963. This was followed by other theoretical work on "effective protection" and "domestic resource costs." See also E. Hagen, "An Economic Justification of Protectionism," *Quarterly Journal of Economics*, vol. 72 (1958); and Gottfried Haberler, "Some Problems in the Pure Theory of International Trade," *Economic Journal*, June 1950. It is perhaps surprising that this advance waited so long for an author. It can now be seen as a standard second-best welfare theorem, analogous to the argument, made over a decade earlier, that the merits of direct and indirect taxation cannot be established a priori.

always provide any desired incentive to manufactures, while maintaining neutrality between the domestic and the export markets. This led to Nicholas Kaldor's advocacy of a dual exchange rate,[16] still a second-best solution. Whether it is a good second-best solution would seem to depend on the extent of the domestic links between primary production and manufactures. Better solutions do not seem to have been much discussed in a policy context until Little, Scitovsky, and Scott (LSS), whose work laid considerable emphasis on the inherent export bias of protectionism.[17]

Aside from the purely theoretical contributions, an early, if not the opening, shot in the battle for more open policies was fired by D. B. Keesing.[18] By 1970, the extraordinary average heights and variability of effective protection had been exposed in books by Little, Scitovsky, and Scott, Bela Balassa, and their attendant authors, together covering ten countries.[19] LSS also discussed the inhibiting effects of general control regimes, which had spread from simple import controls. Both LSS and Balassa laid some stress on promoting rather than protecting industry so as to achieve, as far as possible, neutrality between the domestic market and exports. The LSS volume also made some suggestions for a transition to more liberal trade, which would be more favorable to exports, and suggested that it would be very difficult to justify effective promotion of industry of more than 20 percent. In this connection, it should be noted that none of the challenging authors has wanted to deny that an industrial promotion policy may be justified. It was difficult, however, to justify the effective protection exposed, which was over 100 percent for Argentina, Brazil, Chile, India, and Pakistan.

Some exceptions and anomalies that were swept under the carpet by the broad brush used in the above few paragraphs should be noted. They occur mostly in the Far East. Hong Kong has always pursued pure free trade—no controls, no tariffs (it had virtually no primary production and thus no grounds for protection). By 1954, K. Y. Yin, who was to become the economic czar of Taiwan—then still a predominantly agricultural country pursuing import substitution policies—was ques-

---

[16] Nicholas Kaldor, "Dual Exchange Rates and Economic Development," *Economic Bulletin for Latin America*, September 1966.

[17] I. M. D. Little, Tibor Scitovsky, and Maurice FG. Scott, *Industry and Trade in Some Developing Countries* (New York: Oxford University Press, 1970).

[18] D. B. Keesing, "Outward Looking Policies and Economic Development," *Economic Journal*, June 1967.

[19] Little, Scitovsky, and Scott, *Industry and Trade*; and Bela Balassa and others, *The Structure of Protection in Developing Countries* (Baltimore: Johns Hopkins University Press, 1971).

tioning the value of excessive protection and the control regime.[20] From 1954 to 1959, when their advocacy bore fruit, T. C. Liu and T. S. Tsiang argued in Taiwan for a liberal trade regime (neither economist was part of the development establishment). Korea, Singapore, Israel, and, to some extent, Spain and Greece were making successful liberalization moves well before the academic challenge to the controlled trade orthodoxy. And a few countries, such as Lebanon and Malaysia, were never locked into high protection regimes.

At this point, we turn to the massive ten-country study of trade regimes, directed by Jagdish Bhagwati and Anne Krueger. Each entrepreneur-author has summarized different aspects of the studies in separate volumes.[21] They will, I hope, forgive me for doing the same in a few paragraphs.

First, there can be no doubt that the open or relatively open countries have grown faster—faster than when they were less open, and faster than the chronically "closed."[22] The Bhagwati-Krueger countries were Brazil, Chile, Colombia, Egypt, Ghana, India, Israel, the Philippines, Korea, and Turkey, with Israel, Korea, and Brazil the stars (listed in order of the number of years of stardom). How much more conclusive would this be if Taiwan, Hong Kong, and Singapore had been in the list!

The main reasons given for the superior performance of the open countries run somewhat as follows. Exports proved to be highly responsive to the reduction or elimination of the bias against them. The partly consequential increase in imports has reduced the chaos in the pattern of import substitution incentives and has ensured a freer flow of inputs with benefits for capacity utilization and the size of stocks

---

[20] K. Y. Yin, "Adverse Trends in Taiwan's Industrial Development," *Industry of Free China*, August 1954. Yin blamed the "unrealistic foreign exchange rate," "too much reliance on protection," and "manipulation and monopoly." He proposed lifting restrictions on establishment of new factories, auctioning imported raw materials, specifying the period of protection for any industry, and promulgating an antitrust law. It is interesting that he had read James Meade's *Planning and the Price Mechanism* (London: Allen and Unwin, 1948).

[21] Jagdish Bhagwati, *Anatomy and Consequences of Trade Control Regimes* (National Bureau of Economic Research, forthcoming); Anne O. Krueger, *Liberalization Attempts and Consequences* (New York: National Bureau of Economic Research, 1978).

[22] Other works show that, over the range of all LDCs for which figures are available, opening an economy is related to faster growth. See, for example, Michael Michaely, "Exports and Growth," *Journal of Development Economics*, 1977. Michaely finds a positive relationship between changes in the proportion of exports to GNP and growth in GNP. Numerous studies find a positive relation between exports and GNP growth—but these may be criticized on the ground that exports are part of GNP.

held. The greater value of exports has also made it easier to borrow. More direct foreign investment is attracted, and it is attracted to the relatively labor-intensive export sector.

I would put rather more stress than Bhagwati does on the supposition that exports are simply good business for the country.[23] Social (that is, shadow-priced) profits and savings are higher than they are with import substitution at the margin. That restrictive regimes result in more investment in capital-intensive sectors and plants is empirically clear for a number of countries both within and outside the Bhagwati-Krueger ten, and this has implications for the spread of the benefits of growth as well as for growth itself.

Krueger deals primarily with the conditions under which liberalization attempts have been made and with the resultant game of snakes and ladders (almost as many snakes descended as ladders climbed—unfortunately). Twenty-two liberalization efforts are reported for the ten countries between 1950 and 1972—one per annum. All involved packages. Devaluation was combined with import liberalization, reduction of tariffs and export subsidies, and deflation, in varying degrees. In some cases, after allowance was made for the changes in tariffs and subsidies, the effective exchange rate change was very small. Most efforts were made in periods of crisis and from a position of government commitment to an overvalued exchange rate. The crisis usually involved loss of reserves or debt rescheduling but sometimes arose less critically from the fact that the country was plainly import starved, although there was no immediate payments problem. Many efforts were combined with attempts at stabilization.

Of course, if a simple devaluation was to be effective inflation had to be stopped. It was the consequent deflationary measures and the foreign (or IMF or World Bank) involvement that often made these attempts unpopular and resulted in a reversal. It must be remembered that the IMF norm was then a fixed rate. But a floating rate or a sliding peg was used in several countries on and off. Except for Chile, where the sliding peg rate always remained overvalued, greater success was achieved where stopping inflation was not thought a necessary condition for maintaining liberalization. Brazil, Korea, Israel, and Colombia all used either floating rates or sliding pegs or other means of maintaining a reasonable exchange rate for exports, and all had liberalized substan-

---

[23] In some articles, Bhagwati has argued that export promotion has been as higgledy-piggledy as import substitution. This could be true of India, but I doubt that it is true of many others, and I am sure it is far from the truth in the case of Korea, Taiwan, Singapore, and Hong Kong. The argument has, however, been weakened if not suppressed in Bhagwati's summary volume.

tially by the middle or late 1960s and maintained this position—although of the ten only Israel achieved single-figure inflation in the decade. Of the ten, however, only Korea appears to have altogether eliminated the bias against exports.[24]

There are several reasons for failure. The effective devaluation was inadequate, or the bias against exports was not removed nor much reduced (for example, India, the Philippines), so that exports did not respond sufficiently. Inflation and a fixed rate continued or were reimposed (Chile under Allende). There was insufficient political and intellectual commitment (India, Chile) or an actual reversal for political reasons (Ghana) or bad luck (India again). Needless to say, manufacturers require some expectation of continuing profitability for exports if they are to invest for export production, make products designed for export, and spend money on a marketing organization. In only a few countries was the government commitment to the change of policy sufficient for this expectation.

But although failure has been frequent, there has been progress among the ten. The Bhagwati-Krueger phase analysis suggests an increasing degree of liberalization after the mid-1960s. Evidently the manifest inefficiency and other problems to which the control regimes gave rise were driving events, more so than were the challenges of the 1960 generation of economists, described earlier. (Of course one can also exaggerate the effect of an earlier generation; it was events at least as much as thought that established the control regimes.) Whether the new challenge is having an effect will be seen only after the Bhagwati-Krueger period, which ended in 1972.

Bhagwati ends by recalling the debate of 1959 between Ragnar Nurkse and Gottfried Haberler,[25] quoting A. K. Cairncross's typically cautious review: "We know what most countries have done; it would be interesting if we could be told, by an economist of the standing of Nurkse or Haberler, what the results have been and what they should have done."[26] Bhagwati comments, "the results of the present project, as well as the earlier analysis in the well-known OECD project directed by I. M. D. Little, Tibor Scitovsky, and Maurice Scott, do contain

---

[24] Taiwan liberalized successfully with a fixed rate, but its rate of inflation from 1963 to 1973 was less than the world average, and the Taiwanese dollar was probably becoming undervalued as productivity rose rapidly. There was also no bias against exports. The case of Singapore is similar.

[25] Ragnar Nurkse, *Patterns of Trade and Development*, Wicksell Lectures (Stockholm: Almquist and Wicksell, 1959); and Gottfried Haberler, *International Trade and Economic Development* (Cairo: National Bank of Egypt, 1959).

[26] A. K. Cairncross, *Factors in Economic Development* (London: Allen and Unwin, 1960), p. 208.

an answer to Cairncross's celebrated query and it seems to come down in favor of the Export Promotion Strategy."[27] It should be noted that, for reasons best known to himself, Bhagwati means by "an export promotion strategy" one that is neutral between the domestic and export markets.

Balassa has added and will add further relevant evidence in his World Bank studies of "Export Incentives and Export Performance in Developing Countries" and the "Development Strategies of Semi-Industrial Countries." I here draw on his preliminary report,[28] where he discusses Argentina, Brazil, Chile, Colombia, Mexico, Israel, Yugoslavia, India, Korea, Singapore, and Taiwan, and also on two chapters (by myself and Maurice Scott) in a new book on Taiwan.[29] A few major points seem to me to emerge from the addition of a few countries and from still more recent information:

1. Only Korea, Taiwan, and Singapore have created "virtually free trade regimes" for exports. This means, in brief, that exporters can buy not only imports but also domestic inputs at world prices.[30] The home market remains protected in Korea by tariffs and licensing and in Taiwan and Singapore by tariffs.[31] The tariffs, however, are often redundant, the average effective protection of manufactures is low, and exchange rates are not overvalued. There is no significant bias against exports. Taiwan and Singapore are now as much free traders as most developed countries. These three countries sustained GNP growth rates of around 10 percent for as long as a decade prior to 1973—a performance shared only by Israel, Hong Kong, and Japan.

2. Although Israel is fully liberalized, tariffs still result in a significant bias against exports. None of the other countries is fully liberalized, and none has created the free trade regime for exports of Korea, Taiwan, and Singapore (and, of course, Hong Kong). All, however, have made some effort at export promotion. The staggering export performance of the above four hardly bears repetition. The

---

[27] Bhagwati, *Trade Control Regimes*.

[28] Bela Balassa, "Export Incentives and Export Performance in Developing Countries," World Bank Staff Working Paper, no. 248, January 1977, and "Development Strategies of Semi-Industrialized Countries" forthcoming.

[29] W. Galenson, ed., *Economic Growth and Structural Change in Taiwan* (Ithaca, N.Y.: Cornell University Press, forthcoming).

[30] The manner in which this is effected differs among the three countries and need not be described here.

[31] In Taiwan, the only remaining quantitative import restriction on manufactures is on cars (apart, of course, from arms, narcotics, and imports from Communist countries). No doubt the reason for maintaining the restriction on cars is that a tariff which would keep the domestic industry alive would look shamefully high.

manufactured exports of Argentina, Brazil, and Colombia have also grown rapidly, at around 30 percent per annum from 1967 to 1973, but from very low levels—thus, the proportion of manufactured output exported remains very low (in 1973 it was 3.6, 4.4, and 7.5 percent, respectively, compared with 49.9 percent and 40.5 percent for Taiwan and Korea).

3. The highly open economies of Taiwan, Korea, and Hong Kong have all weathered the world recession of 1974–1975 very well, despite their extreme dependence on imported energy. Korea's growth rate never dipped below 8.3 percent. Taiwan's and Hong Kong's were brought below 3 percent, but they have recovered and achieved 11.9 and 16.2 percent in 1976. Despite continued sluggish world demand and increasing protection in many industrialized countries—some of it specifically directed against them—the dollar value of the exports of these three rose by 52.5, 56.2, and 39.4 percent in 1976. The *increase* for Korea in 1976 was about equal to India's total manufactured exports, and as late as 1960 India had still accounted for half the manufactured exports of LDCs.

One thing at least is certain. The more labor-intensive manufactures of the now semiindustrialized countries need no protection. Of course, it will still be argued that the least industrialized countries need considerable promotion of manufactures, if not protection, to get going. This may be true. But need it be very heavy? And need it result in a bias against exports; that is, need it be protective rather than promotional? I would think that these are mistakes that should be avoided. It will also be argued that the semiindustrialized countries will require protection (or promotion) in order to manufacture instruments and machines, which should be their next area of specialization. I would guess that the removal of such disadvantages as overpriced or low-quality domestic steel, the lack of export credit, and so on, plus access to technical assistance and training, might well be enough.

Of course, liberalization and reduced protection cannot achieve for all nations the miracles it has produced for the four Far Eastern countries. Obviously, the speed of the consequential changes in industrialized countries has some limit. But the fact that there is a limit to the degree of market penetration that will be permitted at any one time by the industrialized countries (and even a limit to the size of their markets) should not be regarded as a reason to continue a bias in favor of import substitution. There are still gains to be made by all countries, even if only a few more miracles can be expected.

The developed countries still produce a very high proportion of the labor-intensive manufactures they consume. Clothing imports from

LDCs account for little more than 5 percent of consumption. The range of labor-intensive goods for which there has been any significant market penetration is still quite limited. Yet, for fifteen years the quantity of manufactured exports from LDCs has increased at 15 percent per annum. With reasonable goodwill and appropriate policies on the part of the DCs, this could be maintained for a very long time. Since the growth from Korea, Taiwan, Hong Kong, and Singapore is certain to slow down (they export such a high proportion of their output now that exports must soon asymptotically approach their overall growth rate, which is unlikely to exceed 10 percent), there should be plenty of room for other countries to grow.[32] It must be remembered that these countries are now far from small in manufactured export markets (the *growth* of exports from them in 1976 was about $7 billion).

Furthermore, there is little trade between LDCs, and such trade is greatly inhibited by their own import substitution policies. Of course, this is of secondary importance because the LDC market is so much smaller than the DC market. Its importance is increasing, however, because LDC markets for tradables are growing faster than those of the DCs. Regional trading arrangements are very much a second-best solution, and they are difficult to negotiate. General liberalization and reduced protection can do far more, and with far less fuss and use of scarce administrative talent. Yet, organized and controlled regional trading remains the conventional wisdom of LDC leaders when their own intratrade is under discussion.

I have focused on manufactures, but it also seems likely that considerable gains could result from more intratrade in agricultural products and even minerals, although this seems to have been relatively little studied. At any rate, there is no doubt that liberal trade regimes would help even if exports did not increase greatly. All the benefits arising from greater use of the price mechanism—the reduction in administration, in delays, in stocks, in corruption, and the increase in competition—accrue in any case.

The present decade has seen a recrudescence of attacks on trade and foreign investment, most of them stemming from England. The attack has changed slightly, in that it concentrates now more on the evils of inappropriate technology and its inappropriate products, on the multinationals, and indeed on the transfer of capital in any form—including aid. It is related to the increased emphasis on income distribution and poverty. But trade is involved: it is claimed that trade has harmed the poor in LDCs; if there were no trade, none of the other

---

[32] The importance of this was pointed out to me by Martin Wolf.

alleged evils could result. If the no-trade conclusion is too extreme, then trade and the transfer of technology should be carefully controlled, just as they have been for twenty-five years. Only, I suppose, they should be better controlled.

Fortunately, I need not say much about the multinationals here, as they are covered in another paper. I will make only two assertions. First, the poor (say, the lowest 40 percent) are far better off in countries where there has been a high concentration of foreign enterprise and capital, which in the past largely developed minerals and plantation crops. Compare Malaysia and even Sri Lanka with India and Burma. Compare Libya, Gabon, Iraq, Jamaica, and Trinidad with Benin, Ecuador, Haiti, Ethiopia, Afghanistan, and so on. One can doubt that the former groups would have developed their resources so quickly by themselves. In the long run, of course, many such mineral and plantation investments are, in any event, nationalized with little compensation.[33]

Second, foreign investment in manufacturing has increased greatly. Here the experience of the Far Eastern countries compared with that of Latin America makes it clear that, as one would expect, foreign investment follows the dictates of the market mechanism as it is doctored by the host countries' governments and policies.[34] In Korea and Taiwan, foreign investment has gone into labor-intensive activities; in Latin America, it has gone largely into capital-intensive activities.

This brings us to the attack based on the dominance of foreign technology. Singer now thinks his earlier emphasis on enclaves and the alleged inhibition of industrialization was wrong: the dominance of foreign technology has meant that LDCs gain little from industrialization, that a duality is created here, too, and that the poor do not benefit. "Singer II now would see salvation not in industrialization, but rather in the building up of indigenous scientific and technological capacities."[35] Probably we can all now agree that industrialization has been too capital intensive and that dual labor markets have been reinforced, even if not created. But anyone who sees foreign technology as the chief cause is wearing blinkers.

---

[33] It has been estimated that in the 1956–1972 period nationalization of foreign assets was about 25 percent of the stock at the end of the period and that compensation was 40 percent of the book value of assets. See M. L. Williams, "The Extent and Significance of the Nationalization of Foreign-Owned Assets in Developing Countries, 1956–62," Oxford Economic Papers, July 1975.

[34] In practice, the host country often first decides it wants a plant and then doctors the price mechanism to suit.

[35] "The Distribution of Gains Revisited, IDS May 1971," published in H. W. Singer, *The Strategy of International Development* (New York: International Arts and Sciences Press, 1975).

PART FOUR: TRADE POLICIES

The Far Eastern countries have shown that a highly labor-intensive development is possible using almost entirely (inappropriate) foreign technology. Korea and Taiwan have very little indigenous technology and very low capital-labor and capital-output ratios. India and Brazil have much more scientific and technological capacity and very high capital-output and capital-labor ratios. They have avoided the extremes of industrial duality because they have traded furiously. The desire to point the finger at the foreigners for any failure, instead of looking at national policies, is at the heart of the matter. The advice implicit in Singer's paper (and in that of K. B. Griffin and others) is to forswear trade until scientific and technical expertise is equalized (and indeed until wealth is equalized—for, in general, trade between "unequal partners" is held to create inequality and even absolute impoverishment).[36] I can think of nothing more disastrous for the poor of the world.

The technology argument for suppressing or controlling trade has been embellished by Griffin.[37] He claims that growth in DCs depends largely on increases in primary factor productivity and that growth in LDCs depends almost entirely on capital and labor growth.

This result is arrived at by examining a collection of Denison-type analyses of growth and finding that the average residual is much larger for developed countries. One's confidence is shaken, however, by the fact that "growth in output attributable to growth in factor productivity" was *minus* 43 percent in Argentina (1955–1964) and negative also in Venezuela, Ghana, India, Sri Lanka, and Malaysia (1950–1965). Most of the developing country analyses come from Angus Maddison, who with slightly greater plausibility attributed the residuals to policy differences.[38] The main point, however, is that capital additions in LDCs not only incorporate technical change but probably incorporate it to a greater extent than in DCs because of the technical gap.

In Griffin's analysis, rapid technical change in DCs causes rapid changes in comparative advantage in LDCs, leaving factors unemployed as a result of their immobility. This is not a situation I can recognize among primary products in the post–World War II world. Synthetic fibers have not, in general, resulted in actual declines in the output of the natural competitors—only in slow growth in some instances. Nor

---

[36] No advice on how to trade or not to trade is made explicit by these authors or by most of the radical challengers.

[37] K. B. Griffin, "The International Transmission of Inequality," *World Development*, vol. 2, no. 3 (March 1974).

[38] Angus Maddison, *Economic Progress and Policy in Developing Countries* (London: Allen and Unwin, 1970).

can I recognize this situation in the industrial sphere. Wigs went out of production in Hong Kong, but this was due partly to fashion and partly to lower wages in Korea. Moreover, labor mobility was very high. Although the opposite is constantly repeated, I myself would think that labor is in general more mobile in developing countries than in the rich countries. This is not to say that grave problems have not resulted in the past from changing comparative advantage—the Northeast of Brazil is, perhaps, the worst example. But I do not think that rapid technical change, which supposedly resulted from elevated expenditure in recent decades on research conducted almost exclusively in the DCs, has presented severe adjustment problems for LDCs.

How is it that backward countries have grown so rapidly—by 5.6 percent in 1960–1965 and 6.0 percent in 1965–1973?[39] Within these averages, half a dozen countries have grown, without special benefit from minerals, at rates that would have been deemed inconceivable twenty years ago. The industrialized countries do not grow at this rate, nor do the centrally planned economies.[40] With all their technology, only one, Japan, has ever achieved even half the growth rate of the half-dozen LDC leaders. And for nearly a hundred years Japan's high growth was based primarily on foreign technology, designed for countries with higher wage levels. I suggest that the basic reason is plain. By fair means or foul, cheaply or expensively, the LDCs have been importing technology. The result, *pace* Mr. Griffin, is technical change. Although this technology is relatively inappropriate—and no one can be against making technology more appropriate—this should not blind one to the fact that foreign technology can and has produced miracles, not only in the agricultural and industrial spheres but also in the health sector.

We can all agree that the poor in LDCs have not benefited from growth as much as could be desired. But the claim that the mass of the poor (the lowest 40 percent) has not benefited at all is rhetoric. Even in Brazil, where income distribution is especially unequal and where inequality increased with fast growth, it is clear that the poorest 40 percent have benefited.[41] The benefits might have been greater if Brazil's development had been less dominated by import substitution and if its policies had been more conducive to labor intensity. In the more open, fast-growing economies in the Far East, the standard of living of the

---

[39] World Bank, *World Tables, 1976.*
[40] Ibid.
[41] See E. L. Bacha and Lance Taylor, "Brazilian Income Distribution in the 1960s: 'Facts,' Model Results, and the Controversy," mimeographed, World Bank Workshop, Bellagio, April 1977.

relatively poor has been revolutionized in a period of fifteen years. If one wants to look for millions who have scarcely benefited, or who have even lost out in the postwar period, there can be little doubt that one would find them most easily in the slow-growing, low-trading countries, principally South Asia and the Sahel. To attribute this primarily to foreign technology is the greatest absurdity.

Griffin, having established to his satisfaction the theory that growth in LDCs is due to increased quantities of capital and labor and not to technical change, suggests that trade impoverishes LDCs because it results in a drain of scarce capital—both human and financial—from LDCs to DCs. This is presented as being contrary to economic theory.

The brain drain is, of course, a problem, but it conforms with economic theory that says people tend to go where they earn most. It arises because, if skilled people were paid their worth, the inequality in many LDCs would appear too glaring. If their productivity is not higher than their earnings, there is, prima facie, no loss to the LDCs. To assess the net loss from human capital movements, one has to put in the balance such factors as these: (1) many of the skills are acquired in DCs, often with the latter's assistance; (2) skilled people are provided by the DCs; (3) remittances are made; (4) some skills have been overprovided in LDCs (for example, engineers in India); (5) some emigrants are not wanted in their own countries. I think also that the brain-drain figures have to be put in the context of total emigration—for instance, relatively skilled adults comprise about one-twentieth of the total legal immigration into the United States (about 200,000 out of 4 million from 1962 to 1971)—and in the context of the approximately 3 million migrant LDC workers in the EEC (not including those from Spain, Greece, and Portugal).

It is when it comes to the nonhuman capital drain that the argument is hardest to follow. Savings, Griffin says, flow from poor countries to rich ones.[42] Some figures follow, however, that make no attempt to establish the facts. I need not go into this. The truth is that there is and has been for a century, even apart from official aid, a net flow of savings from developed to developing countries, despite expropriation,

---

[42] This seems to go beyond even the "suction pump" thesis, which argues that, if total dividends and interest come to exceed the current flow of new capital, then resources are being drained from developing countries. In a balance of payments sense, this would be true, of course (actually there was still a net transfer of about $20 billion in 1975). But this has nothing to do with whether the host benefits (or even with the balance of payments effect—though this is the wrong question to pose). One might as well argue that no one can ever benefit from a loan, except by default. On this, see, for example, G. C. Hufbauer, "The Multinational Corporation and Direct Investment," in P. B. Kenen, *International Trade*.

political uncertainty, some reverse capital flight, and radical protest. Of course, capital flow to LDCs cannot occur without trade. And with trade, and despite almost universal exchange control, some illegal reverse flow is certain. But as far as I know, before 1973 no one put a higher figure on this than a few billion dollars, a reasonably small fraction of the recorded flow to developing countries. Naturally, after 1973, the position has been different with the oil exporters' investment—some long-term, but mostly short-term—in developed countries. But the argument, in any case, was that savings flow from poor to rich—not from "developing" countries to developed.

Finally, there is the neo-Marxist argument of "unequal exchange." A. Emmanuel of the University of Paris has claimed to refute Ricardo and show that, with introduction of profit, a poor, low-wage/high-profit country will suffer a reduction in real wages as a result of trade (which also equalizes profit rates) with a high-wage/low-profit country. This is not merely counterintuitive; it has been shown to be necessarily wrong by Paul Samuelson, using Emmanuel's own assumptions.[43] In another article, Samuelson has shown—apparently to the temporary satisfaction of some Marxists—that, in a time-phased system, perverse specialization can in theory occur with competitive international trade, even with equal profit rates; but although the world is then stuck in a relatively low-level stationary state (or "golden" age), it cannot move to a superior state without passing through a period in which at least one country would necessarily lose. Therefore, when all time periods are taken into consideration, the low-level state is Pareto-optimal. Assuming unequal profit rates, Samuelson shows that a low-level stationary state is possible that is not Pareto-optimal—but international capital movement would then permit the transition to a Pareto-optimal world.[44] One might add that possibility does not imply probability.

I do not think that the kinds of challenges outlined above, prevalent since 1968, have much effect on leaders in the developing world, since such challenges violate common sense. Even the hatred and fear of the multinational, and the feeling of being "dominated," seem to be dying down, as developing countries come to realize their strength. The trend appears to be favorable and should be reinforced by greater familiarity with fluctuating exchange rates. Many countries in Latin America

[43] Paul A. Samuelson, "Illogic of Neo-Marxian Doctrine of Unequal Exchange," in *Inflation, Trade, and Taxes: Essays in Honor of Alice Bourneuf* (Columbus: Ohio State University Press, 1976).

[44] Paul Samuelson, "Trade Pattern Reversals in Time-Phased Ricardian Systems and Intertemporal Efficiency," *Journal of International Economics*, November 1975.

are trying to struggle out of the excessive import substitution trap in which they have landed. The problem is that change takes many years if it is to be relatively painless for all. At the same time, potential exporters need confidence that exports will remain profitable, and this in turn requires confidence that a government committed to change will remain in power. The tragedy is that, elsewhere, a number of countries, especially in Africa, seem to be falling into the old trap of anything goes, provided it is import substitution.

The greater challenge is from those who, like Paul Streeten, encourage "enlightened discrimination" in regard to trade and the acceptance of foreign capital and technology.[45] Of course, such a position always puts the critic at some disadvantage, because he seldom wants to advocate laissez faire, and the policies described will usually contain some elements that he would himself advocate—for example, export taxes or hard case-by-case bargaining in the case of mineral exploitation. Nevertheless, the picture of "enlightened discrimination" drawn by Streeten seems to me to come too close to Indian policy over the past twenty years, and too close to maximum surveillance and control, for it to be likely to do anything but retard growth without any offsetting benefit. There is a mass of evidence, in works already cited and elsewhere, that discrimination is seldom very enlightened.

The pessimists are wrong. The developing world has, with some black spots, done remarkably well. But both a priori reasoning and the experience of the past quarter of this century strongly suggest that with less controlled trading policies, and with a somewhat lower degree of encouragement of industrialization than prevalent in most LDCs, in the form of promotion rather than protection, progress would have been still faster and the quality of growth would have been higher. There is good reason to suppose that there are still many opportunities for socially profitable trading. The presently increasing protection in DCs —and pessimism as to its course—may do far more harm than is likely to be justified by its actual incidence. It is already creating new ripples, if not waves, of export pessimism in LDCs.

---

[45] See Paul Streeten, "Changing Perceptions of Development," *Finance and Development*, September 1977.

The New Protectionism: An Evaluation and Proposals for Reform

Bela Balassa

The postwar period saw a rapid growth of world trade. This expansion, in turn, contributed to economic growth in developed and developing countries alike. For one thing, export expansion favorably affected the growth performance of the developed nations. For another, economic growth in the developed nations was transmitted to the developing countries through trade and provided opportunities to these countries for successfully carrying out export-oriented policies.

These developments occurred in an atmosphere marked by progressive trade liberalization on the part of the developed nations and by the adoption of export-oriented policies, accompanied by reduced protection, in several developing countries. The atmosphere was marred only by the imposition of quantitative import restrictions, pertaining chiefly to Japanese exports, and by the adoption of the Long Term Arrangement Regarding International Trade in Cotton Textiles and, subsequently, the Multi-Fiber Arrangement. Nevertheless, the MFA provided for an annual growth of 6 percent in the exports of textiles and clothing and, as a result of increases in their quota allocation and upgrading of their export products, the developing countries' exports of textiles and clothing rose substantially faster.[1]

The opinions expressed in this paper are those of the author and should not be interpreted as reflecting the views of the World Bank. Some of the ideas underlying the paper were first presented at this conference. Subsequently, the paper was presented at a seminar on "The Role of World Trade in the Present Economic Situation," sponsored by the Instituto Bancario San Paolo di Torino and held in Milan on March 31, 1978. The author is indebted to participants at the seminar for helpful discussions and to Geza Feketekuty, Nicholas Pless, and Jan Tumlir for valuable comments. He is further indebted to Kishore Nadkarni for preparing the statistical data. This is a somewhat abbreviated version of the paper published in the September 1978 issue of the *Journal of World Trade Law* under the title, "The 'New Protectionism' and the International Economy." The *Journal of World Trade Law* kindly gave permission for the use of published material.

[1] D. B. Keesing, "World Trade and Output of Manufactures: Structural Trends and Developing Countries' Exports" (Washington, D.C.: World Bank, February 1978).

PART FOUR: TRADE POLICIES

The situation changed as the quadrupling of oil prices aggravated the recession that followed the 1972–1973 world economic boom. In adding to inflationary pressures, the oil price increase led to stronger antiinflationary measures on the part of the developed countries than otherwise would have been the case. The recession was further aggravated by policy reactions on the part of the developed countries to the increase in their combined balance of trade deficit vis-à-vis OPEC from $17.2 billion in 1973 to $66.6 billion in 1974.[2] And, while the United States has maintained a steady rate of expansion since mid-1975 without regard to its balance of payments consequences, in the other developed countries the desire to lower inflation rates or to reduce balance of payments deficits has not permitted economic expansion to proceed at a rate approaching capacity growth following the recession. As a result, unemployment has continued to increase in Western Europe and Japan, while it has not yet declined to pre-1973 levels in the United States.

High unemployment and unused capacity in a number of industries of the developed countries have contributed to the emergence of protectionist pressures, which were intensified by reason of the continued existence of trade deficits in most developed countries. The protectionist measures proposed and actually applied, if not the extent of their application, have a certain resemblance to those observed during the depression of the 1930s.[3] They may be subsumed under the heading, "new protectionism," and they include various forms of nontariff restrictions on trade, government aids under the aegis of the "rationalization of industry," and attempts to establish worldwide market-sharing arrangements.

This paper will first examine the practical application of the measures of the new protectionism in the developed countries. This will be followed by an evaluation of the effects of the measures applied, with further consideration given to the employment argument for protection. Finally, recommendations will be made on the national and international policies that would need to be followed to redress the situation and to ensure rapid growth in the world economy.

The Emergence of the New Protectionism

Nontariff Restrictions. As noted above, the Multi-Fiber Arrangement, the principal case outside agriculture where nontariff measures were applied prior to the oil crisis, provided for a 6 percent annual rate of

---

[2] United Nations, *Monthly Bulletin of Statistics*, August 1976.
[3] On this point, see Jan Tumlir, herein.

growth in the textiles and clothing exports of the individual countries. The new agreement, pertaining to the 1978–1982 period, is more restrictive. While notionally setting a 6 percent annual rate of growth for the exporting countries in the aggregate, it leaves considerable scope for the importing countries to set lower limits through bilateral negotiations.

In fact, the European Common Market that forced the adoption of the revised rules at the behest of France and the United Kingdom has required that the largest developing country exporters reduce their 1978 exports of textiles and clothing to the EEC to below the 1976 level (the relevant figures are −9 percent for Hong Kong, −7 percent for Korea, and −25 percent for Taiwan). Although better overall terms are provided to very poor countries, the total imports of eight sensitive products, accounting for 62 percent of EEC imports of textiles and clothing from developing countries, will decline below the 1976 level in 1978 and will increase slowly afterward, with growth rates in the 1978–1982 period ranging from 0.3 percent a year for cotton yarn to 4.1 percent a year for sweaters.[4] Import growth rates were also set at less than 6 percent a year for another important group of clothing products, so that the rate of growth of the imports of textiles and clothing into the EEC will remain much below 6 percent.

The United States reached agreements with Hong Kong, Korea, and Taiwan to freeze their 1978 exports of textiles and clothing to the United States at the 1977 level and to increase the exports of a number of sensitive items, accounting for about 70 percent of exports in the case of Korea, at a rate substantially less than 6 percent afterward. If further account is taken of bilateral agreements negotiated with other countries, it is apparent that the 6 percent annual rate of growth of the imports of textiles and clothing under the MFA will not be attained in the United States either.

In regard to steel, the European Common Market established guideline prices for five product groups and a mandatory minimum price for reinforcing bars in 1976. As of January 1978, basic or reference prices were set for all products based on the lowest foreign (namely, Japanese) production costs adjusted for transport costs. Imports below the reference price come under antidumping rules, with a levy imposed in the amount of the price difference. This scheme is assumed to be temporary, to be replaced by bilateral agreements negotiated with steel-exporting countries. The EEC Commission has since negotiated agreements with some twenty countries to accept the same share in the EEC

---

[4] *Economist*, December 24, 1977.

market in 1978 as they had in 1976,[5] implying an average cut in steel imports by 8 percent from the 1977 level. The cuts would be larger for the new developing country exporters that increased their steel exports to a considerable extent between 1976 and 1977.

In establishing reference prices for steel, the EEC Commission drew on the U.S. Solomon plan that came into effect in February 1978. Under the plan, the reference or trigger prices have been set on the basis of assumed Japanese production costs and the cost of shipping to U.S. markets. Correspondingly, the reference prices rise, and the chance of effective import competition declines, as one moves from West to East.[6]

The adoption of import restrictions in regard to textiles and steel is a manifestation of protectionist tendencies that have emerged in recent years. In the United States, the practical application of the provisions of the 1974 Trade Act also points in this direction. Under the act, the U.S. Treasury has to reach a decision within one year after petitions are filed requesting the imposition of countervailing duties on exports that are allegedly subsidized by foreign countries, and countervailing action has been extended to duty-free imports, including those entering under the generalized preference scheme. In turn, dumping has been redefined as selling at less than full production cost, including a margin for profit, rather than at less than the domestic sales price as beforehand.

The Trade Act has also weakened the conditions for escape-clause action by requiring only that imports be "a substantial cause of serious injury, or the threat thereof," while previously such action could be taken only if imports were the "major cause" of serious injury *and* if the increase in imports causing or threatening the injury was the result of previous trade concessions. Furthermore, orderly marketing agreements, representing negotiated restrictions on exports to the United States, have been added to the arsenal of protectionist measures. Finally, the two houses of Congress can overrule the president if he rejects recommendations made by the International Trade Commission on antidumping and escape-clause action.

While the Trade Act of 1974 has also liberalized the conditions for granting adjustment assistance to domestic industries adversely affected by imports, it provides possibilities for the use of protective measures that have come to be increasingly utilized. To begin with, there has been a substantial increase in positive findings in countervailing duty cases— thirty-four positive findings in 1974–1977 as compared with thirteen in

---

[5] *Economist*, May 13, 1978.
[6] *Wall Street Journal*, February 23, 1978.

the preceding eleven years. And, in at least one case, the criteria for imposing countervailing duties have been modified to the detriment of foreign exporters.[7] The Treasury plans even stricter enforcement in the future, although in many developing countries subsidy measures compensate only for the effects of domestic protection.

The number of antidumping cases has also increased since 1974, and the recent interpretation of production costs in the exporting countries is likely to give impetus to further increases. Thus, the Treasury has established a formula for steel based on the "constructed value" of Japanese production costs plus an arbitrary markup of 10 percent for general expenses and another 8 percent for profits, both of which are much above the industry average.[8]

At the same time, the International Trade Commission has become active in its investigation of complaints that imports are harming domestic industries—even when this involves encroaching on the territory of other governmental organizations.[9] The ITC issued forty-two decisions in 1976 as compared with fifteen in 1975, with the amount of imports affected rising from $248 million in 1975 to $1.9 billion in 1976 and surpassing $5 billion in 1977.[10] Finally, although President Carter overruled ITC recommendations in several cases, some important decisions have favored protectionist interests.

Apart from steel and textiles, particular instances are orderly marketing agreements with Japan on color television sets and with Korea and Taiwan on footwear, both in 1977. In the first case, imports were limited to 1.75 million sets a year until 1980, representing a 40 percent reduction from the 1976 level. In the second case, import limitations apply until 1981 and, despite annual increases in quotas, the 1976 level would not be reached by the end of the four-year period of the agreement. The application of protectionist measures in these well-

---

[7] The Treasury has countervailed the imports of bromide and bromide products from Israel that benefit from regional aids, although only 3 percent of total production is exported to the United States.

[8] *Business Week*, November 14, 1977.

[9] It has been reported, for example, that the ITC found the Japanese steel producers guilty of "predatory pricing," which has been defined similarly to dumping violations that are ruled on by the Treasury (*Washington Post*, January 15, 1978). It has also been reported that the White House objected to the ITC negotiating consent orders between domestic and foreign color TV makers on its own initiative (*Wall Street Journal*, November 25, 1977). Note further that the message from the chairman, introducing the 1976 report of the ITC, speaks of "an innovative approach to our substantive and administrative duties and . . . considerable progress in meeting the objectives which the Commission had set as a result of its increased role in international trade."

[10] *Wall Street Journal*, November 25, 1977.

publicized cases has, in turn, contributed to demands for protection in industries such as citizen band radios, electric ovens, railroad equipment, bicycle tires and tubes, copper, and zinc; among these, tariffs have already been increased on citizen band radios.

The taking of protectionist measures by the Carter administration has been rationalized on the ground that they help to forestall more drastic action by Congress. At the same time, according to the *Wall Street Journal* (December 29, 1977), "the sentiment in Congress for protectionism is rising again." This reflects increased protectionist pressures emanating largely from labor, with labor and industry joining forces whenever they perceive a common interest.[11]

It should be emphasized that, whatever the outcome, protectionist demands create uncertainty for exporters. Thus, demands for countervailing or antidumping action may induce foreign producers to limit exports to the United States, because they fear a financial loss in the form of additional duties for which they have to put up a bond.[12] More generally, even if they ultimately prove unsuccessful, protectionist demands are reportedly initiated in the expectation that foreign producers will cut back their expansion plans for the U.S. market.[13]

Protectionist pressures have also increased in Western Europe, particularly in Britain and France. In Britain, the Cambridge Group has provided theoretical justification for the protectionist attitude taken by the Labour government,[14] while in France protectionism has political backing from the Right as well as from the Left. Notwithstanding the

---

[11] "Although organized labor lost its last big fight for import protection only three years ago [when the Burke-Hartke bill went down in defeat], AFL-CIO officials say that much has changed since then. The steel, electronics, shoe, textile, and apparel industries have been badly hurt by imports, unemployment has soared, and multinational operations have suffered a black eye for overseas bribery. The 'new reality,' says a union economist, is that the public no longer perceives protectionism as a bad thing" (*Business Week*, December 26, 1977).

In response to pressures, the House of Representatives has organized a 150-member steel caucus and a 229-member fiber caucus to defend the interests of the steel and textile industries (*Wall Street Journal*, December 29, 1977). More recently, in a joint appeal, business and labor "called on the Carter Administration and Congress to take 'strong and immediate' action to counteract a 'stunning increase' in textile, apparel and fiber imports" (*Washington Post*, June 30, 1978).

[12] A case in point is the imposition of antidumping duties amounting to $46 million in March 1978 on Japanese-made television sets imported in 1972 and 1973.

[13] An example of apparent harassment of foreign exporters is the simultaneous initiation of countervailing, antidumping, and escape-clause action against imports of bicycle tires and tubes from Korea.

[14] See *Le Monde*, April 4, 1978; and *Wall Street Journal*, April 24, 1978.

generally liberal attitudes in Germany and Italy,[15] the position taken by these two countries has apparently greatly influenced the Common Market Commission, as evidenced by the imposition of strict limits on the importation of textiles and clothing as well as by increased reliance on countervailing and antidumping legislation.[16]

At the same time, while the application of protectionist measures in the United States is circumscribed by legislation, in Western Europe as well as in Japan protectionism often takes the form of discretionary measures by national governments. Such "occult" measures, which do not find their origin in legislation, present a particular danger for foreign countries, and especially for developing countries, both because legal recourse is lacking and because they create additional uncertainty.

Limiting attention to protectionist measures actually taken by the industrial countries, one may cite an estimate by the GATT secretariat, according to which the application of these measures over the last two years has led to restrictions on 3 to 5 percent of world trade flows, amounting to $30–50 billion a year.[17] Reference may further be made to a list prepared by the Taiwanese government on restrictions affecting manufactured exports. The list includes one item for 1975, nine items for 1976, and thirty-three items for 1977, of which seven are still under investigation.

Government Aids to Industry. Prior to the oil crisis, government aids were principally used in the major European countries as well as in the United States in favor of the shipbuilding industry. Furthermore, regional aids provided in Western Europe benefited certain industries concentrated in depressed regions.

Government aids, often granted under the heading of "rationalization," have come into greater use since the 1974–1975 recession. They take a variety of forms, including direct subsidies as well as preferential tax and credit treatment. These aids provide indirect protection to domestic industry by reducing its production or sales costs.

The German government provides 75 to 90 percent of the difference between the full-time wage and the wage earned by workers who had to be put on a part-time basis because of unfavorable business conditions. This scheme subsidizes weak industries indirectly as they

---

[15] See the favorable reactions in the Italian press to the author's speech on the new protectionism on March 31, 1978.

[16] *Economist* (December 24, 1977) reports on the increasing number of anti-dumping cases in the EEC and the increase in the "Commission's antidumping staff from three to 10 to cope with the burgeoning work load."

[17] *New York Times*, September 23, 1977.

are likely to have proportionately more part-time workers. In turn, other European countries have directly or indirectly subsidized employment. These measures, together with the introduction of regulations making it difficult to fire workers, have contributed to labor hoarding.

A case in point is the British Temporary Employment Subsidy Scheme that compensates firms for keeping workers on the job who would otherwise be no longer needed. In 1977, about half the benefits under this scheme accrued to textiles, clothing, and footwear industries that reportedly received a subsidy equivalent to about 5–10 percent of their total production cost. At the same time, as the *Economist* (January 14, 1978) notes, little effort has been made to put pressure on subsidized companies to rationalize their operations. It would appear, then, that the subsidy provides an additional protection to the three industries without contributing to adjustment.

While employment schemes are not industry specific, they tend to benefit labor-intensive industries which have higher than average unemployment rates. In several countries, government aids have also been provided to specific industries. In France, for example, the automobile, data-processing, pulp and paper, steel, and watch industries have received various forms of government aid. Whatever their avowed purpose, these aids will shore up, and hence protect, weak industries that find it difficult to face foreign competition. The takeover of insolvent firms by the government and the financing of their deficits as well as the deficits of other state-owned firms from public funds have had similar effect in Italy.

Government aids applied by the individual Common Market countries discriminate against imports from member as well as from nonmember countries. In turn, several actions have been proposed, or have actually been taken, on the Common Market level. To begin with, the EEC steel industry has a legalized cartel, Eurofer, which ensures compliance with minimum prices and also sets quotas for market sharing among producers. Furthermore, the Common Market has provided financial aid to the steel industry under the treaty establishing the Coal and Steel Community; the regional fund will reportedly be doubled between 1974 and 1981, in large part to provide assistance to the steel industry; and the EEC Commission is preparing a sectoral policy for steel.

The Common Market countries have also taken, or contemplate, joint action on shipbuilding and synthetic fibers. For one thing, the EEC Commission has demanded that Japan cut back its exports of ships, and proposals have been made for establishing a credit scheme aimed at financing domestic shipbuilding. For another thing, a proposal has been made to establish a production cartel for synthetic fibers, and "a common market plan to ease the financial pain of redundancies" is reportedly in preparation.[18]

Apart from shipbuilding, where subsidies have long been used, the United States will aid the domestic steel industry under the Solomon plan, using a variety of measures including loan guarantees, accelerated depreciation provisions, and subsidies for research. Several export promotion measures are also reportedly under consideration.[19]

In Japan, a bill containing special measures for aiding certain industries in difficulty was introduced in February 1978. Its aim is to provide assistance to the aluminum, shipbuilding, steel, and synthetic fiber industries, formalizing and extending aids that have been provided in the past. Its application may also be extended to other industries, some of which have been beneficiaries of government assistance in the past.[20]

International Cartels and Market Sharing. While government aids under the guise of the rationalization of domestic industries have led to moves aimed at cartelization in the steel, shipbuilding, and synthetic fiber industries in the European Common Market, suggestions have further been made for cartelization on the world level. In this connection, reference may be made to calls by Raymond Barre, the French prime minister, "to define collective rules for an orderly growth of international trade" in the framework of "a genuine organization of international trade" and "organized liberalism."[21] It has been proposed that the definition of "collectively defined and applied rules that will generate conditions for growth security and dependability in trade . . . should be

---

[18] *Economist*, October 15 and December 31, 1977.

[19] According to the *New York Times* (April 2, 1978), these include "fast write-offs when companies develop new facilities to serve export markets, tax credits for those that establish foreign sales offices, a new tax program on exports tailored principally for medium-sized companies, a system of information-exchange to promote greater exports, a Government loan program for companies that introduce a new product line for exports, and a beefed-up operation (in money and personnel) for the existing Commerce State export-development activities."

[20] It has been reported, for example, that "when the fast-growing computer firms in Japan began to have difficulties with their cash flow situation, the Japanese government organized a leasing company to buy computers and handle the leasing, thus providing a fast injection of cash and reducing the ongoing capital burden" (H. B. Malmgren, *International Order for Public Subsidies*, Thames Essay, no. 11 [London: Trade Policy Research Centre, 1977], p. 24).

[21] Raymond Barre, in a statement made at the National Press Club, Washington, September 16, 1977, and quoted in the press release of the French embassy; Foreign Trade Minister André Rossi in *Le Monde*, July 27, 1977; and Raymond Barre in *Journal de Genève*, September 15, 1977.

one of the main objectives of the international negotiations to be held in the coming months; they must not simply repeat the negotiations of the last twenty years.[22] Negotiations on the organization of international trade would cover a variety of industries, including steel and shipbuilding, that have experienced worldwide overcapacity; some sophisticated industries, such as aircraft and computers, where the United States is in a particularly strong position and infant-industry arguments are invoked in favor of European producers; as well as industries such as textiles, shoes, and electronics, where competition from developing countries and Japan is feared.[23]

The French government proposals may have aimed at taking the wind out of the sails of the domestic opposition, and they have not been voiced since the parliamentary elections held in March 1978, but moves toward the establishment of worldwide cartels have been made in the shipbuilding and steel industries. In the shipbuilding industry, market-sharing arrangements have been proposed in the framework of the OECD that would entail a division of new orders between the European countries, Japan, and the developing countries, together with increases in the prices charged by Japanese producers.[24] In the steel industry, earlier reports that a steel working group established in the framework of the OECD is "planning to unveil a model for an international system to monitor prices, trade, and structural changes in steel industries in the member countries [that] could provide the basis for 'sectoral' talks on steel"[25] have been given credence by meetings of U.S., Common Market, and Japanese officials allegedly aiming to establish a "world steel agreement."[26]

---

[22] *Journal de Genève*, September 15, 1977. As noted above, the negotiations of the last twenty years have led to a considerable expansion of trade and economic growth through trade.

[23] According to Raymond Barre, "when a country develops a sector that is indispensable to the structural equilibrium of its economy but unable to meet normal competition until it reaches a sufficient size, that country may rightfully take such steps as are necessary to protect this activity from being destroyed while it is vulnerable."

He further said: "France cannot allow international competition to develop under conditions that would throw its economic structures into confusion, bring about the sudden collapse of whole sections of its industry or agriculture, put thousands of workers out of work, and jeopardize its independence by eliminating essential activities." Ibid.

[24] *Business Week*, December 5, 1977.

[25] *Business Week*, November 28, 1977.

[26] *Economist*, April 29, 1978.

The New Protectionism

Effects of Protectionist Measures. As noted above, the new protectionism that has emerged in the developed countries since the oil crisis and the 1974–1975 recession is characterized by the employment of nontariff restrictions on trade and the granting of government aids to domestic industries, with further attempts to organize world trade. This contrasts with the "old protectionism," which involves placing reliance primarily on tariffs. Various considerations indicate the superiority of tariffs over the measures employed, or proposed, under the aegis of the new protectionism.

To begin with, tariffs are instruments of the market economy. Consumers make a choice between domestic and imported goods and among alternative foreign suppliers on the basis of price, quality, delivery dates, and other product characteristics, and domestic as well as foreign producers compete in the market without government interference or quantitative limitations. Also, tariffs do not inhibit shifts in trade patterns in response to changes in comparative advantage that are reflected by changes in relative costs.

In turn, nontariff measures interfere with the operation of the market mechanism by restricting consumer choice and limiting competition between domestic and foreign producers. The use of nontariff measures also involves administrative discretion that introduces arbitrariness in the decision-making process, when the decisions actually taken are affected by the relative power position of various groups. Since consumer groups generally have less influence on decision making than pressure groups representing various segments of labor and business, the new protectionism involves a bias toward restrictive measures.

At the same time, limiting imports in quantitative terms increases the market power of domestic producers and thus enables them to raise prices when restrictions applied to raw materials and intermediate products spread forward as users seek to offset the higher prices of their inputs.[27] Incentives for improvements in productivity are reduced as a result, and there is a tendency to freeze production patterns, thereby obstructing changes in international specialization according to shifts in comparative advantage.

---

[27] These conclusions also apply to the use of reference prices as an instrument to limit imports, as evidenced by the 5.5 percent increase in trigger prices on steel as of July 1, 1978, and the demands for the imposition of trigger prices on wire products in the United States. It has been suggested that steel-using industries will also request increased protection, since "distortions arising in steel affect the international competitive position of all steel users—from producers of nuts and bolts to manufacturers of sophisticated machinery" (*New York Times*, May 11, 1978).

PART FOUR: TRADE POLICIES

Quantitative limitations on trade interfere with the market mechanism in the exporting countries, too. With allowed exports falling short of the amount producers would like to sell at the going price, they may collude, or the government may apportion among them the amount that can be exported. This, in turn, may entail discriminatory pricing, with higher prices charged in export than in domestic markets. Foreign firms may also attempt to evade the restrictions through additional processing (steel, for example), changing the basic material used (textiles), or shifting the place of production to countries that enjoy preferential treatment (television sets).

Apportioning quotas among exporting countries also involves interference with the market mechanism. Maintaining historical market shares in the allocation process discriminates against new exporters, and changing market shares is subject to discretionary decision making. At the same time, the decisions taken will be influenced by the bargaining power of the importing country and the actual and potential exporters, respectively, generally favoring large countries over small ones.

In cases where both parties can inflict damage, the possibility of retaliation will arise. An example is Australia's threat of an embargo on uranium in retaliation to European restrictions on steel imports. A retaliatory motive is also apparent in the imposition of antidumping duties by the Common Market on kraft liner imported from the United States in early 1978; the United States had used similar measures against European steel products.

There is the further danger of a cumulative process. Thus, while George Meany, the secretary-general of the AFL-CIO, called for "fair trade—do unto others as they do to us, barrier for barrier, closed door for closed door,"[28] measures taken by the United States in response to alleged offenses by others are bound to elicit foreign reactions. Apart from retaliation, some form of imitative action may be taken, as in the case of the imposition of trigger prices in the framework of the so-called Davignon plan for the Common Market steel industry.

International trade is also affected by government aids to domestic industry, which have come into increased use in recent years. Apart from distorting competition among firms located in different countries, such aid represents a further increase in the role of the state in economic life and extends the scope of bargaining. Thus, the government may wish to obtain a quid pro quo for its aid in the form of stipulated levels of employment, regional allocation of production, and so on. At the same time, within particular industries inducements are provided for collusive

---

[28] *Business Week*, December 26, 1977.

action to divide up the "spoils" and to increase bargaining power vis-à-vis the government.

Moreover, government aids become the subject of policy competition in the international arena, as has occurred in the case of shipbuilding where, Japan excepted, substantial subsidies have been provided in all producing countries. Policy competition has since been extended to new technologically advanced industries, such as computers and integrated circuits, and, more recently, to some "old" industries, such as steel and textiles.

In addition, implicit subsidies are provided in the form of preferential export credits where policies have not been coordinated, despite efforts to do so. In fact, export promotion measures are coming into increasing use, as evidenced by a statement made by K. H. Beyen, state secretary for economic affairs in the Netherlands: "Rather reluctantly, we have been forced to give a certain amount of assistance to our exporting industry when it is threatened with distortion of competition by measures taken in other countries."[29]

The dangers of policy competition were first recognized by Richard Cooper in the mid-1960s, when such competition existed only in an embryonic form.[30] More recently, Assar Lindbeck pointed to the dangers of the trend toward greater government intervention and policy competition. In Lindbeck's view,

> It could be reasonably argued that future conferences on international trade should perhaps concentrate on reducing various selective subsidies rather than cutting tariffs. That would have the additional advantage of perhaps stopping, or even reversing, the enormous concentration of economic powers to central planning administration and politicians, which is perhaps the major consequence for our societies of selective interventions.[31]

The international organization of trade has been proposed, in part, in order to limit policy competition. It also represents a natural outgrowth of collusive action on the national level, inasmuch as national cartels would have limited power in an international economy characterized by strong trade ties among the countries concerned. Orderly marketing arrangements and other forms of quantitative restrictions,

---

[29] *Barron's*, April 24, 1978.
[30] Richard N. Cooper, *The Economics of Interdependence: Economic Policy in the Atlantic Community* (New York: McGraw-Hill, 1968).
[31] Assar Lindbeck, "Economic Dependence and Interdependence in the Industrialized World," in *From Marshall Plan to Global Interdependence*, Lincoln Gordon, ed. (Paris: OECD, 1978), p. 82.

entailing the division of markets among exporting countries, also gave an impetus to the international organization of trade.

These developments are apparent in the European Common Market, where measures taken on the national level to provide financial aid to particular industries and to limit imports have given rise to cartelization efforts and trade restrictions on the Common Market level. Proposals for cartelization have come from the EEC Commission in the guise of the rationalization of industry as well as from industries that expect to benefit from cartelization. Apart from the shipbuilding, steel, and synthetic fibers industries, such proposals have been put forward in regard to automobiles, chemicals, shoes, and, more recently, zinc, pulp and paper, and even hosiery.[32]

The Common Market experience points to the tendency of cartelization to spread among industries, either along the chain of input-output relationships as the cartelization of an input-producing industry affects the costs of the input-using industry, or in the form of imitative behavior. At the same time, cartelization tends to engender price increases,[33] while hindering long-run improvements in productivity that may have been its raison d'être in the first place. Under market-sharing arrangements, producers would derive little benefit from improving productivity because they are enjoined from expanding their sales, whereas higher-cost firms can continue their operations without fear of competition from lower-cost rivals.[34]

An oft-cited example is the limitation imposed on the sales of small and medium-scale steel producers in Italy's Brescia region, who make reinforcing rods and various other products in the framework of the EEC steel cartel. In an effort to maintain market shares, larger firms in the EEC countries with higher production costs objected to the Bresciani producers' low prices. The process of bargaining, in turn, has been affected by political considerations, in part because several of the high-cost firms are state owned and in part because the governments of the individual countries wish to defend the interests of their national industries.

Similar problems are bound to arise in the framework of the recently established cartel of the eleven largest EEC producers of synthetic fibers, which would freeze existing market shares. Since small European producers and the European subsidiaries of American companies are not

---

[32] *Business Week*, March 27, 1978; and *Economist*, May 27, 1978.
[33] Prices actually paid for steel, as opposed to list prices, reportedly increased by 7 to 20 percent in the EEC between November 1977 and April 1978 although there was little change in sales (*Economist*, May 13, 1978).
[34] For an excellent discussion, see Tumlir, herein.

parties to the agreement and since non-European producers have different objectives, the potential for conflict is considerable.[35]

The difficulties multiply when the organization of trade or production is attempted on the world level, where the decisions concern the division of markets not only among the producers of a single country or of the European Common Market but also among producers of the major developed and developing countries. Bargaining and international politics will now increasingly take the place of market forces, tending to freeze existing patterns and thereby discriminating against new producers, obstructing changes in comparative advantage, and forgoing the benefits that may be obtained from shifts to lower-cost sources.

The Employment Argument. The deficiencies of national and international cartels are well illustrated by the experience of the depression of the 1930s.[36] Just as in the 1930s, however, the argument has been put forward that cartelization is needed for the sake of employment threatened by foreign competition.

In recent years, employment arguments have been directed largely to the developing countries that are said to be encroaching on the markets of the developed nations and contributing to unemployment in the latter. This contention leaves out of account the increase in employment generated in the developed nations through their exports of manufactured goods to the developing countries. In fact, since the oil crisis, these exports have increased more than the imports, leading to a substantial improvement in the trade balances of the developed nations with the non-oil-producing developing countries in manufactured goods. The relevant figures for 1973 and 1976 are $3.0 and $5.3 billion in the United States, $11.3 and $16.5 billion for the European Common Market, and $7.7 and $13.2 billion for Japan.[37]

It may be conjectured, then, that during the period of the 1974–1975 recession and its immediate aftermath employment in the developed nations actually benefited from trade in manufactured goods with the non-oil-producing countries. This result reflects the fact that the developing countries spent practically all their foreign exchange earnings and borrowed additional amounts on foreign financial markets. Such borrow-

---

[35] According to press reports, while "one commission official closely involved in the arrangement said he hoped that the United States companies would abide by the rules," the manager of one of the subsidiaries stated that he "will operate on the basis of a free market" (*New York Times*, May 17, 1978).

[36] See C. D. Edwards, "International Cartels as Obstacles to International Trade, *American Economic Review*, March 1944, pp. 330–39; and B. F. Hoselitz, "International Cartel Policy," *Journal of Political Economy*, February 1947, pp. 1–28.

[37] GATT, *International Trade, 1976–77* (Geneva, 1977).

ing and continued economic growth are in turn predicated on LDC success in exporting. In addition, developing countries have assumed increasing importance as markets for the manufactured exports of the developed nations. In 1976, the share in these exports (excluding trade between the United States and Canada as well as within and between EEC and European Free Trade Association) was 27.9 percent for the non-oil-producing developing countries and 45.7 percent when exports to the oil-producing developing countries are added.[38]

It appears, then, that the developed nations have benefited from the continued economic growth of the developing countries during and after the 1974–1975 recession. Since these conclusions refer to export- and import-competing industries combined, one must further consider the employment effects of trade on import-competing industries. Available data indicate that fears of loss of employment in these industries, too, have been exaggerated.

The findings of various studies indicate that the decline in employment because of import competition is generally small compared to that because of technological change. According to studies sponsored by the International Labor Organization, the total elimination of barriers to imports from developing countries would lead to a 1.5 percent decline in manufacturing employment spread over five to ten years in the developed countries.[39] By contrast, technological change associated with increases in productivity entails an annual displacement of labor of 3 to 4 percent.

These findings have been confirmed by studies of British industries that are particularly sensitive to import competition. "Detailed analyses of the Lancashire cotton textile industry and Dundee jute point to the dominant role of technical change—in the form of competition from synthetics in both cases and, for cotton textiles, from labor-saving investment—as a cause of labor displacement."[40] On the basis of more recent data, the conclusion is reached that "it is difficult to suggest that any labor-intensive sector except men's shirts and suits suffered between 1970 and 1975 from exceptionally damaging import growth" and that in the textile yarn, fabrics, clothing, and shoe industries, taken together,

---

[38] United Nations, *Monthly Bulletin of Statistics*, February 1978.

[39] C. Hsieh, "Measuring the Effects of Trade Expansion on Employment: A Review of Some Research," *International Labor Review*, January 1973.

[40] Cited in Vincent Cable, "British Protectionism and LDC Imports," *ODI Review*, vol. 2 (1977), p. 38. The relevant references are Caroline Miles, *Lancashire Textiles: A Case Study of Industrial Changes* (Cambridge: At the University Press, 1968), and Stuart McDowell, Paul Draper, and Anthony McGuinness, "Protection, Technological Change, and Trade Adjustment: The Case of Jute in Britain," *ODI Review*, vol. 1 (1976), pp. 43–57.

"productivity growth emerges as twice as important as trade factors in job replacement," when "the job loss annually from LDC import competition (less exports to LDCs) is little more than 1.5–2 percent in the worst case, clothing, 0.8 percent annually for cotton textile fabrics, 0.4 percent for footwear, and negligible for textile yarn."[41]

During the 1963–1971 period in the United States, "The loss in job potential in import-competing industries due to foreign trade has averaged about 44,000 jobs per year—about 0.2 percent of total manufacturing employment and an even more minute fraction of the total U.S. labor force. The loss of job potential due to increased labor productivity was about six to nine times as great as the loss due to foreign trade in import-competing industries."[42] At the same time, half the estimated job loss was related to imports from developing countries.

Employment losses associated with increased imports from developing countries are likely to have been larger in recent years. However, it should be recognized that, with these countries spending practically all their foreign exchange earnings, restrictions on imports from the developing countries only shift unemployment from import-competing to export industries in the developed nations. Now, as the developing countries rely more on unskilled labor and the developed countries on skilled labor, the upgrading of the labor force of the latter is obstructed as a result, leading to losses in real incomes. As Jan Tumlir eloquently expressed it,

> Unemployment is fungible; the jobs which protection could save at the import-competing end of the industrial spectrum would be balanced out by the jobs forgone at the exporting end. The latter are higher productivity jobs requiring better education [and] high skills. . . . Protection thus restricts an economy's capacity to provide adequate employment for the higher skilled and better educated.[43]

Conclusions and Recommendations

Policies for Long-Term Growth. We have seen that the high rate of unemployment in the developed nations cannot be attributed to international trade. Nor can one expect that protection would reduce unemployment; it will only shift unemployment from lower-skilled labor in import-competing industries to higher-skilled labor in export indus-

---

[41] Cable, "British Protectionism," pp. 38–41.
[42] Charles R. Frank, Jr., *Foreign Trade and Domestic Aid* (Washington, D.C.: Brookings Institution, 1977), p. 36.
[43] Jan Tumlir, "Can the International Economic Order Be Saved?" *World Economy*, October 1977, p. 18.

tries. Nevertheless, protectionist measures have been invoked on employment grounds. The desire of the individual countries to improve their balance of payments position has also created pressures for the application of such measures. There is a "fallacy of composition" here, as protectionist actions taken by any one country can improve its position only temporarily because the OPEC surplus must be matched by the collective deficit of the non-oil-producing countries.

At the same time, protectionist actions taken simultaneously by a number of countries cannot fail to be detrimental to all. National incomes will be lower as a result, since resources are not used to best advantage and potential economies of scale obtainable in export industries are not exploited. Furthermore, protection reduces the pressure for productivity improvements in import-competing industries, whereas possible improvements in export industries are forgone.

The application of protective measures is also likely adversely to affect investment activity in the developed nations. While protection may not lead to increased investment in high-cost import-competing activities that have a precarious existence, it may discourage investment in low-cost export activities that suffer discrimination under protection. The direct subsidization of high-cost activities from government funds will have similar effects by siphoning off funds that could otherwise have been used for investment in low-cost activities.

While protection tends to lower the rate of economic growth through its adverse effects on national income and investment activity, measures aimed at accelerating economic growth would lessen pressures for protection. Such measures, which would increase inducement to investment and lessen the rigidities introduced through government measures and labor legislation, would have to be carried out with special vigor in the surplus countries, particularly Germany and Japan, both to offset the deflationary effects of the appreciation of their currencies and to reduce asymmetries in the balance of payments of the developed countries.[44] At the same time, it should be recognized that the deficit vis-à-vis OPEC is not immutable; there are possibilities for reducing energy imports. This would require, in particular, the adoption of appropriate policies in the United States to lower the consumption and increase the production of energy.

Problems of Adjustment. It has been concluded that, in leading to higher incomes and employment, growth-oriented policies would reduce

---

[44] For a detailed discussion, see "Resolving Policy Conflicts for Rapid Growth in the World Economy," *Banca Nazionale del Lavoro Quarterly Review*, September 1978.

protectionist pressures in the developed countries. In turn, the avoidance of protectionism would contribute to economic growth that requires a continuing transformation of the industrial structure, entailing shifts from lower to higher productivity activities.[45] This conclusion also applies to the developing countries, whose economic growth depends to a considerable extent on the availability of trade opportunities in the developed countries as well as on their own policies for making use of these opportunities.

More generally, trade permits economic growth to proceed in the world economy through shifts in product composition. This entails increasing specialization in research- and technology-intensive products in the developed countries; upgrading of exports that are now based largely on unskilled labor in the semiindustrial developing countries; and exporting of unskilled-labor-intensive manufactures in the less developed countries.[46]

Structural transformation cannot proceed smoothly and will create problems of adjustment in industries that decline in absolute or in relative terms. Such problems, in turn, have often given rise to efforts to reduce the speed of adjustment. This has been the case, in particular, when adjustment in developed countries was presumed to have been triggered by increased imports.

The objective of reducing the speed of adjustment has been pursued by the measures of the new protectionism as well as by adjustment assistance as it has been applied in practice in most developed countries. Thus, in reporting the results of a comparative study, Goran Ohlin concludes that "adjustment assistance seems in practice often designed to bolster the defences against imports rather than to clear the ground for them [and] public policy has sought to delay the transfer of resources."[47]

In this connection, several questions should be raised, including the appropriate purpose of adjustment policies, the choice between import restrictions and adjustment assistance, and the choice of the particular measures to be employed. These concerns will be taken up briefly in the context of the industrial transformation of the developed countries.

Adjustment policies that artificially bolster employment and raise profitability in high-cost industries by reducing the cost of labor and

---

[45] On this point, see Richard Blackhurst, Nicolas Marian, and Jan Tumlir, *Trade Liberalization, Protection, and Interdependence*, GATT Studies in International Trade, no. 5 (Geneva, November 1977).

[46] See Bela Balassa, "A 'Stages' Approach to Comparative Advantage," World Bank Staff Working Paper, no. 256 (Washington, D.C., May 1977).

[47] OECD Development Research Centre, *Adjustment for Trade: Studies on Industrial Adjustment Problems and Policies* (Paris, 1975), pp. 9, 11.

other inputs or by increasing the price received by producers run counter to the process of industrial transformation that is necessary for continued growth. Policies should aim at promoting the movement of resources from lower to higher productivity activities.

Nor should one single out imports as the cause of reduced employment and profitability; more often than not, the cause has been technological change. Also, it is incorrect to argue that losses suffered by domestic nationals because of increased imports require different treatment than losses because of technological change on the grounds that the beneficiaries are foreign nationals in the first case and domestic nationals in the second. In fact, with higher imports leading to increased exports in the process of adjustment, the beneficiaries will be domestic nationals in both cases.

In view of these considerations, it is preferable to use adjustment assistance rather than import restrictions to ease the problems of adjustment to changing conditions in domestic industry. There is still the question, however, of what kind of adjustment measures, and government aids in general, should be utilized for this purpose.

It has been suggested that the measures applied should promote the movement of resources from lower-productivity to higher-productivity industries. This is in the interest of the developed countries, because it contributes to improved resource allocation and rapid economic growth. It is also in the interest of the developing countries because of the gains they can obtain through international specialization. The community of interests is further enhanced by the fact that, in contributing to the foreign exchange earnings of the developing countries, the application of the proposed measures would permit them to avoid high-cost import-substitution policies that would have adverse effects for all.

The described objectives would be served if, rather than subsidizing production and employment in high-cost industries, the developed countries were to encourage the expansion of efficient activities and ensure the transfer of resources to these activities. Appropriate measures include reducing government-induced rigidities in labor markets, retraining workers, and promoting research and development.

Establishing an International Code of Good Conduct. While adjustment assistance is preferable to import restrictions for easing the adjustment of domestic industries, such assistance may not carry the entire burden, especially if sudden changes in trade flows necessitate the use of safeguard measures to limit the growth of imports. The application of these measures should be made subject to internationally agreed-upon rules.

Article 19 of GATT provides an international code for the application of safeguard measures. This article has rarely been applied, however, in part because a country invoking it risks retaliation and in part because import restraints must be imposed in a nondiscriminatory fashion. Instead, countries have invoked safeguard measures by unilateral action or on a bilateral basis.

Article 19 would have to be reinterpreted in order to become a credible instrument to replace presently applied national safeguard measures. It should not, however, be made overly restrictive. Finally, safeguards should remain temporary, which is not the case under Article 19.

These objectives would be served by retaining the "injury clause" in Article 19 while leaving it to appropriately constituted institutions in the individual countries to judge whether injury has been sustained or threatened and to determine the measures to be employed. Decisions by national bodies should, however, be subject to multilateral surveillance in the sense that exporting countries would have the right to retaliate if an international committee established for this purpose finds that safeguard action was not warranted or that the measures used were excessive.

While it would be desirable to maintain the nondiscriminatory application of safeguard measures, at the minimum no exporter should be required to reduce its share in the domestic market of the country concerned. Imports from new developing country producers should not be subjected to limitations. Finally, the temporary nature of the safeguard measures would be expressed by their limited duration in time, the progressive liberalization of import restrictions during the time period of their application, and the exclusion of their reimposition.[48]

Export subsidies, too, are subject to international rules under Articles 6 and 16 of GATT. However, it would be necessary to establish stricter obligations for developed countries and to introduce exceptions for developing countries. At the same time, these exceptions would be circumscribed to ensure that the subsidies applied by developing countries compensate for, but do not create, distortions, with progressively stricter rules applying when developing countries show superior competitiveness in some products. In regard to export subsidies other than those for which developing countries are granted exceptional treatment, it would be desirable to make claims for injury subject to internationally agreed-upon rules, with international surveillance of their administration.

It would further be desirable if, in addition to safeguard measures

---

[48] On the last point, the paper follows suggestions made in an unpublished memorandum by Isaiah Frank.

PART FOUR: TRADE POLICIES

and export subsidies, the international code of good conduct covered adjustment assistance and government aids in general. Government aids affect foreign producers in domestic and foreign markets, and they have increasingly become subject to international policy competition.

As for adjustment assistance, governments may agree to forgo measures that hinder the movement of resources from low-productivity to high-productivity industries. In turn, positive measures aimed at encouraging the movement of resources should have general incidence, affecting all industries in the same way, so that the choice among alternative activities is left to the market mechanism.

There may be times, however, when the market does not fully anticipate future needs, and the application of measures affecting specific industries could not be forgone. In addition, assistance to depressed regions could be considered admissible to the extent that such assistance corrects for existing distortions or serves social goals. Finally, whatever the rationale, most countries have rules of government procurement favoring domestic industry.

An international code of good conduct should provide, first of all, for transparency in the matter of government aids. First, it should make explicit the measures actually applied by incorporating them in public regulations whenever this is not already the case. Second, the budgetary cost of aids provided to specific industries and regions should be estimated, as in the report on subsidies in Germany and in economic impact statements in the United States. Third, commitments to freeze the status quo in relation to government aids, just as tariffs are bound in GATT, would be desirable. Finally, some general rules on the use of government aids by individual countries should be defined.

These moves would provide a basis for negotiating reductions in government aid. Such negotiations may be initially undertaken by the developed countries, patterned on actions taken in the framework of the European Common Market. They would necessitate establishing machinery, possibly in the framework of the OECD, to provide international surveillance of the application of government aids as well as a forum for continuing discussions and negotiations.

The Tokyo Round negotiations provide an opportunity for establishing an international code on safeguards, export subsidies, and government aids. This may take the form of an interpretation of GATT regulations, so that the difficulties involved in changing the existing provisions of the General Agreement might be avoided. Parallel with these efforts, agreement should be reached on across-the-board reductions in tariffs and on lessening disparities in tariffs on individual products. It would also be desirable to liberalize trade in agricultural commodities, in particular in products of export interest to the developing countries.

Developing Country Policies. Developing countries have a considerable interest in establishing acceptable and credible international rules on the application of measures affecting their exports. Their exports have been repeatedly curbed by the imposition of restrictions by the developed countries; they have little bargaining power to forestall the application of new restrictions on particular commodities; and the threat of the imposition of restrictions creates considerable uncertainty for them. Developing countries need a stable environment in which the shifts in the international division of labor necessary for their rapid economic growth can take place.

Developing countries would be well advised to avoid demanding unilateral concessions that would jeopardize the establishment of international rules, for they stand to lose more through the continuation and the extension of the new protectionism than they may gain from any concessions. Nevertheless, while individual developing countries have little bargaining power, they could be influential if they adopted a joint position. The same observation applies to tariff reductions in the Tokyo Round, where developing countries could press for reductions on items of export interest to them.

In this connection, it should be emphasized that developing countries have much more to gain from multilateral tariff reductions than from maintaining preferential margins, on which UNCTAD efforts have concentrated in recent years. Tariff reductions do not involve quantitative limitations on trade and are not reversible, while imports under preferences are subject to quantitative limitations and can be revoked on short notice.

Semiindustrial developing countries would also be well advised to reduce existing protection. To begin with, the existence of high protection in some of these countries is used as an argument for protection in the developed nations. Furthermore, offers made to reduce trade barriers would strengthen the bargaining position of the developing countries in the Tokyo Round. Finally, lowering protective barriers would lessen the need for (explicit) export subsidies that are threatened by countervailing action. This would mean putting greater reliance on the exchange rate, since one may compensate for reductions in import tariffs and export subsidies by a devaluation.[49]

---

[49] For a detailed discussion, see Bela Balassa, "Export Incentives and Export Performance in Developing Countries: A Comparative Analysis," *Weltwirtschaftliches Archiv*, March 1978.

PART FOUR: TRADE POLICIES

Semiindustrial developing countries might also enter into bilateral agreements with developed nations on liberalizing trade, as in the recent agreement between the United States and Mexico. This would be especially important in the case of trade with Western Europe. In this connection, it should be recognized that several of the semiindustrial countries have sufficiently large markets to offer meaningful concessions.

At the same time, the chances for avoiding the imposition of restrictions would be increased if semiindustrial developing countries upgraded and diversified their exports. It would be particularly desirable to expand the exports of commodities in cases where firms in developed countries can respond by changing their product composition, which is not possible in industries consisting largely of one-product firms, such as textiles, clothing, and shoes. The possibility of expanding exports without encountering restrictions would be further increased if export markets were diversified, in particular, if export outlets were sought in the rapidly growing OPEC countries.

Finally, semiindustrial developing countries might gradually abandon the exports of simple, unskilled-labor-intensive manufactures for the benefit of countries at lower levels of development. The latter countries would then have to follow appropriate policies that would not discriminate against exports.

COMMENTARY

Jagdish N. Bhagwati

For me to comment on Ian Little's paper seems somewhat incestuous. Over the last several years, we have played very similar roles in the field of trade theory and policy. He and I have shared, as he notes, the responsibility of codirecting two major projects that have analyzed the trade and industrialization policies of selected LDCs in considerable depth: his OECD project preceded mine for the National Bureau of Economic Research and, in fact, provided the intellectual stimulus for it. In regard to trade theory, while he credits the 1963 Bhagwati-Ramaswami paper with having laid the foundations of the modern theory of tariffs and welfare that has done much to clarify the limited case for tariff protection, I could equally credit his 1969 *Manual* with James Mirrlees as having powerfully extended the basic insights of trade theory to the field of project evaluation in open economies.[1]

If anything divides us, therefore, it is less the main thrust of his arguments than the cutting edge with which he delivers them. And this difference would seem to follow mainly from the pleasure he evidently derives from what he considers to be the final rout of the Gang of Four —Gunnar Myrdal, Raul Prebisch, Hans Singer, and Thomas Balogh— who, to his discomfort, dominated the field for over two decades; I, on the other hand, consider their intellectual contributions in a somewhat more benign fashion.

Little's paper divides essentially into two related sets of arguments: the intellectual challenges to the LIEO in the LDCs; and the empirical evidence now available from numerous studies on whether these challenges are sound. The intellectual challenges are set into a proper perspective with the profoundly correct observation that the LIEO has hardly been in place in several LDCs during the postwar period and that the question we must therefore address is why this has been so.

---

[1] I. M. D. Little and James Mirrlees, *Manual of Industrial Project Analysis in Developing Countries*, vol. 2 (Paris: OECD, 1969).

PART FOUR: TRADE POLICIES

Little notes correctly that the protectionist and antiexport-biased nature of the foreign trade regimes in these LDCs must be traced basically to their exchange controls, *not* to industrial pressures for tariffs. The exchange controls, in turn, reflected the postwar doubts about the efficacy of exchange rate adjustments, which came largely from elasticity pessimism of one variety or another. I think that Little exaggerates, at least for countries outside Latin America, the role of the Prebisch-Singer thesis of the secularly declining terms of trade in defining this elasticity pessimism: for the countries of South Asia, at least, it was simply a case of inability to foresee the enormous potential for export growth in both primary exports and, more importantly, in manufactures.

This brings me to the need to distinguish between two main types of wrongheaded LDCs: those where the overvalued exchange rate regime had the central initiating role in defining the pattern and degree of import substitution and those where it was used in a *permissive* fashion to accommodate what Little describes as the obsession with quantities rather than prices in planning. In the latter group, I would place the countries of South Asia and the earlier Egypt and Ghana, to mention the principal victims of this approach. Thus, in India, a country Little cites as the living—he really means dying—proof of the disastrous results of structural thinking, the notion that one must structurally transform the economy had taken deep root. This led to detailed licensing of industrial activities, with targets derived from increasingly sophisticated consistency and optimization models of the modern planning theory that dates back, in one tradition, to the seminal writings of Ragnar Nurkse and Rosenstein-Rodan on balanced growth and coordinated investment decisions, and in a *separate* tradition, to the heterogeneous capital goods models, the turnpike theorem, and so on, of Paul Samuelson, Robert Solow, Roy Radner, and others. In practice, this implied that trade had to be regulated in such a way as to make the targets feasible *and* production profitable: hence, the preference for the automaticity of protection often implied by quantitative restrictions, the unwillingness to look at current excess costs of domestic production, and so forth.

I make this distinction not merely for intellectual reasons but also because it perhaps explains, in some degree, the tenacity with which some of these countries have held on to foreign trade regimes that produce chaotic incentives for the allocation of economic activity and a bias against exports. On the other hand, where all this was rather an "inadvertent" outcome of the reluctant exchange rate mechanism, countries have managed to shift gears to more successful trade and payments regimes with much greater ease.

I also allude to the more reputable traditions in economic theory that underline the importance of structural thinking in its most sophisticated version, because it helps to underline the lesson that economic theory can be detrimental to economic policy unless the economist has common sense. Thus, I have heard an Indian welfare theorist of some eminence defend the indefensible losses in some Indian public enterprises, on the well-known theoretical ground that they could represent social gain, and successfully browbeat the lesser economists with impenetrable language à la Gerard Debreu.

The question therefore is really whether one can usefully subscribe to the many undoubtedly valid theoretical arguments made in the classroom against the policy option of free trade. Though they enrich economic science, can they also enrich the LDCs? Little seems sufficiently fed up with those who are silly-clever to write at times as if the theoretical arguments do not matter: and here I part company with him. But, in my judgment, he is dead right in suggesting that one must go to the evidence to choose the desirable policy framework and that here, "by and large," "more or less" (two splendid English phrases!), the lessons are clear. The outward-looking or export-promoting countries *have* done better than others cross-sectionally; the shift from protectionist to liberal trade and payments policies has *also* helped individual countries, according to time series evidence.

My reading of the situation today is that these lessons are now widely understood and will probably influence those who are just starting on their way to industrialization. Admittedly, as Little notes, there are new questions and new intellectual challenges: there will always be. The dialectic will not disappear. But my impression is that the intellectual challenges of the 1950s and 1960s were more substantial and real: we really had little clue, if we were to be truthful, as to which trade and payments regime options for LDCs would yield superior economic performance. The new intellectual challenges seem, for the most part, to be essentially derivative, and uninteresting or wrong. Thus, for example, it is old hat to us that trade may damage long-run growth or result in lower welfare for any intertemporal objective function in the presence of second-best savings decisions. However, the Metcalfe-Steedman-Mainwaring-Emmanuel argument that trade may be characterized, in the steady state, by lower per capita consumption will not justify the assertion that free trade is Pareto-inferior to autarky—as clarified by several trade theorists recently. If one really wants to be bamboozled, one has to turn to esoteric theory where, I am told, in the case of an infinite time horizon one runs into the possibility that competitive equilibrium may not be Pareto-optimal and hence free trade may not be

Pareto-optimal. But then I am sure that neither Little nor I will lose sleep over this!

The really serious challenge to the LIEO from the LDCs seems to me to stem from the increasingly widespread feeling that the LIEO is hardly subscribed to by the DCs themselves when it comes to their own interests. Quite aside from the traditional agricultural protectionism of the DCs, there have been increasing sentiments for protection against imports of manufactures—sentiments that are alarming, in fact, if we are to take Jan Tumlir's account seriously, as I am afraid we must. Moreover, the DCs have selectively used immigration quotas throughout recent history to prevent free and "liberal" inflow of manpower from LDCs (and elsewhere as well). It is not entirely without significance that the DC-based human rights groups that worry about the freedom of human beings to locate where they wish are far more concerned about the freedom to exit than the freedom to enter. Nor, finally, can one ignore the increasing evidence that much of modern trade goes through MNCs and probably results in lesser gains from trade by the LDCs who face few and large MNC buyers than would arise from competitive trade. Here, however, I feel that one cannot ignore the economic theory that fewness of numbers is compatible with "as if" perfect competition due to free entry, and the jury is by no means in. All such perceptions by LDCs of the DCs' own lapses from the LIEO, on a number of dimensions, must surely reinforce their cynicism and their efforts to manipulate the international economic system so as to gain more from the total pie.

In particular, the attempts at raising bargaining power via formation of producer cartels have surely an important basis in the perception that this provides the countervailing power against MNCs in DCs that hold prices of LDC goods below the competitive levels. The answer to this specific and all-important challenge to the LIEO will have to come from a systematic attempt to show that the DCs are, in fact, trading competitively despite the MNC structure of their trade. If that fails and DCs are unable to come up with systematic policies to increase competitiveness, the LDC departures from the principles of free trade will have to be put down as a second-best policy designed to protect themselves against the effects of a nonliberal international economic order that is stacked against them. Then we may well have LDCs that have learned Little's lessons about the advantages of free trade in manufactures while the DCs retreat from it, whereas the LDCs retreat from free trade in primary goods through cartelization while the DCs set themselves to fight these moves! If so, the prospects for the LIEO in trade are not too exciting!

Nat Weinberg

I have only limited space in which to present the views of the victims of trade, even though I am the only contributor to this volume with any credentials to do so. I will, therefore, have to omit most of the supporting data and arguments, the qualifications, and much else that I would otherwise include.

I assume that when someone with a labor background is invited to participate in a conference such as this, a labor point of view is expected. It should be stressed, however, that mine is *a* labor viewpoint, not *the* labor viewpoint. My position differs in important respects from that of the AFL-CIO, and while my views are essentially those of the United Auto Workers (UAW), that organization is not responsible for what is expressed here.

On one point, however, the labor movement is united. It is not willing to permit workers to be sacrificed on the altar of economists' dogma, even if the dogma be as hallowed as the theory of comparative advantage. The conclusions of individual unions may vary, but they will all examine trade policy issues, not on the basis of abstract and questionable theories but in terms of their practical consequences for people.

The fact is that the assumptions underlying comparative advantage are ridiculously irrelevant to the realities of the modern world. Among those assumptions are: (1) full employment which, particularly in the United States and the economically underdeveloped countries, has been more notable for its absence than for its presence; (2) immobility of the factors of production which, as applied to capital, is utter nonsense in the era of the transnational corporation; (3) competition which is belied by the prevalence of oligopoly and cartels; and (4)—implicit in Ricardo's original statement of the theory—international equality of wages. As if all that were not enough, there are the further departures from the theory resulting from tax havens, dirty floats, tax deferrals, transfer price manipulations, and the vast array of concessions and subsidies that transnational corporations extort from host countries.

Despite the theory's irrelevance, I am convinced that we must work toward a rational international division of labor in which all peoples are allowed and assisted to participate to their fullest capacities and in which all share equitably in the fruits of their joint efforts. I fear the international political, as well as economic, consequences of efforts by each country to export its unemployment to others.

Protectionism cannot be exorcised by incantation; it must be attacked at its source. It is rooted in and derives most of its political muscle from the insecurity of workers. It is not a coincidence that both protectionist sentiment and unemployment are at postwar highs throughout the industrialized democracies.

As some economists are fond of saying, there is no such thing as a free lunch. Those who seek liberal trade policies must be prepared to pay the price by safeguarding workers against the hazards to which such policies expose them. The focus must not be on faceless statistical aggregates but on the individuals and families who suffer the shocks of trade displacement.

The first requisite is to stop treating the welfare of those workers as expendable. How many people would volunteer to sacrifice their jobs, or even any fraction of their families' living standards, if by so doing they could make lower-priced imports available to their neighbors? Yet, such sacrifices are exactly what our government expects of workers under our present miserable excuse for trade adjustment assistance. Workers with less than average earnings are compensated for only 70 percent of their wage loss. One might say that they save part of the difference because the benefits are tax free; but a large part of those saved taxes represents a loss of social security pension credits that will haunt the workers throughout their retirement years. And what of the high-wage workers? A displaced steel worker who was paid the *average* wage in his industry takes a cut of 42 percent in his income when he goes on adjustment assistance; more highly skilled workers, earning above the average wage, take even deeper cuts. The benefits are limited, with minor exceptions, to one year, although most steel workers will *never* find other jobs paying wages comparable to the wages paid on the jobs they have lost. Workers receive no compensation for loss of valuable seniority rights or for loss of nonvested pension credits. No provision is made for continuation of vitally important fringe benefits. The loss of company-paid health insurance, for example, means disaster for some families.

If we want the benefits of liberal trade policies, we should be willing to bear our full share of the costs of achieving them. No group of workers should be required to bear a disproportionate share of those costs.

There are precedents we can apply to make that principle a reality for trade-displaced workers. The Regional Rail Reorganization Act is one of several laws already on the statute books that indicate the kind of safeguards that can and should be provided for trade-displaced workers. Among other things, it assures displaced railroad workers with five or more years' seniority of the full wages and fringe benefits applicable to their lost jobs plus subsequent wage rate increases and fringe

COMMENTARY

benefit improvements until they reach age sixty-five and qualify for pensions. There is no basis in logic or justice for providing less to trade-displaced workers.

With rare exceptions, however, workers strongly prefer jobs to benefits. The second requisite for overcoming resistance to trade liberalization is, therefore, an effective full employment policy. That should present no problem for the devotees of comparative advantage since, as I have noted, full employment is one of the assumptions of their theory. Yet I find some of them engaged, simultaneously, in arguing comparative advantage and supporting the destructive, futile, and immoral policy of attempting to suppress inflation by deliberately creating unemployment.

Full employment would reduce the cost of 100 percent adjustment assistance to negligible proportions because displaced workers would be able to find new jobs quickly. Full employment is an indispensable precondition for opening DC markets to the manufactured products of the LDCs. Full employment would facilitate the orderly transfer of labor-intensive industries to the job-hungry LDCs. Sweden was able deliberately to wipe out its low-end textile industry without any opposition from the workers or their union because full employment made it possible to give those workers *better* jobs.

Adequate adjustment assistance and full employment are not purely national problems. Every exporting country has an interest in keeping open its markets in other countries. It therefore makes sense to propose amendments to the GATT charter that would require all member nations, under penalty of restrictions against their exports, to provide railroad-type adjustment assistance to their workers and to take all practicable steps to establish and maintain full employment. (If I remember correctly, lip service is presently paid to full employment in the GATT agreement.)

It would be logical to create under GATT an internationally pooled fund to pay adjustment assistance benefits. Since the interest of each nation in keeping its foreign markets open is roughly proportional to its exports, it would be reasonable to finance such a fund, to be administered by GATT, by an internationally uniform, small tax on exports. Because the United States is constitutionally prohibited from imposing such a tax, its contribution would have to be raised by other means, possibly by having other GATT members impose a special tariff on imports from the United States equal to the export tax levied elsewhere, with the revenues to be paid into the pooled fund. Such a tariff would offset any advantage U.S. exporters might otherwise gain from the absence of the export tax.

PART FOUR: TRADE POLICIES

Another concern that impels workers toward protectionism is the danger that their standards may be undermined by competition from imports produced by exploited labor. The validity of that concern was acknowledged at the intergovernmental level as long ago as 1948 in the fair labor standards article of the Havana Charter for a United Nations International Trade Organization.

More recently, both the Roth report of 1969 and the report of the Williams Commission in 1971 urged that the United States seek international agreement on an enforceable code of fair labor standards.[2] Those who are disturbed by challenges to liberal trade policies should press the administration to act on those recommendations.

The labor movement is also concerned, of course, with other forms of unfair trade practices, such as subsidies for exports and nontariff barriers to imports. A further concern of American workers is job loss resulting from failure of corporations in some major industries to engage in effective competition against foreign producers. This has cost jobs related both to domestic and to potential export sales.

It is well known that American steel corporations have lagged far behind their foreign competitors technologically while raising their prices unconscionably. Had they kept up in the technological race, they might well have been able to obtain higher profits at lower prices while blocking the invasion of their markets by imports.

The auto industry provides another example. As early as January 1949, the UAW began to urge the U.S. manufacturers to produce small cars. There was already strong evidence that there would be a sizable domestic market for such cars as well as substantial export possibilities. The industry procrastinated for two decades, while imports took a growing share of the U.S. market and exports dwindled to a trickle. The auto corporations compounded the problem by setting prices at levels that yielded industry average rates of return that in most years were far above the average for all U.S. manufacturing corporations. Even now, with overseas imports taking a fifth of its home market, the industry is raking in profits grossly in excess of the manufacturing average. It would be hard to find clearer evidence of failure to compete than super profits side by side with a huge loss of market share. If they were willing to accept lower profits, the American auto corporations could turn back

---

[2] Report to the President submitted by Special Representative for Trade Negotiations, *Future United States Foreign Trade Policy* (Washington, D.C.: Government Printing Office, January 14, 1969), pp. 44 and Commission on International Trade and Investment Policy, *United States International Economic Policy in an Interdependent World* (Washington, D.C.: Government Printing Office, July 1971), pp. 64–65.

COMMENTARY

the tide of imports by providing higher-quality small cars to be sold at competitive prices.

Those failures to compete, which probably can be matched in other industries, are responsible for the quest for quotas by the steel workers' union and for the rank-and-file pressure for protectionism within the UAW. The UAW leadership may not be able to resist that pressure for very long if the kinds of remedies I am proposing here are not put into practice promptly.

Those who seek liberal trade policies, as well as those who are disturbed by the U.S. trade deficit, should put their minds to devising means to compel corporations to compete when they refuse to do so on their own initiative. The UAW, some years ago, proposed a penalty tax on the profits of corporations guilty of the auto industry type of noncompetition. The formula for calculation of the tax would take into account both the excess of the firm's profit over the average manufacturing rate and the proportion of its industry's market taken over by imports. I commend this proposal to your attention.

Ultimately, the problems raised by the growth and spread of transnational corporations will have to be dealt with by an international agreement establishing an enforceable regulatory code—because national governments, acting individually, cannot cope with them. Space does not permit me to spell out in detail the labor provisions of such a code. In general, I would support the wide-ranging recommendations and suggestions that appear in the labor chapter of the report of the United Nations' so-called Group of Eminent Persons.

Meanwhile, the home governments of the TNCs should apply such leverage as lies within their power. The investment decisions of the TNCs are clearly not market determined; they do not normally go to the market to raise the capital involved. Their allocational decisions diverge from what the market might dictate because of the web of concessions, subsidies, tax deferrals, and other distorting factors that I have already mentioned.

Serious externalities arise when those decisions cause displacement of home-country workers. In addition, direct foreign investment decisions often have important international political dimensions that the home governments involved cannot afford to ignore. It is therefore appropriate to propose that the United States and other home countries establish a license requirement for TNC foreign investments. Workers should have a voice in licensing decisions, as they now do in foreign investment decisions in Germany and Sweden.

Among the conditions for issuance of a license could be: (1) that the investment would have no adverse international political repercus-

311

sions; (2) that the TNC commit itself, subject to penalities for violation, to adherence to a code of good behavior in the host country, including compliance with the International Labor Code—the conventions and recommendations of the International Labor Organization (ILO); (3) that the potential host country agree to exempt the TNC from compliance with national laws in conflict with the home-country and ILO codes—for example, laws requiring racial discrimination or prohibiting bona fide unions and free collective bargaining; and (4) that the TNC obligate itself to maintain the wages and fringe benefits of home-country workers displaced as a result of the investment. If the investment does not yield returns sufficient to pay the social cost of displacement, it cannot be considered economically sound. Let me sum up by saying that the obstacles to liberal trade policies can be overcome only if those policies are given a human face.

DISCUSSION

Juergen Donges took exception to Nat Weinberg's statement that the theory of comparative advantage was irrelevant. Comparative advantage today, he said, is not the naive version that critics like Weinberg attack. He pointed out that there has been considerable development since Ricardo. If comparative advantage is so irrelevant, he asked, how is it that by using comparative advantage one can in fact predict which industries will cease to be competitive? He also questioned why labor unions should differentiate between imported and domestic competition for jobs.

Ronald Findlay argued that the declining-terms-of-trade argument, though incorrect in the past, may be true in the future because some of the LDCs are growing more rapidly than the DCs and the terms of trade will turn against the faster-growing region. He pointed out that the highly differentiated manufactured goods which the LDCs should produce need large home markets and are precisely the goods they find hardest to get into production.

Stanley Black argued that the academic community has not been forceful enough in its advocacy of free trade. He also pointed out that antiliberal policies in the developed countries will elicit arguments from the less developed countries.

Dragoslav Avramovic argued that it is in practice very difficult to move to a more open society. To do this quickly, he argued, would require a police state because people would be thrown out of work, wages would be depressed, and trade unions would be smashed. The challenge, he argued, is to increase international trade without throwing anyone out of work.

The authors were given a chance to respond. Robert Baldwin suggested that the various constituencies—government, labor, and academics—get together and try to understand one another's arguments concerning trade and trade barriers. Baldwin went on to argue that it is possible to open our markets gradually without causing large amounts of unemployment. The objective for the long term, he said, should be opening up our markets for the developing countries. He argued that the present program of adjustment assistance is entirely inadequate.

Jan Tumlir said that the idea that the LDCs should subsidize their exports might make sense economically but that this subsidization generates protectionist pressures in the importing countries. A related point was that it made sense for the LDCs to diversify exports to other developing countries rather than directing them to the developed markets. Tumlir's second major point was that the labor challenge to the LIEO was a more serious challenge than many thought. Retraining programs, he said, do not make a significant dent in the problem. He thought that any solution would have to include educational reform.

I. M. D. Little supported Bela Balassa's idea that the developing countries should diversify into areas that cause fewer political problems in the importing countries. He thought there were many labor-intensive and skill-intensive lines of production they could get into. He disagreed with Avramovic that a move to a liberal order must entail smashing the trade unions. He pointed out that this has not happened in those countries that have successfully opened to trade, because there were no powerful unions in many of these countries. In Singapore, even though there were unions, it was not necessary to smash them.

Jagdish Bhagwati argued that the successful LDCs like Taiwan and Korea should move into engineering so that less successful LDCs can move into textiles.

Nat Weinberg responded to Donges by arguing that comparative advantage does have peripheral validity, but when the assumption of full employment is removed, different results are obtained. He pointed out that workers are more insecure in the United States than in Europe where firms deal with layoffs differently. He argued that full employment would remove labor's insecurity. Weinberg disagreed with Little, arguing that Singapore did, for all practical purposes, smash the trade unions. In response to Tumlir's point that export subsidies encourage protectionism, Weinberg said he felt that this would be a problem only when there was not full employment. Indeed, Weinberg pointed out that full employment would solve many of the problems that create challenges to the LIEO.

PART FIVE

THE LIBERAL'S DILEMMA:
POLICY RESPONSES TO
FOREIGN MONOPOLIES

Countervailing Foreign Use of Monopoly Power

Jacob S. Dreyer

> *The threat of mutual destruction cannot be used to deter an adversary who is too unintelligent to comprehend it.*
> Thomas C. Schelling, *The Strategy of Conflict**

To a proponent of a liberal international economic order, an axiomatic truth beyond controversy is that worldwide free trade redounds to the greatest benefit of the greatest number. With every individual free to produce whatever he wishes and to exchange his products with whomever he pleases, and with all individuals, whatever their citizenship, considered by all governments to be equally deserving, it would be both purposeless and impossible to determine the gains from international trade or their distribution among individual economic agents. Even in a world of less than perfect competition in individual national markets, the free trade arrangement would be the best of all alternatives—were it the only objective of governments to maximize the aggregate real income of their respective national communities and of the international community as a whole.

This, patently, is not the case. It is here that contradictions begin, which impinge upon the foreign economic policies of all nations.

The case for free trade often succumbs to other arguments. The primary and secular policy objectives of nations have appeared to be to increase national power, to protect sovereignty, and, most notably, to safeguard the existing domestic sociopolitical order against disruptive forces, especially against foreign and domestic economic shocks and dislocations. These objectives were cited in a long list of arguments in justification of exceptions to free trade: considerations of national security, protection of infant industries, achievement of fuller employment, prevention of undue hardship in a particular sector or region, assured availability of essential staples and raw materials to domestic consumers and producers, and so on. These arguments have been in-

---

* Cambridge, Harvard University Press, 1960.

PART FIVE: THE LIBERAL'S DILEMMA

voked by governments all over the world to justify tariffs, quotas, subsidies, rebates, norms, standards, procurement preferences, offset agreements, domestic ownership requirements, differential taxes, foreign exchange controls, and many other barriers restricting and diverting international trade and investment flows.

To be sure, most governments are on record as being opposed to trade and investment restrictions, especially, of course, when those restrictions are maintained or contemplated by other governments. Every government tends to believe that its own case for interfering with free trade is demonstrably valid while the restrictive practices of other governments reflect their mercantilist proclivities. Even the governments in the vanguard of the post–World War II thrust for freer trade are guilty of applying the double standard. It is illustrative that when the United States fathered the International Trade Organization for the purpose of maintaining "an 'open' or multilateral system of trade relations between [its] members," the U.S. government at the same time (1948) advised the U.N. General Assembly that export controls imposed by the United States were "for the purpose of securing an equitable distribution of commodities in short supply and of assisting the European Recovery Program in the interest of national security."[1] As was noted sarcastically by one observer at that time, since national security is a subjective criterion, "the difficulty of applying any principles of general validity and of reaching agreements on economic practices can easily be envisaged."[2] The same remark applies to most other arguments used by governments to justify policy measures contradicting the liberal trade principles to which the same governments allegedly subscribe.

Clearly, government intervention is not the only source of divergence between the perfectly competitive free trade ideal and the existing reality. Departures from the pattern of prices, output levels, and trade flows that would have prevailed in perfectly competitive domestic and international markets can occur without government intervention on behalf of selected domestic groups of consumers or producers. The pristine beauty of a perfectly competitive world could be spoiled by monopolies that arise through acquisition of a superior technological know-how (with or without patent protection), as a result of prohibitive entry costs, as a consequence of ownership of a specialized input or information, and through formation of domestic cartels, legal or

---

[1] United Nations, General Assembly, *Official Records*, Plenary Meetings, 3rd session, Pt. 1, September 27, 1948, p. 169.

[2] Werner Levi, *Fundamentals of World Organization* (Minneapolis: University of Minnesota Press, 1950), p. 92 n.

illegal, effectively restricting imports even in the absence of tariffs and quotas imposed by the government. In today's world, however, government-owned or promoted monopolies are no less prevalent than monopolies created by private parties.[3] The aim of the latter is to extract a monopoly rent, that is, to secure a higher profit than could be earned under more competitive conditions. The aim of government monopolies is not necessarily limited to securing commercial advantages. As mentioned above, governments use their foreign economic policies to achieve a variety of goals, some economic, others not. In the process, they inflict injury on their trading partners, usually hurting their economies but not infrequently affecting adversely their social, political, and strategic interests.

If *all* governments were to promote indiscriminately the use of monopolistic or monopsonistic power in world trade, the fate of a liberal economic order would be doomed. If *some* countries were to promote such use, the survival of a liberal order would largely depend on the response of the other countries. Eye-for-an-eye retaliation against foreign use of monopolistic power would certainly lead to disintegration of the world trading system, as happened in the 1930s.

While it is not true that retaliation is beneficial to the retaliating country under all circumstances, it is clear that on some occasions countervailing policies may limit the damage done to national interests of the offended country. It ought to be recognized, however, that policies designed to countervail foreign use of monopoly power may result in further departures from the free trade arrangement and therefore may become a source of further distortions in the national economies concerned and in the world economy as a whole. Thus, a country espousing a liberal economic philosophy faces a philosophical and practical dilemma when confronted by foreign use of monopoly power.

The purpose of this paper is to explore the free trader's dilemma in some detail. The variety of monopolistic practices in international trade is dazzling, and an enumeration, let alone an analysis, of all of them would, unfortunately for the case of free trade, take volumes. Compelled to be selective by the relative brevity of this study, I chose to concentrate on instances of monopoly deliberately created or promoted by national governments.

I shall start with a critical survey of theoretical issues. The consequences of monopoly power in international trade and policies aimed at counteracting it are analyzed first from a national and then from a

---

[3] Unless specified otherwise, such terms as "monopoly," "monopolistic elements," "monopolistic power," and so on, refer to monopsony as well.

global point of view. Some attention is given to the peculiarities of foreign investment.

Central to this study is a review of relationships between selected categories of domestic monopolies and the international market and an analysis of the evolution of the legal doctrine regarding the exercise of market power, as reflected in the American antitrust legislation. Possible applications of a judicial approach to the problem of foreign monopolies are explored.

After a survey of the characteristics of state trading and their consequences, two very distinct specific instances of heavy government involvement in commercial dealings are described. The description is accompanied by an assessment of the costs and benefits of government intervention.

Finally, a postscript enumerates some basic guidelines for dealing with foreign use of monopoly power.

A Summary of Theoretical Issues

One basic tenet of the international trade theory is that free competition in all markets is a necessary condition for achievement of an efficient allocation of resources. If other necessary conditions, such as full employment of resources, flexibility of prices, and equality of prices and social opportunity costs, are met, then (if second-order conditions are satisfied) any restrictions on output and exchange will lead to losses in allocative efficiency.

What would be a rational policy when all conditions for Pareto optimality are not met? It has been shown that when a market failure occurs in the domestic economy a tax-cum-subsidy policy is generally more efficient than direct foreign trade intervention. The reason for the superiority of tax-cum-subsidies over outright restrictions on trade via tariffs or quotas is that, in principle at least, the former policy may restore the equality of marginal values violated by market imperfections, while trade restrictions via tariffs or quotas are bound to fail in attaining this objective.[4]

---

[4] See, for example: James E. Meade, *Trade and Welfare: Mathematical Supplement* (Oxford: Oxford University Press, 1955), chapter 8; Jagdish Bhagwati and V. K. Ramaswami, "Domestic Distortions, Tariffs, and the Theory of Optimum Subsidy," in Jagdish Bhagwati, *Trade, Tariffs, and Growth* (Cambridge, Mass.: M.I.T. Press, 1969); Harry Johnson, "Optimal Trade Intervention in the Presence of Domestic Distortions," in Robert Baldwin and others, *Trade, Growth, and the Balance of Payments* (Chicago: Rand McNally, 1965); Jagdish Bhagwati and T. N. Srinivasan, "Optimal Intervention to Achieve Non-Economic Objectives," *Review of Economic Studies*, vol. 30 (1969); Jaroslav Vanek, "Structural Aspects of Optimal Policies toward Non-Economic Objectives," Discussion Paper, no. 3 (Cornell University, Department of Economics, April 1971).

Benefits and Costs: A National Point of View. Suppose that country *A* does not wish to correct the distortion caused by the presence of a domestic monopoly. Alternatively, we may assume that this monopoly power is curbed at home or its rent is taxed away, but the government of country *A* finds it advantageous to give its monopoly complete freedom of maneuver abroad. In fact, the government of country *A* may actively promote the monopoly position of its industries or be itself a monopolistic owner of such industries.

What does the situation look like from the point of view of country *B*, against whom the monopoly or monopsony power is exercised? If the foreign monopoly price exceeds the marginal social costs of producing the good in question at home, no damage is inflicted; monopolized industry of *A* is unable to sell output in country *B*.[5] If the foreign monopoly price is higher than it would have been under competitive conditions, and country *B* is an importer of the output of monopolized industry, clearly, country *B* will be hurt by the foreign monopoly. Even in this case, however, country *B* may benefit from trade with the monopolist in *A* if *B*'s social cost of producing imports domestically would exceed the cost of purchasing them abroad at the monopoly-set prices.

On the export side, the argument is analogous. If there is a monopsonist in *A* offering for *B*'s exports less than the price that would have been paid by perfectly competitive buyers, *A*'s exporters are hurt by the monopsony of *B*. Even in this case, however, *B* may benefit from trade with *A* if the social cost of producing imports domestically would exceed the cost of exchanging them for exports at the monopsony-set prices.

For country *B* to benefit from trade with *A*, it is thus not necessary at all that prices in *A* correspond to *A*'s social marginal costs. But if monopolistic behavior by one's partner does not invalidate the conclusion that trade is beneficial, why should one worry about the existence of noncompetitive elements in the world economy? From a national point of view—that is, leaving aside the questions of worldwide efficiency—it is obvious that, given finite elasticities of demand, foreign profit-maximizing monopoly will charge higher prices and foreign cost-minimizing monopsony will offer lower prices for a country's imports and exports, respectively, than would have prevailed under competitive

---

[5] If the competitive country is an exporter of the monopolized good, it will be better off under foreign monopoly than it would have been under perfect competition. For elaboration, see Richard J. Sweeney, "Monopoly, the Law of Comparative Advantage, and Commodity Price Agreements: A Simple General Equilibrium Analysis," *Weltwirtschaftliches Archiv*, vol. 110 (1974), pp. 259–87.

conditions. In other words, even though the benefits of international trade to the competitive economy are not wiped out completely, under foreign monopoly or monopsony they are reduced.

Another worry stems from concern about full employment. In today's world, foreign monopolies often persist in charging lower prices for their exports than would have prevailed under competitive conditions. In a static framework, and if a high level of aggregate consumption is considered the only aim of economic activity, such pricing by foreign monopolies would have to be regarded as an expression of their charitable instincts. In a more realistic setting, every country is understandably concerned that foreign predatory pricing practices may drive domestic producers out of business, even though such practices enlarge the importing country's gains from trade in the short run.

How would a country confronted with foreign use of monopoly power and contemplating retaliation go about assessing the expected benefits and costs of this retaliation? On an abstract level of discussion, a handy tool for analyzing these questions is the theory of optimum tariff.[6]

Several pertinent points should be noted in connection with the optimum tariff argument. First and foremost, the offended country itself must have the requisite potential market power to retaliate. If before the retaliation the offended country's exporters or importers were perfect competitors, the government, by interceding on their behalf, cartelizing them, or substituting for them, must be able to acquire sufficient weight in the market to countervail the power of the foreign monopolist. This is a necessary condition for every successful retaliation. Countries too small to affect their terms of trade are helpless victims of foreign monopolies.

Yet, even if a country confronted by foreign monopoly does possess the requisite market power and is determined to use it, the gross benefit of such a retaliation cannot be ascertained. Because of the indeterminancy of the solution under a bilateral monopoly, the most that can be said is that the expected gains from the terms of trade improvement can be presumed to be positively related to the potential market power of the offended country relative to that of the foreign monopoly.

On the other hand, one has to reckon with the cost of retaliation. First, there is the loss caused by the contraction of the volume of trade. Given the elasticities of the reciprocal offer curves of the two countries,

---

[6] An incomparable discussion of the normative implications of the optimum tariff relative to free trade from the national and international point of view may be found in Jagdish Bhagwati, "The Pure Theory of International Trade: A Survey," in *Trade, Tariffs, and Growth*.

this cost is determined by the magnitude of the shift of the offer curve of the retaliating country; that is, it is determined by the potential monopoly power of this country relative to the other country. Next, unless the foreign monopoly constitutes the only departure from Pareto optimality, the retaliation may aggravate other distortions in the retaliating country's economy and create new ones.[7] If the retaliation assumes the form of an optimum tariff, the analysis of various domestic imperfections, such as unemployment or rigidity of prices, shows that the Bickerdike-Kahn formula for the optimum tariff has to be adjusted appropriately.[8] Parenthetically, it is worth noticing that underemployment of resources calls for a lower rate of the optimum tariff than the full employment optimum.

The distribution of income in the retaliating country would also be affected, which may—albeit, admittedly, it need not—cause a decrease in the society's total welfare. The outcome would depend on whether the weights attached to the utility of various groups are the same and, if they are not, on whether intrasociety transfers (import adjustment assistance?) take place.

In spite of all these costs, the retaliating country may be able to derive net advantage from its action. It may come out ahead even if its action provokes another round of retaliations by its trading partners,[9] especially if the scope and intensity of secondary retaliations are likely to be limited. Conceivably, the retaliating country may end up even better off than it would have been under free trade. Insofar as the argument is applicable to both the country using its monopoly power first and the retaliating country, the point is important in explaining the incentives for using commercial policy to gain national advantage at the expense of the rest of the world.

Benefits and Costs: An International Point of View. From the cosmopolitan point of view, it may be noted that the countervailing country can enhance its welfare only at the expense of its trading partners. Unless the monopoly-using country is defined as less deserving, the de-

---

[7] The welfare implications of such a possibility are discussed by Meade in *Trade and Welfare*, chapter 7.
[8] On unemployment, see Jacques Polak, "The 'Optimum Tariff' and the Cost of Exports," *Review of Economic Studies*, vol. 19 (1950–1951). On price rigidity, see Gottfried Haberler, "Some Problems in the Pure Theory of International Trade," *Economic Journal*, vol. 60 (June 1950). For a concise review, see Richard E. Caves, *Trade and Economic Structure* (Cambridge: Harvard University Press, 1967), chapter 8.
[9] Harry Johnson, "Optimum Tariffs and Retaliation," *Review of Economic Studies*, vol. 21 (1953–1954).

PART FIVE: THE LIBERAL'S DILEMMA

terioration in its terms of trade because of retaliation by the offended country may lead to income redistribution in favor of the virtuous—that is, originally competitive—but on various ethical grounds, perhaps, less deserving country. In no case, however, would the use of monopoly power and the ensuing retaliation be the globally optimal solution. The best solution for the country harboring a monopoly and thus generating negative externalities would be to receive from its trading partners a transfer in the amount of subsidy needed to internalize them.[10]

On the other hand, if the retaliating country is concerned with the well-being of its trading partners, in spite of their use of monopoly power, the increase in its welfare following the retaliation would be smaller than it would have been had the country in question been indifferent in this regard.[11] This qualification is not so abstract as it appears at first sight. If a country has a strong interest in the economic well-being of its trading partner, the former is less likely to retaliate even when injured by the latter. An oblique example is provided by the U.S. attitude toward the commercial policies of the young EEC or Japan in the late 1950s and early 1960s. The obverse, of course, is also true, and the discrimination by NATO, especially by the United States, against imports from (as well as restrictions on exports to) the Soviet bloc during most of the post–World War II period can be interpreted in this light.[12]

Given all the ambiguities and indeterminacies, what prescriptions can international trade theorists offer to a country confronted with foreign use of monopoly power? Most frequently, such prescriptions

---

[10] Game-theoretical concepts of the core and imputation make this point clear. The imputation resulting from retaliation is supposed to be equivalent to the imputation that would have prevailed in the absence of externalities. The same imputation is achievable through elimination of externalities coupled with a side payment by the country responsible for them to the country injured by them. The latter solution belongs to the core; that is, loosely speaking, it is Pareto-optimal, while the tariff solution is not.

[11] A related question was rigorously examined by J. Marcus Fleming, "The Optimal Tariff from an International Standpoint," *Review of Economics and Statistics*, vol. 38 (1956).

[12] The last point raises the possibility of an interesting extension of the so-called prisoner's dilemma or any other mixed-motive game. One can postulate that prisoner *A* who confesses and goes free has his opportunities for subsequent bank robberies reduced as a result of the execution of his partner *B*. Of course, even with this modification, the game remains of the nonconstant-sum variety; that is, the sum of payoffs will vary from one outcome to another. But if the disutility to *A* arising from the disappearance of *B* is large enough, the game becomes *determinate*. If each of the prisoners would rather spend a year in jail (neither confesses) than go free but be permanently deprived of a partner (one confesses and the other does not), both prisoners would confess.

accompany discussions of price discrimination,[13] and some are subsequently incorporated into international treaties and the commercial codes of various countries.

Most of the policy recommendations have been put forward in connection with dumping, but some analyses of measures designed to counter reverse dumping have also been undertaken.[14] Historically, nondiscriminating monopoly has received somewhat less extensive coverage in the international trade literature, although in recent years a number of authors have devoted considerable attention to this problem.[15]

Generally, economists have recommended countering foreign dumping with tariffs, but they have been more circumspect in prescribing optimum policies to be adopted by a country facing a simple monopoly or victimized by reverse dumping.[16] Recently, Richard Sweeney analyzed these questions in a general equilibrium framework. He found that under simple monopoly the competitive country lacks the ability to reach a Pareto optimum; assuming no secondary retaliation, the best it can do is to stabilize the price of its import (for example, by means of stockpiling) and use a tariff. Under discriminating monopoly, the optimal response by the dumpee is more complex; the rate of the tariff should be varied, depending on the spread between prices in the monopolist's home market and the dumpee's market.[17]

Sweeney's model is of a two-country variety. When a number of countries face a monopolist, countervailing policies undertaken by one of them will affect other importers. The problem was investigated by Philip Cummins and others in an attempt to devise an optimal policy toward OPEC. Not surprisingly, they found that a policy globally optimal "requires concerted action [by the countries faced by OPEC's monopoly power] to avoid accumulation of external diseconomies."[18]

---

[13] A classical reference is Jacob Viner, *Dumping: A Problem in International Trade* (Chicago: University of Chicago Press, 1923). An extensive analysis can be found in Gottfried Haberler, *The Theory of International Trade and Its Applications to Commercial Policy* (London: Hodge, 1936); and in Joan Robinson, *The Economics of Imperfect Competition* (London: Macmillan, 1964).

[14] See, for instance, Robert Kudrle, "A 'Reverse Dumping' Duty for Canada?" *Canadian Journal of Economics*, vol. 8 (1975).

[15] W. Max Corden, "Monopoly, Tariffs, and Subsidies," *Economica*, vol. 34 (1967); and Jagdish Bhagwati, *The Theory and Practice of Commercial Policy: Departures from Unified Exchange Rates*, Special Paper, no. 8 (Princeton University, International Finance Section, 1968).

[16] From the point of view of bargaining theory, in the context discussed, reverse dumping and simple monopoly are identical.

[17] Richard J. Sweeney, "Dumping: International Price Discrimination in a Simple General Equilibrium Analysis," OASIA Research Discussion Paper (U.S. Treasury, 1975).

[18] Philip Cummins, Michael Finger, Dennis E. Logue, Richard J. Sweeney, and

PART FIVE: THE LIBERAL'S DILEMMA

The common motive of those policy recommendations echoes earlier pronouncements about the ranking of various policies in the order of their distortionary effects on resource allocation: production and consumption subsidies are preferable to all tariffs; ad valorem tariffs are preferable to specific tariffs; tariffs are preferable to quotas. An important recent addition to the roster of trade policies is the price stabilization program, such as maintenance of buffer stocks.

Special Features of Monopoly in Foreign Investment. Apart from a different time framework, most issues of monopoly in foreign investment are analogous to those of monopoly in foreign trade. There is no need to repeat the case for liberal investment policies; with due regard to the nature of goods involved, the same conditions are required as in the argument for unimpeded trade in outputs. Similarly, the recommendations for restrictive foreign investment policies parallel the arguments for restricting trade flows. National advantage is one of them, and it is philosophically and theoretically akin to the optimum tariff argument. Indeed, the two are complementary.[19]

The two substantial arguments against unimpeded foreign investment flows that have no exact counterparts in the normative theory of commercial policy applicable to foreign trade arise from the fact of dealing with income-producing goods located outside the national territory. The first argument refers to the degree of social risk on foreign relative to domestic investment from the point of view of the investing country. Recently, this argument has been gathering strength in the wake of widespread nationalization of American assets abroad. The second argument invokes revenue losses to the national treasury of the investing country as compared with the alternative of having the same amount of private savings invested at home. The validity of these arguments for restricting the flow of foreign investment rests on the existence of negative externalities; social costs of investing in foreign lands exceed private costs of doing so.[20]

Thomas D. Willett, "The Price Effects of Alternative Tariff and Quota Systems in the Face of Foreign Monopoly," OASIA Research Discussion Paper (U.S. Treasury, 1975).

[19] This complementarity was recognized by Abba Lerner, "The Symmetry between Export and Import Taxes," *Economica*, vol. 3 (1936). For a more extended discussion and derivation of the best combination of import tariffs and taxes on foreign investment, see G. D. A. MacDougall, "The Benefits and Costs of Private Investment from Abroad: A Theoretical Approach," *Bulletin of the Oxford University Institute of Statistics*, vol. 22 (1960).

[20] A brief but lucid discussion of these issues is contained in Robert Tollison and Thomas Willett, *Problems of Economic Interdependence*, Pt. 3, "Trade and Investment Policy" (manuscript in progress).

From the point of view of the investment-receiving country, the attitude toward foreign investors is bound to be ambivalent. Foreign investment generates employment, income, tax revenues, possibly export earnings, and bestows other benefits upon the host country. The other side of the coin reflects the concerns of the host governments about local ownership, national sovereignty, status, and prestige.

These concerns are heightened when foreign investment involves high technology. While some arguments about the necessity of independent technological capabilities for national power are appropriate, former Prime Minister Harold Wilson's now famous remark about Britain becoming a "hewer of wood and drawer of water" bespeaks a deep concern for status. In a slightly different but still relevant context, a recent study of West German, French, and U.K. policies toward foreign direct investment "failed to uncover any (solidly based) official economic rationale" for the mix of policies adopted and concluded that its most satisfactory explanation was the concern over the "technology gap" and the advanced technology required for great power status in the age of the scientific state.[21]

These aspects make the issue of foreign investment more intractable than it would be if confined solely to questions of welfare or efficiency. The latter questions tend to be positive-sum matters; generally, potential arrangements exist that will make all partners better off in absolute terms than they would be without the interaction. Status gains, being inherently relative in nature, are more appropriately viewed as resulting from zero-sum contests. In a world where one's own perceived status depends on the degree of control of high technology, any erosion in that control can be seen as a diminution of national prestige.[22]

The issues facing the investment-receiving country confronted with the monopoly power of the investing country have been dealt with in the literature mainly in the context of less developed countries interacting with multinational corporations. From the point of view of an

---

[21] Robert Gillespie, "The Policies of England, France, and Germany as Recipients of Foreign Direct Investment," in Fritz Machlup and others, eds., *International Mobility and Movement of Capital* (New York: National Bureau of Economic Research, 1972), p. 430.

[22] An article in *Business Week* (May 17, 1976) entitled, "France: Seizing Control of Technical Industries," illustrates several points made here. "Giscard is determined to break US domination in high-technology industries that he considers important for national economic independence. . . . But rather than develop French alternatives—the disastrous policy followed by former President Charles de Gaulle—Giscard is buying American technology and using it to help push French industry into world markets."

LDC, it should be utterly irrelevant whether the corporation it is dealing with is a foreign government or a privately owned monopoly.[23] In reality, political considerations may render the task of countering the monopoly power of a privately owned MNC somewhat less complex than the power of a similar company owned by a foreign government. But whatever the legal status of the investing company in its home country, the host governments have legal powers over the movement of investment into, and returns on investment out of, their own countries. These governments operate a system of general controls, exchange controls, tariffs and taxes, requirements of equity participation in concerns initiated by foreign firms, and so on, all designed to encourage local reinvestment of locally generated funds. Even though in many instances the economic power of the investing MNC may exceed that of a local government, the relationship between the investing MNC and the host country more closely resembles a bilateral monopoly. Countervailing each other's monopoly power under these circumstances is tantamount to increasing one's power at the expense of the other, and, consequently, the free trader dilemma acquires in this situation a different focus.

Monopoly and Monopsony Elements in International Trade and Investment

Monopoly power has a number of alternative bases: control over naturally fixed resources, control over process or product technology, organizational and operational skills, spatial monopoly, and preferential treatment by the authorities. It is the latter type of monopoly that we are mostly concerned with here.

Sources of Monopolistic Power. The term *monopoly* is used in this paper in the broadest sense: a monopolist (monopsonist) is any group of sellers (buyers) having a significant degree of discretion over the price at which it sells (buys) and whose quantity sold (bought) varies inversely with the price it selects. On this definition, monopoly includes oligopoly and nonoligopolistic competition among a number of suppliers of differentiated products, as well as situations when (even though individual agents display purely competitive behavior) there are artificial restrictions on their numbers or on the quantities they are allowed to sell or purchase. A monopoly, then, is any agent for whom

---

[23] In fact, a typical MNC has at least one more source of economic power than a comparable corporation owned by a single foreign government. The former can practice transfer pricing more easily, thus extracting greater after-tax profits from its operations. Moreover, it is probably more flexible in shifting its surpluses of funds between locations.

Abba Lerner's measure of monopoly power is greater than zero, that is, whose average revenue exceeds his marginal cost.[24] In the sense of the definition given above, some degree of monopoly power is widespread in many walks of economic life and is probably unavoidable. Furthermore, whenever the degree of monopoly power is small, it is safe to assume that the cost of analysis, detection, regulation, and enforcement would largely exceed the welfare loss arising from the implied departure from the optimal output.

Monopolistic power becomes a matter of public concern when its exercise leads to *significant* price distortions with such corollaries as misallocation of resources and maldistribution of income in favor of the monopolist. In the international sphere, this concern is magnified by the recognition of institutional constraints on the possibility of alleviating the deleterious effects of monopoly through regulation or taxation.

Sources of monopoly power are countless: it can be purchased, inherited, extorted, acquired as a result of inventive genius, war bounty, or revolutionary victory; it can be given by the government explicitly as an exclusive right or implicitly by means of various taxes, subsidies, procurement policies, preferential access to information, concessionary terms of credit, and other deliberate policies; it can result from a merger, a takeover, the formation of a visible cartel, or the conclusion of a tacit agreement; finally, it can derive from the sheer size of an economic agent. Among national monopolies active in international trade, one can distinguish technological monopoly; patent-protected or trademark-protected monopoly; resource-ownership monopoly; monopoly derived from state ownership in a centrally planned economy; monopoly derived from state ownership or from an explicit or a tacit state control in a market-type economy; monopoly derived from state-granted exclusivity rights; state-owned monopolistic industry in a market-type economy; legal or illegal cartels of producers in a market-type economy; cartels of producers in a centrally planned economy; and monopoly based on size.

In addition to this very incomplete enumeration, an important source of monopolistic power in international trade derives from intermittent or temporary privileges granted to private firms by their governments in order to carry out particular deals (for instance, large arms sales) or from intercession by the governments on behalf of privately owned companies (for example, West German nuclear exporters).

---

[24] Abba P. Lerner, "The Concept of Monopoly and the Measurement of Monopoly Power," *Review of Economic Studies*, vol. 2 (1934).

PART FIVE: THE LIBERAL'S DILEMMA

All these categories of monopoly power differ from one another, not only with respect to legal standing and price distortions—hence, the allocative inefficiency they cause—but, more importantly, with respect to the policy measures likely to be most effective in counteracting their undesirable effects in the world markets.

Domestic Monopolies in the World Markets. Monopolization of a particular industry in a particular country need not automatically become a cause for concern for its trading partners. More often than not, the prime sufferer, especially if the industry is unregulated, is the society hosting the monopolized industry. As it happens, when a domestic monopoly enters the international market the degree of its monopoly power usually declines: a domestic monopolist (narrowly defined) becomes an oligopolist in the world market, and a domestic oligopolist may be so small relative to the world market that it becomes a price taker. Generally, the degree of monopoly power retained by a domestic monopoly, aside from its own size relative to the size of the world market for its product, depends on the competitiveness of the world market and the extent of its segmentation.[25] One can distinguish among several typical situations.

Thus, a monopolized industry X in country A, especially if it is a small country, is just one of the competitors in the world market. In the absence of trade restrictions, industry X would be a price taker in both the domestic and the foreign markets. Even if industry X is protected at home by a barrier, it is compelled to behave competitively in the world market. That would be the case, say, of the Israeli printed circuits monopoly, which must compete in the world market with suppliers from North America, Western Europe, and Japan.

The situation is different in country A (especially if A is large) if industry X is able to capture a substantial share of the world market otherwise supplied by a large number of competitive firms from various countries. In the absence of trade barriers, the degree of monopoly power enjoyed by X is greater than zero, and it may easily become the price leader in the world market. Unless it selects the price that would have prevailed under perfect competition, it will either drive its perfect competitors out of business (if it enjoys a cost advantage) or cause output to be restricted. If industry X is protected at home by a barrier,

---

[25] An analysis of the relationship between the nature of various monopolies in the world market and their structure is given by Richard E. Caves in *International Trade, International Investment, and Imperfect Markets*, Special Papers in International Economics, no. 10 (Princeton University International Finance Section, 1974).

it will discriminate between the home and foreign markets. This situation is exemplified by the Japanese shipbuilding consortia as exporters and the Soviet grain-purchasing agency as an importer.

Further, monopolized industry X in country A may compete in the world market with a limited number of large competitors from other countries. If none of the producers is protected at home, the situation amounts to an oligopoly. If one producer is protected at home, it will behave as a monopolist in the protected market and as an oligopolist in the world market. An example of such a monopolist-oligopolist is the British Leyland (Truck Division).

Not infrequently, one encounters instances, mainly in a free trade zone or a customs union, of a home monopoly competing with another national monopoly enjoying a preferential access to the home market and a number of other competitors having a more restrictive access to that market. This is approximately the case of the West German Siemens competing with the Dutch Phillipps, as well as with a host of Japanese, U.S., and other non-German producers of electronic components. Such configuration implies that some firms have relatively stronger monopolistic positions in one segment of the world market than in another. At the extreme, the same competitors may behave as oligopolists in the protected segment of the world market and as perfect competitors in the unprotected one.

To cite another example, firm X in country A may enjoy a considerably greater monopoly power in country B, where it has been granted special privileges, than in either its home market or other markets. For instance, the exclusivity privileges granted to Pepsi Cola in the Soviet Union or Coca-Cola in India give them virtual monopoly in locally producing and distributing soft drinks of a particular variety. This kind of monopoly, instead of restricting the degree of competition in the world market, restricts the size of the world market (for soft drinks) itself.

Monopolized industry X in country A may be the sole producer of its product in the world. Naturally, its price-setting policy would be totally determined by the demand curve for this product, which in turn would be influenced by the availability of functionally appropriate substitutes. Such monopolists are, for instance, Control Data Corporation with regard to its CYBER 176 line, or the U.S. Department of Defense as the supplier of the AWAC systems.

Finally, and in today's world perhaps most significantly, monopolists or oligopolists from various countries may combine into cartels. OPEC, of course, is the most notorious example, but such venerable international institutions as International Air Transport Association (air fares) or North-Atlantic Conference (freight schedules) belong to the same class of cartel-based monopolies.

The very variety of relations between national monopolies and other participants in the world market implies that countering every manifestation of monopoly, whether or not officially sponsored or condoned, is neither practicable nor even desirable. What, then, are the instances of monopoly power that a "free trader" would consider countervailing? Should the criteria for countervailing be based on the source of monopoly power, its extent, the cost of countervailing relative to the benefit from thus weakening the monopoly, or on some political considerations? In other words, when does the presence of a monopoly become harmful enough to justify efforts to counteract it?

Market Structure, Conduct, and Performance: The Judicial Point of View. In the United States—by far the most experienced country in devising, enacting, interpreting, and enforcing antitrust legislation—economists, legal scholars, and the courts have been groping for answers to the questions posed above since well before the Sherman Act came into force. Even though there are many indisputable differences between the questions raised by the presence of monopolistic elements in the domestic economy and problems arising from the exercise of monopoly power in international markets, the parallels are sufficiently close to devote some attention to the interplay of economic and legal theories in this area.

The first step in the analysis of antimonopoly policy is to identify those phenomena in the marketplace that must be affected by public policy to bring about the desired results. Generally, the interrelationship between market structure and market conduct and the resultant consequences have been the focal points of attention of both lawyers and economists.[26] Examination of such interrelationships ought to form the basis for deciding what would be a *desirable* policy; analysis of the legal and, especially in the case of foreign monopolies, the political environment ought to form the basis for deciding what may be a *feasible* policy.

Market structure refers to particular components of an individual

---

[26] The standard reference for economists is still Joe S. Bain, *Industrial Organization*, 2nd ed. (New York: Wiley, 1968). Law students turn frequently to Carl Kaysen and Donald F. Turner, *Antitrust Policy* (Cambridge: Harvard University Press, 1959). For a long time there has been little cross-fertilization between the two groups. Fortunately, as William A. Lovett reports in "Economic Analysis and Its Role in Legal Education," *Journal of Legal Education*, 1974, Bain's volume has become required reading in most law and economics courses taught in leading law schools.

industry, such as (1) the degree of seller concentration as determined by the number and size of firms in a particular industry; (2) the degree of product differentiation as determined by the extent to which buyers distinguish sellers' outputs as being dissimilar; (3) the conditions of entry as determined by the ease with which new sellers may enter the market.

Market conduct "refers to the pattern of behavior that enterprises follow in adjusting to the market in which they sell or buy,"[27] generally reflected in the method and mode of interaction in pricing decisions and other matters of collective interest.

The traditional nexus between a structural factor, the possession of market power, and the resultant behavioral factor, the monopolistic conduct, has caused trouble in consistently applying in legal practice the seemingly unchallengeable conclusions of economic theory.[28] Apparently, U.S. courts did not share economists' infatuation with the perfectly competitive paradigm. At the time of the Standard Oil case (1911), the American industrial structure was swept by a wave of mergers, so that even then the market structure was a far cry from that described by the "pure" competitive model. Consequently, judges were reluctant to become extensively involved in an analysis of market power and saw little value in basing their decisions even partially on what they perceived as an irrelevant theoretical construct. This attitude had a tremendous influence on the manner in which antitrust legislation was initially interpreted.

The Sherman Act is (deliberately?) ambiguous in providing a clue to what kind of monopoly power is deemed socially undesirable—just the kind resulting from a particular type of conduct or the kind due to the structure of the market as well?[29] In the early application of the antitrust law, the Supreme Court interpreted the act as having the purpose of prohibiting the types of conduct whose aim was to restrict competition. "Monopolizing," in Section II of the act, meant in fact the acts incident to attempts to acquire or maintain substantial monopoly power,

---

[27] Bain, *Industrial Organization*, p. 9.

[28] A good summary of the interplay of legal and economic theories in this area can be found in Dale F. Rubin, "Competition Policy and the Caribbean Community," *Journal of World Trade Law*, 1975.

[29] The Sherman Act reads in its pertinent part: "Section I—Every contract, combination in the form of trust or otherwise, or conspiracy, in restraint of trade or commerce among the several States, or with foreign nations, is hereby declared illegal. . . . Section II—Every person who shall monopolize, or attempt to monopolize, or combine or conspire with any other person or persons to monopolize any part of the trade or commerce among the several States, or with foreign nations, shall be deemed guilty of a MISDEMEANOR."

not its mere possession. This interpretation was encompassed by the so-called rule of reason enunciated by Chief Justice Byron White in the landmark case of *Standard Oil Company of New Jersey* v. *United States.* The significance of the rule of reason becomes evident when one admits that monopoly power can be achieved by conduct consonant with competitive behavior. A firm may ascend to dominance in a particular market as a result of "fair" competition—for example, as a consequence of the discovery and introduction of a new process or product. Since the firm can hardly be condemned for that, it follows that mere possession of market power should not be deemed socially undesirable, let alone unlawful.[30] In the early days of application of the Sherman Act, it was the *act* of monopolizing that was taken to mean an *unlawful* exertion of monopoly power. It may be noted, however, that Section I concerns the activities of groups of firms whose goal is usually accomplished by agreement, explicit or tacit. This agreement is unequivocally prohibited by law. But, clearly, a single firm monpolizing the market need enter into collusive agreements with no other firm. As was noted, this interpretation of antitrust law meant that "firms with no preponderant place in total sales are forbidden to take *collective* action to fix prices, restrain output or boycott outsiders. A single firm that covers the same portion of total sales may (within limits) set its own prices, restrict its own output or withhold its goods from whomever it chooses."[31]

As it has become apparent that this interpretation of the intent of the antitrust legislation is too restrictive, the rule of reason has been applied ever more frequently for assessing a firm's "general course of action." The courts recognized that "even without particular, identifiable acts of exploitation or predation, a firm's general course of policy and behavior may be such as to give rise to an inference of monopolistic intent."[32]

---

[30] Legal scholars describe "justifiable accumulation" of monopoly power as a condition where such power was "thrust upon" the firm. Bowman, for instance, isolated four instances of "thrust upon" situations: (1) the "natural" monopoly situation, where the market will support only one plant if a technically efficient level of production is to be achieved; (2) the "dying industry" situation, where a shift toward substitutes so reduces demand for the industry product that all but one firm is eliminated; (3) when a firm "gets the jump" on other firms by introducing a new product or process; (4) when a firm is able to attract and keep "the best brains" and is thus able to "outcompete its competitors." For a fuller elaboration of a lawyer's point of view, see Ward S. Bowman, "Toward Less Monopoly," *University of Pennsylvania Law Review*, vol. 101 (1953).

[31] Corwin D. Edwards, "Control of the Single Firm: Its Place in Antitrust Policy," *Law and Contemporary Problems*, 1965 (emphasis added).

[32] A. D. Neale, *The Anti-Trust Laws of the U.S.A.*, 2nd ed. University Press, 1970.

Two developments gradually led the courts to focus on the interrelatedness between market structure and market conduct. First, as industrial structures grew more complex, so did the task of isolating the opprobrious pattern of conduct. Second, there was growing unease among economists about the dogmatic utilization of the competitive paradigm in solving problems derived from a structural framework almost totally unrelated to this paradigm. Recognizing the need for development of a competition policy suited to the realities of a given industrial structure, John M. Clark pioneered the "workable competition" concept.[33] Clark's objective was to identify those particular conditions under which the market position and the conduct of firms were such as to secure a "desirable level" of effective competition.

Although some economists and lawyers have viewed this concept as involving primarily a structural approach, the more widely accepted view appears to require an analysis of the interrelatedness of workably competitive structures, specific conduct, and acceptable performance. Joe S. Bain states that "knowledge of what structures and patterns of conduct, or combinations thereof, are and are not workably competitive requires a knowledge of the association of structure and conduct to performance."[34] Acceptable performance, in Bain's view, is determined primarily by its "efficiency dimensions." These are (1) technical efficiency, "how closely it [a firm] approaches (or by how far it misses) the goal of supplying whatever output it produces at the minimum attainable unit cost of production"; and (2) allocative efficiency, "judged by the long-run relationship between its selling price and its marginal cost of production that results from the particular rate of output it produces."

It is not entirely clear how much the efforts by economists to devise more realistic models contributed to the willingness of the courts to pay more attention to market structure and its effect on conduct. It is clear, however, that the courts have in fact espoused more comprehensive rules, the effect of which was to circumscribe the business practices of those who happen to possess market power. The "mere" possession of market power ceased to be unassailable.

The evolution toward the new approach was exemplified by the decisions in two famous cases: *Aluminum Company of America* v. *United States* (1945) and *United Shoe Machinery Corporation* v. *United States* (1953). In the Alcoa case, the Supreme Court asserted that the possession of monopoly power cannot in and of itself constitute an offense under the antitrust law and indicated those situations

---

[33] John M. Clark, "Toward a Concept of Workable Competition," *American Economic Review*, vol. 30 (1940).

[34] Bain, *Industrial Organization*, p. 17.

in which monopoly ought to be tolerated.[35] But the burden of demonstrating that its monopoly power arises from one of such situations was placed squarely on Alcoa's shoulders.

In the United Shoe case (the defendant was accused of having illegally exercised its market power in leasing shoemaking machinery), the Court spelled out most explicitly the inherent evils of possession of monopoly power:

> In one sense, the leasing system and the miscellaneous activities just referred to . . . were natural and normal for they were . . . "honestly industrial." They are the sort of activities which would be engaged in by other honorable firms. And, to a large extent, the leasing practices conform to long-standing traditions in the shoe machinery business. Yet, they are not practices which can be properly described as the inevitable consequences of ability, natural forces, or law. They represent something more than the use of accessible resources, the process of invention and innovation, and the employment of those techniques of employment, financing, production, and distribution, which a competitive society must foster. They are contracts, arrangements, and policies which, instead of encouraging competition based on pure merit, further the dominance of a particular firm. In this sense, they are unnatural barriers; they unnecessarily exclude actual and potential competition; they restrict a free market. While the law allows many enterprises to use such practices, the Sherman Act is not construed by superior courts to forbid the continuance of effective market control based in part upon such practices. Those courts hold that market control is inherently evil and constitutes a violation of Section 2 unless economically inevitable, or specifically authorized and regulated by law.[36]

This statement, in conjunction with the delineation (in the Alcoa case) of situations in which market power will be tolerated, implies that monopoly obtained or maintained by other means is per se unlawful even in the absence of an identifiable, specific, condemnable pattern of business conduct. Combined with the earlier "conduct approach," the latter decisions seem to indicate the courts' readiness to adopt the rule that even "normal" or "innocuous" business practices, *if combined with monopoly power*, can be held to be offensive under the antitrust law.

Application of the U.S. Antitrust Doctrine to Foreign Monopoly. From the preceding discussion, it appears that the U.S. antitrust doctrine pro-

---

[35] These situations are virtually the same as those enumerated in n. 30 above.
[36] Quoted in Neale, *Antitrust Laws*, p. 145.

vides an adequate conceptual framework for identifying foreign monopolies whose presence causes social damage, although the ability to identify such monopolies clearly does not imply that countervailing their power would be either advisable on the cost-benefit criteria or practically possible. Apart, however, from the considerations of advisability and feasibility, additional complications arise from such factors as the national identity of a given foreign firm and the economic organization of many foreign countries engaged in commercial exchanges with the United States. The former factor refers to the limited domain of sovereignty of the U.S. authorities over foreign firms, the latter to the fact that in most foreign countries state ownership or control of individual firms or entire industries is incomparably more common than in the United States.

As far as the national identity of a foreign monopolist is concerned, to the extent that the offensive behavior takes place in the U.S. market it is legally inconsequential: foreign firms are subject to the same laws as any domestic company. The adverb "legally" is of importance here since, potentially at least, behind every foreign firm found guilty by U.S. courts or regulatory agencies of exercising monopoly power looms the might of the respective foreign government. Thus, every attempt to curb foreign use of monopoly in the courts, be it initiated by the authorities or the foreign firms' domestic competitors, entails not just legal but also diplomatic maneuvering. When foreign monopoly is exercised against U.S. companies outside the national territory, recourse by the injured parties to the U.S. judiciary is likely to be entirely futile. It is certain to be so when the monopoly power is exercised by foreign authorities themselves.[37] Thus, redress before the U.S. courts being ineffectual or outright impossible, the burden of counteracting foreign monopoly power, not surprisingly, is placed upon the shoulders of the executive and legislative branches.

The second factor—the prevalence of state-owned enterprises in many foreign countries—limits the applicability of U.S. antitrust legislation considerably. Since the sociopolitical structures of many countries give birth to state monopolies, it would seem to make little sense to invoke against those countries the antimonopoly criteria adopted by the U.S. courts. Pushed to its logical conclusion, such a policy would amount to asking, say, the Czechoslovakian government to divest itself

---

[37] This is the consequence of the Act of State Doctrine, which precludes courts of one country from inquiring into the validity of the public acts that a recognized foreign sovereign power commits within its own territory. See Richard N. Swift, *International Law: Current and Classic* (New York: Wiley, 1969). The doctrine was interpreted by the Supreme Court in the Sabbatino case as applicable not only to foreign governments but also to their instrumentalities.

of part of the country's steel industry. Even in dealings with market-type economies, it would be narrowly parochial and highly presumptuous, but most of all entirely purposeless, to expect, say, Japan to abandon its policy of encouraging concentration in certain industries. For better or worse, differences in political, social, and economic arrangements, not to mention economic philosophies, between the United States and other nations are real and permanent. Therefore, U.S. policies aimed at countervailing foreign use of monopoly power ought to treat the peculiarities of economic organization in other countries as fixed parameters, not as variables to be influenced.

Given these limitations, criteria for selection of foreign use of monopoly power subject to countervailing intervention by the United States should be based more on the conduct approach described in the preceding section, rather than on the current attitude displayed by the U.S. courts in domestic antitrust litigation. The "conduct" in this context is somewhat more encompassing than the concept implied by the Sherman Act and the subsequent precedents. It would include elements of what industrial organization experts call "performance" and would be evaluated against the market structure in the United States but *not* against the market structure in the home country of the foreign monopolist. In other words, one should disregard the fact that an exporter of a given product to the United States may be owned or controlled by the state and concentrate instead on how much its conduct and performance in the U.S. market departs from the standards prevailing in the corresponding U.S. industry.

State Trading

In assessing the conduct of enterprises owned or tightly controlled by the state (whether or not they are monopolized), account must be taken of the possibility that their mandate includes pursuit of certain *national* objectives. This is a feature of state trading important enough to merit more detailed treatment.[38]

Characteristics. GATT recognizes that state trading firms "might be operated so as to create serious obstacles to trade."[39] The threat to

---

[38] There exist several comprehensive treatments of this problem: Kenneth Dam, "State Trading," in *The GATT: Law and International Economic Organization* (Chicago: University of Chicago Press, 1970), chapter 18; John H. Jackson, "State Trading and Monopolies," in *World Trade and the Law of the GATT* (New York: Bobbs-Merrill, 1969), chapter 14; K. R. Gupta, *A Study on General Agreement on Tariffs and Trade* (New Delhi: S. Chaud, 1967). See also the spring and summer issues of *Law and Contemporary Problems*, vol. 18 (1959), devoted entirely to various aspects of state trading.

[39] GATT, Art. 17, para. 3.

the world trading arrangement does not arise so much from state ownership of trading enterprises as from some constraints on purely enterpreneurial decisions by an entity manifestly responsive not only to commercial considerations but also to other factors.

State trading, whether conducted by market-type economies (MTEs) or centrally planned economies (CPEs), may be directed toward various objectives. Their attainment may induce state trading firms to (1) aim at improving the terms of trade by raising export prices or lowering import prices or both; (2) improve the balance of payments by directly determining the components of the current account; (3) protect domestic production from imports, promote exports, discriminate in favor of certain trading partners through determination of either the domestic or the external prices of traded goods and the quantities traded; (4) manipulate incomes of particular groups by controlling prices of exports or imports; (5) serve fiscal objectives by channeling profits from trade into budget revenues; (6) enhance national security by monopolizing trade in military items; (7) protect public health and safety or public morals by controlling imports and distribution of such items as pharmaceuticals, alcohol, or narcotics.

The main differences between state trading in MTEs and in CPEs are the extent of coverage and the degree of state control over the rest of the economy. The extent of coverage determines the scope for the exercise of monopoly power by the state, while the degree of state control determines the ease and effectiveness of that exercise. In practice, in centrally planned economies state trading alone is sufficient to attain all objectives listed above (subject, of course, to various constraints) without resort to more familiar instruments of commercial policy. In market-type economies this is usually not the case.

Objections to state trading are predicated upon the validity of the presumption that they commonly pursue objectives other than securing normal profits made from trade for the government. Were this presumption erroneous, a state trading monopoly would be functionally indistinguishable from a privately owned enterprise, although the usual objections against the noncompetitive market structure would still apply. If, however, state trading monopoly, in conjunction with a substantial degree of control over the rest of the economy, is used to drive a wedge between world and domestic prices, objections to state trading become equivalent to the objections raised by the theory of commercial policy against state intervention in trade, production, or consumption.[40] The implications for international welfare are the same

---

[40] For elaboration, see Bhagwati, *Trade, Tariffs, and Growth*, pp. 68 ff.

whether such intervention is carried out through state trading or through more traditional means of commercial policy. Finally, state trading makes it much easier to conceal government intervention in the process of production and international trade and thus enables the government to nullify the effect of reciprocal concessions in the area of trade and investment.

The State of Evidence. Systematic evidence regarding the effects of the use of state monopoly power against U.S. interests is conspicuously lacking. There are well-known instances of foreign cartels or state trading monopolies that succeed permanently or intermittently in exporting to or importing from the United States at prices more advantageous than those presumed to prevail under perfect competition. The press provides daily examples permeated by circumstantial evidence of foreign monopolists hurting U.S. businesses, but comprehensive cross-sectional studies are yet to be published.

Admittedly, it is not easy to come up with a well-documented conclusion about the degree of harm, if any, inflicted by foreign monopolies operating in U.S. markets. Even though the relevant theoretical concepts are familiar and empirical methods commonly used in economics can be employed, the pertinent data are usually unavailable, at least in a usable form.

In what follows, two very different cases of state intervention in the process of international trade are selected for discussion and evaluation of possible policy responses. Clearly, a much more sustained effort is needed to develop a policy-oriented methodology for assessing the extent of damage caused by the presence of noncompetitive elements in international trade.

Case 1: The incidence of monopsony power of centrally planned economies in the market for U.S. homogeneous exports. Studies of Soviet pricing practices have a venerable history. Some fifteen years ago, a lively debate took place on the question of Soviet price discrimination against other members of the Council for Mutual Economic Assistance (COMECON).[41] The debate was enlightening in that it pointed out the conceptual ambiguities related to using any set of prices to measure

---

[41] Franklyn Holzman, "Soviet Foreign Trade Pricing and the Question of Discrimination," *Review of Economics and Statistics,* vol. 44 (May 1962); "Soviet Bloc Mutual Discrimination: Comment," ibid., November 1962; "More on Soviet Bloc Trade Discrimination," *Soviet Studies,* vol. 17 (1965). Horst Menderhausen, "Terms of Trade between the Soviet Union and the Smaller Communist Countries, 1955–1957," *Review of Economics and Statistics,* vol. 41 (1959); "The Terms of Soviet-Satellite Trade: A Broadened Analysis," "Mutual Price Discrimination in the Soviet Bloc Trade," and "A Final Comment," ibid., 1960.

the extent of discrimination. More recently, Ryan Amacher's work on Yugoslavia provided additional clues to what the determinants of power of a state trading monopoly may be.[42] However, no attempts have been made in these studies to examine the extent, if any, of the effects of the monopoly power of socialist trading enterprises on their dealings with American businesses.

As a modest beginning in analyzing the extent to which state trading monopsonies are able to buy U.S. exports below prices paid by other importers, I compared prices paid for 126 U.S. export products in eight consecutive quarters, from first quarter 1975 through fourth quarter 1976. In order to make price comparisons, the selected commodities had to be fairly homogeneous. The a priori assumption was that such goods would command world market prices so that state trading monopsonists would be unable to exercise their power.

The data base consisted of over 2 million pairs of observations on unit values and quantities of U.S. exports shipped, as reported by thirty regional districts of the U.S. Customs. The commodities were classified at the seven-digit level of the Standard International Trade Classification as reported in the so-called Schedule B (*U.S. Exports*) published by the Department of Commerce. The goods examined were split into three groups: forty-two agricultural commodities; forty-six chemicals, minerals, and ores; and thirty-eight industrial products.

Alternative control samples were used, one consisting of nine Western European countries (West Germany, the United Kingdom, France, Italy, Spain, the Netherlands, Belgium-Luxembourg, Sweden, and Norway), the other consisting of the "Big Three" (West Germany, the United Kingdom, and France). COMECON countries were grouped in three alternative test samples—all European members (USSR, Poland, East Germany, Czechoslovakia, Romania, Hungary, and Bulgaria); European members less USSR; and the Soviet Union alone. Prices paid by any country in each period were weighted by the quantities it purchased. Prices paid by the presumed monopsonistic buyers were regressed on prices paid by the presumed competitive buyers. Cross-section, time series, and pooled cross-section–time series regressions were run, both uncorrected and corrected for heteroscedasticity.

As could be expected, the results were somewhat mixed. For instance, for some reason the COMECON countries always pay lower prices for, say, lemons and uniformly higher prices for corn. But the overall tendency for the COMECON importers to pay lower, often significantly lower, prices for U.S. agricultural products than their

---

[42] Ryan C. Amacher, "State Trading and the Question of Discrimination: The Yugoslav Case," *Economic Inquiry*, vol. 13 (1975).

Western European counterparts is unmistakable. The tendency is unaltered by the exclusion of smaller Western European countries from the test sample and is generally stronger for the USSR than for the smaller Communist countries. Thus, the results would suggest the prevalence of competitive buyers in Western European countries and a higher degree of monopsony power enjoyed by the Soviet Union than by other members of COMECON.

The same tests performed on forty-six basic chemicals, ores, and minerals revealed no clear pattern; if anything, the COMECON countries paid slightly higher prices for American exports in this category than did importers from Western Europe. In the third commodity group, prices paid for industrial products were generally lower for the COMECON members than for Western European importers. On average, the former paid 8 percent lower prices than the latter for agricultural products, 11 percent lower for the industrial products in the sample, and 6 percent higher prices for chemicals, minerals, and ores.

Even though these results should be treated with caution, they indicate that, not infrequently, state-owned, centralized purchasing agencies are able to extract price advantages over competitive buyers. Still, in my opinion, this finding does not constitute a casus belli calling for countervailing policies by the U.S. government.

First, there is no certainty that lower prices are necessarily a reflection of monopsony power. It is conceivable, for instance, that the price differentials reflect storage costs: faced with foreign exchange constraints, Eastern European importers may take early delivery of bulky or perishable goods and devote additional domestic resources to storing those goods at home, thus saving on foreign exchange expenditures. Lower prices paid by COMECON importers for industrial products may reflect either lower quality of products purchased by them or purchases of very large amounts of standardized products, enabling U.S. producers to lower their unit costs.

More to the point, countervailing policies would be extremely costly if they were to cover a substantial range of goods, and intercession by the government would be the worst possible solution. The cost of additional bureaucracy definitely would exceed the computed total of $70 million "underpaid" in 1975 by the COMECON countries relative to the Western Europeans. Setting up cartels of U.S. exporters of the Webb-Pomerene type (which are legal under U.S. antitrust law) would be only slightly more desirable. Recent analyses show that their most conspicuous consequence is restriction of domestic competition among their members.[43] Finally, any exercise of the countervailing power by the United States would imply discrimination against foreign buyers. Textbook assertions of perfect competition in the domestic U.S. market for agricultural products notwithstanding, it is well known that large American grain-trading companies purchase agricultural commodities, both spot and forward, on behalf of foreign and domestic clients. Although some of these clients are foreign monopolies, either state owned (COMECON countries) or state controlled (India, Ghana, Tongsun Park of South Korea, for example), they are frequently quite small in relation to many domestic purchasers of a particular crop (for instance, Interstate Brands Corporation has annual purchases of wheat of the same magnitude as the largest foreign monopolies). Finding a foreign importer to be a state monopoly cannot by itself justify initiating countervailing policies against it.

This does not preclude, however, the desirability (and the feasibility) of counteracting monopolisticlike conduct by state trading companies, especially when the stakes are high. The "great grain robbery" of 1972 and its repetition in miniature in 1977 indicate that under propitious circumstances state trading enterprises do behave as monopsonists, considerably damaging U.S. interests in the process. It is possible that the Winnipeg Wheat Board is better suited to prevent the Soviet Union from exerting its monoposony power in the Canadian wheat market than the competitive American grain suppliers are to prevent it from doing so in the U.S. market. But probably the same outcome can be secured by imposing very strict reporting requirements on both foreign importers and domestic grain brokers, supported by the threat of heavy fines and revocation of licenses for noncompliance. This solution would have the advantage of making the policy of countervailing the power of state trading monopolies nondiscriminatory and rooted in law, it would not involve the U.S. government, except to enforce the law, and it would give rise to no additional distortions anywhere in the economy.

Case 2: Foreign military sales. Sales of military goods and services to foreigners (on the so-called agreement as distinct from delivery basis) account for about 8 percent of total U.S. exports of goods and services. Over 95 percent of military exports is administered by the Department of Defense (DOD) under the Foreign Military Sales (FMS) program. In fact, DOD acts as an intermediary, contracting for particular items with private domestic firms at prices mutually agreed upon and selling

---

[43] For a frontal attack on such cartels, see David A. Larson, "An Economic Analysis of the Webb-Pomerene Act," *Journal of Law and Economics*, vol. 13 (1970).

PART FIVE: THE LIBERAL'S DILEMMA

those items to foreign customers. It acts as a monopsonist on one side of the market and as a monopolist or an oligopolist on the other side. The buyers of U.S. military exports are always foreign governments and hence also monopsonists.

Most of the information on pricing of military exports is either proprietary or classified, so that the subject cannot be discussed with any degree of specificity. Enough is known, however, about general pricing patterns to draw certain conclusions. First, an R&D surcharge of about 4.5 percent is applied to the value of most exports of high technology items. The surcharge is not turned over to the producer; it is retained by DOD. Since DOD is funding about 50 percent of all basic research done in the United States, the R&D surcharge on FMS can be viewed as partial recoupment of the social cost of producing a weapons system. Had the producer been selling the items directly to the foreign government, those social costs would not have been internalized.

Further, although military exports are supposed to be priced on a cost-plus basis, prices actually charged to foreign buyers differ, both up and down, from procurement prices paid by the U.S. services. Generally, for items most advanced technologically and of most recent design, foreign importers of American weapons have to pay more than U.S. armed forces; for items of older design, prices charged to the foreigners are lower than domestic procurement prices. Nonetheless, and despite appearances to the contrary, profit maximization is hardly the motive of the FMS administrators. (If it were, they could have done even better by discriminating among their foreign customers.[44] The discrimination would have been effective because one stipulation attached to all arms export deals and vigorously enforced by the U.S. government prohibits unauthorized transfers of U.S.-made equipment to third parties.) Differences in prices charged to the U.S. armed forces and foreign buyers reflect the understandable preoccupation of the Pentagon, a state trading enterprise, with other than purely commercial objectives. In effect, it uses "excess" profits earned on the sale of most advanced types of equipment to subsidize U.S. producers of less modern hardware still being used by the services. Its aim is to keep the industrial mobilization base "warm," that is, ready to resume full-scale production on short notice.

The Pentagon's concern with noncommercial considerations is even more apparent when arms export deals are large and involve transfers

---

[44] Such policy would not be in violation of Art. 17, para. 1(b) of GATT, which exempts from nondiscriminatory treatment goods exported by state trading enterprises, provided that "different prices are charged for commercial reasons, to meet conditions of supply and demand in export markets."

of advanced technology. (Its direct control over transfers of military technology has been acquired rather recently. Before the FMS program was set up, the U.S. government had exercised such control through strict licensing of exports of military items.)

A typical example of large-scale government involvement in a commercial deal was the sale of the light-weight fighter F-16 to four North Atlantic Treaty Organization (NATO) countries: Belgium, Holland, Norway, and Denmark. Initially the competition involved two American firms, one French, and one Swedish, but ultimately the choice was between the U.S. plane produced by the General Dynamics Corporation and the Mirage F-1 produced by Marcel Dassault of France. The deal involved 348 aircraft at close to $10 million apiece. Far more substantial sales loomed on the horizon, since it was expected that other NATO countries would follow suit. Even though the technical performance of the American aircraft was universally judged superior to that of its French competitor, the French government stepped in, offering the potential buyers a number of "sweeteners": coproduction arrangements and offset agreements. General Dynamics was in no position to match the offer made by Dassault at the instigation of the French government. As it became obvious that the choice, instead of being made on the basis of price and quality, would be determined by the concessions offered by the seller, the U.S. government intervened on behalf of the American company.

Eventually, a complex arrangement involving specific and general offsets and coproduction agreements was negotiated between a specially formed consortium of the four European countries and the U.S. government. While some parts of those agreements could have been negotiated by General Dynamics, subject to approval by the U.S. government, the company could not commit the U.S. Air Force to purchase certain electronic components from the Phillipps of Holland or the U.S. Army to equip its M-60 tanks with guns manufactured by the Societé Générale de Belgique. Thus, in this case, countervailing the monopoly power of a foreign government by using the monopoly power of the U.S. government was the only alternative to forgoing "the sale of the century."

Eventually, the American manufacturer won the contract, but the official involvement in this deal was not costless. Given the virtually insurmountable overall technological superiority and greater cost efficiency of the United States in the manufacture of advanced military hardware, coproduction and offset agreements with Europeans imply that the United States is willing to accept inferior goods at higher prices. According to some military analysts, the magnitude of these costs may

PART FIVE: THE LIBERAL'S DILEMMA

exceed the economies of larger-scale production.[45] It is obvious that the benefits to the nation and the international community—standardization of parts, training, and so on, with their corollaries of enhanced military effectiveness for the NATO alliance and political goodwill—outweighed, in the judgment of the U.S. government, the various costs of the open government involvement in the deal. From a global point of view, however, government involvement in such deals is justifiable only if the international community accepts the premise of legitimacy of the government's pursuit of the enumerated objectives.

Postscript

Readers who looked for a precise prescription of how a country adhering to a liberal economic doctrine should behave when exposed to the use of monopoly power by other countries must feel disappointed. The diversity of situations encountered in international relations precludes a uniform policy approach, even when the economic theory is able to provide definitive answers. Nonetheless, several principles enunciated in various sections of this study may be useful guidelines. In my opinion, they at least deserve some consideration.

First, a distinction should be made among the various sources of market power. Market power derived from sheer size or from the economic system of a given country should not be automatically regarded as exploitative or predatory. On the other hand, cartelization of domestically competitive industry for the sole purpose of dealing with foreign buyers or sellers should be viewed as an attempt to increase one's market power at the expense of other countries. The emphasis should be on the motives of the monopolist, as reflected in his conduct and performance, and definitely not solely on his ability to exercise monopoly power.

Second, the legitimacy of certain national objectives ought to have a seal of international approval, with the aim of limiting the gray areas of differing interpretations of this concept by national authorities. An international agreement on this subject, although very remote at present, could be incorporated in principle into GATT. The range of internationally agreed-upon "legitimate" national interests would probably be wider than the U.S. government would advocate, but there is no reason to fear that any attempt to reach such an understanding is doomed to failure. GATT or the IMF Articles of Agreement pro-

---

[45] See Michael D. Eiland, "Some Observations on Comparative Advantage, Economic Efficiency, and the 'Two-Way Street,'" Discussion Paper (Department of Defense, Directorate for International Economic Affairs, 1976).

vide an example of how divergent national economic philosophies can be accommodated.

Third, retaliation should be contemplated only against manifestations of monopoly power aimed demonstrably at objectives not considered legitimate. In particular, unadulterated pursuit of national advantage through better terms of trade or beggar-thy-neighbor predatory pricing would be denied legitimacy.

Fourth, the damage caused by foreign use of monopoly power should be carefully assessed by the national authorities, since consecutive rounds of retaliation are bound to be more costly than the initial real losses arising from foreign misbehavior or the opportunity losses of nonretaliation.

Fifth, if the injury inflicted by the exercise of monopoly power by a foreign government is clear and serious enough to justify countervailing policies, the scope and intensity of retaliation should be geared to the "seriousness of the offense." Generally, retaliation should be "compensatory" rather than punitive, and it should be ceased as soon as the reason for it disappears.

Sixth, the application of countervailing policies should be consistent rather than undertaken on an ad hoc basis. This would make the threat of retaliation credible and at the same time present potential offenders with an "estimate" of the opportunity cost of their intended action. In order to make the threat even more credible, retaliation in response to the most blatant abuses of monopoly power by foreign governments should be mandated by the Congress. The certainty of retaliation, which would wipe out all the offender's initial gains, is likely to be a much more effective deterrent than a Draconian but uncertain retribution.

Even though adherence to the above principles appears to make some uses of countervailing policies justifiable, it should not be forgotten that retaliation is an expression of force, and force is not a source of law. If trade and investment wars are to be avoided, machinery to adjudicate disputes would have to be established, such as an international tribunal or an arbitration agency. It is not clear how those bodies can be made impartial in the very diverse world of today. It is clear, though, that the degree of success in creating an atmosphere of impartiality will determine the extent to which the international community will resolve some of the most intractable trade and investment issues amicably rather than through unilateral use of economic power.

COMMENTARY

Franklyn D. Holzman

I shall restrict my comments on Jacob Dreyer's paper to the part on state trading. I shall first consider the exercise by the Soviet bloc foreign trade organizations (FTOs) of monopsony power—the issue considered by Dreyer—and then broaden my remarks to consider briefly some of the other challenges to the liberal order posed by these nations.

The belief that Eastern FTOs exert monopsonistic power in East-West trade is fairly common among Western economists and has several sources. First, because the FTOs all have monopolies in their own countries of trade in particular products, it is assumed that they therefore have monopsonistic power in dealing with the West. Obviously, there is no basis in either economics or logic to support this reasoning. Second, at the time of the so-called great grain robbery of the early 1970s, the Russians bought an enormous amount of grain from the United States and other nations to supplement the very poor harvest of 1972. By very cleverly making simultaneous secret purchases from many different American grain exporters, they were able to hide the size of their total purchase and thereby avoid driving up the price. This was a clever end run around the price system that was possible only because one giant buyer could coordinate the operation. It was, however, an exceptional case, and the U.S. government has taken steps that should prevent the recurrence of such an event in the grain market. Third, fuel was added to the belief that Eastern FTOs exercise monopsonistic power when the U.S. government's General Accounting Office (GAO) asserted that this is indeed true.[1] In no uncertain terms, the GAO attributes monopsonistic powers to the FTOs and contends that U.S. commercial and banking interests are manipulated, with the result that profits are lower than they should be and both products and tech-

---

[1] General Accounting Office, *The Government's Role in East-West Trade: Problems and Issues*, February 1976.

nology are transferred at much too low a price. So serious does the GAO consider the problem that it proposed that:

> The Secretary of the Treasury, in his capacity as Chairman of the East-West Foreign Trade Board should . . . review all transactions involving . . . national interests, such as commodity price stability and supply, technology seepage and security of investments, as well as transactions requiring credit or export licenses. Criteria for involvement could include size of transaction and credit, nature of product or technology, number of firms competing, and structure of transaction (product payback, for example). *The intensity of involvement could vary from indirect guidelines for the firms, to observer status at commercial negotiations, to direct negotiations with Soviet officials, to disapproval of the transaction.*[2]

Dreyer attempts an empirical assessment of Soviet FTO buying power by comparing the prices at which the USSR imports a wide range of products from the United States with the prices Western European importers paid us in 1975–1976. He finds very little difference, but where differences exist the Soviets appear to pay less. He correctly notes, however, that these lower prices might well reflect quantity discounts, lower quality of imported products, and substitution of domestic for American storage facilities. He concludes, in direct contrast with the GAO (whose report he does not mention), that intervention by the U.S. government is not called for.

The Department of Commerce Advisory Committee on East-West Trade came to similar conclusions. In the publication mentioned in note 2, above, hearings on the so-called whipsaw controversy are reported.[3] These hearings consider the returns on a questionnaire sent out to some 500 American enterprises exporting to the USSR. The majority of the respondents reported generally profitable trade with the USSR and either no whipsawing or no more whipsawing than experienced in other markets. Bankers on the advisory committee further reported that they did not experience any significant amount of whipsawing. In conclusion, most members of the committee took the same position Dreyer takes—that U.S. government interference with U.S. sales to the Eastern bloc is not generally warranted since the evidence of exercise of monopsonistic buying power is not very strong.

---

[2] Ibid., p. 66. Quoted from U.S. Department of Commerce, *US-USSR Trade and the Whipsaw Controversy*, August 1977, p. 6; emphasis in original.

[3] "Whipsawing" is defined "as the ability of a large buyer to play off potential sellers against one another to obtain maximum price breaks or other contractual concessions." Department of Commerce, *US-USSR Trade*, p. 3.

PART FIVE: THE LIBERAL'S DILEMMA

Dreyer does not consider the possiblity that American importers may be hurt in dealing with Soviet exporter FTOs. This omission may be for the very good reason that Eastern exporter FTOs appear to possess much less monopolistic power than the importer FTOs possess monopsonistic power. In a pair of studies by this writer cited by Dreyer, it was shown that Soviet and other Eastern European exports usually had to be sold at below world prices in order to break into Western markets in the 1950s and early 1960s. While the situation may have improved in recent years, no one to my knowledge has ever claimed that Eastern FTOs were extracting monopoly profits. To the contrary, any complaints have been directed at alleged Soviet dumping. The potential for dumping by a state-owned exporting agency is much greater than for a private exporter, of course. The obstacles to adjudicating a dumping charge against an Eastern FTO are substantial because of the unavailability of cost and price information. Even if such information were available, the fact that internal costs and prices are not rational or market clearing and that exchange rates are not real prices but simply units of account would make it almost impossible to interpret the information. Under the U.S.-USSR Commercial Agreement of 1972, the USSR simply agreed to withdraw exports that cause distress to domestic American producers. While this arrangement sidesteps the problems mentioned above, it is important to realize that any solution which in effect automatically rules out the import of goods that compete with domestic products is protectionist to the extreme.

I should like to consider briefly a number of potential challenges to a liberal economic order posed by the Communist nations which do not fit into the topic of Dreyer's paper.

First, central planners are faced with the task of fitting foreign trade into their overall plans. From an administrative standpoint, this is done most "conveniently" by means of trade agreements with other nations that specify the total exports and imports to be traded during the year. In intra-COMECON trade, each pair of nations holds a gigantic barter session each year in which most of its mutual trade is specified in detail and sealed by contracts. The Communist nations would like to have such arrangements with capitalist nations—but the latter cannot commit their exporters and importers. However, under trade agreements, many Western capitalist countries have brought their traders into similar meetings and have facilitated deals by various kinds of preferential treatment. From the standpoint of the liberal economic order, large "barter-type" deals of this sort hide many discriminatory purchases and sales that would never have been made in open competition. For example, Alec Nove argued that the reason one sees Italian cars but not British cars in Budapest was probably "because the Italians demanded a quota for cars in their bilateral agreement and the British did not."[4] (He also points out that Polish, Czech, and East German cars outnumber the Italian.)

That such transactions represent deviations from the optimal pattern of trade is clear. If East-West trade amounted to 25 percent of world trade and all of it were conducted under the umbrella of trade agreements as described above, the problem for the West could be serious. However, East-West trade amounts to less than 5 percent of world trade, and most of it is not conducted as described. Further, given the size of the Communist debt to the West, it seems unlikely that East-West trade will grow faster than world trade. It is my feeling, therefore, that, while undesirable, discrimination arising out of East-West trade is not quantitatively a serious problem; it is probably less serious than the analogous phenomenon that characterizes much of the multinational corporation, intrafirm international trade.

Second, in order to consummate sales to the East, many Western exporters have been more or less forced to accept all or part payment in kind—so-called buy-back or countertrade agreements. The acceptance of Soviet vodka for American Pepsi Cola is a well-known case in point. The same has been true of Western investments in the East—repayment has often involved accepting the products produced by these investments or even other products instead of currency. Such reversions to barter clearly represent a retrogressive trend when viewed in terms of Western objectives of achieving a more liberal international economic order. Why do the Communist nations press for buy-back arrangements? Partly because much of their intrabloc trade is handled on such a basis, that is, trade between bloc countries is bilaterally balanced. With the West, it is primarily because of the hard-currency shortage—vodka substitutes for dollars. Since the hard-currency shortage is likely to be a long-run phenomenon, attempts at this kind of barter are probably here to stay.

If buy-back arrangements were caused by a virus that might spread and infect capitalist trade, they might be a cause for concern. They are not and, in fact, many Western exporters even in East-West trade refuse to accept payment in kind. So there does not appear to be much to worry about even if the number of barter deals increases somewhat over time. In fact, one might look at these deals as a kind of second-best solution to a serious disequilibrium situation. That is to say, because of the hard-currency shortage, the Eastern nations have a large repressed

---

[4] Alec Nove, "East-West Trade," in Paul A. Samuelson, ed., *International Economic Relations* (New York: St. Martin, 1969), p. 111.

demand for Western products. Ability to arrange buy-back deals expands their purchasing power and the level of East-West trade—although not necessarily by the full amount of the barter since some of the Eastern exports-through-barter might have been sold for hard currency anyway. So the Eastern nations gain—and presumably so do the Western enterprises, although perhaps not by as much as if they had been paid in cash. This second-best argument for buy-back is similar to the argument prevalent after World War II that it made sense for the nations of Europe to discriminate against the United States, the cheapest market, and trade with each other, because of the "dollar shortage." By discriminating, they were able to engage in a higher level of trade than would otherwise have been possible.[5]

Third, perhaps the major distortions introduced into the trading practices of the United States and to a lesser extent into those of the Western European nations have resulted from responses to the cold war. The cold war led the Communist nations, under Soviet persuasion, to concentrate their trade among themselves to an extraordinary degree. The implicit equivalent tariffs to their hidden quotas on most Western products, especially in the earlier postwar period, would have made Smoot-Hawley look like a pygmy, I am sure. However, part of the responsibility for COMECON autarky must be laid at the feet of the Western nations, especially the United States, with their rigorous controls over exports to the bloc, not to mention quotas on many imports, controls on credits, and in some cases lack of MFN treatment. The situation at present (1977) is much freer than it was in the past, and in some cases (subsidized export credits, for example) it might be argued that the pendulum has swung too far. My main point here is that the cold war has led this country to distort its trade significantly and to engage in illiberal practices in what I believe to have been a relatively fruitless attempt to deprive the USSR of economic and military gains from trade. U.S. losses in exports have clearly amounted to many billions of dollars in the postwar period. This can be shown by projecting our share of Communist bloc trade and comparing it with the actual trade realized *or* by looking at our market share in general of various industrial products and then comparing that share with our share of Western exports of the same products to the Communist nations. A major reason we failed to hurt the USSR and lost so many billions of dollars in exports was the unwillingness of Western Europe to join

---

[5] See Ragnar Frisch, "Forecasting a Multilateral Balance of Payments," *American Economic Review*, vol. 37 (September 1947); Franklyn D. Holzman, "Discrimination in International Trade," *American Economic Review*, vol. 39 (December 1949).

fully in our embargo. Another fallacy of our policy was the overestimation of the damage that could be imposed on the USSR, an economy which for most of the postwar period imported only 3 percent or less of its GNP. Several other fallacies of our policy are discussed elsewhere.[6]

Finally, most distressing, to me at least, were the provisions of the Trade Reform Act of 1974 which *explicitly* linked the granting of MFN status to the USSR and Eastern Europe to their emigration policies and also limited Export-Import Bank loans to the USSR to $75 million annually, an amount more appropriate to a nation the size of Luxembourg. These provisions represent an interruption in the gradual U.S. trend of trade liberalization toward the Eastern nations. Like the controls of the 1950s and 1960s, these have already proven ineffective in achieving their goals. Emigration from the Soviet Union, which had reached a peak in 1973, declined almost immediately, and the USSR and Eastern Europe have received enormous amounts of credit from other Western nations since 1974. Furthermore, the USSR was moved by these provisions of the Trade Reform Act to annul the U.S.-USSR Commercial Agreement, so laboriously put together in 1972, and accordingly ceased repayment of its Lend-Lease debt.

Robert D. Tollison

Jacob Dreyer sets out to analyze the following type of problem. Some monopolies spring from purely private action and represent a category of behavior that is well understood in terms of the postulates of profit (or, more generally, utility) maximization. Other monopolies are set up by government and represent a category of action that is less well understood—presumably even less well understood if it is set up on foreign soil. A country espousing free trade is thus placed in a dilemma when it faces the exercise of foreign monopoly power; it must uncover the true intent of the foreign monopoly in order to decide upon an optimal response to its actions. If the intent is simply beggar-thy-neighbor, then some form of controlled retaliation is called for. If the monopoly is pursuing some broadly legitimized goal, then the dilemma is resolved by an understanding nonresponse.

Dreyer attacks this problem in two ways. First, he reviews the extensive theoretical literature broadly centered around the theory of an optimum tariff. The conclusion of this discussion is that there is no conclusion. Everything depends on everything else; apart from trying

---

[6] Franklyn D. Holzman, "East-West Trade and Investment Policy Issues," in *United States International Economic Policy in an Interdependent World*, Williams Commission Report to the President, July 1971.

PART FIVE: THE LIBERAL'S DILEMMA

to maximize own-country national income at the expense of world economic efficiency, a policy that does not seem compatible with the spirit of resolving the free trader's dilemma, the theoretical literature offers no particularly appealing or practical resolution to the type of problem Dreyer addresses. Dreyer also looks for a solution to the dilemma in terms of judicial doctrine in the antitrust area. I find his discussion here somewhat dated, but that is not really crucial since he finds no answer here either. At best, foreign businesses operating within our jurisdiction are subject to whatever legal contraints domestic firms face. Since many of the manifestations of the free trader's dilemma are in foreign jurisdictions, judicial doctrine is not likely to be of much help in resolving the issue.

This is not, of course, to argue that I have an answer to the dilemma but only to show the types of approaches that, as Dreyer demonstrates, do not hold answers. At the bottom line, Dreyer resorts to a basically ad hoc discussion of how to respond to foreign monopoly, and I must confess that this appears to be the only feasible way to address such an issue. In the following remarks, I seek to embellish the ad hoc line of reasoning initiated by Dreyer.

In a general sense, the United States cannot expect completely liberal policies abroad with respect to international trade and investment. As Dreyer points out, desires for national economic autonomy may derive from broad political goals, where economic gains are sacrificed for autonomy, or they may be due to special-interest pressures in the domestic political process. Especially in the area of investment and technology flows, laissez faire may simply not be feasible. Many countries will object to it on grounds of national security, and others will have objections based on domestic political considerations. If we are to avoid the possibility of trade and investment wars, there is a critical need to explore ways of determining when countries are pursuing legitimate national objectives in limiting trade and investment flows and to consider means of controlling any retaliatory responses. This sort of challenge is what is termed a free trader's dilemma, and it raises the question of how a liberal should respond to illiberal actions.

One possible course of action would be to let countries completely gratify their pursuit of "national interests" without any quarrel. We must reject this posture because it can lead to a serious danger of illiberal solutions and, more fundamentally, because it is hard to avoid facing up to such foreign actions when domestic political groups perceive them to be costly to the United States.

Perhaps, for the United States, the best general response to an illiberal environment is concern that the exercise of monopolistic and monopsonistic power by foreign governments does not act to the substantial detriment of the U.S. interest. Such a policy, compensating for or defending against beggar-thy-neighbor policies abroad, would seem to be much more defensible than overt beggar-thy-neighbor policies exercised in the context of pursuing national advantage. When governments abroad institute national-advantage policies, the appropriate but second-best response might be to pursue similar policies at home. The moral of the story for the free trader, however, would be not to adopt active international policies to secure short-run national advantages but, rather, to limit such actions to cases where a foreign government acts first and hope that counteraction to sanction such shortsighted behavior leads to a general reduction in its incidence. I would also stress that such retaliatory actions should not be undertaken hastily. Attempts to negotiate should come first, although a country must have a viable ultimate threat of retaliation.

However, while we may be able to identify policies motivated by pure national-advantage aspirations or policies at the other extreme of trading off national autonomy in the interests of international cooperation, there is a wide gulf between the extremes where questions of what constitutes legitimate behavior in gratifying national autonomy may arise. It is thus important for countries to reach a consensus on the principles of legitimacy in this area.

As a general rule, it would be better to institutionalize mechanisms for controlled retaliation that minimize the danger of further rounds of retaliation and ultimately of general trade warfare. Automatic compensation for increases in trade barriers is a potentially useful principle, and GATT contains a good example of how it might work in practice. If a country removes a trade benefit by raising a tariff, then either the offending country has to lower an equivalent amount of tariffs on other items or other countries can raise tariffs against the offender by an equivalent amount. This type of system confronts domestic decision makers with reasonably well-defined opportunity costs for deviations from liberal trade and helps contain incentives for general retaliation and trade conflicts. This approach might be fruitfully extended to nontariff barriers and export controls, although I acknowledge the considerable difficulties involved in doing so.

Foreign investment and technology flows present additional difficulties in searching for general principles of legitimacy in the pursuit of national interest because of the type of problems outlined above and because disagreements over issues in this area are so fundamental. It thus does not seem to be a particularly good time to attempt to reach a consensus on legitimate deviations from liberal principles in this area.

PART FIVE: THE LIBERAL'S DILEMMA

However, in searching for general principles, one might suggest a nondiscretionary approach to limiting inward flows of foreign investment and technology. A good example exists in U.S. policy toward inward investment, where only a limited percentage of foreign ownership is allowed in certain designated industries related to national security (for example, communications). Another example might be a requirement that an industry employ x percent of indigenous labor or that y percent of basic industries be locally owned. Such nondiscretionary rules would not be supportive of large terms of trade advantages and could be treated as substantively different in nature from cases involving foreign investment review boards. Thus, so long as no special concessions were offered to particular trading partners, the presumption would be that such policies were not motivated primarily by a desire to beggar-thy-neighbor. In the case of investment review boards, however, where discretion is used to discriminate among foreign investors, a beggar-thy-neighbor motivation would be presumed and would invite some form of controlled retaliation. In general, then, under this approach certain industries could be placed out of bounds or certain broad rules about percentages of local employment and ownership in certain industries could be instituted without the need for engaging in policies to gain large terms of trade advantages.

I should stress that this discussion is only meant to suggest an approach to a very complicated problem. It is by no means intended as a detailed consideration of the difficult economic and political trade-offs involved in devising the appropriate policy and institutional framework for pursuing liberal trade and investment principles. I hope, of course, that something on the order of this approach, stressing liberal principles with appropriately defined deviations, will prevail in the international economic system, because it will be increasingly difficult for the United States to maintain liberal policies if other countries continue to pursue blatant forms of national advantage in areas of foreign investment.

After all, the problem Dreyer raises is closely analogous to a parent's proper response to a naughty child. At one level, the parent can ignore naughty behavior and hope that the shining example of tolerance will lead to improved behavior. This approach would imply that it is best to ignore foreign monopoly and stick to liberal trade principles, no matter what. At the other extreme, the parent can punish naughty behavior to the maximum extent and hope that the fear of retribution will lead to better behavior in the child. This is equivalent to the optimum-tariff argument. Or, finally, the parent can judiciously mix tolerance with taxation by trying to interpret the naughty behavior of the child case by case. It is this type of response to foreign monopoly that I think Dreyer has in mind.

Let me close with an afterthought: a plea that we forget about predatory pricing and dumping. It is well known among economists that such activity is irrational; we would generally expect to see mergers rather than negative-sum games in the marketplace. Predatory pricing generally only means low foreign prices, and so much the better for consumers. We should concentrate on ways (such as adjustment assistance) to take advantage of low foreign prices rather than on provisions that handicap foreign in favor of domestic competition.

Richard E. Caves

Jacob Dreyer's paper touches on a number of issues and thereby presents the discussant with an amorphous target. I confess to a rather pervasive dissatisfaction with it. Parts of it summarize information that is readily available elsewhere and only tangentially relevant, and the analysis contains a number of theoretical propositions that are incorrectly stated or inadequately developed. The opening paragraph, for example, incorrectly implies that worldwide free trade optimizes the distribution of income as well as maximizes its total amount and that maximization of national income and of world income are equivalent objectives for a government. Rather than pursue such flaws, I shall concentrate on Dreyer's main theoretical conclusions about the use of monopoly power in international trade and the possibilities for countervailing it.

It is useful to recognize at the start the central relevance of the theory of optimal tariffs and retaliation, developed by Tibor Scitovsky, H. G. Johnson, and others.[1] This analysis is simply a translation of bilateral monopoly into general equilibrium, and, under certain assumptions about the policy instruments used by the parties, it applies equally to the manipulation of the terms of trade by tariffs, state trading monopolies, or commercial monopolies that perceive the general equilibrium consequences of their pricing decisions. Here are a few of the central propositions of this analysis: (1) A country with monopoly power can always secure an immediate gain by manipulating its terms of trade away from a competitive outcome and may gain even when the possibility of retaliation is recognized. (2) If the victim of this manipulation

---

[1] Tibor Scitovsky, "A Reconsideration of the Theory of Tariffs," *Review of Economic Studies*, vol. 9, no. 2 (1942), pp. 89–110; H. G. Johnson, "Optimum Tariffs and Retaliation," *Review of Economic Studies*, vol. 21, no. 2 (1953–1954), pp. 142–53.

can improve his situation by retaliating, he would in general also have improved his welfare by taking initial aggressive action; who takes aggressive action is a matter of morals, not opportunity. (3) Successive retaliation leads to a Cournot equilibrium in which at least one party is worse off than with free trade. (4) Terms of trade manipulation in general does not deny the victim some gains from trade unless he is confronted with an all-or-nothing offer, such as a state trading agency might contrive. Dreyer's material generally recognizes this analysis, though I cannot reconcile some of his passages with it; for instance, he proposes some conditions for the monopoly/monopsony price and the victim's social marginal cost which seem to assume that marginal cost is a given datum rather than something that adjusts to the prevailing terms of trade along with the victim's output structure.

I said that this analysis of optimal tariffs and retaliation applies equally to tariffs and to the direct exploitation of a country's monopoly/monopsony power in trade. That statement does not necessarily hold when the potential aggressor nation's policy choice is to use a single industry as an instrument for increasing its gains from trade, if the rest of its economy remains competitive. Allowing or enforcing the monopolization of a single exporting industry in partial equilibrium is a policy inferior to imposing an export tax but keeping that industry competitive. This is because the monopoly exacts a deadweight loss from its domestic customers as well as exploits the foreigners. Furthermore, it can be shown in 2 x 2 general equilibrium that the actions of a single profit-maximizing monopoly industry can actually leave the would-be monopolizing country worse off than in the absence of trade—a fate that cannot befall a "victim" country that is a price taker on world markets.[2] For these and other reasons, there are limitations on the ability of an aggressor country to maximize its gains from trade by fostering commercial monopoly.

Nonetheless, the optimal-tariff analysis generally leads one to expect that such commercial monopolies would be used as instruments to raise one country's income at the expense of world income as a whole. That raises the question of the scope for evasive action by the country or countries that are the immediate victims. And it also leads to the possibility of international agreements of the GATT variety to curb the use of commercial or state trading monopoly in ways harmful to world income and international harmony. Dreyer's position that a nation may or may not gain from retaliation is surely a safe one, but it is also an

---

[2] Antoine A. Auquier and Richard E. Caves, "Monopolistic Export Industries, Trade Taxes, and Optimal Competition Policy," *Economic Journal*, vol. 89, no. 3 (1979).

empty one unless the repertory of retaliatory measures and the market situation of the victim are specified. Let me attempt a more systematic inventory of retaliatory measures than Dreyer provides and indicate some of their properties.

Tariff adjustment. The Scitovsky-Johnson model indicates that a tax on either exports or imports is an effective retaliation when our terms of trade are worsened by a foreign monopoly or monopsony, making us better off than before. But that improvement could be erased by further actions of the monopoly/monopsony, and it might be inferior to some strategy leading back to a Pareto equilibrium. In principle, the retaliatory tax is easy to calculate. But the principle is hard to apply when one market is involved among many—a consideration that tempts one to retreat to partial equilibrium and consider whether the victim of a monopoly can gain from further taxing imports of the monopolized good. The answer is yes, under the following reasonably general assumptions. Suppose that we can view the foreign monopolist as maximizing his profit by selecting a percentage to mark up price over his marginal cost (or supply price, if the producing industry is in fact atomistic). Use of a constant markup percentage would be rational for the monopolist if demand elasticity is constant and less than infinity. The victim can in the first instance increase his national welfare by taxing imports of the commodity, if the monopolist's supply or marginal cost curve is upward sloping. A very small tax causes the loss of an incremental triangle of consumer's surplus but a nonincremental gain on all units of the commodity still imported, because the foreign monopolist rationally lowers his pretax price as his sales fall. The victim country's government gains revenue that is more than sufficient to offset the loss of consumers' surplus. An optimal retaliatory tax on monopolized imports thus is generally positive. Of course, a full treatment of this case again requires us to consider the possibility of further moves by the monopolist; the difference between myopic and all-knowing behavior in this case, however, is not generally different from the general equilibrium case analyzed by Scitovsky.[3]

Retaliatory state trading. In theoretical terms, using a national trading agency to cope with a foreign monopolist differs only in institutional terms from using a tax, unless the use of the state trading agency brings access to additional bargaining instruments such as the all-or-nothing offer. The institutional choice between state trading and taxes as a retaliatory device is hardly a trivial one, but I shall not go into the issues here.

---

[3] Scitovsky, "Reconsideration."

PART FIVE: THE LIBERAL'S DILEMMA

Counterspeculation. Abba Lerner once proposed, as a method for dealing with monopoly, that the government hold a stock of the monopolized commodity and offer to buy or sell unlimited quantities at the equilibrium "shadow" competitive price.[4] A. L. Nichols and R. J. Zeckhauser have recently revived this notion in their investigation of stockpiling and cartel behavior, going beyond Lerner by dealing in dynamic terms with the problem that the government must first acquire the stock before it can be used for counterspeculative sales. They show that such stockpiling is theoretically capable of raising the welfare of the victim country, even if the foreign monopolist is fully aware of what is going on.[5] A useful feature of their analysis is an investigation of "competitive" stockpiling by multiple victim countries. It leads to the conclusion that stockpiling will be underprovided without collusion among the victims.

Antitrust policy. Dreyer's analysis of antitrust policy unfortunately deals with its general development in the domestic market and not with the interesting experience with actual cases involving foreign companies.[6] Antitrust action could potentially erase the offending monopoly and restore optimum conditions. Of course, Dreyer is right that national antitrust policies are generally useless against companies domiciled in foreign nations. He might have added that foreign monopolists in practice find it difficult to operate without owning some assets in the market they are exploiting, and those assets become hostages to the victim country's antitrust laws. The United States was able, for instance, to stop a British chemical company from colluding with its U.S. competitor in exploiting the Canadian market! Furthermore, injunctive relief under the antitrust laws can take the form of an all-or-nothing offer, which is generally a useful defensive asset. Finally, effective exertion of monopoly power by foreign companies often requires collusion with their home-market competitors, and antitrust policy can take action against this collusion. I do not wish to imply that antitrust is a finely honed instrument for dealing with foreign monopolies, but there is more potential than Dreyer's paper indicates. An incidentally interesting feature of antitrust policy, which confirms the reality of the problem of monopoly in international trade, is that all countries give some exemption to their export industries in order to permit collusion and monopolistic practices in foreign markets. Interestingly, the least gen-

---

[4] Abba P. Lerner, *The Economics of Control* (New York: Macmillan, 1944).

[5] A. L. Nichols and R. J. Zeckhauser, "Stockpiling Strategies and Cartel Prices," *Bell Journal of Economics*, vol. 8 (Spring 1977), pp. 66–96.

[6] See Kingman Brewster, *Antitrust and American Business Abroad* (New York: McGraw-Hill, 1958).

erous exemptions tend to be given by countries whose domestic markets are large relative to their export markets; for these nations, the clandestine spillover of collusion from export markets to domestic markets extracts a relatively high social cost.[7]

"Extraneous" bribes and threats. Economic theory indicates that the victim of a monopoly can gain by bribing his tormenter to sell at marginal cost. This is because the victim can pay the monopolist a sum equal to his profits and still be better off by recapturing the erstwhile triangle of deadweight loss. The proposal that a country pay tribute to a foreign monopolist is perhaps not one likely to win elections; however, a monopolist can be brought to heel by threats as well as bribes. An effective threat, in this context, is one that will eliminate the monopolist's profits at an opportunity cost to the victim that is no larger than those profits plus the deadweight loss. The bribe or threat can take any form that is available to the victim country, and the choice between paying a bribe and incurring the cost of implementing a threat should be made to minimize the net expected cost of the action. The bribe-or-threat strategy has the advantage over some other retaliatory strategies of leading to a Pareto rather than a Cournot equilibrium. That advantage is global, however, and the retaliatory strategy having the maximum present value for the victim need not be that with the greatest chance of restoring Pareto optimality.

Overall, economic theory indicates that various types of responses to foreign monopoly potentially make the victim country better off than in a monopoly-ridden situation. Furthermore, it is in principle possible to rank those available in a given instance in terms of their net effectiveness (benefits and costs). Dreyer is welcome to conclude that in general retaliation may or may not be effective, when uncertainty, irrationality, and political feasibility are taken into account. But he should have recognized that economic theory is not so indecisive.

The paper concludes with a set of principles for dealing with situations of international monopoly. Unfortunately, Dreyer does not indicate whether these are principles for national unilateral adoption or an agenda for proposed international agreement. They make some sense to me if they look toward a GATT-type international agreement, but none if they are proposed to foster national welfare through unilateral adoption. He proposes that action against a foreign monopoly should turn on the presence of the motive of exploiting outsiders and, by implication, that possession and use of monopoly power against domestic and foreign

---

[7] See Organization for Economic Cooperation and Development, *Export Cartels: Report of the Committee of Experts on Restrictive Business Practices* (Paris, 1974); and Auquier and Caves, "Monopolistic Exporting Industries."

customers alike should be ignored. This might make sense in terms of diplomatic niceties, but it does not correctly address the feasible options for the victim. Dreyer proposes that retaliation should be "compensatory" rather than "punitive." This has the ring of some familiar GATT provisions, but it has no economic logic. Any retaliation, if it is effective, makes the aggressor worse off than he was after his initial move (that is, it punishes him), and yet an effective retaliation generally does not fully "compensate" the victim by restoring his initial level of real income. That is, retaliation will in general be punitive without being compensatory. If Dreyer means that the retaliation should leave the aggressor no worse off than he was before his aggressive action, then he would confine retaliation to threats or bribes that restore the initial competitive conditions, but at no net cost to the victim (because any cost eats into his compensation). This is likely to be an empty set.

A more charitable reading can be given to Dreyer's suggested principles if we treat them as an approach to a GATT-type agreement on international policies toward monopoly. The common international interest in competitive markets creates an abstract case for such an agreement, just as in the case of tariffs. Unilateral national policies to make markets more competitive in general provide spillover benefits to other countries, and therefore international cooperation is necessary. One could even devise a scenario for reciprocal monopoly-busting agreements closely analogous to the bilateral and subsequently multilateral agreements on tariff cutting that have followed from the U.S. reciprocal-trade-agreements program. This is the proper direction for our efforts to draw up principles of conduct.

Carlos F. Diaz-Alejandro

Discussions of the new international economic order have become a bit of a debating game, so I will try to score a few points for the side not widely represented here.

We agreed at this conference that one of the most serious departures from a liberal economic order is the monopsonistic restrictions by rich countries against inflowing unskilled labor. With OECD bureaucrats on the borders keeping away workers, one could view many LDC actions as exercises in countervailing power. If the monopsonistic actions of the rich countries drive the price of LDC labor down, and that labor has to be embodied in commodities, then attempts by the LDCs to try to drive those prices up by one means and another may not seem so reprehensible.

To give a concrete example: Would it be so bad for either efficiency or equity if the Mexican government tied the price of its oil and gas to the number of Mexican workers allowed into the United States? Would that kind of exercise of monopoly power by the Mexican government reduce world welfare?

One of the first things I learned as a student of Robert Bishop was the way businessmen decline the verb "to compete": I compete, you chisel, he cuts throats. Such grammar is often found not just in North-South debates but also among those who argue, for example, that the Japanese really do not compete fairly (and I am sure many people in Japan do not think U.S. businessmen compete fairly). But this game of deciding who is the monopolist and who is not has reached extremes in the North-South debates.

A few years ago we read that Jamaica was cartelizing bauxite markets. My first reaction was to look in the telephone directory under "bauxite auctioneers." No such category could be found because the bauxite auctioneer is kept in a closet without a telephone by Alcan. The OECD public is being told that the LDCs are cartelizing non-existent markets. This is a new high or a new low in the art of accusing the foreigner of being a monopolist and presenting ourselves as the noble Siegfried who always competes like a good sport.

Far-from-perfect OECD markets abound. The business of technology could be viewed as a gigantic cartel run by developed countries. Technology is a messy commodity, with low marginal and high average costs. So one cannot really have perfect competition. One needs patent laws to encourage new knowledge; but many LDCs have raised the modest question, Who wrote the patent laws that exist in the world? Is it not reasonable to question whether the right price for technology is being charged in world markets today?

Let me turn to the way leadership is often presented in northern discussions, including this one. First of all, it is not called leadership. Only the rich countries have leadership; the LDCs have "elites," who are presented as either crazies or economic illiterates or babies who have to be disciplined. One could follow the infant-leader argument and say that only after 200 years of learning by doing could one hope to produce leaders as selfless and as worried about the welfare of their people as Richard Nixon, Spiro Agnew, and John Mitchell. There is hope, however. It took many years of high culture and industrialization for Germany to produce Adolph Hitler; Uganda has turned the trick more quickly. Generally, these discussions remind me of J. Edgar Hoover's argument that Martin Luther King wanted only power for himself, that he really did not care about the welfare of the blacks.

PART FIVE: THE LIBERAL'S DILEMMA

There is much of that tone in remarks about who really cares about the very poor.

Another, often overlooked example of extreme monopoly and monopsony power is that represented by commercial embargoes undertaken unilaterally by major industrial countries. For example, the U.S. embargo against Cuba has been going on for more than fifteen years.

A more general point concerns the classic case of liberalism, which has markets as the means and freedom as the end. Capitalism and freedom together are supposed to be the name of the game. Now, it happens that the few "good guys" found by liberal economists in the LDCs are, for the most part, quite illiberal in their politics; one thinks of South Korea, Taiwan, and post-1973 Chile. At the same time, the few besieged LDC democracies get a rather bad press from liberal economists. One suspects that many liberal economists who talk about capitalism and freedom turn Fabian when faced with LDC reality. If they cannot get capitalism *and* freedom, they will settle for capitalism.

Finally, let me suggest that the North-South debate is not so much advocates of free markets versus planners and bureaucrats; at bottom, the debate reflects the fight between new, rising oligopolists and the old, established oligopolists.

We are seeing the successful response to the call for "two, three, more Japans," as the developing countries elbow their way into the world economy. Yet the shah of Iran did not care about the poor *that* much (who does?). He wanted a cut; he wanted a piece of the action. Making that point is fair enough, but saying that the new Japans are destroying otherwise atomistic competitive markets is self-deceptive. And this can be dangerous; let us not forget that the other side in World War II was made up of three newcomers to world markets. Referring to the prewar situation, Lord Robbins wrote words that are very apt in 1978: "Let us be under no illusion. So long as the richer powers practice exclusion, so long can the poorer say with truth: 'Our poverty is greater because of their policy. Our misery would be less if their barriers were shattered.' It is not a pleasant thought."[1]

Roger E. Shields

Jacob Dreyer presents a number of interesting issues in his paper, including the problem of externalities. That is one of the issues to which I would like to direct my comments.

---

[1] From an essay written during the winter of 1936–1937, reproduced in Lord Robbins, *Money, Trade, and International Relations* (London: Macmillan, 1971), p. 249.

COMMENTARY

There is general agreement, I think, on the rules of the international trade game when the world is characterized by atomistic markets and free enterprises trading with each other across international boundaries. We understand fairly well what economic efficiency means in that context. Our traditional theory can handle that satisfactorily.

The principles of GATT recognize the special problems that may be raised by state trading enterprises and require in general that, where state trading enterprises exist or state intervention in foreign trade occur, the state should act in accordance with normal market considerations. In other words, it should let its foreign trade activities be governed by normal commercial considerations. Trade decisions should then be based on such considerations as price, availability, credit terms, and quality of product.

The GATT principles recognize, of course, that some state trading agencies would be concerned with national procurement, as, for example, military arms, and suggest that departures from normal commercial practices would be in line in such cases because of the considerations that may apply with regard to issues involving national security, however that may be defined.

These exceptions to the general rule may be interpreted very broadly. Indeed, a legitimate case can be made, and I believe ought to be made, that economic strength and well-being is a vital part of national security. Nevertheless, such an interpretation of national security should not support wholesale deviations by state trading entities from the GATT stipulation that the general criteria for international trade should follow the inherent economic and commercial aspects of the individual transactions themselves.

This implicitly recognizes the proposition that, although governments are broadly responsible for economic welfare and all of the component parts of the economy that contribute to that end, internal macroeconomic and structural policies are better suited to the attainment of these goals than manipulation of international trade. Deviations from this approach, though, seem to be increasing and in the process are creating some very important problems, especially for private enterprise economies.

Jacob Dreyer mentions, for example, the recent case of the so-called arms deal of the century, in which the F-16 aircraft produced by General Dynamics in the United States was eventually sold to a NATO consortium of four countries. This case, of course, does relate directly to state procurement for national security issues and so falls within the pale of exceptions to the normal commercial criteria permitted by GATT rules. Nevertheless, it illustrates clearly how tenuous the relationship

PART FIVE: THE LIBERAL'S DILEMMA

between national defense and nonnormal economic and commercial criteria imposed as conditions of sale can be.

Initially, there were two American competitors for the sale of the tactical fighter aircraft to the consortium countries. The two were also competing for the sale of their respective aircraft to the U.S. Air Force. Because common logistical support, common training, and so on, among NATO allies would result in considerable cost savings, it was obvious that, in the event the consortium chose a U.S. aircraft, it would in all likelihood be the same aircraft chosen by the U.S. Air Force. Thus, the U.S. Air Force selection of the General Dynamics aircraft prior to the consortium decision effectively eliminated its U.S. competitor from consortium consideration.

France, with its Dassault F-1 aircraft, was the other serious competitor for the consortium sale. After a long and exhaustive examination and comparison of the French and American entries, it was generally conceded that the American aircraft was superior in terms of performance and lower in terms of purchase price and operating costs. Normal considerations of a commercial character would, therefore, have dictated that the U.S. aircraft would be an easy winner. However, complex peripheral but, nonetheless, key factors unrelated to the primary questions of cost and military suitability of the aircraft—for example, technology transfer and coproduction, which would generate employment within the consortium countries—entered heavily into the final procurement decision. The French government, which had been closely involved from the beginning, became even more heavily involved as the consortium neared its decision. This ultimately led to the heavy involvement of the U.S. government on behalf of the U.S. competitor.

Although it was clear that costs of production were greater in Europe than in the United States, the Air Force, partly as an inducement but also in its own economic interests, eventually agreed to buy part (10 percent) of its aircraft from the NATO countries, believing that the economies resulting from the larger production runs made possible by the European selection of the F-16 would result in cost reductions that would more than offset the increase in costs due to the substitution of higher-cost production of that portion of the Air Force planes purchased from European sources. As an added inducement, the NATO consortium countries were promised production of 15 percent of all F-16 aircraft sold to third countries and 40 percent of their own purchases.

The outcome, as is well known now, was that the U.S. competitor, the F-16, won the field. In addition to the U.S. Air Force purchase, the U.S. producer was rewarded with a sale of 348 aircraft to the NATO consortium and the near certainty of future large sales to third countries, or an aggregate likely sale of more than 2,000 planes. For their part, the NATO allies were assured that they would recoup, through their share of F-16 production, a substantial portion of their own procurement costs. In fact, they will recoup 100 percent of their procurement costs if F-16 sales reach the 2,000 mark, as they almost certainly will. Economic efficiency, on the other hand, suffered by the outcome. Clearly the countervailing intervention by the U.S. government did not merely offset the French government intervention. It did not produce a result close to what would have been realized in the absence of intervention.

Unfortunately, cases like this are becoming more prevalent. In the past, when governments have considered intervention in trade, they have generally aimed at such things as changing the terms of trade through tariffs or protecting domestic industries through quotas but not at direct intervention in industrial transactions. That may be changing.

From one standpoint, the belief in free trade based on the principle of comparative advantage my be viewed as suboptimizing. A government organized to carry on international trade through a state trading monopoly may very well believe that it, being responsible for the general economic welfare of the country, might obtain a more efficient national economic package by introducing policies that would produce some inefficiencies in international trade but would also promote employment and industrial activities that otherwise would require different policies. That, of course, presents some problems for U.S. trade policy, and we can expect to see far more of these problems in the future.

The Commerce Department put out a paper earlier this year that discussed the idea of a national benefit tax on U.S. private exports of high technology or of high-technology items. This paper also considered the possibility of requiring licensing for the export of technology or high-technology items.

Under the law, there are currently only three purposes for which exports can be controlled. Only one has anything to do specifically with economic goals, and that relates to control for purposes of dampening inflationary pressures on items in domestic short supply. For example, when soybeans are in short supply in the United States and their export would raise the price domestically, their export may be controlled under the law, as was done a few years ago.

The remaining legal reasons for controlling exports relate to foreign policy and national security. The Department of Commerce paper discusses extending those licensing and control procedures to all exports of high technology which may, in some way, affect the ability of the United States to compete in international markets.

PART FIVE: THE LIBERAL'S DILEMMA

Developments along these lines, if taken very far, can only result in substantial misallocation of resources on a worldwide scale. If state trading monopolies are going to be guided in individual trade transactions by goals relating to larger macroeconomic aggregates, then those traders on the other side of the market will have to formulate new strategies that emphasize factors other than cost, quality, ability to meet delivery schedule, and so on.

A private firm in the United States is not in a position to internalize the economies or diseconomies relating to national employment or to the balance of payments implications of changes in the nation's ability to meet future competition overseas. For example, consider the impact on a country's competitive position in international trade of the export of technology unique to the country. If the technology is also a monopoly of the exporting firm, then presumably it will protect its own and also the country's economic interests by either withholding the technology or holding out for a price that provides adequate compensation for the loss of the monopoly. If, on the other hand, the technology is common to many firms within the country, the nation's monopoly may be broken through the export of the technology by a firm that sees itself as only one of many competitors. In this case, only through control of the terms and conditions of the technology export can the government ensure that the compensation received will take into account the future effects on the country of a likely reduction in its competitive position in world trade (unless antitrust laws were amended to allow collaboration by all the firms in the industry).

Concern by state trading enterprises with national economic priorities at the individual level in international transactions is thus likely to lead to state involvement in such transactions. This will, as in the case of the F-16, lead to state intervention on the other side of the market as well. In this process, the principle of comparative advantage as a guide to trade, and the long-run benefits that derive from free trade, are likely to be sacrificed for short-run economic benefits that are themselves unlikely to be attained to the hoped-for extent.

Movement away from the normal economic and commercial considerations that provide the general framework for international trade in fact constitutes an increase in protectionism through greater use of nontariff barriers. And, just as we all recognize today with the more conventional forms of trade barriers, this can only lead to less economically efficient trade and to the loss in world economic well-being that entails.

COMMENTARY

Edward Tower

The paper by Jacob Dreyer reminds us of the various ways in which one nation can increase its own welfare, frequently at some cost to its trading partners: tariffs, limits to price movements, monopolization, monopsonization, and state trading. It also reminds us that the standard Scitovsky-Johnson analysis of retaliation is too narrow, focusing as it does solely on economic gains while ignoring all the other collective preferences countries might wish to use trade policies to satisfy. Dreyer reminds us, too, that retaliation may not be as bad as Johnson visualized if countries have some goodwill for one another—in other words, if they maximize a collective utility function. He also notes that some of the issues involved are the same, whether the foreign monopoly power is exploited through commercial policy or through state trading, and that state trading is difficult to deal with for it is not so visible and clear-cut as a tariff or a quota.

Richard Caves's comments add more precision to Dreyer's analysis. He summarizes the basic theory; discusses various techniques of retaliation, noting that in principle it is possible to rank them according to their effectiveness; and draws some additional conclusions about appropriate responses to foreign use of market power.

The following comments on the Dreyer and Caves papers will be accompanied by a summary of some of the major conclusions drawn from recent work on retaliation, some of which was stimulated by the Dreyer and Caves pieces. My comments touch on various issues, but my most important message is that the efficacy of retaliation depends strongly on the type of trade barrier used. In conclusion, I summarize some of my own work on ranking and choosing the appropriate levels of such restrictions, closing with a suggestion for a reform of GATT designed to reduce the need to rely on retaliation.

Retaliation, the Terms of Trade, and Employment

Dreyer writes: "Eye-for-an-eye retaliation against foreign use of monopolistic power would certainly lead to disintegration of the world trading system, as happened in the 1930s," and he seems to have in mind a system motivated by the desire for gains from terms of trade improvement.

This seems implausible to me. In the 1930s fuller employment was the target of commercial policy, except in Germany. But, today, most

---

Michael Finger and Thomas Willett have made valuable comments on this paper.

governments use tariffs to alter the structure of production, preferring to assign macroeconomic policy to the maintenance of employment in the aggregate. Moreover, as R. A. Mundell and Edward Tower have shown, under flexible exchange rates across-the-board tariffs may not increase employment at all; the result will depend in part on what the government does with the tariff revenue.[1] Furthermore, as Tower and Thomas Willett have shown, under flexible exchange rates in a Keynesian world with the consumption function fixed in real terms and no capital movements, an increase in one country's tariff will increase its trading partner's employment while leaving the partner's real consumption unchanged.[2] This is because when countries cease to produce according to comparative advantage it takes more labor to produce the same real output, and with consumption functions constant in real terms each country's real income and expenditure are insulated under flexible exchange rates from developments abroad. Thus, the disintegration of trade in the 1930s was an effective, if not the best, way to bring about the goal of spreading a given amount of real income among more of the population.

In this connection, M. W. Crain, T. H. Deaton, and R. D. Tollison have recently concluded from examining data on congressional turnover that American voters are considerably more concerned about aggregate unemployment than about inflation and that they are unconcerned about aggregate real income.[3] I believe this result explains a great deal about the bleak outlook for freer trade. However, Bruno Frey and Friedrich Schneider in a similar study for the United Kingdom found all three variables important.[4] Ironically, the optimal use of trade policy should be to create unemployment rather than fight it; then, any resulting unemployment could be mopped up through the appropriate expenditure-changing policies. In other words, the production gains from freer trade come only when trade liberalization frees resources that can then be used elsewhere.

---

[1] R. A. Mundell, "Flexible Exchange Rates and Employment Policy," *Canadian Journal of Economics and Political Science*, 1961, pp. 514–15; Edward Tower, "Commercial Policy under Fixed and Flexible Exchange Rates," *Quarterly Journal of Economics*, 1973, pp. 436–54.

[2] Edward Tower and Thomas D. Willett, *The Theory of Optimum Currency Areas and Exchange-Rate Flexibility* (Princeton University, International Finance Section, 1976).

[3] M. W. Crain, T. H. Deaton, and R. D. Tollison, "Macroeconomic Determinants of Tenure in the U.S. House of Representatives," *Atlantic Economic Journal*, vol. 6 (1978), pp. 79–83.

[4] Bruno S. Frey and Friedrich Schneider, "A Politico-Economic Model of the United Kingdom," *Economic Journal*, vol. 88 (1978), pp. 243–54.

COMMENTARY

Eye-for-an-Eye Retaliation

Studies by Ivor Pearce; Tower, H. J. Baas, and Alain Sheer; and Tower and Sheer have all explored eye-for-an-eye retaliation in the sense of what would happen if both countries in a two-country world simultaneously levied equal taxes or subsidies on trade.[5] Pearce showed that the winner from a small matched tariff would be the country with the lower compensated import demand elasticity. The latter two studies also determine what country A's best tariff is when it knows that its partner will retaliate by mirroring its tariff. In these studies, real income maximization through tariff-induced improvements in the terms of trade was assumed to be the goal. As these papers showed, there is a limit to the extent that trade will contract; it may even be in the interest of one country to start a dumping war if it knows that such a policy will induce its trading partner also to sell below marginal cost, which will cause trade to expand. Thus, it is conceivable that one country could exploit its trading partner's willingness to subsidize exports to foster the liberalization of trade and an improvement in its own welfare.

The Cessation of Trade

In the Scitovsky-Johnson model of tariff retaliation, where each country expects no further tariff change on the part of its partner, H. G. Johnson noted, "That the adjustment process will never end in the elimination of trade is a logical consequence of the proposition that some trade is always better than no trade."[6] This does not, however, exclude the possibility that when both countries retaliate by imposing optimum tariffs the system could approach autarky in the limit, or come within an ϵ of autarky for any ϵ, given sufficient time. Tower demonstrates that even this is impossible if in autarky neither country would be completely specialized and community indifference curves are strictly convex.[7] This is because, under these assumptions, higher tariffs cause excess demands and supplies to become more and more elastic in the limit as trade shrinks to zero.

---

[5] Ivor F. Pearce, *International Trade* (New York: W. W. Norton, 1970); Edward Tower, H. J. Baas, and Alain Sheer, "Alternative Optimum Tariff Strategies as Devices for Transferring Real Income," *Southern Economic Journal*, 1978, pp. 18–31; Edward Tower and Alain Sheer, "How to End Tariff Wars" (manuscript, 1978).

[6] H. G. Johnson, "Optimum Tariffs and Retaliation," *Review of Economic Studies*, vol. 21, no. 2 (1953–1954), pp. 142–53.

[7] Edward Tower, "The Optimum Tariff Retaliation and Autarky," *Eastern Economic Journal*, 1976, pp. 72–75.

PART FIVE: THE LIBERAL'S DILEMMA

The Importance of the Retaliatory Instrument

Studies by C. A. Rodriguez and Tower have shown that, when quotas are used as the retaliatory instrument by either country, in a Cournot policy equilibrium autarky will always be approached in the limit.[8] That the instrument used may have an important bearing on the final outcome has also been illustrated by Murray C. Kemp and Michihiro Ohyama, who built "a model of an asymmetric world composed of resource-poor and resource-rich countries" and used it to examine "the scopes of 'economic imperialism' and 'resource nationalism.'" They show that "self-seeking resource-poor countries will completely exploit their resource-rich trading partners but that the latter will exploit the former only partially," and "in the special case in which international indebtedness is independent of policy, the [resource-rich] colonial economy loses all power to exploit by means of taxes."[9] Tower shows that this result is true only because Kemp and Ohyama assumed that the tax was an ad valorem export tax levied by the colonial economy; other instruments (export quotas, import quotas, an export tariff specified in units of the import per unit of the export, and destruction of the raw material by the government of the colonial economy) may restore the colonial economy's ability to exploit the imperial one.[10]

Caves on Monopoly

Caves notes that, from an individual country's standpoint, allowing or enforcing the monopolization of an industry is a policy inferior to imposing an export tax while keeping the industry competitive. If a firm is granted a monopoly on exporting, it will maximize its profit by setting up the price differential that would be implied by the maximum revenue tariff, which, as is well known, will always be in excess of the optimum welfare tariff.[11] This is why monopolization can cause domestic welfare to fall. Other forms of industrial organization and their implications

---

[8] C. A. Rodriguez, "The Non-Equivalence of Tariffs and Quotas under Retaliation," *Journal of International Economics*, 1974, pp. 295–98; Edward Tower, "The Optimum Quota and Retaliation," *Review of Economic Studies*, 1975, pp. 259–87.

[9] Murray C. Kemp and Michihiro Ohyama, "On the Sharing of Trade Gains by Resource-Poor and Resource-Rich Countries," *Journal of International Economics*, vol. 8 (1978), pp. 93–115.

[10] Edward Tower, "Economic Imperialism and Resource Nationalism: Comment on Kemp and Ohyama," *Journal of International Economics*, vol. 9 (1979).

[11] See, for example, W. Max Corden, *Trade Policy and Economic Welfare* (London: Allen and Unwin, 1974).

for welfare in an internationally trading economy are explored by Johnson.[12]

The Optimal Retaliatory Tax on Monopolized Goods

Caves notes that the optimal retaliatory tax on monopolized imports is generally positive and mentions that for a full treatment of this case one must consider the possibility of further moves by the monopolist. This I have done in a paper stimulated by the Dreyer and Caves pieces.[13]

One intuitively appealing conclusion is that a monopolistic or monopsonistic country that trades with another imperfect competitor will wish to present its trading partner with as elastic an effective supply or demand curve as possible, thus robbing its partner of as much market power as possible and encouraging the partner to *expand* its participation in the market. Such a country will find that its best price floor or ceiling is preferable to its best tariff, which in turn will be preferable to its best quota (the term "best" is used to mean the level of the restriction that maximizes a country's welfare in the presence of retaliation, as opposed to the term "optimum," which means the same but in the absence of retaliation). Moreover, some price floor will always be preferable to free trade, and there may be an ad valorem or specific tariff that is preferable to free trade. However, free trade will be preferable to any binding quota. Interestingly enough, in these cases a price floor or ceiling can be used to achieve Pareto optimality in the world economy because, as R. G. Lipsey and P. O. Steiner show, price floors and ceilings can be used to move an imperfectly competitive system to Pareto optimality.[14] This work builds on Willett and R. J. Sweeney, both of whom have pointed out that a monopolist exporter, when confronted by an import tariff, will lower his price, and when confronted by an import quota, will raise it.[15]

However, a duopolist or duopsonist—that is, a market participant who must compete with a non–price-taking rival—will be more successful when he uses an instrument that makes his own effective excess

---

[12] H. G. Johnson, "Alternative Maximization Policies for Developing Country Exports of Primary Products," *Journal of Political Economy*, 1968, pp. 489–93.

[13] Edward Tower, "On the Best Use of Trade Controls in the Presence of Foreign Market Power" (manuscript, 1978).

[14] See, for example, R. G. Lipsey and P. O. Steiner, *Economics* (New York: Harper and Row, 1975), p. 390.

[15] Thomas D. Willett, "Oil Imports Are Not the Answer," *Journal of Energy and Development*, Spring 1976, p. 240; R. J. Sweeney, "Alternative Tariff and Quota Mechanisms in the Face of a Monopolistic Exporter of a Non-Renewable Resource," *Weltwirtschaftliches Archiv*, heft 1, (1977), pp. 104–24.

supply or demand less elastic, thereby forcing his rival to face a less elastic excess demand or supply. He will thus encourage the rival to *contract* participation in the market, thereby exploiting the rival's power to set prices more fully and leaving more of the market for the duopolist or duopsonist. Thus, for the latter, the best quota will be preferable to the best tariff, which in turn will be preferable to the best price floor or ceiling.

The latter two conclusions are exceptions—in addition to those found by Rachel McCulloch[16]—to the rule that in the presence of imperfect competition tariffs are superior to quotas. Moreover, these four conclusions reaffirm the adage that anything a tariff can do something else can do better: for a monopolist or a monopsonist that something else is a price floor or ceiling, and for a duopolist or a duopsonist that something else is a quota. Finally, in each case there is an explicit transfer combined with free trade by both countries which would be better for both countries than any of these policies, a point ignored by H. G. Johnson, who seems to argue that the optimum tariff is a first best policy for increasing a country's welfare.[17]

In my recent paper, I also derive the appropriate levels of trade restrictions geometrically under all four types of market structure.[18] This leads to the conclusion that the best level of trade for a buyer or seller in bilateral monopoly or for a duopolist or duopsonist is determined by the intersection of his own demand or supply curve with the curve that is marginal to the foreign reaction curve drawn for the particular type of restriction (tariff, quota, or limit to price movement) being considered. Expressing the same idea mathematically, the proportional difference between the domestic and the world price which he should maintain (that is, the ad valorem equivalent of his best trade restriction) is given by the standard formula for the optimum import or export tariff when the elasticity of foreign supply or demand is replaced by the elasticity of the foreign reaction curve.

Foreign Price-Setting Behavior: An Argument for Protection?

When the trading partner of a buyer or seller ceases to be a price taker and becomes an imperfect competitor, the appropriate price ceiling of the buyer or price floor of the seller is unchanged, because such floors

---

[16] Rachel McCulloch, "When Are a Tariff and Quota Equivalent?" *Canadian Journal of Economics*, vol. 6 (1973), pp. 503–11.
[17] H. G. Johnson, *Aspects of the Theory of Tariffs* (London: Allen and Unwin, 1971), p. 119.
[18] Tower, "Best Use of Trade Controls."

and ceilings present the competitor with a perfectly elastic demand or supply, thereby negating any meaningful monopoly or monopsony power. Therefore, in this circumstance, the reaction curve coincides with the foreign supply or demand curve in the relevant range, so the best differential between the domestic and the world price (that which maximizes domestic welfare in the presence of retaliation) will be given by the standard formula for the optimum import or export tariff. However, the adoption of price-setting behavior by a trading partner may cause the appropriate ad valorem or specific tariff to rise or fall, and the best quota is nonbinding.

Thus, if the instrument of protection is a price floor or ceiling, imperfect competition abroad does not constitute an argument for protection that is logically distinct from the standard optimum tariff argument. If a tariff is used as the instrument, imperfectly competitive behavior by a trading partner must be reckoned with, but it may cut in either direction; that is, the best ad valorem or specific tariff may lie above or below the optimum one, and such foreign behavior should always cause any quota to be scrapped. Of course, all this analysis assumes that the foreign country believes the level of the home restriction to be fixed and maximizes utility subject to that constraint. However, as Sweeney, Tower, and Willett have shown in the context of domestic monopoly, if the monopolist realizes that commercial policy is an instrument used to maximize the policy maker's welfare function rather than a goal in itself, the equivalence of all of these instruments reemerges.[19]

A Proposal to Foster a More Liberal International Order

Alain Sheer and I have a proposal to foster a more liberal international economic order.[20] Why do we worry about an illiberal international economic order? We do so because the system we have fails properly to internalize externalities associated with the use of illiberal policies. To some extent, GATT rules already internalize externalities. The raising of a tariff that has been bounded at a lower rate by a GATT negotiation is termed nullification of the concession, and restriction of trade in that product by some other technique such as a quota or a quality standard is termed impairment of it. Under Article 23 of GATT, when a country nullifies or impairs a concession, the injured party has the right to a consultation with the offender and a right to compensation, which is

---

[19] Richard J. Sweeney, Edward Tower, and Thomas D. Willett, "The Ranking of Alternative Tariff and Quota Policies in the Presence of Domestic Monopoly," *Journal of International Economics*, 1977, pp. 349–63.
[20] Tower and Sheer, "How to End Tariff Wars."

undefined, however. Traditionally, compensation is an equal tariff reduction on an equal volume of trade, although this compensation very rarely occurs. If a country does not get satisfactory compensation, then under the same Article 23 the GATT council (consisting of representatives from all member countries) can vote to authorize retaliation. Rarely, if at all, has retaliation been authorized, however; most disputes are resolved with orderly marketing agreements.

The rules for an optimum world commercial-policy system should merely internalize externalities. Such rules should not necessarily foster free trade. After all, some countries may have legitimate reasons for imposing tariffs unrelated to the terms of trade argument, and their policy makers will have the proper incentives to use efficient policy mixes from the world standpoint only if externalities are internalized. Thus, Sheer and I propose that GATT require all import and export licenses to be auctioned off in competitive markets and that each country be required to remit some fraction of all revenues from tariffs and quotas on imports and exports to their trading partners or to international agencies. Ideally, this fraction should be different for countries possessing different degrees of monopoly power, and its calculation should recognize other external effects of tariffs as well, for example, their effects on the transmission of disturbances between economies,[21] and the adjustment costs foisted on one country by changes in its partners' tariffs or quotas.

In practice, what is needed is a club called SATT (special agreement on tariffs and trade). Members would be obliged to remit a given fraction of their revenues from tariffs and quotas on all trade with other SATT nations to the SATT directorate for redistribution among the members. This fraction might depend on the average level and structure of tariffs. Each SATT country would be empowered to extend to all other SATT countries whatever discount on its tariffs it chooses. With part of revenues from its tariffs on SATT trade given away, it would be in each country's interest to extend some sort of discount. Thus, each country would have a uniform tariff schedule applying to all GATT countries and a uniform discount on all tariffs applying to all SATT nations. Countries would join SATT to reap a share of the community's tariff revenue, take advantage of the efficiencies generated by the relatively distortionless decision making on tariffs within the group, and benefit from the lower tariffs afforded to members. Thus, if SATT

---

[21] Tariffs and quotas tend to bottle up disturbances within the country of origin but to insulate countries from disturbances originating abroad. When disturbances are transmitted between countries, the insurance principle of risk bearing assures that they will at least partially cancel out, thereby increasing the stability of the world economy. Thus, each economy's stability is enhanced by each cut in its partner's tariffs.

expanded rapidly, the gains from trade creation would outweigh the losses associated with the diversion of trade from GATT to SATT nations.

GATT could permit such arrangements, even if it did not take an active part in their negotiation. We would suggest, for example, that the United States offer Canadian goods free entry into the United States in exchange for two-thirds of the revenue collected from the Canadian tariff on U.S. goods. With the externalities due to the Canadian tariff fully or more than fully internalized, Canadian tariff policy would be decided within the Canadian Parliament, and diplomats would be free to focus their energies elsewhere. Canadian MPs would be able to explain to their constituencies that the use of commercial policy to foster special interests or industrialization would come at an even higher cost than before to the rest of the Canadian economy, which should mitigate protectionist pressure to some extent. South of the border, U.S. congressmen could explain to their constituencies the benefits to Americans from the Canadian tariff and the costs of retaliating in kind, which would, again, serve to tip the political scales toward free trade. Finally, academic economists in their pleas for freer trade would no longer have to reckon with what H. G. Johnson characterizes as "the only valid argument for protection as a means of maximizing economic welfare": the optimum tariff argument.[22]

---

[22] Johnson, *Aspects*, p. 119.

DISCUSSION

Roger Shields was asked to comment on Franklyn Holzman's statement that the security restrictions on East-West trade were unjustified. Shields replied that we have inconsistent policy in this area because there are no well-established criteria for what relates to national security. Shields agreed with Holzman that in some cases we have harmed domestic producers—without strengthening national security. Shields felt that in relative terms the volume of prohibited items has been very small. Holzman replied that it is relatively small now but historically it has been large. He again stated that the government has been overprotective and over-security conscious.

Marina Whitman commented that a type of protectionism seems to be springing up in the United States that was not discussed in Dreyer's paper—a national security argument against the export of front-end technology. Jan Tumlir picked up on Whitman's point and asked Shields whether the discussions surrounding the limitation of technology exports have any effect on patent conventions. He argued that this was an important point because export of patentable technology would undermine the patent law, resulting in a loss to the exporting nations. Shields replied that most of the technology concerned is not patentable and said that the National Security Council is presently conducting a study of U.S. policy with regard to the export of technology. Shields pointed to the external diseconomy associated with a decline in a country's ability to compete and argued that subsidized state trading monopolies can alter the terms at which technology can be offered. Holzman interjected a comment on the Soviets' inability to use the technology in an efficient way. An example, he said, was the Soviet purchase of an automated Pepsi Cola bottling plant, which could have been operated by five persons; after building the plant, Pepsi engineers returned to find more than a hundred workers wandering around. Tumlir pointed out that the technology argument for intervention has a long history: the British in the nineteenth century worried about the export of the spinning jenny.

DISCUSSION

Paul Streeten argued that the rhetoric of the bureaucrats of the freer access to markets. The demand for radical restructuring comes new order is simply that. What they really want is a bit more aid and from the third world intellectuals and not from the international bureaucrats. It is not at all clear, he said, where the masses in the LDCs stand on these issues. He argued that it is important to separate the different sources of the challenges to the LIEO.

Peter Kenen and Theodore Moran both drew attention to the lack of correlation between liberal economic and liberal political orders in the LDCs. Kenen felt that illiberality in both political and economic regimes is widely distributed. He went on to say that the exercise of market power by nonmarket actors and the exercise of political power by market actors are the two most serious threats to liberal trade policy. The exercise of market power by nonmarket actors is the intrusion of governments as buyers and sellers. The exercise of political power by market actors is represented by the multinational corporations.

Richard Sweeney pointed out that successful cartels and other monopoly practices often require government help. The developed world is trying to get governments to intervene, and we are trying to offset this by having governments negotiate with each other on how to overcome the other type of intervention. As a result of governmental intervention for different reasons, the entire world is victimized.

In the time given Jacob Dreyer to respond, he indicated that he was well aware that the main victim of monopoly was the country monopolizing the industry. He had, however, for the sake of this paper, disregarded that issue. With regard to Robert Tollison's discussion of behavior modification, Dreyer agreed with the intent but doubted that much good would come of it.

Dreyer commented on the technology discussion, pointing out that the COCOM list cost the United States exports because the German, British, and French replaced the United States as exporter. He argued that we must decide how much it is worth to us in terms of lost exports to slow the technological growth of the Soviet Union. Dreyer disagreed with Holzman's point about Soviet inability to use technology. He argued that just because they cannot use Pepsi technology effectively does not mean they will not use military technology effectively.

Dreyer felt that Edward Tower's SATT suggestion was a clever theoretical construct, but he questioned it on a practical basis. Again, he said, the critical factor is the difference between stated costs and social costs of production. The Soviets, Dreyer argued, would not divulge their costs even if they knew them.

PART FIVE: THE LIBERAL'S DILEMMA

Finally, referring to Whitman's comments, Dreyer pointed out that there are two kinds of externalities associated with technology export. One results from loss of competitive position; the other results from the fact that much development of technology is publicly funded.

PART SIX

STRATEGIES FOR A MORE LIBERAL AND EQUITABLE INTERNATIONAL ECONOMIC ORDER

International Resource Transfers: The International Financial System and Foreign Aid

Richard D. Erb

AEI

A word of warning is in order about the scope of this paper, given its title. When the subject of resource transfers is discussed, the focus is usually on net transfers of goods and services (as measured by the current account balance excluding unrequited public and private transfers) from developed to developing countries—and, in particular, transfers financed by foreign aid. In this paper, however, resource transfers are broadly defined to cover the net exports of goods and services among all countries, developed as well as developing. In addition, although the role of foreign aid in financing resource transfers is discussed, the primary focus of this paper is on the international financial system that underpins resource transfers among countries, including developing countries. This is not meant to downgrade the desirability of increasing resource transfers to developing countries, considering the wide income disparities between developed and developing countries. Rather, it is this author's view that the future growth of resource transfers to developing countries will depend importantly, if not primarily, on a growing and efficient international financial system.

Another word of warning is offered about the focus of this paper, given the title of this conference. When talking about the challenges to a liberal international economic order, there is a tendency to think about trade and, to a lesser extent, direct investment. However, the philosophy of a liberal international economic order—with its emphasis on the achievement of economic efficiency and thus higher world output through decentralized, competitive, market-oriented transactions—is as appropriate a guide for the workings of the financial sector as it is for the trade sector. Economic efficiency and world output is enhanced if those countries with the potential for earning relatively high rates of return on domestic investments attract net inflows of resources while those countries with relatively low rates of return are net exporters of resources. Since it is generally believed that developing countries have higher rates of return, international resource transfers enable income levels in those countries to rise in relation to other countries and

PART SIX: STRATEGIES

thereby reduce income disparities among nations. Thus, the objective of improving the efficiency of the international financial system is consistent with the objective of achieving a more equitable world order.

During the postwar period, not only has the magnitude of resource transfers grown, but the pattern of resource transfers among countries has been dynamic. In the early postwar years, net resource inflows contributed to a rapid reconstruction and advance of the economies in Europe and Japan. Some countries, such as Italy, Japan, and Germany, eventually became major net exporters while other countries, such as Canada, France, and Australia, continued to be net importers of goods and services. At that time, resource transfers to developing countries were financed primarily by official development assistance and direct investment flows. During the last decade, however, many developing countries such as Korea, Brazil, Mexico—the list goes on—have increased their net resource inflows by borrowing in the international financial markets, thus providing those countries with the potential to grow more rapidly.

In order to understand how resource transfers are financed among countries, it is necessary to examine all financial inflows and outflows, since a resource transfer is basically the *net* result of a large number of *independent* inflow and outflow transactions. Financial flows to and from a country take place through a large number of entities including banks, multinational corporations, trading firms, international bond markets, government-to-government facilities—including aid institutions—and official international institutions such as the World Bank and the IMF. Because money flows into and out of a country in many different forms, and from many different directions, it is impossible to determine the exact means by which a country's resource transfer is financed. In effect, the ability of a country to be a net importer of goods and services depends on the judgments of a large number of financial decision makers who evaluate not only the risk and return of the specific transaction they are financing but also the overall ability of a country to accumulate resource transfers over time, that is, to become a net debtor country.

The first section of this paper is devoted to a brief discussion of how the international financial system works. Although the international financial system can be characterized as a market-based system, and although the financial system has weathered a number of major shocks in recent years—including the oil-related financial flows that some warned would bring down the financial system—there remain a number of challenges confronting the growth and stability of that market system. Included among these is the seeming inability of most domestic economies to find a stable growth path at a low rate of inflation. As discussed in the second section, the future growth and liberal character of the international financial sector will depend, for a number of reasons, on the ability of governments to achieve stable growth rates.

Although the growth and efficiency of the international financial system will depend heavily on the future course of domestic economic policies, a number of specific international policy steps could be taken to strengthen the liberal nature of the system. As Thomas Willett pointed out in the introduction, a liberal philosophy does not require the belief that there is never a need for government intervention. Thus, in addition to supporting an expansion of the conditional lending facilities of the IMF, a proposal is made in this paper to establish a lender of last resort facility within the Fund. Also proposed is an approach for supervising commercial bank international lending activities. In addition, the need for government steps to provide greater financial and real-sector economic information about countries is cited.

Although the international financial system is market oriented, there exist government regulations and practices that inhibit or subsidize financial flows among countries and thus are inconsistent with the principles of an LIEO. It is interesting to find, however, that many of the government subsidies inadvertently, and in some cases, advertently, operate in favor of the developing countries by encouraging larger financial flows to those countries. This result contrasts with government interference by developed countries in the trade sector, which more often is biased against developing countries.

Although much of the analysis in this paper considers ways of improving the liberal character of the international financial system, at stake also is the equitable character of that system since access to a growing international financial system enables developing countries to improve their relative income levels. The financial system not only enables them to facilitate the exports and imports that are vital to the expansion of their domestic economies but also enables many to sustain larger levels of net resource inflows. Should the financial system falter or fail, such countries would find it not only difficult to finance import and export transactions but virtually impossible to finance resource transfers. To be sure, there are many low income countries that finance only small levels of export–import transactions and are not able to be net borrowers in the international financial markets, but they too would be damaged from the backwash should the financial system suffer severe disruptions.

The final section of this study focuses on the roles of official lending and official assistance in increasing the flow of resource transfers

PART SIX: STRATEGIES

to developing countries. As normally defined, official lending takes place on relatively hard terms while official assistance consists of grants or lending on concessional terms. Developing countries are not homogeneous and range from relatively high income per capita countries to countries with per capita incomes below $100.00. Thus, an attempt is usually made by governments to relate magnitudes of lending and assistance, as well as the mix between lending and assistance, to country income levels, with low income countries designated primarily for assistance and higher income countries designated for lending.

During the past fifteen years, and especially since 1970, loans to developing countries from official lending institutions, primarily the developing banks, have grown rapidly. From a level of $2.5 billion in 1970, lending by the three major development banks rose to $7.8 billion in 1977. Currently, each of the major institutions has plans to increase its capital base substantially in order to permit further real growth of lending. Before such an expansion is underwritten by the major industrialized countries, however, a number of issues concerning the development banks should be examined and debated, including the desirability of general development lending versus project lending, the relationship between the IMF and the development banks, the relative size of the existing institutions, the desirability of creating new institutions versus expanding existing institutions, the relationship between official lending and private-sector lending, and the absorptive capacity of developing countries. The first two items are addressed in this paper.

In contrast to the dramatic growth in official lending, official assistance, which amounted to $8.9 billion in 1976, has not been growing rapidly. In fact, when adjusted for inflation, official assistance from developed to developing countries has declined slightly since the mid–1960s. Among the industrialized countries, the largest inflation-adjusted decline occurred in the U.S. assistance program. Although a real increase in assistance flows could serve to meet the needs of some of the extremely poor countries, as well as to strengthen the international leadership role of the industrialized countries, it would be a mistake to raise expectations in the developing countries that larger real flows are likely to be forthcoming. Public attitudes toward development assistance, especially in the United States, are not likely to turn around and support large real increases within the next five years.

Foreign aid in the United States has never been popular, but during much of the postwar period aid was pulled along by a foreign policy that emphasized national security objectives and sought to avoid the economic conflicts of the interwar period. Thus, the United States played a strong leadership role in building postwar economic institutions, including the concept of development assistance.

The decline in the preeminent role that national security plays in guiding U.S. foreign policy, as well as a decline in the relative economic strength of the United States, have both contributed to the decline in U.S. assistance programs. Since the Vietnam War and the collapse of the Bretton Woods system, the United States has been a country in search of a foreign policy. Until such a policy emerges, and until development assistance is viewed as an integral part of that policy, it is not very likely that U.S. development assistance programs will expand in the near future.

The International Financial Markets

During the postwar period, and especially since 1970, the international financial system evolved at a dramatic rate in terms not only of its size but also of its structure. International financial flows now take place through a plethora of public, private, and mixed public-private entities located throughout the world. Some of those entities specialize in financial transactions, while for others international financial transactions are simply an adjunct to a nonfinancial business. In addition to national entities, there is a host of multilateral institutions, including the IMF–World Bank group, the regional development banks, and institutions such as the recently established International Fund for Agricultural Development.

Limited only by imagination, an almost infinite variety of public and private international financial instruments has been created. In addition, financial instruments are denominated in any one of a number of individual currencies, ranging from the long-established pound to the four-year-old dirham of the United Arab Emirates. Alternatively, financial assets may be denominated in any one of a number of currency combinations, such as a special drawing right, a European currency unit, and an Arab currency-related unit.[1]

Although a large number of distinct markets exist, ranging from currency markets to money markets to long-term debt and equity markets, all markets have become more closely integrated, so that a development in one market immediately influences transaction prices in others. Although markets may be identified with major financial centers, such as London, Hong Kong, and New York, the international

---

[1] Marc Huybrechts and Robert Di Calogero, "Recent Development of Units of Account Designed to Serve Borrowers and Lenders," *IMF Survey* (November 7, 1977), pp. 346–47.

PART SIX: STRATEGIES

financial market is in reality a worldwide system of telephone and teletype communications. From the most remote parts of the world it is possible to pick up a phone, survey current bid/offer prices for almost any type of financial security, and strike a deal. Central bankers and finance ministers can communicate with each other instantaneously and regularly, thus keeping each other abreast of their own actions in the market and, perhaps as important, their outlook and objectives. In addition, from any location in the world, the principals of a financial negotiation or the heads of central banks and finance ministries can be brought together within twenty-four hours by air travel. During February 1973, when the major industrialized countries were forced by capital flows to abandon fixed exchange rates, the transition in government policies was facilitated by daily telephone communications among central banks and finance ministries as well as personal meetings among officials made possible by jet travel. Through such communications, some of the pitfalls of previous periods of international crises, such as the early 1930s, were avoided.

The growth in the international financial system during the postwar period not only facilitated rapid growth in trade among countries but also facilitated the growth in the magnitude of resource transfers among countries. In the immediate postwar period, direct public-sector financing dominated international financial flows, but as time passed the role of private-sector institutions grew. In part, the growth in private-sector financial activity was stimulated by government credits and guarantees, but during recent years an increasing portion of private-sector lending has taken place without special government incentives. Commercial banks and foreign international bond markets perform intermediation services not only for industrialized countries[2] but also for a growing number of countries normally classified as developing countries. For example, between 1973 and 1976, developing countries, excluding the major surplus oil-producing countries of Kuwait, Qatar, Saudi Arabia, and the United Arab Emirates, borrowed on average $1 billion a year (gross) in the international bond markets and $12 billion a year (gross) in the eurocurrency markets.[3]

During the postwar period, not only did the financing of resource transfers among industrial countries grow with countries such as Japan,

---

[2] For the purposes of this study, the following countries will be classified as industrialized countries: Australia, Austria, Belgium, Canada, Denmark, Finland, France, West Germany, Italy, Japan, the Netherlands, New Zealand, Norway, Sweden, Switzerland, United Kingdom, and the United States.

[3] World Bank, *Borrowing in International Capital Markets*, December 1977, table 2.1, p. 15.

France, Canada, and Australia importing large amounts of capital,[4] but the financing of resource transfers between industrialized countries and developing countries also grew rapidly. For example, from an average of $10 billion for the period 1964–1966, resource transfers from industrialized to developing countries almost doubled to a level of $19.7 billion in 1972, as shown in Table 1. Private-sector flows, excluding government-guaranteed export credits, more than tripled between the 1964–1966 average and 1972, with bank lending emerging as an important source of funds for developing countries. Official lending experienced the largest jump, from a level of $0.5 billion in 1964–1968 to $2.2 billion in 1972. Official assistance, that is, grants and loans provided on concessional terms, increased by 56 percent.

The oil price increases of late 1973 not only increased the magnitude of resource transfers that needed to be financed but also led to major shifts in the distribution of resource transfers among countries. During the period from 1974 to 1976, net resource outflows from the major oil-exporting countries as a group, all of which have been classified as developing countries in Table 1, averaged $48.6 billion a year.[5] From 1974 to 1976, the industrialized countries financed average current account deficits of $28 billion.[6] For the non-oil developing countries, resource transfers averaged $46 billion a year for the period 1974–1976.[7]

Although a large portion of the OPEC surpluses have been invested in other countries through established financial institutions—primarily commercial banks and investment banks—a growing proportion is being managed within the OPEC countries as public and private-sector institutions develop financial expertise. There also has been a proliferation of multilateral institutions, especially among the Arab oil-producing states. Thus, in addition to increasing the magnitude of international financial transactions, the growth in the OPEC surplus has diversified and multiplied the number of financial decision makers who manage international financial assets.

During the course of a year, public and private entities within a country continuously carry out foreign financial transactions. Some lend abroad, and others borrow. Because inflows and outflows of financial assets take place in complex ways, it is impossible to link the

---

[4] International Monetary Fund, *Balance of Payments Yearbook*, various volumes: vol. 26 (1976), vol. 27 (1977), vol. 28 (1978).
[5] International Monetary Fund, *Annual Report*, 1977, table 7, p. 15.
[6] *Ibid.* Industrialized countries category plus current account balances for New Zealand, Australia, and Finland found in Balance of Payments Yearbook.
[7] *Ibid.*

PART SIX: STRATEGIES

TABLE 1

NET FLOWS OF FINANCIAL RESOURCES FROM
MAJOR INDUSTRIALIZED COUNTRIES TO DEVELOPING COUNTRIES

(billions of dollars)

	Average 1964–1966	1972
Private flows[a]		
Direct investment	2.1	4.5
Bank lending	0.9	1.4
Export credits (guaranteed)	3.0	7.4
Official lending[b]	0.5	2.2
Official assistance[c]	5.7	8.9
Other[d]	—	1.0
Total	12.2	25.4

Dash (—): negligible.
Definitions:
[a] Primarily government guaranteed export credits.
[b] The net flow of funds from industrialized country public and private sources such as the IMF and the major development banks.
[c] Grants or loans provided on concessional terms for promotion of welfare and development.
[d] Grants by voluntary agencies.
SOURCE: OECD Development Assistance Committee, *Review*, 1975, p. 217, table 17.

financing of a country's positive or negative resource transfer to any one financial entity or instrument. Thus, contrary to popular perceptions,[8] it is not evident that a so-called balance of payments loan by a commercial bank helps a country finance a larger deficit any more than does an export credit or project loan decision by some other commercial entity. To the extent that different sources of finance are close substitutes, an increase in financing by one will reduce the level of financing by others. On the other hand, if alternative sources of financing are complementary, an increase in financing by one will induce others to increase their financing. Unfortunately, relatively little is known empirically about the degree of substitution or complementarity among international sources of funds.

Under the current system, large numbers of individual decision

---

[8] U.S. Congress, Senate, Subcommittee on Foreign Economic Policy of the Committee on Foreign Relations, Staff Report, *International Debt, The Banks, and U.S. Foreign Policy*, 95th Congress, 1st session, August 1977, p. 5.

makers in the private and public sectors make judgments about the expected risks and returns of foreign investments. Although lenders evaluate the *specific* risks and potential returns involved in any individual foreign investment—whether an export credit, project loan, or some other category of investment—lenders also make judgments about a country's general creditworthiness. While a project may be an economic success within an economy, there is the risk that an economy may not generate sufficient foreign exchange to enable the borrower to repay a loan.

Foreign lenders evaluate the general creditworthiness of a country differently and attach different degrees of importance to a country's general creditworthiness, depending on the nature and maturity of a loan. To cite extreme examples, a bank considering a nonguaranteed three-month loan to the independent subsidiary of a U.S. corporation will have little concern about that country's long-term economic prospects, but an institution considering the possibility of granting a long-term loan, whether to finance a project or to finance government expenditures in general, will give much greater weight to a country's long-run economic prospects.

Although a country's creditworthiness is only partly related to its net external debt, the jump in country debt since 1973 has significantly increased the amount of time and resources devoted to evaluating the general creditworthiness of countries. Multinational corporations, commercial banks, and export-import banks in recent years have expanded their staffs of economists—and political analysts—to carry out what is popularly called country risk analysis. The art of analyzing and forecasting general country risk, however, is in a formative stage of development. There is often a wide range of views about an economy's current performance, to say nothing about its future performance.

As experience has shown, debt ratios and econometric studies are of limited help when forecasting future economic performance and when forecasting the likelihood that a country will experience external financing problems. The latter is especially difficult because it requires judgments about how the rest of the financial market will judge the performance and prospects of a country in the future. Currently, lending institutions rely heavily on eclectic judgments based not only on economic analysis but also on analysis of social and political factors and their impact on government policies. Judgments also are made about international political factors, including, for example, the likelihood that developing countries might revolt and declare a moratorium on debt payments. Forecasts of economic developments in industrialized countries are full of unknowns and uncertainties, but these factors increase

PART SIX: STRATEGIES

exponentially for countries in more preliminary stages of development. Not only do analysts face gaps in historical and current economic data in most developing countries, including the more advanced, but they come face to face with the fundamental and unanswered question of what determines economic development.

Although commercial bankers and other multinational institutions may not want to admit it, especially since they have some very skeptical stockholders and government officials looking over their shoulders, learning is by doing. Except for some individual theoretical tools that provide some help, the existing economic theory of country borrowing is too general to be of much practical value, and there is even less empirical work.

In addition to standing on the early portion of the learning curve with respect to evaluating the risks and returns of investing in foreign financial assets, banks and other institutions are grappling with the question of how to structure their total foreign investment portfolios. There are many different dimensions to risk, and overall portfolio risk can be varied by changing not only the levels and mix of countries represented in the portfolio but also the composition and maturity structure of loans within each country.[9]

Thus, the current state of the international system financing resource transfers can be characterized in the following manner: the international financial system consists of a large number of private and public decision makers, each making judgments about the expected return and the specific and general risks associated with foreign financial assets and each making decisions about the levels and composition of foreign assets in their portfolios. Collectively, these decentralized decisions determine not only the financing of specific transactions but also the ability of a country to finance net resource transfers. Thus the distribution of resource transfers among countries is determined through a decentralized process involving public and private decision makers.

The performance of the financial markets to date provides evidence of efficient lending behavior,[10] including the lending experience with

---

[9] For insights into the approaches to credit risk analysis being developed by banks, see the following: Antoine W. van Agtmael, "Evaluating the Risks of Lending to Developing Countries," *Euromoney* (April 1975), pp. 16–29. A. Bryce Breakenridge, "Evaluating Country Credits," *Institutional Investor* (June 1977), pp. 13–16. Stephen Goodman, "How the Big U.S. Banks Really Evaluate Sovereign Risks," *Euromoney* (February 1977), pp. 105–10. S. M. Yassukovich, "The Growing Political Threat to International Lending," *Euromoney* (April 1975), pp. 10–15.

[10] Robert R. Davies, "Tests Show Banks Are Rational, Efficient in Granting LDC Credit," *The Money Manager* (August 1, 1977), p. 9.

developing countries. When various measures of risk are used, it has been found that borrowing costs increase and the amount of lending declines. A large number of instances can be found where countries—for example, Brazil, Taiwan, and Indonesia—undertook internal adjustment programs because they found it increasingly costly and difficult to finance their external deficits. Contrary to the often expressed fears that political pressures can be used to force banks to lend, or that bankers are so deeply involved in a country that they cannot say no,[11] it is the financial market as a whole that appears to be pressuring political decision makers to change their policies, as the experience of countries such as Italy, Mexico, Portugal, and numerous others suggests. In each case, those countries found it necessary to implement economic programs, including their domestic policies and foreign exchange policies, in order to reduce the magnitude of their net foreign borrowing.

As many countries have discovered, however, the current decentralized system has its advantages. Since for most countries there exists a wide range of judgments not only about how effectively an economy is being managed but also about the future prospects of that economy, a country may find it possible to increase its net external liabilities even if some lenders with negative judgments are unwilling to acquire financial assets in that country. Thus, while some bankers are not very bullish on countries like Brazil, Mexico, and Indonesia, others are. Under a centralized system, where a more limited range of judgments would influence lending decisions, a country might find it difficult at times to borrow externally.

A decentralized system also has economic advantages from a global resource allocation perspective. In a world of major unknowns and uncertainties, the fewer the number of judgments affecting lending decisions, and the broader the impact of any one decision, the greater the likelihood of a serious misallocation of resources if an error in judgment should occur. To be sure, mistakes are made under the current decentralized system, and many examples can be found of both private and public institutions lending money to foreign corporations and governments only to find themselves with problem loans. However, because any one investor or, more accurately, any one syndicate of investors, finances only a small portion of the total amount of financing that takes place, the potential aggregate impact of a wrong judgment is significantly smaller than under a centralized system.

In addition, pressures for adjustment are likely to develop more

---

[11] Senate, Subcommittee on Foreign Economic Policy of the Committee on Foreign Relations, Staff Report, *International Debt, The Banks, and U.S. Foreign Policy*, p. 61.

quickly and smoothly under a decentralized system because some lenders will realize—or make judgments—that a problem has developed before other lenders do. Thus, pressure for adjustment builds up slowly through the impact of lender decisions on the exchange rate or because it becomes more difficult for the public and private sectors to find external sources of funds, or the borrowing cost rises relative to the borrowing costs of other countries.

Although a decentralized financial system possesses a number of advantages over a centralized system, the comparative advantages should not imply that there are no major problems or risks inherent in the present decentralized system. In later sections of this paper, institutional proposals are examined for improving the strength and stability of the international financial system. Before examining these proposals, there is a brief discussion of the relationship between domestic economic policies and the growth of international resource transfers.

Domestic Economic Policies and the Stability of the International Financial System

Although the oil price increases of 1973 and the oil-related financial surpluses contributed to world economic instability, the effects of the increases were exaggerated because the world economy was already in a highly unstable condition. By mid–1973, double-digit inflation was closing in on a number of industrial countries, shortages of raw materials and finished goods were encouraging speculative activity, and domestic economic growth rates exceeded the long-run growth rates of most countries. Current account deficits had already expanded sharply in some countries, and in others governments were embarking on ambitious domestic expenditure programs that were about to result in larger current account deficits.

By 1974, most governments were frustrated by a sense that they had lost control of their economies and that old economic solutions no longer worked. During the mid–1970s, the word "adjustment" found its way into the speeches of central bankers and finance ministers.[12] As is common—and necessary—with words or ideas that become centerpieces of policy discussions, the theme had many variations. Since the price of oil had increased fivefold, adjustment meant that significant shifts in the patterns of energy supply and consumption were necessary. Since most economies suffered from double-digit inflation, adjustment meant that domestic economic policies had to give inflation fighting

---

[12] International Monetary Fund, *Summary Proceedings Annual Meeting* 1974, 1975, 1976.

first priority. Since many countries had expanded private and public consumption at the expense of investment, adjustment meant a reorientation of domestic priorities. Since non-OPEC countries would experience higher levels of foreign debt, adjustment meant that higher levels of domestic investment were necessary in order to create the economic base that would sustain those larger debt levels.

Although the word "adjustment" took on different meanings in different contexts, it was a word that bound policy makers together for it became a way of saying that the world had changed and that old norms and old policies had to change; yet it was vague enough to allow each government a high degree of flexibility in finding its way through the transition.

In response to higher oil prices, most governments allowed energy prices to rise to world market levels and encouraged the development of energy production.[13] Unfortunately, the government of the largest oil-consuming country in the world, and the third largest oil-producing nation in the world, did not allow oil demand or supply prices to adjust to the world price level for oil. In addition, controls were maintained on the price of gas, both for producers as well as for consumers. Thus, U.S. oil imports rose sharply from 6.5 million barrels a day in 1973 to 9.2 million barrels a day in 1977. Had U.S. oil supply and demand been allowed to adjust more quickly, OPEC would have found it difficult to raise the price of oil since 1974, and OPEC financial surpluses would have been less.

In response to high rates of inflation, a number of countries, including Japan, Germany, and the United States implemented deflationary policies. Deflation policies, however, overshot the mark and contributed significantly to bringing about the worst economic recession since the depression of the 1930s. Inflation was reduced, but with a high cost in lost output and extraordinarily high rates of unemployment. In addition, the boom of 1973 and the recession of 1974–1975 set the stage for developments that were to have a significant impact on international financial flows during 1976 and 1977.

As the major industrialized countries exited from the recession, they did so with different rates of growth, thus complicating adjustments in the distribution of international resource transfers. For example, by early 1977, the U.S. growth rate was substantially above that of its major trading partners, instead of below as is normal. This shift in relative growth rates is one reason for the rapid increase in the U.S.

---

[13] For a review of national energy policies since 1975 see Organization for Economic Cooperation and Development, *Energy Conservation in the International Energy Agency*, 1976.

goods and services deficit during 1977 and the increase in the goods and services surpluses of Japan and Germany. As a consequence, more than a little conflict and confusion ensued—within and among countries—over the appropriate mix of domestic policies and exchange rates.

Within the U.S. government, for example, the secretary of the Treasury in early 1977 made statements implying that the U.S. deficit was a good thing because the U.S. was leading world economic growth.[14] At almost the same time, other agencies of the U.S. government interpreted the U.S. deficit as evidence that the United States was losing its competitive edge. Meanwhile, some members of the U.S. Congress and a number of special interest groups saw the large deficit as generating unemployment.[15] Externally, there was controversy among Japan, Germany, and the U.S. government over the appropriate mix of domestic policies and exchange rates. Japan and Germany were concerned about avoiding another inflationary surge and were reluctant to pursue expansionary policies that might have reduced the U.S. deficit.

In addition to the economic shifts among the three major industrial countries during 1975 to 1977, which complicated international adjustments, some industrialized and developing countries went off on their own economic paths, creating additional international adjustment problems. During 1974 and 1975, a number of countries did not implement domestic deflationary policies, and thus maintained relatively high rates of real growth as well as high inflation rates.[16] In part, these countries maintained higher growth rates by financing larger goods and services deficits. Eventually, however, the deficits were judged by the markets to be excessively large. This brought external pressures to bear on those countries to "adjust." The type of adjustment proposed and adopted included heavy doses of traditional deflationary fiscal and monetary policies along with major exchange rate devaluations. By 1977, many of these countries had substantially improved their external payment positions but at the cost of negative domestic real economic growth rates. The sharp decline in the deficits of such countries also contributed to the large deficit of the United States.

---

[14] U.S. Congress, Senate, Subcommittee on International Finance of the Committee on Banking, Housing, and Urban Affairs, *Hearings on International Debt*, 95th Congress, 1st session, August 1977, pp. 5–9.

[15] U.S. Congress, House, Subcommittee on Trade of the Committee on Ways and Means, *Hearings on Causes and Consequences of the U.S. Trade Deficit and Developing Problems in U.S. Exports*, 95th Congress, 1st session, November 1977, pp. 262–71.

[16] Included among these countries were industrialized countries such as Italy, Sweden, Canada, the United States, and semiindustrialized countries such as Brazil and Mexico.

It is difficult to determine when exchange rates and the distribution of resource transfers among countries will become more stable, if at all. As of early 1978, it is impossible to find a country on a stable economic growth path with a declining rate of inflation. Since governments are attempting to guide their economies with inadequate tools and, even worse, a limited understanding about the workings of their domestic economies and the interaction among national economies, there no doubt will be both under- and overshooting of economic growth and inflation targets. As a consequence, a relatively stable distribution of deficits and stable exchange rates may not be possible for some time, since fluctuations in domestic and economic activity and fluctuations in foreign economic activity contribute to current account shifts.

Because of the high level of net external debt relative to domestic GNP and foreign exports in many developing countries (and in a few industrialized countries), some nations are vulnerable if their domestic economies stray too far from stable growth-inflation paths or if declines in world business activity should sharply reduce their export growth potential. Those who fear the collapse of the international financial system often cite the possibility that another decline in economic activity among the industrialized countries may trigger a series of defaults among developing countries suddenly confronted with declining export markets.[17]

This should not imply, however, that industrialized countries with strong balance of payments positions should err on the side of higher growth rates. Although high world growth rates and inflation rates may benefit developing countries in the short run—since high world growth rates expand their export markets and high inflation rates reduce the real value of their debt—the inability of industrialized countries to sustain excessively high growth rates ultimately brings about a reaction. In 1973–1974, many countries simultaneously had excessively high growth rates; as the recession of 1974–1975 showed, the reaction can be extreme, even if no one consciously planned or desired such a decline in world output.

In sum, essential to the future stability of the international financial systems and the further growth of international resource transfers is a return to a more stable pattern of domestic growth and inflation rates. If most countries are on stable growth-inflation paths, a deviation by one or two countries may cause financing problems for those countries but not for the system as a whole. If most countries find themselves off

---

[17] Senate, Subcommittee on International Finance of the Committee on Banking, Housing, and Urban Affairs, *Hearings on International Debt*, pp. 3–26.

stable growth-inflation paths, then the risk to the system as a whole is greater should one or two countries meet with external financial problems.

A return to a more stable pattern of domestic growth and inflation rates can also contribute to the stability and growth of international resource transfers in another way. When countries experience excessively low growth rates and high unemployment rates, import restrictions are often intensified.[18] On the other hand, when countries experience shortages and inflation because of a rapid growth in domestic demand, export controls are sometimes imposed.[19] Either way, international trade is threatened. When trade is threatened, so are international resource transfers. The ability of developing countries, in particular, to finance net resource transfers depends importantly on an open and growing international trade system. The proliferation of trade restrictions, motivated in part by balance of payments deficits, will only work to reduce foreign borrowing opportunities and, thus, increase external financing pressures for developing countries since international lenders will shift their lending to lower-risk industrialized countries.

This section emphasized the fundamental role of domestic economic policies in maintaining a stable and growing international financial system—and thus maintaining a growth in international resource transfers. The following sections will include proposals for changes and modifications in the structure of the existing financial system, with emphasis on stability and efficiency. Many steps that would improve the stability and efficiency of the system, in most instances, will also result in larger resource flows to developing countries, thereby contributing to a more equitable system.

IMF Conditional Lending

Contrary to some predictions that the end of the Bretton Woods system would reduce the role of the International Monetary Fund, the activities of the IMF have expanded since the early 1970s. During the period from 1973 to 1977, use of IMF resources increased from $1.1 billion in 1973 to $6.6 billion in 1976 and $4.9 billion in 1977. Those countries that used IMF funds ranged from industrialized countries (for example, Italy and the United Kingdom), to semiindustrialized coun-

---

[18] General Agreement on Tariffs and Trade, *International Trade 1976/77*, 1977. The growth in protectionism during 1977, a year of low growth and high unemployment, was noted frequently in the GATT report.

[19] During 1973, a year of rapid growth and accelerating inflation, a number of countries, including the United States, restricted exports of some products.

tries (Mexico and the Philippines), to low-income developing countries (Peru and Egypt).[20] As required under IMF conditional lending programs, borrowing governments agree to undertake domestic adjustment programs and agree to specific economic policy targets as conditions for access to IMF funds. The extent and stringency of the conditionality agreements increase with the amounts borrowed.

In 1977, because existing IMF resources were considered inadequate, a number of governments agreed to establish a special $10 billion supplemental financing facility, commonly called the Witteveen facility. According to IMF managing director, Johannes Witteveen, "It recognizes that a number of Fund members are experiencing external imbalances that are very large in relation to their economies, and it allows the Fund to encourage these members to adopt programs of adjustment by making available much larger amounts of financing than under the Fund's normal credit transfer policies."[21] The facility is not so large as originally desired by IMF management, but it can be expanded over time.

Attacks on the IMF lending programs came from two directions. There are those who argue that IMF lending is inefficient and leads to a misallocation of international resources.[22] Others argue that the resources of the IMF should be increased and the conditionality requirements eliminated so that more funds can be made available to developing countries.[23]

From a static economic perspective, a case can be made that IMF lending is inefficient. In effect, the IMF is lending money to governments that have been deemed by public and private international lenders as unable to utilize effectively larger amounts of external funds at market rates of return. Since an IMF program enables those countries to draw resources at a subsidized rate away from other countries that use the resources more effectively, a misallocation of resources is encouraged and world growth and output is potentially lowered. In effect, countries that manage their economies well are being asked to transfer resources to countries that manage their economies poorly.

---

[20] IMF, *Annual Report*, 1977, pp. 50–58.

[21] Johannes Witteveen, "Strategy Has Aimed at Adequate Growth to Cut Unemployment," *IMF Survey* (October 10, 1977), p. 36.

[22] U.S. Congress, House, Subcommittee on International Trade, Investment and Monetary Policy of the Committee on Banking, Finance and Urban Affairs, *Hearings on U.S. Participation in the Supplementary Financing Facility of the International Monetary Fund*, 95th Congress, 1st session, September 20, 29, and 30, 1977, pp. 242–45.

[23] Mahbub ul Haq, *The Third World and the International Economic Order* (Washington, D.C.: Overseas Development Council, September 1976), p. 36.

There is, however, a dynamic perspective from which the IMF program of conditional financing is consistent with the principles of economic efficiency. Given the current high degree of accessibility to the international financial system, countries are significantly more vulnerable to external financial pressures if their domestic economies get off the track. Faced with a sudden surge in capital outflows, or a reduction in capital inflows, a country has two basic alternatives: to allow its exchange rate to fall or to adjust its domestic economic policies. A major exchange rate devaluation is not likely to contribute to exchange rate stability unless other policies are implemented, and for political reasons a government may find it difficult to change its domestic policies sufficiently rapidly to improve the judgments of the financial market. Special borrowing arrangements with other countries and the IMF may buy enough time for a government to develop political support for a change in domestic policy. Alternatively, and perhaps more importantly, negotiations with the IMF may strengthen the ability of a government— or elements within a government such as the finance ministry or central bank—to generate political support for economic policy changes that would otherwise be difficult because of purely domestic political pressures.

Thus, in a dynamic sense, IMF conditional lending programs contribute to world economic efficiency by facilitating adjustment and avoiding extreme responses by governments under severe external financial pressures. If a country is forced to declare a moratorium on its debt service, or if external economic instability generates domestic political instability, the world economic consequences might be significantly more negative than the economic cost of short-term subsidized lending through the IMF.

The IMF's ability to assist a country in times of financial stress depends not so much on the magnitude of funds available, but on the credibility of the economic program adopted by the country as a condition for borrowing from the Fund. As the experience of many countries reveals, adoption of an economic program acceptable to the Fund often means that public and private sources outside a country become willing to increase their lending because they accept the judgment of the IMF that a country will in fact improve its domestic economic policies. As a consequence, drawings from the IMF are often less than originally expected. In effect, by maintaining stringent conditions, the IMF expands its power to assist countries, given its available resources.[24]

---

[24] House, Subcommittee on International Trade, Investment and Monetary Policy, *Hearings on U.S. Participation in the Supplementary Financing Facility of the International Monetary Fund*, p. 243.

If it were to relax those conditions, IMF lending would become a substitute for alternative sources of funds rather than a complementary source. As a consequence, the Fund would need access to substantially greater financial resources in order to provide the same degree of assistance that it now provides with its current level of resources.

The credibility of the IMF judgment is a fragile commodity and international financial decision makers keep a close watch on the performance of the Fund. The demands on the management, as well as the demands on the political structure of the IMF increased significantly during the mid–1970s. In many ways, the IMF is also on the early part of its learning curve, and much more time is required to evaluate the long-run success of the major IMF programs carried out in recent years. Thus, it would be a mistake to over-extend the institution by expanding too broadly the scope of its operations, as is often demanded by developing countries.

There were fears in 1975 and 1976 that the nature of the Fund was being changed by the adoption of special subsidy facilities for developing countries, including the Subsidy Account[25] and the Trust Fund.[26] In addition, the expansion of the Compensatory Financing Facility[27] meant larger flows of IMF funds to developing countries with less stringent conditionality requirements. However desirable larger flows of funds to developing countries may be on other grounds, when the IMF becomes a channel for these flows, it detracts from the positive role the IMF can play in providing conditional financing. Thus, further expansion of existing IMF subsidy accounts or the creation of new subsidy facilities for developing countries would be undesirable. To the extent that such facilities are deemed necessary, they should be created within the context of the development banks.

Aside from the question of the desirability of the IMF conditional lending programs, two related issues ought to be mentioned. The first concerns the magnitude of resources that should be available to support the IMF conditional lending programs. In part, the answer to that question depends on the state of the world economy. If many countries are off their long-run growth paths and experiencing high rates of inflation, a higher level of IMF resources may be necessary. The magnitude of

---

[25] IMF, *Annual Report*, 1976, p. 58. The Subsidy Account was established on August 1, 1975 to assist the Fund's most seriously affected members to meet the borrowing costs of the oil facility.

[26] IMF, *Annual Report*, 1975, p. 60. The Trust Fund was established on May 5, 1976 to provide special balances of payments assistance to developing members with profits generated by IMF gold sales and special contributions.

[27] IMF, *Annual Report*, 1975, pp. 52–53. See for details on the expansion of the Compensatory Financing Facility.

resources available to the IMF should also depend on the levels and structure of country debts. The larger the debt levels and the shorter the term structure for all countries, the greater the financial requirements of the Fund. In addition, IMF requirements will be larger the greater the level of international resource transfers. There is, however, no objective way of estimating the amounts required. To an extent, it is a matter of judgment—taking into account, inter alia, the items cited above. Thus, there may be times when the financial resources available to the Fund should be increased and times when the available resources should be decreased.

The second issue concerns the method by which the Fund should acquire resources. Since IMF requirements may vary over time with general economic conditions, and since even a relatively small country, as measured by GNP, may have a large short-run need for funds because of large debts, special facilities provide the IMF with a more flexible means of doing its job than general quota increases. Special facilities enable the IMF to increase or decrease the magnitude of funds available depending on world economic conditions and to shape a lending package to a country's needs rather than its quota.

The IMF as a Lender of Last Resort

Within most countries, it is assumed that the central bank can and will act in a time of extraordinary crisis to prevent a dominolike collapse of the financial system. In other words, should a crisis lead financial decision makers to suddenly contract the amount of lending they are willing to provide to individuals and corporations, the central bank stands ready to provide both liquidity and encouragement to financial institutions so that they will continue lending. Otherwise, economically healthy individuals and corporations might suddenly find themselves on the brink of bankruptcy because of an inability to borrow additional money to roll over existing debt. Although no one really knows if such a crisis will occur (or has occurred), and no one knows what criteria would precipitate a central bank action, there is a sense of confidence within most countries that the central bank has the authority, the power, and the will to act if necessary.

A similar sense of confidence, however, does not exist with respect to the international system. A question that is frequently asked both inside and outside the financial community is what would happen if a major crisis—for example, a Middle East war or a default by a major borrowing country—led to a sudden shift in the supply of international liquidity causing a series of defaults among the weaker countries and, thus, the collapse of a large number of public and private financial institutions with large levels of foreign risk exposure. Contrary to popular perceptions, it is not only the major international banks that would be affected by such a development but also any private corporation and any public institution that holds large amounts of foreign assets. Public institutions vulnerable to a collapse of the international financial system range from national institutions such as the U.S. Export-Import Bank to multilateral institutions such as the World Bank and the regional development banks.

The issue of lender of last resort raises two questions. The most fundamental is whether there should be, in fact, an international lender of last resort. In other words, should there be a sense of confidence that some institution has the financial power and authority to provide large levels of liquidity, directly or indirectly, to foreign borrowers in a time of crisis? The second question follows from the first. If it is determined that such an authority should exist, where should the power reside?

With respect to the first question, it can be argued that the fear of an open-ended international financial crisis provides a healthy check on the growth of international lending. Although post–World War II country lending experience suggests the risks are low, country lending experience prior to World War II suggests the risks may be high especially if a major war or a major recession should occur.[28] If there were confidence that some institution had the power and authority to act immediately to prevent a major financial crisis from developing, more international lending would take place and more lending would flow to higher-risk countries because a lower probability would be assigned to the possibility of a collapse in the system. For example, banks might be under less stockholder pressure to reduce the relative magnitude of their international lending, and especially their lending to developing countries, if there were more confidence in the long-run ability of the system to weather a political crisis. Therefore, such a facility might end up *increasing* the risk exposure of the system.

The cost of the latter risk, however, must be weighed against the potential cost inherent in the risk that some event will precipitate a financial crisis. Although national authorities no doubt would eventually mobilize themselves and put the pieces back together, such a rescue effort would take time, causing a significant contraction in real economic activity. In addition, there would be political costs should the

---

[28] Charles P. Kindleberger, "Debt Situation of the Developing Countries," *Financing and Risk in Developing Countries*, a symposium by the Export-Import Bank (August 1977), edited by Stephen H. Goodman, forthcoming.

crisis lead to domestic unrest within the more unstable countries of the industrialized and developing world.

With respect to the second question concerning what institution should serve as a lender of last resort, it can be argued that central banks currently have the ability to serve as the lender of last resort in the international economy. However, it is not likely that any single central bank would be willing, or have the financial capability, to provide sufficient liquidity to foreign borrowers. In effect, the central bank would need to be able to persuade national banks to continue making loans to foreigners, even as other national banks were reducing their foreign exposure. In the United States, Arthur Burns, then chairman of the Federal Reserve Board, and Representative Henry S. Reuss (D.-Wis.) have insisted publicly that the United States is not the lender of last resort on an international basis and that the role should be borne by the International Monetary Fund.[29] Nor is it likely that other central banks would be willing to step in where the Federal Reserve feared to tread.

One institutional approach would be an explicit agreement among central banks identifying the circumstances and conditions under which they would jointly act as international lenders of last resort. Alternatively, it could be done under the IMF umbrella. Current and proposed IMF facilities, however, are not designed to serve such a need. One approach would be to establish a special facility within the IMF that could be activated quickly in a time of crisis and managed by a small standing subcommittee of the IMF Interim Committee, including Japan, Germany, the United States, and Saudi Arabia. The facility would need to have access to very large amounts of funding to give it credibility in a time of crisis, but the guidelines for the facility would make it clear that the facility could only be used in extraordinary circumstances.

Bank Supervision. Because of the growing international lending role and the exposure of commercial banks, bank supervisors among the major industrialized countries have been attempting to develop a set of principles and guidelines for bank examinations. Since there are many different dimensions of risk, and relatively limited historical experience with which to evaluate risk, bank supervisors face the same questions as commercial bank portfolio managers: How should those risks be evaluated in the context of a bank's portfolio? The resolution of these questions by bank supervisors will have an important impact on the efficiency and equity of the international banking system. From an effi-

---

[29] *Ibid.*

ciency perspective, supervisory limits on lending may prevent the flow of resources to countries that can use them most effectively. From an equity perspective, excessive supervisory concerns about risk are likely to have a limiting effect on the flow of funds to developing countries.

Estimating and classifying foreign asset risks pose political as well as economic dilemmas for bank supervisors. To the extent that the country's dimension of risk is emphasized in classifying international asset risks for bank examiners, downgrading a country's creditworthiness results in political protests from that country, especially since it is impossible to keep such information confidential. More important, when bank supervision is managed by a central bank or a finance ministry, there may sometimes be a conflict between the responsibility of the central bank or finance ministry as a bank supervisor and its responsibility to maintain a stable domestic and international monetary system. This conflict occurs when the central bank or finance ministry receives confidential information about the economic or political health of a country which, if fed into the supervisory process, might in itself be a cause of international economic instability. One way to resolve this conflict is to separate supervisory from monetary policy responsibilities for both central banks and finance ministries.

With respect to efficiency considerations underlying individual bank supervision, the following general principle is suggested: bank supervisors should avoid setting country limit standards. There are two basic reasons for this view. For any given level of lending to a country by a bank, the degree of risk will vary with the mix of specific assets held from that country. In addition, different distributions of lending among countries may also produce the same level of portfolio risk. For both reasons, country limits reduce the bank's overall flexibility in finding its optimal risk/return mix. If such a supervisory practice is followed throughout the system, the inefficiency of such an approach will be compounded.

The impact of bank supervision practices on international banking flows and thus on resource transfers among countries is a complicated subject that requires more detailed analysis, not only of bank supervisory practices in this country and other countries but also of the structure of the international banking system. For example, a large multinational bank with a domestic office, foreign branches, and foreign subsidiaries has the flexibility to move foreign assets around, depending on the degree and nature of supervisory restrictions—or lack of them—in different national jurisdictions. Thus, supervisory restrictions may have an effect on the channels of financing flows to countries but not on the levels of the flows or on the level of net borrowing. Since there exist a relatively large number of such international banks, the impact of supervisory restrictions on the flow of resources may not be very significant.

Although bank regulators have a legal responsibility for bank supervision, it is often forgotten that individual bank risk is monitored by the investment community and major bank depositors. When the stock market value of a bank drops because of concern about its international lending, that signal is reflected in the bank's decision about where to direct its capital for future growth. In addition, major depositors can influence the degree of risks assumed by individual banks. Thus, supervisory authorities should not become overly myopic about their role, and thus overly restrictive in their supervisory practices, since market judgments about risk will, over time, act as a check on the behavior of banks and on the degree to which they are involved in international lending.

Information. Although a great deal of economic and financial information is collected by countries, significant gaps remain. Thus, there is substantial room for improving the efficiency of the international financial markets by improving the amount and quality of reported financial and economic data. In addition, the stability of the international financial system will be enhanced since the likelihood of major lending mistakes will be reduced.

With respect to financial data, it would be desirable to have an external financial balance sheet for every country, including not only public and private-sector foreign liability data, by maturity category, but also public and private-sector foreign asset data, by maturity. While the ideal may not be necessary, current financial reporting practices deviate too far from the ideal.

The country debt data generally reported do not include government borrowing for less than one year or short-term or long-term private-sector borrowing not guaranteed by some government agency. For industrialized and semiindustrialized countries, both gaps result in a significant loss of information; for developing countries, the private-sector gap is not as significant since there is relatively little unguaranteed borrowing. Even less data are available on the magnitude and distribution of foreign assets held by residents. Such data reported over time, of course, would provide some insights into the relative importance of domestic outflows for different countries, information that would be especially valuable during times of financial crisis.

Over the last three years, a significant effort has been made by individual governments as well as by multilateral agencies to organize and to coordinate systematically their financial data collection and reporting efforts. Conceptual as well as collection problems make it difficult to develop a consistent international short-term debt-reporting system, but the Bank for International Settlements is experimenting with different survey approaches. No doubt major improvements in liability reporting will take place during the next few years, resulting in better lending decisions by financial institutions.[30]

Although a considerable amount of attention has been focused on financial data gaps, there are even greater gaps in domestic economic data, especially for developing and semiindustrialized countries.[31] Without such data, it is difficult to carry out an economic analysis of what is happening, let alone what might happen in the future. Although it is recognized that high levels of country borrowing are sustainable if there are sufficient levels of domestic investment, government and private-sector expenditure data for many countries are either lacking or reported only after long lags. Domestic economic data gaps tend to be larger among semiindustrialized and developing countries. Given the growing recognition that such data are necessary for lending decisions, it is in the interest of those countries to improve substantially the depth and quality of their economic reporting, a development that would improve the quality of their own economic decision making as well as their access to foreign resource transfers.

International Capital Controls. Within most countries there is a variety of controls and regulations affecting inward and outward financial flows. A relatively detailed report of such controls for member countries is provided annually by the International Monetary Fund.[32] While it is debatable whether government restrictions distort the flows of money and capital among countries more or less than tariff or non-tariff barriers, the existence of government restrictions on financial flows is inconsistent with the general principles of a liberal international economic order. In recognition of this, the membership of the Organization for Economic Cooperation and Development adopted in 1961 a Code of Liberalization of Capital Movements, but as others have pointed out, the code has had limited impact on the policies of individual members.[33]

---

[30] Henry C. Wallich, "How Much Private Bank Lending is Enough?" *Financing and Risk in Developing Countries*, forthcoming.
[31] *Ibid.*
[32] International Monetary Fund, *Twenty-Eighth Annual Report on Exchange Restrictions*, 1977.
[33] Marina v. N. Whitman, "Coordination and Management of the International Economy: A Search for Organizing Principles," *Contemporary Economic Problems* (1977), p. 338.

PART SIX: STRATEGIES

In addition to creating economic inefficiencies, controls on financial flows are also inconsistent with the objective of achieving a more equitable international economic system. To the extent that currency and capital controls inhibit financial flows to high-rate-of-return developing countries, they prevent those countries from improving their relative economic position. In 1975, the Joint Ministerial Committee of the Boards of Governors of the World Bank and the International Monetary Fund on the Transfer of Real Resources to Developing Countries – –or, as it is usually called for obvious reasons, the Development Committee—established a working group to review regulatory and other constraints affecting the developing countries access to capital markets and to study further proposals to support their access to private markets, including the use of multilateral guarantees. Although the working group found that the most important factor limiting the access of developing countries to foreign capital markets was market perceptions about creditworthiness, they also found that regulations and practices tend to inhibit access.[34] While some countries, such as the United States, have relatively liberal policies, other countries do not. Thus, many developing countries that have established their creditworthiness find that national regulations prevent them from diversifying their sources of borrowing.

Subsidies That Influence International Financial Flows. Although there are controls and restrictions on international financial flows, there are also government policies and programs—including export finance programs, foreign investment guarantees, and tax regulations—that directly or indirectly provide subsidies and guarantees for certain types of financial transactions. Because such policies and practices for the most part are followed by industrialized countries, they work to increase the magnitude of resource transfers from industrialized to developing countries. (Although the direction of impact on resource transfers to developing countries is positive, it is difficult to estimate how much such programs increase resource transfers since it is not known to what extent they substitute or complement other types of financial inflows or to what extent they are offset by capital outflows from the developing countries.) Some of these subsidies deserve to be mentioned since it is often implied by new world order advocates that developed countries only restrict financial flows to developing countries.

At the end of 1975, the stock of official and private export credits provided by industrialized countries to developing countries amounted

---

[34] M. M. Ahmad, "The Developing Countries and Access to Capital Markets," *Finance and Development* (December 1976), p. 26.

to $45.5 billion.[35] Of that total, the United States accounted for 18 percent, or $8.4 billion. During 1976, the *net* flow of export credits to developing countries amounted to $6.7 billion.[36] Since most export credits are directly or indirectly guaranteed by developed country governments, export credits provide funds at substantially lower borrowing costs than the cost of direct borrowing by developing countries.

Aside from export financing subsidies, direct investment financing also is encouraged. As of 1976, fifteen OECD countries had programs that guaranteed foreign direct investments against political risks. In addition, a number of OECD countries have established development finance corporations that provide financial inducements to direct investments in developing countries.[37]

With the possible exception of political guarantees, the programs cited above are inconsistent with the efficiency objectives of a liberal international economic system for two basic reasons: they subsidize the accumulation of foreign financial assets relative to domestic assets and they tie incentives to specific types of investment flows and thus encourage one form of investment over other forms. In particular, to the extent that capital goods exports are subsidized, developing countries are encouraged to establish more capital-intensive industries. In the case of programs that support direct investment flows, there also are noneconomic considerations, for example, a type of investment may be encouraged that conflicts with nationalistic and ideological objectives of many new international economic order advocates. Thus, from a political perspective, such subsidies tend to increase the potential for international conflicts. Within the United States, political opposition to the Overseas Private Investment Corporation has developed because labor unions object to guarantees on foreign investment that may eventually compete with U.S. industries.

Political guarantees can be viewed as inefficient because they substantially reduce the need for an investor to evaluate political risks. Thus, more resources will flow to high-risk countries than otherwise would have occurred. From a different perspective, however, a case can be made that political guarantees (in addition to those that might be provided by private-sector insurers) are efficient. In a world of

---

[35] Maurice J. Williams, *Development Cooperation: Efforts and Policies of the Members of the Development Assistance Committee* (Paris: Organization for Economic Cooperation and Development, 1976), table III-13, p. 75.

[36] Maurice J. Williams, *Development Cooperation: Efforts and Policies of the Members of the Development Assistance Committee* (Paris: Organization for Economic Cooperation and Development, 1977), table A.17, p. 188.

[37] Williams, *Development Cooperation* (1976), p. 72.

PART SIX: STRATEGIES

independent nation-states, a political guarantee serves as an alternative to forming a political-economic union. Thus, political guarantees provide governments with a method for removing an artificial political constraint on real resource flows. However, this argument suggests that a multilateral guarantee system along the lines of the International Investment Insurance Agency (IIIA) system would be more appropriate than the system of national investment schemes that has been developed.[38]

Few subjects generate as much confusion, controversy, and contrary claims as the impact of taxes on international financial flows. Although it is beyond the scope of this study to analyze systematically the efficiency implications of tax policies as they affect international financial transactions, two major issues should be mentioned. The first concerns the treatment of income earned on foreign direct investments. A number of industrialized countries, including the United States, not only allow domestic corporations to credit foreign taxes paid against domestic taxes on foreign income but also allow corporations to defer the payment of taxes on foreign income until it is repatriated. From the point of view of world economic efficiency, it has long been recognized that tax deferral is inefficient. Given the possibility of deferring taxes and assuming equal pretax rates of return, an investor will have an incentive to invest in countries with lower tax rates since the aftertax rate of return will be higher. As a consequence, resources will flow to countries with lower marginal rates of return.

On the other hand, it is generally argued that the tax credit is efficient. If an investor were to be taxed again on foreign source income, a foreign investment that earned an equal pretax rate of return would not offer as high an aftertax return. Thus, private-sector resources would be discouraged from flowing to countries with equal and, in some cases, higher marginal rates of return. However, opponents of the tax credit argue that the credit method violates national economic interests because the social rate of return on a dollar invested abroad is not as high as the social rate of return on a domestic investment. From a national point of view, the social rate of return on domestic investment is the pretax rate, but the social rate of return on foreign investment is the posttax return.

No doubt, other tax practices can be found that affect financial flows among countries. As a general principle, the greater the differ-

---

[38] For a brief history of the proposed International Investment Insurance Agency, see OECD, *Investing in Developing Countries*, third revised edition (Paris: OECD, 1975), pp. 103–04.

ences in tax systems among countries, the greater the likelihood of inefficiencies. Even if inefficiencies do not occur, different tax systems will lend credence to perceptions that there are inequities and thus encourage nationalistic approaches to taxation of foreign financial investments. Thus, to the extent that countries can move in the direction of harmonizing their taxes, economic efficiency will be enhanced.

Official Lending and Assistance

Although private-sector lending and investment in developing countries has increased in recent years, many developing countries either do not borrow from private sources or borrow only very small amounts. There are, of course, many reasons why. Some countries may lack a stable economic-political structure; others, with relatively stable economic-political structures, may lack specific investment opportunities because of inadequate economic and human resources; in yet other countries, private sources of capital may be discouraged or even prohibited for political and ideological reasons. For many developing countries, official sources of funds are the primary, if not the only, means of financing net resource transfers. Although official sources of funds cover a spectrum from pure grants to loans at market rates of interest, the discussion below will follow the conventional practice of drawing a dichotomy between official *assistance* and official *lending*.

Official assistance, as normally defined, includes bilateral or multilateral grants and loans as well as technical cooperation. To be classified as assistance, a loan must have at least a 25 percent grant element. Bilateral assistance flows directly between two countries, while multilateral assistance is channeled through a range of institutions, including the United Nations and the soft lending windows of the development banks. In 1976, bilateral and multilateral assistance flows to developing countries amounted to $18.9 billion, including $13.7 billion from the major industrialized countries and $5.2 billion from the major oil-producing countries.[39]

Official lending usually refers to loans that are provided on relatively hard terms (i.e., loans in which the grant element is less than 25 percent). Although some official lending takes place through bilateral channels, most flows through multilateral institutions such as the World Bank and the major regional banks, the Asian Development Bank, and the Inter-American Development Bank. In recent years, other multilateral lending institutions have been established including the

---

[39] Williams, *Development Cooperation* (1977), table IV-7, p. 67; table IV-14, p. 85.

African Development Bank and a number of development banks by major Arab oil-producing countries.

During 1976, the World Bank and the two major regional banks disbursed $3.1 billion to developing countries. In addition, those banks committed $7.5 billion for new loans.[40] These commitments will result in a higher flow of funds to developing countries in the future as the loans are actually disbursed. Other multilateral institutions, including those established by the major oil-producing countries, provided a net flow of funds to developing countries during 1976 of around $0.6 billion.[41]

The three major multilateral banks serve as an intermediary by borrowing in international capital markets and relending to developing countries at a lending rate that is based on the bank's borrowing cost plus a spread to cover administrative and liquidity costs. Although bank loans are provided at relatively hard terms, a subsidy is implicit in bank lending; the banks can borrow in the international capital markets at favorable rates because they are backed primarily by paid-in and callable capital provided by industrialized countries. More significant than the implicit subsidy, however, is the access to foreign funds provided by the banks. Even if developing countries were willing to pay substantially higher rates, many would still have trouble finding foreign lenders.

Before examining specific methods of providing official lending and assistance, I would like to outline a number of justifications, in the context of a liberal international economic order, for providing financial flows to developing countries through government institutions. I make no attempt to elaborate on these justifications or to compare the justifications with other philosophical arguments for or against development assistance and multilateral lending. As Thomas Willett indicated in his introduction to this conference, extensive literature examines the philosophical issues underlying various justifications for subsidized resource transfers, and it would require a study in itself to effectively compare and critique those justifications.[42]

One justification is based on a recognition that, as a practical matter, developing countries are not integrated into the formal and informal political linkages that guide economic relations among the major industrialized countries. The lack of integration is not of design or a result of discrimination but rather a reflection of the fact that political-economic ties develop as economic transactions grow among countries.

---

[40] See Annual Reports of World Bank, Inter-American Development Bank, and Asian Development Bank.
[41] Williams, *Development Cooperation* (1977), table IV-4, p. 65.
[42] See introduction by Thomas D. Willett.

As the major OPEC countries discovered, their bilateral and multilateral political ties with the major industrialized countries increased in number and intensity following the price increases of 1973 and 1974. Development lending, as well as development assistance, provides a means of bringing countries into the "system" not only by stimulating their economic development but also, and perhaps more important, by reinforcing behavior within developing country governments that is consistent with the principles of a liberal international economic order. As the negotiators who established the World Bank during the Bretton Woods conference believed, the multilateral lending institutions in particular provide a means for accomplishing that objective.

Official lending and assistance also provide a means of reinforcing those countries that share similar economic, social, and political values with the donor countries. Bilateral assistance provides the most direct way of accomplishing that objective and allows each donor country to establish its own criteria independently of the values of other donor countries. For example, to the extent that the United States wishes to strengthen those countries that embrace U.S. values involving human rights, the bilateral aid program eliminates the need to involve other donors who may disagree with U.S. concerns or who may define human rights differently. On the other hand, recent attempts by the U.S. Congress to impose human rights conditions on development bank lending is a deviation from the spirit of multilateralism characteristic of the postwar liberal economic order.

Humanitarian motives provide a third justification for subsidizing resource transfers, although individuals will differ over the amount of foreign assistance that can be justified on humanitarian grounds. Although significant support usually can be generated for assistance to those who are confronted with natural catastrophies such as a drought or an earthquake, support for assistance declines as the concept of humanitarian assistance broadens. Each country, through its own political process, needs to come to terms with the questions of what humanitarian goals should be served by development assistance, what portion of domestic resources should be devoted to that effort, and what means should be utilized to accomplish the objective. With respect to the latter issue, for example, the U.S. Congress has sought to develop bilateral policies and programs aimed more directly at meeting the needs of the very poor in other countries.

A final justification concerns primarily the role of official lending programs in a liberal international order that places a premium on market-oriented systems for making economic decisions. The existence of nation-states with different political, legal, and social systems adds another element of risk that must be taken into account by private-sector (and, in some instances, public institutions such as public corporations) decision makers when comparing foreign investment opportunities with domestic investment opportunities. Development lending, through bilateral or multilateral institutions, enables governments to tap the economic benefits of political integration without forming a single political union. Economic benefits are derived by both the investing countries as well as the recipient countries if development lending is directed to countries where the marginal rate of return on additional investments is higher than in the developed country but lower than the rate of return required by private entities because the latter must take into account political and other risks associated with investment in a foreign country.

The advantage of official lending through bilateral or multilateral institutions over political guarantees, discussed earlier,[43] is that such institutions can selectively chose investments that earn a marginal rate of return below the rates required by private entities (but above the rate of return on domestic capital in the donor countries). Guarantees, however, would apply to all investments, including those that would have taken place anyway (because the rate of return more than justified the noneconomic risk associated with investing in a foreign country). An important assumption underlying this justification for development lending is that official lending agencies will choose those investments that earn a rate of return greater than the rate of return on investments in the donor countries but not those investments with a return and character that will attract foreign private (or public) investment capital.

The justifications cited above for development lending and assistance will not be acceptable to those who either oppose the concept of official development lending and assistance or to those who call for a new system for providing development lending and assistance. With respect to the latter category, many advocates of a new international economic order not only seek greater automaticity of assistance flows from developed to developing countries—with the level of flows determined by an internationally agreed upon target or tax system—but greater automaticity with respect to where the assistance should be directed.[44] The first two justifications cited above, on the other hand, require that developing countries meet conditions established by donor countries. In addition, many advocates of a new approach to develop-

---

[43] See page 409.

[44] See, for example, Jan Tinberger (coordinator), *Reshaping the International Order*, A Report to the Club of Rome (New York: E. P. Hutton and Company, Inc., 1976); and Mahbub ul Haq, "Toward a New Framework for International Resource Transfers," *Finance and Development* (September 1975), pp. 6–9 passim.

ment lending and assistance place great emphasis on achieving a more "equitable" world order in terms of not only a more equal distribution of wealth among nations but also a more equal distribution of political power.[45] The humanitarian objective cited above, however, does not imply that a more equitable distribution of wealth is desired but only that extreme forms of poverty should be eliminated.

In sum, the justifications cited above are based on the preferences and not the obligations of the donor countries. Donor countries should not be defensive about using development lending and development assistance to meet individual or collective national values and interests but should be flexible and respond with sensitivity to the values and interests of other countries. Otherwise, a development assistance strategy based on national values and interests will detract from the principles of cooperation, multilateralism, and open-markets that are at the heart of a liberal international economic order. Indeed, if such a strategy is implemented with a heavy hand, it is likely to backfire and stimulate even greater hostilities among the developing countries. In addition, donor countries should be more than a little humble about what economic and political policies are likely to bring about economic development. Unfortunately, the history of foreign aid has been too often marked by government policies driven by the latest development fad. Finally, donor countries should also remember that their own domestic policies and their own adherence to the principles of a liberal international economic order leave more than a little room for improvement.

Official Lending: Some Specific Issues. Lending commitments by the major banks have increased dramatically since 1970, even after taking inflation into account. World Bank lending increased almost 300 percent from a level of $1.6 billion in 1970 to a level of $5.8 billion in 1977.[46] Lending by the Inter-American Development Bank increased from $195 million in 1970 to $1.1 billion in 1977,[47] and lending by the Asian Development Bank rose from $106 million in 1970 to $615 million in 1977.[48]

Each of these institutions has plans to increase its capital base within the next few years to allow for continued growth in lending levels. In part because of their dramatic expansion in recent years, multilateral institutions face a number of issues concerning their role

---

[45] Tinberger, *Reshaping the International Order*. Equitable political power is discussed throughout. See, for example, pp. 42–45.
[46] World Bank, *Annual Report*, 1977, p. 4.
[47] Inter-American Development Bank, *Annual Report*, 1977, p. 1.
[48] Asian Development Bank, *Annual Report*, 1977, p. 3.

and performance. These issues should be further defined and debated before a decision is made by governments to support the proposed capital increases.

One issue, which is related to earlier sections of this paper, concerns the implications of larger levels of developing country debt on the lending policies of the multilateral banks. For one thing, the growth in country debt poses the same kinds of credit evaluation requirements for the development banks as it does for other public and private lending institutions. Not only must the risks and expected returns of individual projects be evaluated, but more attention must be given to evaluating a country's overall economic policies. The latter analysis is necessary not only for judging the potential of an individual project but also for determining the overall exposure of a bank to an individual country.

Although the bank staffs currently carry out country economic analyses as part of their lending procedures—with the intensity and quality of effort varying from institution to institution—growing emphasis will need to be placed on this function in the future. In addition, members of the executive board of each institution need to give more attention to the overall economic policies of borrowing countries when deciding on individual loans. For example, U.S. government decisions on whether to vote yes or no on a loan focus primarily on the economics of the individual loans and not on the overall economic performance of the recipient country. Executive directors tend to consider the overall economic policies of a country only when that country is experiencing severe economic problems.

The growth in lending activities of the World Bank, as well as the International Monetary Fund, has tended to blur the traditional distinction between the two institutions. The conventional view regarding the roles of the two institutions assigns the IMF responsibility for balance of payments financing and the World Bank responsibility for financing development, mainly by providing funds for specific projects. In fact, the World Bank articles specify that loans be made only for projects except under special circumstances. Thus, the World Bank has provided only a limited amount of general development lending—or program lending, as it is called. The policy of concentrating on project lending has led to a considerable amount of debate over time, and the arguments for and against such a policy are numerous.[49]

In this author's view, the distinction between balance of payments

---

[49] For a good discussion of the issue of program lending, see Raymond F. Mikesell, *The Economics of Foreign Aid* (Chicago: Aldine Publishing Company, 1968), pp. 169–83.

lending and development lending—or project lending and program lending—is not analytically very meaningful since development is much more than the sum of projects in a country and since the economic potential of an individual project depends importantly on the overall economic performance of a country. As a practical matter, however, it is much easier for a multilateral institution to make decisions on project loans since there is much greater concensus about what technical criteria should be used when evaluating a project. In addition, the criteria can be put into relatively concrete or objective terms (although some would disagree with this view) so that decisions are less subject to modification by political pressures. No such consensus criteria exist yet for program or balance of payments lending, and thus such lending is subject to political pressures. It would be desirable, however, to give the World Bank greater flexibility to make general development loans and, in addition, the flexibility to make loans to developing countries facing short-run external financing problems. It would be necessary, however, for the bank to develop a consensus on more explicit criteria to be used in making such loans. The IMF, on the other hand, would concentrate on those countries whose economic situations have reached a crisis state—and in particular, concentrate on developed countries that do not have access to development bank financing and those advanced developing countries that are being weaned away from the development banks.

The division of responsibilities outlined above is a matter of degree, and IMF-World Bank programs will continue to overlap in many countries. While the opportunities and the need for cooperation will continue, so will the inevitable conflicts. Official protests aside, the street running between the World Bank building and the IMF building is often referred to as the Grand Canyon of the East, and on more than a few occasions the staffs have disagreed over what conditions should be imposed under the IMF programs in developing countries. This is not meant as a criticism of either institution. Since there is room for differences of view about what domestic economic policies are appropriate for a country, conflicts are expected and, within limits, desirable.

Although most official lending to countries takes place through multilateral facilities, consideration should be given to providing bilateral lending on relatively hard terms, particularly to meet circumstances in countries that are facing short-term financing problems. Bilateral lending under such circumstances could be linked to multilateral lending programs or provided independently. The recent loan package for Portugal, which involved not only loans by the IMF but also bilateral loans from the United States and other developed countries, provides an example of how such bilateral lending might be used.[50] Within the United States, steps could be taken to build such a lending program into its overall bilateral-multilateral lending programs. However, the use of such a bilateral facility ought to be limited, perhaps by requiring congressional approval for each loan. Otherwise, the president will be tempted to use such a lending capacity too quickly.

Official Assistance. In 1961, John Kenneth Galbraith wrote, "From the beginning, foreign aid has become sharply controversial."[51] Although Galbraith was advocating larger levels of foreign assistance, the quote cited above was more prophetic of foreign aid's future prospects, especially in the United States. In 1966, the major industrialized countries provided assistance amounting to $6.1 billion. In 1976, the level was $13.7 billion, slightly more than double the 1966 level. If, however, the 1966 level is adjusted for inflation, using the U.N. export price index for manufactured goods, official assistance from the major industrialized countries has declined slightly in real terms. Among the industrialized countries, U.S. foreign assistance, after adjusting for inflation, declined by almost 30 percent and amounted to $4.3 billion in 1976.

Given that GNP was growing rapidly while development assistance was growing more slowly during that period, official development assistance as a percentage of GNP for the major industrialized countries declined from an average level of 0.42 percent for the 1965–1967 period to 0.33 percent in 1976. The 0.33 percent falls substantially below the 0.75 percent aid target sought by the developing countries and accepted in principle by most developed countries, with the exception of the United States. As shown in Table 2, seven industrialized countries have increased the percentage of GNP devoted to foreign aid since the mid-1960s, but six of the largest countries have reduced the percentages. The steepest drop occurred for the United States, from 0.45 percent of GNP in 1965–1967 to 0.25 percent in 1976. Thus, it is not surprising that the United States has been subject to extensive foreign criticism, not only from developing countries, but from other developed countries.

Although official assistance can be designed to serve a number of the objectives, as listed at the beginning of this section, humanitarian concerns, at least in the United States, currently appear to be the basis on which the general public is willing to support foreign assistance. The humanitarian motive also has worked to change the focus of U.S. assist-

---

[50] See National Advisory Council, *Annual Report* to the President and to the Congress for 1977. (Washington, D.C.: GPO, 1978), p. 42.
[51] John Kenneth Galbraith, "A Positive Approach to Economic Aid," *Foreign Affairs* (April 1961), p. 444.

TABLE 2

Official Assistance

	Assistance Flows (billions of dollars)		Percentage of GNP	
	Average 1965–67	1976	Average 1965–67	1976
Sweden	0.1	0.6	0.23	0.82
Netherlands	0.1	0.7	0.44	0.82
Norway	—	0.2	0.17	0.71
France	0.8	2.1	0.72	0.62
Australia	0.1	0.4	0.56	0.42
Belgium	0.1	0.3	0.49	0.51
Canada	0.2	0.9	0.28	0.54
Denmark	—	0.2	0.18	0.56
Germany	0.5	1.4	0.38	0.31
United Kingdom	0.5	0.8	0.45	0.38
United States	3.4	4.3	0.45	0.25
Japan	0.3	1.1	0.29	0.20
Switzerland	—	0.1	0.08	0.19
Other[a]	—	0.3	—	—
Total (Average)	6.1	13.7	0.42	0.33

Dash (—): Zero or negligible.
[a] Austria, Finland, Italy, New Zealand.
SOURCE: Organization for Economic Cooperation and Development, *Development Cooperation Review*, 1976, p. 82.

ance programs. Since 1973, U.S. aid legislation has required that aid be directed toward meeting the needs of the very poor in developing countries. Thus, U.S. bilateral aid now emphasizes helping small farmers and improving nutritional levels. In addition, funds are used for population and health programs as well as education and manpower projects.[52]

Although the shift in U.S. aid toward human investments—as distinct from past aid appropriations that emphasized physical infrastructure and physical plant and equipment—was desirable given the importance of human capital in economic development, the shift may have gone too far. Major physical investments also contribute to higher income levels and better standards of living. If anything, what is needed

[52] Agency for International Development, Department of State, *Development Issues: U.S. Actions Affecting the Development of Low-Income Countries* (Third Annual Report of the Development Coordination Committee, April 1978), p. 49.

PART SIX: STRATEGIES

are diversified, and in many cases, experimental approaches to development assistance. Following a specific development strategy presumes that there is much more knowledge of the development process than is actually possessed. Unfortunately, the "basic human needs" concept assumes too much.

Should more official assistance be provided by developed countries, including the United States? Given the relatively small amounts of money that are allocated to development assistance, the opportunity exists for the industrialized countries to employ larger levels of development assistance not only to assist those who live in extreme poverty, but also to strengthen the international leadership role of the developed countries. In particular, the United States is in a good position to deploy larger levels of foreign aid over the next five to ten years to strengthen its international leadership role. Given the relative size of the U.S. economy, a gradual increase in the percentage of GNP devoted to foreign aid would have a significant impact on total world aid flows. For example, assuming a real GNP growth of 4 percent through 1985, if the United States were to gradually increase the percentage of GNP devoted to development assistance from 0.25 percent to 0.40 percent, U.S. aid flows in 1985 would be $10 billion in 1977 dollars. If the development assistance percentage remains at 0.25 percent, U.S. aid flows would be $6.5 billion (in 1977 dollars).

It is doubtful, however, that the humanitarian motive for giving foreign assistance will be strong enough to sustain the 0.25 percent level, let alone bring about an increase in the percentage. Thus, it will be necessary to justify foreign assistance on other grounds. As already indicated, it is this author's view that foreign aid can be used not only to serve humanitarian concerns, but also as a means of strengthening the international leadership role of the United States—if employed with more than a little sensitivity and sophistication. However, in order to serve in a leadership capacity, a country needs to decide its interests and objectives.

Given the end of the cold war as we once knew it, and given the Vietnam debacle, the United States can be characterized as a country trying to determine the nature of its interests and goals. Until those interests and goals become more clearly defined, it is not very likely that we will have a foreign policy context within which to fit an expanding development assistance program. For this reason, it is vital that we maintain a liberal financial system underpinning resource transfers, for that will be the primary means by which developing countries will have access to growing levels of the transfers. Otherwise, it is the developing countries that will suffer the most harm.

Trade Liberalization: A Public Choice Perspective

J. M. Finger

It is not difficult to find incidents that suggest that the trading system is becoming less liberal. In the last year the United States has unilaterally imposed quotas on imports of specialty steel products and has negotiated orderly marketing agreements with exporters of footwear and television receivers which will reduce the levels of U.S. imports of these products.

There is, of course, a general tendency for protectionist interests to dominate when trade problems are approached on an industry-by-industry or a day-to-day basis. Producer interests are concentrated in a few firms while consumer interests are divided among millions; hence, it is easier for producers than for consumers to aggregate sufficient resources to have an impact on the decision process.[1] Proponents of liberal trading regimes can hope at best to minimize the setbacks that the handling of day-to-day trade issues will bring.

Trade liberalization has a much better chance when it is approached (as at the GATT negotiations) on an economywide and reciprocal basis. Negotiations that cover many industries mute somewhat the imbalance between the concentrations of producer and of consumer interests. An exchange of concessions allows for some netting out of displaced production and places the interests of exporting producers on the side of trade liberalization.

Trade liberalization should thus be viewed in net terms. It is achieved (or a liberal trading system is maintained) when the pace of advance of general liberalization is more rapid than the tendency for protectionism to dominate day-to-day trade questions.

As often noted, general economic conditions are at present not favorable to trade liberalization. For several years, economic growth

---

I wish to thank my colleagues Stephen Golub and Joanna Shelton for fruitful discussions of many of the topics covered in this paper. I retain, however, sole responsibility for all information presented and opinions expressed here. This paper is not an expression of the official views of the U.S. Treasury Department.

[1] See Mancur Olson, Jr., *The Logic of Collective Action* (Cambridge: Harvard University Press, 1965), esp. pp. 141–48.

PART SIX: STRATEGIES

has been below desired levels, and unemployment has been a significant problem. Attempts in certain industries (notably steel) to maintain operating rates in the face of slack demand have generated charges of unfair international competition, which have, in turn, been used to justify requests for limits on imports. In addition, slow economic growth and oil import bills have intensified concerns about trade balances. Further, during the 1970s trade has increased considerably relative to GNP, leaving little "room" in the economic expansion that did take place for the increased trade that additional liberalization would bring. Given this general worsening of factors that determine the demand for, or the political will to achieve, further trade liberalization, "supply conditions" become that much more important. An important question, thus, is how institutional arrangements have evolved and whether this evolution will make additional production of a public good, trade liberalization, more or less likely.

This paper applies the analytic insights of public choice theory to that question. The record of the GATT tariff negotiations is reviewed from a public choice perspective and an attempt is made to isolate those factors that contribute to a successful outcome. The analytical apparatus thus developed is then used to examine the likelihood that the negotiating format carried over from the Kennedy Round will bring additional rounds to successful outcomes. It also serves as the basis for suggestions for format changes that might make international agreement to trade liberalizing measures more likely.

Improved Market Access as a Public Good

In form, all GATT rounds except the 1965–1967 Kennedy Round and the ongoing Tokyo Round were collections of bilateral negotiations. In pairs, countries agreed to exchanges of "concessions"—reductions of tariff rates or bindings of tariff rates at existing levels. The most-favored-nation (MFN) provision requires a GATT contracting party to grant the products of all other GATT contracting parties the same treatment on importation that it grants the products of any one of them. Because of the MFN provision, all GATT contracting parties shared in the fruits of each of the bilateral exchanges of concessions.

Under this system, trade liberalization, defined as access to export markets, displays both of the characteristic properties of a public good. First, it is *nonexclusive*. If the United States receives from Norway a pledge to allow trucks to be imported at a lowered rate of duty, the MFN provision requires that other suppliers receive access to the Norwegian market on the same terms. Second, access to the Norwegian market has the characteristic of *nonrivalness*. The GATT rules allow no limit to the amount of imports that enter at the agreed-upon terms. Hence, the export of trucks to Norway by one country at these terms does not affect the availability of these terms to another exporter.[2]

The nonexclusive property of market access is clearly a result of the MFN provision. If Norway were to apply the lower tariff rate only to imports from the United States, then improved market access would not be a public good. It would be available only to the country that "produced" it—in this example, the United States.

Analysis of Past GATT Negotiations

By any reasonable standard, the past performance of GATT, summarized in Table 1, must be considered a success. At the first negotiating round (Geneva, 1947), the United States exchanged concessions with twenty countries, colonies, or customs areas, which supplied 65 percent of U.S. imports.[3] At these negotiations, the United States made tariff concessions on 93 percent of (prewar) imports from the negotiating partners and tariff reductions on 74 percent of imports from participants. Relative to imports from all sources (participants and nonparticipants), U.S. tariff reductions affected 56 percent of dutiable imports, and reductions plus bindings affected 78 percent of total imports.[4] At the next round (Annecy, France, 1949), the United States negotiated with ten acceding governments. Two years later, at Torquay, England, Germany and Austria (plus Korea, Peru, and Turkey) became contracting parties to GATT, and after the accession of Japan in 1955 all of the major non-Communist developed countries were contracting parties. In this sense, the Annecy Round and the negotiations with the acceding governments at the Torquay Round can be viewed as the completion of the first round (Geneva, 1947) rather than as separate rounds.

Concessions granted at the earlier rounds were in large part bindings of tariff reductions. But by the Torquay Round, a large share of the lines in the tariffs of the GATT contracting parties had been bound, and negotiations concentrated on tariff reductions. Thus, the last three rounds have dealt almost entirely with tariff-cutting (row C, Table 1).

---

[2] The public good is represented by the terms of access to the Norwegian market, not the *size* of that market. Similarly, the playing of a radio does not diminish the signal available to another radio.

[3] Participants are listed in Table 11 at the end of this Chapter.

[4] Because the GATT procedures emphasized balanced concessions (discussed below), it is very likely that a similar volume of U.S. exports was affected. But because not all countries to whom the U.S. exports were active GATT participants, the percentage of U.S. exports affected may have been lower.

TABLE 1

INDICATORS OF THE OUTCOME FOR THE UNITED STATES OF GATT TARIFF NEGOTIATIONS

Variable (all calculated from U.S. imports and exports)	Geneva 1947 (1939 data)	Annecy 1949 (1948 data)	Torquay 1951 (1949 data)	Geneva 1956 (1954 data)	Dillon 1960–1961 (1960 data)	Kennedy 1964–1967 (1964 data) Major participants[a]	Kennedy 1964–1967 (1964 data) All participants
A. Concession imports (reductions and bindings) as percent of total imports[b]	78	39	7	9	12	n.a.	46
B. Tariff reductions							
Reduction imports as percent of dutiable imports[b]	56	6	15	20	19	n.a.	64
Average depth of cut (per-cent reduction of ad valorem rate)	35	37	26	15	20	n.a.	44
C. Balance (affected exports less affected imports as percent of affected exports)[c]							
Overall	−27	−29	59	n.a.	n.a.	5	5
With participants							
Bilateral	n.a.	73	75	−68	18	n.a.	n.a.
Multilateral	4	76	74	n.a.	n.a.	12	5
D. Tariff reductions as percent of all concessions							
Imports from participants	32	43	91	100	95	95	93
Imports from all countries	29	20	88	100	95	93	93

E. Imports from participants as percent of imports from all countries						
Dutiable	65	6	34	66	68	72
Dutiable and duty free	63	5	42	59	58	73
F. Internalization (percent of concession imports originating in participating countries)[c]						
All concession						
Bilateral	n.a.	16	56	69	n.a.	n.a.
Multilateral	76	18	62	96	78	94
Tariff reductions						
Bilateral	n.a.	35	58	69	n.a.	n.a.
Multilateral	84	39	64	96	81	91

n.a.: Not available.

[a] EEC, Canada, Japan, United Kingdom, Austria, Denmark, Norway, Finland, Sweden, Switzerland.

[b] Based on figures for imports from all countries, GATT participants and nonparticipants.

[c] The export and import values used in the formulas for the measures of balance and of internalization are:

X = U.S. exports on which concessions were made by other countries, made up of two parts: Xa, concessions given directly to the United States; and Xb, concessions exchanged among other countries but extended to the United States according to MFN provisions. M = U.S. imports on which the United States made concessions, divided into three parts: Ma, imports from the country with whom a concession was negotiated; Mb, imports from other participating countries; Mc, imports from nonparticipating countries.

The formulas for balance are: overall, $[(X - M)/X](100)$; with participants: bilateral, $[(Xa - Ma)/Xa](100)$; multilateral, $[X - (Ma + Mb)]/X](100)$.

The formulas for internalization are: bilateral, $(Ma/M)(100)$; multilateral, $[(Ma + Mb)/M](100)$.

SOURCE: Calculated from data given in Table 6 below and in official U.S. reports of GATT negotiations (see Table 10 at the end of this Chapter).

PART SIX: STRATEGIES

Negotiating with countries which supplied at the time of each round approximately two-thirds of U.S. dutiable imports,[5] the United States reduced tariffs at the Geneva 1956 and Dillon rounds on over one-fourth of dutiable imports from participants, and at the Kennedy Rounds on four-fifths of such imports. As percentages of dutiable imports from all countries, the coverage of U.S. tariff reductions at the Geneva 1956, Dillon, and Kennedy rounds was 20 percent, 19 percent, and 64 percent, respectively.

The Role of Internalization. A major determinant for the success of a collective decision process is the extent to which there will be "free riders"—that is, the benefits of the public good produced will spill over to countries that do not share in the costs of producing it. The larger this spillover, the lower the benefit-cost ratio to participants and the lower the likelihood of a successful outcome.

The record of the GATT negotiations indicates a strong desire to minimize free riding or, in GATT terms, to assure reciprocity or a balance between the concessions participants made and the concessions they received. This was accomplished by concentrating concessions on those products exported only by participants—which sometimes required that new product categories be developed. For example, the United States, in negotiating with the United Kingdom, would request concessions on products for which the United States was principal, or only, supplier of exports to the United Kingdom, and would offer concessions on imports supplied principally or exclusively by the United Kingdom. In this way, the "benefits" and the "costs" tended to be internalized.

The last rows of Table 1 use data for U.S. concessions to measure the degree of internalization achieved at each GATT round. Internalization is measured bilaterally as the sum over participating countries of U.S. imports from each country of those goods on which the United States granted a concession in bilateral negotiations with that country. Multilaterally, internalization includes the spillover to other participants of the concessions granted in each bilateral session; it is the sum of all concession imports orginating in countries with whom the United States exchanged concessions, expressed as a percentage of imports from all countries, participants and nonparticipants, of concession items. The measure of bilateral internalization uses the same denominator.

The difference between the percentage of imports originating in participating countries and the percentage of internalized concessions

---

[5] For the Kennedy Round, only "major participants" are counted.

indicates the degree to which product selection managed to internalize the benefits of U.S. concessions to countries that granted concessions to the United States in exchange. The participating countries with whom the United States exchanged concessions at the Geneva 1947, Geneva 1956, Dillon, and Kennedy rounds supplied in each case just under 70 percent of dutiable U.S. imports. At the first of these rounds, judicious selection of products managed to internalize 84 percent of U.S. concessions, and by the Dillon Round product selection had become a fine art, internalizing 96 percent of U.S. concessions.

At the Kennedy Round, the major participants adopted a multilateral, across-the-board form of negotiation rather than the bilateral form used at previous rounds. These negotiations did, however, include determination of an "exceptions list," which managed to internalize 81 percent of U.S. tariff reductions. (Because not all countries represented at the Kennedy Round participated on a fully reciprocal basis, it is not strictly appropriate to consider all of the 94 percent of U.S. concession imports as internalized, or as part of the one-for-one exchange of concessions.)

The Most Favored Nation Provision. The evidence cited above is a strong indication that the negotiators attempted to minimize spillover or free riding on the concessions. This was accomplished by judicious product selection, though it could have been achieved by eliminating the MFN provision. Without this provision, the tariff reductions agreed to could have been applied only to imports from countries that gave up concessions in return; the benefits produced could have been completely internalized. However, the trade and payments systems put together immediately after World War II tended to be bilateral arrangements, and the multilateralization as well as the expansion of trade as recovery progressed were generally accepted objectives. Thus, the multilateralization of concessions through the MFN provision should be viewed (especially at the early rounds) as an objective rather than as an instrument to help achieve the single objective of trade expansion.

General Economic Conditions. While the ability of judicious product selection to internalize the benefits of concessions contributed significantly to the success of the GATT rounds, it was certainly not the only contributing factor. As Table 2 shows, the GATT rounds began when the proportion of production entering into world trade was low by historical standards. Further, through the 1960s, covering the time span of completed GATT rounds, there was no significant increase of the ratio of trade to GNP. This was a period of almost continuous eco-

PART SIX: STRATEGIES

nomic expansion in the major industrial countries, few of which experienced significant inflation. And even with the completion from 1947 to 1967 of six GATT rounds, the ratio of trade to output did not increase over the period. It seems, thus, that trade was inelastic relative to economic expansion, that is, that economic expansion of output itself brought a less than proportional increase of international trade, leaving room for the trade-expanding effects of trade liberalization.

TABLE 2

EXPORTS PLUS IMPORTS AS A PROPORTION OF NATIONAL PRODUCTION OF MAJOR TRADING COUNTRIES AT CURRENT PRICES: HISTORICAL TRENDS AND RECENT YEARS
(percent)

Period[a]	United States	United Kingdom	France	Germany	Italy	Japan
Nineteenth century	13	22	18[b]	37[d]	21	10
Pre–World War I	11	44	54[d]	38[d]	28	30
1920s	11	38	51[b]	31[d]	26	36
1950s	8	30	41[b] 20[c]	35[d] 29[c]	25	19
1970s	11	38	29[c]	37[d] 36[c]	37	21
Recent						
1951	8	45	25	24	22	21[a]
1955	7	26	20	28	19	19
1960	7	23	22	30	24	20
1965	7	30	21	31	25	19
1970	9	33	23	34	28	19
1975	15	42		39		23

[a] Years for which data were used for each country are: United States, 1804–1813, 1834–1843, 1918–1928, 1954–1963, 1970–1974; United Kingdom, 1809–1813, 1837–1845, 1924–1928, 1957–1963, 1970–1974; France, 1805–1813, 1845–1854, 1920–1924, 1957–1963 and 1954–1963, 1970–1974; Germany, 1872–1879, 1919–1923, 1925–1929, 1955–1959 and 1954–1963, 1970–1974; Italy, 1861–1870, 1911–1913, 1925–1929, 1957–1963, 1970–1974; Japan, 1878–1887, 1908–1913, 1918–1927, 1950–1956, 1970–1974.

[b] Exports plus imports as a percentage of value added in agriculture and manufacturing (including mining and handicraft and some construction).

[c] Exports plus imports as a percentage of GNP.

[d] Exports plus imports as a percentage of the sums of private and government consumption and net domestic capital formation.

[e] Figures for 1952.

SOURCE: Robert Solomon and Anne Gault, "The Economic Interdependence of Nations: An Agenda for Research" (Washington, D.C.: Brookings Institution, June 1977; processed), tables 1 and 3.

Changing "Supply Conditions" and Future Prospects

The evolution of several "supply side" factors since the GATT rounds began will have a significant influence on prospects for continuing trade liberalization through such negotiating rounds. In this section, I will attempt to analyze these changes within a framework developed for the purpose.

Number of Participants. Common sense suggests that, as the number of participants in a negotiation grows, attaining agreement will become more difficult. Table 1 indicates that at each of the first and the last three GATT rounds the United States negotiated with countries that supplied approximately two-thirds of U.S. imports. But the number of participating countries has increased from round to round. At Geneva 1947 the United States negotiated with sixteen countries, several of which negotiated for their colonies as well. Negotiating with the United States at Geneva 1956 were nineteen governments and the High Authority of the European Coal and Steel Community, and at the Dillon Round the United States negotiated with the EEC as a unit, plus eighteen country governments. By the Kennedy Round, there were, besides the United States, thirty active participants, again counting the EEC as one.

Negotiating Format Changes at the Kennedy Round. The Kennedy Round represented several significant departures from the negotiating procedure followed at previous rounds. Among major participants, the bilateral, product-specific form was replaced by multilateral, across-the-board (with exceptions) negotiations. Also, LDCs were allowed to participate on a less than fully reciprocal basis.

Bilateral versus multilateral. Comparison of the bilateral and multilateral internalization figures indicates that the switch to multilateral balancing probably took place before it was formally acknowledged at the Kennedy Round. Through the Torquay Round, the bilateral and multilateral internalization figures are quite similar, indicating that the major effort to internalize the benefits of concessions was at the bilateral level. The difference between imports from participants as a percentage of imports from all countries (row E of Table 1) and the internalization figures is between row E and the bilateral, not the multilateral, measure of internalization. At Torquay, more so at Geneva in 1956, and very markedly at the Dillon Round, the difference between row E and the internalization figures is at the multilateral, not the bilateral, level. Thus, while the *form* of negotiation remained bilateral through the Dillon Round, *objectives* were obviously viewed in multilateral terms long before the Kennedy Round.

Across-the-board versus product selection. The shift at the Kennedy Round to an across-the-board approach seems to have been a significant departure from the previous format. Whereas the high degree of product selection applied at the Dillon Round achieved almost complete internalization, tariff reductions made there touched only 28 percent of dutiable U.S. imports from participants and only 19 percent of dutiable imports from all sources. Cuts at the Kennedy Round touched 64 percent of U.S. dutiable imports (from all countries), but almost 20 percent of the coverage of U.S. cuts spilled over to nonparticipants—countries that did not give concessions in exchange.

It is clear that the "exceptions list" at the Kennedy Round was clearly not the equivalent of the product selection applied at the Dillon Round. At the Dillon Round, product selection pushed the percentage of imports from participants from 66 percent (all dutiable goods) to 96 percent (goods on which tariffs were reduced). The Kennedy Round exceptions list pushed this percentage from 68 to 81 (relative to major participants).

Nonreciprocity from LDCs. The major participants in the Geneva 1956, Dillon, and Kennedy rounds were the United States, Canada, Japan, and the Western European industrial countries. There was, however, a basic difference between the position of nonmajor participants at the Kennedy Round and their position at earlier rounds. At earlier rounds, a balanced exchange of concessions among all participants was expected. At Geneva 1947, for example, the United States negotiated with seven nonmajor participants, receiving from them concessions (mostly reductions) on $135 million (1939 data) of U.S. exports. In exchange, the United States reduced tariffs on $115 million of imports from them and bound, duty free, an additional $185 million.

The Kennedy Round, however, was a balanced multilateral exchange of concessions only among the major industrial countries. Within this group, the United States "gave" concessions on $6.7 billion of imports and received concessions on $7.6 billion (1964 data). Counting only tariff reductions, the figures are $6.7 billion "received" and $6.4 billion "given." Though negotiations with other developed countries were on a bilateral basis, full reciprocity was expected from them; that is, concessions exchanged with them were expected to "balance." The United States negotiated with seven countries on this basis, granting concessions (in all negotiations) on $443 million of imports, of which $418 million were tariff reductions. Such countries made concessions on $486 million of U.S. exports, of which tariff reductions covered $112 million.

Full reciprocity was not expected from LDC participants. U.S. tariff reductions affected $546 million of imports from active LDC participants (total concessions, $571 million), while the LDC participants agreed to reduce tariffs on only $15 million of U.S. exports and to bind tariffs on an additional $190 million. The impact of this format change will be analyzed in the following section.

The Internalization-Coverage Trade-off. Since the number of commodities imported only (or in major part) from a given list of sources is limited, there is obviously a trade-off between the coverage (concessions imports as a percentage of total imports) and the degree of internalization that can be achieved. The outcomes of different GATT rounds can be viewed as movements to different positions on this trade-off. For example, product selection at the Dillon Round produced a high degree of internalization but at the cost of low coverage, while across-the-board cuts at the Kennedy Round covered a larger fraction of imports but achieved a substantially lower degree of internalization. When other conditions are favorable, negotiators can aim for high coverage; but when other conditions turn sour, they may have to emphasize internalization in order to achieve any agreement at all on concessions.

Changes in the underlying pattern of trade or in the negotiating format can be viewed as shifts of the internalization-coverage trade-off line. For example, if this curve is defined for a given list of participants, then an increase (as was observed from the earliest to the most recent GATT round) in the number of countries that provide a given percentage of U.S. imports will worsen this trade-off—shift the curve to the left. Allowing the LDCs to participate on a less than fully reciprocal basis represents a worsening of the coverage-internalization trade-off. Of a given amount of concessions, the larger the number of countries allowed to free ride, the larger the proportion of concession imports originating in countries that do not reciprocate—in other words, the larger the proportion of concessions not internalized.

This shift of the coverage-internalization trade-off obviously did not prevent agreement from being reached at the Kennedy Round. But this does not mean that under less favorable conditions than those prevailing at the time of the Kennedy Round such a shift would not be critical. Furthermore, since 1964 (the base year for the Kennedy Round), the role in world trade of Kennedy Round nonparticipants and partial participants has increased. This means that the gap has grown between the coverage-internalization trade-off lines with and without a fully reciprocal role for LDCs.

Table 3 attempts to quantify this increase. In this table, manufactured goods (Standard International Trade Classification [SITC] 5–8) is taken as an approximation of the coverage of U.S. concessions at the Kennedy Round.[6] If concessions were exchanged in 1976 among Kennedy Round participants on this basket of goods, only 74 percent of the concessions given up by the United States would be received by countries that gave up concessions in return. In 1964 this figure would have been 82 percent. The eight-percentage-point decline in the major participants' share reappears as an eight-percentage-point increase in the LDC share—almost all of which is accounted for by LDCs who were nonparticipants in the Kennedy Round.

How the Prospects for Trade Liberalization Might Be Improved

Format from the Kennedy Round. The negotiating format carried over from the Kennedy Round is not likely to produce substantial advances for trade liberalization so long as the general economic conditions that determine the "political will" for trade liberalization are not extremely favorable. An increase in the number of countries (particularly LDCs) playing a significant role in world trade, along with acceptance of a nonreciprocating role for LDCs in trade negotiations, have substantially worsened the internalization-coverage trade-off. Further, across-the-board (rather than product-specific) bargaining may not be able to achieve the degree of internalization necessary to reach agreement when other conditions are unfavorable. Ten years have passed since the completion of the Kennedy Round. Previously, the longest span from completion of one round to completion of the next was six years.

The Kennedy Round included, and the format of the present round includes, a provision for sectoral or industry-specific negotiations—intended to find ways to reduce such industry-specific trade restrictions as the "American selling price" system used in this country to value for

---

[6] There were, of course, exceptions across the manufactured goods list, and concessions were made on some materials, particularly processed materials. The coverage of Table 3 includes $9.1 billion of U.S. imports in 1964, while the Kennedy Round concessions covered $8.5 billion. The distribution of imports by country group of origin is approximately the same in Table 3 as for actual Kennedy Round concessions. According to data in Table 9 at the end of this chapter, imports of items actually reduced came 81 percent from major participants, 5 percent from other developed participants, 7 percent from active LDC participants, and 7 percent from nonparticipants. Thus, Table 3 understates slightly the importance of nonparticipants and major participants while overstating slightly the role of other participants.

TABLE 3
U.S. Manufactured Goods Trade with Various Groups of Kennedy Round Participants, 1964 and 1976
(values in millions of dollars)

Country Group	Imports (f.o.b.)				Exports (c.i.f.)			
	1964		1976		1964		1976	
	Value	Percent of total	Value	Percent of total	Value	Percent of total	Value	Percent of total
All countries	9,097	100.0	66,154	100.0	16,389	100.0	77,249	100.0
Major participants	7,491	82.0	49,030	74.0	8,708	53.0	40,630	53.0
Other developed participants	344	4.0	2,537	4.0	1,036	6.0	4,459	6.0
Active LDC participants	522	6.0	3,932	6.0	1,446	9.0	5,224	7.0
All participants	8,356	92.0	55,489	84.0	11,262	69.0	50,313	65.0
All LDCs	1,214	13.0	14,043	21.0	6,738	41.0	28,496	37.0
Nonparticipant LDCs	692	8.0	10,120	15.0	2,292	32.0	23,232	30.0
Nonparticipant developed countries	48	0.5	544	0.8				

SOURCE: U.S. Bureau of the Census, *Highlights of U.S. Export and Import Trade* (FT990), December 1964 and December 1976.

PART SIX: STRATEGIES

customs purposes certain chemical products. Sectoral sessions for chemicals, cotton textiles, and steel were held at the Kennedy Round, but the degree of trade liberalization agreed to was no longer than that achieved in across-the-board negotiations.

Sectoral negotiations present the potential for mutating the GATT rounds into a net protectionist rather than a trade-liberalizing influence. The tendency for producers' interests to dominate is not decreased by making *industry* discussions multicountry. The representation of each country at each sector negotiation would be tilted toward its interests as a producer, and the results of such sessions would tend toward organizing markets in ways producers find useful rather than toward trade liberalization. Given the upper hand producer interests tend to have in industry-specific negotiations, these interests will push to increase the relative importance of such sessions. Thus, as the Tokyo Round began, U.S. industry groups began to build support for the position that sectoral negotiations for an industry *automatically* put that industry on the exceptions list for the general negotiations. As the relative importance of sectoral negotiations grows, the GATT rounds will become less effective in promoting trade liberalization.

While sectoral negotiations may be the only way to "get at" industry-specific, nontariff trade restrictions, such sessions should perhaps be held separately from the general negotiations. This might make it more difficult for protectionist interests to erode the coverage of the general negotiations by expanding the list of sectoral negotiations.

A further problem is that as tariffs have been reduced the relative importance of nontariff protective measures has increased. The form such measures take varies widely, but a significant part are quantitative restrictions (import quotas). There is, however, no apparent reason why the GATT bargaining process could not be applied to liberalization of such measures. Reciprocity inherent in an exchange of quota enlargements could be measured at least as precisely as a comparison of base-year imports measures the relative increases of imports resulting from an exchange of tariff reductions. Mixed exchanges—quotas for tariffs—would require prior agreement as to what percentage change on what coverage of tariff reductions would be equivalent to a given percentage quota enlargement.

Potential for Product-Specific Negotiations. With conditions for trade liberalization generally bad, it might be a strategic move to limit negotiations to the major industrial countries and shoot for a high internalization—low coverage outcome, that is, to move down the internalization-coverage trade-off. But there are several problems with this strategy. First, high internalization at the Dillon Round (which included six developing countries) cut coverage to only 19 percent of dutiable U.S. imports, and there is considerable evidence that the coverage-internalization trade-off curve has shifted backward (worsened) since then. Hence, getting back to Geneva 1956 or Dillon Round (or perhaps even Kennedy Round) levels of internalization for this group of negotiators would probably push coverage so low that the degree of trade liberalization generated would not be sufficient to offset the tendency toward protectionism inherent in day-to-day trade issues.

Further, the negotiators would be aware of the growing importance of nonparticipants, as illustrated in Table 3. Concessions that were completely balanced and internalized in terms of 1976 trade flows would probably not be so in terms of 1980 flows. Awareness of this would be a further impediment to agreement or a further drag on coverage.

The Role of the LDCs. It is clear from the discussion that the role the LDCs play in trade negotiations will be critical. Their significance in world trade has become such that further trade liberalization depends on their active participation. Further, barriers to trade flows between developed and developing countries have been less reduced through the GATT mechanism than have barriers to trade among developed countries, and hence they are the most significant remaining impediments.

Reciprocity pays. Unfortunately, the third world and its spokespersons and institutions have taken a vocal position against a reciprocal role for the LDCs. The Kennedy Round, however, provides strong evidence that reciprocity pays. There, the United States made concessions (almost entirely tariff reductions) on $571 million or 33 percent of its (1964) imports from the nine active LDC participants (Table 4). Of some $6 billion of U.S. imports in 1964 from other LDCs, only 5 percent was subject to concessions.

TABLE 4

U.S. Imports, 1964, Affected by Kennedy Round Concessions (Reductions plus Bindings) as a Percentage of Total Imports

Country Group	Percentage
Major participants	70
Other developed participants	49
Active LDC participants	33
Other LDCs	5

Source: Table 9.

PART SIX: STRATEGIES

The exports of the active LDC participants received this increased coverage in exchange for much less than full reciprocity. Active LDC concessions were almost entirely binding and covered only $205 million of 1964 U.S. exports to these countries. In several cases, the "concession" extended by an LDC participant was to bind under GATT tariff reforms that were implemented because of their benefit to the LDC —in other words, the LDC governments received concessions in exchange for taking actions they would have taken anyway. For example, trade reforms made by Argentina and Brazil were part of general economic policy reforms. Chilean tariff reforms bound at the Kennedy Round were not part of general economic reform but were in any case taken for their own sake rather than in exchange for benefits received.[7] Indian concessions consisted primarily of reducing "official" rates of duty to the levels actually being collected.[8] Thus, if the Kennedy Round is taken as a guide, the extension of trade liberalization to products exported by LDCs would be significantly increased by minimal acts of reciprocity by the LDCs.

But third world spokespersons often express concern that multilateral reductions of trade barriers in industrial countries would not benefit LDCs. Part of their argument is the infant-industry argument applied to exporters: if concessions are not extended *preferentially*, LDC export suppliers will be "squeezed out" by industrial country exporters to whom *multilateral* tariff reductions would also apply. The LDCs already enjoy tariff preferences on many goods imported by developing countries; hence, reducing tariffs multilaterally would erode the preference margin they presently enjoy. As to the first point, analysis of the increase of imports resulting from concessions made at the Dillon Round by the United States,[9] as well as of concessions made by the United States, the EEC, and Japan at the Kennedy Round,[10] demonstrates that imports from LDC suppliers increased by at least as large a percentage as did imports from industrial country exporters. LDC suppliers were not squeezed out. A limited number of LDCs are exporters of manufactured goods (on which the Dillon and Kennedy rounds concentrated); hence, these results do not exclude the possibility

---

[7] U.S. Office of the Special Representative for Trade Negotiations, *General Agreement on Tariffs and Trade, 1964–67, Tariff Conference, Geneva, Switzerland,* vol. 1, pt. 1, pp. 132–43.

[8] Ibid., p. 147.

[9] J. M. Finger, "GATT Tariff Concessions and the Exports of Developing Countries: U.S. Concessions at the Dillon Round," *Economic Journal*, vol. 84 (September 1964), pp. 566–75.

[10] J. M. Finger, "Effects of the Kennedy Round Tariff Concessions on the Exports of Developing Countries," *Economic Journal*, vol. 86 (March 1976), pp. 87–95.

that potential exports by less advanced countries have been squeezed out. They do imply that if "fourth world" countries are being squeezed out of world markets, the pressure is coming from third world as well as from developed country suppliers. If this is the case, fourth world suppliers require preferential treatment relative to third world as well as to developed country suppliers in world markets.

As to the erosion of preferences, a careful examination by Robert Baldwin and Tracy Murray indicates that the effect of multilateral tariff reductions on LDC exports would be a net increase.[11] Multilateral reductions would have broader product coverage, would apply to imports from LDCs not eligible for preferences, and would be free of the limits applied to the volume of imports that can be entered at preferential rates. The expansionary effects of these factors on LDC exports would substantially outweigh the negative impact that erosion of existing preferences would have.

Political obstacles. These factors suggest an active, reciprocal role for at least the major LDCs in multilateral tariff negotiations. Unfortunately, positions to the contrary have already solidified. The demand for "special and differential" treatment is a prominent brick in the wall of solidarity the third world is attempting to maintain. A developing country that saw the advantage of a reciprocal role in trade negotiations would come under considerable political pressure to maintain third world solidarity. And the industrial countries have publicly accepted the idea of special and differential treatment for LDCs at the Tokyo Round. Thus, progress might depend on getting away from global forums, which provide an optimal climate for posturing but are too unwieldy to allow the attention to details necessary to assure each participant that a proposed action will be to his net benefit. As indicated before, negotiations in response to industry problems will be, at best, injury minimizing; hence, what is needed is identification of manageable possibilities that are of clear mutual benefit to developed and developing countries. Several such possibilities are examined below.

Reciprocal Negotiations between the United States and Major LDCs. An approach to consider is a return to the format of the old reciprocal trade negotiations, concentrating, however, on exchanges between a major industrial country and its major LDC trading partners. The feasibility of such an approach depends on there being substantial bilateral, *principal supplier* trade flows between the proposed participants that are

---

[11] Robert E. Baldwin and Tracy Murray, "MFN Tariff Reductions and LDC Benefits under GSP," *Economic Journal*, vol. 87 (March 1977), pp. 30–46.

PART SIX: STRATEGIES

subject to negotiable trade restrictions. Gerald Lage has explored in some detail the possibility of such negotiations between the United States and ten major LDC trading partners: Mexico, Brazil, Colombia, Israel, India, Singapore, the Philippines, Korea, Hong Kong, and Taiwan.[12] In 1974, in the case of products of which one of these ten countries was the largest (principal) supplier, U.S. dutiable imports from all sources totaled approximately $4 billion, about 4 percent of total U.S. imports.[13] Of this $4 billion, 42 percent came from the principal supplier country and another 33 percent from other countries in this group. In terms of agreements reached by the United States at the Kennedy Round in bilateral negotiations with "minor" participants, this is an "acceptable" degree of internalization. As Table 5 indicates, 77 percent of U.S. concession imports from the nine active LDC participants were goods principally supplied by these countries.

Lage also identified products imported by each of the ten countries principally from the United States.[14] This list covered some $5 billion of 1974 U.S. exports. The ratio of imports for which the United States is the principal supplier to total imports from the United States exceeded 50 percent for each of the ten countries except Israel (39 percent), India (44 percent), and Taiwan (49 percent). Available figures (Table 5, last column) indicate that the United States was the principal export supplier of somewhat higher percentages of imports of products on which LDC participants granted concessions to the United States at the Kennedy Round.

The $4 billion of LDC principal supplier exports to the United States and $5 billion of U.S. principal supplier exports to these ten countries define the area for possible negotiation rather than the ultimate outcome. Of items on which LDCs finally agree to make concessions, the percentage of their imports supplied by the United States might easily equal the figure achieved at the Kennedy Round. And while the Lage study concentrated on the possibility of reciprocal tariff concessions, negotiations might focus on nontariff restrictions applied by each side to these principal supplier exports.

While the range of the internalization figures for U.S. concessions indicates that agreement might be reached, the product composition of the list of goods the United States imports principally from these ten LDCs suggests that special problems might be encountered here. Sub-

---

[12] Gerald M. Lage, "The Feasibility of Mutually Beneficial Trade Negotiations between the U.S. and Advanced LDCs" (U.S. Treasury Department, Office of Policy Research, February 1977).
[13] Based on seven-digit Schedule A classifications.
[14] Based on four-digit SITC data.

stantial amounts are in textiles, footwear, and apparel. Even with full reciprocity from the LDCs, it might be impossible to overcome domestic resistance to reducing U.S. import restrictions on such items.

Extending Preferential Concessions. In another approach designed to get around the concentration of LDC principal supplier exports on import-sensitive goods, the United States might, as its part of the bargain, extend the present tariff preferences to other, less import-sensitive goods. If the MFN provision is not applied to U.S. concessions to LDCs—or is applied only to imports from other LDCs (or only fourth world countries)—the benefits of the concessions could be concentrated on the countries willing to make concessions in return.[15]

Objections to this approach might be raised on two grounds. First, the LDCs' comparative advantage certainly lies more in those products principally supplied by them in world markets than in other products. This increases the likelihood that these preferential tariff reductions would be more trade distorting than trade creating and hence would have undesirable efficiency effects.

Second, administering preferential tariffs involves certification of country of origin, which is not necessary when the same rate applies regardless of origin. Providing such certification might be costly and might cause administrative problems, although several years' experience with existing preferences has brought no major problems to the surface.[16]

For the United States to negotiate with one or several LDCs preferential concessions that are extended to *all* LDCs would certainly enhance the negotiating countries' positions in the third world. This would give the United States considerable influence over the makeup of third world leadership and would provide a noneconomic incentive for the LDCs to bargain seriously.

LDC Export Taxes and DC Tariff Escalation. It is often noted that developed countries protect their processors of primary materials by imposing higher import duties on processed than on raw materials. Unilateral reduction by the developed countries (DCs) of these "escalated" tariffs is often proposed as a way to improve the economic lot of the LDCs, but little has been done to implement such proposals.

---

[15] Present negotiating authority granted by the Trade Act of 1974 does not include such preference bargaining.

[16] The "competitive need" criterion in the U.S. preference scheme excludes from preferential treatment exports from any country that supplies more than 50 percent or a specified value of U.S. imports of the product in question. This criterion also serves to limit the incentive for a country to provide false certificates of origin in order to capture the preferential margin on goods produced in other countries.

TABLE 5

UNITED STATES CONCESSION TRADE WITH SELECTED KENNEDY ROUND MINOR PARTICIPANTS
(millions of dollars, 1964 data as available)

Participant	U.S. Imports from Listed Country Affected by U.S. Concessions			Listed Country Imports from U.S. Affected by Listed Country Concessions		
	Total country exports affected (1)	Country "principal supplier" exports (2)	b as percent of a (3)	Total U.S. exports affected (4)	U.S. "principal suppliers" exports (5)	c as percent of d (6)
Greece	38.0	31.0	82.0	—[a]	—[a]	—[a]
Poland	47.0	2.0	4.0			
South Africa	71.4	6.9	10.0			
Israel	44.6	0.2	0.4	40.6	34.6	85
Portugal	36.6	18.4	50.0			
Spain	71.8	39.6	55.0	47.8	34.4	72
Yugoslavia	40.8	3.2	8.0	28.4	14.0	50
Total, available data	350.2	101.3	29.0			
All LDCs	900.0					
Participating LDCs	700.0					
Nine active participants	570.0	439.0	77			
Brazil	62.5	49.5	79	31.1	28.1	90
Chile	68.5	64.4	94			

Dominican Republic	16.6		4.6	28	
India	235.4		193.0	82	
Jamaica	95.1		83.3	88	
Korea	12.0		3.6	30	
Peru	26.6		8.9	33	
Trinidad and Tobago	1.7		0.8	50	
		18.0			17.2	96
		2.8			2.3	82
		5.1			4.7	92
		0.9			0.4	50

NOTE: The countries listed are those for which data were given in the cited source.

[a] Poland agreed to increase its imports from GATT members by at least 7 percent a year.

SOURCE: U.S. Office of the Special Representative for Trade Negotiations, *General Agreement on Tariffs and Trade, 1964-67, Tariff Conference*, vol. 1, pp. 93–164.

TABLE 6

Values of U.S. Imports of Goods on Which the United States Granted Tariff Concessions at GATT Negotiations

(values in millions of dollars)

Round	Year for Which Data Are Given	Imports from Countries to Whom Each Concession Was Granted — Value	Percent of Concession and Non-concession Imports[a]	Imports from Other Participants (Value)
Geneva 1947				
All concessions	1939	n.a.	n.a.	n.a.
Tariff reductions	1939	n.a.	n.a.	n.a.
Annecy 1949				
All concessions	1948	143	37	19
Tariff reductions	1948	61	33	8
Torquay 1951				
All concessions	1949	266	10	30
Tariff reductions	1949	241	26	27
Geneva 1956				
All concessions	1954	677	13	134
Tariff reductions	1954	677	22	134
Dillon 1960–1961				
All concessions	1960	1,225	14	491
Tariff reductions	1960	1,163[a]	20	466[a]
Kennedy 1964–1967				
All concessions	1964	n.a.	n.a.	n.a.
Tariff reductions	1964	n.a.	n.a.	n.a.

n.a.: Not available.
[a] Dutiable or all imports, as appropriate.
Source: Official U.S. reports of GATT negotiations (see Table 10) and Table 8.

Less often noted is the extensive use of export taxes by LDCs. These export taxes tend to be escalated in the opposite direction—that is, they are lower on processed than on primary goods. Thus, LDC export taxes tend to encourage processing in the LDCs, while DC tariffs tend to shift processing toward the DCs, offsetting one another as far as the

Total Imports from Participants		Imports from Nonparticipants		Total	
Value	Percent of Concession and Nonconcession Imports[a]	Imports[a]	Percent of concession and Non-Concession Value	Value	Percent of Concession and Nonconcession Imports[a]
1,337	93	430	53	1,767	78
429	74	79	24	508	56
69	42	721	38	883	39
162	38	109	4	178	6
296	11	212	6	478	7
268	29	151	8	419	15
811	15	100	2	911	9
811	26	100	7	911	20
1,715	20	71	1	1,786	12
1,629[a]	28	67[a]	2	1,696	19
8,000	n.a.	500	n.a.	8,500	46
n.a.	n.a.	n.a.	n.a.	7,900	64

division of the processing pie is concerned. But both increase the price of processed goods to DC consumers, thereby reducing the size of that pie. It should be possible to reduce LDC export taxes and DC import tariffs simultaneously in such a way that processing will expand in the LDCs but not contract in the DCs.

TABLE 7
VALUES OF U.S. EXPORTS OF GOODS ON WHICH OTHER PARTICIPANTS GRANTED CONCESSIONS AT GATT TARIFF NEGOTIATIONS
(values in millions of dollars)

Round	Year for Which Data are Given	Concessions granted to U.S.A.		Concessions Exchanged among Other Participants (value)	Total	
		Value	Percent of imports from United States		Value	Percent of imports from United States
Geneva 1947	1939	1,192	63	200[a]	1,392	74
Annecy 1949	1938	108	n.a.	n.a.	n.a.	n.a.
Torquay 1951	1947	537	39	100[a]	637	46
Geneva 1956	1949	1,058	19	100[a]	1,158	21
Dillon 1960–1961	1954	398	6	n.a.	n.a.	n.a.
Kennedy 1964–1967	1960	1,496	15	n.a.	n.a.	n.a.
Major participants[b]	1964	n.a.	n.a.	n.a.	7,600	70
All participants	1964	n.a.	n.a.	n.a.	8,100	42

n.a.: Not available.
[a] Bindings and reductions.
[b] EEC, Canada, Japan, United Kingdom, Austria, Denmark, Norway, Finland, Sweden, Switzerland.
SOURCE: Official U.S. reports of GATT Negotiations (see Table 10) and Table 6.

TABLE 8
U.S. Imports, Dutiable and Duty Free, Selected Years
(millions of dollars)

		Dutiable		Total	
Year	Duty Free	All countries	Participants	All countries	Participants
1939	1,397	879	581	2,276	1,438
1948	4,175	2,918	182	7,092	382
1949	3,883	2,708	931	6,592	2,792
1954	5,668	4,572	3,078	10,240	5,332
1960	5,780	8,870	5,891	14,650	8,588
1964	7,029	11,572	n.a.	18,601	10,811

n.a.: Not available.
SOURCE: Bureau of the Census, *U.S. Historical Statistics, Colonial Times to 1970*, Series U 207–212.

In a separate study, Stephen Golub and I estimated the effects of simultaneous elimination of DC tariffs and LDC export taxes on eight commodities—copra, rubber, cocoa, cotton, wool, leather, wood, and coffee.[17] Our estimates indicate that world consumption of the eight commodities in the study would increase by 0.8 percent. Processing would increase by 8.7 percent and primary production by 4.1 percent in the LDCs. In the DCs, primary processing and production would fall by 1 percent or less.[18] For the products studied here, the 8.7 percent increase in LDC processing amounts to about $1.1 billion at 1973 prices and based on 1973 levels of activity. On the same basis, the 4.1 percent increase of production of primary products comes to a total of $0.9 billion for the eight studied here. Because world consumption increases, the corresponding declines in the DCs are about one-third as large as the volume increases in the LDCs. Over the eight commodities, the increase of LDC export earnings is about 11 percent, which, relative to trade levels in 1973, amounts to just over $1 billion. As policy alternatives go, this is a significant increase. Tariff preferences, by comparison, are estimated to have increased LDC export earnings by less than $500 million.[19]

---

[17] Stephen Golub and J. M. Finger, "The Processing of Primary Commodities: Effects of Developed Country Tariff Escalation and Developing Country Export Taxes" (U.S. Department of the Treasury, Office of Policy Research, June 1977).

[18] "Fine tuning" of the extent of concessions could theoretically keep the net change of DC processing at zero.

[19] Baldwin and Murray, "MFN Tariff Reductions and LDC Benefits," p. 37.

TABLE 9
VALUE OF 1964 U.S. IMPORTS AND EXPORTS AFFECTED BY KENNEDY ROUND CONCESSIONS
(millions of dollars, c.i.f.)

Participants	Concession and non-concession items		U.S. Imports from Country Listed					
					Items on which U.S. made concessions			
	Dutiable and nondutiable (1)	Dutiable (2)	Bindings and tariff reductions				Tariff reductions	
			Value	Percent of (1)		Percent of (2)	Value	Percent of (2)
Major participants								
EEC	2,948	2,677	2,216	75			2,170	81
Canada	3,993	1,655	1,443	36			1,257	76
Japan	1,907	1,833	1,463	77			1,458	80
United Kingdom	1,193	929	959	72			836	90
Austria	61	59	53	87			53	90
Denmark	133	110	102	77			53	48
Finland	81	35	33	41			33	94
Norway	131	108	104	79			103	95
Sweden	218	175	161	74			160	91
Switzerland	252	231	161	64			160	69
All (sums and % of sums)	10,917	7,812	6,595	70			6,283	80
Total major participants[a]	10,811	n.a.	6,700	n.a.			6,400	n.a.
Other DC participants								
Greece	n.a.	41.0	38.0	n.a.			38.0	n.a.
Iceland (acceded)	n.a.	15.0	12.1	n.a.			12.1	n.a.
Ireland	n.a.	n.a.	14.0	n.a.			14.0	n.a.

New Zealand (1966 data)	152.6	n.a.	12.5	n.a.	12.4	n.a.
Poland (acceded)	n.a.	n.a.	47.0	n.a.	47.0	n.a.
South Africa	n.a.	n.a.	71.4	n.a.	71.4	n.a.
Turkey	n.a.	59.0	54.0	n.a.	54.0	n.a.
Israel	53.8	n.a.	44.6	n.a.	44.6	n.a.
Portugal	56.8	40.6	36.6	n.a.	29.9	n.a.
Spain	110.6	n.a.	71.8	n.a.	58.9	n.a.
Yugoslavia (acceded)	49.5	n.a.	40.8	n.a.	36.0	n.a.
Total[a]	911.3	n.a.	442.8	n.a.	418.3	n.a.
Active LDC participants						
Argentina	105.9	n.a.	52.1	n.a.	40.7	n.a.
Brazil	533.0	87.0	62.5	n.a.	53.7	n.a.
Chile	221.6	n.a.	68.5	n.a.	67.9	n.a.
Dominican Republic	123.9	n.a.	16.6	n.a.	16.3	n.a.
India	306.4	n.a.	235.4	n.a.	233.1	n.a.
Jamaica	111.5	n.a.	95.1	n.a.	95.1	n.a.
Korea (acceded)	30.0	23.8	12.0	n.a.	12.0	n.a.
Peru	195.3	n.a.	26.6	n.a.	25.6	n.a.
Trinidad and Tobago	117.6	n.a.	1.7	n.a.	1.7	n.a.
All (sums and % of sums)	1,745.2	n.a.	570.5	33	546.1	n.a.
Total[a]	1,769	n.a.	n.a.	n.a.	n.a.	n.a.
All participating LDCs[a]	2,200	1,000	700	33	n.a.	n.a.
All LDCs[a]	5,800	3,140	900	16	n.a.	n.a.
All participating countries (sums above)	n.a.	n.a.	7,738	n.a.	7,176	n.a.
All participating countries[a]	n.a.	n.a.	8,000	n.a.	n.a.	n.a.
All countries, participating and nonparticipating[a]	18,601	11,572	8,500	n.a.	7,900	n.a.

TABLE 9 (continued)
VALUE OF 1964 U.S. IMPORTS AND EXPORTS AFFECTED BY KENNEDY ROUND CONCESSIONS
(millions of dollars, c.i.f.)

Listed Country Imports from U.S.

Participants	Concession and non-concession items		Items on which listed country made concessions					
	Dutiable and nondutiable (3)	Dutiable (4)	Bindings and tariff reductions			Tariff reductions		
			Value	Percent of (3)		Value	Percent of (4)	
Major participants								
EEC	4,616	3,150	3,029	66		2,724	86	
Canada	4,744	2,346	1,405	30		1,403	69	
Japan	2,334	1,265	1,177	50		886	70	
United Kingdom	1,562	1,161	981	63		889	77	
Austria	98	57	49	50		31	54	
Denmark	195	80	118	61		73	91	
Finland	88	65	70	80		59	91	
Norway	124	58	72	58		48	83	
Sweden	364	227	303	83		211	93	
Switzerland	305	287	263	86		228	79	
All (sums and % of sums)	14,430	8,696	7,467	52		6,552	75	
Total major participants[a]	14,617	n.a.	7,600	n.a.		6,700	n.a.	

Other DC participants				
Greece	150.0	n.a.	50.0	n.a.
Iceland (acceded)	n.a.	n.a.	5.2	1.4
Ireland	65.0	n.a.	27.0	10.0
New Zealand (1966 data)	117.5	11.8	16.4	11.8
Poland (acceded)	n.a.	n.a.	0.0	0.0
South Africa	n.a.	n.a.	6.3	6.3
Turkey	155.9	n.a.	155.9	0.7
Israel	212.2	n.a.	40.6	11.2
Portugal	80.6	n.a.	8.8	8.6
Spain	526.7	n.a.	47.8	47.4
Yugoslavia (acceded)	173.0	n.a.	28.4	14.6
Total[a]	1,902.4	n.a.	486.4	112.0
Active LDC participants				
Argentina	n.a.	n.a.	88.3	0.0
Brazil	n.a.	n.a.	31.1	0.0
Chile	n.a.	n.a.	6.1	5.0
Dominican Republic	n.a.	n.a.	6.3	0.0
India	n.a.	n.a.	18.0	0.0
Jamaica	n.a.	n.a.	2.8	2.5
Korea (acceded)	n.a.	n.a.	46.6	2.0
Peru	n.a.	n.a.	5.1	5.0
Trinidad and Tobago	n.a.	n.a.	0.9	0.0
All (sums and % of sums)	n.a.	n.a.	205.2	14.5
Total[a]	2,546	n.a.	n.a.	n.a.

(continued on next page)

TABLE 9 (continued)

VALUE OF 1964 U.S. IMPORTS AND EXPORTS AFFECTED BY
KENNEDY ROUND CONCESSIONS
(millions of dollars, c.i.f.)

Listed Country Imports from U.S.

Participants	Concession and non-concession items		Items on which listed country made concessions			
	Dutiable and nondutiable (3)	Dutiable (4)	Bindings and tariff reductions		Tariff reductions	
			Value	Percent of (3)	Value	Percent of (4)
All participating LDCs[a]	n.a.	n.a.	n.a.	n.a.	n.a.	n.a.
All LDCs[a]	n.a.	n.a.	n.a.	n.a.	n.a.	n.a.
All participating countries (sums above)	n.a.	n.a.	8,159	n.a.	n.a.	n.a.
All participating countries[a]	n.a.	n.a.	8,100	n.a.	n.a.	n.a.
All countries, participating and nonparticipating[a]	n.a.	n.a.	8,100	n.a.	n.a.	n.a.

n.a.: Not available.
NOTE: This table is the result of an attempt to consolidate into a common format information presented (in the cited source) in various tables (not numbered) with different formats. A good deal of numerical information was also taken from the text of the report. The overall results given in the text often do not equal the sums built up from the available country-by-country figures. Giving the page on which each figure was found would require as many footnotes as there are figures.
[a] These "total" figures were found in the text of the source and are not sums of the column.

SOURCE: U.S. Office of the Special Representative for Trade Negotiations, *General Agreement on Tariffs and Trade, 1964-67, Trade Conference*, vol. I, pt. 1.

TABLE 10

OFFICIAL REPORTS ON U.S. PARTICIPATION IN MAJOR GATT ROUNDS

Round	Report
Geneva 1947	U.S. Department of State, *Analysis of General Agreement on Tariffs and Trade, Signed at Geneva, October 30, 1947.* Pub. 2983, Commercial Policy Series, no. 109, November 1974.
Annecy 1949	U.S. Department of State. *Analysis of Protocol of Accession and Schedules to the General Agreement on Tariffs and Trade, Negotiated at Annecy, France, April-August 1949.* Pub. 3651, Commercial Policy Series, no. 120, October 1949.
Torquay 1951	U.S. Department of State. *Analysis of Torquay Protocol of Accession, Schedules, and Related Documents, General Agreement on Tariffs and Trade, Negotiated at Torquay, England, September 1950–April 1951.* Pub. 4209, Commercial Policy Series, no. 135, May 1951.
Geneva 1956	U.S. Department of State. *General Agreement on Tariffs and Trade, Analysis of United States Negotiations, Sixth Protocol (Including Schedules) of Supplementary Concessions Negotiated at Geneva, Switzerland, January-May 1956.* Pub. 6348, Commercial Policy Series, no. 158, June 1956.
Dillon 1960–1961	U.S. Department of State. *General Agreement on Tariffs and Trade, Analysis of United States Negotiations, 1960–61, Tariff Conference, Geneva, Switzerland.* 4 vols. Pub. 7349, Commercial Policy Series, no. 186, March 1962 (vols. 1 and 2), June 1967 (vol. 3), May 1963 (vol. 4).
Kennedy 1964–1967	U.S. Office of the Special Representative for Trade Negotiations. *General Agreement on Tariffs and Trade, 1964–67, Tariff Conference, Geneva, Switzerland.* Vol. 1 (General Summary), pts. 1 (Concessions by Country) and 2 (Special Multilateral Negotiations); vol. 2, pts. 1 and 2 (List of Tariff Concessions Granted by the United States), 1967.

TABLE 11
COUNTRIES WITH WHOM THE UNITED STATES EXCHANGED CONCESSIONS AT GATT NEGOTIATIONS

Geneva 1947	Annecy 1949	Torquay 1951	Geneva 1956	Dillon 1960–1961	Kennedy 1964–1967
Australia	*Acceding countries*	*Acceding at Torquay*	Australia	EEC	*Major participants*
Belgium and colonies	Denmark	Austria	Austria	Austria	EEC
Brazil	Dominican Republic	Germany	Benelux	Cambodia	Canada
Canada	Finland	Korea	Canada	Canada	Japan
Chile	Greece	Peru	Chile	Denmark	United Kingdom
China (Hong Kong and Kwantung)	Haiti	Turkey	Cuba	Finland	Austria
Cuba	Italy	*Acceding before Torquay*	Denmark	Haiti	Denmark
Czechoslovakia	Liberia	Benelux	Dominican Republic	India	Finland
France and colonies	Nicaragua	Brazil	Federal Republic of Germany	Israel	Norway
India	Sweden	Canada	Finland	Japan	Sweden
Lebanon (Syro-Lebanese Union)	Uruguay	Denmark	France	New Zealand	Switzerland
Netherlands and colonies		Dominican Republic	Haiti	Norway	*Other DC participants*
		France	Italy	Pakistan	Greece
		Indonesia	Japan	Peru	Iceland
		Italy	Norway	Portugal	Ireland
			Peru	Sweden	New Zealand
			Sweden	Switzerland	Poland
				United Kingdom	

New Zealand	Norway	Turkey
Norway	Sweden	United Kingdom
Union of South Africa		Hong Kong
United Kingdom and colonies		Bahamas
		High Authority of the European Coal and Steel Community
Burma		
Ceylon		
Newfoundland		
		South Africa
		Turkey
		Israel
		Portugal
		Spain
		Yugoslavia
		Active LDC participants
		Argentina
		Brazil
		Chile
		Dominican Republic
		India
		Jamaica
		Korea
		Peru
		Trinidad and Tobago

A Survey of Proposed Changes in World Trade Institutions
An Appendix to J. M. Finger's Paper

Stephen Golub and Joanna Shelton

Report of the American Society of International Law

Deficiencies of the GATT. The world trading system is in a period of crisis, according to a panel of experts organized by the American Society of International Law. According to their report, "if new efforts are not made [to remake world trade institutions] we are likely to move . . . towards further disintegration of the international economic order."[1]

The main threat to the international trading system is the rapid change in products, countries, and commercial policies that play key roles in trade. GATT was meant to deal with developed country tariffs on trade in manufactured products. The growth of North-South and East-West trade, concern over commodities and agricultural products, access to supply issues, and nontariff barriers are viewed by the panel as intractable in the framework of GATT, thus imperiling the climate of free trade. Furthermore, the panel seems to believe that the world trading system is likely to face rapid changes and unpredictable shocks in the future, many of which GATT may be unable to deal with promptly and effectively.

A second underlying problem is flagging political will on the part of GATT members. "Many of the weaknesses of GATT are directly related to the failure of governments to take their commitments seriously." The report implies that to some extent this is due to the institutional defects of GATT. "The connection between methods and forms, on the one side, and political will, on the other, is important."[2] The main criticism of GATT is that it has evolved from a restricted group of developed nations where the one country–one vote rule was viable to a large organization where less developed countries constitute a

---

[1] American Society of International Law, *Remaking the System of World Trade: A Proposal for Institutional Reform*, Studies in Transactional Legal Policy, no. 12 (Washington, D.C., 1976), p. 1. This report was prepared by a panel chaired by Anthony Solomon.

[2] Ibid., pp. 3 and 4.

majority and the voting system misrepresents interests in world trade. GATT is also criticized for carrying out periodic rather than continuous negotiations.

Proposed Institutional Changes. The institutional reform proposed by the report is the creation of a World Trade Organization (WTO), an "umbrella" organization that would gather together all international institutions concerned with trade. The precise relationship of the WTO to UNCTAD, the World Bank, and the OECD is never made clear, however. The WTO would presumably include them as suborganizations that could be decentralized to some extent.

> The Panel recommends uniformity to the extent of one umbrella organization, one Secretariat, and one dispute settlement procedure. However, it recommends that norm formulation and the establishment of new obligations be left to a variety of specific procedures, which could be tailored to particular subject matter.[3]

The types of "subcodes" that would be grouped under the WTO umbrella are a "General Commodity Code," which would include commodity agreements; a nontariff barrier (NTB) code; and arrangements for trade liberalization between a subgroup of GATT nations along the lines suggested in the *GATT Plus* proposal of the Atlantic Council.[4]

Five arguments are advanced in favor of an umbrella organization: (1) It would simplify coordination and liaison between institutions. (2) There may be some economies of scale—for example, in personnel management. (3) "Forum shopping" by nations with a particular idea or ideology would be reduced. (4) The umbrella organization would have a broader jurisdiction and greater flexibility in anticipating new issues. (5) The institutional structure to deal with unexpected shocks would not have to be created from scratch.

The first three are not very convincing, as no reason is provided for expecting economies of scale or curtailment of forum shopping. The latter two are associated with the panel's view that the problems confronting the world trading system are increasingly diverse and subject to rapid and unpredictable change. A broad and flexible organization is required to respond to these problems.

Disadvantages of the umbrella organization cited by the report are: (1) some nations might prefer to participate in ad hoc organizations and (2) governments may be fearful of an overly powerful WTO.

---

[3] Ibid., p. 35.
[4] See below for a discussion of the *GATT Plus* proposal.

PART SIX: STRATEGIES

The contents of the WTO "codes" are not discussed with much specificity. It is the view of the panel that MFN treatment should be made conditional on accepting obligations. On the other hand, the report endorses differential treatment for LDCs. The discussion of the NTB code is little more than a list of problems: (1) technical standards; (2) government procurement; (3) export controls; (4) safeguards; (5) subsidies; (6) countervailing duties.

Critique. The focus of the panel was on "structural and institutional problems of international trade as opposed to substantive economic problems."[5] It is difficult to see how institutional considerations can abstract from the underlying economic problems, and this undoubtedly contributes to the vagueness of the recommended institutional changes.

The lack of specificity as to the functioning and purpose of the WTO is viewed by the authors as an asset in dealing with the unpredictable problems of the future but also has the effect of finessing most of the important issues—the WTO's relationship with other international organizations, for example. It seems most unlikely that the OECD and UNCTAD would be willing to be subordinated to the WTO. "Substantive economic problems," such as the role of the LDCs in trade liberalization, are addressed in very general terms, if at all.

Report of the Atlantic Council

Deficiencies of the GATT. The Atlantic Council panel singles out, explicitly or implicitly, several key weaknesses of the GATT as it is currently structured.[6] The most crippling weakness, the panel suggests, is the existence of a double standard for developed and developing countries. Developing countries are beneficiaries of GATT's trade liberalizing provisions, but due to their special trading problems they often are unable to reciprocate and open their own economies to their industrialized trading partners.

A second, related problem, according to the panel, is that the decision-making machinery for the international trading system is inadequate for dealing with today's major trading problems. The one country–one vote principle "has [given] the controlling voice in all GATT decisions, even those affecting trade among the industrialized nations, to countries with a smaller volume of trade and a lesser ability,

---

[5] ASIL, *Remaking the System*, p. 11.

[6] Atlantic Council, *GATT Plus: A Proposal for Trade Reform*, Report of the Special Advisory Panel to the Trade Committee of the Atlantic Council (New York: Praeger, 1975). The panel was chaired by John M. Leddy.

at their present stage of development, to assume new trade obligations." The new effect of this situation is a tendency on the part of industrialized countries to take their GATT commitments less and less seriously. "Stronger rules must be established for the conduct and further liberalization of trade among these countries," the panel concludes.[7]

Proposed Solution. The panel advocates the creation of a Code of Trade Liberalization, a supplementary agreement among the industrialized countries of GATT. Trade benefits of the code would be extended to all GATT countries through the MFN clause, and all countries capable of reciprocating would be free to join. Reciprocity would not be expected of less developed countries. Decision making would be responsive to the economic weight of the participants, and code obligations would be enforced exclusively by those nations that adhere to it. These provisos, the panel believes, will prevent weakening or abuse of the code by nonmembers while avoiding any taint of discrimination against LDCs.

The overall aim of the code is to "(1) liberalize trade through the substantial further reduction of tariffs and other trade barriers, (2) tighten and improve existing GATT trade rules along more equitable lines, and (3) provide a more effective international enforcement mechanism for trade commitments than is now available under GATT."[8]

Specific provisions, dealing with such issues as nontariff barriers, agricultural and commodity trade, dumping and antidumping practices, and "voluntary" arrangements to restrict imports, are set out by the panel. Prior international consultation on trade matters affecting many countries is a recurrent theme throughout.

Organization. The code would be administered within the GATT framework, if possible, or, alternatively, under the OECD. The organization's structure would include a Trade Council, comprised of government ministers, and an Executive Committee of senior trade officials, as well as a director and a staff. The Trade Council would interpret all rules; the Executive Committee would hear all complaints brought by members. These and other provisions would aim at facilitating dispute settlement.

Critique. The *GATT Plus* proposal offers a solid, detailed approach to some of the major institutional and trade problems currently facing GATT, as seen by the panel. The proposal's strength is reinforced by its comprehensiveness and its specificity.

---

[7] Ibid., pp. 5 and 6.
[8] Ibid., p. 11.

PART SIX: STRATEGIES

One potential stumbling block to the success of the plan, as noted by the panel, is the possibility that GATT members may not welcome the code within the GATT framework. Such a move could erode the credibility and effectiveness of any reform measures set forth by the code members.

A more serious flaw in the report concerns the existence of what the panel calls a double standard, whereby one set of trade rules and obligations applies to the so-called developed countries and a separate set applies to the less developed countries. The panel's proposal fails to show how an MFN principle that does not require reciprocity of even the most advanced LDCs will help solve the problems stemming from a double standard. As more LDCs move up the scale of development and their exports capture growing shares of developed country markets, stress on the trade system will continue to mount. Where no cost is involved in maintaining a consistently aloof stance in trade negotiations and in maintaining consistently high barriers to trade, LDCs have little incentive to play a more active role in international trade matters. While *GATT Plus* is detailed and comprehensive in most areas, it would be strengthened by a closer examination of the double standard and alternative solutions to that problem.

Partial Reforms

Most studies do not attempt to evaluate GATT as a whole; they focus on a few problem areas that can be dealt with case by case. The following discussion is not meant to be exhaustive.

Nontariff Barriers. Much attention has been devoted to nontariff barriers as they have increased in importance relative to tariffs.[9] Their relative prominence is due to a large extent to the declining tariff rates that have been the main target of postwar multilateral trade negotiations. Some countries, however, appear to be erecting new NTBs, so that the increase is absolute as well as relative. The United States in particular, but other countries also, has resorted to quantitative restrictions in the form of "voluntary" export control agreements or "orderly market agreements." Even more alarming, according to Robert Baldwin, is the widespread use of government measures to promote domestic industries,

---

[9] Among the many studies devoted to NTBs, see in particular Robert E. Baldwin, *Nontariff Distortions of International Trade* (Washington, D.C.: The Brookings Institution, 1970); and Harold B. Malmgren, *Trade Wars or Trade Negotiations: Nontariff Barriers and Economic Peacekeeping* (Washington, D.C.: Atlantic Council, 1970).

mainly in the form of government procurement practices and subsidies.[10] More generally, NTBs include any government practice that has the effect of discriminating between foreign and domestic goods.

NTBs are less susceptible than tariffs to liberalization through multilateral trade negotiations. Defining NTBs operationally is itself no simple matter, since any policy that affects traded goods could conceivably be classed as an NTB. Many NTBs serve domestic policy objectives and only indirectly discriminate between foreign and domestic goods (for example, safety and health standards). Reciprocity and balance in granting concessions are difficult enough to resolve in tariff negotiations and will be still more problematical in NTB discussions.

Detailed studies and discussions must precede any successful attempt at liberalization. Good candidates for liberalization among the NTBs are government procurement practices and subsidies. Quotas are technically the easiest to liberalize, but politically they are among the most difficult.

Safeguards. Another reform that has widespread support aims at altering the safeguard provisions (Article 19) so that countries will stop using "voluntary" export control agreements as a means to evade them. There is much less agreement on how this objective is to be realized. John Renner proposes a system whereby import relief could be granted with or without international approval.[11] Import relief with international approval would not entail retaliation. International approval would be granted if present GATT requirements for import relief are met and if the measures are temporary and nondiscriminatory. Import relief without approval would be subject to compensation or retaliation, as all import relief comes under the present Article 19. The rationale is that elimination of the threat of retaliation would eliminate the incentive to conclude voluntary export control agreements. Jagdish Bhagwati proposes a harsher approach.[12] In his view, exporters (mainly LDCs) should be paid financial compensation, not only when they are forced into these "voluntary" agreements but also when they are merely threatened with such an action, on the ground that the threat of restrictive measures reduces the exporting country's economic welfare. This would be made operational by establishing a list of items eligible for "restraint." The amount of the compensation owed to the suppliers of

---

[10] Baldwin, *Nontariff Distortions*, p. 170.

[11] John C. Renner, "Trade Barriers, Negotiations, and Rules," *Columbia Journal of World Business*, Fall 1973, pp. 56–57.

[12] Jagdish N. Bhagwati, "Market Disruption, Export Market Disruption, Compensation, and GATT Reform," *World Development*, vol. 4, no. 12 (1976).

these products would rise if the restraints are in fact imposed on exporters. The compensation owed would be still higher if restrictive action is taken on a product not on the "List of Potentially Restrainable Items." Bhagwati's proposal reflects his view that in most cases the trade restrictions imposed on LDC suppliers had more to do with the political clout of the industries seeking protection than with the severity of the market disruption caused by increasing imports.

There are several serious flaws in Bhagwati's approach. First, it is not necessarily true that the export control agreements are damaging to the LDCs involved in them. These LDCs are in a position to garner scarcity rents from their quotas because they are shielded from potential competition. Second, if the lack of political clout accounts for their being forced to accept the export control agreements, there is no reason to believe that Bhagwati's compensation scheme could be imposed on the developed countries. If the developed countries wanted to aid the LDCs for moral reasons, they could simply desist from organizing the export control agreement. Third, since the developed countries have been unable to devise a satisfactory domestic compensation system, the prospects for a scheme to compensate foreigners are rather bleak.

Renner's approach is predicated on the assumption that making safeguards multilateral will result in less damage to free trade by ensuring that escape-clause actions are temporary and take a less restrictive form, tariffs instead of quotas, for example. Since escape-clause actions are taken in response to political pressures in various countries, it could be argued that multilateralization will not have much effect as long as those pressures persist. Renner contends that the availability of an internationally sanctioned alternative (import relief with international approval) could be helpful to governments faced with a difficult political situation.

Trade Measures for Balance of Payments Purposes. Finally, C. Fred Bergsten points out that banning trade distortions for balance of payment purposes is a plausible option in the current flexible exchange rate regime. Even under fixed exchange rates, trade restrictions were widely regarded as an inferior means of dealing with balance of payments disequilibrium, so there should be little opposition to a total ban. Exceptions could be granted for LDCs that still maintain rates fixed to their major trading partner's currency. Of course, one runs into the usual problem of deciding where to draw the line between developed and developing countries. Bergsten favors a total ban not only for its own sake but also for the purpose of "demonstrating anew the momentum towards freer world trade."[13] If such a step proves to be unacceptable, Bergsten suggests an alternative four-point proposal that would result in closer supervision of trade measures justified on balance of payments grounds: (1) Quantitative measures would no longer be the only allowed measure. (2) All actions would require prior authorization. (3) All "internal" measures with substantial balance of payments effects would have to be justified in terms of those effects. (4) The IMF would decide whether a country's balance of payments justified special measures, while GATT would retain jurisdiction over the particular measures used if the IMF ruled that trade restrictions were justified.

---

[13] C. Fred Bergsten, "Reforming the GATT: The Use of Trade Measures for Balance of Payments Purposes," *Journal of International Economics*, February 1977, p. 6.

COMMENTARY

Peter T. Bauer

Signpost to Disorder

The proposals of the current advocacy of a New International Economic Order are incompatible with even a tolerably liberal international economic order. They should be taken more seriously than has been suggested by some participants in this conference. In the NIEO proposals for massive wealth transfer to less developed countries, the primary emphasis is on redistribution and restitution, rather than on development or poverty. The demands for politically promoted, far-reaching international egalitarianism represent a major challenge to any economic order; they are a signpost to a Hobbesian war of all against all.

According to the 1974 United Nations Declaration on the Establishment of a New International Economic Order, "There should be the broadest cooperation of all member States of the international community based on equity whereby the prevailing disparities in the world may be banished and prosperity secured for all." Acceptance of this declaration implies a completely open-ended commitment by the West. While large-scale transfers can despoil donors, they cannot ensure any substantial specific level of income, rate of growth, or reduction of international income differences, since these depend largely on domestic factors. If these are unpropitious, no amount of external donations can secure any specified level of income.

Equality and Equity

It is not clear why income differences as such should be inequitable, regardless of how they have come about. This is one reason we should talk about income differences and not about inequalities or disparities; that is, we should use a neutral term that does not prejudge the issue as do these other expressions, which plainly suggest that income differences are inequitable. Why is it inequitable that incomes in the United States or Germany or Japan should be much higher than in Afghanistan or East Africa, or that the Chinese in Southeast Asia should have incomes higher than those of the Indians or Malays there or higher than those of Indian villagers or African tribesfolk?

Especially in the context of policy, it is not sensible to discuss income differences and changes without considering how they have come about. For instance, incomes can be equalized through a voluntary or enforced reduction in the birth rate of the poor; or an increase in their mortality; or the expropriation, expulsion, or destruction of relatively prosperous people; or an increase in capital; or technical change; and so on. These differences are plainly pertinent to policy.

Anomalous Practices and Policies

In recent years governments have persecuted, expelled, or even massacred relatively productive and prosperous groups, especially, but not only, ethnic minorities in many parts of Asia and Africa. Countries in which minorities have been maltreated on a large scale include, among others, Algeria, Burma, Burundi, Egypt, Ethiopia, Ghana, Indonesia, Iraq, Kenya, Malawi, Malaysia, Nigeria, Sri Lanka, Tanzania, Uganda, Zaire, and Zambia. Because the victims' incomes were above the national average, their maltreatment promptly reduced average incomes and thereby widened income differences between these countries and the West. Such policies brought about greater equality within these countries, a situation perversely described as improvement in distribution. The policies have often resulted in a reversion to subsistence production over large areas, a situation or sequence aptly termed one of disdevelopment. These policies have often been supported or even made possible by Western aid. Should the results serve as ground for further aid to these governments? And if this aid facilitates and encourages such policies, should the resulting further impoverishment justify further assistance?

The large-scale, brutal, compulsory sterilization program in India in 1975–1977 bore harshly on the poor, on whom it inflicted acute emotional and physical suffering. Should a reduction in their number and a resulting so-called improvement in distribution serve as ground for increased aid? Should aid to Tanzania be increased if agricultural productivity is reduced and the country impoverished by the enforced collectivization of farming and the herding of millions of unwilling people into so-called brotherhood or freedom villages, a process accompanied by mass destruction of homesteads and removal of social amen-

PART SIX: STRATEGIES

ities and civil rights from those who are unwilling to comply? Many types of policy pursued systematically by governments of LDCs reduce incomes and retard development and thereby extend international income differences. The converse situation is also possible. An increase in age-specific mortality in LDCs compared with that in DCs would reduce income differences. Should assistance be curtailed to the afflicted societies?

Large-scale maltreatment of productive minorities; enforced collectivization of farming; penal taxation of small-scale farmers; proliferation of wasteful state monopolies; severe restrictions on the inflow and deployment of private capital—these are among the many economically damaging policies widely pursued in LDCs. Their aim is not to help the poor or reduce income differences but to extend the power of the rulers over the population by enfeebling actual or potential opponents, placating supporters, and eliminating all differences that do not favor the rulers.

Sources of Income Differences

Government policies are of course not the only determinants of income levels, differences, and changes. Economic attainment depends greatly on aptitude, motivation, mores, political arrangements, and objectives. Natural resources, climate, and accessibility to different societies also play a part, although their utilization depends on the personal, social, and political factors just noted. Throughout most of the world people differ radically in these matters. Pronounced group differences in economic performance are evident in many LDCs, as for instance those between the Chinese and Indians (both recent immigrants) and the Malays in Malaysia, the Indians and the Singhalese in Sri Lanka, and between tribal and ethnic groups in East and West Africa, as well as between different ethnic groups in the Middle East, the Caribbean, and Latin America. Mores that manifestly affect economic performance include the refusal to allow women to work outside the home (North Africa, the Levant, and the Middle East) or the reluctance to take animal life and the treatment of cattle as inviolable (South Asia).

The world is not divided into two distinct collectivities, separated by a wide gap reflecting external exploitation. The world comprises a very large number of societies that have emerged in varying degrees from a base of material poverty. The earlier emergence or greater progress of some groups does not retard but facilitates the progress of others, who can take advantage of skills, knowledge, and markets of the more developed groups.

COMMENTARY

Egalitarians are apt to reinforce their case by arguing that the incomes of the prosperous have been extracted from the poor so that the case for redistribution is compounded by the need for restitution. The advocates of the NIEO habitually imply or even state explicitly that the prosperity of the West has been achieved at the expense of LDCs. In fact, the prosperity was generated by the peoples of the West, not taken from LDCs. References to colonialism as the cause of the poverty of LDCs is a red herring, as is immediately obvious when one looks at North America, Australasia, Switzerland, Scandinavia, West Germany, and Japan, on the one hand, and Afghanistan, Tibet, Ethiopia, and Liberia on the other hand. The former group either had no colonies to speak of or were themselves colonies of other countries and yet were even then very prosperous; the latter group of very poor countries had never been colonies.[1]

Central Thrust of the NIEO

Substantial reduction or even removal of income differences worldwide is the explicit major objective of the NIEO. When these differences reflect aptitudes, mores, motivations, and institutions, attempts to reduce them substantially imply extensive coercion. The rigor of the coercion depends on the degree of standardization to be attempted and on the strength of the force behind the differences in economic performance. Because these are often deep-seated, both among societies and within them, political action designed to reduce differences in incomes and living standards over large areas of the world, or even worldwide, implies forcible remolding of peoples and societies, far-reaching coercion, and wholesale politicization of life. Substantial moves in that direction postulate world government with totalitarian powers.

The coercive policies of enforced egalitarianism have already spilled over from the international to the domestic scene in LDCs. Such policies, supported by Western resources or even made possible by them, have vastly increased the prizes of political power and the stakes in political conflict. Who has the government has become paramount, often a matter of life and death, to large numbers of people in many LDCs. Whether from choice or from necessity, the energies and ambitions of many people are diverted from economic and cultural activities to political life. This sequence exacerbates political tensions, promotes conflict, and encourages centrifugal forces. It has contributed greatly to the frequency and extent of the often literally murderous intensity of political

---

[1] Ethiopia was for a short period of six years an Italian colony in the course of its very long history.

PART SIX: STRATEGIES

conflict, including large-scale civil war, in Asia and Africa in recent decades. These developments have inflicted massive hardship both on ethnic minorities and on the indigenous populations. Pursuit of the NIEO will reinforce these sequences.

What Should Be Done about the NIEO?

The demands of the advocates of the NIEO should be resisted. Any substantial move toward worldwide egalitarianism implies large-scale coercion and promotes far-reaching tensions. These tensions can be expected to be pronounced, not only between Western donors and LDCs but also between relatively prosperous and less prosperous LDCs. The spread of politically inspired egalitarianism would also exacerbate political tensions within LDCs. And even if wealth transfers reduced international income differences appreciably, which is by no means certain, this would not appease demands for further redistribution either internationally or on the domestic level. Tocqueville has already observed that when social differences have narrowed appreciably those that remain are felt as especially irksome.

Official aid is certain to continue for many years ahead. How can it be improved? In the space available, I can do no more than make a few bald assertions.

Aid should take forms that allow its volume, cost, and incidence to be identified. This rules out commodity agreements and debt cancelation, which in any case are open to other major objections. I favor cash grants as opposed to loans or tied aid. Cash grants do not confuse investment and handouts as do the heavily subsidized loans that have become a prominent feature of aid arrangements. And cash grants do not confuse subsidies to exporters with subsidies to foreign governments as do tied aid and aid in kind.

I favor bilateral grants as against multinational grants. Bilateral grants are less likely to become instruments of worldwide egalitarianism. They are subject to some measure of budgetary control by the legislatures of the donors. They are also more likely to be productive than multinational grants, because bilateral grants retain some contact between the supplier of capital and its user, which promotes its effectiveness.

It is often thought that, in contrast to bilateral aid, multinational aid is likely to be disinterested and objective. But multinationalization of aid does not ensure its objectivity. Like the rest of us, staff members of the international aid organizations and the individuals and groups associated with them have political, personal, and professional interests of their own to promote. Since their constituents are mostly governments of LDCs, they increasingly regard themselves as spokesmen for the less developed world and understandably press for persistent expansion of aid. They also favor governments committed to extensive economic controls, as this suits both their own interests and those of their constituents.

Finally, a major advantage of the bilateral system is its greater flexibility. It can be adjusted much more readily to the policies of the recipients than can multilateral aid, and thus it can act more effectively as a check on wasteful or barbarous policies. If aid had been entirely bilateral, the policies pursued over the last ten years or so in many LDCs, notably including Tanzania, Ethiopia, Uganda, and more recently India, would have been scrutinized more carefully.

I think grants should go primarily to governments that, as far as possible, try to perform the necessary but difficult and complex tasks of government without resorting to close control of the economy and politicization of their societies. The performance of the essential tasks of government would stretch the resources of all governments of LDCs. It is now apparent that many aid recipients neglect their primary governmental functions, while they attempt to control their economies closely. By the same token, aid should be withheld from governments that pursue policies that plainly obstruct the development of their own societies, that often inflict large-scale hardship both on minorities and often on the population at large, and that also exacerbate the problems both of other aid recipients and of aid donors. Such criteria would promote relatively liberal systems in the less developed world, minimize coercion, and favor material progress, notably improvement in living standards. Their adoption would also reduce political tension in recipient countries.

These criteria would favor liberal societies and effective but limited governments. They reflect political preferences clearly implicit in the subject matter of this conference, and we need not hesitate to acknowledge this. Official aid is taxpayers' money and therefore cannot be removed from politics. Suggestions for depoliticizing official aid are a contradiction in terms.

Although I think that adoption of these criteria would benefit ordinary people in both donor and recipient countries, they are very unlikely to be accepted in the contemporary political climate, as they go counter to some of the most effective and influential groups operating in this area.

Kenneth W. Dam

At the cost of slighting Richard Erb's excellent paper, the constraints of space forced me to limit myself to trade issues.

PART SIX: STRATEGIES

The discussion of trade at this conference has involved two prescriptions for dealing with the growing challenges to the international trading system. One is to think straight. I have nothing against thinking straight, other than to note that it is harder than it sounds. The second prescription, represented by the latter part of J. M. Finger's careful analysis, consists of suggestions for concrete changes in international procedures or substantive rules. I found Finger's suggestions for new GATT negotiating constellations excellent, but of course they do not carry us very far toward meeting the growing protectionist threat.

Of the two approaches, the second is by far the more promising. Protectionist pressures do not yield to intellectual arguments, as generations of economics teachers could surely testify. What we need are institutional arrangements that will pull the political teeth of the autarkic beast. These new institutional arrangements are needed at both the domestic and the international levels.

Two classes of approach to institutional reform may be distinguished at this conference. Robert Baldwin advocated wage subsidies. On examination, it turned out that he was not advocating a specific program but merely throwing out an idea. If we have learned anything from our experience over the last fifteen years in social programs, it is that we should not start them without great attention to programmatic detail, to cost, and to the crucial question of how and when they are to end.

Nat Weinberg advocated an expansion of adjustment assistance—essentially a cradle-to-grave, 100 percent guarantee against loss of jobs through trade. The difficulty here, again, is that adjustment assistance is simply a categorical income security program and, as such, is subject to all of the limitations and complications that have plagued our other categorical income security programs. The truth is that a Weinbergian adjustment assistance program would surely deter adjustment. Workers respond to incentives, as we have learned to our sorrow in welfare programs. If adjustment assistance payments are to equal wages, then the implicit marginal tax rate on going to work is 100 percent (or even more if adjustment assistance is not taxable and if the costs of commuting to work are not subtracted from benefits). Workers, like capitalists, know how to respond to such tax rates.

Adjustment assistance also creates further complications in our social programs and stands in the way of thoroughgoing reform, say, along negative income tax lines. Why should such especially high benefits be paid only for trade-induced unemployment? Why not also for unemployment brought about by environmental regulations, technological change, even bad management—none of which is the fault of the worker? Quite aside from the equity questions, such munificence has a cost beyond the transfer payments involved. It is seldom clear when a particular job is lost because of trade, but when the amount of the benefits depends on the cause, then adjudication of the cause is going to chew up a considerable volume of resources.

A second class of institutional measures, which I believe we need to work on, would strike at the political foundations of protectionism. Protectionist sentiment will always be with us, but if it is true that the country as a whole gains from freer trade and loses by giving in to the special pleas of adversely affected industries, then the explanation must lie in our political institutions and the nature of the political process.

The passage of the Smoot-Hawley tariff of 1930 is an instructive episode. It demonstrated that Congress could not effectively deal with the political fact that the few who have much to gain (from protection) can organize at lower cost than the many who would each lose a little. It showed further that Congress cannot deal with the psychological fact that people fight harder to avoid a certain capital loss (from foreign competition in this instance) than to achieve an uncertain capital gain, even though—taking into account the probabilities—the expected gain is equal to the expected loss.

Cordell Hull's approach to these twin problems through reciprocal trade agreements permitted a vote in the Congress at a time when it was not yet clear who was going to lose from lower trade barriers. Hence, the congressional decision could be made on the basis of national gain with relative freedom from constituency pressures. This approach has now become institutionalized in the successive postwar trade acts and in GATT, although its advantages are being watered down by the more extensive protectionist safeguards in each successive trade act.

These acts make possible a delegation to the president, who is able (in large part because he is elected by all of the people rather than by a particular geographical constituency) to act on the basis of national rather than special interest. It is true that the president's willingness to pursue a liberal foreign trade policy is partly attributable, as Baldwin suggested, to considerations of foreign policy. But in my view Baldwin fails to recognize that international politics, though clearly of great influence on trade outcomes, is not unambiguous in the direction of that influence. In particular, his reference to a recent episode should not go unchallenged. He suggested that President Nixon's proposal of the recent 1974 Trade Act was an "aberration," and he implied that the proposal was the result of Henry Kissinger's efforts. That is not at all my recollection.

PART SIX: STRATEGIES

During the crucial debates within the executive branch about whether to propose a trade bill, Kissinger was on the whole opposed. He feared, and quite rightly, that when the ensuing trade negotiations reached their climax and each side was threatening to pick up its marbles and go home (a stage that is inevitably reached in any serious negotiation) the resulting tensions and recriminations would be likely to spread to the political and security spheres. Since Kissinger had little interest in the gains from trade, he saw no reason to mortgage his future with such contingencies. In the end, however, international political factors drove Nixon to support a trade proposal. The crucial factor at the decisive moment was the compelling personal argument of Prime Minister Edward Heath in favor of more outward-looking policies in the developed world.

Though presidents tend to be more liberal than Congress in trade matters, they too must make compromises. Compromises are not to be decried. We are interested in *net* liberalization: better three steps forward and one back than immobility. Moreover, presidents do not act alone. A key institutional question concerns the way the executive branch makes a decision in the context of what George Shultz and I in our recent book, *Economic Policy Behind the Headlines*, called the advocacy process. Here again I must quarrel with Baldwin's history. I agree that the State Department has usually been the most liberal of the departments, but it might not be forgotten that during the recent past State has also been the driving force for such illiberal proposals as commodity agreements and a seabed authority. The State Department represents institutional, not intellectual, interests.

This brings me to the inevitable question of whether we have reached the end of the line in GATT trade negotiations. GATT negotiations today have perhaps a greater value in enabling the executive branch to resist protectionist pressures during the period of negotiations than they do in actually lowering barriers. But will that be true next time? I am worried about the tendency of each new trade bill to be more protectionist than the one before. If President Nixon was hesitant about proposing the most recent trade act, it was because he had freshly in mind the near disaster of the 1970 trade bill. That bill became so loaded with protectionist riders that when it fell of its own weight everyone with any interest in trade liberalization breathed a sigh of relief.

As several conference participants have suggested, the availability of antidumping and countervailing duties helps to contain protectionist arguments based on the unfairness of foreign practices. But here again the value of these procedures is declining, because trade legislation and judicial decisions have constrained executive branch flexibility. If the "judicialization" of these procedures goes much further, they may themselves become engines of protection. I invite my lawyer colleagues to consider the experience under the Robinson-Patman Act, a price discrimination statute that bears a remarkable resemblance to the substantive rules in antidumping and countervailing duty legislation.

I am also concerned about the institutional strategy, already suggested, that would involve a renegotiation of GATT. I shudder to think where such a process might end, particularly in a one nation–one vote organization such as GATT.

My basic point, then, is that our prime concern should be to avoid worsening the situation. If we can devise strategies, particularly institutional strategies, that will avoid new protection, the international economy will inevitably move in a more liberal direction. This apparent anomaly may be explained, first, by the fact that market forces tend to circumvent regulation, as we have learned in domestic economic policy but have forgotten in trade policy. Second, as time passes, new products become important in international trade and old, heavily protected products decline in importance. Third, inflation tends to lessen the impact of some barriers, particularly specific duties. Consequently, standstill agreements, which are relatively easy to negotiate, may have a great long-range role to play. The Committee of Twenty declaration forswearing escalation of trade and other current account restrictions was a notable success. It appears, for example, to have played a role in Britain's decision not to impose import controls to support sterling.

I should perhaps apologize for being so pessimistic, but it has always seemed to me that rational pessimism was better than emotional optimism. One of my University of Chicago colleagues has pointed out that rational optimism is more palatable than rational pessimism and has the advantage, if one is truly rational, of being substantively the same. So let me end on the rationally optimistic note that, for the reasons sketched earlier, achieving a stalemate in the battle against the current protectionist offensive would actually be a sign of great progress in the direction of a more liberal international economic order.

William R. Cline

J. M. Finger and Richard Erb have provided us with stimulating and thoughtful papers. Finger's analysis has a great deal of formal appeal. The free rider problem is one that has bothered policy advisers, such

PART SIX: STRATEGIES

as the authors of *GATT Plus*,[1] and it is helpful to formulate the issue in terms of the theory of public choice.

I do have doubts about the importance of the free rider problem, however, and I suspect that the paper overstates its role in determining the liberality of the outcome of trade negotiations. At the conceptual level, the problem is that reciprocity from LDCs (or Communist countries, for that matter) is largely illusory. Their import functions are based primarily upon the availability of foreign exchange earned from exports. So when their exports rise from a free ride in trade negotiations, they spend more on imports from the industrial countries. The industrial countries gain the exports on this indirect round in any event, so they are losing nothing from the absence of LDC reciprocity in the negotiations themselves. This point does not mean that LDCs could not benefit their own economies by reducing their protection, but it does mean that potential export gains to industrial countries through LDC reciprocity are an illusion. Therefore, any major strategy of the negotiations based on circumventing the free rider problem is not on solid ground.

At the practical level, free riding by LDCs also appears to be unimportant to the negotiations, as is the increase in the number of participants, emphasized by Finger. The Tokyo Round has been principally a U.S.-EEC affair, as the tentative agreements on the Swiss formula for cutting tariffs illustrates. Canada and Japan, to say nothing of the LDCs, have had difficulty making themselves heard. There was some fear at first that LDC opposition to tariff cuts, for fear of erosion of preferences, would frustrate liberalization attempts, but that threat has proven to be relatively unimportant. It probably did help matters somewhat that some major LDCs such as Brazil recognized the flaws in the UNCTAD position, which opposed deep tariffs cuts in the name of preserving preference margins, and recognized that their own interests lay in the direction of deep cuts in the preferential treatment of MFNs, as shown by the studies of Robert Baldwin and Tracy Murray and others.

I would suggest that the depth of liberalization is not so much a function of the free rider problem as it is one of sensitive industries. Textiles, shoes, electronics, and steel are prime candidates for exemption, not because all sourcing comes from free riders but because these industries are sensitive to imports generally. It is true that many of these imports come from LDCs, but the relevant reason for exemption is that these products are labor intensive and tend to hit the sensitive industries —not that they come from nonreciprocating participants.

---

[1] Atlantic Council of the United States, *GATT Plus: A Proposal for Trade Reform* (New York: Praeger, 1975).

A few technical points: first, "coverage" of liberalization is an unsatisfactory measure, since it places no weight on the degree of change in the level of protection. Second, one wonders how Finger's central hypothesis could be tested empirically. If low coverage and high internalization in the Dillon Round constitutes one observation confirming the importance of internalization and therefore that of the free rider problem, then why does not the high coverage–low internalization of the Kennedy Round constitute an observation rejecting the hypothesis that free riding is an important problem? Finally, Finger's proposal to extend preferences only to reciprocating LDCs seems unpromising. Any change in preference legislation at the present time would open Pandora's box to protectionist revisions. More importantly, the LDCs that would benefit would be precisely those that do not need concessional measures: the middle-income LDCs.

Despite these qualifications, I find Finger's paper novel and thoughtful.

The paper by Richard Erb surveys the network of financial flows to LDCs. This paper also makes many perceptive observations. One section grapples with the question of whether the current system of international credits and OPEC surpluses is viable over time. It is useful to raise this issue again, and it is honest to admit, as the paper does, that the answer is not clear. The paper does have a certain air of admiration for the wonderful challenges posed by the oil price increases and the seeming sophistication of the private financial markets in meeting them, as if the cloud were welcome for its silver lining. Nevertheless, I agree with the central conclusions in this area: alarmist reports such as that by the Committee on Foreign Relations are overstated. New laws imposing rules of thumb limiting bank lending abroad would be counterproductive. In this area, I think Erb could have emphasized more the findings of recent studies by the IMF,[2] and by others including Gordon Smith,[3] to the effect that LDC debt is not outrageously high and that LDC deficits are about what one would expect under historical patterns before the oil price rise, after accounting for inflation. As the IMF has pointed out, the real swing in current account has been in the industrialized countries. And, contrary to Erb's concern that lending may be diverted from LDCs to developed countries, I would argue that it is stabilizing for the system as a whole for much of the OPEC surplus to be reflected by increased debt in the industrial countries—those with

---

[2] International Monetary Fund, *Annual Report, 1977* (Washington, D.C., 1977).
[3] Gordon W. Smith, *The External Debt Prospects of the Non-Oil-Exporting Developing Countries: An Econometric Analysis*, Monograph no. 10 (Washington, D.C.: Overseas Development Council, 1977).

the creditworthiness to absorb it. This is just what happened after 1974 and 1975, when LDC borrowing was too high to be sustainable, even though it was temporarily helpful to the system as a whole by providing a source of foreign demand during the trough of the world recession.

Erb has usefully raised the issue of whether the IMF is doing the right things in its lending to LDCs. Are the narrow balance of payments criteria relevant once the institution moves further into developmental areas (especially in the case of the Trust Fund); are they relevant in a world context of the requirement for large aggregate deficits on the part of non-OPEC countries? There does seem to be a need for greater developmental policy input—or else a need to channel the new longer-term financial flows through other institutions. Program loans through the World Bank come to mind.

As for Erb's long discussion of the desirability of making more resources available to the IMF, one is relieved that he finally emphasizes the analogy to the domestic central bank as lender of last resort. He thereby recognizes that shoring up the stability of the overall system, including the reliability of outstanding loans to LDCs, matters more than alleged loss of static efficiency from channeling resources to countries that might be wasting them.

Erb's treatment of concessional flows is marked by skepticism. His concern that the amounts are too small for a sizable impact should lead to the conclusions that aid needs to be increased and that it should be more narrowly focused by recipient groups, however, not to the conclusion that aid is secondary. Peter Bauer has told us that the world's poorest one or two billion people justifiably may be ignored by the rich nations because civil war and political repression have occurred in LDCs. Craig Roberts has told us that all aid advocates are out to line their pockets. These two positions deserve to be taken equally seriously. Did Bauer immediately advocate aid to India upon the replacement of Indira Ghandi's "emergency" by a democratic regime?

The small amount of attention devoted to concessional transfers is the main weakness of Erb's paper and, I would argue, of this conference as a whole. After a review of the various elements in any new international economic order, I have become increasingly convinced that a dynamic program of concessional aid is far more important than the other proposals for reform in the North-South dialogue. In particular, if the developed countries were suddenly to double aid and achieve the U.N. target of 0.7 percent of GNP, the additional flow of concessional resources would be approximately $16 billion annually. By contrast, commodity price stabilization would generate only about $700 million in annual benefits to LDCs in terms of static changes in producer and consumer surplus, based on estimates by Jere Behrman—although benefits would presumably be considerably larger after including dynamic effects.[4] Trade liberalization might raise LDC exports by about $5 billion (using a 1974 base), on the basis of our recent study at the Brookings Institution, and these exports would not be at zero resource cost.[5] Debt relief would be counterproductive for, and rejected by, the middle-income countries; it might provide some incremental aid for the poor LDCs, but the maximum would be the current flow of repayments to official sources, or about $2.5 billion yearly.

What is needed is a return to the leadership the United States exercised in aid efforts over the whole postwar period until 1966. Throughout that period, U.S. aid stood at half of 1 percent of GNP or higher; recently, our aid effort has been only about one-quarter of 1 percent of GNP. The United States has turned inward. We have multiplied fivefold the real value of federal spending on our domestic social problems since 1966, while we have steadily reduced the real value of our foreign aid. Germany and Japan have also lagged far behind the U.N. target for aid effort. It is no wonder that the developing countries have become increasingly militant—by now an increase in our aid might temper that militance but would not necessarily eliminate it.

For the increasingly prosperous middle-income countries, or third world, the types of market-related financial flows described by Richard Erb are sufficient. For the poorer fourth world, larger flows of concessional resources are necessary if there is to be a more equitable international order, or even one as equitable as a decade ago if we consider U.S. aid programs alone. For both sets of LDCs, perhaps the other crucial "reform" will be merely to preserve the degree of entry that the industrial countries now permit in their import markets, in order to make possible the growth of exports advocated by I. M. D. Little and others. Preserving this degree of openness will require political honesty on the part of legislatures and executive branches and in particular a willingness to assess import injury on a factual basis. Recent estimates by the World Bank and others indicate that the displacement of jobs from the future growth of manufactured imports from LDCs will be extremely small, despite the outcry for protection against goods produced with cheap labor in LDCs. More fundamentally, however, the main condition

---

[4] Jere R. Behrman, *International Commodity Agreements: An Evaluation of the UNCTAD Integrated Commodities Programme*, Monograph, no. 9 (Washington, D.C.: Overseas Development Council, 1977).

[5] William R. Cline, Noboru Kawanabe, T. O. M. Kronsjo, and Thomas Williams, *Trade Negotiations in the Tokyo Round: A Quantitative Assessment* (Washington, D.C.: Brookings Institution, 1978).

PART SIX: STRATEGIES

for preserving liberal access to markets will probably be the achievement of economic recovery in the industrial countries.

Juergen B. Donges

At most good conferences, the major issues have been discussed once the last discussant of the last theme has had his turn, and this applies to the trading system area, on which I have been asked to comment. Furthermore, I find myself in a dilemma in that J. M. Finger's excellent paper embraces the most important aspects and contains little with which I would disagree. As a matter of fact, some of my recent work and that of my colleagues on these issues coincide well with his analysis and findings. Nevertheless, I will try to take up some of the points mentioned and comment particularly on the medium- and long-term perspective of the paper. The strategic issues that I consider crucial in this context are (1) the responsibility of industrial countries to take the lead in further developing an international framework based on liberal trade principles; (2) the type of reciprocal role developing countries should play within the international framework in order to enhance the development prospects of their own economies; (3) the manner in which the special characteristics of trade with primary commodities can be accommodated within a liberal trading system.

One general point worth mentioning at the outset is that intellectual efforts with respect to recommending improvements in the international framework for trade, based on the principle of market mechanism with active competition, will not have great appeal to representatives of LDCs as long as they can hope to gain more from political confrontations or—to state it more politely—in North-South dialogues. However, the experience since 1974, when LDCs started to insist unanimously and resolutely on the need for a New International Economic Order, does not lend much support to such expectations. There is growing recognition among developing countries that the zero-sum game mentality behind the NIEO concept is inferior to positive-sum game prescriptions, that it has more emotional appeal than capacity to really solve problems. This is especially true when we consider the positive effects on economic development, employment, and manufactured export expansion achieved by LDCs that liberalized their trade regimes in the 1960s and early 1970s. Under such circumstances, it is worthwhile to emphasize how much can be gained from a well-functioning international system with decentralized decision-making processes. The trading system is the key to achieving those gains. The same holds for DCs, provided that long-term economic growth with high levels of employment is desired.

As to the first strategic issue, Finger shows in his paper that the results of past GATT negotiations have been satisfactory, referring to substantial reductions of U.S. import tariffs. I may add that this positive evaluation also holds for the case of the Federal Republic of Germany and other Western European countries. He further stresses that the applied principle of reciprocity, which contributed to balancing the benefits of tariff concessions among the industrial countries, was a major determinant of the positive outcome of the six GATT rounds preceding the Tokyo Round. Another important factor was the rapid and sustained economic growth of the world economy, to say nothing of the relatively small number of participants in the trade negotiations. From this analysis Finger concludes, somewhat agnostically, that in light of less conclusive conditions (increasing heterogeneity of export interests, LDC demands for special and differential treatment, uncertain prospects of economic growth, widespread and persistent unemployment) further improvements in the trading system will be very difficult to achieve in practice.

I think that Finger is right in stressing the danger of creeping protectionism in DCs. He explicitly refers to the United States, but the gap between free trade rhetoric and protectionist behavior seems to be widening in the European Economic Community too, as Jan Tumlir has pointed out in his paper. If such tendencies are not stopped and then reversed, the liberal trading order will certainly be undermined from within the DCs. Moreover, one can expect a growing mistrust on the part of LDCs in a trading system that works through the market mechanism. Demands will be reinforced for an NIEO based on centralized and politically determined worldwide decision making. No one will be convinced that such a system will work efficiently, since the present one does not—not because of an inherent weakness but because of too much state intervention for the sake of political compliance with internal pressure groups, which refuse to adjust themselves to (rapidly) changing supply and demand conditions in the world economy. A disintegration of the world economy, a return to economic isolationism, and a deceleration of economic growth, followed by a proliferation of political conflicts among countries, would be the most likely result. Whether the serious threat to a liberal international trading system will be of a passing nature depends in the last analysis upon the availability of statemanship in DCs. Protectionists will be the more successful, the less skilled the governments that have to make trade policy decisions in a democratic society. They will follow the easiest way of coping with increased import competition, and they will also trust that the costs of such behavior will be overlooked by most citizens. This is morally

PART SIX: STRATEGIES

objectionable and violates the constitutions of democratic societies, according to which policies must serve the public interest rather than particular demands. If, however, governments are highly skilled, imaginative, and politically open-minded, further trade liberalization may become feasible. At the moment, there is a serious lack of supply of this type of statemanship. It is hoped that this will change in a not too distant future.

If this assumption is realistic (this is a big "if"), the question arises of how to deal with the trade liberalization issue in practice. Finger provides some answers that clearly show a preference for a piecemeal approach. In practical trade negotiations, it probably makes much sense to look at specific items. In order, however, not to lose the overall perspective—and to make further developments in the trade policy area predictable rather than uncertain—I want to stress the importance of DC agreement on some basic rules. Fundamentally, the choice is between a status quo variant and a forward-looking strategy. Maintaining the status quo implies that DCs refrain from both increasing effective tariff protection and introducing new quantitative import restrictions. The forward-looking strategy means, on the one hand, that import tariffs are further reduced on as many products as possible, with a larger reduction for the higher stages of fabrication in order to mitigate the negative impact of the tariff escalation on LDC-manufactured exports. On the other hand, additional nontariff barriers are not substituted for reduced tariffs, while existing NTBs are reduced and eventually phased out. In order to overcome resistance from affected workers and entrepreneurs, the implementation of a liberalization program should be gradual, taking place over a period of, say, ten years. And in order to strengthen LDC confidence that the implementation will in fact take place, the DCs should negotiate an advanced time schedule with the LDCs (analogous to the formula adopted when the EEC was created). Deviation from the fixed time schedule to the disadvantage of LDCs should be permitted only in well-founded, exceptional cases, that is, subject to the condition that increasing imports have caused serious damage to domestic production and employment. In any case, safeguards should be applied in a nondiscriminatory manner. In order to avoid abuses, resort to escape clauses should be subjected to strict criteria of time limitation, of definition of "market disruption," and of international approval and surveillance (for instance, through a standing committee rather than a panel). An adjustment assistance policy at a sectoral and regional level should be linked with the liberalization program. Not only would domestic opposition to trade liberalization be further weakened; the LDCs' confidence in an improved trading system will also probably be enhanced significantly.

Whether the status quo or the forward-looking strategy is pursued, we are left with two "special cases": one relates to agricultural trade, the other to the demand of LDCs for differential treatment. Finger has referred only to the latter issue, although the former has been declared a major concern in the Tokyo Round. Probably he is skeptical about the possibility of integrating agricultural trade into the framework of principles that already governs trade in manufactures in this ongoing round. Indeed, it seems to be very difficult to lessen the conflict between international farm support measures and international trade requirements, including commitments on better market access of exporters of both temperate-zone products and tropical commodities. However difficult policy changes in this area may be, they are not impossible. Tactically, the countries participating in the multilateral trade negotiations can put their domestic support schemes, in the first instance, on an "exception list," thus bidding up the amount of concessions to be made by others if the support schemes are to be made negotiable at a later stage of the bargaining. The prospects for improved conditions of world agricultural trade are not so bad as we used to think, simply because governments in DCs are now more conscious of the need of a stable trading system for agricultural products as a necessary condition for internally pursuing farm-support policies.

Finger is critical, and so am I, of the LDCs' demand for special and differential treatment. The heart of the problem is that differential rules for LDCs in (a reformed) GATT would reduce the adaptability of the trading framework when conditions change. This becomes particularly evident in connection with the eligibility of LDCs for the special and differential treatment. Making this question a matter of negotiation might conflict with the principle of national sovereignty. If, alternatively, LDCs are allowed from the outset to decide whether they are eligible, there is no mechanism to assure that they would elect themselves out at a later stage, as soon as they have a competitive trade sector by conventional standards. A "graduation" formula that automatically strips successful LDCs of their special privileges could help, provided it is evolutionary in nature. The prospects for agreement on such a formula, however, are gloomy, for consensus is required on the definition of "success," which must be as acceptable now as it would be some years later. If, on the contrary, the trading system were based on an equality of contractual rights and obligations between DCs and LDCs, it would be easier to decide on ad hoc adjustments, if required. For instance, participating countries could even now think of ways to

PART SIX: STRATEGIES

assure that LDCs have an advantage in realizing benefits from MFN trade liberalization—possibly by reducing the tariffs (and the tariff equivalent of nontariff barriers) for LDCs at a somewhat faster rate than for DCs.

The second strategic issue is the role LDCs should play for the sake of improving the international trading system. Finger's paper does not deal with this in detail, except for the question of reducing LDC export taxes (together with DC import protection) and some remarks on trade reforms in selected LDCs. In my view, their role is broader, as I. M. D. Little has also shown in his paper. LDCs need to proceed toward outward-looking policies that promote both import substitution and export diversification; that is, they should try to get a production structure (including the industrial sector) suitable to the country's particular factor endowment.

Programmatically, two lines of action are warranted: First, LDCs should dismantle their own import protection, reducing tariffs to moderate levels and softening import licensing schemes (including import prohibitions based on criteria of domestic availability). Import liberalization may be more difficult in most LDCs than in DCs because the former would start with higher levels of protection and enjoy less sophisticated economic management capabilities than the latter. A too sudden liberalization could stop industrialization, thereby incurring substantial social and political costs. Hence, a gradual approach over years is also warranted here; the liberalization has to be predictable in any case. The second line of action would be directed toward import liberalization in relation to other LDCs. Intercountry differences in the level of development may result in serious dislocations in existing industries when barriers on intra-LDC trade are reduced. An appropriate approach to this problem would be to allow LDCs at lower levels of development both to reduce protection on a slower time path and to grant, on infant-industry grounds, subsidies to new exports into more advanced LDCs. Again, the practical difficulties of implementing such a program are enormous, but serious attempts to overcome them will pay off because, as Finger points out correctly, they will be regarded by DCs as an application of reciprocity.

It is sometimes argued that many LDCs will not be prepared to participate actively in the establishment of a liberalized trading system because of the socialist or nationalist philosophy to which they have subscribed. This philosophy is not market oriented and calls for direct state intervention in economic affairs, including those of trade (the same holds for the centrally planned economies in Eastern Europe and Asia). While the tendency of such LDCs not to participate in more liberalized trading cannot be doubted, there is no reason for countries with market-oriented economies to refrain from steps toward further trade liberalization just because of such behavior. The implication is only that those governments that want to manipulate their trade in a discriminatory way cannot expect to qualify for whatever improved and nondiscriminatory market access other countries have agreed upon. Bilateral trade arrangements, with special safeguard rules, will continue to govern trade between these two groups of countries.

Finger has not focused on the third strategic issue, how to improve the framework for trade with primary commodities. However, many important aspects have been treated in Gordon Smith's paper (Part 2, herein) and in the discussion that followed it; therefore, I can be very brief. I assume that the rationale of alleviating the economic difficulties arising from price instability in primary commodity markets is beyond any question.

Nevertheless, the UNCTAD proposal to serve this objective primarily by the integrated commodity program is questionable for at least three reasons. First, this program implies that effective price stabilization will also lead to a stabilization of export revenues, although this is not at all sure. Second, the program presupposes the ability of an international buffer stock organization under intergovernmental surveillance to make sufficiently accurate predictions of future equilibrium commodity prices in an uncertain world. Experience with past commodity agreements does not lend support to such an expectation. Third, the program aims, in the final analysis, at fixing prices at a "remunerative" and "just" level, that is, at a level above market equilibrium. The consequence will naturally be serious inefficiencies, at both country and world levels.

I want also to emphasize the need for correcting a basic deficiency in the world trading system for primary commodities: it provides rules only for nondiscriminatory and competitive access to import markets; there is no effective provision to assure access to export markets, particularly to supplies of raw materials. Such rules have to be agreed upon. They must also include prohibitions and safeguards against the unilateral imposition of export controls or of export taxes, for the same reason that import restrictions must be removed. Although export restrictions instituted as a last resort to lessen sharp domestic inflationary pressures or abrupt physical shortages of critical primary commodities could be authorized, exporting countries should show the greatest restraint in imposing such restrictions. The use of escape clauses should be subjected to the same strict standards as in the case of import protective measures.

PART SIX: STRATEGIES

Let me conclude by saying that the formulation of a trade liberalization program does not pose great difficulties to an economist. In particular, the economic criteria essential for improvement can clearly be stated. The problem remains, however, of how to sell the idea to those who are responsible for economic policy making. In answer to this question, I can only stress the importance of conducting empirical research in an accurate and comprehensive way, so as to provide policy makers with solid evidence they can hardly ignore—in the hope that Say's law will function. If the liberal idea can be sold, the next difficulty relates to achieving agreements that entail as much of the idea as possible. For the sake of political acceptability, two things will then be important: First, each signatory country must achieve some negotiating success on at least one major trade issue. Second, the constituency must be able to regard the liberalization program and the complementary burden of additional domestic adjustment as equitable among participating nations. In the short run, the requirements of internal political stability in DCs may not allow for significant headway. If this is the case, I would not worry about the Tokyo Round being behind schedule, provided that our governments take the opportunity effectively to resist protectionist pressure groups, arguing that no measures can be taken until the negotiations have been completed, even if this is later than the end of 1979 (when the present negotiating authority of the United States expires). Without such resistance, it will be politically difficult for DCs to continue to substantiate the legitimacy of advocating a liberal international trading system.

DISCUSSION

Donald Syvrud argued that the most serious threat to the liberal order comes not from the developing countries but from within the developed world itself. The growing protectionism in the postwar period is caused by stagflation, and Syvrud argued that neither the monetarists nor the Keynesians offer a solution to the twin evils of inflation and stagnation. Stagflation, in turn, is largely a result of the severe blows to the economy of 1973 and 1974—the oil price increase, the shortfall in output of many commodities in many countries, and the longer-term rise in inflationary pressures. These blows to the system altered the existing price structure and created the need for fairly sharp adjustments in almost every major country. The key threat to the liberal economic order, according to Syvrud, arises from the inability of the Western democratic industrial countries to adjust to these changes in real prices. The difficulty of achieving a U.S. energy program is a good example. It is much easier, politically and economically, to adjust in the context of a growing economy than it is in a stagnant economy.

In response to this situation, Syvrud suggested that we might (1) accept the greater risks of inflation or (2) accept some form of incomes policy. He said that there are other alternatives, but they would focus on individual markets and would be less acceptable because of ideological constraints. Policy makers in the major countries focus on macro economics on the grounds of past experience and ease of implementation. Moreover, macro economics avoids the difficult political-economic issues of demographics, cultural trends, distribution, and allocation within the economy. In dealing with payments imbalances, Syvrud argued that we have recognized the need for structural adjustment, which means a shift in the productive structure of the economy and therefore in the allocation of resources and the distribution of income, yet we are unwilling to consider the full implications of structural adjustment in terms of policy changes and greater involvement of the government in the economy.

Wilson Schmidt was puzzled by Richard Erb's comment that the

PART SIX: STRATEGIES

IMF was in an early stage of its learning curve. Schmidt felt the IMF has had enough time (thirty-one years) to have evolved from any early stage. He also disagreed with the need for the IMF to be a lender of last resort, saying that the New York Federal Reserve Bank does the job very well.

Thomas Willett asked Peter Bauer to elaborate on his own preferred strategy for foreign aid, and in the case of cash transfers to the poor Willett asked whether Bauer would prefer the aid to go to governments or to individuals and whether the aid should be general or directed toward certain programs. Bauer responded that he would like to phase out official aid altogether, but that was not realistic. He argued that, contrary to the general view, more aid does not necessarily promote development. This is because aid can benefit the development process only marginally, at best. Aid is not manna from heaven, he argued; it sets up all sorts of repercussions that can far outweigh any benefits from the inflow of resources. One such repercussion is the politicization of the recipient country. His preference is to channel aid in such a way as to promote a more liberal society. Bauer argued that bilateral aid is superior to multilateral aid because it is more flexible. The people who allocate multinational aid have their own special interests to promote, while bilateral aid is subject to parliamentary control by the legislature of the donor country. This is good, he argued, because policies can be more quickly adjusted. As an example, he pointed out that British aid to Idi Amin has been terminated, but the EEC is still wrangling about reducing aid to Amin because of all kinds of multinational problems. On all these grounds, he favored bilateral, straight cash grants to governments that perform the essential tasks of government without controlling the economy too closely and without trying to politicize life in their countries.

Dragoslav Avramovic agreed with Erb that capital markets had done a remarkable job of shifting resources to the developing countries in the last few years, but this was done, he said, at the cost of steady deterioration in these same countries' debt structure. He wondered whether these international lending agencies would be enough in the future, because the debts are enormous and growing. Erb responded that there is too much emphasis on the imminent collapse of the system. He thought that there was a high probability that some country would default in the next few years, and at that time it might be necessary for the IMF or World Bank to step in as a lender of last resort. At this stage, Erb said, we would have to face the question of either increasing the role of the IMF or the World Bank or developing some other institution. How deficits are to be allocated would also have to be decided. He felt that the current system does a better job of financing deficits (and in effect allocating deficits) than would a centralized system.

Erb responded to Schmidt by saying that the IMF is still in the early stages of its learning curve because the full effect of many of its newer programs has not been felt in the developing countries. On the question of the Federal Reserve acting as lender of last resort, it is Erb's feeling that a multilateral lender should handle that role.

Erb agreed with Bauer that bilateral aid can better achieve country-specific objectives. He argued that experimentation with different types and forms of aid is needed because there is much to learn about how to accomplish the objective of raising very low income levels.

J. M. Finger, in the time given to respond, emphasized the very real danger that trade liberalization can be perverted into trade de-liberalization. The fact that negotiations are going on does not mean that there is nothing to worry about. The forum of the negotiations can be exploited by those who want more protection of domestic markets.

Finger disagreed with William Cline's argument that reciprocity was not necessary because LDCs spend all their export earnings. This is not the point, he said, because most protection is not aimed at reducing imports relative to exports but at reducing the traded goods sector relative to the domestic sector.

LIST OF PARTICIPANTS

Amacher, Ryan C., *Arizona State University*
Anton, Ian, *Institute of World Economy, Romania*
Arndt, Sven, *United States Treasury*
*Avramovic, Dragoslav, *The World Bank*
*Balassa, Bela, *Johns Hopkins University and the World Bank*
*Baldwin, Robert E., *University of Wisconsin*
*Bauer, Peter T., *London School of Economics*
*Bhagwati, Jagdish N., *Massachusetts Institute of Technology*
Black, Stanley, *Department of State*
Bryant, Ralph, *The Brookings Institution*
*Caves, Richard E., *Harvard University*
*Chenery, Hollis B., *The World Bank*
*Cline, William R., *The Brookings Institution*
Cooper, Richard N., *Department of State*
*Dam, Kenneth W., *University of Chicago*
*Diaz-Alejandro, Carlos F., *Yale University*
*Donges, Juergen B., *Kiel Institute of World Economics*
*Dreyer, Jacob S., *United States Treasury*
*Erb, Richard D., *American Enterprise Institute*
Feketekuty, Geza *Office of Special Representative for Trade Negotiations*
*Fellner, William, *American Enterprise Institute*
*Findlay, Ronald, *Columbia University*
*Finger, J. M., *United States Treasury*
Finkel, E. Jay, *Inter-American Development Bank*
Fisher, Richard, *United States Treasury*
Frank, Isaiah, *Johns Hopkins University*
Fried, Edward R., *The World Bank*
*Gillis, Malcolm, *Harvard University*
*Haberler, Gottfried, *American Enterprise Institute*
*Hawkins, Robert G., *New York University*

---

* Conference panelist

LIST OF PARTICIPANTS

*Holzman, Franklyn, *Tufts University*
*Horst, Thomas, *United States Treasury*
Houthakker, Hendrik S., *Harvard University*
*Hufbauer, Gary C., *United States Treasury*
Junz, Helen B., *United States Treasury*
Katz, Samuel I., *Georgetown University*
*Kenen, Peter B., *Princeton University*
Krauss, Melvin, *New York University*
Levy, David, *National Planning Association*
*Little, I. M. D., *The World Bank*
*MacBean, A. I., *University of Lancaster*
*Machlup, Fritz, *New York University*
Meigs, A. James, *Booz, Allen, and Hamilton, Inc.*
Moran, Theodore H., *Department of State*
Nackmanoff, Arnold, *United States Treasury*
Rares, Petru, *Institute of World Economy, Romania*
*Roberts, Paul Craig, *Office of Senator Orrin G. Hatch*
*Schmidt, Wilson E., *Virginia Polytechnic Institute and State University*
Sewell, John W., *Overseas Development Council*
*Shields, Roger E., *Chemical Bank*
*Smith, Gordon W., *Rice University*
Solomon, Robert, *The Brookings Institution*
*Stern, Robert M., *University of Michigan*
*Streeten, Paul P., *The World Bank*
*Sweeney, Richard James, *Claremont Men's College*
Syvrud, Donald, *United States Treasury*
*Tollison, Robert D., *Virginia Polytechnic Institute and State University*
Tower, Edward, *Duke University*
Truman, Edwin, *Federal Reserve System*
*Tumlir, Jan, *General Agreement on Tariffs and Trade, Geneva*
*Walter, Ingo, *New York University*
*Weinberg, Nat, *Economic Consultant, Sumner, Maryland*
*Whitman, Marina v. N., *University of Pittsburgh*
*Willett, Thomas D., *Claremont Men's College*
Zschock, Dieter K., *State University of New York at Stony Brook*

---

* Conference panelist

AEI Associates Program

The American Enterprise Institute invites your participation in the competition of ideas through its AEI Associates Program. This program has two objectives:

The first is to broaden the distribution of AEI studies, conferences, forums, and reviews, and thereby to extend public familiarity with the issues. AEI Associates receive regular information on AEI research and programs, and they can order publications and cassettes at a savings.

The second objective is to increase the research activity of the American Enterprise Institute and the dissemination of its published materials to policy makers, the academic community, journalists, and others who help shape public attitudes. Your contribution, which in most cases is partly tax deductible, will help ensure that decision makers have the benefit of scholarly research on the practical options to be considered before programs are formulated. The issues studied by AEI include:

- Defense Policy
- Economic Policy
- Energy Policy
- Foreign Policy
- Government Regulation

- Health Policy
- Legal Policy
- Political and Social Processes
- Social Security and Retirement Policy
- Tax Policy

For more information, write to: AMERICAN ENTERPRISE INSTITUTE
1150 Seventeenth Street, N.W.
Washington, D.C. 20036

Selected AEI Publications

The AEI Economist, Herbert Stein, ed., published monthly (one year, $10; single copy, $1)

The Distribution of the Tax Burden, Edgar K. Browning and William R. Johnson (84 pp., $3.25)

A Conversation with Friedrich A. von Hayek: Science and Socialism (21 pp., $1.75)

A Treatise on Markets: Spots, Futures, and Options, Joseph M. Burns (145 pp., $4.75)

The Multilateral Trade Negotiations: Toward Greater Liberalization? Robert E. Baldwin (30 pp., $3)

Forming Multimodal Transportation Companies: Barriers, Benefits, and Problems, Clinton H. Whitehurst, Jr., ed. (181 pp., paper $4.75, cloth $10.75)

Reflections of an Economic Policy Maker: Speeches and Congressional Statements, 1969–1978, Arthur F. Burns (485 pp., paper $6.75, cloth $14.75)

Econometric Model Performance in Forecasting and Policy Assessment, W. Allen Spivey and William J. Wrobleski (77 pp., $3.25)

Contemporary Economic Problems 1978, W. Fellner, project director (353 pp., $6.75)

Notes on Stagflation, Howard S. Ellis (23 pp., $1.25)

Swiss Monetary and Exchange Rate Policy in an Inflationary World, Fritz Leutwiler (14 pp., $1.25)

LIBRARY OF DAVIDSON COLLEGE

Books on regular loan may be checked out for **two weeks**. Books must be presented at the Circulation Desk in order to be renewed.

A fine is charged after date due.

Special books are subject to special regulations at the discretion of the library staff.

OCT 12 1980			
FEB 16 1981			
NOV 17 1981			
FEB 22 82			
NOV -7 1982			
JAN 28 1983			
FEB -6 1984			
MAY -2 1984			
MAY 16 1984			